COMPUTER SCIENCE
Research and Applications

COMPUTER SCIENCE
Research and Applications

Edited by
Ricardo Baeza-Yates
University of Chile
Santiago, Chile

and
Udi Manber
University of Arizona
Tucson, Arizona

Springer Science+Business Media, LLC

Library of Congress Cataloging in Publication Data

Computer science: research and applications / edited by Ricardo Baeza-Yates and Udi Manber.
   p.   cm.
   "Proceedings of the Eleventh International Conference of the Chilean Computer Science Society, held October 15–18, 1991, in Santiago, Chile" — T.p. verso.
   Includes bibliographical references (p.   ) and index.
   ISBN 978-1-4613-6513-6   ISBN 978-1-4615-3422-8 (eBook)
   DOI 10.1007/978-1-4615-3422-8
   1. Computer science — Research — Congresses. I. Baeza-Yates, R. (Ricardo) II. Manber, Udi. III. Chilean Computer Science Society. International Conference (11th: 1991: Santiago, Chile)
QA76.27.C673   1992   92-13842
004′.072 — dc20   CIP

Proceedings of the Eleventh International Conference of the
Chilean Computer Science Society, held October 15–18, 1991,
in Santiago, Chile

ISBN 978-1-4613-6513-6

© 1992 Springer Science+Business Media New York
Originally published by Plenum Press, New York in 1992
Softcover reprint of the hardcover 1st edition 1992

Preface

The articles in this collection were presented at the 11th International Conference of the Chilean Computer Science Society held in Satiago, Chile on October 15 - 18, 1991. A record number of 85 submissions were received this year in response to the call for papers. They came from 19 countries in four continents. The articles presented here were selected by the program committee whose members were

> José Balcázar (Polytechnic University of Catalunya)
> Francois Bancilhon (ALTAIR/INRIA)
> Marcos R.S. Borges (Universidade Federal do Rio de Janeiro)
> Ignacio Casas (Universidad Católica de Chile)
> J.L. Encarnaçao (Zentrum fuer Grafische Datenverarbeitung)
> Hector Garcia-Molina (Princeton University)
> Michael Langston (University of Tennessee)
> Raphael Finkel (University of Kentucky)
> Tom Maibaum (Imperial College)
> Udi Manber, Chairman (University of Arizona)
> Michael Robson (Australian National University)

The criteria for selection was based primarily on quality; we also considered relevance, clarity and the potential benefit to the community.

In a time of great specialization, it is refreshing to see a conference devoted not to particular narrow fields but to all areas of computer science. Included are papers in algorithms, artificial intelligence, computer architecture, computer networks, databases, data structures, distributed systems, graphics and user interface, object-oriented systems, operating systems, programming languages, and the theory of computing. It was a pleasure reading high-quality papers in so many different areas of computer science.

The purposes of every scientific conference are to foster cooperation between scientists and to advance the state of the art. This conference, being one of the oldest and highest quality computer science conference in Latin America, is serving many facets of these purposes: It helps to bring the work done in Latin America to the attention of computer scientists from around the world; it helps to keep Latin American scientists and computer professionals up to date with major advances in the field; and it helps the cross fertilization between different areas of computer science. The latter is essential to the growth of our field, which, even though it is already so important in the lives of so many, is still a very young field.

I wish to thank the organizing conference chairman, Ricardo Baeza-Yates, the program committee, and the other anonymous reviewers for their work and dedication.

Udi Manber

Tucson, Arizona, USA
September 1991

v

Contents

Object-Oriented Systems

Distributed Systems

Complexity and Parallel Algorithms

Computer Architecture and Networks

Introduction

The International Conference of the Chilean Computer Science Society (SCCC) is an annual event which is held in Santiago, Chile. Since its inception in 1981 it has grown to become one of the most important events of its type in Latin America. The official language of the conference is English. During 1991, the SCCC became a sister society of the ACM and the IEEE Computer Society.

The SCCC seeks to facilitate the interchange of knowledge and experience among academics and professionals who work in the field of computing. This year 85 papers were received from 19 countries on 4 continents. From these the program committee selected only 35 for presentation, which indicates the conference's selectivity and the high quality demanded of participants.

The accepted papers were selected by the following program committee:

José Balcazar (Polytechnic University of Catalunya)
Francois Bancilhon (ALTAIR/INRIA)
Marcos R.S. Borges (Universidade Federal do Rio de Janeiro)
Ignacio Casas (Universidad Católica de Chile)
J.L. Encarnaçao (Zentrum füer Grafische Datenverarbeitung)
Hector Garcia-Molina (Princeton University)
Michael Langston (University of Tennessee)
Raphael Finkel (University of Kentucky)
Tom Maibaum (Imperial College)
Udi Manber, Chairman (University of Arizona)
Michael Robson (Australian National University)

The proceedings are organized in seven areas (number of papers in parentheses):

Databases (3)
Artificial Intelligence, Logic and Functional Programming (6)
Algorithms and Data Structures (8)
Object-Oriented Systems (5)
Distributed Systems (5)
Complexity and Parallel Algorithms (3 plus 2 invited)
Computer Architecture and Networks (5)

The conference also included six tutorials:

- Expert Systems, *Miguel Nussbaum, Pontificia Universidad Católica, Chile (in Spanish).*

- Design of Algorithms, *Udi Manber, Univ. of Arizona, USA (in English).*

- Hypertext and Applications, *Marcos Borges, Univ. Fed. de Rio de Janeiro (in Spanish).*

- Distributed Operating Systems and Software, *Raphael Finkel, Univ. of Kentucky, USA (in English).*

- Distributed Databases, *Héctor García-Molina, Princeton Univ., USA (in Spanish)*.

- Automatic VLSI Design, *Raúl Camposano, Univ. of Paderborn/GMD, Germany (in Spanish)*.

Three talks were invited (the first two are included in the proceedings):

- Complexity of Algorithmic Problems on Succinct Instances, *José Balcázar, Univ. Politécnica de Cataluña, Spain*.

- Parallel Algorithms for NP-Complete Problems, *Michael Robson, Australian National Univ., Canberra, Australia*.

- Categoric Aspects of Computer Science, *Jose Luis Freire, Universidad de La Coruña, Spain*.

A panel discussion regarding the software industry in Chile was also organized, as well as one dealing with the ACM/IEEE 1991 CS curriculum.

This year the conference was organized by the Department of Computer Science of the University of Chile and took place at the central campus of the university. The organizing committee was composed of the following:

Juan Alvarez
Ricardo Baeza-Yates, Chairman
Andrés Pavez
José A. Pino
Patricio V. Poblete

The SCCC conference was held jointly with the Ibero-American Congress on Computer Science in Higher Education, the first of its type in Latin America.

These events are jointly sponsored by the Chilean Software Association (ACS), the Latin American Center for Studies in Informatics (CLEI), the National Council of Research in Science and Technology (CONICYT), the IEEE Computer Society, and SONDA (Digital representative). Collaborating sponsors include the British Council, the Chile-France cooperation program, and the Andes Foundation.

Underwriting these events are Apple Chile, Cientec S.A. (Sun distributor), the Chilean Telephone Company (CTC), IBM Chile, UNISYS, XXI magazine of El Mercurio, Informática magazine, Difusión Publishing (Addison-Wesley), and Ciencia and Técnica Distributors (McGraw-Hill).

About 140 people attended the conference (50% of them students), mainly from Chile, but also about 50 from Argentina, Australia, Brasil, Canada, Colombia, England, France, Germany, Israel, Mexico, Panama, Paraguay, Spain, Switzerland, USA, Uruguay and Venezuela.

Finally, I wish to acknowledge the staff at the Computer Science Department of the University of Chile, as well as David Fuller of the Pontifical Catholic University of Chile, the organizing chairman of the 1990 conference.

Ricardo Baeza-Yates

Santiago de Chile
December 1991

Historical Overview

The International Conference of the Chilean Computer Science Society started more than 10 years ago as an ambitious project for developing computer science research in Chile. This conference has also provided a way to meet researchers from Latin America and the rest of the world.

During this time we have been sponsored by many international computer companies (or their representatives) such as IBM, Digital, NCR, Unysis, and Xerox, as well as institutions such as IEEE, ACM, CREI (Regional Centre for Computer Science Studies, Spain), and CLEI (Latin American Center for Studies on Informatics).

We strongly believe that our conference is one of the most important computer science events in Latin America, and has the highest technical level in the region. This belief is supported by several facts:

- A fully international program committee. Among the persons that have participated in the program commitee or as invited speaker, we can mention:

    Prof. Ernst Leiss, University of Houston, 1979, 1982, 1983, 1984, 1986, 1990.
    Prof. Daniel Berry, University of California at Los Angeles, 1982.
    Prof. Larry Kerschberg, University of South Carolina, 1982.
    Dr. David Smallberg, University of California at Los Angeles, 1982.
    Prof. Domenico Ferrari, University of California at Berkeley, 1983.
    Prof. J. Ian Munro, University of Waterloo, 1983, 1987, 1990.
    Prof. Eduardo Fernández, University of Miami, 1983.
    Prof. Raúl Camposano, Paderborn, 1983, 1991.
    Dr. Luis Felipe Cabrera, IBM Almaden Research Center, 1983, 1989, 1990.
    Dr. Agustín Araya, Corporate Technology Center, Santa Barbara, 1983, 1984, 1990.
    Prof. Gaston Gonnet, ETH Zurich, 1984, 1985, 1986, 1988, 1989.
    Prof. Alberto Mendelzon, University of Toronto, 1984, 1988, 1990.
    Dr. Ernest Chang, University of Victoria, 1984.
    Dr. Luis Osin, Centre for Educational Technology, Israel, 1984.
    Prof. Malcolm Atkinson, Glasgow University, 1985.
    Prof. Hector García-Molina, Princeton University, 1985, 1987, 1991.
    Dr. Philippe Flajolet, INRIA, France, 1986, 1987, 1989.
    Prof. Jurg Nievergelt, ETH Zurich, 1986.
    Dr. Edward Coffman Jr., Bell Laboratories, 1986.
    Prof. Richard Bartels, University of Waterloo, 1987.
    Dr. Jorge Vidart, ESLAI, Argentina, 1987, 1989, 1990.
    Prof. Jean Villemin, INRIA, France, 1987.
    Prof. D. Jensen, Carnegie Mellon Univ., 1987.
    Prof. A. L. Furtado, Catholic University of Rio de Janeiro, 1987.
    Prof. Ugo Montanari, Universita di Pisa, 1988.
    Prof. Don Batory, Univerity of Texas at Austin, 1988.
    Dr. Jorge Bocca, European Computer Research Center, Munich, 1988.
    Dr. Alfred Pietrasanta, IBM Hawthorne, 1988.
    Dr. Jorge Sanz, IBM Almaden, 1988.
    Prof. Hugo Scolnick, Universidad de Buenos Aires, 1988.
    Prof. Ken Sevcik, University of Toronto, 1988.

Prof. Brian Barsky, University of California at Berkeley, 1989.
Prof. Josep Diaz, Politechnic University of Catalunya, 1989.
Prof. Tony Marsland, University of Alberta, 1989.
Prof. Paulo Veloso, Catholic University of Rio de Janeiro, 1989.
Dr. Jean-Jacques Lévy, INRIA, France, 1989.
Prof. Joachim von zur Gathen, University of Toronto, 1990.
Prof. Samson Abramsky, Imperial College, London, 1990.
Prof. Pere Botella, Politechnic University of Catalunya, 1990.
Prof. C.C. Gotlieb, University of Toronto, 1990.
Prof. Dana Nau, University of Maryland, 1990.
Prof. Alberto Marchetti S., Universita La Sapienza, Roma, 1990.
Prof. Udi Manber, University of Arizona, 1991.
Prof. José Balcázar, Polytechnic University of Catalunya, Barcelona, 1991.
Dr. Francois Bancilhon, ALTAIR/INRIA, Paris, 1991.
Prof. Marcos R.S. Borges, Universidade Federal do Rio de Janeiro, 1991.
Prof. J.L. Encarnação, Zentrum füer Grafische Datenverarbeitung, Darmstadt, 1991.
Prof. Michael Langston, University of Tennessee, 1991.
Prof. Raphael Finkel, University of Kentucky, 1991.
Prof. Tom Maibaum, Imperial College, 1991.
Prof. Michael Robson, Australian National University, 1991.

- Current policy is that all accepted papers are written in English and are thoroughly reviewed by several referees (see Table 1). The high number of papers received in 1989 is because the conference was jointly organized with the XV Latin American Conference on Informatics.

Table 1. Statistics summary (research contributions).

Year	Program Committee	Papers Accepted	Language		
			English	Spanish	Portuguese
1979	4	17	7	10	-
1982	4	13	11	-	2
1983	4	11	9	2	-
1984	4	17	11	4	2
1985	6	10	5	5	-
1986	7	16	13	3	-
1987	9	19	15	4	-
1988	10	21	17	3	1
1989	8	37 of 103	31	4	2
1990	9	30 of 66	30	-	-
1991	11	35 of 85	35	-	-

- Submissions come from all parts of the world: North and South America, Europe, Asia and Australia (see Table 2). This year 85 papers were submitted from 19 countries and 4 continents. For 90% of the papers, three or more reviews were used. Based on those reviews, 35 papers were accepted as technical presentations (see Table 3).

Table 2. Geographical distribution of accepted papers.

Year	Chile	USA	Canada	Brasil	Argentina	France	UK	Others
1979	13	3	1	-	-	-	-	
1982	1	6	-	4	-	-	-	2 (Israel, Belgium)
1983	-	2	2	2	-	-	1	5 (Japan, Malaysia, Mexico, Spain, Taiwan)
1984	3	1	2	4	-	4	1	3 (Denmark, Israel, West Germany)
1985	6	4	-	-	-	-	1	-
1986	3	4	5	1	-	1	-	5 (Israel, Japan, Taiwan, Venezuela, West Germany)
1987	4	5	-	2	2	4	1	6 (Australia, Italia, Malaysia, Sweden, Venezuela(2))
1988	-	6	1	2	3	2	-	7 (Austria, Denmark, Korea, Spain(2), Sweden, West Germany)
1989	5	5	5	4	3	6	4	11 (Australia, Austria, Israel, Mexico, Spain(2), Sweden, Uruguay(3), Venezuela)
1990	3	8	2	6	6	2	1	6 (Cameroon, Italy(2), Mexico, Sweden, Venezuela)
1991	4	5	4	6	-	4	1	11 (Germany(3), Israel(4), Spain, Switzerland, Uruguay, Venezuela)

Table 3. Geographical distribution of papers for 1991.

Country	Submitted	Accepted	Country	Submitted	Accepted
Brazil	19	6	Spain	2	1
United States	9	5	Colombia	1	-
Mexico	8	-	Venezuela	1	1
Chile	7	4	Portugal	1	-
Argentina	6	-	Sweden	1	-
France	6	4	Switzerland	1	1
Canada	5	4	Malasya	1	-
Germany	4	3	South America	40	12
Israel	4	4	North America	22	9
Uruguay	3	1	Europe	18	10
Paraguay	3	-	Asia	5	4
United Kingdom	3	1	Total	85	35

Databases

OFFICE INFORMATION SYSTEMS ENGINEERING

José Palazzo M. de Oliveira
Duncan D. Alcoba Ruiz

Universidade Federal do Rio Grande do Sul
Instituto de Informática
Caixa Postal 15064
91501 Porto Alegre - RS
Brazil
E-mail: palazzo@vortex.ufrgs.br

ABSTRACT

The paper presents an engineering model for developing socio-technical systems such as office applications. This model is composed of a methodology for analysis of the office work based in the structure of their components, the Tasks, Activities and Actions Methodology (T.A.& A.). A view mechanism on objects of the database is employed to represent user transactions. The relationship between the concepts of T.A.& A. methodology, objects and database views on objects are described.

1. INTRODUCTION

The modeling of the reality into an conceptual model for the development of conventional data processing systems starts when the designer knows what part of the system will be materialized as automatic procedures. This means that the decision on what segment of the office work will be left to the human activities and what will be automated is previous to the software engineering specification process.

In conventional systems, as an inventory system, the starting point for the development is a decision taken by the organization and methods group on what parcel of the system will be automated. E.g., the sales would correspond to a manual update of the database, or it would be associated with the invoice printout and the data on the product might be obtained via an optical code bar scanner. This kind of modeling is a partial, and often very partial, modeling of the reality.

Office systems are socio-technical systems [Voss 86] which integrate human actions and automated procedures. Continuing improvement in computers system allows us to build more complex and closely tied interactions between the automated and human parcels of office work as a consequence of new human interfaces and more complex processing. This kind of system needs a comprehensive design methodology. However, the traditional methodologies used in software engineering are dedicated to the description and the development of the automated procedures, not for the description of a complete information system including the automated and the human parts of work. If this traditional modeling is accepted a big amount of information will be lost during the process. Worse, some important decisions about the automation of some parcel of the activities are taken without a clear statement of why this has happened.

Why are the actual limits of information systems modeling is so restricted? One of the first answers is that this kind of system is so complex that we are not able to create appropriate models. Now arrives the next question: Can we improve the modeling methodologies? The response seems to be YES if we are able to use new requirements collection and analysis tools and additionally to apply formal verification methods to help to develop the correct representation of the reality.

The difficulties found in systems analysis methodologies in terms of passing from reality to a conceptual model are well-known. On one hand this model must be validated by the users and, on the other, the same model must be clear and non-ambiguous for the systems analysts. In this context, an environment for the development of Office Information Systems (OIS) must be able to support alternative and equivalent representations in view of the difficulty to support these two conflicting needs with one single model.

From the reality to a working and reasonably reliable system a collection of techniques, tools and formalisms is needed. In an engineering environment the use of formal specifications to validate the design is an essential characteristic. The real problem to get a good system is:

> The reason why it is so hard to say what we want is that we do not really know what we want (at least not in a complex system, which is where the problems are). One way of discovering what we want is to draw up a formal specification, derive a program conforming to it, and run it. (...) it is necessary to run the programs, *not to debug the programs, but to debug the specifications* - M. H.. van Emden, in [Denning 89].

The purpose of our research is to develop both a conceptual model and an environment for the analysis, design and implementation of systems including human tasks in offices as an integrated part of the computerized environment.

In section the relations between net modeling, action of the user and the automated system are described; in section a representation of office work derived from the concepts of hierarchical decomposition of Structured Analysis [DeMarco 78] is shown; in section the use of Pr-T nets as a tool to represent the dynamics of the systems is described; and finally in section the correspondence between the representation of office work and the database schema is derived. This integration generates a conceptual model able to represent a complete environment in which not only the computerized but also the human actions are described.

2. ENGINEERING OF AN OFFICE SYSTEM

The full engineering cycle of a office system consists of five phases:
- requirement analysis,

- T.A.& A. modeling,
- model formalization by Pr-T nets,
- system synthesis,
- system acceptance.

Figure1 illustrates graphically the stages and processes.

The purpose of *requirement analysis* is to catalog the characteristics and aspirations of the users. As a result, it has a collection of data and functions.

The T.A.& A. *modeling* (section) aims to organize and to consolidate the data and functions found in the analysis stage of requirements and to produce a model of reality. This model is substantiated by the contextual diagram (task), by the data flow diagram (DFD level 1) of activities and respective functional primitives, and by the description of the data obtained in consolidating the actions, mainly the result of the study of documents manipulated in the office environment. With these (semiformal) specifications, *model validation* is performed together with the user.

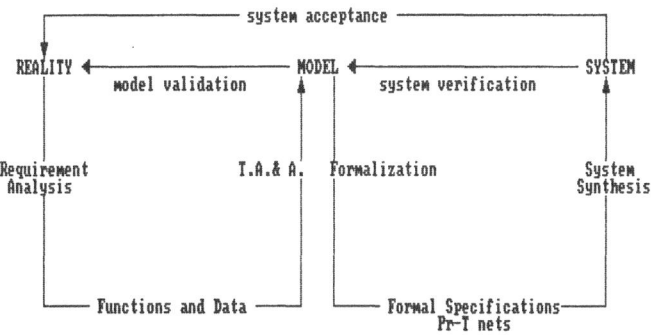

Fig. 1. Full Cycle in the Engineering of a System

In this stage it is possible to evaluate the degree of structuring of each activity which is classified according to three categories:
- automated;
  * self performable;
  * with user interaction;
- assisted;
- helped.

An automated and self performable activity is one whose formal specification in a Pr-T net (section 4) is complete, and independent from user interaction. It has the greatest degree of structuring and will happen each time it is enabled. This enabling may depends on system timers (activities with deadline). An example of this kind of activity is the printing of delayed devolution of cars in an renting agency.

An automated activity with user interaction is one whose formal specification is complete but the execution depends on the interaction with the user. In other words, modeling in Pr-T nets defines the types of data which the user must feed into the activity, when enabled, for it to take place. An example is the rent of a car, the user must *decide* from a list of available cars what car he or she would like to rent after this decisitio the system will generate a rental form.

An assisted activity is one whose formal specification is complete, but in which the user has different alternatives of methods and, thus, can produce different results with the same set of objects. The alternatives available to the user are known in the modeling of an application. An example is the alternatives for a rental: weekend rate, free mileage or special rates. Each alternative corresponds to a method.

A helped activity is an activity whose formalization is incomplete. The user is free to treat the objects available to him. It has the least degree of structuring. The decision-making process is a typical example of this kind of activity. In the case of a leasing different alternatives may be evaluated by the user using a decision support system based in a spreadsheet model.

At the end of this stage the formal specification of all of the office application is compleated. In this specification, the definition of the activities which will be automated and which objects will be electronically stored has not yet been made.

The purpose of the stage of synthesis is to select, specify and implement the automated part of the application. For this purpose, the synthesis is the decision regarding which objects will be electronically stored, and which will remain on paper. In other words, which documents must, for some reason, retain physical existence (legal requirements) or subsets which have not been automated due to economic reasons.

The next step in the modeling process is to delimit the set of activities (transitions) which should be automated in the Pr-T net of the application, since they possess entry and exit objects to be stored electronically. It should be observed there will be activities with electronically stored objects and material (paper) objects. This means that, in the Pr-T sub-net corresponding to system implementation, some activities may be less structured. For this step some net rules have being derived to help the decision.

The final step of synthesis is to describe the objects to be stored electronically in the DDL of the data base and describe the activities to be implemented as views on the objects. The activities which continue being automated and self performable even in the implementation sub-net Pr-T, will not have a presentation. The other activities will be defined with presentation to enable easier interaction with the user.

When the system has been implemented, it is verified, with the user, against the model produced by the T.A.& A. modeling. Finally there is the acceptance process of the implemented system by the user. The validation, verification and acceptance processes will permit possible corrections of the model and the system.

3. T.A.& A. METHODOLOGY

The development cycle of an information system begins with the requirement collection, assembled by the users and the system's analysts jointly. The second phase is the requirement organization, these two phases together compose the requirement analysis. This step gives origin to an informal or semi-formal system specification, where the manipulated objects and the possible transactions on these objects are identified.

The characteristics of OIS that motivate the proposal of a new methodology are
- emphasis on activities performed;

- the occurrence of structured and less-structured activities;
- coexistence of human activities and automated activities;
- extremely dynamic systems.

The T.A.& A. [Hoppen 88] methodology is used for this requirement analysis. It unfolds the office analysis in three basic hierarchical levels: the tasks, the activities and the actions. Office entities like documents, books, messages and texts are all perceived as objects.

The T.A.& A. methodology is based on two previous studies: Structured Analysis [DeMarco 78] and Distributed Systems Design [Santos 86]. The justification for choosing these studies as a point of departure in defining an OIS analysis methodology is related to the characteristic of these types of systems: integration of human and automated procedures. The concept of decomposition found in Structured Analysis presents a strong correlation with the perception of office work by the system users. On the other hand, the OIS are, in themselves, distributed systems, since they consist of different persons, working in different places, interacting among themselves and with the OIS through workstations.

The problem in using the traditional top-down data flow decomposition to analyze office work is the lack of certainty regarding the number of levels required and the lack of significance in the real world of each model level. In the structured analysis, the criterion of how many levels the decomposition takes is a consequence of the system analyst's perception.

When the T.A.& A. methodology was developed, the above mentioned hierarchical decomposition criteria were used in case studies and three levels were identified, each one representing a description level of the reality: the level of tasks, the level of activities and the level of actions.

A *Task* is an office application to be modeled. It has a well-defined significance and consolidates a group of activities which, together, can produce a specified result. In the structured analysis, it corresponds to the contextual diagram. A rent-a-car service is a typical example.

An *Activity* is an interaction between the user and the application, it represents an user's transaction. An activity has aggregate semantics, it means the transformations of elementary data should be executed in a limited time period. All changes of elementary data should be carried out in a step perceived by an external observer as a single transaction. It is similar to a process in Data Flow Diagram (DFD): the objects of the application correspond to the data deposits. The difference is in the temporal aspect of the activity. It, in fact, corresponds to a function or to a consolidation of functions which represent the users interaction with the application system, and the corresponding functional primitives. It is composed of (1) an ordered set of actions and (2) a pre and post-execution conditions set. The resulting diagram is equivalent to a first level DFD. The "rent-a-car" or the "return-a-car" transaction are examples.

Actions are elementary changes of data, which possess external significance. From the actions, it is possible to identify the types of data of the application and their semantics. For instance, a client's change of address.

An OIS schema consists of the description of the office objects and the office activities. The activities are performed on the objects. At each workstation, one or more activities of an application and activities of a set of applications can be carried out.

As a result, a Contextual Diagram (CD) of the task, some DFD to represent the activities, the corresponding functional primitives and the description of data obtained by consolidation of actions are obtained. This phase is supported by a software tool running on an IBM AT compatible computer that assist the requirements collection and organization phase and produces as output a compleat system description.

Up to this stage in the OIS modeling it has not yet been defined what parcel of the office work will be implemented by computer programs: this corresponds to the requirement of a conceptual model of the application [ISO 82]. The step of defining what portion will be implemented on the computer corresponds to the synthesis of the application and will be discussed in section .

4. MODELING WITH PR-T NETS

There are two main aspects in office modeling: the application structure and the application dynamics. This modeling is difficult due to the close interaction between the user and the automated system, and the complexity of the information which flows in offices. More sophisticated support tools and models are required to model the tasks of an office environment. Much research has been done on methodologies to model both the static properties (structure) and dynamic properties (behavior), of Information Systems [Bravoco 85]. Some methodologies are available to model the system dynamics and the static part of industrial systems [Geoffrion 87]. In offices, the less concrete nature of the work performed points toward greater difficulty in modeling applications effectively.

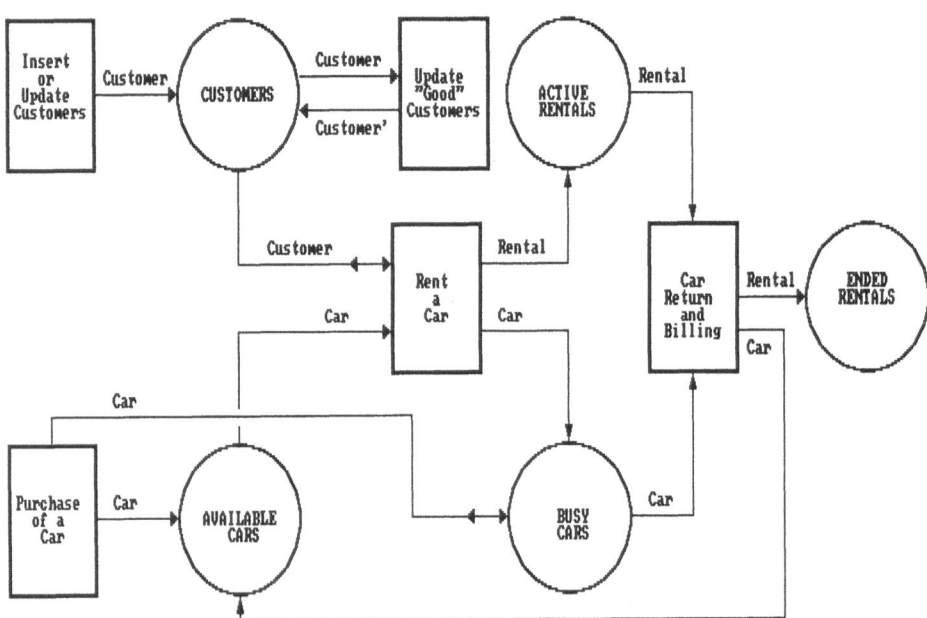

Fig. 2. Rent-a-Car Service modeling in Pr-T nets

Additionally to the activities, the flow control process among this activities must be modeled. The activities executed on the objects are controlled by the arrival of the objects at a workstation, fulfilling certain requirements which enable the activity.

One consequence of including information about the dynamic aspects of office work in the conceptual schema is the possibility of the introduction of automated procedures executing the succession and the control of office work. GOFOR [Richter 87] presents a proposal of a pattern for modeling office applications. In that work various aspects to be taken into account in modeling are described, and a scheme is proposed on how to model office activities. The tool suggested is Predicate-Transition nets (Pr-T nets) [Genrich 87], a class of Petri nets.

Petri nets are suitable to represent asynchronous and discrete tasks since they render feasible two important aspirations in systems modeling: an convenient graphic representation, and a strong formal foundation. We have decided to use Pr-T nets to represent the dynamics of office applications because they allow the graphical representation of more information on the applications than the Petri nets.

A Pr-T net is composed of predicates, graphically represented by circles, transitions represented by rectangles and branches which connect predicates to transitions and vice-versa[1]. A predicate cannot be connected directly to another predicate, nor can a transition be connected directly to another transition. Objects flow through the net. The types of objects present in the net are defined by the predicates. In other words, a predicate defines a class of objects: only objects belonging to that class can enter or exit a predicate (corresponding to the data deposit in the DFD).

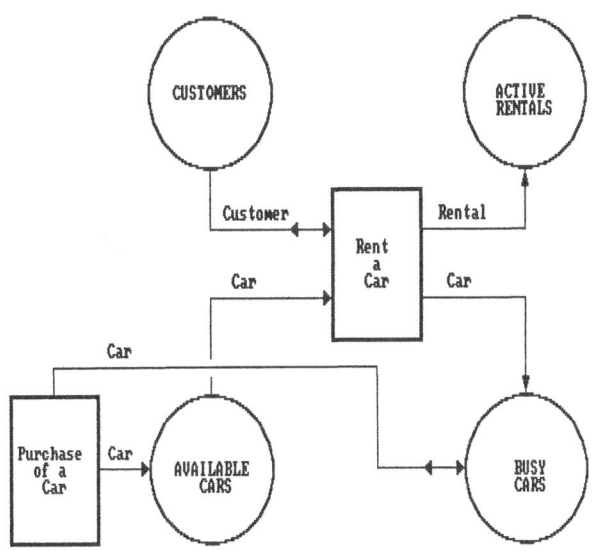

Fig. 3. Examples of Pr-T nets branches

The transitions define the rules that the objects must satisfy to flow through the net and the transformations to be performed on the objects. The arcs between predicates and transitions are called branches, the arcs which go from the predicates to the transition being called entry branches, and those going from the transition to predicates, exit branches. The

---

1 For a more complete description of Petri Nets see [Petri 80], for Predicate-Transition Nets see [Genrich 87].

branches can also be of two types: altering and restoring. A branch is altering when the object really flows through the branch: if it is an entry branch, the object is consumed; if it is an exit, the object is generated. A branch is restoring when it only finds the presence (if an entry) or the absence (if an exit) of the object in the predicate. For a transition to occur, it is necessary that object occurrences be present in the entry predicates and absent in the exit predicates. Figure 2 shows a Pr-T net diagram that models a Rent-a-Car application.

Figure 3 shows a Pr-T net diagram with the four types of branches: from AVAILABLE CARS to Rent-a-Car, altering entry; from CUSTOMERS to Rent-a-Car, restoring entry; from Rent-a-Car to BUSY CARS and from Purchase-of-a-Car to AVAILABLE CARS, altering exit; from Purchase-of-a-Car to BUSY CARS, restoring exit.

Furthermore, each transition is associated to a formula and a term. The transition formula defines the integrity constraints to be satisfied by the objects, so that the transition may occur: the transition be enabled. The assignment of a transition specifies what transformations should be made on the entry objects to produce the exit objects. Figure 4 shows an example of condition and assignment of a transition.

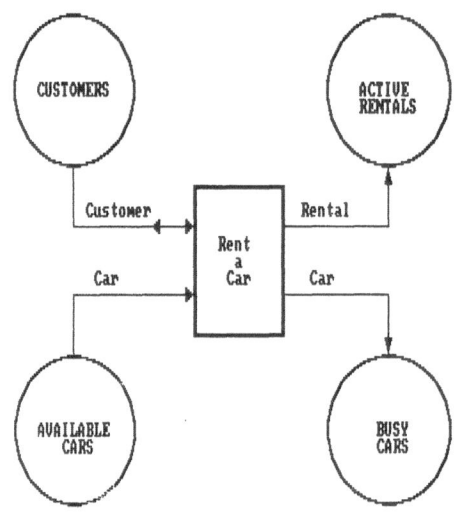

```
condition (Rent-a-Car) => Customer.Cust-Good = "YES"

assignment (Rent-a-Car) => Rental.Cust# := Customer.Cust#
                           Rental.Car# := Car.Car#
                           Rental.Miles-Exit := <ue>
                           Rental.Insurance := <ue>
                           Rental.Sched-Return-Date := <ue>
                           Rental.Deposit := <ue>
                           Car.Actual-Miles := <ue>

       where <ue> means an user interaction, with the
       transition, to get some data, and Cust#, Car#,
       Miles-Exit, Insurance, Sched-Return-Date, Deposit
       and Actual-Miles are attributes of the predicates'
       tuples.
```

Fig. 4. Example of condition and assignment of a transition

In the Pr-T net nomenclature, a transition is enabled and may occur if: (1) its condition returns the true logical value; (2) the occurrences of entry predicates are present (keys of the objects specified by the user); and (3) the occurrences of the exit predicates are absent. In the example in Figure 4, transition Rent-a-Car is enabled when there is the selected (by Cust#) occurrence on CUSTOMERS in which the value of attribute Cust-Good is equal to "YES", there is the selected (by Car#) occurrence on AVAILABLE CARS, there are no occurrences on BUSY CARS with the same value for the key attribute Car#, and there are no occurrences on ACTIVE RENTALS in which the key values (Cust# and Car#) are the selected by the user.

When a transition is triggered the assignment specifies the changes to be made in the objects related to view. Each assignment also specifies which data are obtained from the user, and which data result from the operation on other fields. In the same example of fig.4, the transition assignment defines how to produce the correspondent occurrences on predicates ACTIVE RENTALS and BUSY CARS, when it occurs: Rental.Cust# receives Customer.Cust#; Rental.Car# receives Car.Car#; Rental.Miles-Exit, Rental.Insurance, Rental.Sched-Return-Date, and Rental.Deposit receive values supplied by the user; finally, Car.Actual-Miles receives Rental.Miles-Exit. The transitions which do not depend on user data, when enabled, occur automatically: they correspond to the completely automated activities (they are triggers for the application system).

An important feature of the Pr-T nets is that the possible state of enabled transition, which requires obtaining data from the user, does not imply its occurrence. The triggering of a transition occurs only on the occasion of user-system interaction. In other words, the model in Pr-T nets controls the correct flow of information, but the information really flows (a transition is fired) in this case by decision of the user.

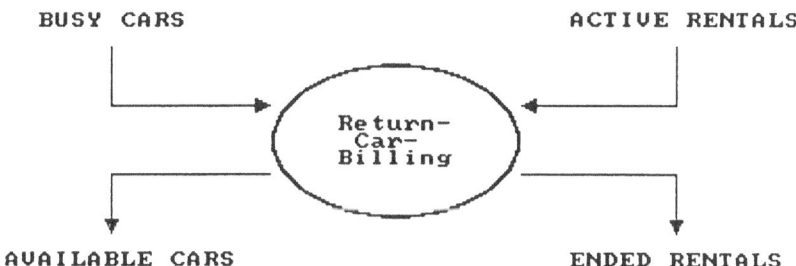

Fig. 5. DeMarco's D.F.D. representation

In database data definition language, predicates are defined as object types. The transitions are defined as views on the objects. Views define the objects involved in each activity and include the specifications in Pr-T nets.

The DFD process Car-Return-Billing (fig. 6) is formalized by Car Return and Billing transition (fig. 6 (a)). The condition (fig. 6 (b)) and the assignment (fig. 6 (c)) complete the description of the transition. Note that there is a natural mapping of a DFD sub-diagram to Pr-T subnet. The restriction is the obligation of the DFD process to represent a complete and consistent interaction user-application: one transaction.

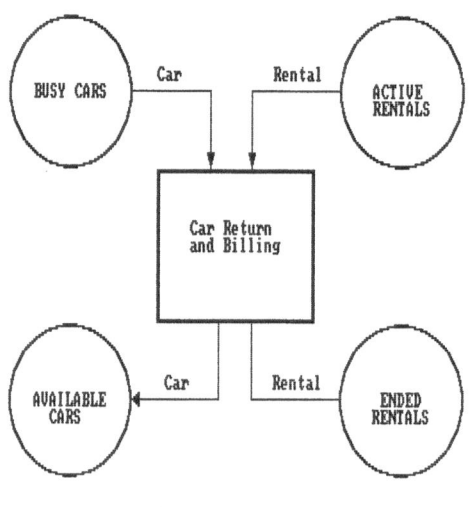

(a) Pr-T net representation

```
condition (Car Return and Billing) =>   Rental.Cust# = ⟨ue⟩
                                         Rental.Car# = ⟨ue⟩
                                         Rental.Car# = Car.Car#
```

(b) Pr-T net transition condition

```
assignment (Car Return and Billing) =>   Rental.Return-Date := ⟨ue⟩
                                          Rental.Return-Miles := ⟨ue⟩
                                          Rental.Fuel-Gallons := ⟨ue⟩
                                          Rental.Credit-Card := ⟨ue⟩
```

(c) Pr-T net transition assignment

Fig. 6. Pr-T net representation

5. VIEWS AND OBJECTS

The dominant characteristic of the object paradigm is the fact that the application objects can only be manipulated by the methods associated to them - an object is seen by what can be done on it, and not by its structural definition. This agrees with data-flow oriented methods, where emphasis on modeling is on the processes executed not on the data manipulated.

The identification of application objects is done mainly by the study of documents (in a broad sense: forms, texts, guides, invoices), existing in the environment, and of the possibly already existing magnetic files. Our approach is equivalent to the first specification stage of one office task the collection of the OTM project [Lochovsky 88]. The representation of objects in the data definition language (DDL) aggregates its semantics. All operations and integrity constraints are defined together with the definition of the object structure. This aggregated semantics corresponds to the static properties of the objects; properties which the object must satisfy permanently.

The dynamic application properties are represented by views on the objects. The concept of view used here comes from data base. The user's interaction with the application is always performed through a view. Therefore, it represents the dynamic properties of the application - its transactions. Through the views the user employs object-associated methods: figure 7.

The definition of a view in DDL relates the objects to be manipulated by the user, specifies the transaction semantics (its behavioral restrictions), and defines its most convenient presentation. Presentation is a component of object semantics. Different presentations associated to the same object, or to the same set of objects, correspond to different forms of manipulating the objects [Ruiz 87].

Information flow in the office is represented, in modeling, by the DFD (level 1) of activities. Thus, the same object is manipulated sequentially by different employees. Each presentation is adapted to the particular form of work being performed. The presentation shows only the obligatory fields in the view, enables the subset of actions of the object(s), and emphasizes the most significant information using formatting rules.

----- Modeling -----		---- Synthesis ----	
	---- Formalization ----		
User Perception	T.A.& A.	Pr-T Nets	DL
Application	Task	Pr-T Model	Schema
Transaction	Activity	Transition	View
Field fill-in	Action	Assignment	Method
Document	Object	Condition	Object

Fig. 7. Interrelationship between description levels

6. CONCLUSION

The engineering method presented is centered on the application dynamics, a point to be emphasized in Office Information Systems. The use of Pr-T nets provides the support for the representation of these dynamics. The three levels of representation in the methodology, each with its own meaning, give greater precision and simplify the specification debugging process. Each task corresponds to an application to be modeled.

Therefore, the task isolates a sub-set of the reality to be analyzed. Activities, represented by views, correspond to user transactions of the application. Actions are the transformations of the fields performed by the users. The data structures, the objects, are the predicates of the Pr-T nets application model.

The main contribution of the present research is the mapping between those various contexts: user's perception, T.A.& A. methodology, Pr-T nets and DDL of the object-oriented support system. This mapping makes the office applications development process simpler, more direct and allows the validation of this process through the formal foundation offered by Pr-T nets.

At present, some CASE tools are operational; requirement collection and analysis. There is a data model of objects (and their methods), views on the objects (with specifications of the transition conditions and assignments) and the respective presentations, this definitions are the products of two M.Sc. thesis. The requirements collection and analysis process is under evaluation as another M.Sc. thesis. The object-oriented approach to model office tasks is the theme of an Phd dissertation. The formal specification of the analysis method is the subject of a second Ph.d. dissertation. The project has consumed an estimate amount of five persons years in the last three years.

At the present stage we are evaluating the concepts in real world cases as a shared work developed by the Graduate Program in Computer Science and the Graduate Program in Management at the Universidade Federal do Rio Grande do Sul, Brazil.

REFERENCES

[Bravoco 85] A.M. Bravoco, "A Methodology to Model the Dynamic Structure of an Organization", Information Systems, 10(3), Pergamon Press, mar 85. pp 299-317.

[DeMarco 78] T. DeMarco, Structured Analysis and System Specification. New York, Yourdon Inc., 1978.

[Denning 89] P.J. Denning ed., "A Debate on Teaching Computing Science", Communications of the ACM, dec 89, v 32, n 12, p. 1397-1414.

[Genrich 87] H. Genrich. "Predicate-Transition Nets". in W. Brauer et alii (eds.) Petri Nets: Central Models and Their Properties. Advances in Petri Nets 1986, Part I. Lecture Notes in Computer Science 254, Springer, Berlin-Heidelberg, 1987. pp 207-47.

[Geoffrion 87] A.M. Geoffrion, "An Introduction to Structured Modeling", Management Science, USA, 33(5), may 1987. pp 547-588.

[Hoppen 88] N. Hoppen, J. Palazzo Oliveira & L.M.R. Lima, "Metodologia para a Modelagem de Escritório Baseada no Nível de Estruturaçao das Atividades". In: Proceedings of the XII reuniao Anual da Associaçao dos Programas de Pós-graduaçao em Administraçao, Natal, RN, Brazil, Sep. 26-28, 1988, p 247-263.

[ISO 82] J.J. van Griethuysen (ed.). Concepts and Terminology for the Conceptual Schema and the Information Base. Publication Number ISO/TC97/SC5-N695, ANSI, New York, 1982.

[Lochovsky 88] F.R. Lochovsky, et alii. "OTM: Specifying Office Tasks", in Proceedings of COIS88 - Conference on Office Information Systems, 1988, pp 46-54.

[**Petri 80**] C.A. Petri. "Introduction to General Net Theory", in Net Theory and Applications, Ed. W. Brauer, Springer Verlag, 1980.

[**Richter 81**] G. Richter. "IML - Inscribed Nets for Modeling Text Processing and Data(Base) Management Systems", in Proceedings of VLDB'81, Cannes, France, 1981. pp363-375.

[**Richter 87**] G. Richter, et alii. Generic Office Frame of Reference: GOFOR. GMD, St. Augustin, F. R. Germany, 1987. (Esprit Project 56: Functional Analysis of Office Requirements).

[**Ruiz 87**] Ruiz, D.D.A. Interface de Usuario para Manipulaçao de Formulários Eletrônicos. Porto Alegre, Brasil, CPGCC da UFRGS, 1987. (M.Sc. Dissertation) .

[**Santos 86**] S.A. Santos, J.P.M. Oliveira, M. Tazza. "Projeto de Sistemas Distribuídos: uma Soluçao Integrada", in Anais do XIX Congresso Nacional de Informática, Rio de Janeiro, Brazil, SUCESU, 1986. pp 245-54.

[**Tsichritzis 82**] D. Tsichritzis. "Form Management". Communications of the ACM 25(7), July 1982, pp 453-78.

[**Voss 86**] K. Voss, "Nets in Office Automation", in Advanced Course on Petri Nets, Bad Honnef, Germany, 8-19 Sep. 86, paper n 6.

UPDATE LANGUAGES vs. QUERY LANGUAGES

R. Asher Hasson and Johann A. Makowsky

Department of Computer Science
Technion - Israel Institute of Technology
Haifa 32000, Israel

INTRODUCTION

Two kinds of basic operations can be performed on a database: *update* it, i.e. modify the data values stored in it, and *query* it, i.e. ask questions about its data value. In this work we deal with update and query languages for the *relational database model*, introduced by Codd in [1]. Some query languages were developed since the origin of this model, e.g. the *first–order relational calculus* and the *relational algebra*. A precise concept of *completeness*, based on computability, for relational query languages was defined by Chandra and Harel in [2]. Updates in the relational database model were considered systematically as a research topic in [3]. Restructuring of relational databases was considered in [4, 5]. In [6, 7] a family of relational update languages was defined. The languages introduced in [6, 7] are *complete* update languages (deterministic and non–deterministic). By completeness it follows that these languages are also capable of expressing all computable queries, as defined in [2]. However, the constructs chosen in [7] do not necessarily reflect this, but capture the essence of update operations. The completeness proof in [7] is very detailed and built from scratch.

In this paper, we focus the attention on complete query languages And update languages for relational databases. We first observe a strong relationship between queries and updates, namely that every update consists ultimately of computing some queries and then performing a global replacement operation. This is spelled out precisely in the theorem 8. We use this observation to introduce a new way of proving completeness of update languages in any data model, for which complete query languages were introduced before. It consists in proving that all computable queries and the global simultaneous replacement operation are expressible in the update language. If a complete query language is available, this is done easily by structural induction over its constructs. Hence, it allows us also to shorten *completeness proofs of update languages* considerably by avoiding the coding of Turing machine capabilities and Gödel numbers, as in [7].

COMPUTER SCIENCE, Edited by R. Baeza-Yates
and U. Manber, Plenum Press, New York, 1992

The method described above suggests a simple way of extending a complete query language into a complete update language. This is conceptually very transparent, but introduces a basic construct (the global simultaneous replacement) which may have arbitrary high computational complexity, that is, the implementation of such construct is very expensive due to its high resources requirements.

In [3] it is argued that updates (in the relational model) cannot be viewed as just being queries in relational calculus augmented by tuple assignment. We agree with [3], but we think that this remark is misleading. Our view is that updates are computable queries followed by a global simultaneous replacement operator for the interpretation of relations. The power of this observation lies in its applicability to other data models, such as, the complex object data model [8, 9], the logical data model [10], the hierarchical model based on directories [11, 12], etc.

The rest of this paper is organized as follows. In the following section relational databases are defined, we also define the concepts of computable queries and updates, their interrelations, finally, we define completeness criteria for relational database languages. Then we describe deterministic languages that satisfy these criteria, and we state and show theorems about the completeness of those languages. Next, we describe a non–deterministic complete update language. Finally, in the last section we present our conclusions and discuss some possible extensions and further research.

PRELIMINARIES

We start by reviewing some basic definitions, such as *relational databases, (deterministic/non–deterministic) computable queries and updates*. Then we introduce fundamental concepts relating updates and queries. Finally, we define completeness criteria for relational (query/update) languages.

Relational Databases

Let U denote an infinity, countable and nonempty set, called the *universal domain*. Let $D \subset U$ be finite and nonempty, we call D the *domain*. Let $AS = \{A_1, A_2, \ldots\}$ be a set of *attributes*, such that $U \cap AS = \emptyset$.

1 Definitions

A **relation scheme** *(with domain D) RS_i is a finite set of attributes. The arity or rank a_i of RS_i is its cardinality, i.e. the number of attributes. An* **instance** *over a relation scheme RS_i is a subset of D^{a_i}. The set of instances over a relation scheme RS_i is denoted by $inst(RS_i)$. A* **tuple** *over a relation scheme RS_i is a mapping from RS_i into D.*[1]

A **relational database schema** *(with domain D)*[2] *DS is a finite set of relation schemes. An* **instance** *I over a relational database schema DS is a mapping from DS such that for each RS_i in DS, $I(RS_i)$ is an instance over RS_i. The set of instances over a relational database schema DS is denoted by inst(DS).*

---

[1]In the following sections we will relax this definition allowing also variables as values of some attributes in a tuple.

[2]From now on, every relation scheme and relational database schema will have domain D, unless otherwise stated.

C–genericity

We note that an update is understood like any change made to some instance of certain database schema, hence, also structural changes (restructuring of databases) are considered as updates (in those cases the input and output schemas of the update are different). The difference between updates and queries can be viewed primarily in the interpretation of the results, rather than in the computation involved. Therefore, to define *computable updates*, we basically start from *computable queries*. The precise relationship between queries and updates will be given in the lemma 6. For updates (queries) we require that instances over a fixed database schema be mapped to instances over another fixed database (relation) schema, and that constants be essentially viewed as uninterpreted, although it is allowed for a finite number of constants to be interpreted. Lastly, we require that the result of a query, or an update, should be independent of the representation of the data in a database, i.e. the implementation of a particular database should no affect the result of a given query or update. The following fundamental property, called *C–genericity*, captures the consistency criterion described above [2, 13, 11, 3].

2 Definitions

Let C be a finite set of constants in D. Let h be a permutation of D leaving C invariant, i.e. a bijection over D which is the identity on C. Let DS be a relational database schema. Let SCH be a relation scheme or a relational database schema.

1. *A mapping φ from inst(DS) to inst(SCH) is **C–generic** if φ commutes with every h, i.e., for every $I \in inst(DS)$ we have $\varphi(h(I)) = h(\varphi(I))$.*

2. *A subset Γ of inst(DS) × inst(SCH) is **C–generic** if for every h we have $(I, J) \in \Gamma$ iff $(h(I), h(J)) \in \Gamma$.*

Computable Queries and Updates

Next, we define the notions of (non–deterministic) computable queries, deterministic computable queries, (non–deterministic) computable updates and deterministic computable updates. We have to remark that the concept of computable query from [2] corresponds to our *deterministic* computable query.

3 Definitions *Let DS, $DS^{\#}$ be relational database schemas. Let RS_k be a relation scheme. Let C be a finite set of constants in D.*

1. *A **deterministic computable query** (from DS to RS_k) is a partial recursive function from inst(DS) to inst(RS_k) which is C–generic for some finite C.*

2. *A (**non–deterministic**) **computable query** (from DS to RS_k) is a recursive enumerable, C–generic subset of inst(DS) × inst(RS_k), for some finite C.*

3. *A **deterministic computable update** (from DS to $DS^{\#}$) is a mapping from inst(DS) to inst($DS^{\#}$) which is partial recursive and C–generic for some finite C.*

4. *A (**non–deterministic**) **computable update** (from DS to $DS^{\#}$) is a recursive enumerable, C–generic subset of inst(DS) × inst($DS^{\#}$), for some finite C.*

In the traditional database systems, the non–determinism in queries or in updates is not permitted, but it arises in many applications in a natural way. Consider, for example, the query: "Find a participant in the Eleventh Conference of the Chilean

Computer Science Society that also participated in the Tenth Conference." Without surprises there should be different answers (assuming that some persons satisfy both conditions). We now illustrate the notions defined above with several examples:

4 Examples

1. *Any query expressed in the relational algebra is a deterministic computable query.*

2. *Let r_1, r_2 be two instances over a given relational schema. The query that computes $r_1 \vee r_2$ (whose meaning is to non–deterministically choose r_1 or r_2 as its result) is a non–deterministic computable query.*

3. *The transformation "change the contents of R_1 by the contents of R_2, and let unchanged the rest of the relations", is a deterministic computable update.*

4. *The transformation "add a tuple composed by randomly selected new values to R_1, and let unchanged the rest of the relations", is a non–deterministic computable update.*

Using all the kinds of transformations (queries or updates) defined before, we now define four classes of transformations, that will be used in the last subsection to introduce completeness criteria for relational database languages.

5 Definitions

1. *The class **DQ (DU)** corresponds to all the relational database transformations that are deterministic computable queries (updates).*

2. *The class **NDQ (NDU)** corresponds to all the relational database transformations that are (non–deterministic) computable queries (updates).*

Decomposition of Updates

Note that the results of queries are always relations. On the other hand, an update returns an instance of some relational database schema. The above is formalized by the next lemma (which can be derived straightforwardly from the respective definitions).

6 Lemma (Updates Normal Form)

Let DS, DS' be two relational database schemas: $DS = \{RS_1, \ldots, RS_n\}$ and $DS' = \{RS'_1, \ldots, RS'_m\}$. Let t be a (deterministic/non–deterministic) computable update from $inst(DS)$ to $inst(DS')$. For every update t there exist m (deterministic/non-deterministic) computable queries $q_1, \ldots, q_m$ such that for every instance $I = (O_1, \ldots, O_n)$ the result of the update is

$$t(I) = I' = (O'_1, \ldots, O'_m) = (q_1(I) \ldots, q_m(I)).$$

In other words, the lemma says that if I is the result of any deterministic (non–deterministic) computable update, then I consists of a tuple of results of deterministic (non–deterministic) computable queries.

We define next a construct for *global simultaneous replacement*. This construct, jointly with the above lemma, gives us a powerful theorem, which shows the essential difference between updates and queries.

7 Definition (Global Simultaneous Replacement)

The next abstract operator receives two arguments, a relational database instance I and a vector with an even number of components.

Syntax: *$Replace_I(R_1, q_1, \ldots, R_m, q_m)$.*

Semantics: *compute simultaneously the queries $q_1, \ldots, q_m$ over the instance I, and then assign those results simultaneously into the relation schemes $R_1, \ldots, R_m$, respectively.*

Note that the set $J = \{R_1, \ldots, R_m\}$ can be regarded as a database instance (of not neccesarily the same database schema of I).

8 Theorem (Update Computation)

Every (deterministic/non–deterministic) computable update can be computed as a finite number of (deterministic/non–deterministic) computable queries, whose results are simultaneously computed and assigned to the components of the output relational database schema.

Proof: From the lemma 6 (*updates normal form*), we can decompose an update as a tuple of queries. Therefore, using such queries we construct the vector which is the argument of the abstract operator defined above (*global simultaneous replacement*), and then we apply it (consider that I is an instance of DS and J is an instance of DS'). □

Query and Update Languages

A *relational database language* L consists of a *set of expressions* E, and a *meaning function* (or *effect*) M, such that for any expression $e \in E$ and for any instance I of some relational database schema DS, the effect or meaning of e is either undefined, or is a relation (or an instance of some relational database schema, in the case of an update). We say that L *defines* the transformation t if there is some expression $e \in E$ whose meaning is equivalent to t. Following, we define some completeness criteria for query and update languages.

9 Definition (Completeness Criteria)

Let L be a relational database language. L is **deterministic query complete (query complete, deterministic update complete, update complete)** *if it defines exactly all the members of the class DQ (NDQ, DU, NDU).*

In the following sections we will describe several relational database languages that fulfill the above completeness criteria. In the next section we focus the attention on deterministic languages. Non–deterministic languages are studied in section 4.

DETERMINISTIC LANGUAGES

First, we define the languages QL [2] and UL, and then we describe the language detTL [7]. Secondly, we give some results about the completeness of those languages.

The Language QL

In the sequel we describe briefly the language QL (for a more formal and complete presentation of QL, see [2]). The basic operations of QL are the equality, complementation, intersection, a test for emptiness, and simplified versions of projection and cartesian product.

10 Definition(Syntax)
- $y_1, y_2, \ldots$ are variables in QL.
- The terms of QL are defined inductively in the following way:
    1. **E** is a term, and for $i \geq 1$, **rel**$_i$ and **y**$_i$ are terms.

2. For any terms e_1 and e_2, $(e_1 \cap e_2), (\neg e_1), (e_1 \downarrow), (e_1 \uparrow)$, and $(e_1 \sim)$ are terms.

- The set of programs of QL is defined inductively the following way:
  1. $y_i \leftarrow e$ is a program for a term e and a variable y_i.
  2. For programs P_1 and P_2 and some variable y_i

$$(\mathbf{P_1}; \mathbf{P_2}) \quad \text{and} \quad \text{while } \mathbf{y_i} \text{ do } \mathbf{P_1}$$

  are programs.

Note that a variable in QL can hold a relation of arbitrary arity, i.e. the variables are untyped. Following, we define, informally, the semantics of QL.

11 Definition(Semantics)

The term E is a fixed relation (the equality), given by $E = \{(a, a)/a \in D\}$. The value of rel_i is given by $I(RS_i)$ (where I is an instance of the input database schema) if RS_i is in the database schema, otherwise rel_i is defined to be the empty relation. The operators $\cap, \neg, \downarrow, \uparrow, \sim$ mean intersection, complementation, projection out of the first coordinate (i.e. projection of all components except of the first one), projection in on the right (i.e. extension of the relation by one last component), and the exchange of the two rightmost components of the tuples, respectively. The programs in QL act in the natural way (i.e. assignment, composition, and a while–loop). The result of a program is defined to be the value of the variable y_1 if the program terminates, otherwise it is undefined.

The Language UL

The language UL is defined as a superset of QL. The only construct that is added to the language is the *global simultaneous replacement* (see definition 7), that is, an operator that receives an unbounded number of pairs *(relation scheme, QL program)* and an instance I over a database schema DS. The semantics of this construct is defined in the following manner: execute in parallel all the QL programs over I, and then replace their results simultaneously into the given, respective, relation schemes.

The Language detTL

In this subsection we describe concisely the language detTL (see [7] for a more detailed description). First, we have to define some auxiliary concepts. We assume the existence of an infinite set V of symbols called *variables*, these variables range over D. Let DS be a database schema. A condition over DS is a conjunction of basic formulas of the forms $RS_i(s), \neg RS_i(s), x = y, x \neq y$, where RS_i is in DS, s is a tuple (that may contain variables), and x, y are constants or variables.

Next, we define the concepts of parameterized program (p–program) and program. Informally, p–programs are programs with variables not bound to any condition.

12 Definition (P–programs)

Let DS be a database schema, let RS_k be a relation schema in DS, and s a tuple over RS_k. The set of P–programs of detTL over DS is defined inductively as follows:

1. $i_{RS_k}(s)$ *(insertion),* $d_{RS_k}(s)$ *(deletion),* erase_{RS_k} *are* **p–programs** *in detTL over DS.*

   If t and t' are **p–programs** *over DS, Q a condition over DS, and z a variable, then the following are* **p–programs** *over DS:*

2. $t ; t'$

3. **while** Q **do** t **done**

4. **with new** z **do** t **done**

13 Definition (Free Variables)

The set of **free variables** *of a detTL program P (denoted by Free(P)) is defined inductively as follows:*

1. *Free$(i_{RS_k}(s))$ = Free$(d_{RS_k}(s))$ is the set of variables appearing in s.*

2. *Free$(erase_{RS_k})$ = $\emptyset$.*

3. *Free$(t \, ; \, t')$ = Free(t) $\cup$ Free(t').*

4. *Free(while Q do t done) = Free(t) $\setminus$ var(Q)[3].*

5. *Free(with new z do t done) = Free(t) $\setminus$ $\{\, z \,\}$.*

14 Definition (Programs)

A **program** *P in detTL is a p–program with no free variables, that is, it holds Free(P) = $\emptyset$.*

We present now the concept of *valuation* of p–programs and conditions. The valuations are used for defining the semantics of programs in detTL.

15 Definition (Valuations)

Let t be a p–program in detTL or a condition over a database schema. Let X be the set of the free variables in t. A **valuation** *v of X is a mapping from X into D. The* **valuation** *v is extended to t in the natural way: vt corresponds to t replacing each free variable $x \in X$ by $v(x)$.*

16 Definition (Semantics of detTL)

The semantics of a detTL program t is defined as a binary relation between database instances, denoted **eff(t)** *(i.e. the* **effect** *of the detTL program t). The meaning of insertions, deletions and erase are the intuitive ones. The program $t; t'$ is interpreted as the product of the binary relation corresponding to t and t'. The semantics of (while Q* **do** *t* **done***) is as follows: the result of one iteration is the union of the results of all valuations satisfying the condition Q, the body of the loop is executed until no valuation that satisfy Q can be found. Next, $(I, J) \in$* **eff***$(t' \equiv$* **with new** *z* **do** *t* **done***) if $(I, J) \in$* **eff***(vt) for some valuation v of z, such that vz does not occur in I nor in t', with the restriction that we forbid the insertion of invented values in an output relation.*

Completeness of the Deterministic Languages

In this subsection we give theorems about the expressiveness of the languages defined in the previous subsections, and we show their completeness with respect to the criteria defined in the previous section.

17 Theorem [2]

The language $\mathcal{Q}L$ is deterministic query complete.

18 Theorem

The language UL is deterministic update complete.

---

[3] The set of variables in the condition Q.

Proof: This theorem is a direct consequence of the previous theorem (completeness of QL) and the theorem 8 (update computation). □

19 Theorem [7]

The language detTL is deterministic update complete.

Proof: The first step in this proof is to prove that every QL–program can be translated into a detTL one. This is done by structural induction over the constructs of QL, so we construct a program in detTL for every operation in QL:

- `Variables`. They can hold relations of arbitrary arity, so they are used to simulate *counters* (using the number of attributes of a relation). In detTL we can use *relation variables* (with fixed arity), and *counters* are simulated using chains of invented domain values [7], i.e. applying the *with–new* construct.

- `Equality`. Program that computes $\mathbf{E}$ in R_o:

    $erase_{R_o}$;
    while $\neg R_o(x, x)$ do $i_{R_o}(x, x)$ done

- `Intersection`. Program that computes $R_1 \cap R_2$ in R_o:

    $erase_{R_o}$;
    while $R_1(s) \wedge R_2(s) \wedge \neg R_o(s)$ do $i_{R_o}(s)$ done

- `Complementation`. Program that computes $(\neg R_1)$ in R_o:

    $erase_{R_o}$;
    while $\neg R_1(s) \wedge \neg R_o(s)$ do $i_{R_o}(s)$ done

- `Project out`. Program that computes $(R_1 \downarrow)$ in r_0:

    $erase_{R_o}$;
    while $R_1(x_1, \ldots, x_n) \wedge \neg R_o(x_2, \ldots, x_n)$ do $i_{R_o}(x_2, \ldots, x_n)$ done

- `Project in`. Program that computes $(R_1 \uparrow)$ in R_o:

    $erase_{R_D}$;
    while $\neg R_D(x)$ do $i_{R_D}(x)$ done;
    $erase_{R_o}$;
    while $R_D(x) \wedge \neg R_o(x_1, \ldots, x_{n-1}, x)$ do
        while $R_1(x_1, \ldots, x_{n-1}) \wedge \neg R_o(x_1, \ldots, x_{n-1}, x)$ do
            $i_{R_o}(x_1, \ldots, x_{n-1}, x)$
        done;
    done

- `Exchange the two rightmost components`. Program that computes $(R_1 \sim)$ in R_o:

    $erase_{R_o}$;
    while $R_1(x_1, \ldots, x_n) \wedge \neg R_o(x_1, \ldots, x_{n-2}, x_n, x_{n-1})$ do
        $i_{R_o}(x_1, \ldots, x_{n-2}, x_n, x_{n-1})$
    done

- `Assignment`. Assume the term e was computed in R_1, and y_i is represented by R_o. The program that computes $R_o \leftarrow R_1$ is the following:

    $erase_{R_o}$;
    while $R_1(s) \wedge \neg R_o(s)$ do $i_{R_o}(s)$ done

30

- Composition("`;`") and `while-loop`. Those constructs are also present in detTL.

The next step of the proof is to show that we can simulate the behavior of the abstract operator *Replace* using a detTL program, this can be done as follows:

$Aux_1 \leftarrow R_1; \ldots; Aux_n \leftarrow R_n;$
Compute q_1 and put its result in T_1
$$\vdots$$
Compute q_n and put its result in T_n
$R_1 \leftarrow T_1; \ldots; R_n \leftarrow T_n;$

Finally, we use the fact that QL is deterministic query complete (theorem 17) and the theorem *Update Computation* (theorem 8), to deduce the desired result, i.e. the deterministic update completeness of detTL. □

NON–DETERMINISTIC LANGUAGES

In this section we deal with non–deterministic languages. We show the language TL, a non–deterministic variant of detTL, whose complete definition can be found in [7]. The syntax of TL is the same of detTL. The semantics remains unchanged in most of the cases, following we describe the changes. In TL we allow the insertion of invented values in an output relation, and the other change is in the semantics of the while: there is made an arbitrary choice of a valuation, formally we can define the *effect* of the while construct in the following way: $(I, J) \in$ eff(while Q do t done) *iff* there is a sequence of instances $I = J_0, \ldots, J_n (n \geq 0)$, and some valuations $v_0, \ldots, v_{n-1}$ of the variables in Q such that

- $\forall i : 0 \leq i \leq n-1, v_i$ is a valuation that holds: $J_i \models v_i Q$, and $(J_i, J_{i+1}) \in eff(v_i t)$.

- for each valuation $v, \neg(J \models vQ)$.

20 Theorem [7]

TL is (non–deterministic) update complete.

The above theorem can be proven with the same technique as the theorem 19, that is, showing by structural induction over the constructs of a *complete non–determinitic query language* that every program in it can be expressed in TL, and showing that the *global simultaneous replacement* is also expressable in TL. We do not give the complete proof here because of the lack of a known complete non–deterministic relational query language.

CONCLUSIONS AND FURTHER RESEARCH

We have established a close relationship between computationally complete query and update languages in the relational data model. This relationship holds more generally for arbitrary data models, as in [8, 12, 14, 10]; a first step in this direction was done in [9]. We have used this as the basis for proving computational completeness of update languages and have exemplified the method with the update languages UL and detTL.

We have described in the paper two deterministic update complete languages. One of them, UL, is just an extension of QL, hence its definition is very transparent from a theoretical point of view, but its implementation may be very expensive (because of the simultaneous replacement operator); therefore, we agree with the necessity of the introduction of update languages that emphasize the elementary update operations (detTL is a good example of such a language).

The section about non–determinitic languages should be completed with a completeness proof of TL by reduction to a non–deterministic complete query language. We are still working on a satisfactory natural definition of such a language.

Database updates and restructurings may be computationally very expensive. In this paper complexity issues were avoided. It would be beneficial for real applications, to examine which update operations and queries fit together, to get update languages complete for some realistic complexity class. Realistic complexity classes should take into account both low time and space complexity, such as LogSpace, but also considerations such as hierarchic and distributed memory and storage.

References

[1] E.F. Codd. A relational model of data for large shared data banks. *Communications of the ACM*, 13(6):377–387, 1970.

[2] A. Chandra and D. Harel. Computable queries for relational data bases. *Journal of Computer and Systems Sciences*, 21:156–178, 1980.

[3] S. Abiteboul. Updates, a new frontier. In *Proceedings of the 2nd. International Conference on Database Theory, LNCS 326*, pages 1–18, 1988.

[4] V.E. Markowitz and J.A. Makowsky. Incremental reorganization of relational databases. In *VLDB '87*, pages 127–135, September 1987.

[5] V.E. Markowitz and J.A. Makowsky. Incremental restructuring of relational schemas. In *Proceedings of the 4th International Conference on Data Engineering*, pages 276–284, February 1988.

[6] S. Abiteboul and V. Vianu. A transaction language complete for database update and specification. In *Proceedings of the 6th ACM SIGACT-SIGMOD-SIGART Symposium on Principles of Database Systems*, pages 260–268, 1987.

[7] S. Abiteboul and S. Vianu. Procedural languages for database queries and updates. *Journal of Computer and Systems Sciences*, 41:181–229, 1990.

[8] S. Abiteboul and C. Beeri. On the power of languages for the manipulation of complex objects. Research Report 846, INRIA, April 1988.

[9] R.A. Hasson and J.A. Makowsky. Updates in the complex object data model, 1991. (Unpublished manuscript).

[10] G.M. Kuper and M.Y. Vardi. A new approach to database logic. In *Proceedings of the 3rd ACM SIGACT-SIGMOD Symposium on Principles of Database Systems*, pages 86–96, 1984.

[11] E. Dalhaus and J.A. Makowsky. Computable directory queries. In P. Franchi Zannettacci, editor, *Proceedings of CAAP'86 (11th Colloquium on Trees and Algebra in Programming), LNCS 214*, pages 254–265, March 1986.

[12] E. Dalhaus and J.A. Makowsky. Query languages for hierarchic databases. Technical Report 652, Department of Computer Science - The Technion, Haifa, Israel, 1990. To appear in *Information and Computation*.

[13] R. Hull and C.K. Yap. The format model: A theory of database organization. *Journal of the ACM*, 31(3):518–527, July 1984.

[14] S. Abiteboul and P. Kanellakis. Object identity as a query language primitive. In *Proceedings of the 8th ACM SIGACT-SIGMOD-SIGART Symposium on Principles of Database Systems*, pages 159–173, 1989.

OPUS: AN EXTENSIBLE OPTIMIZER FOR UP-TO-DATE DATABASE SYSTEMS

Rosana S.G. Lanzelotte[*] , Rubens N. Melo, Alexandre Ribenboim

PUC-RIO, Departamento de Informática
22453 - Rio de Janeiro - Brasil
Email: rosana@inf.puc-rio.br, rubens@inf.puc-rio.br, alerib@inf.puc-rio.br

Abstract

New deductive and object-oriented database systems (DOODBs) aim to offer declarative interfaces to users. Query optimization is, then, a critical component to guarantee declarativeness and efficiency. As implementing an optimizer is a complex task, it should be extensible to cope with different DB models and execution environments. In this work we describe the design of OPUS, an extensible OPtimizer for Up-to-date database Systems. Its extensibility is achieved by isolating the specification of the search space from that of the search strategy. The optimizer search strategy is specified by means of a set of extensbility primitives, which capture common aspects of known search strategies. Thus, OPUS implements four different search strategies with a great degree of code reusability.

1   Introduction

The availability of declarative interfaces is recognized as a major benefit issued from relational DBMSs. However disagreeing in many respects, statements of intentions concerning object-oriented or extended relational DBMSs [Atkinson89, Stonebraker90] confirm the convenience of offering declarative interfaces.

To support declarative interfaces, the DBMSs rely on their component called the optimizer. Its main goal is to find an *optimal execution plan* for a DBMS query. An *execution plan* is a sequence of the storage system primitives which have to be executed to provide the desired results. An *optimal* execution plan is the best among all investigated in terms of a *cost function*, which associates a cost estimate to each possible plan. So, key issues for an optimizer concern the design of the cost model and of its control engine, the *search strategy*, which guides the exploration of the space of all possible plans (i.e., the optimizer search space).

Developing a query optimizer is a complex task and the optimizer is affected by any change in the environment. This motivates the need for extensible optimizers. In particular, the optimizer search strategy must adapt to different problem sizes (small

---

[*] Visiting INRIA-Rocquencourt (France)

or large queries) as well as to different uses (single versus multiple query executions). Previous work on extensible relational query optimization did not take into account the requirements of new DOODBs and did not focus on the extensibility of the search strategy [Graefe87, Lohman88].

This work describes the design of OPUS, an extensible OPtimizer for Up-to-date database Systems [Lanzelotte90]. For "up-to-date" we mean object-oriented or deductive DBMSs. The key issue for OPUS extensibility is the isolation between the descriptions of its search space and search strategy. Although the search space description depends on the conceptual and physical DB models, OPUS provide for a translation step which encapsulates all environment-dependent features. The result of this translation constitutes the initial step for search. OPUS search strategy is specified by means of a set of *extensibility primitives*, which capture common aspects of different known search strategies. Thus, we were able to implement four different search strategies with a great degree of code reusability: that of System R [Selinger79], Augmentation Heuristics [Swami89], Iterative Improvement [Swami89] and Simulated Annealing [Ioannidis87].

The rest of this work is as follows. Section 2 describes the requirements for designing the optimizer search space. The search strategy issues are discussed in Section 3 and Section 4 concludes and describes the current status of implementation.

2   Specifying the Optimizer Search Space

The optimizer search space depends on the descriptions of its input and output. To describe the input to the optimizer (i.e., the input query and related schema information), a conceptual and physical DB models are assumed. A model for queries is developped based on the conceptual DB model, which encompasses most of the features required by DOODBs. We also develop a model for the output of the optimizer (i.e., query execution plans), as well as all investigated states of the search space, based on Processing Trees [Krishnamurty86].

2.1   The Conceptual Model

The input conceptual model for OPUS has been designed to support queries involving path traversals and recursion, as required in DOODBs. The DB conceptual schema is constituted of classes. To each class there corresponds a type and a set of all its instances (i.e., its *extension*). The instances of a class are objects and to each object there corresponds a unique object identifier (oid) and a value of the same type of the class. The following schema will serve as a basis for the sample queries of the paper. In the type definitions for classes, we use [], {} and <> for denoting respectively the tuple, set and list constructors.

class Composer =	[name:	string,
	birth:	date,
	birthplace:	string,
	master:	Composer,
	works:	{Composition}]

```
class Composition = [ title:          string,
                      composer:       Composer,
                      movements:      <string>,
                      duration:       float,
                      instruments:    <Instrument>]

class Instrument =  [ name:           string,
                      family:         string]

class Concert =     [ program:        <Composition>,
                      date:           date,
                      city:           string ]
```

2.2 A Model for Queries

The model used to express the input query to OPUS allows for queries involving path traversals, associative joins, accesses to oid's and recursion. It is well-adapted to be an intermediate representation for query languages of different DOODBs [Bancilhon89, Abiteboul90]. Also it is a better support for the optimizer input than other proposals (e.g., [Kim89, Kemper90]) in the sense that it enables the recognition of overlapping path expressions on objects (see [Lanzelotte91b] for a comparison between the proposed representation and that of the mentioned previous proposals).

A query is represented by a *query graph*. A query graph is constituted by predicate nodes represented by squares, name trees and directed dataflow arcs connecting name trees to predicate nodes. A *predicate node* has one or more input *name trees* (e.g., NT1, NT2, ..., NTk) and one output name tree (OutputNT). Figure 1 shows an example of a query graph with one predicate node.

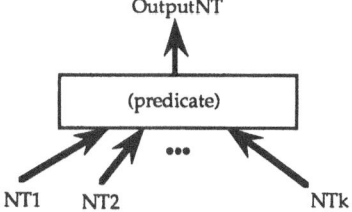

Figure 1. A Query Graph

Figure 2 shows the query graph for a query that retrieves "the name and the birthdate of composers such that a concert has been held in their birthplace including a composition of Bach using a harpsichord".

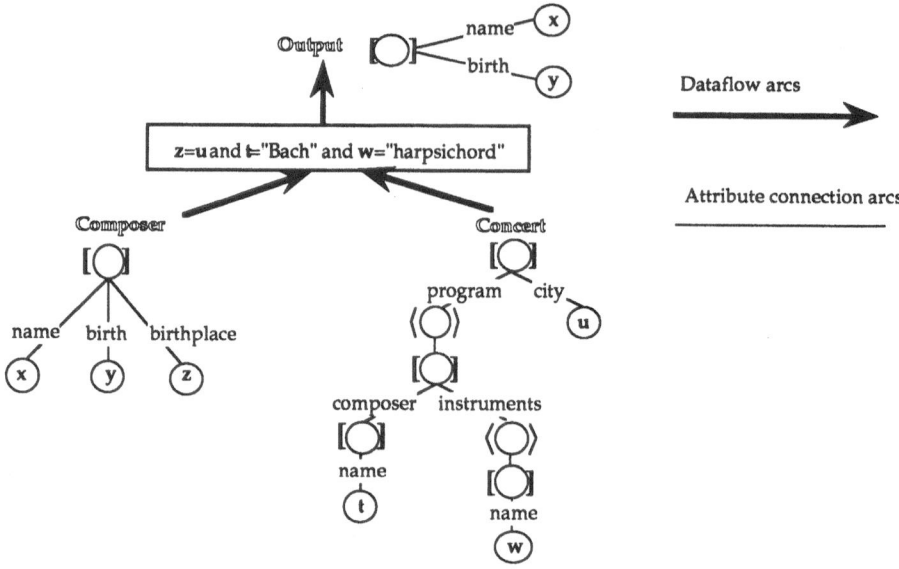

Figure 2. The query graph for the sample query

An *input name tree* is a tree whose root corresponds to a class of the conceptual schema (e.g., Composer and Concert in Figure 2) and whose nodes, labelled with variable names (e.g., x, y, v, w), are class attributes needed in the predicate node or the output projection. A variable labelling a set- or list-valued node assumes each possible value in the set. The undirected arcs of name trees capture the connection between objects and their attributes and bear the attribute names. The *output name tree* is rooted at a new class name (e.g., Output) and specifies the type of the query result and the output projection. The predicate node contains a conjunctive predicate on variables that label nodes of the input name trees. Since we do not address the problem of views or recursive queries in this paper, the query graph reduces to a single predicate node. However, this definition of query graph is general enough to capture queries on sets of rules, as required in deductive DBMSs. When the query involves more than one rule, one predicate node is used for each rule (see [Lanzelotte91c] for examples of recursive queries and views).

In the rest of the paper, we call *implicit joins* the joins corresponding to the implicit connections between class instances and their attributes (e.g., Composer and Composition through the *works* attribute) and *explicit joins* the joins for which there is a join predicate in the predicate node (e.g., z=u).

2.3 Translating the Query onto the Physical Schema

The input query is expressed on the conceptual schema while the optimizer output, i.e., an execution plan, is expressed on the physical schema. A first step of the optimizer, then, consists in translating the input query onto the physical DB schema. Of course, this is dependent of the physical DB model. The result of this translation constitutes the data over which are performed the actions controlled by the optimizer search strategy.

Many proposals exist for physical OODB models [Valduriez86, Kemper90]. The aim of OPUS is to specify the result of the translation to the physical DB schema in an independent way from the particularities of each physical model. Thus, extensibility is improved by isolating in this translation phase all the system-dependent features.

The main objective of an optimizer is, for a given query, to find an optimal ordering of the operations to be performed on entities of the physical DB schema involved in the query (e.g., a join permutation in relational query optimization). For each operation (e.g., an access to an individual entity or a join between two entitites), it must choose the best algorithm. Then, the translation of the input query onto the physical schema must identify the required physical entities from which execution plans are built, as well as the existing "connections" (i.e., operations) between them. In relational query optimization, a connection is a join, while in OODBs, connections are due to either explicit or implicit joins. Relation Connection Graphs (RCGs) [Wong76] are useful for representing the relations involved in a query and the connections between them. OPUS uses an extended representation based on RCGs, called Extension Connection Graph, to represent the result of the translation of the query onto the physical DB schema. Figure 3 shows the Extension Connection Graph for the query of Figure 2.

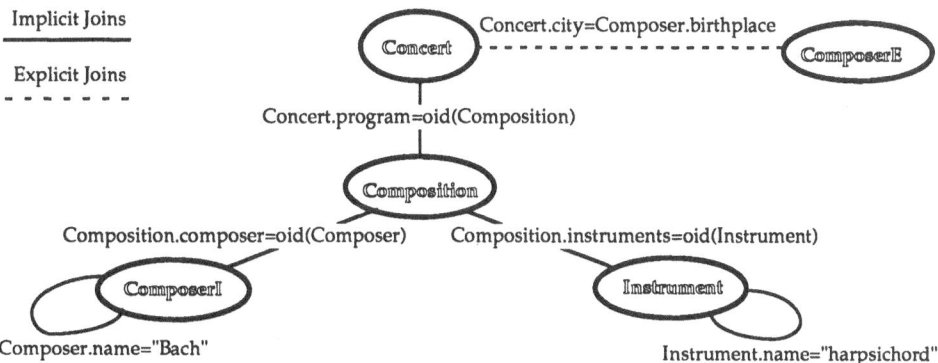

Figure 3. Extension Connection Graph for the Query of Figure 2

In the extension connection graph, the nodes denote class extensions referred to in the query and the arcs denote the implicit joins (by full arcs) or explicit joins (by dashed arcs). As in a relation connection graph, selections are denoted by arcs around a single node (e.g., Instrument.name="harpsichord"). Note the double occurrence of the Composer class extension. They are treated as different entities when generating permutations and are distinguished by appending the suffix I (for the Composer class extension connected by an implicit join) and E (for the Composer class extension connected by an explicit join). The class connection graph provides a non-navigational representation of the query. Furthermore, it provides a means for recognizing the atomic entities (from the physical schema point of view) useful for the query execution plan.

Often physical OODB models allow for *clustering* in the same file the instances of several classes. When clustering is specified (e.g., Composer and Composition through the *works* attribute), the instances of the component objects (e.g., Composition) are stored close to the owner object record (e.g., in a same or neighbor disk page) usually by depth-first placement. Thus, accesses to entire objects (i.e., retrievals of an object and its clustered component objects) are more efficient. In spite of this, the class extension, and not the clustered file, is considered as an atomic physical entity[1] in the Extension Connection Graph. This enables the investigation of plans in which the sequence of implicit joins does not necessarily follow the clustering sequence. This may seem unworthy, but is justified by the presence of selective predicates matched by indexes on the inner class of a clustering sequence. It is up to the search strategy, supported by the cost model, to decide the best scanning sequence. For example, if the physical schema contains a selection index on Instrument.name, then a candidate for optimal plan could specify first the retrieval of Composition and then Composer. This would not be possible if the file Composer/Composition were considered as one atomic entity (i.e., a single node in the Extension Connection Graph).

The Extension Connection Graph is also affected by the presence of *decomposition* in the physical DB model [Copeland85]. For example, suppose a physical DB schema specifying that file Concert is vertically fragmented into two files Concert1 and Concert2. Then, the extension connection graph would contain two different nodes, for Concert1 and Concert2, and one implicit join between them. So, it would be possible to investigate plans where they were not necessarily accessed together, if this is considered to be worth from the point of view of the cost.

Existing indices (e.g., value or path indices [Maier86]) are not represented in the extension connection graph. They are entities from which query execution plans are built and, rather, constitute a possible way of implementing one access.

2.4 Modeling Execution Plans as Processing Trees

Execution plans are abstracted by means of Processing Trees (PTs) [Krishnamurty86]. A *processing tree* (PT) is a labelled tree where the leaf nodes are entities of the physical schema (i.e., nodes of the Extension Connection Graph) and each non-leaf node represents an operation to be performed on the operand nodes resulting in a temporary file. Figure 4 shows three different PTs for the query of Figure 2.

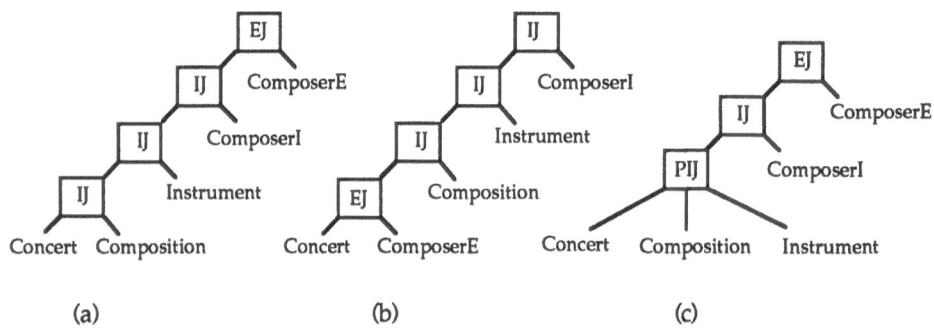

Figure 4. Processing Trees for the query of Figure 2

---

[1]   A clustered file can be scanned for the instances of any one of its contained classes. This is similar to the access to multi-relation segments in some relational DBMS (e.g., System R).

PTs specify the order in which implicit and explicit joins are to be performed and the join algorithm to apply. As PT nodes serve to express path traversals as well as all the other query operations, it is possible to build PTs where a *path* through a complex object is interleaved with other operations. For instance, the PT in Figure 4.b specifies that the explicit join is to be performed prior to follow the path from Concert to its components. Also, it is possible to express PTs where the path traversal starts from the "middle" of a path and not only from its extremes. Thus, PTs can express more general solutions than other proposed representations [Kim87, Kemper90].

When used in the present context, the original definition of PTs has to be modified as follows:

- Non-leaf nodes of PTs in the original definition represent only joins (selections and projections are assumed to be applied on-the-fly when accessing the files). Here they may represent also selections and projections, treated as isolated operations due to their possibly expensive cost (e.g., when involving method calls).

- As opposed to the original PTs, where special nodes were introduced to indicate pipelining, any non-leaf PT node in the present context may indicate pipelining or materialization. The PT shape does not change as a consequence of pipelining and we are able to express the pipelining of heterogeneous operations (e.g., a join and a selection or a projection).

- We use n-ary PIJ (Path Implicit Join) nodes, with n≥2, to represent a n-ary implicit join through a path index [Maier86]; Figure 4.c shows a PT where the implicit joins through Concert, Composition and Instrument are performed through an existing path index through *program.instruments*.

For clarity, we did not show the explicit join predicates, the implicit joins attributes, the join algorithm and the materialization or not of the intermediate results. However, they must be captured in the PT nodes.

The optimizer proceeds by applying operations on PTs, which are controlled by its search strategy. Two main approaches for exploring the search space can be distinguished, which imply two different kinds of optimizer actions:

- solutions are built *bottom-up* by enumerating permutations of the nodes of the extension connection graph; this process is called PT *generation* and one of its steps, called *expansion*, is to connect a PT to a new node by adding a node of the extension connection graph, as shown in Figure 5.

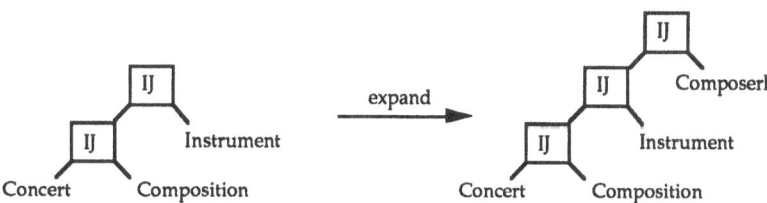

Figure 5. An *expand* action in PT generation

A PT generation stops when a PT is *complete*, i.e., when it involves all the nodes of the extension connection graph;

- solutions are obtained by applying modifications to a solution previously obtained; this process is called PT modification and is performed in rule-based optimizers [Graefe87, Kemper90]; such a modification can be an exchange of two extensions in the PT, as illustrated in Figure 6.

Note that all the PTs shown here are such that there always exists a connection (i.e., an arc in the extension connection graph) between the right-hand and the left-hand operands of each PT node. This corresponds to the heuristics which avoids unnecessary Cartesian products [Selinger79].

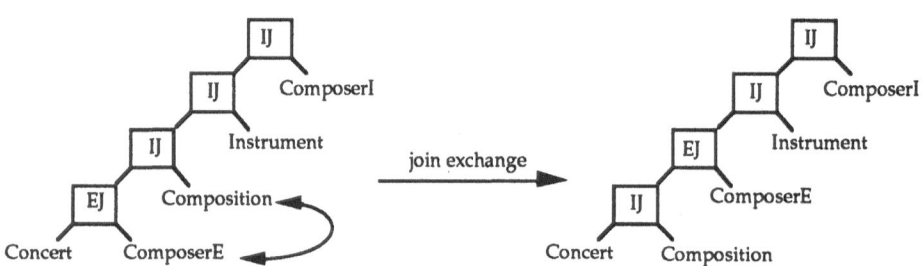

Figure 6. A Join Exchange as a PT modification

3   Specifying the Optimizer Search Strategy

The search strategy of the optimizer controls the exploration of the search space, i.e., the application of actions on PTs. Relational query optimizers either applied an *enumerative* or a *randomized* strategy. Both approaches have been implemented in OPUS. To achieve a great degree of extensibility and reusability, the common aspects of the search strategies have been captured in *extensibility primitives*.

3.1 Enumerative Strategies

Enumerative strategies *build* PTs from the nodes of the extension connection graph. This characterizes a *generative* approach, used, for example, in System R [Selinger79] and STARBURST [Lohman88]. Enumerative strategies depart from an initial state consisting of individual nodes of the extension connection graph. Successor nodes are generated by *expand* actions until complete PTs are generated. The search strategy controls the order in which states are visited for being expanded, as well as how many successors are retained in the search space. Algorithm 1 implements an enumerative search strategy based on a generic branch-and-bound algorithm.

Algorithm 1: Enumerative Search (branch-and-bound)
begin

```
        type state = PTnode;
        declare current : state;                    // the current state
        declare Open, Closed, Goal, Succ : {state}  // variables of type set of states

        Open := setInitState ();                     // initialize the Open set
        while not stopCond ()                        // usually Open = {}
        begin
                current := setNextState (Open);      // choose next to apply an action
                Open := Open - {current};
                if      goal (current)               // testing for goal
                then    Goal := Goal ∪ {current}
                else    begin
                        Closed := Closed ∪ {current};
                        Succ := action (current);    // generate a set of successors
                        Succ := prune (Succ);
                        Open := Open ∪ Succ
                        end
        end;
        return leastCostly (Goal)
end
```

The extensibility primitives (in bold) change the behavior of the basic algorithm. The Open set is initialized with (some or all) PT nodes that correspond to individual physical entities. The choice of the next state to apply an action on is performed by the **setNextState** primitive, which determines in which direction the search space is going to be explored. If its implementation is such that the least recent state is chosen, then the search strategy is breadth-first (e.g., System R). The primitive **action** (i.e., implementing an expand) decides the number of successors to be generated. Heuristics are used to reduce the search space by discarding the *bad* states. Bad states are recognized by comparison with other states (the comparison is based on the cost; see [Lanzelotte91c] for details on the cost model). The search space is reduced using the **prune** method, which removes the bad states from Succ. Figure 7 shows a snapshot of the search space generated for the sample query by Algorithm 1 implementing the breadth-first search strategy of System R [Selinger79].

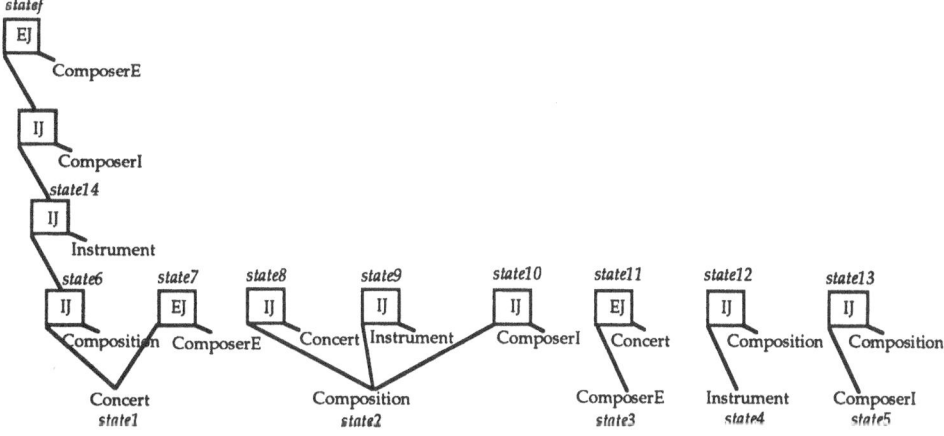

Figure 7. A Snapshot of the Search Space generated by System R

Algorithm 1 may alternatively implement Augmentation Heuristic [Swami89]. In this case, the **setNextState** primitive selects the most recently generated state and **prune** leaves only the successor with least cardinality. Then, one PT is generated by depth-first search.

3.2 Randomized Strategies

Randomized strategies (i.e., Iterative Improvement (II) [Swami89] or Simulated Annealing (SA) [Ioannidis87]) depart from a set of complete PTs, usually built by depth-first search, and modify them by applying modifications (i.e., like the one illustrated in Figure 6) until a local minimum is reached. They differ in some aspects:

- the number of start states (several in II or one in SA)
- the criterion for accepting a modification (those producing only less costly PTs in II and "bad" modifications producing higher costly PTs with a little probability in SA)
- the criterion for reaching a local minimum
- the global stopping criterion (related to the number of start solutions in II and related to a "temperature" parameter in SA)

The same comprehensive approach has been adopted for modelling randomized strategies. A basic algorithm has been designed in which extensibility primitives model the specific aspects of each strategy, which is not shown here for space reasons (see [Lanzelotte91a]).

4   Conclusion

This work described the design of OPUS, an extensible optimizer for DOODBs. Its extensibility is guaranteed by the isolation of the search space from the search strategy and by a translation step, which produces an initial state for search that is environment-independent. Although we did not discuss it here, the presented framework is straightforward extensible to cope with inheritance and method calls, as required in DOODBs.

The proposed solution has been validated by the implementation in C++ of an optimizer prototype. The code corresponding to the search space class hierarchy for PTs as defined in this paper with a sketched cost model (a single join algorithm and one access path for each relation) consists of about 800 lines of code. Another implementation of the search space class hierarchy for coping with an object-oriented database model and language was implemented where 400 of those were replaced by 600 lines of code. Two search strategies implementing the branch-and-bound algorithm and Iterative Improvement incurred only 60 additional lines of code each. The prototype spends approximately 1 second to optimize a query like that of Figure 2 using the almost exhaustive branch-and-bound algorithm. Although this optimizer prototype is quite limited, these numbers are encouraging. The prototype will be enhanced with other strategies and extended to cope with more general cost models (e.g., considering the cost of evaluating complex predicates involving method calls).

Overall, we plan to use it as an experimental vehicle to measure the effectiveness of other randomized search strategies.

5   References

[Abiteboul90]   S. ABITEBOUL: "Towards a Deductive Object-Oriented Database Language", *Journal of Data and Knowledge Engineering*, Vol. 5, N° 4, October 1990.

[Atkinson89]   M. ATKINSON et al.: "The Object-Oriented Database System Manifesto", In *Proc. 1st Int. Conf. on Deductive and Object-Oriented Databases*, Kyoto, Japan, December 1989.

[Bancilhon89]   F. BANCILHON , S. CLUET, C. DELOBEL: "Query Languages for object-oriented database systems: the O2 proposal", In *Proc. Int. Conf. on Database Programming Languages*, Salishan Lodge, Oregon, June 1989.

[Copeland85]   G. COPELAND: "The Decomposition Storage Model", In *Proc. ACM SIGMOD Int. Conf. on Management of Data*, May 1985.

[Graefe87]   G. GRAEFE, D.J. DEWITT: "The EXODUS Optimizer Generator", In *Proc. ACM SIGMOD Int. Conf. on Management of Data*, 1987.

[Ioannidis87]   Y.E. IOANNIDIS , E. WONG: "Query Optimization by Simulated Annealing", In *Proc. ACM SIGMOD Int. Conf. on Management of Data*, San Francisco, USA, 1987.

[Kemper90]   A. KEMPER, G. MOERKOTTE: "Advanced Query Processing in Object Bases Using Access Support Relations", In *Proc. 16th Int. Conf. on Very Large Data Bases*, Brisbane, Australia, 1990.

[Kim87]   W. KIM et al.: "Features of the ORION Object-Oriented Database System", MCC Technical Report n°ACA-ST-308-87, 1987.

[Kim89]   W. KIM: "A Model of Queries in Object Oriented Databases", In *Proc. 15th Int. Conf. on Very Large Data Bases*, Amsterdam, 1989.

[Krishnamurty86]   R. KRISHNAMURTY, H. BORAL, C. ZANIOLO: "Optimization of Nonrecursive Queries", In *Proc. 12th Int. Conf. on Very Large Data Bases*, Kyoto, August 1986.

[Lanzelotte90]   R.S.G. LANZELOTTE: "OPUS: an extensible OPtimizer for Up-to-date database Systems", *Ph. D. Thesis*, Computer Science, PUC-RIO, 1990, available at INRIA, Rocquencourt, n° TU-127.

[Lanzelotte91a]   R.S.G. LANZELOTTE, P. VALDURIEZ: "Extending the Search Strategy in a Query Optimizer", In *Proc. 17th Int. Conf. on Very Large Data Bases*, Barcelona, Spain, 1991.

[Lanzelotte91b]   R.S.G. LANZELOTTE, P. VALDURIEZ, M. ZIANE, J.P. CHEINEY: "Optimization of Nonrecursive Queries in OODBs", In *Proc. 2nd Int. Conf. on Deductive and Object-Oriented Databases*, Munich,1991.

[Lanzelotte91c]   R.S.G. LANZELOTTE, J.-P. CHEINEY: "Adapting Relational Optimisation Technology to Deductive and Object-oriented Declarative Database Languages", In *Proc. 3rd Int. Workshop on Database Programming Languages*, Nafplion, Greece, August 1991.

[Lohman88]   G. LOHMAN: "Grammar-like Functional Rules for Representing Query Optimization Alternatives", In *Proc. ACM SIGMOD Int. Conf. on Management of Data*, 1988.

[Maier86]   D. MAIER and J. STEIN: "Indexing in an Object-Oriented DBMS", In *Proc. Int. Workshop on Object-Oriented Database Systems*, Asilomar, California, September 1986.

[Selinger79]   P.G. SELINGER et al.: "Access path selection in a relational database management system", In *Proc. ACM SIGMOD Int. Conf. on Management of Data*, Boston, May 1979.

[Stonebraker90]   M. STONEBRAKER et al.: "Third-Generation Database System Manifesto", *Memorandum N° UCB/ERL M90/28*, University of California, Berkeley, 1990.

[Swami 89]   A. SWAMI: "Optimization of Large Join Queries: combining Heuristics and Combinatorial Techniques", In *Proc. ACM SIGMOD Int. Conf. on Management of Data*, Portland, USA, 1989.

[Valduriez86]   P. VALDURIEZ, S. KHOSHAFIAN, G. COPELAND: "Implementation Techniques of Complex Objects", In *Proc. 12th Int. Conf. on Very Large Data Bases*, Kyoto, August 1986.

[Wong76]   E. WONG, K. YOUSSEFI: "Decomposition - A Strategy for Query Processing", *ACM Transactions on Database Systems*, Vol. 1, N° 3, September 1976.

Artificial Intelligence,
Logic and Functional Programming

A HYPERICON INTERFACE TO A BLACKBOARD SYSTEM FOR PLANNING RESEARCH PROJECTS

Patricia Charlton, Christopher Burdorf

School of Mathematical Sciences
University of Bath
Bath
Avon
United Kingdom

Abstract

We introduce a novel interface to the blackboard architecture using research projects as the application. This graphical interface, HyperIcons, inherits many ideas from hypertext and is used to assist in the using and building of a planning tool. We use the typical blackboard structure design for the foundation of the planning system, but this structure differs through its interface which is to move more towards a planning language based on the blackboard architecture, hypertext and recent planning research.

1 Introduction

A new kind of interface is described to integrate blackboard systems and planning. The initial application is to develop a planning system for research projects. Research is concerned with investigating areas in depth to provide *an original contribution to knowledge* [Philips & Pugh 1987]. The independent nature of research can encourage people to work without communicating their ideas to others which may present an unorganised environment for the group members. Many times research projects are purposely ill-defined to allow free investigation and openness resulting in an environment that allows ideas to flower and develop from thoughts to product. Although independence should be encouraged, the sharing of ideas and information is often not inspired by this environment. Members of the projects may find in this free and open structure less co-ordination towards the specified goals, which can then lead to project overruns [Brooks 1982]. For this and several other reasons given below, a tool to assist in planning research projects is being developed.

A blackboard system for planning a research project can prove useful for managing such an open structure. A blackboard system can help researchers to focus on their goals. It will also assist in avoiding expensive overruns and project cancellation. This system not only provides assistance in managing projects more efficiently through better co-ordination, but also helps to enrich the researcher's environment. This mechanism of planning will record historical knowledge which will be available to new project members. The blackboard system will give the research domain breadth as well as assisting in memory recall for the members of the project about previous ideas.

The design of the system is being developed from typical blackboard structures and hypertext ideas. There are existing planning systems which use a blackboard model [Hayes-Roth & Hayes-Roth 1979, Tate & Currie 1990, Ambros-Ingerson & Steel 1990]. The system is based upon some of this work and expert system design [Wielinga *et al.* 1987].

The different approach to planning occurs from two positions:

1. *HyperIcons*

2. Interactive System

The use of this model is to assist in the breaking down of projects with the result of a system which can develop plans to achieve the project goals. The *HyperIcon* use is two fold: interface assistance for application use and, planning language level on system use. The bootstrap [Terry 1990] effect on both a model and implementation, is to move closer towards a better understanding of planning and the developing of plans for projects.

2 Hypertext and HyperIcons

We introduce the use of *HyperIcons* as an interface mechanism to our blackboard system. As the name suggests, *HyperIcons* have grown from the idea of hypertext [Barlow *et al.* 1990]. In this implementation of the blackboard system, *HyperIcons* are used to assist in improving the use of the system. A similar approach is taken to Expertext [Barlow *et al.* 1990] in sharing of intelligence between the user and the Expertext system.

A hypertext process can be used to navigate through a network of concepts in order to obtain specific information or to acquire a better general understanding of a particular knowledge domain. *Control of hypertext systems is left very much with the user, rather than the machine, contrary to the usual philosophy in AI* [Samuals 1991].

HyperIcons are bitmapped pictures that represent ideas internally as knowledge sources. This "idea" capturing method has the advantage of improving recall by presenting pictorial images that have meaning to the user. Pictorial representation can also improve the performance of user interaction with the blackboard system by being simple to use in comparison to using a database query language. This pictorial approach should shorten the learning curve required in using the system, hence there is the potential for the tool to be more useful and productive at an earlier stage. *HyperIcons* solve problems involved with hierarchical menu systems where the user must navigate several hierarchies to get to the selection they desire. This type of user interface can present all the information at the top level, so there is no need to search what appears to be an endless hierarchy of menus [Barlow *et al.* 1990].

The initial nine icons are attached to their respective knowledge sources (KSs)[1]. The

---

[1]Knowledge source is a specific term to the blackboard architecture and the nine KS used for this system are explained in more detail in future sections.

general planning system uses the icons as both an ease of use facility and a tailoring utility to move towards the application specific system. The ability to network icons, to see the network, allow user interaction and fire KS relates to hypertext. The icons are a different approach for blackboard systems as the blackboard structure shows a different architecture for hypertext.

Like hypertext, the *HyperIcon* system is trying to present to the user an initial impact of information that can assist recall and ease of interaction [Nielsen 1990]. Hypertext allows graphical as well as textual information to be presented in an attempt to present information in a form where location as well as detail has meaning. Although there are some user problems [Nielsen 1990] with the system, it is what hypertext is trying to achieve that is important to this paper. The use of the term *HyperIcon* is to present the reader with two connections:

1. The relationship to hypertext

2. More than an Icon interface

Solving planning problems has long been under investigation [Tate *et al.* 1990] presenting many interesting questions. In projects which are difficult to define for planning purposes they could be assisted by an interactive tool such as hypertext. Hypertext has its disadvantages in navigating problems [Nielsen 1990] and is passive in interaction [Barlow *et al.* 1990]. The *HyperIcon* tool is built specifically towards planning issues and so the design considerations are those that should provide more understanding of planning and the problems, although a better solution is hoped for it is difficult to measure. Initially the *HyperIcon* is less active in the planning architecture than it is intended, the tool will become more powerful as the planning language is developed. SPRINT [Carlson & Ram 1990] is a planning system which uses hypertext ideas in the development of a strategic planning system. However knowledge acquisition still remains a problem and the multi-user system does not appear to be considered.

The enthusiasm about hypertext is dampened by the experience that readers tend to get lost when they are presented with complex networks. Hopefully the *HyperIcon* system is less guilty of this.

3   HyperIcons and Blackboards

HyperIcons are used as a visual interface that link to knowledge sources stored in the blackboard. There is an icon database which stores the bitmap representation of the icon which is mapped to the display when an icon is accessed. Knowledge sources are represented as frame structures [Bundy 1990]. Icon bitmaps are stored in a database which contains the bitmap and a pointer to the knowledge source. Knowledge sources contain knowledge structures and pointers to their respective icon bitmaps. New icons can be created using an icon editor. Once the new icon has been created it can be linked to the knowledge source that it is related to. Slots can be added to the knowledge source by using the **Icon Rules** (see section 3.1).

Keywords connected to icons allow the user to navigate the icon database. The user can enter a keyword and instigate a search resulting in the system displaying the icons of all knowledge sources that correspond to the keyword. The user can then click on the various icons to cause procedures to execute which will generate information based upon what is stored in the knowledge source in the form of graphical or textual output. An icon browser will allow the user to examine the various icons that are accessed by the system and execute the knowledge source associated with them.

New knowledge sources can be attached to icons automatically when electronic mail is received. When the mail file is received, it can become part of a KS or create a new KS. The classification and storage of the mail file is either decided by the system or the user.

3.1 Blackboard Design and HyperIcons

Users are presented with a default set of icons which are attached to KS's which can be tailored. Tailoring the system is done via a rule interpreter which also allows the addition of new icons and rules. All the necessary bindings between the new *HyperIcon*, the KS and the blackboard are done by the rule set. The rule interpreter uses a language called **Icon Rules**.

The functions allowed by the **Icon Rules** are:

1. define a new KS

2. attach an icon to KS

3. modify a KS

The following format is used to activate an **Icon Rule**:

```
(define-new-KS project-name KS-name Level-certainty-factor facet value)
```

The `project-name` will be allocated at system initialisation. The `KS-name` is user defined. The `level-certainty-factor` is used to decide how this new KS should influence the overall plan. To establish this value the systems priority feature[2] can be used and the value altered accordingly to get the desired effect. To use the priority feature, the new KS should be compared to an existing KS to determine where this structure should be placed. The `facet` is either a user defined symbol or a link to trigger existing rules and/or KSs. The `value` can take the format of either a value, data, rule triggers (user or system defined) or a KS to be triggered.

The blackboard system is built in four layers. This differs from other planning blackboard models [Hayes-Roth & Hayes-Roth 1979, Tate & Currie 1990, Ambros-Ingerson & Steel 1990] although the essential structure is similar. This layered structure is based on an knowledge acquisition techniques for expert systems [Wielinga *et al.* 1987]. As the blackboard architecture in principle is the bringing together of many experts using the blackboard as communication [Englemore & Morgan 1988]. The dividing line between the layered structure is not as easy to define in comparison to an expert system. However this structure has its advantage for the vertical modelling of planning and still fits well with the blackboard architecture in terms of abstraction.

Strategy

This level shows the concept abstraction and represents the plans and meta rules.

Task

Again this level shows concept abstraction but represents the goals and task structures.

---

[2]The priority feature allows a new feature to take a position in the plan. To establish where this position should be a before and after schema [Fox 1983] is used. The priority function on based existing tasks i.e. its either the same, lower or higher priority.

Inference

This layer contains the knowledge source and applies them to the domain.

Domain

The domain is structured using frames and schema design ideas. The frame paradigm [Luger & Stubblefield 1989] allows active values and triggers to be utilised.

4   Blackboards and Planning

Planning can be ambiguous and may involve inaccurate judgments, because it uses incomplete and imprecise theories. The blackboard architecture is used in modelling incomplete knowledge structures. This architecture works well when building strategies from knowledge which may be inaccurate, unclear and incomplete [Tate *et al.* 1990]. Planning produces a control structure which will assist in either preventing or solving the problem. The blackboard system will use the control structure to produce a strategy which will assist in establishing a direction towards the required result. The basic strategic steps are:

1. The instance

2. The result required

3. The method used to bring about change

A problem arises because these steps start off with uncertain and incomplete definitions. A typical plan will start with an "idea" which may not be well thought out.

Planning systems are built from partial hypotheses which vary from concrete to unclear in various knowledge areas. There are levels of hypotheses formed through abstraction to determine solutions. Solutions can be inadequate because the theoretical model which the system is based upon is insufficient or inaccurate. The intention is to produce the best strategy in the light of the information available at the time. It is important that results are monitored so that the model can be improved upon where necessary.

The more hypotheses can be combined the more likely they will be used to generate a solution [Erman *et al.* 1980]. To avoid combinatorial explosion, a control scheme is needed to exploit the most promising combinations of alternatives. The explosions occur when there is a large amount of uncertainty in the hypothesis.

The control scheme needs to manage diverse knowledge sources which are required in planning systems. The system tailors and trims the strategies to produce a pattern of events leading to a goal.

The knowledge sources identify a type of inference. The inference is an operation from states to states. The relationship between the input state and the output state denotes the type of inference and is expressed by an action like "assemble" or "specify" [Wielinga *et al.* 1987]. For instance, in the relationship "abstraction," the input state consists of one concept and the output state is another concept which has fewer attributes. In other words, in the "abstraction" relationship irrelevant features are deleted and the remaining structure is then the same as an existing concept, otherwise a new concept is created. The KS places constraints on the inference process. This function is important to the internal and external structure of the system.

The design of the inference mechanism is influenced by the Hearsay-II problem solving model. The KS is schematised as condition-action pairs [Erman *et al.* 1980]. The condition component prescribes the situations in which the KS may contribute to the problem solving activity, and the action component specifies what that contribution is and how to integrate it into the current activity. These KS communicate through a shared database called the blackboard.

The planning strategy is built up from the results of the hypotheses which arrive on the blackboard. An internal request from the system or an external request by the user activates the strategy. This request causes access to a KS which starts the building of the strategic planning mechanism. Each time a KS is accessed, a new event node will be created [Rice 1989]. The event node will be either a partial result or a solution component. The event node will then be:

1. made a component of the strategic plan

2. used to evaluate the next task

3. used to change the present event node

4. changed by the next event node

To achieve a plan, a number of stages are required. The first stage is to get the outline. This outline may be as simple as "we have A and we want to change it to B." The next stages will take the expected input and output and build a more detailed path. This path is constructed by taking the nodes from the outline and expanding or completing details where necessary. The information required is accessed via the KS.

Nodes on the path are called tasks. Each task has a certainty factor which may require improvement. In cases where the partial hypothesis is extremely speculative, it has to be analysed for improvements or allow user interaction. The user interaction is to improve permanently or temporarily the defect caused by an uncertain hypothesis. The strategy path is iteratively trimmed to remove irrelevant components. At each stage of the analysis of the plan, the blackboard system must monitor the constraints to ensure they are being achieved.

5   Research Planner

The research planner is the application we choose for the *HyperIcon* blackboard system. The goal of the research planner is to help project members organize tasks related to the specified goal of the project. At the same time, it is important to recognize that good research needs to have a large amount of flexibility. If a project member develops an exceptional idea during the project, the system should allow plan modification to permit time for the idea to be developed. Thus, the planner allows the use of stepwise refinement for periodic modification of the project tasks, subtasks, and goals. The basic research planner system consists of the following elements: title icon, idea icon, bibliography icon, deadline icon, and an expectations icon. The title icon corresponds to the scope and domain of the project. There is an icon for each team member which will plan their individual tasks. The title icon contains the following fields: title, description, tasks, and subtasks. Tasks can be broken down into subtasks using stepwise abstraction [Partridge 1986]. The stepwise abstraction process will take the main task and draw out subtasks. These smaller components of the original task will create a more detailed path to the goal. The goal is achieved via tasks which are made up of subtasks. These subtasks are reached through a cycling process which should result in a refined specification of the goal (in this example producing a plan). The subtasks can be viewed as smaller plans known as subplans. Tasks can include modules of code that need to be written, interfaced, or tested. The writing of papers can also be tasks. The paper writing tasks have information stored in them which include the title, the due date, a list of sections to be written and by whom. A field in the top-level title knowledge source will cause the system to produce a listing of all tasks necessary to finish the paper and their scheduled completion date.

The bibliography icon points to a knowledge source that stores information about the sources of information used for the project. The knowledge source indexes each bibliography entry by author, title, and subject. Queries can be made on the bibliography by using the built-in window interface. Once a user clicks the mouse on the bibliography icon, the system produces a menu asking whether the user wants to add to the bibliography or make a query of it. If the user requests a query, the system will request an author, subject, or title to search upon. If the user wants to add an entry, the system will prompt for authors, title, and all other information pertinent to the subject. All bibliography entries are stored in BibTeX format so that they can be referenced from LaTeX formatted documents.

The expectation icon can be set by the supervisor or other project members. This icon is classed as a constraint. Further input by the user may be required to establish how the constraint objective is to be met. The expectation icon can hold many constraint requirements. The constraints may consist of paper due dates, new modules that need to be specified, already specified modules that need to be implemented, and when the deliverables are due and what they should consist of. These icons can specify knowledge areas that are both known and unknown. Finally, the system will generate a Pert chart of the tasks highlighting the critical path and what needs to be done next. As tasks and the content of the project are refined, the Pert chart can be regenerated automatically showing the new structure of the project. As with the other icons, all information for the input and expectation icons can be entered using the window interface that prompts the user for the required information.

5.1 Research Planner Design

The first level of abstraction for the research planner is done by the blackboard system. The first level of abstraction provides the division into KSs. Each KS has subsequent levels of abstraction which depend upon the domain. These default structures can be altered or removed. There are nine default structures outlined below.

Research

The research domain will be given a title by the user. This title in most instances will be broad. The research domain will have areas to be investigated.

Range

This domain is used to hold more detail about the research

Focus

This domain is more specific with depth about the research

Time

The time structure is used to set the constraints of the system. This structure will influence two levels in the system [Fox 1983]: the domain and the task.

Interface

The interface structure allows the user to set up the relationships across the domain and view the system structure at a low level. The interface domain can allow the user to define links across the blackboard database. This utility allows adjustment towards the specific project requirements. The mechanism is required as the relationships between the subjects under investigation are not always easily defined by the **Icon Rules**. The interface domain gives the user flexibility to generate communications in a less structured but meaningful manner. Even though there is flexibility through this domain the blackboard architecture is adhered to [Craig 1987]. The interface domain complements the *HyperIcon* interface. The *HyperIcons* can also be linked in at this level.

New Ideas

The new ideas domain allows members of the team to enter new thoughts and suggestions which are linked to the project. It is a facility which can hold details of results from experimenting with new ideas. This structure can be thought of in terms of a note book which may be reviewed in respect of the overall project goals. The reviewing is done by the project members. Once an idea moves from being on the fringe of the project a new domain structure will be built. The building of the new domain structure may require some rule instructions of the user. It is not essential that new ideas move into the main stream of the project, but if the priority setting of the task is low, it will have a low impact on the developing plan strategy.

Project Members

The project member component shows each members' involvement in the project and how their work fits together. The details stored about each member are to show the best skill allocation, the subjects each person is working on and their expert areas.

Plan Library

The plan library component is used to store plan outlines for solutions to problems [Cohen *et al.* 1989]. Once a plan has been built it can be used again if the same or a similar problem arises. The plan library helps in reducing some of the searching difficulties making a more efficient system. However it can only be achieved if the plan is adequate. It is not essential to have the best possible plan, but rather one that fits the requirements in an optimistic manner. The plan library helps in resolving some of the combinatorial problems by keeping the system as up to date as possible.

Decision Changes

The "decision changes" component is used to keep backup trace information to show the reasoning behind a certain line of action. This structure is used when a plan is either modified or removed.

5.2 Research Planner and HyperIcons

The integration of the *HyperIcons* into the blackboard structure gives the planning system a graphical interface. The interface allows browsing of the network icon structure which will be either two or three dimensional, this can assist in showing the different levels of abstraction. The structure presents the user with a concise viewing mechanism. It can assist in clarifying concepts by showing an image of the arrangement. The recall aid will assist in focusing the user on the link structure between domain settings. It is expected that a research project's focus and structure will change. A trace can monitor these changes and highlight the focus at each instance. The trace will be able to support decision changes. The trace history will also be useful for the final report. The icon representation will help trigger more ideas from the user.

6 Implementation

The blackboard system is being built using frame structures for the KS and domain areas. Although in the blackboard model these can be represented as separate units, in the implementation they can be seen as one component. This structure is divided into subcomponents showing the varying levels of abstraction. The lowest level of abstraction is matched on terms, facts and triggers (this is termed the parametric level): the highest level is the conceptual level which deals with the concepts such as the initialisation and focus ideas [Craig 1987]. Each KS frame structure has attribute lists at each abstract level. The attributes are the conditions for using the KS. The level associated with the attributes is the action to be taken. Below shows the frame structure of three KSs. The trigger looks at a bibliography search to produce a reading list output.

The system levels are defined by 1 to n labels, they take a numeric value for identification. The other levels that can be defined are fact-level (also a system label), user-level which is defined by the user using the priority level feature and other system considerations, the Icon-level which is to work as part of the interaction and tailoring feature. As seen below a basic initial outline is shown, however for further detail see [Charlton 1991a, Charlton 1991b]. The system is built from nine initial KS (explained in section 5.1), three KS are expanded on. The first level of abstraction of the research planner produces in this case three KS, which are research, range and focus. Having established the first abstraction each KS's detail needs to be defined. At this stage each KS does not know of the existence of the other, their only communication is via the blackboard, this being important to the design of blackboard structures [Craig 1987]. The research KS is further described by more levels of abstractions, these are range, focus and bibliography and research-frame. Both the focus and the range follow a similar pattern.

```
KS-research

level-1      [KS-range]
             [KS-focus]
             [..     ]

level-n      [bib-search] ; search for information on project


Research-frame [text project-title ..] ; rules and text
```

KS-range

```
level-1    [KS-research]
           [KS-focus]
           [..      ]

level-n    [bib-search] ; search more specific

Range-Frame [scope of project ..] ; rules and text
```

KS-focus

```
level-1    [KS-research]
           [KS-range]
           [..      ]

level-n    [bib-search] ;

Focus-Frame [specific expectations, examples] ; rules and text
```

The request for action by blackboard is either by the user or the system. An entry on the blackboard can take the format (project-name, Knowledge-Source-Name, Level-n) e.g. (Constraint-Analysis, Research, (Level-n, Bib-search, nil)). Each entry can take a number of values which are then matched with the appropriate KS and abstraction level(s).

The blackboard takes the first entry (Constraint-Analysis, KS-research, (Level-n, Bib-search, nil)) and matches the project and the KS. The next stage is to take the condition-action pair, this provides a number of combinatorial and semi-pattern matching problems but many have been reduced by the KS arrangement. In this example the matching is simple, the label and rule exist so the KS is fired. In this instance the KS has a number of possibilities:

1. Existing search facts

2. Range search facts

3. Focus search facts

The system defaults are to search all three possibilities but this can be altered by the user. Along with the detail being an entry on the blackboard further KS triggers also arrive, in this instance they are for the focus and the range. The process is repeated with the respective KSs until no more KS can be fired. The result is a list of authors relating to the research. The reading list is prioritised by the system through frequency of occurrence of the author in the subject. Authors that occur in the research frame will take preference over range and focus frame, as this was the initial trigger. The priority system can be altered to highlight a different ordering method. If a pattern matched in all three KS then this result would be high in the reading list. The priority feature is organised by the task layer.

The task layer has both a task scheduler and a task table. The task table knows the conditions that are required before a KS can be fired. When complications occur in firing a

KS due to incomplete pattern matching, a decision action is required. This inference is applied by the scheduler. The scheduler is also used when constraint conflicts require resolving. The strategy layer supervises the scheduler by looking for ways to connect tasks on the blackboard and to improve certainty in the planning strategy.

The blackboard structure is three dimensional. Its design is very similar to the Hearsay-II model [Erman *et al.* 1980]. The dimensions are the time constraint, certainty factor and level of abstraction. This arrangement for positioning the primitive, selection and planning action[3] [Cohen *et al.* 1989] assists in the managing of the overall strategy.

Once a plan has been developed for a task or subtask it is stored as a possible solution in the plan library in an outline format. Each plan or subplan requires an adequacy and certainty factor. As the project progresses, the library will be updated by the removal of redundant plans, the addition of new plans, and the replacement of plans by improved plans. Redundant and improved plans are viewed differently by the system. The information which has been replaced or deleted is stored in the historical frame which is used to show the reason for the action taken or plan deviation. This is to help the project members to avoid routes which are not beneficial to the project goals.

The planning tool may help project members in many ways. The default structures assist the user in breaking down the task in hand into more manageable blocks. It helps move the vague project title to a more tangible format. Using the blackboard system as a guide line in achieving this tangible format and in recording decision changes, may help the project to progress more quickly towards its goals.

The system is currently being implemented in EuLisp [Padget, J. and Nuyens, G. (Eds.)]. FEEL [Concurrent Processing Research Group, University of Bath] is an implementation of EuLisp being done at Bath University. The system will make use of YYonX [Ida *et al.* 1990] window system, which is a toolkit built on X windows and is used to build the user interface. The development of the scheduler will take advantage of work being carried out on concurrent and parallel symbolic processing at Bath University [Padget *et al.* 1991].

7   Future Work

In the system the initial guide lines are set using a blackboard structure using icons to fire KS. The icons can be viewed as a planning language which can be built and added to the system. Ideally the system should be developed into having a planning language similar to Bliss[4]. The system shows a reflective [Smith 1983] structure as the new icons and rules can be added to modify the model. As the model is moulded into the specific problem solver the general planning structure becomes redundant. Instead of a reflective language there is a reflective model which can be self modified. In essence the system monitors change and can reason about the change to provide where necessary an altered solution. The blackboard model could be lost to allow reflective activity and icon networking.

Effective plans would be achieved through solving specific problems. This could possibly be produced through using a general problem solver and modifying it towards the specific planning problem. This architecture assists in providing such solutions using the planning tool

---

[3]These are planning terms: the primitive is computational i.e. fact level, the selection is the choice and relates to the plan library, and the plan actions are the sub-plans or sub-tasks providing the general plan.

[4]Charles Bliss [Hahner 1986] invented an Icon language that is presently used by handicapped people as a form of communicating. The Icons can be put together to form meaningful sentences in a picture format.

icons and rule modification. The new structure that will be created will no longer adhere to the blackboard design hence a new model is provided which may be a closer architecture for planning than the blackboard structure. To attempt to establish this requires further research.

References

[Ambros-Ingerson & Steel 1990] J. Ambros-Ingerson and S. Steel. Integrating planning, execution and monitoring. *Readings in Planning*, pages 735–740, 1990.

[Barlow *et al.* 1990] J. Barlow, M. Beer, T. Bench-Capon, D. Diaper, P. Dunne, and R. Rada. Expertext: Hypertext-expert system theory, and synergy and potential applications. pages 117–127, 1990.

[Brooks 1982] F Brooks. *Mythical man month*. Addison-Wesley Publishing Company, 1982.

[Bundy 1990] A Bundy. *The Catalogue of Artificial Intelligence Techniques*. Springer-Verlag, 1990.

[Carlson & Ram 1990] D. Carlson and S. Ram. HyperIntelligence The Next Frontier. *Communications of the acm*, **33**(3):311–321, March 1990.

[Charlton 1991a] P Charlton. The Blackboard Architecture. Technical report, School of Mathematical Sciences, University of Bath, Bath, Avon, United Kingdom, August 1991.

[Charlton 1991b] P Charlton. The Design of Knowledge Sources for a Research Planner. Technical report, School of Mathematical Sciences, University of Bath, Bath, Avon, United Kingdom, August 1991.

[Cohen *et al.* 1989] R. Cohen, D. Greenberg, D. Hart, and A. Howe. Trial by fire. *AI Magazine*, **10**(3):33–48, fall 1989.

[Concurrent Processing Research Group, University of Bath] Concurrent Processing Research Group, University of Bath. FEEL: An Implementation of EuLisp.

[Craig 1987] I. D. Craig. The blackboard architecture: A definition and its implications. Research report, University of Warwick, 1987.

[Englemore & Morgan 1988] R. Englemore and T. Morgan. *Blackboard Systems*. Addison and Wesley, 1988.

[Erman *et al.* 1980] L. Erman, F. Hayes-Roth, V. Lesser, and D. Reddy. The Hearsay-II speech-understanding system: Integrating knowledge to resolve uncertainty. *ACM Computing Surveys*, **12**:213–253, 1980.

[Fox 1983] M. Fox. *Constraint-Directed search: a case study of job-shop scheduling*. PhD thesis, Carnegie-Mellon University, 1983.

[Hahner 1986] B. Hahner. *Blissymbols for use*. Bliss Symbolic Institute, 1986.

[Hayes-Roth & Hayes-Roth 1979] B. Hayes-Roth and F. Hayes-Roth. A Cognitive Model of Planning. In *Cognitive Science*, 1979.

[Ida *et al.* 1990] M. Ida, T. Kosaka, and K. Tanaka. YY Protocol Specification for YYonX. Aoyama Gakuin University, November 1990.

[Luger & Stubblefield 1989] G. Luger and W. Stubblefield. *Artificial Intelligence and The Design of Expert Systems*. The Benjamin and Cumming Publishing Company, 1989.

[Nielsen 1990] J. Nielsen. The Art of Navigating through HYPERTEXT. *Communications of the acm*, **33**(3):296–310, 1990.

[Padget, J. and Nuyens, G. (Eds.)] Padget, J. and Nuyens, G. (Eds.). The EuLisp Definition.

[Padget *et al.* 1991] J. Padget, R. Bradford, and J. Fitch. Concurrent Object-Oriented Programming in Lisp. *Computer Journal*, **34**(4):311–320, 1991.

[Partridge 1986] D. Partridge. *Artificial Intelligence: applications in the future of software engineering*. Ellis Horwood Limited, 1986.

[Philips & Pugh 1987] E. Philips and D. Pugh. *How to get a Ph.D.* Open University Press, Celtic Court, 22 Ballmoor, Buckingham MK18 1XW, 1987.

[Rice 1989] J. Rice. The Design and Implementation of *poligon*, a High-Performance, Concurrent Blackboard System Shell. report STAN-CS-89-1294, Stanford University, November 1989.

[Samuals 1991] P. Samuals. Hypertext for computational mathematics. In *Artificial Intelligence in Mathematics*. The institute of mathematics and its applications, 1991.

[Smith 1983] B. Smith. Reflection and semantics in lisp. *ACM*, pages 23–35, 1983.

[Tate & Currie 1990] A. Tate and K. Currie. O-PLAN - Control in the Open Planning Architecture. *Readings in Planning*, pages 361–367, 1990.

[Tate *et al.* 1990] A. Tate, J. Allen, and J. Hendler. Readings in planning. *Readings in Planning*, 1990.

[Terry 1990] A. Terry. Using explicit strategic knowledge to control expert systems. *Blackboard Systems*, pages 160–183, 1990.

[Wielinga *et al.* 1987] B. Wielinga, B. Bredeweg, and J. Breuker. Knowledge Acquisition for Expert Systems. In *Lecture Notes in Artificial Intelligence*. Springer-Verlag, 1987.

CHUSAURUS: A WRITING TOOL RESOURCE
FOR NON-NATIVE USERS OF ENGLISH

Osvaldo N. Oliveira Jr.,[1] Sandra M. A. Caldeira,[2] and Niura Fontana[3]

[1]Instituto de Física e Química de São Carlos, USP
   C.P. 369, 13560 São Carlos, S.P. - Brazil
[2]Departamento de Ciências de Computação e Estatística, ICMSC-USP
   C.P. 668, 13560 São Carlos, SP - Brazil
[3]Departamento de Letras, Universidade de Caxias do Sul
   Campus Universitário C.P. 1352, 95070, Caxias do Sul, R.S. - Brazil

ABSTRACT

A novel work of reference is proposed which is to be implemented as a writing aid in the form of software tools. This reference source is named Chusaurus and is based on a compilation of well-written, useful expressions extracted from papers and books which could be used to assist in the generation of scientific text. The expressions have blank spaces (representing missing words) which should be filled in by the user to suit his/her needs. The most important feature of the Chusaurus lies in the help it provides to non-native users of English in coping very rapidly with linguistic difficulties, since it provides pieces of real language in use. For example, it assists them in producing correct phase structuring with adequate vocabulary, which is one of the aspects of English that can be extremely different from their own native language. Two possible implementations are discussed. In the first, the resourse could be implemented as an extra function in word processors. The expressions would be accessed from menus with the compiled expressions being indexed according to their suitability for use in the different sections (and for the subjects) most likely to appear in a paper. The second implementation is more sophisticated and involves the development of a writing environment in which support tools would assist the user in selecting and organizing the material to be written as well as in producing a well-written text.

INTRODUCTION

English has undoubtedly become the international language for business, science and technology, and is currently the most commonly taught second language around the world. It is therefore of fundamental importance that scientists and businessmen alike should be able to use it, particularly in its written form, for the majority of international journals and scientific literature are written in English. For the writing

COMPUTER SCIENCE, Edited by R. Baeza-Yates
and U. Manber, Plenum Press, New York, 1992

of scientific work in general (formal reports, essays, theses, papers, etc.), help can be found in a number of books [1-10] which deal specifically with the question of "How to write in English"or "How to present technical information." Other writing aids such as spelling checkers, Thesaurus dictionaries and software packages [11] aimed mainly at postwriting evaluation also provide significant help.

Several studies are reported in the literature which address a variety of issues relevant to the improvement of non-native speakers' English usage (see for instance refs. 12-15). Nevertheless, there are still enormous difficulties facing those who need to use English on a regular basis. In order to identify these difficulties an informal study was carried out by one of us on the most frequent errors made by a group of Brazilian graduate students in the United Kingdom. One could observe that the errors are not restricted to using incorrect gramatical structures and inadequate vocabulary, but include the misuse or omission of collocations and idiomatic expressions usually employed by native users for specific purposes in a scientific text. This is a consequence of the problems encountered by non-native users in the phrase structuring, as phrase structure in English is obviously different from that of a large number of languages.

After having analysed the difficulties mentioned above we concluded that one writing strategy which could be employed to solve them was to try and write sentences based upon expressions or passages of authentic texts in an attempt to ensure that correct sentences were being produced. This strategy on the part of the foreign language learner is known as "appeal for assistance" [16], i.e. an authority (a native speaker, a teacher, books, dictionaries, etc.) is searched in order to help the learner cope with his/her problem. The strategy is likely to be quite effective, provided that adequate resources are available, which was not the case.

Hence, we decided to compile a list of well-written, useful expressions extracted from papers and books written by competent native speakers of English which could be useful in a writing exercise. In doing so, we realized that a relatively small number of expressions is sufficient to cover a large proportion of the words and phrases needed in our scientific work. This occurs because expressions are employed systematically — sometimes with little variation within a canonical framework — when describing common features such as tables and figures, or even experimental procedures or when making a comparison of results.

We first used the mini-dictionary compiled, named Chusaurus by analogy with Thesaurus dictionaries, together with a word processor (albeit not online). Because of its features, this is just the sort of process ideal to be automated. We now intend to extend this use by developing a writing software environment comprising tools aimed at helping the writer not only to produce a well-written text but also to organize the material to be written. A proposal for such an environment is presented in Section 3, while in Section 2 we discuss a simpler possible application in word processors. (These two applications have not actually been implemented yet.) Section 4 discusses the advantages and disadvantages of the Chusaurus resource.

IMPLEMENTATION OF THE CHUSAURUS INTO A WORD PROCESSOR

As a reference source, the Chusaurus can be implemented as an additional function of word processors, i.e. as an extra option on the processor Main Menu. Since the relationship that holds between linguistic items and specific sections of the scientific text is quite obvious, the list of compiled sentences was indexed according to the divisions of this text type [17], namely Introduction, Problems, Method, Discussion and Conclusion.

Although this division can vary a little in the Teaching of English to Students of Other Languages (TESOL) or English for Specific Purposes (ESP), there seems to be a general agreement in that it covers the basic macro-structures of the scientific text. In addition to the five divisions above some subdivisions were included to make it easier for the user to identify more precisely the subject(s) in each section.

The implementation can be performed so that the compiled expressions would be accessed as follows. Once the option Chusaurus is selected, the user would be presented with a menu containing the names of the different sections, as illustrated in Figure 1.

CHUSAURUS

1. Abstract

2. Introduction

3. Theory

4. Materials and Methods

5. Results

6. Discussion

.

.

.

n. Conclusions

Figure 1. Chusaurus menu containing the names of the various sections likely to appear in a paper.

The user would then be requested to choose one of the sections and a sub-menu containing the subdivisions would appear on the screen. Examples of such subdivisions are given in Figures 2 and 3 for the Introduction and Results Sections, respectively. Also shown are some examples of the compiled expressions which were indexed according to their suitability for a certain part of the written work. Obviously, some expressions will be suitable for more than one section or sub-section.

INTRODUCTION

a) Importance of the field,general interests, etc.

b) Previous reports on related work.
This topic has recently been the subject of two reviews (refs.) both of which dealt with .....

c) What is lacking in the field.
Although .... (a model) has been applied by several authors to the process of ...., a purely .... approach has not so far been presented to describe .....

Although models exist for .... these have not been related to .... results in any detail to show that ....

d) Description of an effect, phenomenon, etc.
The .... technique (method, etc.) for the formation of .... has attracted attention both as a possible method for .... and also as a way of exploring the properties of ....

e) Improvements on previous works,models, etc.

f) What the present work does.
A useful approach for developing ... is described here.

This paper describes the .... (design) and .... (operation) of a .... (system) used to produce (verify) .... Ease of fabrication of .... has been accomplished by ....

g) Outline of the paper.

Figure 2. Examples of subjects which are likely to appear in Introduction. Also given are examples of the compiled expressions.

The blank spaces in the expressions should be filled in according to the user's needs. A word between brackets following the blank space is included in some cases in order to give a hint as to the sort of term which is expected to fill the gap. Facilities should also exist to allow users to select expressions to be automatically inserted into the text.

One of the main objectives of the resource is thus to provide a variety of expressions from which the user can choose when writing about certain aspects of his/her work. Let us take, for instance, the item "Showing and Describing Figures" for which a larger number of expressions were listed in Figure 3. The various sentences will exemplify a number of ways in which the user can present his/her data, and also describe diagrams. Furthermore, the sentences would provide the appropriate adjectives for explaining the curves, graphs, etc. Though it might be straightforward for a competent native speaker to know when to use "large" or "high," for example, the same may not be true of non-native users.

Hitherto we have referred to a sort of "fill-in-the-blank use," which is in fact the more mechanical and simpler way of using the Chusaurus as a reference source. A more cognitive and creative way of approaching the resource is to use it as an aid to plan/organize the writing process. In the next section, we discuss another possible application of the Chusaurus with such characteristics, namely, the develoment of a writing environment.

RESULTS

a) **Showing and describing figures.**

> Reduction of the .... below ..... (certain value) led to an
> appreciable increase in the ....
> A continued decrease is observed at higher....
> The changes in .... (variable) illustred on the right hand
> ordinates of Figs 1 and 2 could be due to ....
> It can be seen from the figures that increased ....
> (parameter) has the anticipated effect of decreasing the....
> The .... curve obtained for .... is identical to that
> presented previously (ref.) and shows a small feature at ....
> Fig. 3 is the .... curve for .... displaying a ....
> The .... (area,other variable) at which the reversal
> (peak, etc) occurs appears reasonably independent of ....
> Fig. 4 gives representative plots, from at least ten experiments
> per compound (sample), of .... as a function of ....
> The ... plots (curves) in Fig. 5 for ... exhibit significant ...
> Fig. 6 shows typical results obtained from the ....
> measurements with .... The broken curve is a control
> measurement showing that ...

b) **Showing and describing tables.**

c) **Comparing data.**

d) **Dependence on several parameters.**

> Increasing the temperature (or other parameter) from ...
> to ....gives minor chances in ....
> Fig. 4 shows that the .... (peak, plateau, etc.) moves to
> lower .... (variable) as the temperature is raised from ....
> to .... Changing the ....(parameter) within the range
> 3-10 did not cause any significant changes in the results.

e) **Numerical analysis.**

> The computed values of .... are given in Fig. 1
> for ... A preferable analysis is made with
> alternative approximations for the ....

Figure 3. Examples of subjects which are likely to appear in Results sections of a paper. Also given are examples of the compiled expressions.

THE CHUSAURUS INTO AN ENVIRONMENT
OF SOFTWARE WRITING TOOLS

A number of software writing tools have been developed recently which could be classified into three main categories:

- (i) postwriting assessment tools using statistical text analysis;

- (ii) pre-writing tools; and

- (iii) writing environments.

Tools of type (i) are the commonest and usually analyze writing style at the word and sentence level [18-20], and allow overused words and expressions to be substituted. Some of them are commercially available such as the Right Writer [20] which is based upon a rule-based knowledge system. Tools of type (ii) are aimed at helping the writer to select and organize the material to be written, an example of which is provided by Beer [21] who proposed the use of flow charts for helping electrical engineering students to organize their laboratory reports. The third kind of tool is, in principle, the most comprehensive as tools are developed to help the writer not only to select and organize the material to be written but also to produce and polish the final version of the text. These environments consist, therefore, of tools of type (i) and (ii). As Carlson [22] has pointed out these environments are only at an embrionary stage, and, as yet, far from being flexible and comprehensive.

In spite of the many tools already presented in the literature, no tool aimed specifically at assisting non-native users of English in composing a text from the very beginning appears to have been proposed. In this context, the implementation of the Chusaurus resource suggested here may prove extremely attractive. The implementation of an extra option into word processors as described in the last section would already be of considerable help. This resource would use techniques such as the earliest employed Natural Language Processing for producing sentences which relied on templates [23]. It would present, therefore, problems of extensibility and flexibility for not allowing intra- and inter-sentential combination, hindering the possibility of producing a large number of different texts using the same database. Since this extra option in word processors would not possess such a flexibility, we have instituted a research programme aimed at developing a writing environment, a model of which is given below.

The Model For The Writing Environment

The writing environment is to include support tools which are flexible and interactive, so that the user may play a participative role in the writing process. It is to assist the writer in the selection of the material to be written as well as in generating and structuring the text. Figure 4 shows the main modules of the environment proposed.

- The Ideas Processor will allow the user to write comments and structure them in a semantic network. It will also be linked to the Knowledge Base for text generation.

- The Linearizer will transform the information contained in the semantic network and the expressions selected from the database into continuous prose.

- The Knowledge Base will consist of the database containing expressions and phrases extracted from books and papers, and also of knowledge base rules which will drive the selection of expressions from the database.

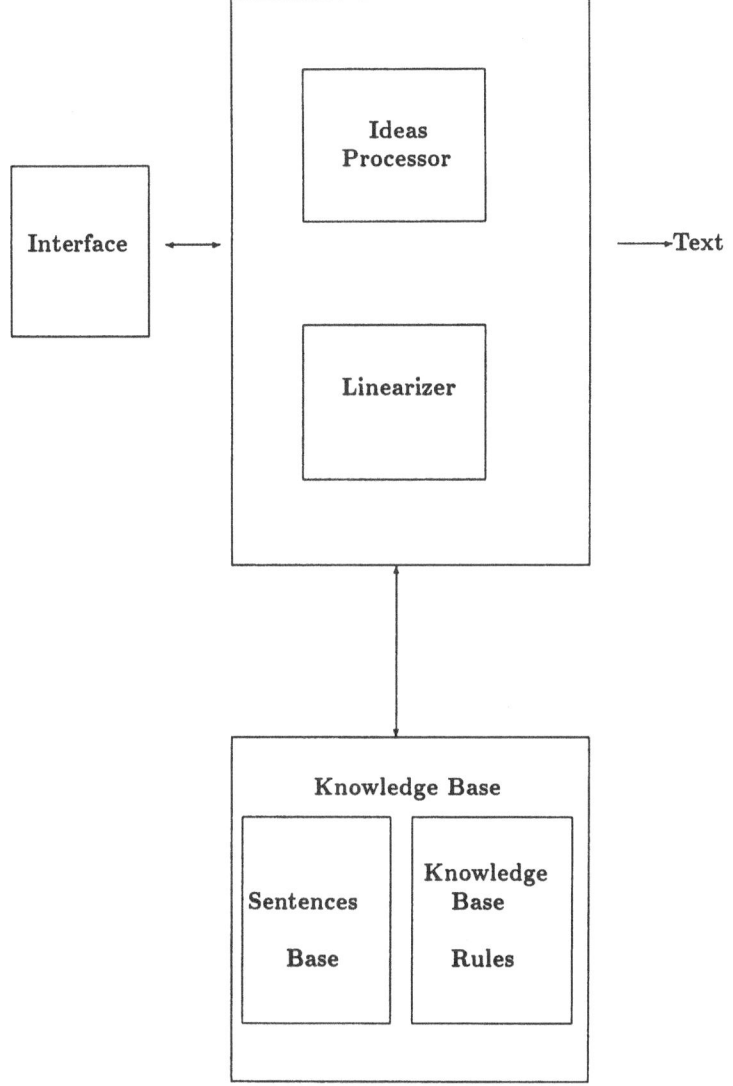

Figure 4. Model of the Environment Proposed.

For the implementation of the writing environment, issues belonging to the realms of software engineering and text generation must be addressed. Hypertext techniques may be used for constructing the semantic network and navegating over it [24]. The indexation system illustrated in Figures 2 and 3 would have to be replaced by another knowledge-representation formalism (such as schemas [25] or rethorical structure theory (RST) [26]) which could encode diverse kinds of information. Unlike the tool discussed in Section 2 where the choice of any sentence rested entirely with the user, the system is to suggest a number of possible sentences or expressions based upon information provided by the user to the Ideas Processor (which could even be in his own language). As for the text generation itself two stages are involved: planning and realization. Our tools will be more closely related to planning as they will help the user in the topic collection and organization. There will also be text realization to some extent, however, as prose will be output from the system even though there may be blanks to be filled in by the user.

It must be stressed that text generation in our context is not completely equivalent to text generation in the Natural Language Processing (NLP) jargon. In NLP, the aim is to produce a syntactically, semantically and pragmatically correct text while in our case the user will ultimately be responsible for the final quality of the text.

DISCUSSION

The two versions of the Chusaurus were conceived with a clear objective in mind, namely to help students/writers solve — as quickly as possible — global problems caused by lack of appropriate lexical, structural, pragmatic and discourse knowledge in academic text production. This is not an easy task, which has just reached the first attempts of partial implementation. So far, we have concentrated our efforts on the study of the techniques for text generation and for computer-aided writing, and on the linguistic aspects of writing strategies. While the development of the writing environment proposed in Section 3 is our long-term goal, the implementation of the Chusaurus resource (a mini-dictionary has already been compiled) into word processors will hopefully be forthcoming in the near future.

In the actual implementations some drawbacks are expected to occur, mainly on the technical, linguistic and pedagogical levels. Nevertheless, the Chusaurus is expected to offer help more effectively than dictionaries and grammar books, because the compiled sentences which comprise the database of the resource present real language in large stretches within the context required for use.

A pedagogical implication deriving from the use of the resource is that after the user has become familiar with the expressions listed in it he/she will use some of the phrase constructions naturally which had previously seemed very unusual.

This is in line with what Hovstad [12] has shown in his so-called gap tests. In these experiments, a fraction of a given text was removed and the students were asked to reproduce the text by guessing the missing words. With regards to Computer Assisted Language Learning (CALL) use can be made of the work by Leffa [27] who built on-line glossaries to help non-native users of English in reading comprehension tasks.

It is clear that while it can help with specific difficulties, the Chusaurus on its own cannot be successfully employed by users without a minimum background knowledge of English. One cannot (or should not) expect an author to write a paper without a certain proficiency in the language. Although it has been targeted primarily at non-native users of English, the Chusaurus resource can also be useful for native speakers who have little experience in writing scientific works in assisting them to structure their documents or to produce a more formal phraseology.

Caution must be advised in using the Chusaurus, however, in spite of its strengths. Three main problems can arise from its inappropriate use: i) the production of wordy sentences, one of the most common undesirable features of many written products [16-20]; ii) overuse of the author's favorite expressions; and iii) misuse of expressions or their misapplication in the wrong context.

We believe, however, that the help this recourse can provide to non-native users of English as well as to inexperienced native writers outweigh these possible disadvantages by far.

ACKNOWLEDGMENTS

We are indebted to a number of colleagues at the School of Electronic Engineering Science, Bangor, U.K. for many helpful discussions. Special thanks are due to Cristina

Oliveira, and David Chapman. The authors acknowledge the financial assistance of FAPESP and CNPq (Brazil).

REFERENCES

1. G.E.Williams. "Technical Literature," George Allen Unwin Ltd., London (1948).
2. C.Turk and J.Kirkman. "Effective Writing," E. F.N. Spon, London (1982).
3. R.Barrass. "Scientists Must Write," John Wiley and Sons, New York (1978).
4. A.D.Farr. "Science Writing For Beginners," Blackwell Scientific Publications, Oxford (1985).
5. J.Kirkman. "Good Style For Scientific And Engineering Writing," Pitman Publishing Ltd., London (1980).
6. J.W.Godfrey and G.Parr. "The Technical Writer," Chapman Hall Ltd. London (1959).
7. R.O.Kapp. "The Presentation Of Technical Information," Constable Company Ltd., London (1948).
8. R.A.Day. "How To Write And Publish A Scientific Paper," 2nd. ed., ISI Press, Philadelphia, PA (1983).
9. R.Schoenfeld. "The Chemist's English," VCH Publishers Ltd., Cambridge, UK (1986).
10. T.McArthur. "The Written Word - A Course In Controlled Composition," Oxford Univ. Press, Oxford (1984).
11. N.Williams, Computer assisted writing software: Ruskin, in: "Computers And Writing: Models And Tools," N.Williams and P.Holt, eds., BSP Ltd, Oxford, England (1989).
12. P.Hultfors. "Reactions to Non-Native English: Part 2: Foreign Role and Interpretation," Almqvist Wiksell Inter, Stokholm (1987).
13. E.E.Evans and C.K.Alexander, Jr., Increasing Aural Skills of International Graduate Students, IEEE Trans. on Education. E-27:167 (1984).
14. J.T.Dennett, Writing Technical English: A Comparison of the Process Native English and Native Japanese Speakers, IEEE International Professional Commun. Conf. 5-7:249 (1988).
15. U.Hovstad, Computer assisted essay-writing: An inter-disciplinary development project at Eikeli Grammar School, in: "Computers and Writing: Models and Tools," N.Williams and P.Holt, eds., BSP Ltd, Oxford, England (1989).
16. E. Tarone, Conscious communication strategies in interlanguage: A progress report, in: "On TESOL 77," Y. C. Brown, ed., Washington (1977).
17. A.F.Deyes, Discourse, science and scientific discourse (the raw material of comprehension in ESP), Working Paper No. 6, Brazilian ESP Project, Pontifícia Universidade Católica de São Paulo, São Paulo (1982).
18. N.H.MacDonald, L.T.Frase, P.S.Gingrich and S.A.Keenan, The Writer's Workbench: Computer Aids for Text Analysis, IEEE Trans. Commun. Com-30:105 (1982).
19. L.Cherry, Writing Tools, IEEE Trans. Commun. COM-30: 100 (1982).
20. J.Matzkin, Grammar Checkers Improve, But Won't Replace Your English Teacher, PC Magazine. March, 13:46 (1990).
21. D.F.Beer, Designing the Electrical Engineering Lab. Report, IEEE International Professional Commun. Conf., 5-7:129 (1988).
22. P.A.Carlson, Cognitive Tools and Computer-Aided Writing, AI Expert. October:48 (1990).
23. E.H.Hovy, Unresolved issues in paragraph planning, in: "Current Research in Natural Language Generation," R.Dale, C.Mellish and M.Zock, eds., London Academic Press, London (1990).
24. P.Wright and A.Lickorish, The influence of discourse structure on display and navigation in hypertexts, in: "Computers and Writing: Models and Tools," N.Williams and P.Holt, eds., BSP Ltd, Oxford, England (1989).

25. K.R.McKeown, Discourse Strategies for Generating Natural-Language Text, in: "Readings in Natural Language Processing," B.J.Grosz, K.S.Jones and B.L. Webber, eds., Morgan Kaufmann Publishers, Inc. New York (1986).

26. W. C. Mann & S. A. Thompson, Rhetorical Structure Theory, in: "The Structure of Discourse,"L. Polanyi, ed., Ablex, Norwood, N.J (1987).

27. V. J. Leffa, O uso do dicionário eletrônico na compreensão do texto em língua estrangeira, in: "Anais do XI Congresso Nacional da Sociedade Brasileira de Computação," São Paulo (1991).

TRENDS IN REPRESENTING THE SEMANTICS OF NATURAL LANGUAGE SENTENCES: A COMPARATIVE STUDY[†]

Harold José Paredes-Frigolett[††]

German Center for Artificial Intelligence
Stuhlsatzenhausweg 3
D-6600 Saarbruecken 11, FRG
e-mail: pepe@dfki.uni-sb.de

Abstract

In the present report, we briefly present a comparison of some of the principal theories for representing the semantics of natural language. The theories considered here are Montague Grammar [Montague 74], Discourse Representation Theory [Kamp 81], Situation Semantics [Barwise & Perry 83] and Situation Schemata Theory [Fenstad et al. 87]. Research trends in Situation Schemata Theory and Discourse Representation Theory, the latter being considered as the most promising candidate for a logic of discourse, are also presented.

INTRODUCTION

In this report, we present a comparison of some representation theories for the semantics of natural language originated in recent research in Computational Linguistics, such as Montague Grammar [Montague 74], Discourse Representation Theory, in one or the other of its versions (cf. [Kamp 81], [Heim 82], [Groenendijk *et al.* 87]), Situation Semantics [Barwise & Perry 83] and Situation Schemata Theory [Fenstad *et al.* 87].

In section 1, the theories mentioned above are succinctly introduced. In section 2, a comparative description of these formalisms is presented and in section 3, some of the main problems to be solved for a successful treatment of discourse as well as future trends in computational semantics are outlined.

[†] This work has been carried on at DFKI, the German Research Center for Artificial Intelligence.

[††] The author is currently working at DFKI as a DAAD (the German Academic Exchange Service) fellow.

1   REVISITING SEMANTIC REPRESENTATION THEORIES

In this section, we present the theories considered for comparison, i.e., Montague Grammar (MG) [Montague 74], Discourse Representation Theory (DRT) (cf. [Kamp 81], [Heim 82], Groenendijk 87]), Situation Semantics (SS) [Barwise and Perry 83] and Situation Schemata Theory (SST) [Fenstad *et al.* 87].

1.1   Montague Grammar - An Overview

> *I reject the contention that an important theoretical difference exists between formal and natural languages.*
>
> **Richard   Montague**

In this section, we introduce a little fragment of Montague Grammar (MG) for representing the semantics of the sentence *every man loves a woman*. There is not much motivation or explanation, but this still is Montague's original theory in the sense that it makes the same predictions as the one presented in Dowty, Wall and Peters' text book.

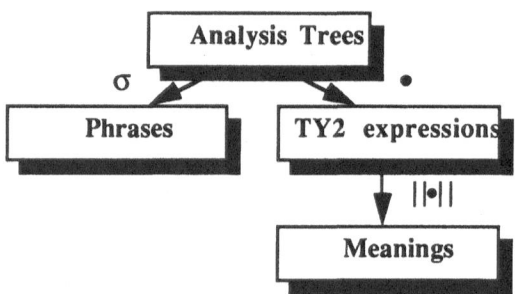

Fig. 1.1. Montague Grammar: Basic set-up

1.1.1   Analysis Trees

Definition 1 (Categories):

 i. *e* is a category; *t* is a category,
 ii. if *A* and *B* are categories then *A/B* and *A//B* are categories.

In table 1.1, we introduce the set of categories available in MG. Their corresponding basic expressions are given by the following definition.

Definition 2 (Basic Expressions for the categories listed in Table 1.1):

 B_{IV} = {run, walk, talk}
 B_{CN} = {man, woman}

$B_{t/t}$	=	{necessarily}
B_T	=	{John, Mary, Bill, he$_0$, he$_1$, he$_2$}
$B_{IV/t}$	=	{believe that, assert that}
B_{IAV}	=	{rapidly, slowly, voluntarily, allegedly}
$B_{IV//IV}$	=	{try to, wish to}
B_{TV}	=	{find, lose, eat, love, date, be, seek, conceive}
B_{DET}	=	{every, the, a}
$B_{IAV/T}$	=	{in, about}
B_A	=	$\emptyset$ if A is any category other than those mentioned above

Table 1.1. Categories in MG.

Category	Abbreviation	Traditional name
t		Sentence
t/e	IV	Verb Phrase/Intransitive Verb
$t//e$	CN	Common Noun
t/t		Sentence Adverb
t/IV	T	Noun Phrase/Proper Name
IV/t		Sentence-Complement Verb
IV/IV	IAV	Verb Phrase Adverb
$IV//IV$		Infinitive-Complement Verb
IV/T	TV	Transitive Verb
T/CN	DET	Determiner
IAV/T		Preposition

Now, we introduce a reduced set of analysis trees, especially those needed for the analysis of our sample sentence.

Definition 3 (Analysis Trees): For each category A the set AT_A of analysis trees of category A is defined recursively with the help of the of the grammatical rules G_1 - G_5.

Basic rule.

G_1. $B_A \subseteq AT_A$ for every category A.

Rules of functional application.

G_2. If $\xi \in AT_{DET}$ and $\theta \in AT_{CN}$ then $[\xi\theta]^2 \in AT_T$,
G_3. If $\xi \in AT_T$ and $\theta \in AT_{IV}$ then $[\xi\theta]^3 \in AT_t$,
G_4. If $\xi \in AT_{TV}$ and $\theta \in AT_T$ then $[\xi\theta]^4 \in AT_{IV}$.

Quantification rules.

G_5. If $\xi \in AT_T$ and $\theta \in AT_t$ then $[\xi\theta]^{5,n} \in AT_t$ (for each n).

This definition produces numbered bracketings for our sample sentence like [[every man]^2[love [a woman]^2]^4]^3 and [[a woman]^2[[every man]^2[love he$_0$]^4]^3]^{5,0} (both elements of AT_t). The results are just analysis trees in Montague's sense.

1.1.2 Phrases

Montague's syntax is awkward and is not the reason for studying Montague Grammar. Fortunately, Montague's semantics can be coupled to much less naive syntactic theories, as shown for example in Generalized Phrase Structure Grammar and in modern versions of Categorial Grammar.

Definition 4 *(Syntactic Operations)*:

$F_{1,n}(\gamma, \delta)$ = $\gamma\delta'$, and δ' is the result of replacing the main verbs, i.e., members of B_{IV}, B_{TV}, $B_{IV/t}$ or $B_{IV//IV}$, in δ by their third person singular present,

$F_{2,n}(\gamma, \delta)$ = $\gamma\delta$ if δ does not have the form he$_n$ and $F_2(\gamma, he_n) = him_n$,

$F_3(\gamma, \delta)$ = $\gamma\delta$,

$F_{4,n}(\gamma, \delta)$ = comes from δ by replacing the first ocurrence of he$_n$ or him$_n$ by γ and all other ocurrences of he$_n$ or him$_n$ by he/she/it or him/her/it respectively, according as the first B_{CN} or B_T in γ is masc./fem. /neuter, if γ does not have the form he$_k$,

$F_{4,n}(\gamma, \delta)$ = comes from δ by replacing all ocurrences of he$_n$ or him$_n$ by he$_k$ or him$_k$ respectively, if $\gamma = he_k$.

Using these functions we can give a compositional analysis for our sample phrase to trees. The main operation is to stipulate which operation is used in what case.

Definition 5 *(Phrases)*: For each analysis tree ξ, define a phrase $\sigma(\xi)$ by induction on the complexity of analysis trees:

$S1.$ $\sigma(\xi) = \xi$ if $\xi \in BA$,

$S2 - 5.$ If g is a rule number and $S(g)$ is as in Table 1.2 below, then $\sigma([\xi\theta]^g) = F_{S(g)}(\sigma(\xi), \sigma(\theta))$.

Table 1.2. Phrase construction.

g	$S(g)$
2	3
3	1
4	2
5, n	4, n

For our sample example we have the following two analysis:

i. $\sigma([[every\ man]^2[love\ [a\ woman]^2]^4]^3)$ =
    $F_1(F_3(every, man), F_2(love, F_3(a, woman)))$ =
    $F_1(every\ man, F_2(love, a\ woman))$ =
    $F_1(every\ man, love\ a\ woman)$ =
    every man loves a woman,

ii. $\sigma([[\text{a woman}]^2[[\text{every man}]^2[\text{love he}_0]^4]^3]^{5,0})$ =

$F_4(F_3(\text{a, woman}), F_1(F_3(\text{every, man}), F_2(\text{love, he}_0)))$ =

$F_4(\text{a woman}, F_1(\text{every man}, \text{love him}_0))$ =

$F_4(\text{a woman}, \text{every man loves him}_0)$ =

every man loves a woman.

1.1.3   Semantics

In this section, we will provide phrases with a semantics. Instead of giving a direct interpretation to the analysis trees defined, we will translate them into type theory. Since type theory has a semantics, our trees will then have a semantics as well. A tree of category A will be translated into a term of category $\tau(A)$, where $\tau(A)$ is obtained according to the following rule.

Definition 6 (Category-to-type rule):

i. $\tau(e) = e; \tau(t) = (st);$

ii. $\tau(A/B) = \tau(A//B) = (\tau(B)\tau(A)).$

The idea is that the meaning of a sentence is a set of possible worlds, so that we associate the type *st* with category *t*.

The type *e* (possible individuals) is associated with the category *e* and a complex category A/B or $A//B$ is linked to the type of functions that expect things of the type linked to B in order to return something of the type linked to A.

In Table 1.3, the values under τ are written out for those categories that are actually used for a little fragment of English, in particular for our sample sentence *every man loves a woman*.

Table 1.3. Term categories.

Category A	$\tau(A)$	Semantic name
t	*st*	*Proposition*
t/e (IV)	*e(st)*	*Property*
t//e (CN)	*e(st)*	*Property*
t/t	*(st)(st)*	
t/IV (T)	*(e(st))(st)*	*Quantifier*
IV/t	*(st)(e(st))*	
IV/IV (IAV)	*(e(st))(e(st))*	
IV//IV	*(e(st))(e(st))*	
IV/T (TV)	*((e(st))(st))(e(st))*	
T/CN (DET)	*(e(st))((e(st))(st))*	
IAV/T	*((e(st))(st))((e(st))(e(st)))*	

We now can translate each expression of the fragment, in particular our sample sentence, into type theory inductively by giving translations to all lexical items and by telling how the translation of a complex expression is to depend on the translations of its parts.

Definition 7 *(Some Constants)*: We consider the constants with types in Table 1.4.

Table 1.4. Constants and its categories.

Category A	$\tau(A)$
john, bill, mary	*e*
man, woman, unicorn	*e(st)*
love, find, lose, date	*e(e(st))*
believe, assert	*(st)(e(st))*
fnd, love	*(e(e(st))*
seek, conceive	*((e(st))(st))(e(st))*
rapidly, slowly	*(e(st))(e(st))*
try, wish	*(e(st))(e(st))*
in	*(e((e(st))(e(st))))*
about	*((e(st))(st))((e(st))(e(st)))*
<	*s(st)*

Definition 8 *(Translation)*: For each analysis tree ξ define its translation $\xi\bullet$ by induction on the complexity of analysis trees. We let x, y, and z range over individuals, i and j over indices, p and q over propositions, P over properties and Q over quantifiers. *T1* to *T5* denote translation rules, *P1* to *P3* denote principles.

T1. John$\bullet$ = $\lambda P(P\ john)$, Mary$\bullet$ = $\lambda P(P\ mary)$, he$_n\bullet$ = $\lambda P(P\ x_n)$ ...
love$\bullet$ = $\lambda Q\lambda y(Q\lambda x(love\ xy))$, ...
man$\bullet$ = *man*, woman$\bullet$ = *woman*, ...
every$\bullet$ = $\lambda P_1\lambda P_2\ \lambda i\forall x(P_1xi \rightarrow P_2xi)$,
a$\bullet$ = $\lambda P_1\lambda P_2\ \lambda i\exists x(P_1xi\ \&\ P_2xi)$,

T2 - 4. $([\xi\theta]^k)\bullet = \xi\bullet\ \theta\bullet$ if $2 \leq k \leq 4$,

T5. $([\xi\theta]^{5,n})\bullet = \xi\bullet\lambda x_n(\theta\bullet)$,

P1. *Lambda conversion:*
$\models\lambda x(A)B = [B/x]A$ *if B is substitutable for x in A,*

P2. *Alpha conversion:*
$\models \lambda x(A) = \lambda y([y/x]A)$ *if y is substitutable for x in A,*
$\models\forall x\phi = \forall y([y/x]\phi)$ *if y is substitutable for x in ϕ,*

P3. *Eta conversion:*
$\models \lambda x(Ax) = A$ *if x is not free in A.*

For *Translation 1* (*every* taking wide scope, *a* taking narrow scope), we first compute the translations for the sentence constituents as follows:

woman$\bullet$	=	$woman_{(e(st))}$
$([a\ woman]^3)\bullet$	=	$\lambda P_1\lambda P_2\ \lambda i\exists x(P_1xi\ \&\ P_2xi)woman\ \Rightarrow$
		$\lambda P\ \lambda i\exists x(woman\ xi\ \&\ Pxi)$

love•	=	$\lambda Q \lambda y(Q \lambda x(love_{(e(e(st)))} xy))$
([love [a woman]2]4)•	=	$\lambda Q \lambda y(Q \lambda x(love\ xy))\lambda P\ \lambda i \exists x(woman\ xi\ \&\ Pxi)\ \Rightarrow$
		$\lambda y(\lambda P\ \lambda i \exists x(woman\ xi\ \&\ Pxi)\lambda x(love\ xy))\ \Rightarrow$
		$\lambda y\ \lambda i \exists x(woman\ xi\ \&\ \lambda x(love\ xy)xi))\ \Rightarrow$
		$\lambda y\ \lambda i \exists x(woman\ xi\ \&\ (love\ xyi)$
every•	=	$\lambda P_1 \lambda P_2\ \lambda i \forall x(P_1 xi \rightarrow P_2 xi)$
man•	=	$man_{(e(st))}$
[every man]2	=	$\lambda P_1 \lambda P_2\ \lambda i \forall x(P_1 xi \rightarrow Pxi)man\ \Rightarrow$
		$\lambda P \lambda i \forall x(man\ xi \rightarrow Pxi)$

And now we compute the translation for the whole sentence:

([every man]2[love [a woman]2]4]3)• $\Rightarrow$
$\lambda P\ \lambda i \forall x(man\ xi \rightarrow Pxi)(\ \lambda y\ \lambda i \exists x(woman\ xi\ \&\ love\ xyi))\ \Rightarrow$
$\lambda i \forall x(man\ xi \rightarrow \lambda y\ \lambda i \exists x(woman\ xi\ \&\ love\ xyi))xi)\ \Rightarrow$
$\lambda i \forall x(man\ xi \rightarrow \exists y(woman\ yi\ \&\ love\ xyi))$

Translation 2 for [a woman]2[[every man]2[love he0]4]3]5,0 with *a* taking wide scope and *every* taking narrow scope goes in similar terms.

1.2 Discourse Representation Theory - An Overview

.. to provide an account of meaning both as that which determines conditions of truth and as that which a language user grasps when he understands the words he hears or reads.

Kamp

Hans Kamp [Kamp 81] developed his Discourse Representation Theory aiming for a formalism capable of providing a good representation for the meaning of indefinite descriptions in pronominal anaphora, especially in donkey sentences, i.e., sentences like *every man who owns a donkey beats it.*

In his logic Kamp replaced the traditional formulas of first order logic by so-called Discourse Representation Structures (DRSs) which are pairs <M,C>, where M is a set of markers and C is a set of conditions. DRT consists of a language L, given by a lexicon and phrase structure rules, and DRS construction rules for constructing DRSs from phrase structure trees, and rules for interpreting DRSs with respect to a model.

A model for Kamp's logic consists of a structure M=<U, F> with universe U and interpretation function F. F assigns an element of U to each of the proper names of the language, a subset of U to each of its basic compound nouns and basic intransitive verbs, and a set of pairs of elements of U to each of the basic transitive verbs. A partial DRS is a pair consisting of a set of discourse referents or markers and a set of conditions. A condition is either:

i.   not fully reduced, or

ii.   an atomic simple condition of the form $u=v$, $u=\alpha$, $\beta(u)$, $\gamma(u,v)$, where u, v are referents, α is a proper noun, β is a noun, and γ is a verb, or

iii. it is a complex condition of the form $s: dr$, $dr_1 \rightarrow dr_2$, etc., where dr, dr_1, dr_2 are DRSs, and s is a discourse referent.

The language used to express the atomic conditions L augmented by the relation symbol '=', the auxiliary symbols ',' '(', and ')', and the set of discourse referents is denoted by L'. If S is a sentence in L, then S' is a sentence in L' where S' is like S except that one or more NPs may be replaced by a referent.

If A is a proper name, $u=A$ is a sentence in L'. If $u\beta$ or $u\beta u'$ are sentences in L where β is a verb and u, u' are referents, then $\beta(u)$ and $\beta(u, u')$ are sentences in L'. A dr is a possible DRS for the discourse D in L if it is constructed from the DRS: $<\varnothing, \{D\}>$ by using the so-called construction rules. The discourse $D = $ *Every man loves a woman* may have the DRS shown in Fig. 1.2. To indicate the construction process, the reduced (canceled) conditions are written between /'s.

The final DRS consists only of conditions that cannot be further reduced. The resulting DRS is inductively interpreted into a first order model. Truth is defined in two stages:

i.   ***Notion of Verification***: Let $f:V\to U$ (f is called an embedding function). Then f *verifies* the DRS $K=<M, C>$, in symbols $f \vDash K$, if and only if $M \subseteq \mathrm{DOM}(f)$ and $f \vDash C$. $f \vDash C$ if and only if for each condition $C_i \in C$, $f \vDash C_i$.

   i.i.   ***Verification*** for atomic conditions is analogous to truth for atomic formulas (relative to an assignment), i.e., if an atomic condition C is of the form $\alpha(\beta)$, $\alpha=\beta$ or $\alpha(\beta, \gamma)$, i.e., of the form $R(\alpha_1, \dots, \alpha_n)$, $f \vDash C$ iff. $<f(\alpha_1), \dots, f(\alpha_n)> \in F(R)$.

   i.ii. ***Verification*** for complex conditions is defined in different ways for the different kinds of conditions .

ii.   ***Notion of Truth***:   A DRS K is made true by a model M if there is some embedding f defined on M such that $f \vDash K$.

/Every man loves a woman/

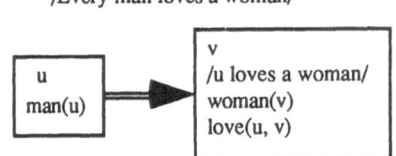

Fig. 1.2. DRS for /Every man loves a woman/

The discourse D above is true with respect to a model $M=<U, F>$, where U is the universe of M, and F is the interpretation function for the lexicon, if (1) follows.

(1) $(\forall f:\{u\}\to U)(F(\mathrm{man})$
      $(f(u)) \Rightarrow (\exists g:\{v\}\to U)(F(\mathrm{woman})(g(v))$ and $\mathrm{F}(\mathrm{love}), (f(u) , g(v))))$

(1) can be paraphrased as for all functions $f:\{u\}\to U$ such that $f(u)$ is a man in M, there is a function $g:\{v\}\to U$ such that $g(v)$ is a woman in M and $f(u)$ loves $g(v)$ in M.

Most of the empirical import of DRT comes from the definition of the DRS construction rules, especially those for the interpretation of NPs and of conditionals.

Three of these rules have been used to build the DRT representation of /every man loves a woman / in Fig 1.2, namely,

i.   **proper names rule**: if α is a proper name, a new marker u has to be added to the outermost DRS, i.e., the one not embedded in any other, and a new atomic condition $\alpha(u)$ has to be added to the same outermost DRS,

ii. **indefinite NPs rule**: if α is an indefinite NP then a new marker u has to be added to the current DRS, and a new atomic condition of the form $\alpha(u)$ has to be added to the same DRS,

iii. **every construction rule**: If *every* α β is a sentence, add to the current DRS a new complex condition of the form $K_1 \Rightarrow K_2$, where K_1 and K_2 are DRSs, adding a new marker u to K_1, adding the conditions for α to K_1, and the conditions for β to K_2.

An embedding f *verifies* a complex condition of the form $K_1 \Rightarrow K_2$ if and only if for every embedding g which extends f and such that $f \vDash K_1$, there is an embedding h that extends g and such that $h \vDash K_2$.

Accessibility in DRT is a way of representing in a geometrical fashion the constraint on anaphora usually called *scope constraint*, which states that no quantified expression can take wider scope than its clause. There is also the other usual constraint that no quantified expression can serve as antecedent of a pronoun outside its scope. In dealing with complex conditions such as $K_1 \Rightarrow K_2$, the accessibility conditions are modified as follows: a marker u is accessible from the DRS K if either u is local to K, or is introduced in a DRS K' such that $K' \Rightarrow K$, or is introduced in a DRS K' which contains K.

1.3 Situation Semantics - An Overview

The linguistic meanings of expressions in a language are conventional constraints on utterances. To study semantics is to attempt to spell out these constraints, to spell out what it is that the native speaker knows in knowing what utterances of his language mean.

Barwise and Perry

Situation Semantics is grounded in four basic domains, namely,

D   the set of individuals,
L   the set of space time locations,
POL the set of truth values true and false, and
S   the set of situations (courses of events).

A fact is of the form *at l; r, d1, ... , dn; pol*, where *l* is a location, *r* a relation, *d1*, ... , *dn* individuals and *pol* a polarity, positive or negative. A fact may hold or it may not hold in a course of events *s*. An event-type is a set of facts where any of *l, r, d1, ... , dn* may be indeterminates. A situation *s* is of a given event-type if there is an anchoring of the indeterminates of the event-type to individuals in *s* such that all of the facts obtained from the facts in the event-type by the anchoring hold in *s*. The situational structure *M* consists of a collection M of courses of events (*coes*), the factual courses of events, with a non-empty subcollection $M0$ of actual courses of events, satisfying the following rules.

    i.   Every $e \in M0$ is coherent,

    ii. $e \in M$ and $e' \subseteq e \Rightarrow e' \in M$,

    iii. $X \subseteq M \Rightarrow \exists e \in M0 \, (\forall e' \in X \, (e' \text{ is part of } e))$,

    iv. if C is any constraint in M, then M respects C.

Let C be a simple constraint, say, $C := (involves, S0, S1; 1)$, let $e0, e1$ be *coes*, then:

    i. $e0$ is meaningful with respect to C, $e0 \in \mathbf{MFc}$, if $e0$ is of type $S0$,

    ii.   if $e0 \in \mathbf{MFc}$, $e1$ is a meaningful option from $e0$ with respect to C, $e0\mathbf{MOc}e1$, if $\forall f \, ((f \text{ total anchor for } S0 \text{ and } S0[f] \subseteq e0) \Rightarrow S1[f] \subseteq e1)$,

    iii. a structure of situations M respects a simple constraint C if $\forall e0 \in M0$ $(e0 \in \mathbf{MFc} \Rightarrow \exists e1 \in M(e0\mathbf{MOc}e1))$, and a structure of situations M respects a complex constraint if it respects each simple part.

In SS, an expression φ expresses a meaning relation, a conventional constraint between utterance situations and described situations. If d,c is an utterance situation of φ, i.e., d,c is in MF[[φ]], then s will be a described situation if s is a meaningful option from d,c with respect to the constraint [[φ]]; d,c[[φ]]s. An statement Φ of an expression φ is an ordered triple $\Phi = <d, c, \varphi>$, i.e., an utterance situation of φ. The interpretation of $\Phi = <d, c, \varphi>$ is [[Φ]]$= \{e \mid d,c[[\varphi]]e\}$, the collection of situations that Φ describes.

1.4 Situation Schemata Theory - An Overview

.. to give an overall framework for relating the linguistic form of utterances and their semantic interpretation which is based on the idea of constraint propagation.

Fenstad et al.

The situation schemata is a theoretical notion convenient for summing up information from linguistic form that is relevant for semantic interpretation. The notion of situation schemata is open; it depends upon the underlying theory of grammar and is susceptible both to emendations and extensions. Situation schemata can also be adapted to various kinds of semantic interpretations; one can give some kind of operational interpretation in a suitable programming language or into a system of higher order intensional logic in a Montagovian sense. A situation schemata is a tabular representation as in (2).

(2) Situation Schema of β (β any declarative sentence)

$$
\begin{bmatrix}
\text{SIT} & - \\
\text{REL} & - \\
\text{ARG1} & - \\
\text{ARG2} & - \\
- & - \\
- & - \\
\text{ARGN} & - \\
\text{LOC} & - \\
\text{POL} & -
\end{bmatrix}
$$

This expresses that the situation schemata of β is a function with arguments *REL*, *ARG.1*, *ARG.2*, ... , *ARG.n*, *LOC*, *POL* (and possibly others). The meaning of a (simple declarative) sentence β is a relation between an utterance situation, u and a described situation, s.

(3) $u[[SIT.β]]s$ (SIT.β is the schema associated with β), where
  u is a moment of speech,
  s is a moment of evaluation.

In interpreting an utterance of β there is a flow of information, partly from the linguistic form, that has been encoded or summarized in the SIT.β schema, and partly from the other contextual factors, that are read off from the utterance situation u.

These combine to form a set of constraints on the described situation s. s is not uniquely determined; given u and an utterance of β in u there will be several situations s that satisfy the constraints. SST is grounded in a set of primitives:

(4) S   situations,
  L   locations, (connected regions of space-time)
  D   individuals,
  R   relations.

It is assumed that the set L comes equipped with two structural relations:

(5) •   temporarily overlaps, <   temporarily precedes.

Primitives combine to form facts that can either be located or unlocated. Let r be an n-ary relation, l a location and $a1$, ... , an individuals. Basic located facts will have the form shown in (6) with the intended meaning that at location l the relation r holds (does not hold) of the individuals $a1$, ..., an, respectively.

(6) *at l: r, a1,... , an; 1*
  at l: r, a1,... , an; 0

Basic unlocated facts will have the form shown in (7).

(7) *r, a1, ... , an; 1,*
  r, a1, ... , an; 0

Unlocated atomic assertions concerning the location structure will have the form shown in (8) expressing the above-mentioned relations of temporal precedence and overlap.

(8) $l < l', l • l'$

The basic format connecting the primitives is in the located case shown in (9). (9) is read as: in s at location l the relation r holds (does not hold) of $a1$, ..., an.

(9) *in s: at l: r, a1, ..., an; 1,*
  in s: at l: r, a1, ..., an; 0

The authors' proposal is an analysis where syntax, phonology and morphology constrain the semantics directly. By viewing the relationship between form and meaning in terms of mutual constraints, one can reflect more directly the intuition that the different aspects of linguistic form all partially determine the interpretation. A situation schema for a given utterance is one that satisfies all the semantic constraints.

There is a construction algorithm for the constraint system which, given a set of constraints in the form of equations, allows one to build, i.e., derive, the semantic representation. Consider the situation in (10) which involves an unlocated fact expressing that 2 is greater than 1. Its associated fact is given in (11).

(10) $< >, 2, 1 >$

(11)

$$\begin{bmatrix} \text{REL} & > \\ \text{ARG1} & 2 \\ \text{ARG2} & 1 \\ \text{POL} & 1 \end{bmatrix}$$

Consider now the situation type described in (12) that characterizes a situation in which *every man loves a woman* at the time of utterance. There is a restriction on the location that it spatio-temporally overlap the location of the utterance, *ld*.

(12)   *Every man loves a woman*

This type of case is handled in the attribute-value representation by introducing an indeterminate for the complex term, and then, as pointed out above, allowing conditions, or restrictions, to be associated with these indeterminates, as in (13).

(13)

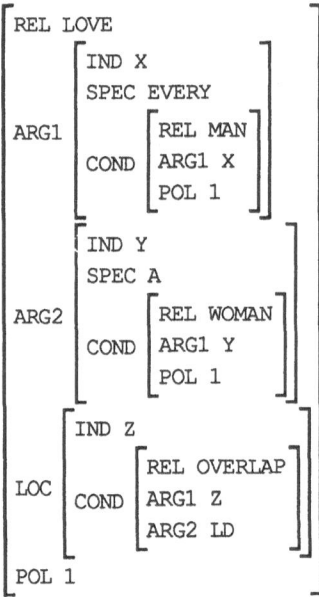

In (13) one recognizes the attribute names from [Barwise and Perry '83]. The indeterminate *ld* is a special indeterminate that is conventionally used to refer to the utterance location of the sentence.

This situation schema is not fully disambiguated. Thus, it can be taken to represent more than one reading of a sentence. From this schema, the basic fact schemata in (14) can be extracted, corresponding to the SIT.SCHEMA and COND parts of the situation schema.

In (14) there are two inequivalent scope orderings of the quantifiers. Through a recursive procedure depending on the relevant quantifier scope chosen (cf. [Vestre 91]), one can construct fact schemata for the full sentence.

$$(14) \quad C_1: \quad love, \ ind_1, \ ind_2; \ 1,$$
$$ C_2: \quad man, \ ind_1; \ 1,$$
$$ C_3: \quad woman, \ ind_2; \ 1$$

Thus, the situation schema above and disambiguation information about quantification given in what Fenstad *et al.* call the Q.MODE yields a so-called fact schema, an expression that is disambiguated with respect to quantification, but not with respect to anaphora and coreference.

From the situation schema and the Q.MODE that ascribes wide scope to *every man* and narrow scope to *a woman* one gets the fact schema in (15). Adding the existentially interpreted time and place reference, one gets the fact schema given in (16).

$$(15) \quad \textbf{\textit{Every}} \ (< x \mid C_2 >)$$
$$ (< x \mid A \ (< y \mid C_3 >)(< y \mid C_1 >)>)$$

$$(16) \quad \textbf{\textit{Every}} \ (< x \mid man, \ x; \ 1> \ )(< x \mid A \ (< y \mid woman \ , \ y; \ 1 >)$$
$$ (< y \mid A \ (< z \mid \bullet, \ z, \ ld \ ; \ 1>) \ (< z \mid \text{at } z: love, \ x, \ y; \ 1>)>)>)$$

(16) is then translated into a situation-fixed model $M_s = <\Lambda, R, D; Ins >$. The sentence holds in M_s if given d,c (utterance situation with speakers connections) (17) follows.

$$(17) \quad \{u \mid (c(man), \ u; \ 1) \in Ins\} \quad \subseteq \quad \{u \mid \{v \mid (c(woman \ ), \ v; \ 1) \in Ins\} \ \cap$$
$$\phantom{(17) \quad \{u \mid (c(man), \ u; \ 1) \in Ins\} \quad \subseteq \quad} \{v \mid (c(love \ ), \ u, \ v; \ 1) \in Ins\} \ \neq \ \emptyset\}$$

The generalized quantifier style of (17) expressions is expressed in (18).

$$(18) \quad (\forall f:\{u\} \rightarrow D)((c(man \ ), \ f(u); \ 1) \in Ins \ \Rightarrow$$
$$ (\exists g:\{v\} \rightarrow D)((c(woman \ ), \ g(v); \ 1) \in Ins \ \& \ (c(love \ ), \ f(u), \ g(v); \ 1) \in Ins))$$

(18) can be paraphrased as, for every anchoring f of *ind1* such that $f(ind1)$ is a man in s, there is an anchoring g of *ind2* such that $g(ind2)$ is a woman in s and $f(ind1)$ loves $g(ind2)$ in s. In (15) and (16) one recognizes the generalized quantifiers syntax of [Barwise and Cooper '81].

On the basis of the structure of the fact schemata, [Fenstad *et al.* 87] give an inductive definition of the meaning relation, the relation between utterance situation and described situation. The full interpretation process is sketched in Fig. 1.3.

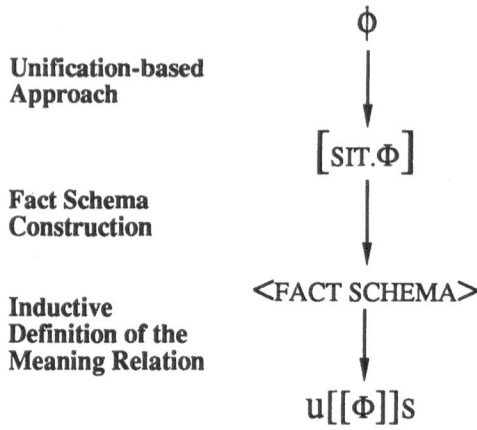

Unification-based
Approach

$$\phi$$

$$\downarrow$$

$$[\text{SIT}.\Phi]$$

Fact Schema
Construction

$$\downarrow$$

$$<\text{FACT SCHEMA}>$$

Inductive
Definition of the
Meaning Relation

$$\downarrow$$

$$u[[\Phi]]s$$

Fig. 1.3. Interpretation Process in situation schemata.

2 REPRESENTING THE MEANING OF NATURAL LANGUAGE UTTERANCES: A COMPARISON

In this section, we present a parallel between the semantic representation frameworks of MG, SS and DRT.

2.1 Preliminaries

Whenever information is conveyed, it is given in a particular form somewhere at some time, it has a source, a destination and a purpose. It has also content, and this content is about entities standing (or changing) in constellations of some sort. Accordingly, some concepts have been proposed, as shown in Table 2.1.

Table 2.1. What kind of information is conveyed?

Setting	The time, source, destination, purpose and form of the information
Content	The facts and courses of events in case of a narrative, the quest for information of a particular kind, the order, or instructions, and
Cast	The actors and entities that the information is about, with their properties and the constellations in which they take part.

Setting and content are parts of the world, whereas the cast is an organization of parts of the information well suited for individuals sorting out information about agents and entities. Part of the content information is contained in the cast, that is, all the actors or entities explicitly mentioned in the previous discourse that are available to be referred to in the later discourse.

Up to now, several representation formalisms for NL Semantics has been put forward, all they differing from each other in the way they formalize setting, content and cast. This point is shown in Table 2.2 for the formalisms presented in section 1. A main issue for text understanding systems concerns the way cast is formalized. In the formalisms of Table 2.2, cast has been formalized with different degrees of sophistication.

Table 2.2. Some representation formalisms for NL Semantics

	MG	DRT	F S	S S	SST
Setting	ignored	almost ignored, indexical information only	almost ignored, indexical information only	utterance situation	utterance situation
Content	possible worlds	set of conditions	not focused	described situation	described situation
Cast	indices	set of referents	set of files	indeterminates	indeterminates

We can observe the opposite approaches taken by Heim's and Barwise's proposals, the former taking an explicit treatment having almost all the information available for the agents in the cast, the latter formalizing cast as anchors and assignments carrying no information beyond the identification of the domain of possible antecedents, a proposal that turns out to be insufficient for an advanced treatment of coreference for dependent elements. We can think of formalizing cast with a high degree of sophistication by putting in the cast all the information available for the agents, but even then one could not choose just one actor in the cast as the most suitable and salient for a certain dependent element and reject the others. This involves not only lexical and structural information, but also knowledge about the world. Among the formalisms presented above one can distinguish between dynamic and non-dynamic systems. In the dynamic ones (cf. [Kamp 81], [Heim 82], [Barwise 87], [Groenendijk & Stockhof 87]) the generation and use of casts come to the focus and play an important role in the interpretation process.

In the non-dynamic ones (cf. [Montague 74], [Barwise & Perry 83], [Fenstad *et al.* 87]) algorithms are given that describe how to compute a meaning from the meaning of the parts, once the way the parts are put together and what they really are had been decided upon. There may be filtering mechanisms on the number of ways different possible basic blocks can be put together to a full meaning construct, but these systems give algorithms for computing meaning after the dependencies have been decided in a correct way.

2.2 Representing Meaning in MG and SS

There are some important differences between the two theories, some of them shown in Table 2.3. Both theories have relations, but in SS, relations are thought of as primitives while in MG they are thought of as sets of ordered pairs or a kind of function. A main difference between the theories is the fact that SS has indeterminate objects that are not present in MG.

Furthermore, there is no construct in MG that plays the role indeterminates play in the model theory, a role that turns out to be very interesting in dealing with partiality of information, as will be seen below.

Table 2.3. Basic constructs in MG and SS

SS basic constructs

Locations, relations, individuals, polarity values, indeterminates

---

MG basic constructs

Time (point/intervals), space, individuals, possible worlds, truth value

---

2.2.1   Interpreting NL Sentences

There are also differences in interpreting sentences, as shown in Table 2.4. In SS, sentences describe situations, i.e., one thinks of a sentence as representing all of the situations it might describe or as the type corresponding to that set of situations.

Model-theoretic objects called facts from which SS can distinguish between located and unlocated facts are shown in (19).

(19) $< l, r, a_1, ... , a_n, i >$
      $< r, a_1, ... , a_n, i >$

Table 2.4. What do sentences represent?

S S

Sentences describe situations and they can represent:

- a set of situations,
- a situation-type,
- a fact(-type).

M G

Sentences are true or false at possible worlds and times, and can represent:

- a truth-value,
- a set of possible worlds, times

There are also fact-types that are objects like facts, except that they may contain in-determinates, i.e., some of the constituents of the fact may not have been determined as in (20) where the indeterminates are represented in boldface.

(20) corresponds to something like "some loving is going on at *l* or not". Once the notion of fact(-type) has been introduced, one can define a situation as a set of facts and a situation-type as a set of fact-types.

(20) $< l,\ love,\ s,\ o,\ i >$

In MG, sentences are true or false at possible worlds or times, and will in a given context represent a truth-value or, in intensional terms, a set of possible worlds and times. Table 2.5 summarizes how to interpret constituents of subsentences.

Montague's propositions, which is what one is aiming for when interpreting a whole sentence, don't carry any information about how they were built up from smaller objects corresponding to subconstituents of the sentence.

Table 2.5. What information is conveyed in interpreting subsentences?

M G

Functions taking as arguments something corresponding to a needed constituent and producing another such function or truth-value.

S S

Smaller parts of a sentence represent fact-types with indeterminacies which may correspond to constituents that are needed to make a sentence representation.

2.3 Representing Meaning in DRT, SS and SST

It is now interesting to look at what is considered by many researchers in Computational Semantics as the two most promising formalisms for representing semantics for natural language, especially when focusing on the dynamics of discourse anaphora and partiality of information. In Fig. 2.1, some of the most important correspondences between DRT and SST are given.

On the one hand, SST introduces static objects called situation schemata that are not very well suited for some discourse phenomena such as pronominal reference, anaphora and scope resolution, for which a rather dynamic system has to be introduced. Some steps in this direction have been put forward under a situation-oriented framework (cf. [Barwise 87]). On the other hand, DRT, in one or the other of its various forms (cf. [Kamp 81], [Heim 82], [Groenendijk *et al.* 87]), incorporates dynamicity and has come to be accepted in Linguistics as the most promising candidate for a logic of discourse.

A DRS has not been thought of as an LF, i.e., as an intermediate and not yet disambiguated representation, as opposed to a situation schema where all kind of ambiguities are left unsolved. On the contrary, DRSs are fully determined with atomic simple conditions of the form $u = v$, with u, v referents, fact conditions and scope conditions.

On the other hand, from a situation schema one gets a set of basic fact schemata that may need a Q.MODE (quantification mode) and an R.MODE (resource situations) to be interpreted. The latter corresponds to situations other than the utterance situation and the described situation that the speaker may refer to in a given discourse.

At the intermediate level there is correspondence 3, which states that in analysing the same sentence from the common lexicon and phrase structure rules, the resulting basic facts of the DRSs and the basic fact schema of the situation schemata correspond.

Intuitively, the relations coming from a shared lexicon are the same for both grammars, and, as long as extra-lexical mechanisms are similar, e.g., whenever every coreference condition is explicitly stated in separate conditions in the DRS and outside the situation schema, only corresponding sets of fact conditions and basic fact schemata can come out of the analyses.

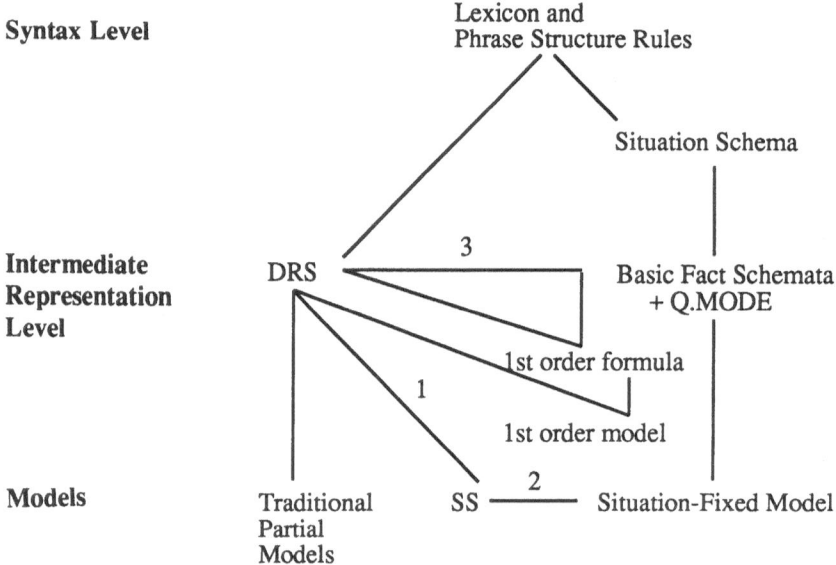

Fig. 2.1. Some correspondences between DRT, SS and SST

Formally, the isomorphism between DR grammars and situation schema grammars was proven in [Sem 88] for languages without relatives and conjunctions by giving a construction procedure from DRT grammars to situation schema grammars and vice versa that are based on the fact that the parts of the construction that have consequences for the fact conditions and the basic fact schemata are always connected to the same nodes in each of the grammar types. The grammars obtained by such a construction procedure do not have scope or coreference conditions. This is because scope conditions and the situation schema/Q.MODE do not enter at the same level in the syntax tree, and coreference conditions do not enter in connection with one phrase structure only.

If one wants isomorphic grammars with the correct scope and coreference mechanisms, one must add these to the grammars separately. This leads to the fact that the basic fact schema of the situation schema(ta) and the basic facts of the DRSs resulting from the analysis of a common sentence correspond, i.e., one gets the same interpretations from the situation schema as from the DRS, provided one starts from a common lexicon and phrase structure rules, and facts and scope are interpreted in the same way into the same model.

As to the correspondence labeled with 1 and 2 in Diagram 2.1, DRSs can be translated into a a first order model as usual in DRT or, as shown in [Sem 88] for the notorious sentence *every man loves a woman*, into a full situational structure in the style of SS, which is what correspondence 1 states.

Situation schemata, on the other hand, is translated into a restricted model, i.e., a situation-restricted model corresponding to a restriction of a situational structure to just one situation (cf. [Fenstad *et al.* 87]). The correspondence labeled 2 in Diagram 2.1 claims that the interpretation of sentences like our famous *every man loves a woman* into a full situational model in the style of SS corresponds to the interpretation into a situation-re-stricted model in the style of SST.

This completes our illustration of some of the connections between DRT, SS and SST. The most important point to note here is the fact that a complete DRS for an expression φ generates substantial parts of the meaning relation $[[\varphi]]$ in SS, giving rise to corresponding interpretations either into a full situational model M as in SS, or into a situation-restricted model M_s as in SST.

3   CONCLUSIONS AND FUTURE WORK

Some of the correspondences between Montague Grammar, Discourse Representation Theory, Situations Semantics and Situation Schemata Theory have been presented. We are now in a position of drawing some of the advantages of one approach over the other.

3.1   Montague Grammar and Situation Semantics

We will start our discussion here with Montague Grammar and Situations Semantics. The latter present a series of advantages over the former, especially when we focus on computational aspects of the theories.

In fact, SS a series of advantages over MG, some of them listed below:

i.   SS provides explicitly for indeterminacy,

ii.   SS provides explicitly for structuring of information in terms of the interplay between various situations in a way that MG does not,

iii.   SS suggests a general unification-based approach for analysing sentences that is absolutely absent in MG.

The use of indeterminacy in SS as opposed to the use of functions in MG represents an important difference in interpreting subsentences constituent, which, apart from being an important ontological difference, may turn out to have a computational significance directly associated with ambiguity.

Recent research has incorporated dynamicity into Montague Grammar. This has resulted in what is called Dynamic Montague Grammar (DMG) whose primary motivation was that of proposing a compositional and non-representational theory of meaning for discourses, as opposed to DRT and SS.

Compositionality is the cornerstone of all semantic theories in the logical tradition, and, as a consequence, it has also been of prime importance in those approaches to NL semantics which use tools based on the logical paradigm. However, compositionality has been challenged as a property of NL semantics. Especially when dealing with the meaning of discourses people have felt, and sometimes argued, that a compositional approach fails.

The days of the hegemony of MG as the paradigm of model-theoretic semantics for NL are over. And rightly so, since the development of alternatives, such as DRT, clearly has been inspired by limitations and shortcomings of MG. These alternatives have enabled us to cover a new ground, and they have brought us a new way of looking at our familiar surroundings. Yet, every expanding phase is necessarily followed by one contradiction, in which, again, attempts are made to unify the insights and results of various frameworks. Recent research in NL semantics is intended as a contribution to such unification.

3.2 Situation Schemata and Discourse Representation Theory

Now, considering Situation Semantics, Situation Schemata Theory and Discourse Representation Theory, we find that these seemingly different approaches to semantic representation have much in common. SST is an intent to combine a well-founded semantic theory, in this case SS, with a well-founded syntactic theory like that of Lexical Functional Grammar, that is, to extend feature structure systems to semantic representation taking as a basis, on the one hand, the proposal for semantic representation of SS, and, on the other, the well-founded functional unification formalism and grammar of LFG. While Fenstad *et al.* succeeded in that, SST in its current stage, is far from being acceptable for application in sophisticated NL systems. SST, while very promising, has to be extended for a better representation of spatio-temporal relations, modality, plurality, non-locative prepositional phrases, complex and vague quantifications, adverbials and genitive attributes.

But that is only one part of the whole enterprise, especially when the focus is on discourse understanding. In order to succesfully deal with NL discourse dynamicity has to be integrated in the system. In fact, situation schemata are static objects that are interpreted into a model restricted to just one situation.

This restriction was imposed on the theory by Fenstad *et al.* in order to simplify it. The focus was not on providing a discourse representation theory, but on combining the proposal for semantic representation of SS with a unification-based syntactic theory, in particular with LFG.

This has been the main contribution of SST so far. Now, moving one step further towards a discourse representation theory, it turns out that SST has to be interpreted into a model of multiple situations, as in SS, and that some of the characteristics of dynamic semantic theories, mainly DRT, must be integrated.

Starting from the observation that DRSs consist of fact conditions, coreference conditions and scope conditions, a comparison between DRSs and situation schemata with scope and coreference conditions was given following [Sem 88], where a construction procedure from DRT grammars to SST grammars that give rise to corresponding basic facts and basic fact schemata for languages without relatives and conjunctions was proposed. The construction procedure can be extended in a straightforward way for more complex languages containing, say, relative clauses.

The translations given to these intermediate representations may vary according to the model chosen to translate into. Here, decisions have to be made regarding what kind of models are best suited for representing the semantics of NL texts and dialogues for different implementation purposes. Also the decision of what kind of information must be represented at an intermediate level will depend on such implementation purposes.

The fact that comparisons of theories of this kind of complexity must be done by taking into account the set of requisites imposed on particular implementations has been repeatedly pointed out in the literature when comparing different theories for NL Semantics representation. Discussion of the general characteristics of the theories alone might be quite interesting and, as shown here, may be of interest in the study of the approaches to phenomena like scope and anaphora that the different theories make use of, but it will not provide the insight one needs to make comparisons in the computational domain.

The theories as they stand now do not give solutions to a great variety of the problems posed by NL discourse. Consider for example problems like segmentation in NL discourse where more flexible structures are required to represent segments. Recent research in DRT suggests extending the usual DRSs by breaking the DRS into smaller DRSs, each one representing one sentence. The main motivation for this is the fact that representing a discourse as a unique DRS forces one to select a unique situation as the interpretation of the dialogue, thus making the representation incapable of handling multiple-situations dialogues (cf. [Grosz & Sidner 86]).

Also in SST, extensions going in very much the same direction (cf. [Sem 88]) have been proposed to deal with some of the problems in NL discourse, especially those posed by segmentation. The question of either representing a discourse as a single situation schema or representing it as a set of situation schemata, each one of them representing the meaning of just one sentence, eventually depends on where in the interpretation process to make use of casts.

There are also reasons to extend the model in SST to more than one situation. This comes from the fact that in interpreting situation schemata into the restricted model proposed in SST, there are only two sources of information, namely, the utterance situation and the described situation. In more complex discourses, coreference conditions may require extending the present model into which situation schemata are interpreted, which is restricted to one situation, to a model containing multiple situations. That is, the described situation and the utterance situation, as well as possible resource situations must be in S, the set of situations.

As opposed to DRT, the main motivation in the proposal of SST was to have at the intermediate representation level a structure where most of the ambiguities remain unsolved. If SST were to be extended continuing this idea, the natural solution would be to keep the situation schemata as small as possible by constructing situation schemata only for sentences. Reasons of simplicity also suggest that this proposal would be the most convenient one for extending SST to discourse.

4 REFERENCES

[Barwise 87]   Barwise, J., 1987. **Noun Phrases, Generalized Quantifiers and Anaphora**, in Gärdenfors, P. *Generalized Quantifiers, Linguistics and Logical Approaches*, Dordrecht.

[Barwise & Cooper '81]	Barwise, J. and Cooper , R., 1981. **Generalized Quantifiers and Natural Language** in *Linguistics and Philosophy* 4, 159-219.
[Barwise & Perry 83]	Barwise, J. and Perry, J., 1983. **Situations and Attitudes**, The MIT Press.
[Dowty *et al.* 81]	Dowty, D., Wall, R., Peters, S., 1981. **Introduction to Montague Grammar**. Studies in Linguistics and Philosophy. Reidel.
[Fenstad *et al.* 87]	Fenstad, J. E., Halvorsen P. K., Langholm, T. and van Benthem J., 1987. **Situations, Language and Logic**, Reidel.
[Groenendijk *et al.* 87]	Groenendijk, J. and Stockhof, M., 1987. **Dynamic Predicate Logic: Towards a compositional and non-representational discourse theory.** Amsterdam ITLI/Department of Philosophy.
[Grosz & Sidner 86]	Grosz, B, and Sidner, C. **Attention, Intention and the Structure of Discourse**, in Computational Linguistics, 12(3).
[Heim 82]	Heim, I., 1982. **The Semantics of Definite and Indefinite Noun Phrases**, PhD dissertation, University of Massachussets at Amherst.
[Kamp 81]	Kamp, H., 1981. **A Theory of Truth and Semantic Representation**, in Groenendijk, J. *et al.* (eds.), *Formal Methods in the Study of Language*, Amsterdam.
[Montague 74]	Montague, R., 1974. **The Proper Treatment of Quantification in Ordinary English**, in Thomason, R. (ed.) *Formal Philosophy: Selected Papers of Richard Montague*, Yale University Press, New Haven.
[Rooth 86]	Rooth, M., 1986. **Noun Phrase Interpretation in Montague Grammar, File Change Semantics and Situation Semantics**, in Peter Gärdenfors (ed.), Generalized Quantifiers - Linguistics and Logical Approaches, pages 237-268. Reidel. Also available as Report No. CSLI-86-51.
[Sem 84]	Sem, H. F., 1984. **Quantification Scope and Coreferentiality**, in Fenstad, J. E. (ed.), report of an Oslo Seminar in Logic and Linguistics, University of Oslo.
[Sem 88]	Sem, H. F., 1988. **Discourse in Situation Schema Theory**, COSMOS Report No. 10, Department of Mathematics, University of Oslo.
[Vestre 91]	Vestre E., 1991. **An Algorithm for Generating Non-redundant Quantifier Scopings**, to appear in: Proceedings of the Fifth Conference of the European Chapter of the Association for Computational Linguistics, Berlin, April 1991.

EXTENDING PARTIAL EVALUATION IN

LOGIC PROGRAMMING

David A. Fuller, Sacha A. Bocic

Departamento de Ciencia de la Computación
Pontificia Universidad Católica de Chile
Casilla 306
Santiago 22
Chile

1. INTRODUCTION

Partial evaluation has been known as a program optimization technique since the early seventies [Futamura71, Ershov78]. Only in the last few years, however, its use has been made possible.

Partial evaluation of a subject program with respect to known values of some of its input parameters will result in a residual program. Running the residual program on any remaining input values will yield the same result as running the original subject program on all of the same input values. A residual program, therefore, is a specialization of a subject program with respect to known values of some of its parameters.

In expert systems and logic programming, this technique is now known as a way of eliminating the extra layers of interpretation produced by meta-interpreters [Takeuchi86, Sterling86, Levi88].

In this section we will describe the equations defining partial evaluation and the meaning they have in the automatic production of compilers and compiler generators.

Let P be a programming language with a semantic function:

$$\mathcal{P}\colon \; D \; \to \; (D \; \to \; D)$$

where D is a set whose elements may represent programs in various languages, as well as their input and output. Note that $\mathcal{P}$ is a partial function, since programs may have infinite loops. A residual program r is defined by:

$$\mathcal{P}(p) \; (<d1,d2>) \; = \; \mathcal{P}(r) \; (<d2>)$$

where d1 is the known parameter, d2 the unknown, and p and r are valid programs in language P. Let *mix* and int be two valid programs in P, where *mix* is a partial evaluator, int is an interpreter for programs in language L, and l a valid program in L. The description of the three residual programs is given in the following equations:

$$\text{target} = \mathcal{P}(mix)(<\text{int}, l>) \qquad\qquad (1.1)$$

$$\text{comp} = \mathcal{P}(mix)(<mix, \text{int}>) \qquad\qquad (1.2)$$

$$\text{cocom} = \mathcal{P}(mix)(<mix, mix>) \qquad\qquad (1.3)$$

The residual program target is generated by running the partial evaluator *mix* with input parameters int and l, and corresponds to the compiled program l into P. It should be noted that this is exactly how partial evaluation is being used in meta-interpretation.

The second equation shows the production of a compiler comp by running *mix* with the inputs *mix* and int. In other words, we are specializing the interpreter int for language L into a compiler for language L. A *mix* partial evaluator with the ability to apply to itself will be called a *mix* self-applicable partial evaluator.

As explained in a latter section, not every partial evaluator has this ability. The third equation describes how to produce the residual program cocom, a compiler-compiler or compiler generator, by running a *mix* self-applicable partial evaluator with its two inputs being copies of *mix* . Thus, when running cocom it will produce a compiler for a language L when an interpreter for language L is given.

We have briefly summarized the theory of partial evaluation and self-application. The first *mix* self-applicable partial evaluator was described in [Jones85], using a first order subset of Lisp. In the case of logic programming, a *mix* self-applicable partial evaluator for Prolog programs was first described in [Fuller88, Fuller89].

In this paper, we present an extended partial evaluator capable of undertaking powerful partial evaluation of logic programs.

First, we present basic operations in a partial evaluator such as expansion and suspension of predicates during the process of building the proof tree.

The following two sections introduce new operations to partial evaluators. Subsequently, a treatment of negated predicates during partial evaluation is presented. Then, local optimizations are introduced in order to optimize the residual program. Finally, conclusions are drawn and further research is outlined.

2. BASIC OPERATIONS

In terms of logic programming, a partial evaluator *mix* attempts to build a proof tree of its first input program with respect to its second one. For example, from equation (1.1), *mix* will attempt to produce a proof tree for int running l. The proof tree thus produced will correspond to the residual target program.

2.1. Expansion

Expansion of a predicate **p** corresponds to building a partial proof tree for **p** [Lloyd89]. The expansion of the user's goal will then produce the residual program.

This can be implemented easily in PROLOG with the help of a predicate pe/2 which receives as first argument a predicate and returns in its second argument the proof tree for the predicate as a list. This is shown in Figure 1.

Note that this implementation does not handle built-in predicates. In fact, if the variable Goal is instantiated to a built-in predicate, the first definition of pe/2 will fail because clause(Goal,true) fails to find a solution for all predicates that are not facts in the PROLOG database.

The second definition of pe/2 also fails because Goal cannot unify with a term like (Goal,Goals). The third definition fails because there is no definition for Goal in the database (since it is a built-in predicate that the user cannot redefine). Even so, extending the definition of pe/2 to handle built-in predicates is trivial. This will be shown later.

The implementation uses the PROLOG unification mechanism to unify variables of predicates that are being partially evaluated.

```
:- mode pe(+,-).
pe(Goal,[Goal]):- clause(Goal,true).[1]

pe((Goal,Goals),Tree):- pe(Goal,Tree1),
                        pe(Goals,Tree2),
                        append(Tree1,Tree2,Tree).

pe(Goal,Tree):- clause(Goal, Body),
                pe(Body,Tree1),
                append([(Goal:-Body)],Tree1,Tree).[2]
```

Figure 1. Expansion in partial evaluation.

An important fact is that the implementation only finds the first solution. Other solutions have to be found using backtracking. As an example, let us consider the definition for the predicate member/2 in Figure 2. This predicate receives, as first argument, an element and second, a list of elements The predicate is true if the element belongs to the list.

```
member(X,[X|_]).

member(X,[Y|Z]):- X \== Y, member(X,Z).
```

Figure 2. Implementation of member/2.

To partially evaluate the predicate member/2 with its first parameter, instantiated to the constant "3" and its second, to a list with three elements, we use the predicate pe/2 previously defined as follows:

```
?- pe(member(3,[_, _, _ ]),Tree).
```

To obtain the instantiation of variable **Tree**:

```
Tree = member(3,[3,Y,Z]).
```

Using PROLOG's backtracking feature, we obtain the instantiations of **Tree** shown in Figure 3.

```
Tree = member(3,[X,3,Z]):- 3 \== X, member(3,[3,Z]).
       member(3,[3,Z]).

Tree = member(3,[X,Y,3]):- 3 \== X, member(3,[Y,3]).
       member(3,[Y,3]):- 3 \== Y, member(3,[3]).
       member(3,[3]).
```

Figure 3. Backtracking the partial evaluation of member/2.

---

1. clause(H,B) is a built-in predicate which is true if there is a clause H:-B in the PROLOG database. If B is the constant "true" then H is a fact.
2. append/3 is true if its third argument is syntactically equal to the concatenation of the first two arguments.

At partial evaluation time we have less information than at execution time. This presents problems for the expansion of the proof tree, especially if the search space is infinite. This, nonetheless, is not an uncommon situation in partial evaluation. Uninstantiated variables can lead us to infinite solutions or infinite depth proof trees. Ways of handling this problem will be discussed in the following sections.

2.2. Suspension

The process of constructing the proof tree for a predicate may not terminate. It seems, therefore, necessary to determine the predicates that are not safe to expand during this process.

These predicates have to be suspended, i.e. expansion has to be avoided. We will define a meta-predicate unsafe/1 to be true if its predicate argument is not safe to expand, i.e. it may lead to a non-termination situation or to incorrect evaluations due to the lack of appropriate information (such as the treatment of negated predicates discussed in a latter section).

Remark 2.2.1: The expansion of a predicate **p** is suspended if **p** is considered **unsafe**.

The problem at this point is how to decide which predicates are **unsafe.** To solve this problem there are several approaches. [Vasak & Potter 86] propose a formal characterization for logic programs which permit us to know if a predicate has a finite set of solutions. The characterization builds a set of safe predicates in bottom-up.

The method builds, starting from the facts, the set of predicates with a proof tree of depth one, proceeding to those which have depth two, until a depth level h. We define as C_i the predicate set whose proof tree has depth i which represents the set of all the predicates that are safe to expand up to a depth level h.

$$C = \overset{i=h}{\underset{i=1}{\cup}} C_i$$

To determine whether a predicate is unsafe, we may check for membership in set C. Predicates not belonging to the set have to be suspended. Depth level h is, obviously, an artificial fence and for this reason we might consider unsafe predicates that are safe.

As a final result a worst quality partial evaluation would be obtained. It is cleaner, easier and a lot less expensive to keep a depth counter, and suspend the expansion of a predicate when depth level h is reached.

We will call this procedure **depth suspension control** (DSC). This method has not yet been used in partial evaluation. In this case, the condition for expansion is checked at partial evaluation time. The previous case was determined before partial evaluation time.

The implementation of a DSC partial evaluator is shown in Figure 4. We add two new parameters to the meta-predicate pe/2. These two new parameters will be used to handle the DSC. The first, has to be initialized to zero The second parameter is a constant corresponding to the depth level h.

A second technique verified at partial evaluation time consists of keeping a record of the predicates that have been expanded. This prevents the expansion of a predicate that can be subsumed to one predicate in the list [Fuller89]. This technique is expensive in terms of time and memory usage. Each predicate has to be checked, at partial evaluation time, from the list being produced.

It seems that the less expensive solution is to specify the unsafe predicates before the partial evaluation process. A manual method would allow the user to specify the predicates to be suspended through a process of user annotations, using a meta-predicate unsafe/1 to be true if its argument is a predicate defined as unsafe. The implementation of meta-predicate pe/2 in Figure 1 only needs to add, as first definition of pe/2, the clause:

```
pe(Goal,[Goal]):- unsafe(Goal).
```

```
pe(Goal,[Goal],H,H):- !.

pe(Goal,[Goal],N,H):- clause(Goal,true).

pe((Goal,Others),Tree,N,H):-
              pe(Goal,SubTree1,N,H),
              pe(Others,SubTree2,N,H),
              append(SubTree1,SubTree2,Tree).

pe(Goal,Tree,N,H):- clause(Goal,Body),
              N1 is N +1,
              pe(Body,SubTree,N1,H),
              append([(Goal:- Body)],SubTree,Tree).
```

Figure 4. Partial evaluation with depth suspension control.

With this extension to `pe/2`, the unsafe predicates will be "captured" and will not be expanded. Consider, for example, a predicate `length/2` as unsafe if its first argument is an uninstantiated variable:

$$\texttt{unsafe(length(X,N)):- \textbackslash+ ground(X).}[3]$$

Note that a predicate might be unsafe to expand under certain conditions, but it could be safe under others. For this reason, it is important to specify the conditions for which it is unsafe to expand a predicate.

The definition of unsafe predicates depends on the context in which a predicate is used. In some cases, it is possible to specify only a subset of all the conditions that make a predicate unsafe in obtaining a successful partial evaluation.

It should be noted that this annotation process involves the users in a programming problem. There is work on automatizing the predicate annotations as a process done before partial evaluation time [Fuller 91] based on abstract interpretation of logic programs, however this is still an open problem.

3. NEW POWERFUL OPERATIONS

3.1. Freezing and Melting

An uninstantiated variable could trigger the suspension of a predicate. Given PROLOG´s resolution mechanism, it is possible that a variable, not instantiated during the process of partial evaluation of a predicate, could instantiate later during the partial evaluation of other predicates. Let us consider the example shown in Figure 5. In this example, `length/2` is considered unsafe (because its argument is an uninstantiated variable). The partial evaluation of this predicate, therefore, is suspended.

```
foo(N):- length(X,N),
         X = ['this','is','an','example'].

unsafe(length(X,_)):- \+ ground(X).
```

Figure 5. Freezing a predicate.

---

3. \+ ground(X) is true if it is not the case that X is instantiated to a ground term.

99

During the expansion of the second predicate in the body of `foo/1`, variable X is instantiated, therefore, `length/2`, at this pont, is no longer unsafe.

This example proposes the necessity of temporarily suspending the expansion of an unsafe predicate, and trying its expansion at a later time.

In logic programming, these techniques are known as **freezing** and **melting** predicates. They, however, have never been used in partial evaluation. A necessary condition for freezing the expansion of a predicate is that there should be the possibility of melting it. In other words, the uninstantiated variables which made us consider the predicate as unsafe, appear in other predicates with a possibility of instantiation.

In order to explore necessary conditions to characterize a predicate as frozen, we need to consider PROLOG´s resolution strategy (such as left-to-right and top-down). Also, we need to use variable modes, either by user annotations (many PROLOG systems allow the user to declare parameter modes) or by an automatic process through static analysis [Mellish87].

Definition 3.1.1: A predicate p is a **descendant** of a predicate q iff p appears in the body of any definition of q; or p is a descendant of any predicate in that body.

Definition 3.1.2: A predicate p is a **right-ancestor** of a predicate q iff q is a descendant of a predicate r; so that r and p belong to the body of any rule, and p is at the right of r in that body.

Thus, we can formulate the necessary conditions for freezing and melting a predicate, as follow.

Definition 3.1.3: A predicate p belonging to the body of a rule R is **freezable**, if for every variable X in the set of variables that make it unsafe (a set denoted by X_u) it is true that:
1. X appears as an output variable in a predicate at the right of p in rule r, or;
2. X is instantiated to an output variable in a right-ancestor of p.

Definition 3.1.4: If all the variables belonging to X_u of the predicate p satisfy the first condition of definition 3.1.3, we say that p can be **locally frozen**.

Definition 3.1.5: If a predicate has been frozen, and at least one of the variables that belong to X_u satisfy the second condition of Definition 3.1.3, we say that p has been **globally frozen**.

Proposition 3.1.6: The condition for melting a predicate p is that that the set X_u of p has been instantiated. Note that this condition is independent of the manner in which a predicate has been frozen.

Remark 3.1.7: Predicate p will **never be melted** if it has been locally frozen and if the partial evaluation of the body of the rule to which it belongs to has no effect on the state of p (it is still unsafe).

Definition 3.1.8: If during the partial evaluation of an input program a predicate p, (which has been frozen) instantiates its arguments so that it is no longer considered unsafe, we say that p has been **melted**.

We now requiere a definition of the algorithm to handle frozen predicates. For those predicates that have been globally frozen, we partially evaluate the input program. Once this process has finished, all the predicates that have been melted are expanded and the process is repeated. If there are no melted predicates, the process stops.

For local freezing, a record of every frozen predicate have to be stored, and each time a predicate is expanded successfully, check if any predicate has been melted. If this happens, the melted predicate is partially evaluated. Those predicates that will never be melted must be eliminated from the frozen predicates record.

3.2. Reflection

Operationally, a partial evaluator translates a program in one meta-level to a lower meta-level. Sometimes, it is possible to directly execute operations in a higher meta-level in a lower level. This is called reflection, and will be considered as an extension to the proposed partial evaluator.

The implementations of partial evaluators, shown in this paper, use the PROLOG unification mechanism to unify terms belonging to the predicates that are being partially evaluated. In other words, the implementations we propose are using a capacity of a lower meta-level (the PROLOG interpreter) to handle predicates of an upper meta-level.

We can use this concept in a more general context. For instance, we can take an operation of a level k, send it to a level j (j < k) execute it, and return the result to level k.

To implement reflection in our partial evaluator, we only have to extend the definition of predicate pe/2 of Figure 1, as shown in Figure 6.

In this definition, we consider as **reflectable** a predicate if it satisfies a certain "reflectability criterion". This is defined using the predicate reflectable/1. It is clear that the evaluation of higher meta-level built-in predicates can be reflected, to the PROLOG meta-level, if all their input mode parameters are instantiated. The reflection of those built-in predicates whose reflection might produce side-effects, should be avoided. Finally, no other necessary conditions to define a predicate as reflectable, have been identified.

```
pe(Goal,[]):- reflectable(Goal),
              call(Goal).
```

Figure 6. Extending partial evaluation with reflection.

4. OPERATIONALIZATION & GENERALIZATION

The techniques of operationalization and generalization are both "borrowed" from the theory of explanation based generalization (known as EBG) [Mitchell et al. 86].

This is an inductive learning technique, which has never before been used in partial evaluation. In this perspective, the operationalization of a predicate is related to its reformulation in terms of other predicates, which are easier to calculate, and are called "operational predicates".

The main idea is to expand the proof tree of a predicate until it reaches the operational predicates, and to obtain a reformulation in terms of these predicates.

This reformulation is the conjunction of all the leaves in the proof tree. As an example let us consider the set of rules of Figure 7 and consider as operational the predicates son/2 and parents/2.

```
relative(X,Y):- cousin(X,Y).
cousin(X,Y)   :- son(X,Z),son(Y,W),brothers(Z,W).
brothers(X,Y):- parents(X,W),parents(Y,W).
```

Figure 7. Set of rules for Operationalization.

Using the EBG algorithm, the reformulation of relative/2 is: relative(X,Y):-son(X,Z),son(Y,W),parents(Z,V),parents(W,V).

In order to apply this technique, it is necessary to define an operational criterion capable of identifying the operational predicates, which will expand or suspend the expansion of predicates in the proof tree.

Obviously we can define as operational all the facts of a given program, or we can use a meta-predicate `operational/1` to define the predicates in its argument as operational. In general, the necessary conditions to define a predicate as operational are still a matter for further research.

In Figure 8, we present the implementation of a partial evaluator extended with the operational capacity (OPE). Note that the satisfaction of the operational criterion is implemented by the meta-predicate `operational/1`, which is defined in terms of the predicate `member/2`. In order to be consistent with the example, in this implementation `son/2` and `parents/2` are considered operational.

During the construction of a proof tree in partial evaluation, it is possible to face the problem of not having enough information to decide which node to expand (in or-nodes).

```
pe(Goal,GoalOut):- operational(Goal),
                   copy(Goal,GoalOut) [4],
                   call(Goal),!.

pe((Goal,Goals),(Tree1,Tree2)):- pe(Goal,Tree1),
                                 pe(Goals,Tree2).

pe(Goal,Tree):- clause(Goal,Body),
                pe(Body,Tree).

operational(Goal):- member(Goal,[son(_,_),parents(_,_)]) [5].
```

Figure 8. Implementation of an OPE.

We can either abort the expansion (meaning that we abort the operationalization) or expand all the possible branches (with the probability of obtaining more than one reformulation). If the number of reformulations is n (n big enough), it is convenient to apply the generalization.

At present we do not know how to predict the number of reformulations obtained from the expansion of a certain predicate. If the operationalization process concludes with m (m < n) reformulations, it is possible to generalize these reformulations in order to obtain a shorter residual program. It is argued that the generalization of many branches will still produce a more specialized predicate than if it were suspended.

Basically, a generalization process replaces constants by variables, but as in P.E. we need to take care of the soundness and completeness of the residual program. Therefore, the generalization process needs to be done carefully. In other words, the generalized version of the operationalized predicate cannot be more general than the original predicate.

5. TREATMENT OF NEGATED PREDICATES

Negation will be treated based on techniques shown in previous sections.

5.1 Expansion and Suspension of Negated Predicates

Expansion of a negated predicate is not equivalent, to the negation of the expansion of the predicate, when uninstantiated arguments are involved.

---

4. copy(Goal,GoalOut) is true if GoalOut is a copy of Goal with fresh variables.
5. member/2 defined in Figure 2.2.

As an example let us analyze the partial evaluation of not p(X) in the context of Figure 9. The expansion of p(X) produces p(1) after elimination of tautologies (which will be shown later). The partial evaluation of not p(X) is, therefore, false. From the logical point of view, this is, obviously, not correct because X was instantiated and then eliminated.

Intuitively, the negation of p(X) is true if X does not unify with "1". It is clear then, that the problem arises because variable X is being uninstantiated during partial evaluation.

```
p(X):- q(X),r(X).

q(1).

r(1).
```

Figure 9. Example of problems for P.E. with Negation.

Definition 5.1: Let $p(X_1, X_2, \ldots X_n)$ be a predicate such that X_i $(1 \le i \le n)$ is an uninstantiated term. The expansion of not $p(X_1, X_2, \ldots, X_n)$ is therefore unsafe.

In other words, if there are uninstantiated terms in a negated predicate, its expansion should be avoided. On the other hand, if all the terms are instantiated, we can always know whether not $p(X_1, X_2, \ldots, X_n)$ is true or false.

This necessary condition can be added to the definition of predicate unsafe/1 as shown in Figure 10. A more formal treatment of negation during partial evaluation is presented in [Chan & Wallace 89].

```
unsafe(not Goal):- Goal =.. [_|Vars]6,
                          \+ allgrounded(Vars).

allgrounded([]).
allgrounded([X|Xs]):- ground(X),
                          allgrounded(Xs).
```

Figure 10. Extension of unsafe/1 for negated predicates.

5.2. Freezing Negated Predicates

Freezing can be used successfully for the treatment of negated predicates. It is possible to freeze negated predicates considered unsafe if variable instantiations during partial evaluation will revert the unsafe situation, allowing predicates to melt. Here the same considerations regarding local and global freezings are valid.

5.3. Reflection in Negation

Reflection can be applied to the treatment of negated predicates, expanding the proof tree as much as possible, in order to obtain better residual programs. Let us consider the definition of a predicate p:

$$p:- L_1, L_2, \ldots, L_n$$

---

6. Term =..List is defined by List being a list whose head is the atom corresponding to the principal functor of Term, and whose tail is a list of the arguments of Term.

where L_i ($1 \leq i \leq n$) is a negated predicate such as `not q`. If the proof of q produces an empty set[7], it is possible to express p as follows:

$$\texttt{p:- } \texttt{L}_1, \ldots, \texttt{L}_{i-1}, \texttt{L}_{i+1}, \ldots, \texttt{L}_n.$$

Note that this is possible since predicate q failed, and therefore, no instantiation of variables is done during the process of partial evaluation.

To determine if the solution set of a predicate q is empty, we define the meta-predicate `noSolution/1` to be true if the proof of the predicate in its argument produces a truth value false.

Here, reflection is used to execute a predicate of a higher meta-level in the lower PROLOG meta-level. A PROLOG implementation is shown in Figure 11. One of the major advantages of this technique is that it is possible to handle part of the negated predicates considered unsafe (according to definition 5.1).

```
noSolution(Q):- call(Q),!,fail.
noSolution(_).
```

Figure 11. Implementation of meta-predicate `noSolution/1`.

If the solution set of q is partitioned into $S_1 \cup S_2 \cup \ldots \cup S_n$ where S_i (S_i not empty) represents the solution i we will have:

$$\texttt{not q = not } \texttt{S}_1 \wedge \texttt{not } \texttt{S}_2 \wedge \ldots \wedge \texttt{not } \texttt{S}_n$$

allowing us to reformulate predicate p as follows:

$$\texttt{p:- } \texttt{L}_1 \wedge \ldots \wedge \texttt{L}_{i-1} \wedge \texttt{not } \texttt{S}_1 \wedge \ldots \wedge \texttt{not } \texttt{S}_n \wedge \texttt{L}_{i+1} \wedge \ldots \wedge \texttt{L}_n.$$

Obviously, this method works for n finite. Unfortunately, we do not yet know how to detect the unsafe cases. As an example let us consider an example from [Mendelzon 88] shown in Figure 12. Even though fat and weight are finite relations, eats has a breadth-infinite solution space. A simple solution to this problem is to consider a breadth counter control (BCC) mechanism.

```
eats(X,Y):- fat(X).

fat(X):- weight(X,Y), Y > 100.
```

Figure 12. Predicate with breadth-infinite solutions.

6. LOCAL OPTIMIZATIONS

Many local optimization techniques can be used in order to reduce the complexity of the residual program.

---

7. An empty solution set means that q is always false.

6.1. Elimination of Tautologies

This technique consists of the elimination of those predicates in the body of a clause of the residual program that are true independently of the input variables. As an example, consider the set of rules shown in Figure 13.

```
p(a,Y):- q(a),r(a,Y),s(Y).

q(a).

r(a,Y):-...

s(Y)  :-...
```

Figure 13. Eliminating tautologies.

It is possible to eliminate q(a) from the body of the first rule without changing the semantics of the residual program.

An implementation for this technique is simple. We only need to define a meta-predicate unique/1 to be true if the predicate in its argument has only one solution.

Please note that it is not necessary to determine if such a predicate has all its arguments instantiated. Also, note that unique/1 needs to take care of unsafe predicates.

6.2. Predicate Specialization

This process is expensive in terms of time. It is performed for each clause:

$$A:- B_1,...,B_m \quad (m > 0)$$

in the residual program. For each B_i with at least one ground term in it, it is necessary to search for all the clauses in the residual program with instances of B_i. These clauses may be of two types, namely:

$$B'_i:- C_1,...,C_j \qquad (j \geq 0)$$
and
$$A'':- B''_1, ..., B''_k \qquad (k > 0)$$

such that B_i matches B'_i and B''_i. If there is at least one clause of the form:

$$B'_i:- C_1,...,C_j.$$

the predicates B_i, B'_i and B''_i can be specialized to their ground values.

This is accomplished by first deetermining the common ground term values to all the predicates to be specialized. For example, the common ground terms of the predicates p(a,Y,f(c)) and p(a,b,f(c)) are the first and the third. Then it is possible to eliminate such values from the predicates and append to the predicate symbols a unique symbol. In our example, the two predicates would become p_it(Y) and p_it(b); respectively. The predicate symbol p_it is unique in the residual program. This will create a new residual program with the specialized clauses for B_i.

This process has also to be carried out for the user's goal. Please observe that if the total number of predicate calls in the residual program is n, the time-complexity of the process of predicate specialization (as described) is $O(n^2)$.

A different approach for the predicate specialization based on abstract interpretation [Abramsky & Hankin 87] which will lead to a much faster algorithm, is now being investigated.

6.3. Transformation of Equality Predicate

Another used transformation is the transference of equalities in the body of a rule to its head.

This is a simple syntactic transformation. As an example, the rule:

```
p(X,Y):- X = Term,body(Term,Y)
```

can be reformulated as:

```
p(Term,Y):- body(Term,Y).
```

7. CONCLUSIONS

In this paper we presented extensions to the technique, known as partial evaluation, which will allow the processing of large complete examples.

The extensions proposed here obey the need of extending not only the functionality of current logic programming partial evaluators (with only two operations, expansion and suspension of predicates using the subsumption criterion), but also allow the obtention of a better performance from the partial evaluator and the residual program.

For example, depth suspension control (DSC) increases the performance of the partial evaluator with respect to subsumption. DSC also gives the user the flexibility to obtain larger or smaller residual programs, depending on his needs, and guarantees termination of the process. The latter does not apply to the subsumption criterion.

The operations of freezing and melting predicates produce more instantiated residual programs and, therefore, more efficient programs.

Reflection allows the partial evaluator to run operations from higher meta-levels into PROLOG's meta-level, and then, return their values. This is obviously a gain in partial evaluation time efficiency.

We also included operationalization and generalization of predicates, two operations "borrowed" from explanation-based generalization learning techniques, which will prove to be very powerful in the construction of the residual program.

The treatment of negated predicates in the input programs was also introduced . This will give the partial evaluator the capacity to analyze real programs, a feature lacking in current partial evaluators. Finally, a number of local optimizations were proposed in order to produce a more efficient residual program.

There are still many open-ended questions that we are currently investigating, such as more necessary conditions to characterize some of the defined meta-predicates.

We have implemented a PROLOG partial evaluator which includes most of the operations here defined, and were able to process large examples of the kind described by Equation (1.1).

We are currently in the process of extending the partial evaluator to the problem of mix self-application as described by Equations (1.2) and (1.3).

ACKNOWLEDGEMENTS

This work was partially supported by the Chilean National Fund for Science and Technology (FONDECYT), grants 90-0688 and 89-0591, and grant CHI/88/022 of the United Nations Development Programme (UNDP).

REFERENCES

Abramsky, S., Hankin, C. (eds.), 1987, Abstract Interpretation of Declarative Languages, Wiley.

Chan, D., Wallace, M., 1989, A treatment of negation during partial evaluation in "Meta-Programming in Logic Programming",H. Abramson and M. Rogers, eds., Chap. 16, MIT Press, London.

Ershov, A. P., 1978, On the essence of compilation in "Formal Description of Programming Concepts", E. J. Neuhold ed., North-Holland, pp.391-418.

Fuller, D., Abramsky, S., 1988, Mixed computation of prolog programs in Workshop on Partial Evaluation and Mixed Computation, Gl. Avernæs, Denmark, 18-24 Oct. 1987, New Generation Computing, Vol. 6, Springer Verlag, Tokyo.

Fuller, D., 1989, Partial Evaluation and Mix Computation in Logic Programming, PhD Thesis, Department of Computing, Imperial College of Science and Technology, London, U.K.

Fuller, D.,1991, Replacing the loop detection scheme in partial pvaluation of logic programs, in preparation.

Futamura, Y., 1971, Partial evaluation of computation process - an approach to a compiler-compiler, *Systems, Computers, Control,* Vol. 2, No. 5, pp. 41-67.

Jones, N., Sestoft, P., Søndergaard, H., 1985, An experiment in partial evaluation: The generation of a compiler generator in "Rewriting techniques and applications", J. P. Jouannaud ed., *Lecture Notes in Computer Science*, No. 202, Springer Verlag, pp. 124-140.

Levi, G., Sardu, G., 1988, Partial evaluation of metaprograms in a "Multiple Worlds" Logic Language, Workshop on Partial Evaluation and Mixed Computation, Gl. Avernæs, Denmark, 18-24 Oct. 1987, *New Generation Computing*, Vol. 6, Springer Verlag, Tokyo .

Lloyd, J.W., Shepherdson, J.C., 1989, Partial Evaluation in Logic Programming.

Mellish, C., 1987, Abstract interpretation of PROLOG programs, in [Abramsky & Hankin 87], pp. 181-198, Wiley.

Mendelzon, A., 1988, Logic and Databases. VIII Conference of the Chilean Computer Science Society, Santiago.

Mitchell, T.M., Keller, R.M. and Kedar-Cabelli, S.T., 1986, Explanation-based generalization: a unifying view in Machine Learning Vol I.

Sterling, L., Beer, R., 1986, Incremental flavor-mixing of meta-interpreters for expert system construction, Tech. Rep. TR 103-86, Center for Automation and Intelligent Systems Research, Case Western Reserve University.

Takeuchi, A., Furukawa, K., 1986, Partial evaluation of prolog programs and its application to meta programming, Information Processing 86 (ed. H. Kugler), Proc. IFIP 86 Conference, North-Holland.

Vasak, T., Potter J., 1986, Characterization of terminatinglogic programs, *IEEE*, pp. 140-147 .

MODULES, MACROS AND LISP

Christian Queinnec[1]* and Julian Padget[2]†

[1] École Polytechnique & INRIA-Rocquencourt, France, `queinnec@polytechnique.fr`
[2] University of Bath, United Kingdom, `padget@maths.bath.ac.uk`

Abstract

Many modern languages offer a concept of modules to encapsulate a set of definitions and make some of them visible from outside. Associated to modules are directives ruling importations and exportations as well as controlling other capabilities like renaming or qualified notation. We propose here a language to handle sets of named locations with the aim of describing precisely which locations are to be shared between modules and under which local names they are known. The language is symmetric for imports and exports. It is also extensible since it provides a framework to handle named locations. Mutability, for instance, can readily be expressed thanks to a simple extension of our language.

Another more subtle extension is to offer a protocol for modules with "macros." Macros allow a user to extend the syntax of a language by providing rewriting rules expressed as computations performed on the representation of programs. Lisp is a language offering macros and much of its extensibility stems from them. However, many problems arise from macros, amongst them being the exact definition of when, where and how the macroexpansion is done to turn the body of a module using extended syntaxes into a regular form in the bare, unextended language.

This paper presents, in the framework of Lisp, a definition of modules offering tight control over module environments as well as a precise semantics of separate compilation and macroexpansion. These new (for Lisp) capabilities definitely add some power relative to the management of name spaces but also justify compiling optimizations (inlining, partial evaluation etc.) and, above all, turn Lisp into a language suitable for application delivery since applications are finite collections of modules. Our proposal contributes to a vision of Lisp composed of a multitude of linked and reusable modules. Our results concerning name space management and macros can also be applied to other languages.

Two different implementations of these concepts exist: in FEEL, the implementation of EuLisp done by the University of Bath and in the idiom of Icsla, a dialect of Lisp designed at INRIA-Rocquencourt and École Polytechnique. This paper reflects the results of the experiments carried out in these systems during the last year.

---

*This work has been partially funded by Greco de Programmation.
†This work has been partially funded by the Science and Engineering Research Council.

1　Introduction

A module encapsulates a set of definitions. Some of these definitions must be made available to clients of the module while others must remain invisible. These definitions can be shared by a number of different methods: name, location or value. Names is the method used in COMMON LISP[Steele, 1990] and implies the existence of a unique name space where two entities from two different modules and bearing a same name cannot be present together. Values is the method used, for example, in Poly [Matthews, 1983] but is of limited worth since this makes modules little different from closures. As in more classical languages, such as C, we feel locations are the right thing to exchange in presence of assignments since they hold (and allow access to) values, but are independent of names and therefore can be alpha-converted on a local basis.

The exportation language must be able to handle sets of locations and to perform the usual set operations on them. Since a location is known by its name within a module, the exportation language must then handle locations through their names. However, there is a restriction which is that no two different locations may have the same name, a situation introducing ambiguity known as *name clash*. Since the programmer's naming convention usually has some semantic import for the value being manipulated, the default behaviour is to maintain the association between the name given and the location when it was defined. Conversely since a location is independent of its name, this association may be changed.

Similarly, the importation language, whether importing locations under their real names or new names, must have equivalent power. In consequence, we have developed a common language for both importation and exportation. The current syntax of this language, as presented below, was chosen to be regular rather than convenient. Abbreviations can be contrived, but are irrelevant to this paper.

A module of Lisp can also contain executable code which will be evaluated when the module is loaded. Hence it is necessary to define very carefully how a module is processed and loaded. The information stored in the importation and exportation directives shows a given module depends on other modules. This dependency shows itself both when processing and loading a module: the modules on which it depends must be processed or loaded beforehand. Introducing macros imposes the additional constraint that to obtain the pure code for the body of a module, a computation is required. Finally, we define how to start a computation, that is, how to invoke a function within a module.

Section 2 introduces modules and how they are processed. Section 3 focusses on the importation and exportation language. An example of an extension, to handle mutability of locations, appears in section 4. The second extension, macros, is presented in section 5. Various examples are given throughout the paper. The results of practical experience with this model are covered in the conclusions.

2　Module

A module comprises four parts: a name, an importation directive, an exportation directive and a body[1]. Whilst it may not be the most suitable form in practice, we will assume the representation of a module in this paper to be a file with the same name as the module, the first two expressions contained therein being the import and export directives respectively, followed by the body. The language we use is lexically scoped, but it is convenient for us to be able to distinguish between the bindings made within a program—such as by `lambda`—and the bindings created by `define` or by importation. We call the former *inner-lexical* bindings and the latter *top-lexical* bindings. Where there is no ambiguity, we simply refer to *lexical* bindings. As an example, the following module defines the fibonacci function:

---

[1]For convenience, we suppose a language for the body which is regular Scheme augmented with an access special form which will be explained later.

```
;;;====== The fibonacci module ======
(expose standard)

(union
  (immutable (rename ((fibonacci bm-fib))
              (except (fib20 fib-max)
                (only-from (fibonacci) (expose fibonacci)))) ))
  (mutable (qualified (only (fib-max) (expose fibonacci)))) )
;;;======          ======

(define (fib n) (if (< n 2) 1 (+ (fib (- n 1)) (fib (- n 2)))) )

(define fib20 (fib 20)) ;better precompute it !

(define (bm-fib n)
  (cond
    ((= n 20) fib20)
    ((> n fib-max) (error "Too big number" n))
    (else (fib n))))
```

A module is processed as follows:

1. The importation directive is processed in order to build the imported part of the top-lexical environment in which to analyse the body of the module.

   For instance, in the above module, the functions <, +, , =, error and > are, among others, imported from the module standard.

2. The body of the module is analysed: all free variables are extracted from it and these define the proper part of the top-lexical environment. The combination of the imported part and the proper part forms the top-lexical environment of the module currently being processed. We will refine this phase when considering macros in section 5.

   In the above module, the variables fib, fib20, bm-fib and fib-max are free. They are thus considered to form the proper part of the top-lexical environment of module fibonacci.

3. The exportation directive is processed to determine the exportations.

   In the above module, only the locations fib, bm-fib and fib-max are exported. The first two are exported as immutable locations: they cannot be assigned to from outside, whereas fib-max can. The location bm-fib is exported under a new and more meaningful name: fibonacci.

4. Finally, the module is then added to the module environment (a disjoint environment). The "real compilation" is done here since anything that can affect the meaning or the behaviour of the module is now known.

   The module environment associates names to processed modules. A processed module comprises the information about its dependencies, importations and exportations. The processed module is presumably also associated to its compiled body, top-lexical environment for debugging, amongst other things. This module environment does not need to be represented within the programming language environment, but can be based on the file system of the underlying operating system.

After a module has been processed it is ready to be imported or loaded. A processed module is said to be dependent on other modules if it imports or exports locations from them. A module, m, is loaded as follows:

1. The modules on which m depends are loaded, but modules already loaded are not reloaded.

These modules either contribute to the imported part of the top-lexical environment of the module or may accompany this module and provide any client of m with the accompanying facilities.

2. The proper part of the top-lexical environment of m is allocated.

Now, the top-lexical environment of the module is complete.

3. The body of the module is evaluated sequentially in this top-lexical environment.

The top-lexical environment can be viewed as a kind of "letrec" form allowing mutual recursive definitions. Note that in the example above, the variable fib20 will be computed at load-time so that faster answers will result when calling the bm-fib function.

After a module is loaded, any location exported from it can be used to start a computation provided it holds a function that can be applied to the arguments of the intended computation. The means to start a computation can be supplied from Lisp itself, or from the shell of the underlying operating system. In this instance, we suppose ourselves to be operating on top of UNIX[2] where we have defined the start-module command to start a computation. Given the above module, we can submit numbers[3] to the fib function:

```
% start-module fibonacci fib 5 ; start-module fibonacci fib 10
589
```

Starting the fibonacci module forces the standard module (and all the modules on which it depends) to be loaded before the contents of the fib location, a monadic function, can be invoked. An error would be signalled if the number of submitted arguments does agree with the arity of the specified entry point.

3 Importations and exportations directives

We give a grammar for import export directives in figure 1.

$$
\begin{array}{lll}
\textit{directive} & ::= & \texttt{(expose} \; \textit{module-name}) \\
& | & \texttt{(only} \; (\textit{name} \; \ldots) \; \textit{directive}) \\
& | & \texttt{(except} \; (\textit{name} \; \ldots) \; \textit{directive}) \\
& | & \texttt{(only-from} \; (\textit{module-name} \; \ldots) \; \textit{directive}) \\
& | & \texttt{(rename} \; (\textit{substitution} \; \ldots) \; \textit{directive}) \\
& | & \texttt{(qualified} \; \textit{directive}) \\
& | & \texttt{(union} \; \textit{directive}\ldots) \\
\textit{substitution} & ::= & (\textit{new-alias} \; \textit{old-alias})
\end{array}
$$

Figure 1. Grammar of basic directives

The language is completely symmetric with respect to importation or exportation except in the case of the expose directive. The expose directive takes the name of a module and produces the set of tuples describing all its exported locations. For the moment, these are quadruples as follows:

$$< alias, name, module\text{-}name, \alpha >$$

Such a tuple represents the location α in the proper part of the top-lexical environment of the module named *module-name*, this location being known as *name* and referred to as *alias*. Initially *name* and *alias* are the same. The standard module produces a large set of tuples

---

[2] UNIX is a trademark of AT&T.

[3] We suppose that arguments given from the shell are submitted as if read by Lisp, fib is then invoked on the number ten and not the string "10". We also suppose that the final result is printed according to Lisp rules. These assumptions are false in real implementations but simplify the examples.

describing all the usual functions that are considered as standard in Scheme such as `cons`, `null?` and so on, as well as the arithmetic functions `+`, `-` amongst others.

Of course, it does not make sense to `expose` the module currently being processed in an importation directive. However, this is reasonable at exportation since its top-lexical environment is completely defined. Thus, `expose`-ing the current module for exportation produces the set of all locations belonging to its top-lexical environment.

Sets of tuples representing locations can be filtered to deliver some subset and the filtering can be done on the name or on the module-name stored in the tuple. The `only` directive accepts the set produced by the enclosed *directive* and only those locations which have an alias belonging to the list of *name* ... are allowed to pass through. The `except` directive allows only those locations whose alias does *not* belong to the list of *name* ... to pass through. The `only-from` directive permits only those locations which are defined in the list of modules *module-name* ... to pass. For the sake of symmetry one can easily imagine the behaviour of the `except-from` directive.

Sets of tuples can be merged by means of the `union` directive provided no name clash occurs. Two tuples are different if they mention different *module-names* or different *locations*. A name clash occurs when two different tuples have the same alias. Note that it is harmless to merge a set of tuples with itself: `(union (expose M) (expose M))` is the same as `(expose M)`.

One way to resolve a name clash is to rename one of the offending tuples. Renaming can be achieved using the `rename` directive. The `rename` directive takes as input a set of tuples and produces a new set of tuples where any original tuple having an alias equal to one of the *old-alias* is rewritten as a new tuple with the associated *new-alias*. All other tuples are unchanged. Note that all directives are functional and do not modify tuples.

It is also interesting in many cases to offer the visiblity of a location without providing any name for it. Modula offers a qualified notation which allows a kind of "absolute name" for a location. We add to the language of module bodies the `access` special form for that purpose: `(access module-name alias)` refers to the location which was exported under *alias* from *module-name*[4]. A location can be referred to using qualified notation only if it is exported, hence `access` forms cannot break the encapsulation provided by a module. When a location is exported (or imported) as qualified, no alias is associated to it so it can only be referred to using qualified notation.

Directive example

Suppose that the exportation directive of the `fibonacci` module was in fact:

```
(union (rename ((fibonacci bm-fib))
         (except (fib20 fib-max)
            (only-from (fibonacci) (expose fibonacci)))) )
       (qualified (only (fib-max) (expose fibonacci))) )
```

The directive `(expose fibonacci)` produces the set of all locations of the top-lexical environment of the `fibonacci` module. This set contains:

$$
\begin{aligned}
\{ \quad &< \texttt{fib, fib, fibonacci}, \alpha_0 > \\
&< \texttt{fib20, fib20, fibonacci}, \alpha_1 > \\
&< \texttt{bm-fib, bm-fib, fibonacci}, \alpha_2 > \\
&< \texttt{fib-max, fib-max, fibonacci}, \alpha_3 > \\
&< \texttt{+, +, standard}, \alpha_{37} > \\
&< \texttt{cons, cons, standard}, \alpha_{21} > \\
&\ldots \qquad\qquad\qquad\qquad\qquad\qquad\qquad \}
\end{aligned}
$$

---

[4] Note that contrary to the definition of tuples, it is not required that *alias* names a location belonging to the proper part of *module-name*. It may also belong to the imported part of the top-lexical environment and then reexported to be visible. Also note that the `access` special form can be implicitly written with a qualified name such as *module-name:name*, if so desired.

Note that since all locations from `standard` were imported, they all belong to the top-lexical environment of the `fibonacci` module. The `only-from` directive filters out of the above set the proper locations of the `fibonacci` module i.e.

```
{   < fib, fib, fibonacci, α0 >
    < fib20, fib20, fibonacci, α1 >
    < bm-fib, bm-fib, fibonacci, α2 >
    < fib-max, fib-max, fibonacci, α3 >   }
```

From which are removed locations `fib20` and `fib-max`. After that, `bm-fib` is renamed as `fibonacci` thus yielding:

```
{   < fib, fib, fibonacci, α0 >
    < fibonacci, bm-fib, fibonacci, α2 >   }
```

And finally, the qualified `fib-max` location is added, but with a null alias. The final result is thus:

```
{   < fib, fib, fibonacci, α0 >
    < fibonacci, bm-fib, fibonacci, α2 >
    < , fib-max, fibonacci, α3 >          }
```

Another directive example

The `standard` module itself is, presumably, not a monolithic module but a composition of more primitive modules gathered in a single module so that the user has only one module to import rather than many. Our directive language allows us to write modules whose only effect is to collect locations in a single module: linkers or partial evaluators can benefit from this situation. A first way to define `standard` would be to import all needed locations then to reexport them in one go:

```
;;;====== The standard module (first attempt) ======
(union (expose arithmetic) (expose pair) ...)

(expose standard)
;;;======                  ======
;;;No body at all
```

A second, less naïve, approach is to gather all needed locations at exportation time:

```
;;;====== The standard module (second attempt) ======
(union)

(union (expose arithmetic) (expose pair) ...)
;;;======                  ======
;;;No body at all
```

It might seem strange to be exporting locations which were not imported, but this facility contributes to the provision of more useful dependency information as will be shown with macros in section 5. In the previous example, the `standard` module depends (at least) on the modules `arithmetic` and `pair`.

4 Mutability

When exporting locations, the writer of a module may provide immutable definitions and also some special locations which can be changed by the user. In our preferred example, the `fib-max` location must be set by the client of the `fibonacci` module before s/he invokes the `fibonacci` function otherwise an "uninitialized location" error would be signalled. Part of the interface is the explicit mutability of this location. Making other locations immutable for clients denies them the right to modify the contents of these locations. The processor can take advantage of that and can analyse the body of the module to determine which locations are initialized for certain and which locations are only assigned once and never again changed thereafter. The results of such analyses are fruitful since constants can be safely propagated and the invocation of the contents of immutable locations can be inlined, for instance.

We therefore want to specify the mutability of exported locations. First we extend the previous tuple definition to a quintuple with an additional field specifying the mutability of the location. Initially, tuples are created with no restrictions on mutability. Tuples become:

$$< alias, name, module\text{-}name, \alpha, \{mutable \mid immutable\} >$$

In consequence we add two new directives.

$$
\begin{aligned}
directive \quad ::= \quad & (\texttt{immutable} \; directive) \\
\mid \quad & (\texttt{mutable} \; directive)
\end{aligned}
$$

The `immutable` directive produces a new set of tuples with a mutability field set to *immutable*. The `mutable` directive is not really legitimate since an immutable location cannot revert safely to a mutable one. The `mutable` directive only serves to emphasize that a location is exported with write access.

The initial exportation directive of the `fibonacci` module therefore now yields the following set of tuples:

```
{   < fib, fib, fibonacci, α₀, immutable >
    < fibonacci, bm-fib, fibonacci, α₂, immutable >
    < , fib-max, fibonacci, α₃, mutable >            }
```

5 Macros

Macros permit the extension of the syntax of the language. A macroexpansion phase translates the body of a module into a regular expression without additional syntaxes. In Lisp, this translation might use all the resources of the language. Macros and macroexpansion present many problems which can be summarised in three words: *when*, *where* and *how*. We mainly focus here on the when and the where rather than how. Given the number of variants that exist, we prefer to offer a macroexpansion protocol allowing the user to decide how macros are represented and how module bodies are expanded. It is then possible to implement the proposal of [Clinger & Rees, 1991] or Expansion Passing Style (EPS) advocated in [Dybvig *et al.*, 1988] as legal implementations of the macroprotocol stated below.

Associated with each macro is a syntax expander, that is a function taking forms using the extended syntax and translating them into more verbose, simpler forms lacking that extension. While most macros are simple rewriting rules, some are very complex and embed specialised compilers: see for example the `loop` macro [Steele, 1990] or pattern matching [Queinnec, 1990]. Macros may also need an internal state like the `define-class` macro which has to manage the inheritance tree of classes. Since using a macro involves a computation, we impose the requirement that macroexpansion be implemented as a module, to be called the macroexpansion module, exporting a location named `macroexpand-module-body`. When it is necessary to macroexpand the body of a module, the macroexpansion module is loaded and the function held in the `macroexpand-module-body` location is invoked with the necessary arguments which are: (i) the body of the module and (ii) the complete syntax that might be used by the module. The result will become the macroexpanded body of the currently processed module.

The remaining problem is how to represent syntaxes. Syntaxes can be additive, allowing rewriting rules to be freely combined. Conversely some syntaxes might want to be locally exclusive. We therefore conclude that the macroexpansion module must export another location named `initial-syntax`, holding a function with a signature similar to `macroexpand-module-body` but whose rôle is to walk its first argument (the module body), check if there are some uses of extended syntaxes and, if so, expand them using its second argument (the syntax). If no macros occur then the macroexpanded body is equal to the initial body i.e.

(macroexpand-module-body *body* initial-syntax) — *body*

A macro is represented by a function which takes three arguments: (i) the current syntax, (ii) the name under which the macro is imported, (iii) the name of the module currently being processed. This function generally enriches the current syntax with a (or some) new rewriting rule(s) and returns a syntax that will be considered as the new current syntax. Hence macros do not exist *per se* but are represented by ordinary functions which "install" new syntaxes. We add a new directive to signal that some locations hold functions that must be considered as macros:

$$directive \quad ::= \quad (\texttt{syntax} \ directive)$$

To explain the **syntax** directive, we again extend tuples, now to become sextuples, with a field specifying whether the location is syntax or not:

$$< alias, name, module\text{-}name, \alpha, \{mutable \mid immutable\}, \{regular \mid syntax\} >$$

The **syntax** directive takes a set of tuples and produces a new set of tuples with the syntax attribute set.

After processing an importation directive, imported locations are sorted into two sets: ordinary and syntax locations. These latter represent the set of syntaxes that might be used in the body of the module currently being processed. These partial syntaxes may then be composed into a single syntax. To macroexpand this body the following actions are taken:

1. The macroexpansion module is loaded and the current syntax is set to the contents of the **initial-syntax** location.

   Various macroexpansion modules can exist, but for now, we have implemented Expansion Passing Style (EPS) and COMMON LISP-like macros with hashtables.

2. For any syntactic location $< alias, name, module\text{-}name, \alpha_i, mutability, syntax >$, the module *module-name* is loaded, the contents of the location α_i is retrieved and applied to the current syntax, the *alias* under which the syntactic location was imported and the name of the module being processed. We remark that the set of macros is not ordered.

   This scheme allows macros to be renamed thus avoiding syntax clashes. The name of the currently processed module is also given so that macros define in the module being processed can generate **access** forms relative to it.

3. The original body of the processed module and the final syntax obtained in the previous phase are submitted to the contents of the **macroexpand-module-body** of the macroexpansion module. The result is the macroexpanded body.

   As with all computations, this operation might not terminate or might yield a syntactically recursive program, see [Queinnec & Padget, 1990] for further details.

4. All the syntactic locations are removed from the top-lexical environment of the module being processed.

   Nothing remains from macroexpansion if it is not needed at run-time.

To resume our discussion of the macroexpansion protocol:

- A module is processed with respect to a specific macroexpansion module. Such a module can be explicitly passed to the processor as a compiler option, assuming a reasonable default value.

- The macroexpansion module exports a location named **macroexpand-module-body** whose signature is:

  (macroexpand-module-body *module-body syntax*) → *macroexpanded-module-body*

- The macroexpansion module exports a location named **initial-syntax** whose signature is:

  (macroexpand-module-body *module-body syntax*) → *module-body*

- A macro is a location with the *syntax* attribute whose signature is:

  (*macro syntax keyword module-name*) → *syntax*

We remark that no constraints exist on the nature of syntaxes. They can be represented by functions as in EPS or using a list of hashtables to provide COMMON LISP-like facilities. A macro may introduce more than one syntax at once or even no syntax at all, but just side-effect the compilation environment. An essential macroexpansion module using EPS is given in the appendix.

Example

Suppose we wish to offer a **fibonacci** macro which when given a natural number expands into the correct fibonacci number. We can write the following **fibmac** module, using the **define-macro** macro of **standard** to hide implementation details[5]:

```
;;;====== The fibmac module ======
(union (expose standard) (expose fibonacci))

(union (syntax (only (fibonacci) (expose fibmac)))
       (qualified (only (fib) (expose fibonacci))) )
;;;======        ======
(define-macro (fibonacci exp)
  (if (integer? exp)
      (fib exp)
      '((access fibonacci fib) ,exp) ) )
```

This module defines a function which respects the macroexpansion protocol courtesy of the **define-macro** macro. The **fibonacci** location is exported as syntax explicitly by the user. Note that since the macro may be invoked on a number, the macro itself requires access to the **fib** function of the **fibonacci** module so this latter is exposed at importation in **fibmac**. Also note that the expansion of a call to the **fibonacci** macro might use the **fib** function of the **fibonacci** module and that therefore must be visible from any client of the **fibmac** module. Since it would be cumbersome to force the user of the **fibonacci** macro to remember to import the **fibonacci** module explicitly, we simply mention it in the exportation directive of **fibmac**. Thus, we completely hide the details of the **fibonacci** macro.

Let us give an example of a client of **fibmac**, say the **fibuser** module, which renames the **fibonacci** macro into **fib**:

```
;;;====== The fibuser module ======
(union (only (define list) (expose standard))
       (rename ((fib fibonacci)) (expose fibmac)) )

(only (test) (expose fibuser))
;;;======        ======
(define (test arg)
  (list (fib 10) (fib arg)) )
```

A lot of standard syntaxes are exported from of **standard**, for brevity here we only show **define**. Two macros are therefore visible within **fibuser**. The set of locations yielded by the importation directive is:

---

[5]See appendix.

```
{   < define, define, standard. a₈₀. immutable, syntax >
    < list, list, standard. a₁₁₇. immutable, regular >
    < fib, fibonacci, fibmac. a₈₃₁. immutable, syntax >
    < , fib, fibonacci, a₀, immutable, regular >          }
```

The official macroexpand module (say `macroexpand`) and modules **standard**, **fibmac** and
fibonacci (on which **fibmac** depends) are then loaded since some macros in these might be
used. The complete syntax that will be used to macrowalk the body of **fibuser** is thus the
result of either:

```
((access fibmac fibonacci)              ((access standard define)
 ((access standard define)               ((access fibmac fibonacci)
  (access macroexpand initial-syntax)     (access macroexpand initial-syntax)
  'define 'fibuser )                       'fib 'fibuser )
 'fib 'fibuser )                         'define 'fibuser )
```

Since macros defined by `define-macro` are additive, the two previous forms give equivalent
syntaxes, that is, the order is immaterial. This final syntax is then used for macroexpanding
the body of **fibuser**. The macroexpanded body is therefore the result of:

```
((access macroexpand macroexpand-module-body)
 '(begin (define (test arg)                          ; the initial body
          (list (fibonacci 10) (fibonacci arg)) ))
 ((access fibmac fibonacci)                          ; the proper name
  ((access standard define)
   (access macroexpand initial-syntax)
   'define 'fibuser )
  'fib 'fibuser ) )                                  ; the alias
```

The result, that is, the macroexpanded body, is:

```
(set! test (lambda (arg)
             (list 89 ((access fibonacci fib) arg)) ))
```

The generated **access** form is legal since it refers to a visible location which has been
imported thanks to the importation of the **fib** macro. After macroexpansion, the top-lexical
environment is shrunk to the set of ordinary locations:

```
{   < list, list, standard. a₁₁₇. immutable, regular >
    < , fib, fibonacci, a₈₃₁. immutable, regular >     }
```

It is then clear that the **fibuser** module only depends on modules **standard** and **fibonacci**
at run-time and no longer on **fibmac**. This last module has been used for syntax only and
has disappeared from the run-time.

6 Related Work

Traditional solutions for information hiding in Lisp were supported by read-time symbol space
management (the packages of COMMON LISP). These facilities are difficult to master, can
be bypassed and were not designed to assist with separate compilation. The main work
on modules was presented in [Curtis & Rauen, 1990]. Many differences exist between that
proposal and ours. In particular, module bodies and interfaces are separated in Curtis's
proposal. Although following software engineering principles, we think that the interface can
be deduced from the module body and its exportation directive, that some optimizations such
as inlining cannot be done if the module body is not provided and finally that their separation
does not fit harmoniously with macros. Macros cannot be used, nor exported, if unknown.
Complex macros cannot be entirely put in the interfaces with all the definition of the utilities
they use which needs to remain hidden. We therefore decided not to invent new concepts but
just to define macros founded on simple modules.

Another big difference is that macros involve computations and therefore, the order in
which macroexpansions are performed matters. The vast majority of macros are very simple

rewriting rules that can be expressed in the restricted pattern language of [Clinger & Rees, 1991] and which do not depend on the exact order of macroexpansions. However complex macros (such as `define-class`) are not amenable to this view yet we still to be able to define them within the module framework. We therefore choose (i) a sequential evaluation semantics for module bodies and (ii) to let the user defines his/her own macroexpansion model. It is then possible to adopt the best of all the solutions to the different problems macros create.

The language we describe differs from other implementations of Lisp or Scheme since it is only a language of modules and not a language of expressions submitted to an interactive top-loop. We describe in [Queinnec & Padget, 1990] an evaluation feature allowing for the definition of modules defining new top levels. This point of view is rather novel for Lisp yet does not restrict its power. Autonomous applications as collections of linked and reusable modules can now be conceived.

7 Conclusions

We presented in this paper simple but useful modules that allow the precise definition of how to share locations. We designed a language to handle sets of named locations which can be used both for importations and exportations. We extended it straightforwardly to deal with mutability.

We defined how modules are processed, loaded and started as well as how collections of modules can be considered as complete applications that may be run autonomously from the underlying operating system.

We proposed a macroexpansion protocol which allows the parameterisation of a compiler giving it the power of macros while retaining a simple semantics. Our protocol does not enforce a particular macroexpansion algorithm nor the exact representation of macros. We therefore complement proposals such as [Dybvig *et al.*, 1988] or [Clinger & Rees, 1991]. We also give additional power to the user to rename macros.

Two implementations of modules using these ideas have been carried out, one at the University of Bath and another at INRIA-Rocquencourt and École Polytechnique. The construction of the `standard` module (which is a single module offering all the needed syntaxes and usual functions) makes use of all the features presented above: (i) renaming can be used, for instance, to export simultaneously `call/cc` and `call-with-current-continuation` as two aliased names for the same location. An assignment to one of these locations is guaranteed to be seen from the other. (ii) Modules form a tree. Mutually recursive functions that are sufficiently important to be defined in separate modules are defined as follows: first a module defines the two locations of the two mutually recursive functions and mutably exports them, the two functions are then defined in their own modules by assignment and eventually these two modules are gathered in a single module. The two initial locations can now be exported as immutable from this last module. (iii) Our module scheme eases interoperability and linking modules to existing C libraries. More complex macros such as `define-class` have also been written and this experience lead to a careful examination of what belongs to macroexpansion-time, load-time and to run-time. To merge syntactic locations with regular locations makes importations of complex macros easier for the user since all irrelevant details dealing with module dependencies are hidden.

We are now considering more interesting analyses such as partially evaluating modules which just collect other modules. A formal denotational semantics of our proposal was out of the scope of this paper but is fully detailed in [Queinnec & Padget, 1990].

Bibliography

[Clinger & Rees, 1991] William Clinger, Jonathan Rees, *Macros That Work*, Eighteenth Annual ACM Symposium on Principles of Programming Languages, Orlando, Florida, January 1991, pp 155–162.

[Curtis & Rauen, 1990] Pavel Curtis, James Rauen, *A Module System for Scheme*, 1990 ACM Conference on Lisp and Functional Programming, Nice, France, June 1990, pp 13-19.

[Dybvig *et al.*, 1988] R. Kent Dybvig, Daniel P. Friedman, Christopher T. Haynes, *Expansion-Passing-Style: A General Macro Mechanism*, Lisp and Symbolic Computation, Vol. 1, No. 1, June 1988, pp 53-76.

[Kohlbecker *et al.*, 1986] Eugene Kohlbecker, Daniel P. Friedman, Matthias Felleisen, Bruce Duba, *Hygienic Macro Expansion*, Proceedings of 1986 ACM Conference on Lisp and Functional Programming, pp 151-161, ACM Press, New York, 1986.

[Matthews, 1983] Matthews D.C.J, *Programming Language Design with Polymorphism*, University of Cambridge Computer Laboratory Technical Report No. 49, 1983.

[Queinnec & Padget, 1990] Christian Queinnec, Julian Padget, *A Model of Modules and Macros for Lisp*, Bath Computing Group Technical Report 90-36, University of Bath, UK.

[Queinnec, 1990] Christian Queinnec, *Compilation of Non-Linear, Second Order Patterns on S-Expressions*, International Workshop PLILP '90, Linköping, Sweden, August 1990, Lecture Notes in Computer Science 456, Springer-Verlag, pp 340-357.

[Rees & Clinger 1986] Jonathan A. Rees, William Clinger, *Revised³ Report on the Algorithmic Language Scheme*, ACM SIGPLAN Notices. 21, 12, Dec 86, pp 37-79, ACM Press, New York, 1986.

[Steele, 1990] Steele G.L. Jr., *Common Lisp the language*, Second Edition, Digital Press, 1990.

A   An example of a macroexpansion module

This module presents the essence of a macroexpansion module. It does not handle errors but just suggests how to define modules implementing the macroexpansion protocol. This module exports a macro, called `defmacro`, to define macros that are coherent with this implementation of syntax. We suppress some details of the exact way in which `lambda` is walked but we give precedence to local variables over macros. This module implements EPS [Dybvig *et al.*, 1988].

```
;;;A simple macroexpansion module

(expose standard)

(immutable
 (union
   (syntax (only (defmacro) (expose macrxpnd)))
   (only (initial-syntax macroexpand-module-body)
     (expose macrxpnd))))

;;;macroexpand: Syntax
;;;keyword: Symbol
;;;expander: Form × Syntax — Form
;;;Build a new syntax similar to macroexpand but where forms whose car
;;;is equal to keyword are expanded thanks to expander.

(set! macro-extend-on-form
  (lambda (macroexpand keyword expander)
    (lambda (e m)
      (if (pair? e)
          (if (eq? (car e) keyword)
              (expander e m)
              (macroexpand e m))
          (macroexpand e m)))))

(set! macro-walk (lambda (e m) (m e m)))
(set! module-body-macro-walk macro-walk)
```

```
(set! macro-walk*
  (lambda (e m)

    (if (pair? e)
        (cons (macro-walk (car e) m)
              (macro-walk* (cdr e) m))
        e)))

(set! initial-syntax
  (lambda (e m)
    (if (pair? e)
        (case (car e)
          ((quote) e)
          ((set!)
           '(set! . ,(macro-walk* (cdr e) m)))
          ((if)
           '(if . ,(macro-walk* (cdr e) m)))
          ((lambda)
           '(lambda
              ,(cadr e)
              . ,(macro-walk* (cdar e) m)))
          ((access) e)
          (else (macro-walk* e m)) )
        e)))

;;; The defmacro form:
;;; syntax: (defmacro name variables  body)
;;; defmacro is itself a macro !

(set! defmacro
  (lambda (s kw modname)
    (macro-extend-on-form s kw
      (lambda (e m)
        (if (if (pair? (cdr e))
                (if (symbol? (car (cdr e)))
                    (if (pair? (cdr (cdr e)))
                        (pair? (cdr (cdr (cdr e)))))
                    #f) #f) #f)
            (m
              '(set!
                ,(car (cdr e))
                ((lambda (expander)
                   (lambda (syntax
                            keyword
                            module-name)
                     ((access macrxpnd
                              macro-extend-on-form)
                      syntax
                      keyword
                      (lambda (expression
                               macroexpand)
                        (macroexpand
                          ((access primitives apply)
                           expander
                           ((access primitives cdr)
                            expression))
                          macroexpand)))))
                 (lambda . ,(cdr (cdr e))))))
              m)
            (error 'defmacro))))))
```

USING FILTERS TO IMPROVE THE EFFICIENCY OF GAME–PLAYING LEARNING PROCEDURES

R. A. Hasson, S. Markovitch, and Y. Sella

Department of Computer Science
Technion - Israel Institute of Technology
Haifa 32000, Israel

INTRODUCTION

Most of the efforts in the machine learning research have been concentrated in finding methods for acquiring knowledge. The possibility that the acquired knowledge can be harmful to the system was paid only little attention. Many systems employed selection mechanisms to filter out knowledge that was estimated to be harmful to the system, but the selection mechanisms (or filters) have never played a major role in those systems. A clear manifestation of that approach is the lack of experimental results that compare the performance of the learning systems with and without the filters.

Minton's research [1] was one of the first to concentrate on the problem of harmful knowledge (which he calls *the utility problem*) and on building selection procedures to eliminate the problem. Markovitch and Scott [2, 3] define knowledge to be harmful if its addition to the knowledge base reduces the system's performance according to a given criterion. They also define a framework that unifies the research efforts concerned with the problem of eliminating harmful knowledge. The framework is based on a view of learning systems as information processing systems where information flows from the experience space through some attention procedure then through the acquisition procedure and the knowledge base and finally to the problem solver. The framework defines five types of filters, according to their location within the information flow: selective experience, selective attention, selective acquisition, selective retention and selective utilization.

We have encountered the problem of harmful knowledge in the context of a learning program that tries to improve its playing performance in a game called *fives*. The program learns by playing against a teacher (an instance of the program that is given more time resources) and modifying coefficients of the evaluation function. Unfortunately, experiments show that some of the modifications can be harmful. We have studied the implementation of information filters to avoid the problem of acquiring harmful knowledge in the context of game playing programs.

COMPUTER SCIENCE, Edited by R. Baeza-Yates
and U. Manber, Plenum Press, New York, 1992

Game playing programs have the advantage of a very clear evaluation criterion associated with them: two programs can be easily compared by letting them play against each other. The availability of a good evaluation criterion enables us to create acquisition filters in the following way. Before making a modification to the knowledge base, compare the performance of two instances of the program: one that uses the knowledge base in its current state, and another that uses the modified knowledge base. Only if the modified state is better than the current state the modification takes place.

Such a test-based acquisition filter was implemented and proved to be useful. The problem with this method of filtering is the high cost associated with its application. Another acquisition selector uses domain specific rules to filter out some of acquired knowledge before it arrives the high cost filter. In addition, an experience filter was inserted before the acquisition procedure in order to allow only learning instances that are likely to be highly informative. These two additional filters reduce the number of times that the test-based filter is applied and thus save learning resources.

The next section of this paper describes the learning system before the filters were inserted. Then we describe experiments performed with that version of the learning systems and shows that some of the learned knowledge was harmful. Afterwards we describe the information filters that were added to the system, and demonstrates their usefulness by experimentation. The last section concludes and discusses some potential extensions.

LEARNING TO PLAY THE GAME OF FIVES

The game of *fives* can be regarded as an extension of the famous game *Tic-tac-toe* or as a reduced version of the game *Go-muku*. The game is played on a square board of 10×10, i.e. there are 100 places in the board where any player can make his move, provided that the place is not already taken. The number of players is two, one of them plays with the x symbol, and the other with the symbol o. The two players place their symbols alternately. The game's objective is to generate a sequence of five consecutive symbols (x's or o's) in any legal direction, where the legal directions are vertical, horizontal and diagonal. The first player who succeeds in creating such a sequence (obviously of his own symbol) is the winner. If none of them achieves that goal the game is tied.

The basic *fives*-playing program consists of an implementation of the *minimax* algorithm with *alpha-beta pruning* [4]. It is a search procedure that generates moves through the problem space until encountering a goal state (i.e. a winning board) or reaching a predefined maximal depth (called *max level*) . This depth is naturally a very important parameter, that affects the playing quality of the problem solver.

In order to speed up execution time, i.e. to improve the effectiveness of the search, we introduced the following variations:

- Improvement of the generation procedure: For a given node (i.e. board), we only generate the children which are inside the *interest zone* of that node. The *interest zone* of a board is defined as the sub-board of that board, which includes every place filled until now, expanded by two columns (one to the left and one to the right) and by two rows (one from above and one from below). The *interest zone* can include the entire board at the most.
- Improvement of the test procedure: From the set of children generated for a given node we select the most promising ones (i.e. best moves) to be further developed in the *minimax* tree.

The size of the set of best children has a major influence on the problem solver's playing quality. Since it actually determines the width of the *minimax* tree, it is designated by a constant named the *branching factor*.

In order to evaluate the leaves (i.e. boards) of the *minimax* tree, and for the purpose of selecting the best children of an internal node, we used a polynomial style evaluation function. In the next subsection, we will show the architecture of a learning system that tries to improve the performance of the player of *fives*. Finally, in the last subsection, we explain the approach taken in the construction of the learning procedure of the system.

Learning System Architecture

The learning system employs two different instances of the problem solver that play a game of *fives*. One instance of the problem solver is the *student* and the other is the *teacher*. The *student* attempts to adapt its strategy to the teacher's one. Therefore we allocate more computing resources to the *teacher* (greater *max level* and *branching factor* values) than to the *student*.

During a *learning game* (i.e. a game of *fives* played between the *teacher* and the *student*), every time the *teacher* has to play, the *student* tries to predict the next move of the *teacher* (called the *expected move*). The *teacher* makes his move (called the *actual move*), which might be the same as the *expected move* or not. The pair formed by the *expected move* and the *actual move* serves as input for the *learning procedure*. The output of the learning procedure are some coefficient modifications which are fed into the knowledge base that holds the coefficients of the evaluation function used by all the instances of the problem solver. Figure 1 shows the architecture of this learning system.

The Evaluation Function of the Problem Solver

We start this subsection by defining some useful concepts related to the evaluation function. We will use $s \in \{x, o\}$ to denote a player's symbol, and "$\sqcup$" to denote an empty place:

1. *five* : five consecutive s.
2. *full open four* : four consecutive s, that can grow to a *five* in two directions. E.g. $\sqcup$ssss$\sqcup$.
3. *half open four* : four consecutive s, that can grow to a *five* in only one direction. E.g. $\sqcup$ssss.
4. *full open three* : three consecutive s, that can grow to a *full open four* in two directions. E.g. $\sqcup\sqcup$sss$\sqcup\sqcup$.
5. *half open three* : three consecutive s, that can grow to a *full open four* in one direction, and in the other they can grow to a *half open four*. E.g. $\sqcup$sss$\sqcup\sqcup$.
6. *quarter open three* : three consecutive s, that can only grow to a *half open four*. E.g. $\sqcup$sss$\sqcup$ or $\sqcup\sqcup$sss.

The evaluation function involves the following board features:
- $five^s$: number of *fives* of the player s.
- $four_1^s$: number of *full open fours* of the player s.
- $four_2^s$: number of *half open fours* of the player s.

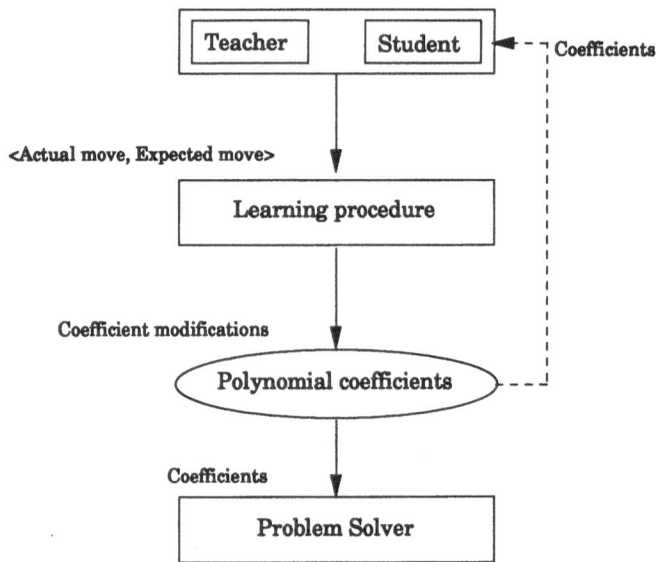

Figure 1. The architecture of the learning system.

- $three_1^s$: number of *full open threes* of the player **s**.
- $three_2^s$: number of *half open threes* of the player **s**.
- $three_3^s$: number of *quarter open threes* of the player **s**.
- $k_i; i = 1, \ldots, 5$: coefficients.

The evaluation function is computed in the following manner (for the player whose symbol is x) [1] :

1. If $five^x \geq 1$ then $F = +999999$.
2. If $five^o \geq 1$ then $F = -999999$.
3. Otherwise

$$F = k_1 * (four_1^x - four_1^o) + k_2 * (four_2^x - four_2^o) + k_3 * (three_1^x - three_1^o) +$$

$$k_4 * (three_2^x - three_2^o) + k_5 * (three_3^x - three_3^o)$$

Note that a legal board created during a legal game cannot include a *five* of both x and o. The vector constructed from the 5 differences above (e.g. $four_1^x - four_1^o$, etc...), will be referred to as the *contents* of the board.

In future versions of the system we intend to introduce more board features in order to increase the expressiveness of the evaluation function. For example, the number of ␣s␣ss␣ for each player.

---

[1] For the opponent the function simply takes the negative sign.

The Learning Procedure

In this section we describe the approach used in the construction of the learning procedure, i.e. the part of the system that attempts to improve the performance of the problem solver. We used a learning procedure which continuously re–evaluates the coefficients of the evaluation function. Hence the knowledge to be learned is the values of the coefficients (the k_i's from the previous subsection) which yield a better performance of the problem solver. This kind of learning technique is sometimes called *learning by parameter adjustement* [5].

As stated above, The learner employs two problem solvers that play a game of *fives* (the *student* and the *teacher*). The starting position of every game (the first 5 paired-moves) is predefined by a human operator. Thus it can be stated, that the learning procedure generates its own experiences by a process, which is mostly automated, but does need some initialization from an external agent (i.e. human).

The learning procedure starts by creating two boards:

- $Board_1$ - the board generated by applying the *actual move*.

- $Board_2$ - the board generated by applying the *expected move*.

The learning procedure then computes the *contents* of the two boards (B_1, B_2 are the *contents* of $Board_1$, $Board_2$, respectively):

1. $B_1 = (t_1, t_2, t_3, t_4, t_5)$

2. $B_2 = (p_1, p_2, p_3, p_4, p_5)$

The difference between these two vectors is then computed. Let us denote this vector by $\Delta = B_1 - B_2 = (\Delta_1, \Delta_2, \Delta_3, \Delta_4, \Delta_5)$. Note that it can include positive integers, negative integers and zeroes. Let us denote by N the negative numbers in Δ, and by P the positive numbers in Δ. The learning process will cause coefficients corresponding to $\Delta_i \in P$ to grow according to the following calculations.

First, the *gain* (GA) is computed by:

$$GA = \frac{\sum_{\Delta_i \in N} | \Delta_i * k_i |}{\sum_{\Delta_i \in P} \Delta_i} * 0.1$$

Second, the *gain* is added to each of the k_i's corresponding to $\Delta_i \in P$.
For example, consider the coefficients:

$$k_1 = 500, \quad k_2 = 400, \quad k_3 = 300, \quad k_4 = 200, \quad k_5 = 100$$

and the Δ vector:

$$\Delta = (1, -1, 2, -1, 0)$$

The updated coefficients will be:

$$k_1 = 520, \quad k_2 = 400, \quad k_3 = 320, \quad k_4 = 200, \quad k_5 = 100$$

The rationale behind the above formulas is that the components corresponding to $\Delta_i \in P$ outweighted (from the *teacher*'s point of view) the components corresponding to $\Delta_i \in N$, and therefore $\Delta_i \in P$ should be increased by a value proportional to the strength of the $\Delta_i \in N$. The division by 10 is done in order to stabilize the learning process, and the other division is simply normalization.

THE PROBLEM OF LEARNING HARMFUL KNOWLEDGE

The system enables two different operating modes, which have different objectives. They allow the system to use its three different instances of the problem solver (i.e. the *fives game-players*). In the previous section we introduced two of them: the *teacher* and the *student*, the third one is the *tester*. The operating modes are:

- *Test Mode*: *Student* confronts *tester*. Learning is off. Its objective is to evaluate the *student* (vs. another *fives* game-player program, the *tester*).

- *Learn Mode*: *Student* confronts *teacher*. Learning is on. Its goal is to allow the *student* to learn how to play *fives* in a better fashion.

Following we describe the parameters of the three instances of the problem solver used by the operating modes.

1. *Student*:
   - Plays with the symbol x
   - *Max Level* = 3
   - *Branching Factor* = 3
   - Coefficients – Initial values read from an external data file. May change during the game.

2. *Teacher*:
   - Plays with the symbol o
   - *Max Level* = 5
   - *Branching Factor* = 10
   - Coefficients – Initial values read from an external data file. May change during the game.

3. *Tester*:
   - Plays with the symbol o
   - *Max Level* = 3
   - *Branching Factor* = 3
   - Coefficients – Fixed in software.

During the experiments we had the system play games in both *test mode* and *learn mode*. Every game was played until one of the players (x or o) won, or until 25 paired-moves were taken without a victory. For the latter case the game is announced tied. The first 5 paired-moves of each game (i.e. the first 5 x's and o's in the board) are predefined through data files. This means that the starting position of each game is fixed.

Let us now define the different kinds of games that were played during the experiment:

- *Learning session*: a game between the *student* and the *teacher*, in which the system acquires knowledge. The *student* always moves first.

- *Test game*: a game between the *student* and the *tester*. The decision concerning who moves first, comes from the data file.

We gathered 5 starting positions together with their 5 duals (i.e. x's are replaced by o's and conversely), to form a set of 10 test games. This set is called the *exam*.

For each *test game* the *student* gets a score in [0,100]. Before calculating the score we set the value of the variable g in the following manner:

- if the game was tied, then $g = 0$

- if the *student* won, then $g = 26 - moves$

- if the *student* lost, then $g = -(26 - moves)$

where *moves* is the rounded up number of paired moves played in the game (e.g. if x moved first and won on his 7th move, the number of paired–moves executed is only 6.5, but it is rounded up to 7).

The score is then computed according to the following formula:

$$Score = g * 2.5 + 50$$

The *student*'s score in the entire *exam* is the average of the scores he got in the 10 games composing it.

The idea behind this scoring scheme is that a victory achieved after n moves worth more than a victory achieved after n+1 moves, and a defeat caused after n+1 moves worth more than a defeat caused after n moves (i.e. better players will win faster and loose slower). The rest is simply normalization of the score to the range [0,100] (consider the fact that we allowed 25 paired moves after which the game is announced tied).

The experiments were conducted in the following manner:

1. The data file from which the coefficients of the evaluation function were read, was initialized with the coefficients that were fixed in software for the *tester* (i.e. 500, 400, 300, 200, 100).

2. A preliminary *exam* (*exam0*) was held. The score of *exam0* was expected to be exactly 50, since at this stage the *student* and the *tester* are identical, and both the *exam* and the scoring-scheme are symmetric.

3. The following steps were repeated five times:
   (a) A *learning session* was held.
   (b) The coefficients in the data file were updated according to the changes made in them during the *learning session*.
   (c) an *exam* was held.

The graph in figure 2 shows the scores of the *student* in the *exams* as learning advanced.

The top score, 66.25, was reached after the second *learning session*. *Learning sessions* carried out from this point on, had a deleterious effect on the system performance which degraded to the score of 55 after the last (fifth) session. It is obvious that some of the knowledge acquired by the system was harmful. In the next section we describe our attempts to solve the problem of harmful knowledge by introducing information filters to the system.

SELECTIVE LEARNING

The poor performance of the learning program that was demonstrated in the last section raises an important question: is the learning technique that we are using inherently bad? Looking closely at the experiment graph reveals that it is not so. There were some learning sessions where the performance of the learning program had improved. On the other hand, there were some sessions where the learning decreased the performance. But how can we differentiate between the cases? The answer is simple: the tests that were performed as part of our research methodolgy can also be performed by the learner itself as a part of its learning techniques. The learner can use

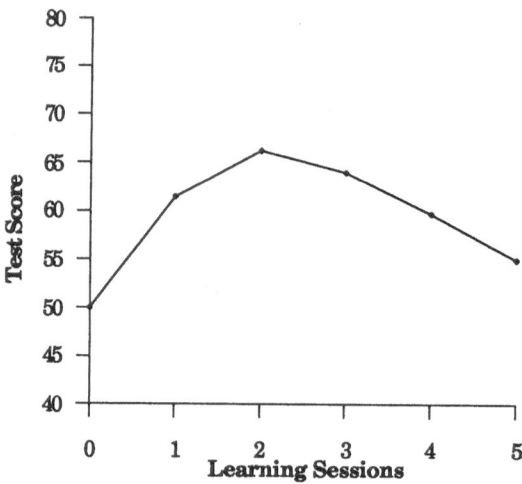

Figure 2. System performance during learning sessions.

this self test to decide whether a particular change in the knowledge base is likely to improve its performance.

The test described above is an example of an acquisition filter: it decides whether to acquire a piece of knowledge which is generated by the acquisition procedure. It is different than most of the filters employed in other works. While most of the other filters try to estimate the utility of a newly generated knowledge by employing a relatively simple (and low-cost) heuristics, the filter that we employ here invests substantial resources for that decision. In that sense, it is similar to the hypothesis filter [6] that performs an extensive set of statistical tests before deciding whether to accept a newly generated classifier.

Specifically, the filter operates in the following way: a set of coefficients is preprogrammed into the filter. Whenever a coefficient modification is generated by the acquisition (learning) program, the filter invokes an *exam* to test the performance of the problem solver with the modified coefficients. The score that the program achieved after the last change is stored. The modification takes place only if the score achieved in the exam is higher than the last score.

One major problem with employing such a filter is its high cost in learning time. In order to reduce that cost we have implemented two other filters that reduces the number of times that the self-test filter is being called. One is another acquisition filter which is inserted between the acquisition procedure and the self-test filter. The filter uses a set of domain specific rules to filter out some modifications that do not make sense. For example, there is a rule that specifies that half open four can not be worse than quarter open three, and any modification that suggests so should be filtered out. This filter reduce the number of modifications that needed to be tested by the self-test filter.

The other filter is an experience filter which is inserted between the learning instance generator and the acquisition procedure. The input to the acquisition program are pairs of actual score and expected score. The experience filter allows only instances

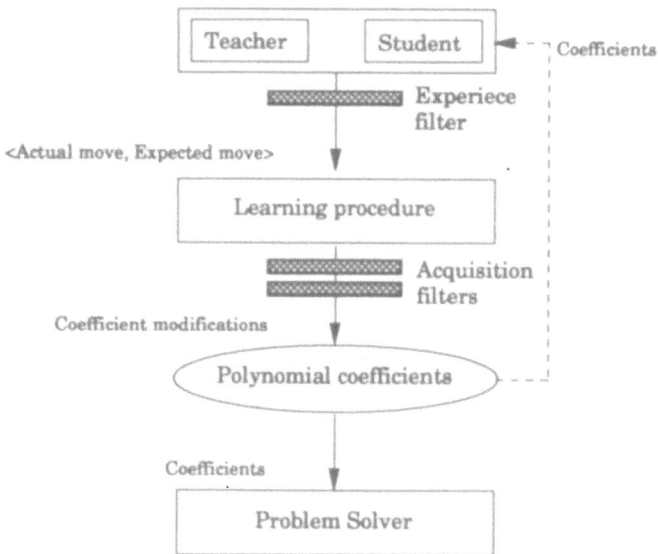

Figure 3. The learning system with its filters.

with significant difference between the actual and expected values to pass through. The architecture of the learning system with the filters is shown in figure 3.

We have repeated the experiment described in the third section, this time with the system that includes the filters. The results of the experiment is shown in figure 4.

The coefficients that were used to achieve the highest score were

$$k_1 = 560 \ , k_2 = 450 \ , k_3 = 300 \ , k_4 = 222.5 \ , k_5 = 122.5$$

The first observation that can be made by looking at the results of the experiment with the system that includes the filters is that the filters were extremely beneficial. While the score achieved by the system that did not employ filters was 55 after five learning sessions, the score achieved after the filters were introduced to the system was 74.2. It is worthwhile to notice that during the third and fourth learning sessions the system performance was not changed. This is due the rejection of all the proposed modifications by the various filters.

DISCUSSION

The work presented in this paper concentrated in the problem of harmful knowledge acquired by learning systems that attempt to improve game playing programs. In the third section we have demonstrated that such a phenomenon indeed occurs in a particular learning system that tries to improve its ability to play the game of *fives*. Some of the acquired knowledge had deleterious effects on the performance of the game playing program.

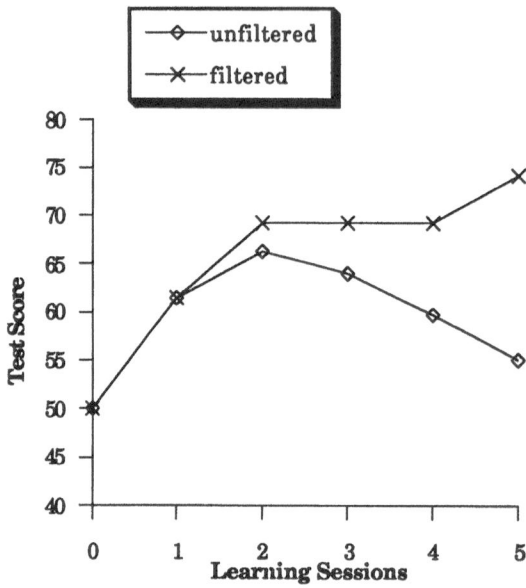

Figure 4. Results of experiments with and without filters.

Using the information filtering model as a guide we were able to build an acquisition filter that only selects acquired knowledge that can pass a performance test. Minton [1] and Markovitch and Scott [2, 3] define the utility of a knowledge element to be the difference in the performance of the system with and without that element. Our filter uses this definition as a functional one and actually tests the system performance under the two conditions.

While the filter proved to be very efficient in blocking harmful knowledge, it has a major drawback of requiring a substantial ammount of learning resources. We had overcome this problem by inserting other filters into the system that reduced the number of times that the expensive filter was invoked.

The combination of filters proved to be very useful and the system achieved a much better performance when using them. The filters also made the learning curve behave more consistently. System performance did never decrease when using the filters.

It is interesting to note some of the ideas discussed here were implemeted as early as 1959 by Samuel [7]. Unfortunately, Samuel did not report any experiment comparing the system's performance with and without the various selection mechanisms.

The research described in this paper is far from being completed. The most important step to follow is to perform a much more extensive experimentation in order to have a better understanding of the roles of the various filters. Particularly, we need to experiment with each filter separately and with every combination of filters so that the relationships between them can be well understood.

References

[1] Steve Minton. *Learning search control knowledge: an explanation-based approach.* Klower Academic Publishers, Boston, Mass, 1988.

[2] Shaul Markovitch. *Information filtering: selection mechanisms in learning systems.* PhD thesis, University of Michigan, 1989.

[3] Shaul Markovitch and Paul D. Scott. Information filters and their implementation in the syllog system. In *Proceedings of the sixth international workshop on machine learning, Ithaca, New York.* Morgan Kaufmann, 1989.

[4] Judea Pearl. *Heuristics: intelligent search strategies for computer problem solving.* Addison-Wesley, 1984.

[5] Elaine Rich and Kevin Knight. *Artificial intelligence.* McGraw-Hill, New York, 2nd edition, 1991.

[6] Oren Etzioni. Hypothesis filtering: a practical approach to reliable learning. In *Proceedings of the fifth international workshop on machine learning, Ann Arbor, MI.* Morgan Kaufmann, 1988.

[7] Arthur L. Samuel. Some studies in machine learning using the game of checkers. *IBM Journal*, 3(3):211–229, 1989.

Algorithms and Data Structures

AN O $(n^{2.5})$ TIME HEURISTIC ALGORITHM FOR A CLASS

OF LARGE WEIGHTED EDGE COLOURING PROBLEMS

Ruy Eduardo Campello

FURNAS-Centrais Elétricas S.A. and
Department of Mathematical Technology
Institute of Logic, Philosophy and
Theory of Science - ILTC

INTRODUCTION

Let $(S_1, S_2, ..., S_n)$ be a sequence of n pairwise edge-disjoint perfect matchings on the complete bipartite graph $\mathbf{K}_{n,n}$ and let $D = (d_{ij})$ be a $n \times n$ matrix whose entries $d_{ij} \geq 0$ for all $i, j = 1, 2, ..., n$ are the edge weights. Denote by $(D^1, D^2, ..., D^n)$ the sequence of matrices $n \times n$ and a scalar T such that:

(i) $D^r = (d_{ij}^r)$ where $d_{ij}^r = \begin{cases} d_{ij}, & \text{if } (i,j) \in S_r \\ 0, & \text{otherwise} \end{cases}$

(ii) $T = \sum_{r=1}^{n} \left(\max_{i,j} d_{ij}^r \right)$.

Next define $W(S_r) = \max_{i,j} d_{ij}^r$ as the weight of a perfect matching S_r. As such,

$$T = \sum_{r=1}^{n} W(S_r)$$

is the sum of the weights of the perfect matchings $S_1, S_2, ..., S_n$.

Consider the following Minimax Combinatorial Optimization Problem (n-BAP): find a partition of the edge set of $\mathbf{K}_{n,n}$ into n perfect matchings $(S_1, S_2, ..., S_n)$ in such a way that the sum of the weights of the matchings in the partition T be minimized. Therefore the minimization of T amounts to determining a Minimax Weight Edge-Colouring of the Bipartite Graph $\mathbf{K}_{n,n}$.

COMPUTER SCIENCE, Edited by R. Baeza-Yates
and U. Manber, Plenum Press, New York, 1992

Areas of application for (n-BAP) include, but are by no means limited to, the efficient time slot scheduling of switching modes that make up a frame period for operating a Satellite Communication Network under the Switched Time Division Multiple Access System - SS/TDMA (see, Balas and Landweer, 1985; Inukai, 1979 and Inukai et al., 1977) and also Drivers Rostering Scheduling Problems (see, Carraresi and Gallo, 1984 and also Paias, 1988).

This problem is NP-Complete and can be formulated either as a 3-index bottleneck assignment problem or alternatively as a set partitioning problem. While the first formulation leads to an optimization problem with $3 \cdot n^2$ constraints and n^2 variables the second has n^2 constraints and $n!$ variables. These formulations are important for they yields algorithmic insights. For further references see for example Balas and Landweer, 1985.

The NP-Completeness of (n-BAP) implies that one cannot hope to be able to solve large problem instances in polynomial time therefore leading to the development of efficient polynomial time heuristic algorithms that are more likely to be of pratical use specially for very large scale problems.

HEURISTIC HBAP

Balas and Landweer (1985) have developed and tested a good polynomial time heuristic algorithm for (n-BAP) that consists of solving a sequence of n bottleneck, or minimax assignment problems.

At the r-th iteration it solves an $n \times n$ bottleneck assignment problem and if S_r is the optimal matching found, defines $d_{ij}^r = d_{ij}$ if $(i,j) \in S_r$ and $d_{ij}^r = 0$ otherwise for $i,j = 1,2,...,n$. Then it sets $d_{ij} = +\infty$ if $(i,j) \in S_r$ leaving unchanged otherwise for all $i,j = 1,2,...,n$. If $r+i < n$ it sets $r \leftarrow r+1$ and repeats the step. Otherwise $(S_1,S_2,...,S_n)$ is the desired sequence of n pairwise edge-disjoint perfect matchings with the heuristic objective function value being

$$T = \sum_{r=1}^{n} \left\{ \max_{i,j} d_{ij}^r \right\} .$$

Many techniques are known for finding an optimal solution to a minimax assignment problem in time $O(n^3)$ and space $O(n^2)$. See for instance Garfinkel (1971), Carpaneto and Toth (1981), Derigs and Zimmermann (1974) and also Derigs (1984). Thus the time complexity of the whole procedure is $O(n^4)$ with space requirements of order $O(n^2)$.

As to the performance, no previous constant-performance bound polynomial-time heuristic for (n-BAP) is known. Nevertheless, a lower bound $\overline{T}$ on the optimal value of (n-BAP) can be easily verified to be the maximum among the row and column sums, that is

$$\overline{T} = \max \left\{ \max_{i} \sum_{j=1}^{n} d_{ij} , \max_{j} \sum_{i=1}^{n} d_{ij} \right\} .$$

That being so, the performance of any heuristic algorithm for (n-BAP) can be defined as the ratio $\overline{T}/T$, where T is the heuristic value. In that respect the Balas and

Landweer heuristic algorithm performed very well on randomly generated problems displaying ratios very close to 1 and obtains consistently better results than earlier methods based on different formulations. However there is a drawback namely, main memory limitations when one has to solve very large instances.

Kurtzberg (1962) proposed a nice heuristic algorithm for the assignment problem that consists of partitioning a very large $n \times n$ problem into many smaller subproblems. Thus a $k \cdot m \times k \cdot m$ assignment problem is decomposed into k^2 subproblems of size $m \times m$. This can always be done without loss of generality by assuming $n = k \cdot m$ for integers k and m such that $k \leq m$. The solution of these k^2 subproblems is then used to solve a $k \times k$ assignment problem that provides an heuristic solution to the original problem.

The computational complexity of this procedure is discussed by Avis and Devroye (1985) and it is quite direct. Since k^2 assignment problems of size $m \times m$ and afterwards a $k \times k$ assignment problem are solved the overall time complexity is $O(k^2 \cdot m^3)$. Besides, another interesting feature is that matrix D may be kept in secondary storage and thus the space complexity is only $O(\max\{m^2, k^2\})$.

The idea behind the heuristic algorithm **HBAP** is fairly simple. Instead to solve a minimax assignment problem of size n at each iteration we apply the Kurtzberg procedure and solve k^2 minimax smaller subproblems of size $m \times m$ and then a minimax assignment problem of size $k \times k$. Notice however that there is no need of solving the k^2 minimax assignment problems at every iteration but the first one. Only those k subproblems that have been penalized have to be solved again. This way the first iteration has time complexity of order $O(k^2 \cdot m^3)$ while the others are $O(k \cdot m^3)$. Since there are $(n-1)$ iterations, because the n-th iteration is straightforward, the overall computational effort of our procedure is at most $O(n^2 \cdot m^2)$. Furthermore, the space requirement of order $O(\max\{m^2, k^2\})$ is preserved.

Let $MinMax(n, d_{ij}, x_{ij}, i, j = 1, \ldots, n, T_r)$ be a procedure that solves a bottleneck or minimax assignment problem of size n on $D = (d_{ij})$. Consider $P(n, k, m, D, R^{ij}, \text{Skip})$ as a procedure that for a given k and m gets in turn the correct problem partition R^{ij} of size $m \times m$, being also able to identify those subproblems that need not be solved again and in that event sets the boolean variable Skip to TRUE, otherwise Skip is FALSE. Besides, let $W(m, R^{ij}, Y^{ij}, t^{ij})$ be a procedure whose time complexity is $O(m^3)$ for solving minimax assignment problems of size m on R^{ij} (see for instance, Carpaneto and Toth, 1981 and Derigs, 1984) whereas Y^{ij} and t^{ij} are the resulting permutation matrix and the threshold associated value.

As a matter of fact there will always be a trade-off between space and time therefore leading to optimal space and time versions. As such the optimal versions of the procedure **HBAP** are as follows:

Optimal Versions	Space	Time
$m = k = \sqrt{n}$ $k = n^{3/4}$	$O(n)$ $O(n^{1.5})$	$O(n^3)$ $O(n^{2.5})$

The description of our **HBAP** heuristic algorithm as outlined follows:

Algorithm HBAP $[(S_1, S_2, ..., S_n)]$
  Begin
    Read D Matrix and **Keep** it in Secondary Storage
    $\{n, d_{ij}, i, j = 1, 2, ..., n\}$;
    Read Parameters $\{k, m\}$;
    $T := 0$;
    For $r := 1$ **To** n **Do**
    Begin
      MinMax$(n, d_{ij}, x_{ij}, i, j = 1, 2, ..., n, T_r)$;
      For $i := 1$ **To** n **Do**
      For $j := 1$ **To** n **Do**
      Begin
        $d_{ij}^r := d_{ij} \cdot x_{ij}$;
        If $x_{ij} = 1$ **Then** $d_{ij} := +\infty$;   {Penalties}
      end;
      $T := T + T_r$;
    end;
  End.

MinMax $(m, d_{ij}, x_{ij}, i, j = 1, 2, ..., n, T_r)$ [Perfect Matching S_r]
  Begin
    For $i := 1$ **To** k **Do**
      For $j := 1$ **To** k **Do**
      Begin
        $P(n, k, m, D, R^{ij}, \text{Skip})$;   {Partitioning}
        If Not Skip **Then**
        Begin
          $W(m, R^{ij}, Y^{ij}, t^{ij})$;   {Subproblem Optimization}
          $A[i, j] := t^{ij}$;   {Master Problem Assemblage}
        end;
      end;
    $W(k, A, H, T_r)$;   {Master Problem Optimization}
    Build the $n \times n$ permutation matrix $X = (x_{ij})$
    from k^2 submatrices $h_{ij} \cdot Y^{ij}$, $1 \le i, j \le k$;
  End.

It is worthy of note that the Balas and Landweer heuristic (1985) has time complexity $O(n^4)$ and space complexity of order $O(n^2)$. In the next section we address the experimental behavior of our heuristic procedure.

NUMERICAL RESULTS

In order to investigate the average performance of the **HBAP** a set of 200 test problems with $n = 20,40,60,80,100,120,140,160,180,200$ (10 replications for each size) and the entries of matrix D integers drawn randomly from a uniform distribution over the interval [50,100].

The experimental results disclose average efficiency $(\overline{T}/T)$ fluctuating in the range (0.93%, 0.96%] when the parameters k and m where chosen around its space optimal version and in the range (0.87%, 0.90%] when k and m where chosen so as to meet its time optimal version. No matter the choice of parameters may be there was a slight increase in the average efficiency as n grows. The sample variances were very small indicating a stable algorithm.

Details on the implementation of the **HBAP** heuristic as well as comprehensive computational results can be found in Garcia, 1990.

CONCLUSIONS

As far as expected performance is concerned our computational results are comparable to those obtained by Balas and Landweer, 1985.

Yet, whatever the choice of parameters may be the **HBAP** procedure displays better time and space complexities than earlier methods and also makes it possible to handle very large scale problems being limited only by secondary storage space which is a mild shortcoming.

REFERENCES

Avis, D. and Devroye, L., 1985, An Analysis of a Decomposition Heuristic For The Assignment Problem, *Operations Research Letters* 3, Nº 6:279-283.

Balas, E. and Landweer, P.R., 1984, Traffic Assignment in Communication Satellites, *Operations Research Letters* 2, Nº 4:141-147.

Carpaneto, G. and Toth, P., 1981, Algorithm For The Solution of The Bottleneck Assignment Problem, *Computing* 127:179-187.

Carraresi, P. and Gallo, G., 1984, A Multi-Level Bottleneck Assignment Approach to the Bus Drivers Rostering Problem, *European Journal of Operational Research*, Nº 16:163-173.

Derigs, U., 1984, *Alternate Strategies For Solving Bottleneck Assignment Problems - Analysis and Computational Results, Computing* 133:95-106.

Derigs, U. and Zimmermann, U., 1987, *An Augmenting Path Method For Solving Linear Bottleneck Assignment Problems, Computing* 119:285-295.

Garcia, S., 1990, *Heurística Polinomial para Obtenção de Seqüência Min-Max Disjunta de n Matchings Perfeitos em* $K_{n \times n}$ *de Grande Porte, Master of Science Thesis of the Military Institute of Engineering-IME.*

Garfinkel, R.S., 1971, *An Improved Algorithm For The Bottleneck Assignment Problem, Operations Research* 119:1747-1751.

Inukai, T., 1979, An Efficient SS/TDMA Time Slot Assignment Algorithm, *IEEE*, Vol. COM-27, Nº 10:1449-1455.

Ito, Y., Urano, Y., Muratani, T. and Yamaguchi, M., 1977, *Analysis of a Switch Matrix for an SS/TDMA System, Proceedings of the IEEE* 165:411-419.

Kurtzberg, J.M., 1962, On Approximation Methods for the Assignment Problem, *JACM* 9:419-439.

Paias, A.M., 1988, Sistema Interactivo para Geração dos Horários de Condutores de Viaturas, *Investigação Operacional* 8, 1:47-53.

RANDOMIZED SORTING OF
SHUFFLED MONOTONE SEQUENCES

Vladimir Estivill-Castro[1] and Derick Wood[2]

[1]Department of Computer Science
York University, North York
Ontario M3J-1P3, Canada

[2]Department of Computer Science
University of Waterloo, Waterloo
Ontario N2L-3G1, Canada

INTRODUCTION

A sorting algorithm is adaptive if it sorts in time proportional to the length and the disorder of the input [6]. That is, when the input is nearly sorted, sorting is fast and only on randomly permuted inputs does it take $O(n \log n)$ comparisons. The main motivation behind adaptive sorting is that, in practice, nearly sorted inputs are more frequent, as opposed to the usual assumption for expected-case analysis that all inputs are equally likely.

Several measures of the disorder in a sequence and several sorting algorithms that adapt with respect to these measures have been proposed. The proposed sorting algorithms are shown to achieve maximal (or optimal) adaptivity in the worst case with respect to some measures. Among the measures of disorder, the minimum number of monotone subsequences (denoted SMS) stands out because it is *algorithmically finer* than other important measures (where a measure of disorder M_1 is algorithmically finer than a measure M_2 if all sorting algorithms optimal with respect to M_1 are also optimal with respect to M_2). Given a sequence X and $k \geq SMS(X)$, *Slabsort* [4] sorts X optimally in $O(|X|(1 + \log[k + 1]))$ time, where $|X|$ denotes the length of X. In general, the value of $SMS(X)$ is unknown, but through *exponential guessing* optimality with respect to SMS can be obtained. However, *Slabsort* is impractical because it requires repeated median finding.

Randomized adaptive sorting algorithms [1] are a practical alternative to worst-case adaptive algorithms since they avoid complex data structures and allow simple implementations achieving the same asymptotic complexity in the expected case and with a smaller multiplicative constant. We propose *Randomized Slabsort* as a practical alternative to *Slabsort* that is adaptive with respect to *SMS* in the expected case.

In this paper we use the following notational conventions. The set of finite sequences of distinct positive integers is denoted by $N^{<N}$. For a sequence $X \in N^{<N}$, the length of X is denoted by $|X|$. For a set S, the cardinality of S is denoted by $\|S\|$. For a real z, the natural logarithm of z is denoted by $\ln(z)$ and the logarithm base 2 by $\log(z)$. Let $X \in N^{<N}$, we denote a subsequence of X by $\langle x_{i(1)}, \ldots, x_{i(s)} \rangle$ where $i : \{1, \ldots, s\} \to \{1, \ldots, |X|\}$ is injective and monotonically increasing. We say that a subsequence $\langle x_{i(1)}, \ldots, x_{i(s)} \rangle$ is an *up-sequence* if $x_{i(1)} < x_{i(2)} < \ldots < x_{i(s)}$. Similarly, we say that a subsequence $\langle x_{i(1)}, \ldots, x_{i(s)} \rangle$ is a *down-sequence* if $x_{i(1)} > x_{i(2)} > \ldots > x_{i(s)}$. A subsequence is *monotone* if it is a down-sequence or an up-sequence. We say that two subsequences $\langle x_{i(1)}, \ldots, x_{i(s)} \rangle$, $\langle x_{j(1)}, \ldots, x_{j(t)} \rangle$ *intersect* if $\{i(1), i(1)+1, \ldots, i(s)\}$ and $\{j(1), j(1)+1, \ldots, j(s)\}$ intersect. For example, if $W_0 = \langle 6, 5, 8, 7, 10, 9, 4, 3, 2, 1 \rangle$, the subsequences $\langle 6, 8, 10 \rangle$ and $\langle 5, 7, 9 \rangle$ intersect but $\langle 6, 8, 10 \rangle$ and $\langle 4, 3, 2, 1 \rangle$ do not.

MEASURES OF DISORDER

In order to express the performance of a sorting algorithm in terms of the length and the disorder in the input we must assess the disorder in the input. Intuitively, a measure of disorder is a function that is minimized when the sequence has no disorder and depends only on the relative order of the elements in the sequence.

Definition. *Letting $M : N^{<N} \to \Re$, we say that M is a measure of disorder if*

1. *X sorted implies $M(X) = \min_{|Y|=|X|}\{M(Y)\}$, and*

2. *$X = \langle x_1, \ldots, x_n \rangle$, $Y = \langle y_1, \ldots, y_n \rangle$ and ($x_i \leq x_j$ if and only if $y_i \leq y_j$ for all $i, j \in \{1, \ldots, n\}$) implies $M(X) = M(Y)$.*

We describe the most common measures of disorder, many others can be found in the literature [1,8]. An *inversion* is any pair of elements in a sequence that are in the wrong order. The total number of inversions in a sequence X is the measure *Inv*. We may consider that, in terms of the disorder it represents, an inversion pair of elements that are far apart is more significant than an inversion pair whose elements are closer. We define *Dis* as the largest distance determined by an inversion. Often local disorder is not as important as global disorder; for example, if books in a library are one slot away from their correct positions, we are still able to find them, since the index will get us close enough; however, a book very far away from its correct position is difficult to find. We define *Max* as the largest distance an element must travel to reach its sorted position. The number of operations required to rearrange a sequence into sorted order may be our first concern. We define *Exc* as the minimum number of exchanges required to sort a sequence. We may also consider that disorder is produced by inserting some records into the wrong positions. We define *Rem* as the minimum number of elements that must be removed to obtain a sorted subsequence. Ascending runs constitute sorted segments of the data. We define *Runs(X)* as the minimum number of contiguous up-sequences required to cover X. A natural generalization of *Runs* is the minimum number of ascending subsequences required to cover the given sequence. We denote this measure by *SUS* for Shuffled Up-Sequences. We can generalize again and define *SMS(X)* (for Shuffled Monotone Subsequence) as the minimum number of monotone (ascending or descending) subsequences required to cover the given sequence. For example $W_0 = \langle 6, 5, 8, 7, 10, 9, 4, 3, 2, 1\rangle$ has $Runs(W_0) = 8$, while $SUS(W_0) = \|\{\langle 6, 8, 10\rangle, \langle 5, 7, 9\rangle, \langle 4\rangle, \langle 3\rangle, \langle 2\rangle, \langle 1\rangle\}\| = 7$ and $SMS(X) = \|\{\langle 6, 8, 10\rangle, \langle 5, 7, 9\rangle, \langle 4, 3, 2, 1\rangle\}\| = 3$.

The examples above show that disorder can be evaluated in many ways and different measures take into account different types of disorder. Researchers strive for sorting algorithms that are adaptive to as many measures as possible. A sorting algorithm that is optimally adaptive with respect to SMS is also optimally adaptive with respect to $Runs$, Max, Dis, and SUS [4], and can easily be modified to achieve optimality with respect to Exc and Rem too [1].

Slabsort — THE ALGORITHM

Slabsort is a sorting algorithm that can be used to achieve optimality with respect to SMS and therefore optimality with respect to Dis, Max, $Runs$ and SUS. Although *Slabsort* is an important theoretical breakthrough it has limited practical value because it repeatedly requires median finding in worst-case linear time.

Slabsort uses a subalgorithm that attempts to sort with a limited amount of resources. If the subalgorithm is not successful with this limited amount, it returns a flag indicating so; otherwise, it returns a sorted sequence. The subalgorithm is a variant of *Melsort* (an adaptive sorting algorithm developed by Skiena [8]). We now describe *Melsort*. When *Melsort* is applied to a sequence Y, it constructs a set of sorted lists called the "encroaching list set" of Y and then, it merges the lists to obtain the elements of Y is sorted order. The encroaching set of a sequence $Y = \langle y_1, \ldots, y_n\rangle$ is defined by the following procedure: We say that y_i fits a dequeue D if y_i can be added to the front or the end of D so as to maintain D in sorted order. Start with y_1 in the first dequeue and repeatedly insert y_i into the first dequeue that it fits. Create a new dequeue if y_i does not fit in any existing dequeue. An example will make this process clear. Consider the sequence $W_1 = \langle 4, 6, 5, 2, 9, 1, 3, 8, 0, 7\rangle$. Initially, D_1 consists of 4, and the second element fits at the end of D_1. 5 is between 4 and 6, so 5 is added to an empty D_2. The next three elements all fit in D_1 and are placed there. 3 does not fit in D_1 but it fits at the front of D_2. Similarly, 8 fits at the end of D_2. 0 fits in D_1, but the last element requires a new dequeue. The final encroaching set is

$$\{D_1 = \lfloor 0, 1, 2, 4, 6, 9\rfloor, \quad D_2 = \lfloor 3, 5, 8\rfloor, \quad D_3 = \lfloor 7\rfloor\}.$$

Skiena [8] observed that the number of lists in the encroaching set is a measure of disorder and denoted it by Enc. For example,

$$Enc(\langle 4, 6, 5, 2, 9, 1, 3, 8, 0, 7\rangle) = 3.$$

In fact, SMS is also algorithmically finer than Enc [4]. Moreover, Skiena [8] pointed out that *Melsort* takes $O(|X|(1 + \log[Enc(X) + 1]))$ comparisons for all sequences X.

Let *Melsort*$(X, k, flag)$ be the variant of *Melsort* used in *Slabsort* where X is the input sequence and k is a bound on the size of the enroaching set it can construct. If during its execution an encroaching set with more than k lists is required, *Melsort*$(X, k, flag)$ halts and flags that it is unable to complete the sorting. Otherwise, it sorts X. The bound k guarantees that for all sequences X, *Melsort*$(X, k, flag)$ takes $O(|X|(1 + \log[k + 1]))$ comparisons.

Slabsort sorts sequences X such that $SMS(X) \leq k$ using $O(|X|(1 + \log[k + 1]))$ comparisons. The input sequence X is stably partitioned into $p = \lceil k^2/2\rceil$ parts of almost equal size using the $\lfloor |X|/p + 1\rfloor$-th, $\lfloor 2|X|/p + 1\rfloor$-th, $\ldots$, $\lfloor (p - 1)|X|/p + $

1⌋-th elements as pivots. These elements are found by repeated median finding in $O(|X|\log[1+p])$ comparisons. Let $X_1, X_2, \ldots, X_p$ be the resulting parts or intervals. For each interval X_i, the subalgorithm $Melsort(X_i, k, flag)$ is applied. The fact that $SMS(X) \leq k$ guarantees that half of these subalgorithms sort successfully [4]. On those parts where $Melsort$ is not successful, $Slabsort$ is called recursively.

Since, in the general setting, the value of $SMS(X)$ is unknown, optimality with respect to SMS is achieved by exponentially guessing $SMS(X)$ [4]. More precisely, we first call $Slabsort$ with an initial guess of $k = 2$. If, during the execution of $Slabsort$, more than half of the calls to $Melsort$ are unsuccessful, the process is aborted, the guess value of k is squared, and $Slabsort$ is started again using this new value.

Randomized Slabsort — THE ALGORITHM

Randomized Slabsort is a randomized version of *Slabsort*. Rather than finding elements that will partition the input sequence X into intervals of almost equal length, a sample of size $p = \lceil k^2/2 \rceil$ elements is chosen at random. These elements are used as pivots to stably partition X.

This division protocol is analogous to *Samplesort* [2]. *Samplesort* is a generalization of *Randomized Quicksort* where rather than choosing a single pivot at random, a sample of several pivots is chosen at random. To select any subset of p elements with equal probability the sample is selected as described by Knuth [3, Algorithm S, page 137] Thus, the stable partitioning can be carried out in $O(|X|(1 + \log[p + 1]))$ comparisons with a much smaller multiplicative constant than with median finding. However, the length of the i-th interval is now a random variable with expectation $(|X| - p)/(p + 1)$ [2].

We now show that *Randomized Slabsort* achieves the same asymptotic complexity as *Slabsort*, but in the expected case. In order to do so we must describe *zig-zag shuffled sequences*. Zig-zag shuffled sequences are important because if Y is a zig-zag shuffle and $SMS(Y) \leq k$, then $Melsort(Y, k, flag)$ sorts Y.

Definition. *A sequence Y is a zig-zag shuffle if there is a cover of Y by $SMS(Y)$ monotone subsequences such that no up-sequence intersecs a down-sequence.*

Let X be a sequence with $SMS(X) \leq k$ and $|X| \leq \lceil k^2/2 \rceil$. Assume that the minimum cover of X has k_1 up-sequences and k_2 down-sequences with $k_1 + k_2 = k$. Thus, the number of intersections between an up-sequence and a down-sequence is bounded by $k_1 k_2 \leq k^2/4$. Since *Randomized Slabsort* stably partitions X into $p = \lceil k^2/2 \rceil$ intervals $X_1, \ldots, X_p$, at least half of these intervals are zig-zag shuffle sequences with $SMS(X_i) \leq k$ and they will be sorted by $Melsort(X_i, k, flag)$ in $O(|X_i|(1+\log[k + 1]))$ comparisons. Unfortunately, we do not know which intervals are successfully sorted by $Melsort$, this makes the analysis different from the analysis of $Samplesort$ [2].

Let $L_Z(X)$ be the sum of the lengths of the intervals that are zig-zag shuffles and let $L_N(X)$ the sum of the lengths of the intervals that are not zig-zag shuffles. $L_Z(X)$ and $L_N(X)$ are random variables over all partitions of X into p intervals with $L_Z(X) + L_N(X) = |X|$. Moreover, by the discussion above $L_Z(X)$ is always larger than the sum of lengths of the $\lfloor p/2 \rfloor$ smallest intervals.

Let $L(X)$ denote the length of the $\lfloor p/2 \rfloor$ smallest intervals. The expected length of the i-th smallest interval when partitioning X into p pieces is

$$\frac{|X|}{p} \sum_{j=1}^{i} \frac{1}{p - (j - 1)} \quad \text{[7, page 66].}$$

Thus,

$$E[L(X)] = \sum_{i=1}^{\lfloor p/2 \rfloor} \frac{|X|}{p}^{i} \sum_{j=1}^{|X|} \frac{1}{p-(j-1)}.$$

Let $H_n = \sum_{i=1}^{n} 1/i$ denote the n-th harmonic number. Algebraic manipulations show that

$$E[L(X)] = |X| \frac{H_{\lfloor p/2 \rfloor} - H_p + 1}{2};$$

therefore,

$$E[L(X)] \geq (1 - \ln(2))|X|/2.$$

Thus, we have proved the following result.

Lemma. *Let $X \in N^N$ and S be a uniform sample of p elements. Then, there is a constant c_0 such that $0 < c_0 < 1$ and the expected length of the smallest $\lfloor p/2 \rfloor$ intervals is at least $c_0|X|$.*

Therefore, there is a constant $0 < c_0 < 1$ such that, $E[L_Z(X)] \geq c_0|X|$ and

$$E[L_N(X)] \leq (1 - c_0)|X|. \tag{1}$$

This allows us to prove the main result of this paper.

Theorem 1. *Let $T_S(X, k)$ denote the number of comparisons taken by Randomized Slabsort(X, k). There is a constant $d > 0$ such that, for all k and for all sequences $X \in N^{<N}$ with $SMS(X) \leq k$,*

$$E[T_S(X, k)] \leq d|X|(1 + \log[k + 1]).$$

Proof: The proof is by induction on $|X|$ and we present only the induction step since the base is immediate. Let $c_1 > 0$ be a constant such that, stably partitioning a sequence X using a sample of p elements takes no more than $c_1|X|(1 + \log[p + 1])$ comparisons. Let $c_2 > 0$ be a sequence such that, Melsort$(Y, k, flag)$ takes no more than $c_2|Y|(1 + \log[k + 1])$ comparisons. Let

$$d > (2c_1 + c_2)/c_0, \tag{2}$$

and assume as the induction hypothesis that if Z is a sequence with $|Z| < |X|$ and $SMS(Z) \leq k$, then

$$E[T_S(Z, k)] \leq d|Z|(1 + \log[k + 1]).$$

Now, let X be a sequence, and $SMS(X) \leq k$ and let $T_S(X, k)$ be the number of comparisons performed by Randomized Slabsort(X, k). Let X_i, for $i = 1, \ldots, p$ be the intervals X is stably partitioned into. $E[T_S(X, k)]$ is the sum of three quantities. The first is the expected value of the comparisons required to do the partitioning. The second is the expected value of the comparisons performed by the Melsorts in the intervals. The third is the expected value of the comparisons performed by the recursive calls on those intervals that the Melsorts were unsuccessful. The first quantity is bounded by $c_1|X|(1 + \log[k^2/2 + 1]) < 2c_1|X|(1 + \log[k + 1])$ comparisons. The second quantity is bounded as follows.

$$\begin{aligned} E[\sum_{i=1}^{p} T_{Melsort}(X_i, k)] &\leq \sum_{i=1}^{p} c_2 E[|X_i|](1 + \log[k + 1]) \\ &= c_2|X|(1 + \log[k + 1]). \end{aligned}$$

Let $J = \{i \mid 1 \le i \le p$ and X_i is not a zig-zag shuffle$\}$. By the induction hypothesis

$$E[T_S(X,k)] \tag{3}$$

$$\le (2c_1 + c_2)|X|(1 + \log[k+1]) + \sum_{i \in J} E[T_S(X_i, k)] \tag{4}$$

$$\le (2c_1 + c_2)|X|(1 + \log[k+1]) + \sum_{i \in J} dE[|X_i|](1 + \log[k+1]) \tag{5}$$

$$= (2c_1 + c_2)|X|(1 + \log[k+1]) + d(1 + \log[k+1]) \sum_{i \in J} E[|X_i|] \tag{6}$$

We analyze the last term in the right hand side. By Equation (1),

$$\sum_{i \in J} E[|X_i|] = E[L_N(X)]$$

$$\le (1 - c_0)|X|.$$

Thus, by Equations (2) and (6),

$$E[T_S(X,k)] \le [2c_1 + c_2 + d(1 - c_0)]|X|(1 + \log[k+1])$$
$$\le d|X|(1 + \log[k+1]).$$

$\square$

OPTIMALITY

Using the terminology introduced by Mehlhorn [6, page 72] we demonstrate that *Randomized Slabsort* is optimal. Since a lower bound for sorting a sequences X with $SMS(X) \le k$ in the worst case is known [4], we translate this worst-case lower bound to an equivalent expected case lower bound for randomized sorting algorithms.

Let M be a measure of presortedness, n and k be nonnegative integers and let $below'(k, n, M)$ be the set of sequences of length n with no more that disorder k according to M; that is,

$$below'(k, n, M) = \{Y \mid Y \text{ is a permutation of } \{1, \ldots, n\} \text{ and } M(Y) \le k\}.$$

Consider sorting algorithms having as input not only the sequence X but also an upper bound k on the value of $M(X)$. We analyze the corresponding decision tree for such algorithms. These trees must have at least $\|below'(k, |X|, M)\|$ leaves, since this is the number of possible inputs; so the height of the tree is at least $\log \|below'(k, |X|, M)\|$. Therefore, the algorithm takes at least $\log \|below'(k, |X|, M)\|$ comparisons in the worst case. The average depth of a decision tree D with at least $\|below'(k, X, M)\|$ leaves is

$$Average\text{-}depth[D] = \frac{1}{\|below'(k, X, M)\|} \sum_{Y \in below'(k,X,M)} depth \text{ of } Y \text{ in } D.$$

This implies that [6] there is a constant $c > 0$ such that, for every sorting algorithm D that sorts a sequences in $below'(k, X, M)$,

$$Average\text{-}depth[D] \ge c \log \|below'(k, X, M)\|. \tag{7}$$

Now, a randomized sorting algorithm corresponds to a randomized decision tree [6]. In a random decision tree there are two types of nodes. The first type of node is the ordinary comparison node. The second type is a coin tossing node. It has two outgoing edges labeled 0 and 1 which are taken with half probability each. Without loss of generality we can restrict attention to finite random decision tress; thus, we assume that the number of coin tosses on inputs of size n is bounded by $t(n)$. However, the leaf reached not only depends on the input but also on the sequence $s \in \{0,1\}^{t(n)}$ of outcomes of coin tosses. For any permutation Y and sequence $s \in \{0,1\}^{t(n)}$ let $d_{Y,s}^T$ denote the depth of the leaf reached on sequence s of coin tosses and input sequence Y. Let X be a sequence and T a randomized decision tree, the expected number of comparisons performed by T on X is

$$E[T(X)] = \sum_{s \in \{0,1\}^{t(n)}} \frac{1}{2^{t(n)}} d_{X,s}^T.$$

That is, the average over all random sequences $s \in \{0,1\}^{t(n)}$ of $d_{X,s}^T$.

Let $\mathcal{R}(n,k)$ be the family of all randomized algorithms that sort sequences X with $|X| = n$ and $M(X) \le k$ and let $R \in \mathcal{R}(n,k)$. We denote by $T_R(X,k)$ be the number of comparisons performed by algorithm R on input X. $T_R(X,k)$ is a random variable. A lower bound on the largest expected value of $T_R(X,k)$ is given by the following equation.

$$\max_{X \in below'(k,n,M)} E[T_R(X,k)] \ge \min_{A \in \mathcal{R}(n,k)} \max_{Y \in below'(k,n,M)} E[T_A(Y,k)].$$

Observe that, once the sequence $s \in \{0,1\}^{t(n)}$ is given, the randomized decision tree becomes an ordinary decision tree D_s that sorts sequences in $below(k,n,M)$. Therefore, by Equation (7), there is a constant $d > 0$ such that,

$$\max_{X \in below'(k,n,M)} E[T_R(X,k)] \ge \min_{A \in \mathcal{R}(n,k)} \max_{Y \in below'(k,n,M)} E[T_A(Y,k)]$$

$$\ge \min_{A \in \mathcal{R}(n,k)} \sum_{Y \in below'(k,n,M)} \frac{E[T_A(Y,k)]}{\|below'(k,n,M)\|}$$

$$\ge \min_{A \in \mathcal{R}(n,k)} \sum_{s \in \{0,1\}^{t(n)}} \frac{1}{2^{t(n)}} Average\ depth[D_s]$$

$$\ge d \log \|below(k,n,M)\|.$$

Intuitively, an adaptive randomized algorithm R is optimal in the expected case if for every sequence X, the expected value of $T_R(X)$ is with in a positive constant of the minimum possible. Thus, for R to be optimal, the largest expected value of $T_R(X,k)$ must be within a factor of the minimum possible for all k. Since

$$\log(\|below(k,|X|,SMS)\|) = \Omega(|X|(1 + \log[k+1]))\ [4],$$

Theorem 1 and the derivation above prove the following result.

Theorem 2. *Randomized Slabsort is optimal.*

FINAL REMARKS

A sorting algorithm is optimally adaptive with respect to a measure M if it sorts a sequence X with maximum adaptivity without knowledge of the value of $M(X)$. This notion was first made precise by Mannila [5].

Definition. *Let M be a measure of disorder and A a sorting algorithm. We say that A is optimal (in the worst case) with respect to M (M-optimal) if, for some $c > 0$, we have, for all $X \in N^{<N}$,*

$$T_A(X) \leq c \cdot \max\{|X|, \|below'(M(X), X, M)\|\}.$$

The notion of optimal adaptivity with respect to a measure of disorder has recently been extended to randomized algorithms [1].

Definition. *Let M be a measure of presortedness and R a randomized algorithm. Let $E[T_R(X)]$ denote the expected number of comparisons performed by R on input X. We say that R is optimal with respect to M (or M-optimal) if, for $c > 0$, we have, for all $X \in N^N$,*

$$E[T_R(X)] \leq c \cdot \max\{|X|, \|below'(M(X), X, M)\|\}.$$

Clearly, if an algorithm is M-optimal in the worst case, it is also M-optimal in the expected case but the converse is not true [1]. However, what is more important is that the relationship of being algorithmically finer is preserved.

Theorem 3. *Let M_1 and M_2 be measures of disorder. M_1 is algorithmically finer than M_2 in the worst case if and only if M_1 is algorithmically finer than M_2 in the expected case.*

Thus, *SMS* is algorithmically finer than *Dis, Enc, Max, Runs,* and *SUS* in the worst and in the expected cases. Therefore the importance of optimality with respect to *SMS*.

In order to achieve optimality with respect to *SMS* in the expected case exponential guessing must be applied or $SMS(X)$ must be approximated to within a constant in $O(|X|(1 + \log[SMS(X) + 1]))$ comparisons. It is unknown if $SMS(X)$ can be approximated within a constant in $O(|X|(1 + \log[SMS(X) + 1]))$ comparisons without using median finding. We conjecture that exponential guessing with *Randomized Slabsort* results in an *SMS*-optimal algorithm in the expected case.

ACKNOWLEDGEMENTS

This work was done while the first author was a Postdoctoral Fellow in the Department of Computer Science at the University of Waterloo. It was carried out under a Natural Sciences and Engineering Research Council of Canada Grant No.A-5692, under an Information Technology Research Centre grant and under the financial support of the Department of Computer Science at York University.

The authors are thankful to Prabhakar Ragde and Venkat Raman for motivating discussions.

References

[1] V. Estivill-Castro. *Sorting and Measures of Disorder.* PhD thesis, University of Waterloo, 1991. Available as Department of Computer Science Research Report CS-91-07.

[2] W.D. Frazer and A. C. McKellar. Samplesort: A sampling approach to minimal storage tree sorting. *Journal of the ACM*, 17(3):496–507, July 1970.

[3] D.E. Knuth. *The Art of Computer Programming, Vol.2: Seminumerical Algorithms*. Addison-Wesley Publishing Co., Reading, Mass., 1973.

[4] C. Levcopoulos and O. Petersson. Sorting shuffled monotone sequences. In J.R. Gilbert and R. Karlsson, editors, *Proceedings of the 2nd Scandinavian Workshop on Algorithm Theory*, pages 181–191, Bergen, Sweden, 1990. Springer-Verlag Lecture Notes in Computer Science 447.

[5] H. Mannila. Measures of presortedness and optimal sorting algorithms. *IEEE Transactions on Computers*, C-34:318–325, 1985.

[6] K. Mehlhorn. *Data Structures and Algorithms, Vol 1: Sorting and Searching*. EATCS Monographs on Theoretical Computer Science. Springer-Verlag, Berlin/Heidelberg, 1984.

[7] F. Mosteller. *Fifty Challenging Problems in Probability with Solutions*. Addison-Wesley Publishing Co., Reading, Mass., 1965.

[8] S.S. Skiena. Encroaching lists as a measure of presortedness. *BIT*, 28:755–784, 1988.

A CLASSIFICATION OF QUADRATIC ALGORITHMS FOR MULTIPLYING POLYNOMIALS OF SMALL DEGREE OVER FINITE FIELDS

Amir Averbuch[1], Nader H. Bshouty[2] and Michael Kaminski[3]

[1]Department of Computer Science, Tel Aviv University, Tel Aviv, Israel
[2]Department of Computer Science, University of Calgary, Calgary, Canada
[3]Department of Computer Science, Technion, Israel Institute of Technology, Haifa, Israel

ABSTRACT: It is shown that any quadratic optimal algorithm for computing the product of two degree-n polynomials over the q-element field, where $n \leq q$, is based on the Chinese Remainder Theorem, with linear and quadratic polynomials presented as the moduli.

1. INTRODUCTION

In infinite fields it is possible to compute the product of two degree-n polynomials by evaluating the multiplicands in $2n+1$ distinct points (including ∞), multiplying the samples, and interpolating the results, cf. [12]. Moreover, each optimal algorithm for computing the above product must be of such form, cf. [13]. This computation can be considered as a computation by means of the Chinese Remainder Theorem with linear polynomials presented as the moduli. However this method fails in finite fields whose cardinality is less than $2n$. We show that if n is sufficiently small relatively to the cardinality of the field q, namely $n \leq q$, then any optimal algorithm for computing the polynomial product is also based on the Chinese Remainder Theorem.

Notice that if n is large relatively to q, then a straightforward application of the Chinese Remainder Theorem does not result in an optimal algorithm, cf. [9]. However it seems to be likely that optimal algorithms are based on a refined version of the Chinese Remainder Theorem, cf. [3].

The proofs are based on the technique developed in [6], but they are shorter and simpler than the corresponding proofs in [6, Section 6] because of a uniform approach to an analysis of Hankel matrices developed in this paper.

The paper is organized as follows. In the next section we state the Chinese Remainder Theorem and show how it can be applyed to polynomial multiplication. Section 3 contains the model of computation, and the classification results are presented in Section 4.

COMPUTER SCIENCE, Edited by R. Baeza-Yates
and U. Manber, Plenum Press, New York, 1992

2. CHINESE REMAINDER THEOREM

Let F be a field. An (integral) *divisor* is an expression of the shape $f(\alpha) = \tilde{f}(\alpha)(\alpha - \infty)^d$, where $\tilde{f}(\alpha)$ is a monic polynomial over F. I.e., a divisor is a polynomial in two variables α and $\alpha - \infty$, and we can in an obvious manner define the greatest common divisor, least common multiple, product, degree, etc.. The factors $\tilde{f}(\alpha)$ and $(\alpha - \infty)^d$ are denoted by $\tilde{f}(\alpha)$ and $\bar{f}(\alpha)$, respectively.

For a divisor $f(\alpha)$ and polynomials $v(\alpha) = \sum_{i=0}^{l} a_i \alpha^i$, $a_l \neq 0$, and $w(\alpha) = \sum_{i=0}^{\deg f(\alpha) - 1} b_i \alpha^i$ we shall say that $w(\alpha)$ is the *minimal residue* of $v(\alpha)$ modulo $f(\alpha)$, denoted by $w(\alpha) = \mathbf{res}(v(\alpha), f(\alpha))$, if

- $v(\alpha) \equiv w(\alpha) \mod \tilde{f}(\alpha)$, and

- $v(\alpha)$ and $w(\alpha)$ have the same $\deg \bar{f}(\alpha)$ leading coefficients, i.e., $a_{l-i} = b_{\deg f(\alpha) - 1 - i}$, $i = 0, 1, \ldots, \deg \bar{f}(\alpha) - 1$. (If $\deg \bar{f}(\alpha) = 0$, then leading coefficients of $w(\alpha)$ may be zero.)

Note that computing the residue modulo $\alpha - \infty$ corresponds to evaluating a polynomial at infinity.

Chinese Remainder Theorem. *Let $f_1(\alpha), \ldots, f_m(\alpha)$ be fixed pairwise coprime divisors. Then for every $v_1(\alpha), \ldots, v_m(\alpha) \in F[\alpha]$ such that $\deg v_i(\alpha) < \deg f_i(\alpha)$, $i = 1, \ldots, m$, there exists a unique polynomial $v(\alpha) \in F[\alpha]$ of degree less than $\sum_{i=1}^{m} \deg f_i(\alpha)$ such that $v_i(\alpha) = \mathbf{res}(v(\alpha), f_i(\alpha))$. The coefficients of $v(\alpha)$ are linear functions of the coefficients of $v_1(\alpha), \ldots, v_m(\alpha)$ over F.*

Applying the Chinese Remainder Theorem for design of algorithms for polynomial multiplication is well-known from the literature, cf. [11].

Let $x(\alpha), y(\alpha) \in F[\alpha]$ be polynomials of degree n with indeterminate coefficients and let $f_1(\alpha), \ldots, f_m(\alpha)$ be fixed pairwise coprime divisors, such that $\sum_{i=1}^{m} \deg f_i(\alpha) > 2n$. Then the product $x(\alpha)y(\alpha)$ can be computed recursively by means of the following procedure:

Compute $x_i(\alpha) = \mathbf{res}(x(\alpha), f_i(\alpha))$ and $y_i(\alpha) = \mathbf{res}(y(\alpha), f_i(\alpha))$, for $i = 1, \ldots, m$. This computation does not require non-scalar multiplications.

Compute $z_i(\alpha) = x_i(\alpha)y_i(\alpha)$, for $i = 1, \ldots, m$.

Compute (by the Chinese Remainder Theorem) $z(\alpha)$ of degree less than $\sum_{i=1}^{m} \deg f_i(\alpha)$ such that $\mathbf{res}(z(\alpha), f_i(\alpha)) = \mathbf{res}(z_i(\alpha), f_i(\alpha))$, $i = 1, \ldots, m$. This computation does not require non-scalar multiplications.

By the Chinese Remainder Theorem, $x(\alpha)y(\alpha) = z(\alpha)$, and we shall say that the above algorithm is a *computation by means of the Chinese Remainder Theorem with the moduli* $\{f_i(\alpha)\}_{i=1,\ldots,m}$.

If all the moduli are linear divisors, then the algorithm essentially is Lagrange interpolation of the product, and in the case of non-linear irreducible moduli the algorithm performs evaluating at a point in an extension field. Also, whereas the algorithm has been described as a recursive procedure, in our case the degree of polynomials is relatively small to the field size and the residues are, at most, linear. Thus the computation is worked out directly, not by a recursive call.

The notation introduced above reflects the symmetry of polynomial multiplication. Namely the sets of the coefficients of the product $\left[\sum_{i=0}^{n} x_i \alpha^i\right]\left[\sum_{i=0}^{n} y_i \alpha^i\right]$ is equal to that of the product $\left[\sum_{i=0}^{n} x_i \alpha^{n-i}\right]\left[\sum_{i=0}^{n} y_i \alpha^{n-i}\right]$. Also this notation allows a more uniform analysis of algorithms for polynomial multiplication than that used in [6]. Our classification result is given by Theorems 1 and 2 in the last section.

3. MODEL OF COMPUTATION

We remind the reader that a *quadratic* algorithm for computing a set of quadratic forms $Q = \{Q_1, Q_2, \ldots, Q_k\}$ in indeterminates $x_1, \ldots, x_n$ is a straight-line algorithm all whose nonscalar multiplications are of the form $L * L'$, where L and L' are linear forms in $x_1, \ldots, x_n$ and every element of Q is a linear combination of the above products.

Quadratic algorithms which compute Q in the minimal number of nonscalar multiplications are called *minimal* (for Q) and their multiplicative complexity will be denoted by $M(Q)$.

Since the coefficients of a residue of a polynomial modulo a fixed divisor are linear combinations of the polynomial coefficients and the coefficients of the product of two polynomials are bilinear forms of the polynomials' coefficients, a computation by means of the Chinese Remainder Theorem can be performed by means of *bilinear* algorithms which constitute a subclass of quadratic algorithms and are defined as follows.

A *bilinear* algorithm for computing a set of bilinear forms $B = \{B_1, B_2, \ldots, B_k\}$ in indeterminates $x = (x_0, x_1, \ldots, x_n)^T$ and $y = (y_0, y_1, \ldots, y_n)^T$ is a straight-line algorithm whose all nonscalar multiplications are of the shape $L * L'$, where L and L' are linear forms in x and y, respectively, and every element of B is a linear combination of the above products.

4. CLASSIFICATION RESULTS

A classification of quadratic algorithm for multiplying polynomials of small degree is given by Theorems 1 and below.

Theorem 1. *Let $q > 2$ be even and let $\frac{q}{2} < n < q$. Then each minimal quadratic algorithm over $\mathbf{F}_q$ that computes the product of two degree-n polynomials is a computation by means of the Chinese Remainder Theorem with the moduli $\{\alpha - c\}_{c \in \mathbf{F}_q \cup \{\infty\}} \cup \{f_i(\alpha)\}_{i=1, \ldots, n-\frac{q}{2}}$, where $f_i(\alpha)$ is an irreducible quadratic polynomial, $i = 1, \ldots, n - \frac{q}{2}$.*

The classification for the case of odd characteristic is more complicated.[*]

Theorem 2. *Let $q > 3$ be odd and let $\frac{q}{2} < n < q$. Then each minimal quadratic algorithm over $\mathbf{F}_q$ that computes the product of two degree-n polynomials is a computation by means of the Chinese Remainder Theorem where the set of the moduli is of one of the following.*

- $\{\alpha - c_i\}_{i=1, \ldots, q} \cup \{f_i(\alpha)\}_{i=1, \ldots, n-\frac{q+1}{2}}$, *where $c_i \in \mathbf{F}_q \cup \{\infty\}$ and each $f_i(\alpha)$ is either an irreducible quadratic polynomials or of the shape $(\alpha - c)^2$, where $\{c\} = (\mathbf{F}_q \cup \{\infty\}) - \{c_1, \ldots, c_q\}$.*

- $\{\alpha - c\}_{c \in \mathbf{F}_q \cup \{\infty\}} \cup \{f_i(\alpha)\}_{i=1, \ldots, n-\frac{q+3}{2}} \cup \{f(\alpha)\}$, *where $f_i(\alpha)$ is an irreducible quadratic polynomial, $i = 1, \ldots, n - \frac{q+3}{2}$ and $f(\alpha)$ is an irreducible cubic polynomial.*

---

[*] However, if $\deg x = n$ and $\deg y = n - 1$, the statement of Theorem 2 is exactly as that of Theorem 1, cf. [2] for technical details.

- $\{\alpha - c\}_{c \in \mathbf{F}_q \cup \{\infty\}} \cup \{f_i(\alpha)\}_{i=1,\ldots,n-\frac{q+1}{2}}$, where $f_i(\alpha)$ is an irreducible quadratic polynomial, $i = 1, \ldots, n - \frac{q+1}{2}$. In this case the algorithm computes only one nontrivial linear combination of the coefficients of the product modulo $f_{n-\frac{q+1}{2}}(\alpha)$, say.

The scheme presented in [7] shows that for $q = n = 2$ and $q = 3$, $n = 2,3$ the above classification results are not true.

Example. Consider the following algorithm for computing the coefficients of the product of two quadratic polynomials $x_2\alpha^2 + x_1\alpha + x_0$ and $y_2\alpha^2 + y_1\alpha + y_0$ over Z_2. Let

$$p_1 = x_0 y_0,$$
$$p_2 = x_1 y_1,$$
$$p_3 = x_2 y_2,$$
$$p_4 = (x_1 + x_2)(y_1 + y_2),$$
$$p_5 = (x_0 + x_1)(y_0 + y_1),$$
$$p_6 = (x_0 + x_2)(y_0 + y_2).$$

Then

$$z_0 = x_0 y_0 = p_1,$$
$$z_1 = x_0 y_1 + x_1 y_0 = p_5 - p_2 - p_1,$$
$$z_2 = x_0 y_2 + x_1 y_1 + x_2 y_0 = p_6 - p_3 + p_2 - p_1,$$
$$z_3 = x_1 y_2 + x_2 y_1 = p_4 - p_3 - p_2,$$
$$z_4 = x_2 y_2 = p_3.$$

The above algorithm requires 6 nonscalar multiplication. Hence it is minimal, cf. [6, Theorem 2]. However the algorithm is not a computation by means of the Chinese Remainder Theorem, because there is no (linear) divisor $f(\alpha)$ such that x_1 and y_1 are the residues of $x_2\alpha^2 + x_1\alpha + x_0$ and $y_2\alpha^2 + y_1\alpha + y_0$ modulo $f(\alpha)$, respectively.

Since computing the product of two polynomials modulo a fixed quadratic polynomial can be performed in three multiplications and there are $\frac{q^2 - q}{2}$ irreducible quadratic polynomials over $\mathbf{F}_q$, cf. [10, Theorem 3.25, p. 93], the above algorithms together with the Chinese Remainder Theorem immediately imply the following upper bound for $n \le \frac{q^2 + 1}{2}$.

$$M_q(n) \le 3n + 1 - \lfloor q/2 \rfloor,$$

where $M_q(n)$ denotes the minimal number of multiplications required to compute the coefficients of the product of two degree-n polynomials over $\mathbf{F}_q$. It was shown in [6] that for $\frac{q}{2} < n \le q + 1$ the bound id tight, and it follows from Theorems 1 and 2 that for $q \ge 4$ and $\frac{q}{2} < n \le q$ all the minimal algorithm for computing the coefficients of the product of two degree-n polynomials are computations by means of the Chinese Remainder Theorem.

References

[1] A. Averbuch, Z. Galil, S. Winograd, Classification of all the minimal bilinear algorithms for computing the coefficients of the product of two polynomials modulo a polynomial in the algebra $G[u]|<Q(u)^l>$, $l > 1$, *Theoret. Comput. Sci.* **58** (1988), 17-56.

[2]   N.H. Bshouty, M. Kaminski, Multiplication of polynomials over finite fields, *SIAM J. Comput.* **19** (1990), 452-456.

[3]   D.V. Chudnovsky, G.V. Chudnovsky, Algebraic complexities and algebraic curves over finite fields, *J. Complex.* **4** (1988), 285-316.

[4]   E. Feig, On Systems of Bilinear Forms Whose Minimal Division-Free Algorithms Are All Bilinear, *J. Algor.* **2** (1981), 261-281.

[5]   E. Feig, Certain Systems of Bilinear Forms Whose Minimal Algorithms Are All Quadratic, *J. Algor.* **4** (1983), 137-149.

[6]   M. Kaminski, N.H. Bshouty, Multiplicative complexity of polynomial multiplication over finite fields, *J. ACM* **36** (1989), 150-170.

[7]   A. Karustsuba, Y. Ofman, Multiplication of Multidigit Numbers on Automata, *Dokl. Akad. Nauk SSSR* **145**, (1962), 293-294 (in Russian).

[8]   S. Lang, *Algebra*, Addison-Wesley, Reading, MA, 1965.

[9]   A. Lempel, G. Seroussi, S. Winograd, On the Complexity of Multiplication in Finite Fields, *Theoret. Comput. Sci.* **22** (1983), 285-296.

[10]   R. Lidl, H. Niederreiter, *Finite Fields*, Encyclopedia of Mathematics and its Applications, Vol. 20, G.-C. Rota, ed., Addison-Wesley, Reading, Massachusetts, 1983.

[11]   R. Moenck, A. Borodin, Fast modular transforms via divisions, *in* "Proc. 13th Ann. Symp. on Switching and Automata Theory", pp. 90-96, The Institute of Electrical and Electronic Engineers, New York, 1972.

[12]   A.L. Toom, The complexity of a scheme of functional elements realizing the multiplication of integers, *Soviet Math. Docl.* **4** (1963), 714-716.

[13]   S. Winograd, Some Bilinear Forms Whose Multiplicative Complexity Depends on the Field Constants, *Math. System Theory* **10** (1976/77), 169-180.

AN ALGORITHM FOR COMPUTING

MULTIVARIATE POLYNOMIAL RESULTANTS [1]

J. Llovet and J.R. Sendra[2], J.A. Jaén and R. Martínez[3]

[2] Department of Mathematics
University of Alcala
28871-Madrid, Spain
[3] Department of Computer Engineering
E.T.S.I.I. Polytechn. Univ. of Madrid, Spain

INTRODUCTION

Resultants of multivariate polynomials are applied to many Computer Algebra and Algebraic Geometry problems, see Buchberger et al. (1983). Therefore, the effective calculation of resultants plays a principal role in Symbolic Computation. Modular methods provide efficient approaches. Collins' algorithm is one of the most important, see Collins (1971).

This paper presents an alternative method –based on Hankel matrices– for the calculation of resultants. The basic idea of this process is to express the resultant by means of the determinant of a Hankel matrix of order equal to the maximum degree of the given polynomials.

The computational feasibility of the algorithm derived from this process is directly related to the construction of an efficient procedure for computing the determinant of a Hankel matrix. For this purpose, the special structure of these matrices is utilized to optimize the computations.

Computing time analysis shows that the modular version of the Hankel approach and Collins' resultant algorithm for have the same complexity. Finally, we describe the partial implementation of this algorithm in Maple. Furthermore, we show a running-time table where the main procedure and the Maple function are compared.

---
[1] This research was partially supported by I.B.M. Study Contract -10.90 and University of Alcala Project 90/A18.

ALGEBRAIC PRELIMINARIES

This section introduces the basic definitions and main results needed to compute resultants of multivariate polynomials by means of Hankel matrices, see Llovet and Sendra (1989,1990).

Let K be a unique factorization domain, and $Q(K)$ its quotient field. Then, we define the $n \times n$ **Hankel matrix** generated by the tuple $(d_1, \ldots, d_{2n-1})$, $d_i \in K$, as the matrix $H_n = (h_{i,j})_{1 \le i, j \le n}$ where $h_{i,j} = d_{i+j-1}$ for $1 \le i, j \le n$. Analogously, one defines the infinite Hankel matrix H_∞ generated by $\{d_i\}_{i \ge 1}$, $d_i \in K$. Let H_m be the $m \times m$ principal submatrix of H_n ($m < n$). If H_m is nonsingular, then one defines the **m−fundamental vector** of H_n as the vector $\omega^m \in Q(K)^m$ that satisfies $\omega^m \cdot H_m = (d_{m+1}, \ldots, d_{2m})$. Likewise, one defines the vector $y^m \in Q(K)^m$ such that $y^m \cdot H_m = (0, \ldots, 0, 1)$. The pair $[\omega^m, y^m]$ is called the **m−fundamental pair** of H_n. When $m = 0$ we assume that H_0 is the empty matrix, that $\det(H_0) = 1$, and that ω^0 is the empty vector. Hence, associated with H_n there always exists a sequence $\{\omega^m\}_{\det(H_m) \ne 0, 0 \le m < n}$, called **fundamental vector sequence**, and one can construct a recursive algorithm for computing this sequence in at most $O(n^2)$ operations. For this purpose, one begins with the construction of algorithm GAP that determines the dimension q of each fundamental vector ω^q.

Algorithm GAP(H_n, w^p, p)

Input: • The dimension p of the fundamental vector ω^p of H_n
Output: • The dimension q of the next fundamental vector ω^q

1. $\sigma := 0$; $q := p$;

2.   **While** $\{ \sigma = 0 \text{ and } q < n \}$ **do**
$\qquad \ll q := q + 1$;
$\qquad \sigma := (w^p, -1) \cdot (d_q, \ldots, d_{p+q})^T \gg$;

3.   **If** $\sigma \ne 0$ **then return** $[q, \sigma]$
$\qquad$ **else return** $[n, \sigma]$;

One continues by designing algorithm LIFT that computes the fundamental pairs of a Hankel matrix.

Algorithm LIFT(H_n, w^p, y^p, p, q)

Input: • The p-fundamental pair $[\omega^p, y^p]$ of H_n
$\qquad\qquad$ • The dimension q of the next fundamental pair
Output: • The q-fundamental pair $[\omega^q, y^q]$ of H_n

1.   **If** $p = 0$ **then** $\ll \bar{w}(0)$ is the q dimensional zero vector;
$\qquad\qquad\qquad$ **go to (4)** $\gg$;

2. $w(0) := w^p$;

3. **For $k := 0$ to $q - p - 1$ do**
$$\ll \rho_k := w(k) \cdot (0, \ldots, 0, 1)^T \; ;$$
$$\epsilon_k := d_{2p+k+1} - w(k) \cdot (d_{p+1}, \ldots, d_{2p})^T;$$
$$w(k+1) := w(k) \cdot I_{p,p}^1 + \rho_k w^p + \epsilon_k y^p \gg;$$

4. $\bar{w}(0) := w(q - p) \cdot I_{p,q}^0;$

5. $\sigma := (w^p, -1) \cdot (d_q, \ldots, d_{q+p})^T;$

6. **For $k := 0$ to $q - p - 1$ do**
$$\ll \alpha_k := \tfrac{1}{\sigma}(d_{p+q+k+1} - \bar{w}(k) \cdot (d_{p+k+1}, \ldots, d_{p+q+k})^T);$$
$$\bar{w}(k+1) := \bar{w}(k) + \alpha_k(w^p, -1) \cdot I_{p+1,q}^{q-p-k-1} \gg;$$

7. $[\, w^q, y^q \,] = [\bar{w}(q-p), \tfrac{1}{\sigma}(w^p, -1) \cdot I_{p+1,q}^0 \,];$

8. **Return $[\, w^q, y^q \,];$**

On the other hand, Hankel matrices are closely related to univariate polynomial over the domain K. To be more precise, let $f, g \in \mathrm{K}[x]$ ($deg(g) = m \leq n = deg(f), n > 0$), and consider the Hankel matrix H_∞ generated by $\{d_i\}_{i \geq 1}$, where d_i are given by the expansion:

$$\frac{g(x)}{f(x)} = \sum_{i \geq 0} d_i x^{-i}$$

Then, one can prove that such an infinite matrix is of finite rank $r = n - deg(\gcd(f, g))$, and that $\det(H_r) \neq 0$. Thus, one can just consider the $n \times n$ principal submatrix. That is, the $n \times n$ Hankel matrix generated by $(d_1, \ldots, d_{2n-1})$. Hence, one need not compute the whole expansion. Therefore, one defines the **K-Hankel matrix** associated with $\{f, g\}$ as the $n \times n$ Hankel matrix generated by $(d_1^\star, \ldots, d_{2n-1}^\star)$, where $d_i^\star = 0$ for $i < n - m$, and $d_{n-m}^\star x^{n+m-1} + \cdots + d_{2n-1}^\star$ is the pseudoquotient of $x^{2n-1}g(x)$ and $f(x)$. Analogously, one defines the **Q(K)-Hankel matrix** associated with $\{f, g\}$ as the $n \times n$ Hankel matrix generated by $(d_1, \ldots, d_{2n-1})$, where $d_i = 0$ for $i < n - m$, and $d_{n-m}x^{n+m-1} + \cdots + d_{2n-1}$ is the quotient of $x^{2n-1}g(x)$ and $f(x)$.

HANKEL DETERMINANTS

The basic idea for computing efficiently the determinant of a Hankel matrix is to obtain every principal minor by means of the fundamental vectors. For this purpose, one presents the following theorem:

Theorem 1. *Let H_n be the $n \times n$ Hankel matrix generated by the elements of the tuple $(d_1, \ldots, d_{2n-1})$; H_p, H_q ($0 \leq p < q \leq n$) are nonsingular principal submatrices such that $\det(H_i) = 0$ for $p < i < q$, and ω^p is the p-fundamental vector. Then, it holds that:*

$$\det(H_i) = (-1)^{\frac{(i-p)(i-p+1)}{2}} \sigma_i^{i-p} \det(H_p) \qquad \text{for} \quad p < i \leq q$$

where $\sigma_i - \omega^p \cdot (d_i, \ldots, d_{i+p-1})^T - d_{i+p}$.

Proof: Let $p > 0$ (if $p = 0$ the theorem is trivial), and $\omega^p = (a_1, \ldots, a_p)$. For every i $(p < i \leq q)$ we consider the matrix of order i:

$$M_i = \begin{pmatrix} 1 & & & & & \\ & \ddots & & & & \\ & & 1 & & & \\ a_1 & \cdots & a_p & -1 & & \\ & \ddots & & \ddots & \ddots & \\ & & a_1 & \cdots & a_p & -1 \end{pmatrix}$$

Then:

$$M_i \cdot H_i = \begin{pmatrix} d_1 & \cdot & \cdot & d_p & d_{p+1} & \cdot & \cdot & d_i \\ d_2 & \cdot & \cdot & d_{p+1} & d_{p+2} & \cdot & \cdot & d_{i+1} \\ \cdot & \cdot & \cdot & \cdot & \cdot & \cdot & \cdot & \cdot \\ d_p & \cdot & \cdot & d_{2p-1} & d_{2p} & \cdot & \cdot & d_{i+p-1} \\ \sigma_1 & \cdot & \cdot & \sigma_p & \sigma_{p+1} & \cdot & \cdot & \sigma_i \\ \sigma_2 & \cdot & \cdot & \sigma_{p+1} & \sigma_{p+2} & \cdot & \cdot & \sigma_{i+1} \\ \cdot & \cdot & \cdot & \cdot & \cdot & \cdot & \cdot & \cdot \\ \sigma_{i-p} & \cdot & \cdot & \sigma_{i-1} & \sigma_i & \cdot & \cdot & \sigma_{2i-p-1} \end{pmatrix}$$

where $\sigma_j = 0$ if $j < q$. Therefore, for every i $(1 < i \leq q)$ it holds that:

$$\det(H_i) = (-1)^{\frac{(i-p)(i-p+3)}{2}} \sigma_i^{i-p} \det(H_p) \det(M_i)$$

$$= (-1)^{\frac{(i-p)(i-p+1)}{2}} \sigma_i^{i-p} \det(H_p). \square$$

The last formula expresses the determinant of every principal submatrix by means of the previous nonzero principal minor and the corresponding fundamental vector. Therefore, using algorithms GAP and LIFT one can design the algorithm:

Algorithm HD(H_n) (Algorithm for Hankel Determinants)

Input: • H_n is the Hankel matrix generated by $(d_i)_{1 \leq i \leq 2n-1}$, $d_i \in \mathrm{K}$;

Output: • The determinant of H_n;

1. $p := 0$; $D := 1$; $W := [\ ]$; $Y := [\ ]$;

2. **While** $p < n$ **do**
 2.1. $[q, \sigma] := \mathrm{GAP}(H_n, W, p)$;
 2.2. $m := q - p - 1$;
 2.3. $D := (-1)^{\frac{(m+1)(m+2)}{2}} \sigma^{m+1} D$;
 2.4. **If** $m < n - p - 1$ **then** $[W, Y] := \mathrm{LIFT}\ (H_n, W, Y, p, q)$;
 2.5. $p := q$;

3. **Return** D;

This algorithm requires at most $O(n^2)$ operations, where n is the order of the matrix. Furthermore, if H_n is an $n \times n$ matrix over $Z[x_1, \ldots, x_r]$, the maximum computing time function of the corresponding modular approach is $O(n^{r+3} \log n \, \lambda^{r+1} \log^2 L)$, where L and λ bound respectively the norm, and the degree -with respect to any variable- of the entries.

MULTIVARIATE POLYNOMIAL RESULTANTS

Multivariate polynomial resultants can be computed efficiently, applying the preceeding ideas. More precisely, the resultant of two polynomials can be expressed as the determinant of the associated Hankel matrix. Hence, resultant computations are reduced to Hankel determinants. To establish this relation, we first prove the following lemma.

Lemma 2. *Let $f, g \in \mathrm{K}[x]$ $(deg(g) = m \leq deg(f) = n, n > 0)$, and let H_n, M be the $\mathrm{Q}(\mathrm{K})$-Hankel matrix associated with $\{f, g\}$ and $\{f, 1\}$, respectively. Then it holds that $H_n = M \cdot g(C)$, where C is the companion matrix of $\frac{1}{f_n} f(x)$, and f_n is the leading coefficient of f.*

Proof: Let us assume that M_{n+k}, $0 \leq k \leq m$, is the $\mathrm{Q}(\mathrm{K})$-Hankel matrix associated with $\{f, x^k\}$. Then, one deduces that $M_n^{-1} \cdot M_{n+k} = C^k$ for $1 \leq k \leq m$. On the other hand, if $g(x) = g_m x^m + \cdots + g_0$, one also obtains that $H_n = g_m M_{n+m} + \cdots + g_0 M_n$. And therefore, $M_n^{-1} \cdot H_n = g(C)$. $\square$

The next theorem shows how to compute the resultant of two polynomials using Hankel matrices.

Theorem 3. *Let $f(x) = f_n x^n + \cdots + f_0$, $g(x) = g_m x^m + \cdots + g_0$ $(m \leq n, n > 0)$ be polynomials over K. Consider H_n and $\bar{H}_n$ to be the Hankel matrices associated with $\{f, g\}$ over $\mathrm{Q}(\mathrm{K})$ and K, respectively. Then it holds that:*

- $res(f, g) = (-1)^{\frac{n(n+3)}{2} + m(n+1)} f_n^{n+m} \det(H_n)$

- $\det(\bar{H}_n) = (-1)^{\frac{n(n+3)}{2} + m(n+1)} f_n^{(n+m)(n-1)} res(f, g)$

Proof: Let us assume that $f(x) = f_n \prod_{i=1}^{n} (x - \alpha_i)$ and $g(x) = g_m \prod_{j=1}^{m} (x - \beta_j)$. Then, applying Lemma 2, one has that:

$$\det(H_n) = (-1)^{\frac{n(n+3)}{2}} f_n^{-n} g_m^n \prod_{j=1}^{m} \det(C - \beta_j I)$$

On the other hand, using that C is the companion matrix of $\frac{1}{f_n} f(x)$, one obtains:

$$\begin{aligned} \det(H_n) &= (-1)^{\frac{n(n+3)}{2} + nm + m} f_n^{-n} g_m^n \prod_{j=1}^{m} \prod_{i=1}^{n} (\alpha_i - \beta_j) \\ &= (-1)^{\frac{n(n+3)}{2} + nm + m} f_n^{-n-m} res(f, g) \end{aligned}$$

To prove the second equality, one just has to use that $\bar{H}_n = f_n^{n+m} \cdot H_n$. $\square$

Theorem 3 can be used to construct a Hankel algorithm for computing the resultant of two polynomial over a unique factorization domain. Essentially, this algorithm has to divide (to form the associated matrix), and has to compute the determinant of the corresponding Hankel matrix.

Algorithm HRES(f, g, x) (Hankel algorithm for **Res**ultants)

Input: • $f(x), g(x) \in K[x]$ $(deg(g) = m \le n = deg(f), n > 0)$;
Output: • The resultant of f and g with respect to x;

1. $A := COEFF(f, x, n)$;

2. $Q(x) := PSEUDOQUOTIENT(x^{2n-1}g(x), f(x), x)$;

3. $S := HD(H_n)$;

   (H_n is the K-matrix associated with $\{f, g\}$)
4. $R :=$ **If** $S = 0$ **then** 0 **else** $(-1)^{\frac{n(n+3)}{2} + m(n+1)} A^{(1-n)(n+m)} S$;

5. **Return** R;

In the complexity analysis we observe that algorithm HD requires $O(n^2)$ operations, and that all the remainding steps are dominated by n^2. Therefore, algorithm HRES requires at most $O(n^2)$ operations. Consequently, the modular version of algorithm HRES for computing multivariate polynomial resultants, and the modular resultant algorithm of *Collins*, see Collins (1971), have the same maximum computing time function.

REMARKS ON THE IMPLEMENTATION

The modular version of algorithm HRES is partially implemented in Maple, see Char et al. (1988). This implementation consists of a set of procedures distributed in three logic levels. The first level contains the main procedure, and the second the procedures associated with the Maple functions **modp1** y **mod**. These procedures construct –over Z_p– the generating sequence of the Hankel matrix associated with the polynomial, and compute its determinant. In the last level, in order to obtain the determinant, one has the procedures that implement algorithms GAP and LIFT.

The feasibility of this implementation is directly related to the construction of an efficient algorithm for computing Hankel determinants over finite fields. For this purpose, all data are represented by lists. In particular, any $n \times n$ Hankel matrix is treated as a list of $(2n - 1)$ elements. On the other hand, univariate polynomials over finite fields are manipulated by means of the function **modp1**. Furthemore, a heuristic analysis shows that matrices associated with polynomials are often strongly regular. Hence, in most of the cases, we use a simpler version of algorithms GAP and LIFT.

Considering all these remarks we have constructed in Maple a very fast procedure that computes the determinant of a Hankel matrix over a finite field. We compare our procedure to the Maple function 'mod/Det' running on a *IBM RISC System/6000*. The following table shows the running time (in sec.) for some random examples given over the finite field defined by $p = 46327$.

TABLE 1. RUNNING TIME

Order of the Matrix	Our Procedure	mod/Det (Maple)
10	0.9	1.6
20	4	9.4
30	9	29
40	18	65
50	29	130
70	66	157
100	165	1133
150	507	4806
200	1184	15172
500	18956	792870

REFERENCES

Buchberger B., Collins G.E., Loos R. (eds); "Computer Algebra: Symbolic and Algebraic Computation", Springer-Verlag, Viena (1983).

Char B., Gonnet G., Monagan M., Watt S. , "Maple Reference Manual, V ed.", Symbolic Computation Group, University of Waterloo (Canada), (1988).

Collins G.E., " The Calculation of Multivariate Polynomial Resultants", J.ACM 19, pp 515-532 (1971).

Llovet J.; Sendra J.R. "Hankel Matrices and Polynomials". Lectures Notes in Computer Science 356 (Springer-Verlag) pp 321-333 (1989).

Sendra J.R., "Hankel Matrices and Computer Algebra", ACM SIGSAM Bulletin Vol. 24, No.3, pp. 17-26 (1990).

NEW ABSORBING AND ERGODIC DOUBLY-LINKED LIST REORGANIZING HEURISTICS

R.S. Valiveti and B.J. Oommen

School of Computer Science
Carleton University
Ottawa, Ontario, Canada, K1S 5B6

Abstract

We study the problem of maintaining a doubly-linked list (DLL) in approximately optimal order, with respect to the mean search time. Move-To-End (MTE) [1] and SWAP [2] are two ergodic memoryless DLL heuristics obtained from natural extensions of the well known Singly-linked-list (SLL) heuristics Move-To-Front (MTF) and Transposition (TR) respectively. We first derive a general sufficient condition which permits comparison of **any** two DLL heuristics. We use this condition as a guideline to identify families of access distributions for which SWAP yields a lower expected cost than the MTE.

We then present an absorbing DLL heuristic. The strategy requires one additional memory location, and is analogous to the scheme presented in [3]. The reorganization is achieved by moving each element **exactly** once to its final position in the reorganized list. The scheme is stochastically absorbing and it is shown to be optimal for a restricted family of distributions. Thus, for these distributions, the probability of the scheme converging to the optimal list order can be made as close to unity as desired.

1 Introduction

In recent years considerable research effort has focussed on the aspect of dynamically reorganizing a sequential list (also referred to as a Singly-Linked List (SLL)), so as to keep it in approximately optimal order[4]. Among the heuristics that have been thoroughly investigated are the Move-To-Front (MTF) and the Transposition rule (TR), and detailed analyses of these schemes can be found in [4, 5].

Although SLLs have been very extensively studied and analyzed, very little work has been done to study the adaptive restructuring of Doubly-Linked lists (DLLs). To the best of our knowledge, the only papers in this regard are [1, 2]. The DLL can be defined as a linear list in which each item in the linked list has pointers to both its successor and its predecessor. This structure facilitates searching the list commencing from either end. Various applications of DLLs are catalogued in [6].

Formally speaking, a DLL, D, consists of the set of N records $\mathcal{R} = \{R_1, R_2, \ldots, R_N\}$ stored in some order. Accesses to the record R_i are made from the left and right with probabilities s_{iL} and s_{iR} respectively. These probabilities obey the constraint that: $\sum_{i=1}^{N}(s_{iL} + s_{iR}) = 1$. We assume that the record accesses are statistically independent and identically distributed. We also assume that the starting position of the search for a record is independent of the record itself. In our case, we will always commence the search for an element from the end at which the element was requested.

It is well known that the permutation which arranges the list in the decreasing order of the difference $s_{iL} - s_{iR}$ results in the lowest expected cost and hence is the optimal order. Our aim is to maintain D in an approximately optimal order with respect to the expected cost. Since we assume that the access distribution S is unknown *a priori*, we will consider the use of heuristics which endeavor to minimize the expected cost.

Two types of heuristics have been studied for SLLs and they can be categorized to be either ergodic or absorbing. In the ergodic schemes, the list is dynamically reorganized according to the heuristic, and it has the property that even asymptotically, the list could be in any one of the $N!$ configurations. For stationary environments, the ideal heuristic would, of course, be one which gradually transforms the initial list into the optimal configuration and then never disturbs it. Absorbing schemes aim to attain this goal.

In this paper we study both ergodic and absorbing DLL heuristics. In connection with ergodic heuristics, we establish a sufficient condition for one DLL heuristic to be better than another, in the sense of lower expected cost. We make use of this condition to compare the DLL heuristics SWAP and MTE, which are obtained by extending the well known SLL heuristics TR and MTF respectively. Specifically, we identify sufficient conditions under which SWAP has a lower expected asymptotic cost than the MTE. The necessary conditions are still being investigated.

We subsequently turn our attention to absorbing rules for reorganizing DLLs. We present an absorbing scheme which is based on using one additional counter, and is a generalization of the SLL absorbing heuristic proposed in [3]. For a restricted family of distributions, this heuristic is shown to be asymptotically optimal. Thus, for these distributions, the probability of converging to the optimal order can be made as close to unity as desired.

It is rather astonishing to discover that the families of distributions for which the above absorbing heuristic is asymptotically optimal happens to be a superset of the family of distributions under which SWAP outperforms the MTE heuristic. We begin our discussion by considering ergodic heuristics.

2   Heuristics for DLL

We begin with a few definitions.

Definition 1 *A memoryless heuristic for a DLL is described by a set of permutations given by $\tau = \{\tau_i^L, \tau_i^R\}$. The permutation τ_i^L (τ_i^R) is applied whenever the element located at position i in the list is accessed from the left (right) [1].*

Definition 2 *Let $C_\tau(S)$ denote the expected cost resulting from the use of the heuristic τ when the access distribution is $S = [s_{1L}, s_{1R}, s_{2L}, s_{2R}, \ldots, s_{NL}, s_{NR}]^T$. A heuristic τ is said to be **more efficient** than another heuristic σ if $C_\tau(S) \leq C_\sigma(S)$ for all distributions S.*

For fixing ideas, let us denote the order of elements in the DLL D, by the permutation $\langle R_{i_1}, R_{i_2}, \ldots, R_{i_N} \rangle$ where $\langle i_1, i_2, \ldots, i_N \rangle$ is a permutation of the integers $1 \ldots N$. Consider the MTE rule described in [1]. This heuristic operates as follows: if the element R_{i_j} is accessed from the left ($j \neq 1$), the accessed element is moved to the left end of the list, resulting in the configuration $\langle R_{i_j}, R_{i_1}, R_{i_2}, \ldots, R_{i_{j-1}}, R_{i_{j+1}}, \ldots, R_{i_N} \rangle$. On the other hand, if the element R_{i_j} is accessed from the right (and $j \neq N$, i.e. the element is not already at the end), the accessed element is moved to the right end, yielding the list:$\langle R_{i_1}, R_{i_2}, \ldots, R_{i_{j-1}}, R_{i_{j+1}}, \ldots, R_{i_N}, R_{i_j} \rangle$.

In this paper, we study the SWAP heuristic, obtained in an intuitive manner, from the TR heuristic. The SWAP heuristic was proposed by Ng and Oommen [2]. For the sake of clarity, a description of the heuristic is given below. The order of elements in the DLL is denoted as before. In the SWAP heuristic, whenever a record R_{i_j} is accessed from the left, the list is reorganized by swapping R_{i_j} with $R_{i_{j-1}}$. We note that no swap is performed if $j = 1$ and the element being accessed is at the left end of the list D. On the other hand, if the search for the element R_{i_j} commenced at the right end, we swap R_{i_j} with $R_{i_{j+1}}$, unless $j = N$. The special case identified corresponds to the case when the R_{i_j} happens to the last element in the list.

Rivest showed that the TR heuristic always has a lower expected cost when compared to the MTF heuristic[5]. Intuitively there is good reason to believe that SWAP should perform better than the MTE rule. Since a rigorous proof of this statement is difficult, in this paper, we establish sufficient conditions which will ensure that SWAP is better than MTE.

We will assume, without loss of generality that $s_{iL} - s_{iR} \geq s_{jL} - s_{jR} \ \forall i < j$. In other words, the optimal order of the records is $R_1, R_2, \ldots, R_N$. We shall make extensive use of the fact that the probability of a given record R_i preceding another record R_j under a heuristic τ (denoted by $b_\tau(i,j)$) determines the cost of using τ. We now state and prove a sufficient condition which allows us to compare the efficiency of any two arbitrary heuristics.

Theorem 1 *Let τ and σ be two DLL heuristics with the property that $b_\tau(i,j) \geq b_\sigma(i,j) \ \forall i < j$. Then τ is more efficient than σ.*

Proof:

We denote the expected cost produced by the heuristics τ and σ as $C_\tau(\mathcal{S})$ and $C_\sigma(\mathcal{S})$ respectively. We can write down the expected cost under the heuristic τ as:

$$
\begin{aligned}
C_\tau(\mathcal{S}) &= \sum_{i=1}^{N} s_{iL} \left\{ 1 + \sum_{j \neq i} b_\tau(j,i) \right\} + \sum_{i=1}^{N} s_{iR} \left\{ 1 + \sum_{j \neq i} b_\tau(i,j) \right\} \\
&= \sum_{i=1}^{N} s_{iL} \left\{ 1 + \sum_{j \neq i} b_\tau(j,i) \right\} + \sum_{i=1}^{N} s_{iR} \left\{ 1 + \sum_{j \neq i} (1 - b_\tau(j,i)) \right\} \\
&= \sum_{i=1}^{N} \{ s_{iL} + N s_{iR} \} + \sum_{i=1}^{N} \sum_{j \neq i} s_{iL} b_\tau(j,i) - \sum_{i=1}^{N} \sum_{j \neq i} s_{iR} b_\tau(j,i).
\end{aligned}
$$

Since the first term is independent of i, we denote it using the constant K, and thus:

$$
\begin{aligned}
C_\tau(\mathcal{S}) &= K + \sum_{i<j} \{ s_{iL} b_\tau(j,i) + s_{jL} b_\tau(i,j) - s_{iR} b_\tau(j,i) - s_{jR} b_\tau(i,j) \} \\
&= K + \sum_{i<j} \{ (s_{jL} - s_{jR}) - (s_{iL} - s_{iR}) \} b_\tau(i,j) + (s_{iL} - s_{iR}).
\end{aligned}
$$

The expression for $C_\sigma(\mathcal{S})$ has an identical form, and hence we can write down the difference between $C_\tau(\mathcal{S})$ and $C_\sigma(\mathcal{S})$ as:

$$C_{\boldsymbol{\tau}}(\mathcal{S}) - C_{\boldsymbol{\sigma}}(\mathcal{S}) = \sum_{i<j} \{(s_{jL} - s_{jR}) - (s_{iL} - s_{iR})\} \left(b_{\boldsymbol{\tau}}(i,j) - b_{\boldsymbol{\sigma}}(i,j)\right). \tag{1}$$

Since we have assumed that $b_{\boldsymbol{\tau}}(i,j) \geq b_{\boldsymbol{\sigma}}(i,j)$ and that $s_{iL} - s_{iR} \geq s_{jL} - s_{jR} \ \forall i < j$, the RHS of (1) is never greater than zero, and the result is proved. $\qquad\square$

2.1 Comparison of the SWAP and MTE heuristics

Because of Theorem 1, a sufficient condition for SWAP to perform better than MTE is that the probability of record R_i being before another record R_j (as viewed from the left) should be greater for the SWAP heuristic than for the MTE heuristic, whenever $i < j$. We wish to identify distributions for which $b_{SWAP}(i,j) > b_{MTE}(i,j) \ \forall i < j$.

Ng and Oommen analyzed the Markov chain for the SWAP heuristic, making use of the fact that it is *time reversible* [2]. The relation obeyed by the Stationary distribution of the chain representing the SWAP heuristic is stated by Lemma 0 below [2]:

Lemma 0 *Consider the two list configurations* $\langle R_{i_1}, R_{i_2}, \ldots, R_{i_j}, R_{i_{j+1}}, \ldots, R_{i_N} \rangle$ *and* $\langle R_{i_1}, R_{i_2}, \ldots, R_{i_{j+1}}, R_{i_j}, \ldots, R_{i_N} \rangle$. *The ratio of the asymptotic probabilities of these two configurations is given by:*

$$\frac{Pr(\langle R_{i_1}, R_{i_2}, \ldots, R_{i_j}, R_{i_{j+1}}, \ldots, R_{i_N} \rangle)}{Pr(\langle R_{i_1}, R_{i_2}, \ldots, R_{i_{j+1}}, R_{i_j}, \ldots, R_{i_N} \rangle)} = \frac{s_{i_j L} + s_{i_{j+1} R}}{s_{i_j R} + s_{i_{j+1} L}}. \tag{2}$$

Proof:

Can be found in [2]. $\qquad\square$

We now formally define the families of distributions examined in this paper.

Definition 3 *An access distribution* $\mathcal{S} = [s_{1L}, s_{1R}, s_{2L}, s_{2R}, \ldots, s_{NL}, s_{NR}]^T$ *satisfying*

$$s_{iL} - s_{iR} > s_{jL} - s_{jR} \ \forall i < j$$

is said to be **Exclusive**[1] *if the following condition holds whenever* $i < j$:

$$s_{kL}(s_{iL} - s_{jL}) + s_{kR}(s_{jR} - s_{iR}) + (s_{iL}s_{jR} - s_{jL}s_{iR}) > 0. \quad \forall \ k \neq i, j. \tag{3}$$

Examples of Exclusive distributions will be given later in this section.

Theorem 2 *Let* $\mathcal{S}$ *be an exclusive distribution, and* R_i *and* R_j *be any two records of* $\mathcal{R}$, *where* $i < j$. *Also let* $\langle k_1, k_2, \ldots, k_m \rangle$ *denote some permutation of m of the integers in the set* $\{1, 2, \ldots, N\} - \{i, j\}$. *Then, the following result holds for the SWAP heuristic:*

$$\frac{Pr(\langle L_1 R_i R_{k_1} R_{k_2} \ldots R_{k_m} R_j L_2 \rangle)}{Pr(\langle L_1 R_j R_{k_1} R_{k_2} \ldots R_{k_m} R_i L_2 \rangle)} \geq \frac{s_{iL} + s_{jR}}{s_{jL} + s_{iR}}$$

where L_1 *and* L_2 *are arbitrary prefix and suffix lists respectively, made up of the elements of* $\mathcal{R} - \{R_i, R_j\} - \{R_{k_1}, R_{k_2}, \ldots, R_{k_m}\}$.

---

[1]The name Exclusive is used merely for want of a better characterizing property of the family of distributions. Indeed if the condition (3) is satisfied, it turns out that ratios of probabilities in which records R_i and R_j are separated by any number of elements has, as its lower bound, the analogous ratio in which records R_i and R_j are adjacent. Thus, in a sense, the influence of the intervening records can be ignored.

Proof:

For the sake of clarity, we denote:

$$\xi_{ij}(\langle k_1, k_2, \ldots, k_m \rangle) = \frac{Pr(\langle L_1 R_i R_{k_1} R_{k_2} \ldots R_{k_m} R_j L_2 \rangle)}{Pr(\langle L_1 R_j R_{k_1} R_{k_2} \ldots R_{k_m} R_i L_2 \rangle)}$$

The theorem trivially holds when $m = 0$ (by (2)) and thus the basis step of an inductive proof is established. We will prove the general result by induction, assuming in the inductive step that the theorem is true for $m = l - 1$. That is, we assume that:

$$\xi_{ij}(\langle k_1, k_2, \ldots, k_{l-1} \rangle) \geq \frac{s_{iL} + s_{jR}}{s_{jL} + s_{iR}}$$

Now, the ratio of the stationary probabilities of the two states in which records R_i and R_j are separated by l elements can be written down using the chain rule as:

$$\xi_{ij}(\langle k_1, k_2, \ldots, k_l \rangle)$$
$$= \frac{Pr(\langle L_1 R_i R_{k_1} R_{k_2} \ldots R_{k_{l-1}} R_j R_{k_l} L_2 \rangle)}{Pr(\langle L_1 R_j R_{k_1} R_{k_2} \ldots R_{k_{l-1}} R_i R_{k_l} L_2 \rangle)} \cdot \frac{Pr(\langle L_1 R_j R_{k_1} R_{k_2} \ldots R_{k_{l-1}} R_i R_{k_l} L_2 \rangle)}{Pr(\langle L_1 R_i R_{k_1} R_{k_2} \ldots R_{k_{l-1}} R_j R_{k_l} L_2 \rangle)} \cdot$$
$$\frac{Pr(\langle L_1 R_i R_{k_1} R_{k_2} \ldots R_{k_l} R_j L_2 \rangle)}{Pr(\langle L_1 R_j R_{k_1} R_{k_2} \ldots R_{k_l} R_i L_2 \rangle)}$$
$$= \xi_{ij}(\langle k_1, k_2, \ldots, k_{l-1} \rangle) \cdot \frac{Pr(\langle L_1 R_i R_{k_1} R_{k_2} \ldots R_{k_{l-1}} R_{k_l} R_j L_2 \rangle)}{Pr(\langle L_1 R_i R_{k_1} R_{k_2} \ldots R_{k_{l-1}} R_j R_{k_l} L_2 \rangle)} \cdot$$
$$\frac{Pr(\langle L_1 R_j R_{k_1} R_{k_2} \ldots R_{k_{l-1}} R_i R_{k_l} L_2 \rangle)}{Pr(\langle L_1 R_j R_{k_1} R_{k_2} \ldots R_{k_{l-1}} R_{k_l} R_i L_2 \rangle)}$$
$$= \xi_{ij}(\langle k_1, k_2, \ldots, k_{l-1} \rangle) \cdot \left[\frac{s_{jR} + s_{k_l L}}{s_{jL} + s_{k_l R}} \cdot \frac{s_{iL} + s_{k_l R}}{s_{iR} + s_{k_l L}} \right]. \quad \text{(By (2))} \qquad (4)$$

Let us denote the term within the square brackets of (4) as f. The difference between the numerator and the denominator of f can be easily seen to be:

$$s_{k_l L}(s_{iL} - s_{jL}) + s_{k_l R}(s_{jR} - s_{iR}) + (s_{iL} s_{jR} - s_{jL} s_{iR})$$

Because of the assumption that S is an *exclusive* distribution, the quantity f is strictly greater than 1. Hence, (4) can be rewritten as follows:

$$\xi_{ij}(\langle k_1, k_2, \ldots, k_l \rangle) \geq \xi_{ij}(\langle k_1, k_2, \ldots, k_{l-1} \rangle). \qquad (5)$$

The Theorem follows because of the inductive hypothesis. $\qquad \square$

Theorem 3 *For all exclusive distributions S, $b_{SWAP}(i,j) \geq b_{MTE}(i,j)$ $\forall i < j$, and hence, the SWAP heuristic is more efficient than the MTE.*

Proof:

Our proof will be a generalization of the proof used by Rivest to prove that TR is better than MTF [5]. We shall show that for all Exclusive distributions, $b_{SWAP}(i,j) \geq b_{MTE}(i,j)$, for $1 \leq i < j \leq N$. We then have:

$$\frac{b_{SWAP}(i,j)}{b_{SWAP}(j,i)}$$
$$= \frac{\sum_{l < m} \sum_{k's} Pr(\langle R_{k_1}, \ldots, R_{k_l}, R_i, R_{k_{l+1}}, \ldots, R_{k_m}, R_j, R_{k_{m+1}}, \ldots, R_{k_{N-2}} \rangle)}{\sum_{l < m} \sum_{k's} Pr(\langle R_{k_1}, \ldots, R_{k_l}, R_j, R_{k_{l+1}}, \ldots, R_{k_m}, R_i, R_{k_{m+1}}, \ldots, R_{k_{N-2}} \rangle)}. \qquad (6)$$

Notice that in (6), the summations are taken over all permutations $k_1, k_2, \ldots, k_{n-2}$ of the integers $1, 2, \ldots, i-1, i+1, \ldots, j-1, j+1, \ldots, N$, for all $1 \le l < m \le N$. Thus from (6) a weak lower bound for the LHS of (6) can be immediately written as:

$$\frac{b_{SWAP}(i,j)}{b_{SWAP}(j,i)} \ge \min_{1 \le l < m \le N} N \frac{Pr(\langle R_{k_1}, \ldots, R_{k_l}, R_i, R_{k_{l+1}}, \ldots, R_{k_m}, R_j, R_{k_{m+1}}, \ldots, R_{k_{N-2}} \rangle)}{Pr(\langle R_{k_1}, \ldots, R_{k_l}, R_j, R_{k_{l+1}}, \ldots, R_{k_m}, R_i, R_{k_{m+1}}, \ldots, R_{k_{N-2}} \rangle)}. \quad (7)$$

Because of Theorem 2, we immediately conclude that:

$$\frac{b_{SWAP}(i,j)}{b_{SWAP}(j,i)} \ge \frac{s_{iL} + s_{jR}}{s_{jL} + s_{iR}}, \quad (8)$$

which implies that:

$$b_{SWAP}(i,j) \ge \frac{s_{iL} + s_{jR}}{s_{iL} + s_{jR} + s_{jL} + s_{iR}}. \quad (9)$$

Observe that the expression on the RHS of (9) is exactly $b_{MTE}(i,j)$, as derived in [1]. Hence we have proved that:

$$b_{SWAP}(i,j) \ge b_{MTE}(i,j) \quad \forall \, i < j.$$

This information, together with Theorem 1, establishes the superiority of the SWAP heuristic, when compared to MTE, for all Exclusive distributions. $\square$

It only remains to show that entire families of Exclusive distributions exist. Two such families are listed below.

Corollary 1 *Consider the families of distributions in which $s_{iL} > s_{jL}$ and $s_{jR} > s_{iR}$ for all $i < j$. A distribution of this type is said to be* **Dually Monotonic.** *All Dually Monotonic distributions are Exclusive and hence, the SWAP heuristic is more efficient than the MTE heuristic for such query distributions.*

Proof:

By virtue of the conditions satisfied by a dually monotonic distribution, we can easily deduce that $s_{iL} - s_{jL} \ge 0$ and $s_{jR} - s_{iR} \ge 0$ for all $i < j$. Moreover, whenever $i < j$, we trivially observe that $s_{iL} s_{jR} \ge s_{iR} s_{jL}$. In other words, this distribution satisfies the condition defined in (3), and hence all dually monotonic distributions are also Exclusive. By Theorem 3, it follows that for this family of access distributions, SWAP performs better than MTE. $\square$

As an example of a dual monotonic distribution, consider the following distribution in which the access probabilities for the left and right directions are based on Zipf's law. Specifically, the probability of accessing a record R_i (for $i = 1, 2, \ldots, N$) from the left and right are given by:

$$s_{iL} = \frac{c_1}{i}$$
$$s_{iR} = \frac{c_2}{N - i + 1}$$

Notice that the constants c_1 and c_2 must be chosen in such a manner that $\sum_{i=1}^{N}(s_{iL} + s_{iR}) = 1$.

Corollary 2 *Consider the family of distributions in which the total probability of accessing record R_i ($1 \le i \le N$) is given by p_i. These probabilities obey the relation $p_i > p_j$ for all $i < j$. Furthermore, the conditional probability of accessing a record R_i from the left is p (where $p > 0.5$) independent of the index i. We call this family of distributions* **Directionally Biased**. *Directionally biased distributions are Exclusive, and hence, the SWAP is more efficient than MTE for such query distributions.*

Proof:

We note that as a result of conditions specified in the statement of the Corollary, the probabilities s_{iL} and s_{iR} can be expressed as $p_i p$ and $p_i (1-p)$ respectively, where p_i represents the total probability of accessing record R_i. For this family of distributions, the condition for their being Exclusive, remains to be verified. Indeed, the LHS of condition (3) can be written down as:

$$
\begin{aligned}
& p_k(p_i - p_j)p^2 + p_k(p_j - p_i)(1-p)^2 + p_i p_j \{p(1-p) - p(1-p)\} \\
&= p_k(p_i - p_j)\left\{p^2 - (1-p)^2\right\} \\
&= p_k(p_i - p_j)(2p - 1).
\end{aligned}
$$

It is clear that because of the condition that $p > 0.5$, this family qualifies as an Exclusive distribution. The claim immediately follows. $\qquad\square$

Note that we have proved the superiority of SWAP relative to MTE, only for Exclusive distributions. Since the TR heuristic is known be better than the MTF for **all** access distributions, we expect SWAP to be always better than MTE. This result (which we conjecture to be true) is by no means trivial to prove. Whenever $b_{SWAP}(i,j) > b_{MTE}(i,j)$ can be established for all $i < j$, SWAP has been shown to be the superior heuristic. However, it is an easy task to construct examples of distributions in which $b_{SWAP}(i,j) < b_{MTE}(i,j)$ at least for one pair of indices i, j where $i < j$. Hence to compare SWAP and MTE, we apparently have to deal with the explicit expression for cost itself and not the asymptotic pairwise precedence probabilities. Indeed, this problem currently remains unsolved and has been stated as a conjecture.

Conjecture 1 *The SWAP heuristic has a lower expected cost when compared to the MTE heuristic, for* **all** *access distributions.*

3 Absorbing schemes for DLLs

In the preceding section, we have examined the memoryless heuristics SWAP and MTE for DLLs. If the environment is known to be stationary, it is better to use an absorbing scheme, which gradually transforms the list until an absorbing state is reached. After this, no further transformations in the list take place. If the probability of converging to the optimal order can be made exactly unity, all subsequent queries will benefit from the lowest possible cost.

We shall now present an absorbing strategy which moves each data element exactly once. In other words, once an element is moved, it is never moved again. After each of the elements in the list have been moved once, the list is considered to have converged to its "final" configuration. In the following section, we explain this procedure in detail and derive some of its asymptotic properties.

3.1 Absorbing-MTE

We have seen earlier that the optimal configuration of records is one which arranges the records in the descending order of the difference $s_{iL} - s_{iR}$. Maintaining estimates of the difference in access probabilities clearly requires $O(N)$ locations. Instead of using $O(N)$ such counters, our scheme is based on the use of *one* additional counter, and a parameter M which determines the accuracy of the scheme.

Let $\mathcal{V}$ be the set of elements that have not been moved from their initial positions. $\mathcal{V}$ is initially set to $\mathcal{R}$ (the set of all records in the list) and is progressively reduced until it is empty. At this point, the data reorganization algorithm is said to have converged, and further reorganizations will not take place with subsequent accesses.

Whenever an element R_i is accessed and $R_i \notin \mathcal{V}$ (i.e. the record R_i has already been moved from its initial position) although the contents of R_i are presented to the user, the data reorganization strategy completely ignores this access. We now consider the case when $R_i \in \mathcal{V}$.

To aid in the understanding of the scheme, let us imagine that a new "conceptual" list is being formed as we decide the final positions of the individual records of $\mathcal{R}$. For simplicity of exposition we shall consider that the new list being formed consists of two sublists, *Front* and *Tail* to be ultimately concatenated.

Initially *Front* and *Tail* are both empty. If a record R_i is accessed M consecutive times from the *left*, it is appended to the end of the list *Front*. As alluded to above, we note that these M consecutive accesses to R_i could be interleaved by any number of accesses to the elements of $\mathcal{R}$ that have been already moved. Analogously, if the record R_i is accessed M consecutive times from the *right*, we add R_i to the list *Tail* as its **first** element. The intuitive explanation is that elements being accessed very frequently from the left are moved to belong to the sublist *Front* and hence appear at beginning of the reorganized list. On the other hand, elements being accessed more frequently from the right are placed at the head of the list *Tail* and consequently appear near the end of the overall concatenated list. When all the elements of the original list have been moved once, the scheme has converged and we can replace the original list by the Newlist consisting of *Front* ∪ *Tail*, where ∪ is taken to represent the concatenation operator. Figure 1 illustrates the operation of this algorithm, for an example list consisting of 5 elements.

Element Accessed M times	Direction	*Front*	*Tail*
R_1	Left	$\langle R_1 \rangle$	$\langle \rangle$
R_5	Right	$\langle R_1 \rangle$	$\langle R_5 \rangle$
R_4	Right	$\langle R_1 \rangle$	$\langle R_4, R_5 \rangle$
R_2	Left	$\langle R_1, R_2 \rangle$	$\langle R_4, R_5 \rangle$
R_3	Left	$\langle R_1, R_2, R_3 \rangle$	$\langle R_4, R_5 \rangle$

Figure 1. Figure shows how the sublists *Front* and *Tail* are gradually built, as elements of the DLL are moved. The initial order of elements in the DLL is $\langle R_3, R_5, R_1, R_2, R_4 \rangle$. The final ordering is $\langle R_1, R_2, R_3, R_4, R_5 \rangle$.

For the sake of brevity, we have omitted the formal statement of the algorithm, referred hereafter as Algorithm Absorbing_DLL_1. This appears in the unabridged paper[7].

The explanation given above is only to aid in the conceptual understanding of the algorithm. To avoid the overhead of $O(N)$ storage required to build the sublists *Front* and *Tail*, we would like to update the list "in place." The in-place update can be achieved by simple pointer manipulations and this more efficient version of the algorithm is also found in the unabridged paper[7].

It is easy to see that the scheme presented above is absorbing. Moreover, the total number of list reorganizing operations performed is exactly N. We now investigate the conditions under which the above scheme converges to the optimal list order. We shall show that for a family of distributions $\{\mathcal{S}\}$, the above scheme is asymptotically optimal. We now state and sketch the proof of an important result, which assists in the computation of the probability that Algorithm Absorbing_DLL_1 converges to the optimal order.

Theorem 4 *Let $\mathcal{S}$ be the access probability vector. Then the* **total** *probability that a record R_u precedes another record R_v in the final list obtained by Algorithm Absorbing_DLL_1 is given by:*

$$Pr(R_u \prec R_v) = \frac{s_{uL}^M + s_{vR}^M}{s_{uL}^M + s_{uR}^M + s_{vL}^M + s_{vR}^M}. \tag{10}$$

Sketch Of Proof:

For the indices $u, v \in \{1, 2, \ldots, N\}$, let $\xi_{uv}(\mathcal{V})$ be the event that either R_u or R_v is the element which is selected from the set $\mathcal{V}$ to be moved, where $\mathcal{V} \subseteq \mathcal{R}$.

The operation of Algorithm Absorbing_DLL_1 is modeled by a conditional Markov chain with $4M - 2$ states. The chain captures the states of two integer counters z_1 and z_2 which record the index of the recently accessed record and the number of times it has been accessed. For $i = 1, 2, \ldots, M$, the state $U_i(U_{-i})$ represents the state in which $z_1 = u$ and $z_2 = i(-i)$. We similarly define the states V_i and V_{-i} for $1 \leq i \leq M$. Additionally, we have a state θ_0 which represents the state of maximum uncertainty $(z_1 = z_2 = 0)$ in which there is insufficient information about which of the records R_u or R_v should be moved first. Also θ_t represents the state in which the elements of $\mathcal{V} - \{R_u, R_v\}$ have been accessed at least once (but not M consecutive times). Transitions between these states are easily defined.

This happens to be an absorbing chain, in which U_M, U_{-M}, V_M, V_{-M} are the absorbing states. Absorption into one of the states U_M or V_{-M} implies that R_u ultimately precedes R_v. The probability of absorption into one these states yields the desired probability. We define the following absorption probabilities, for values of i in the set $\{-M, -(M-1), \ldots, 1, 2, \ldots, M-1, M\}$.

$$
\begin{aligned}
a_i &= Pr[\phi(\infty) = U_M | \phi(0) = U_i; \xi_{uv}(\mathcal{V})] \\
b_i &= Pr[\phi(\infty) = V_{-M} | \phi(0) = U_i; \xi_{uv}(\mathcal{V})] \\
c_i &= Pr[\phi(\infty) = U_M | \phi(0) = V_i; \xi_{uv}(\mathcal{V})] \\
d_i &= Pr[\phi(\infty) = V_{-M} | \phi(0) = V_i; \xi_{uv}(\mathcal{V})]
\end{aligned}
$$

Notice that a_i denotes the conditional probability of getting absorbed into the state U_M given that we start in the state U_i (and $\xi_{uv}(\mathcal{V})$). The quantities b_i, c_i, and d_i can be given a similar interpretation. The required probability can be easily related to the terms a_1, b_1, c_1 and d_1. These terms can be obtained by solving **four sets** of recurrence relations which evaluate the first passage probabilities. By solving these sets simultaneously and applying the boundary conditions, it is possible to conclude that for all $\mathcal{V} \subseteq \mathcal{R}$, the quantity $Pr[R_u \prec R_v | \xi_{uv}(\mathcal{V})]$ is given by the RHS of (10). Using this information and the laws of total probability, the required result follows. The complete proof of this result can be found in [7]. $\square$

We now investigate the conditions under which the probability of the above scheme converging to the optimal order can made arbitrarily close to 1 (by increasing M, the parameter of the scheme). To study this, observe that it is sufficient to attempt to make $Pr(R_i \prec R_j)$ tend to 1, as $M \to \infty$. Our next result examines the distributions which force this limit to unity.

Theorem 5 *Let S be an access distribution. Then the necessary and sufficient conditions that Algorithm Absorbing_DLL_1 converges to the optimal order with probability 1 as $M \to \infty$ is:*

$$\max(s_{iL}, s_{jR}) > \max(s_{jL}, s_{iR}) \ \forall \ i < j. \tag{11}$$

Sketch Of Proof:

For sufficiency, it is enough to show that the ratio $\frac{s_{jL}^M + s_{iR}^M}{s_{iL}^M + s_{jR}^M}$ tends to 0 as $M \to \infty$, and consequently, $Pr(R_i \prec R_j)$ tends to 1 as $M \to \infty$. Note that because of the input conditions, this property holds for all $i < j$. This fact can be used to prove that the optimal order occurs with probability 1. The fact that (11) is necessary, can be proved along similar lines. The proof is omitted for the sake of brevity but can be found in [7]. □

We now show that the families of distributions presented in Corollary 1 and Corollary 2 indeed satisfy condition (11).

Corollary 3 *Let S be a dual monotonic access distribution obeying the conditions of Corollary 1. Then, the probability of Algorithm Absorbing_DLL_1 converging to the optimal order approaches 1 as $M \to \infty$.*

Proof:

Because of the conditions specified in Corollary 1 we have the conditions $s_{iL} > s_{jL}$ and $s_{jR} > s_{iR}$, whenever $i < j$. Combining both these inequalities, we obtain $\max(s_{il}, s_{jR}) > \max(s_{jR}, s_{iR})$, whenever $i < j$. This information, together with Theorem 5 establishes our claim. □

We now state our final result.

Corollary 4 *Let S be a Directionally Biased Distribution, as defined in Corollary 2. Then for this distribution, Absorbing_DLL_1 is asymptotically optimal.*

Proof:

The input conditions are : $p_i > p_j$ for all $i < j$, and that the conditional probability of accessing any record from the left is $p > 0.5$. Since $p > 0.5$, it is clear that $p > p_j/(p_i + p_j)$; as a result we conclude that:

$$\max(s_{iL}, s_{jR}) = \max(p_i p, p_j(1 - p)) = p_i p. \tag{12}$$

We note that $\max(s_{jL}, s_{iR})$ can be $p_j \cdot p$ or $p_i(1 - p)$. In the first case, the term in (12) is greater, since $p_i > p_j$. In the second case, the difference between $p_i p$ and $p_i(1 - p)$ is $p_i(2p - 1)$ which is greater than 0, because $p > 0.5$. Hence, in either case, the conditions of Theorem 5 are met and the required result follows. □

Remark:

The conditions imposed by Corollary 4 are rather strict. In fact it is easy to show that Absorbing_DLL_1 is optimal for a family of distributions for which the following (weaker) conditions are satisfied: $s_{iL} > s_{jL} \quad \forall \ i < j$ and $s_{iL} > s_{iR} \quad 1 \leq i \leq N$.

4 Conclusions

In this paper we have studied the problem of dynamically reorganizing the elements of a DLL. We have compared two DLL heuristics, namely the MTE and the SWAP, which are intuitive generalizations of the well known SLL heuristics MTF and TR. We have identified families of distributions for which SWAP is asymptotically more efficient than MTE. Proving that SWAP is superior to MTE under all access distributions is an open problem.

We have also proposed an absorbing scheme for reorganizing the elements of a DLL. The proposed scheme utilizes a single parameter, denoted as M. In this scheme, each data element is moved into its final position in the reorganized list if it accessed for M consecutive times. Again, it has been shown that for two rather general families of distributions, the probability of our scheme converging to the optimal order can be made as close to unity as desired.

Acknowledgements

Both the authors of this paper were partially supported by the Natural Sciences and Engineering Research Council of Canada. The work of the first author was also supported by a graduate award from Bell-Northern Research.

References

[1] D. Matthews, D. Rotem, and E. BretHolz. Self-organizing doubly-linked lists. *J. Comput. Maths.*, 8(Sec.A):99–106, 1980.

[2] D. T. H. Ng and B. J. Oommen. Generalizing singly-linked reorganizing heuristics for doubly-linked lists. In *Proc. of Conf. on Mathematical Foundations of Comp. Sc.*, pages 380–389, Rytro, Poland, Aug-Sept. 1989.

[3] B. J. Oommen and D. T. H. Ng. Ideal list organization for stationary environments. Technical Report SCS-TR-154, School Of Computer Science, Carleton University, Ottawa, Ont., K1S 5B6, 1989.

[4] J. H. Hester and D. S. Hirschberg. Self-organizing linear search. *ACM Computing Surveys*, 17(3):295–311, 1985.

[5] R. L. Rivest. On self-organizing sequential search heuristics. *Comm. ACM*, 19(2):63–67, 1976.

[6] J. P. Tremblay and P. G. Sorenson. *An Introduction to Data Structures with Applications.* McGraw-Hill, New York, 1976.

[7] R. S. Valiveti and B. J. Oommen. Self-organizing doubly-linked lists. Technical Report SCS-TR-173, School Of Computer Science, Carleton University, Ottawa, Ont., K1S 5B6, May 1990.

Skip Sort - AN ADAPTIVE RANDOMIZED ALGORITHM

OR

EXPECTED TIME ADAPTIVITY IS BEST

Vladimir Estivill-Castro[1] and Derick Wood[2]

[1]Department of Computer Science
York University, North York
Ontario M3J-1P3, Canada

[2]Department of Computer Science
University of Waterloo, Waterloo
Ontario N2L-3G1, Canada

INTRODUCTION

A sorting algorithm is *adaptive* [15, page 224] if it requires fewer comparisons to sort a "nearly-sorted" sequence than to sort a "well-shuffled" sequence. Adaptive sorting algorithms are attractive because nearly sorted sequences are common in practice [10,15]. Recently, adaptive sorting has been the subject of intensive investigation [6,11,12,14,18,19]. However, the proposed sorting algorithms have received limited acceptance because they are adaptive with respect to only one or two measures [2,6,8,12,18], they require complex data structures that have a significant overhead [3,11,14], or their adaptive behavior has eluded analysis [2,4,19]. Moreover, the analysis of the performance of adaptive algorithms has been, so far, based only on worst-case. The notion of optimal adaptivity in the worst case was formalized by Mannila [14] who quantified disorder with measures of presortedness.

In contrast to the pessimistic view of worst-case analysis, expected-case analysis provides practical information, especially when worst-case instances are unlikely to occur. There are two approaches for expected-case complexity [20], the distributional approach and the randomized approach. In the distributional approach a "natural" distribution of the problem instances is assumed and the expected time taken by the algorithm over the different instances is evaluated. This approach may be inaccurate, since the probabilistic assumptions needed to carry the analysis may be false. Based on the distributional approach, we show that sound definitions of optimality with respect to a measure of presortedness can be made; but little new insight is obtained from them.

The difficulties with the distributional approach are circumvented by randomized algorithms because their behavior is independent of the distribution of the instances to be solved. In this paper, we use randomization as a tool in the design of practical sorting algorithms that are adaptive; the first time randomization has been used for this purpose. We introduce *Skip Sort*, and we show to be expected-case optimal with respect to at least five common measures of presortedness. This means that *Skip Sort* is adaptive to many types of existing order. Moreover, we show that *Skip Sort* is a practical alternative to worst-case adaptive sorting algorithms also optimal to these measures. For example, simulation results show that *Skip Sort* is twice as fast as *Local Insertion Sort* [14].

We should point out that although *Skip Sort* is our choice example to demonstrate that randomization is best, we have found that randomization can be applied to design other adaptive sorting algorithms that result in efficient and practical implementations. We mention two more randomized sorting algorithms that are adaptive in the expected case. First, *Randomized Quicksort*, which we have proved [5] to have time complexity $\Theta(|X|[1 + \log(Exc(X) + 1)])$ in the expected case, where $Exc(X)$ is the minimum number of exchanges required to sort X. Second, *Randomized Mergesort*, which we have proved [5] to be expected *Runs*-optimal, but not *Runs*-optimal in the worst case. These randomized sorting algorithms are simple and can be implemented efficiently, in contrast to previous adaptive sorting algorithms that use complex data structures or require median finding.

DEFINITIONS

Informally, a measure of presortedness is an integer-valued function that is zero if there is no disorder. As the disorder grows, the value of the measure grows. Moreover, the value of the measure for a sequence depends only on the relative order of the elements in the sequence.

We now describe the most common measures of presortedness, many others can be found in the literature [5,11,18]. An *inversion* is any pair of elements in a sequence that are in the wrong order. The total number of inversions in a sequence X is the measure *Inv*. We may consider that, in terms of the disorder it represents, an inversion pair of elements that are far apart is more significant than an inversion pair whose elements are closer. We define *Dis* as the largest distance determined by an inversion. Often local disorder is not as important as global disorder; for example, if books in a library are one slot away from their correct positions, we are still able to find them, since the index will get us close enough; however, a book very far away from its correct position is difficult to find. We define *Max* as the largest distance an element must travel to reach its sorted position. The number of operations required to rearrange a sequence into sorted order may be our first concern. We define *Exc* as the minimum number of exchanges required to sort a sequence. We may also consider that disorder is produced by inserting some records into the wrong positions. We define *Rem* as the minimum number of elements that must be removed to obtain a sorted subsequence. Ascending runs constitute sorted segments of the data. We define *Runs* as the number of boundaries between runs.

For a sequence X, $|X|$ denotes its length, for a set S, $\|S\|$ denotes its cardinality.

The standard assumption for a distributional expected-case analysis of the sorting problem is that all permutations are equally likely. With this in mind, Katajainen and Mannila [9] have defined optimality for adaptive algorithms in the expected case, using the distributional approach. Although the definition is sound [5], it is unclear that it provides new insight. Katajainen and Mannila [9] have been unable to construct an example of a sorting algorithm that is optimal in the expected case, but not optimal in the worst case. Moreover, this definition does not illuminate the behavior of Cook and Kim's *CKsort* [2] which has been assumed to be adaptive with respect to *Rem* in the expected case. *CKsort* is an $O(|X|^2)$ worst case algorithm; and, because in the second phase of the algorithm sequences of length at most $2Rem(X)$ provided to *Quickersort* are not equally likely to occur, *CKsort* is not expected-case optimal with respect to any measure and the their definition of optimality.

From the theoretical point of view, Li and Vitanyi [13] have discovered a second difficulty with the distributional approach. They show that the *universal distribution*[1] is as reasonable as the uniform distribution and, in a sense, explain why nearly sorted sequences appear more frequently in practice. Moreover, they show that if an expected-case analysis is carried out for the universal distribution, then the expected-case complexity of an algorithm is of the same order as its worst-case complexity. This means that *Quicksort* requires $\Theta(|X|^2)$ time in the expected case. Therefore, the distributional complexity analysis depends heavily on the assumed distribution. More realistic distributions are usually mathematically intractable and, moreover, we know that nearly sorted files are more likely, but the distribution may change over time. Because of the difficulties presented by the distributional approach we take the randomized approach.

Using the terminology introduced by Yao [20] and Mehlhorn [15, page 72] we extend Mannila's [14] notion of optimal adaptivity in the worst case to optimal adaptivity in the expected case for randomized algorithms. Let M be a measure of presortedness, n and z be nonnegative integers and let $below'(z, n, M)$ be the set of sequences of length n with no more that disorder z according to M; that is,

$$below'(z, n, M) = \{Y \mid Y \text{ is a permutation of } \{1, \ldots, n\} \text{ and } M(Y) \leq z\}.$$

Consider sorting algorithms having as input not only the sequence X but also an upper bound z on the value of $M(X)$. We analyze the corresponding decision tree for such algorithms. These trees must have at least $\|below'(z, |X|, M)\|$ leaves, since this is the number of possible inputs; so the height of the tree is at least $\log \|below'(z, |X|, M)\|$. Therefore, the algorithm takes at least $\log \|below'(z, |X|, M)\|$ comparisons in the worst case. If an upper bound of $M(X)$ is not available, we assume that the algorithm is very lucky and uses the best bound possible, namely, $z = M(X)$. This means that the corresponding decision tree has at least $\|below'(M(X), X, M)\|$ leaves. The average depth of a decision tree D with at least $\|below'(z, X, M)\|$ leaves is

$$Average\text{-}depth[D] = \frac{1}{\|below'(z, X, M)\|} \sum_{Y \in below'(z, X, M)} depth \text{ of leaf for } Y \text{ in } D.$$

This implies that [15] there is a constant $c > 0$ such that, for every sorting algorithm D that sorts a sequences in $below'(z, X, M)$,

$$Average\text{-}depth[D] \geq c \log \|below'(z, X, M)\|. \tag{1}$$

---

[1] A function $w : S \to [0, 1]$ is a semimeasure over S if $\sum_{x \in S} w(x) \leq 1$. We say that w is a measure or a probability distribution, in the discrete case, over the space S, if $\sum_{x \in S} w(x) = 1$. A function is semicomputable if the set $\{(x, r) : x \in S, r \in Q, r < f(x)\}$ is recursively enumerable. A semicomputable semimeasure μ is universal if it multiplicatively dominates every other semicomputable semimeasure μ', i.e. $\mu(x) \geq c\mu'(x)$ for a fixed constant $c > 0$ independent of x. The function $m(x) = 2^{-K(x)}$, where $K(x)$ is the (self-delimiting) Kolmogorov complexity of x is a universal distribution.

Now, a randomized sorting algorithm corresponds to a randomized decision tree [15]. In a random decision tree there are two types of nodes. The first type of node is the ordinary comparison node. The second type is a coin tossing node. It has two outgoing edges labeled 0 and 1 which are taken with half probability each. Without loss of generality we can restrict attention to finite random decision tress; thus, we assume that the number of coin tosses on inputs of size n is bounded by $k(n)$. However, the leaf reached not only depends on the input but also on the sequence $s \in \{0,1\}^{k(n)}$ of outcomes of coin tosses. For any permutation Y and sequence $s \in \{0,1\}^{k(n)}$ let $d_{Y,s}^T$ denote the depth of the leaf reached on sequence s of coin tosses and input sequence Y. Let X be a sequence and T a randomized decision tree, the expected number of comparisons performed by T on X is

$$E[T(X)] = \sum_{s \in \{0,1\}^{k(n)}} \frac{1}{2^{k(n)}} d_{X,s}^T.$$

That is, the average over all random sequences $s \in \{0,1\}^{k(n)}$ of $d_{X,s}^T$.

Let $\mathcal{R}$ be the family of all randomized algorithms and let R be a randomized algorithm. We denote by $T_R(X)$ be the number of comparisons performed by algorithm R on input X. $T_R(X)$ is a random variable. A lower bound on the expected value of $T_R(X)$ is given by the following equation.

$$E[T_R(X)] \geq \min_{T \in \mathcal{R}} \max_{Y \in below'(M(X),|X|,M)} E[T(Y)].$$

Observe that, once the sequence $s \in \{0,1\}^{k(n)}$ is given, the randomized decision tree becomes an ordinary decision tree D_s that sorts sequences in $below(M(X),|X|,M)$. Therefore, by Equation (1), there is a constant $d > 0$ such that,

$$
\begin{aligned}
E[T_R(X)] &\geq \min_{T \in \mathcal{R}} \sum_{Y \in below'(M(X),|X|,M)} \frac{E[T(Y)]}{\|below'(M(X),|X|,M)\|} \\
&\geq \min_{T \in \mathcal{R}} \sum_{s \in \{0,1\}^{k(n)}} \frac{1}{2^{k(n)}} Average\ depth[D_s] \\
&\geq d \log \|below(M(X),|X|,M)\|.
\end{aligned}
$$

Intuitively, an adaptive randomized algorithm R is optimal in the expected case with respect to a measure of presortedness M if for every sequence X, the expected value of $T_R(X)$ is with in a positive constant of the minimum possible. Finally, since testing for sortedness requires linear time, a sorting algorithm should be allowed at least a linear number of comparisons. We capture the notion of optimal adaptivity for randomized sorting algorithms as follows.

Definition. *Let M be a measure of presortedness and R be a randomized sorting algorithm. Let $E[T_R(X)]$ denote the expected number of comparisons performed by R on input X. We say that R is optimal with respect to M (or M-optimal) if, for some $c > 0$, we have, for all $X \in N^{<N}$,*

$$E[T_R(X)] \leq c \cdot \max\{|X|, \log(\|below'(M(X),X,M)\|)\}.$$

In the next section we present *Skip Sort*, a practical sorting algorithm that is optimally adaptive with respect to *Dis*, *Exc*, *Inv*, *Max*, *Rem* and *Runs*. Thus, *Skip Sort* takes advantage of existing order even when it appears in different forms.

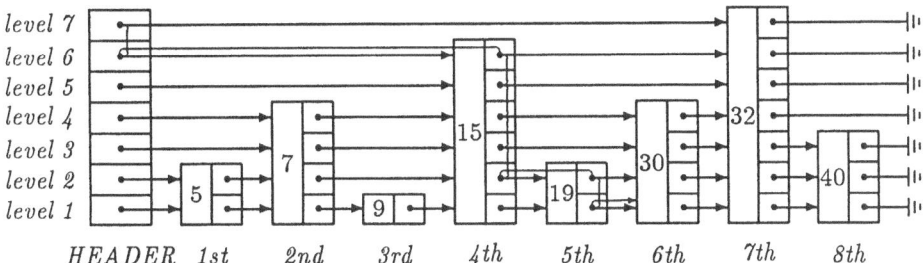

Figure 1: A skip list of 8 elements, and the search path when searching for the *6th* element. *update=[5th,5th,4th,4th,4th,4th,HEADER]* is the finger to the *6th* element.

Skip Sort – THE ALGORITHM

Skip Sort is a variant of *Local Insertion Sort* [14] that uses *skip lists* [17] to represent a sorted subsequence. It is a faster local insertion sorting algorithm that requires less space. A skip list is a simple and practical probabilistic data structure that has the same asymptotic expected time bounds as a balanced tree. The price we pay for this is that performance is no longer worst-case optimal, but expected-case optimal. Note that the same behavior can be achieved with *randomized treaps*[2] [1]; we use skip lists because updates in a treap require rotations and care must be taken to preserve the heap-order of the priorities; thus, skip lists are simpler for our purposes.

Skip Sort is an insertion sort. The elements are considered one at at a time, and each new element is inserted in the appropriate position relative to the previously sorted elements. The sequence of sorted elements is represented by a skip list.

Suppose that $x_1, \ldots, x_{i-1}$ have been inserted and x_i is to be inserted in its correct position with respect to $x_1, \ldots, x_{i-1}$. When looking for the appropriate position to insert x_i in the skip list, the search is started where x_{i-1} was inserted. When searching for the position of x_{i-1}, the insertion routine constructed a vector of pointers (Pugh called it the *update* vector [17]) such that *update*[j] contains a pointer to the right most node of level j or higher that is to the left of the position of x_{i-1}; see Figure 1. The *update* vector allows us to splice the skip list in as many levels as the height of the node being inserted. The *update* vector works as a finger in the skip list for x_{i-1}. The search for the position for x_i uses *update* as a finger and starts by a comparison of x_i with x_{i-1} to determine if the search should go forward in the skip list (past x_{i-1}) or backwards (before x_{i-1}).

We describe the insertion of x_i in the case we must go backwards. We repeatedly increase the level and compare x_i with the nodes pointed by *update*[1], *update*[2], ..., until we find a level such that x_i falls in a suitable range. From there, we go down levels performing the insertion algorithm to place x_i. If we ever surface to the top of the skip list, we insert x_i from the head of the skip list.

For example, suppose we are inserting 18 after 30 has been inserted in the skip list of Figure 1. We compare 10 with 30 and determine that we must go backwards. After comparing 18 with *update*[1] = 19 and *update*[2] = 19, we find that *update*[3] = 15, is smaller than 18. Thus, the insertion of 18 is made from the forth element and down from level 3.

---

[2]Treaps are search trees with keys and priorities stored in their nodes. The keys are arranged in in-order and the priorities in heap-order.

Table1. Comparing *Local Insertion Sort* and *Skip Sort* by *Rem*. CPU time for *Rem*-nearly sorted sequences.

Algorithm	$|X|$							
	64	128	256	512	1024	2048	4096	8192
L I Sort	57.8	120.2	247.0	517.1	1086.56	2191.28	4618.76	9224.77
Skip Sort	25.2	51.2	105.6	224.4	483.11	979.32	2094.97	4181.15

Skip Sort– THEORETICAL AND EXPERIMENTAL RESULTS

To insert an element d positions away from the last insertion takes $O(1 + \log d)$ expected time [17,16]. Denote by $C_I(d)$ the number of comparisons performed by an insertion d positions away from the current finger position and let $T_{SS}(X)$ denote the number of comparisons performed by *Skip Sort* on input $X = \langle x_1, \ldots, x_n \rangle$. Since $E[T_{SS}(X)]$ is the sum of the expected times of the insertions,

$$E[T_{SS}(X)] \quad = \quad O(\sum_{i=1}^{|X|} E[C_I(d_i(X))])$$

$$= \quad O(\sum_{i=1}^{|X|} 1 + \log[1 + d_i(X)]),$$

where $d_i(X) = \|\{j \mid 1 \le j < i \text{ and } (x_{i-1} < x_j < x_i \text{ or } x_i < x_j < x_{i-1})\}\|$. From this point onwards, the proofs of worst case optimality [6,12,14] can be modified to obtain the following theorem.

Theorem. *Skip Sort is expected case optimal with respect to Inv, Runs, Rem, Exc, Max, and Dis.*

Proof: To illustrate the techniques we give the proofs for *Runs*, the others are left to the reader. We analyze $\sum_{i=1}^{|X|} 1 + \log[1 + d_i(X)]$ as in the proofs for the worst case and use

$$E[T_{SS}(X)] = O(\sum_{i=1}^{|X|} 1 + \log[1 + d_i(X)]) \qquad (2)$$

to bound the expected value of $T_{SS}(X)$ by a function of $|X|$ and the disorder in X. Since $\log \|below'(Runx(X), X, Runs)\| = \Omega(|X|[1 + \log(Runs(X) + 1)])$ [14], to show that *Skip Sort* is *Runs*-optimal in the expected case we must show that, for all X, $E[T_{SS}(X)] = O(|X|[1 + \log(Runs(X) + 1)])$. Let $R = Runs(X) + 1$ and $t(r)$ be the set on indices of the r-th run. Thus, $\sum_{r=1}^{R} \|t(r)\| = |X|$. Moreover, for each run r, $\sum_{j \in t(r)} d_j(X) \le 2|X|$.

Now,

$$\sum_{i=1}^{|X|} 1 + \log[1 + d_i(X)] = |X| + \sum_{r=1}^{R} \sum_{j \in t(r)} \log(1 + d_j(X)).$$

For nonnegative integers d_j such that $\sum_{j \in t(r)} d_j \le 2|X|$, $\sum_{j \in t(r)} \log(1 + d_j)$ is maximized when $d_j = 2|X|/\|t(r)\|$. Therefore,

$$\sum_{i=1}^{|X|} 1 + \log[1 + d_i(X)] \le |X| + \sum_{r=1}^{R} \|t(r)\| \log(1 + 2|X|/\|t(r)\|).$$

Table 2. Comparing *Local Insertion Sort* and *Skip Sort* by *Max*. CPU time for *Max*-nearly sorted sequences.

Algorithm	$|X|$							
	64	128	256	512	1024	2048	4096	8192
L I Sort	63.5	127.4	245.6	497.9	1052.76	2163.80	3115.64	9552.80
Skip Sort	27.1	54.2	109.5	234.4	507.61	1080.16	2370.37	4881.20

We analyze the right hand side.

$$|X| + \sum_{r=1}^{R} \|t(r)\| \log(1 + 2|X|/\|t(r)\|) \;=\; |X| + |X| \sum_{r=1}^{R} [\log(1 + 2|X|/\|t(r)\|)]^{\|t(r)\|/|X|}$$

$$=\; |X| + |X| \log \prod_{r=1}^{R} [1 + 2|X|/\|t(r)\|]^{\|t(r)\|/|X|}.$$

Since the geometric mean is no larger than the arithmetic mean we obtain.

$$|X| + |X| \log \prod_{r=1}^{R} [1 + 2|X|/\|t(r)\|]^{\|t(r)\|/|X|} \;\leq\; |X| + |X| \log \sum_{r=1}^{R} [2 + \|t(r)\|/|X|]$$

$$=\; |X|(1 + \log[2R + 1]).$$

This and Equation (2) gives $E[T_{SS}(X)] = O(|X|(\log[1 + Runs(X)]))$ as required $\square$

Furthermore, because of the simplicity of skip lists, *Skip Sort* is a practical alternative to *Local Insertion Sort*. Table 1 presents simulation results that imply that *Skip Sort* is twice as fast as *Local Insertion Sort*.

Both algorithms were coded in *C* and simulations were performed on a *VAX-8650* running UNIX^{TM} 4.3BSD and measured using *gprof* [7]. Each algorithm sorted the same set of 100 nearly sorted sequences for each input length. The *Rem*-nearly sorted sequences were generated using Cook and Kim's method [2,19] with $Rem(X)/|X| \leq 0.2$. The percentage of disorder in Table 2 is given by $Max(X)/|X| \leq 0.2$ and the permutations were generated using that *Max* is a normal measure of presortedness [5].

CONCLUSIONS

Randomization provides practical and efficient adaptive sorting algorithms. It is possible to achieve optimal adaptivity with respect to many measures of presortedness. We match, in the expected case, the asymptotic performance of worst-case algorithms with much simpler algorithms. The mathematical analysis and simulations confirm that the multiplicative constants are small. Therefore, randomized sorting algorithms that are adaptive result in practical and efficient implementations.

ACKNOWLEDGEMENTS

This work was done while the first author was a Postdoctoral Fellow in the Department of Computer Science at the University of Waterloo. It was carried out under a Natural Sciences and Engineering Research Council of Canada Grant No.A-5692, under an Information Technology Research Centre grant and under the financial support of the Department of Computer Science at York University.

The first author wishes to thank Tom Papadakis for helpful discussions on skip lists and for his assistance in drawing Figure 1.

References

[1] C. Aragon and R. Seidel. Randomized search trees. In *Proceedings of the 30th IEEE Symposium on Foundations of Computer Science*, pages 540–545, Research Triangle Park, NC., 1989.

[2] C.R. Cook and D.J. Kim. Best sorting algorithms for nearly sorted lists. *Communications of the ACM*, 23:620–624, 1980.

[3] E.W. Dijkstra. Smoothsort, an alternative to sorting in situ. *Science of Computer Programming*, 1:223–233, 1982.

[4] P.G. Dromey. Exploiting partial order with Quicksort. *Software — Practice and Experience*, 14(6):509–518, 1984.

[5] V. Estivill-Castro. *Sorting and Measures of Disorder*. PhD thesis, University of Waterloo, 1991. Available as Department of Computer Science Research Report CS-91-07.

[6] V. Estivill-Castro and D. Wood. A new measure of presortedness. *Information and Computation*, 83:111–119, 1989.

[7] S. L. Graham, P.B. Kessler, and M. K. McKusik. gprof: A call graph execution profiler. *The Proceedings of the SIGPLAN'82 Symposium on Compiler Construction, SIGPLAN Notices*, 17(6):120–126, 1982.

[8] J. D. Harris. Sorting unsorted and partially sorted lists using the natural merge sort. *Software — Practice and Experience*, 11:1339–1340, 1981.

[9] J. Katajainen and H. Mannila. On average case optimality of a presorting algorithm. Unpublished manuscript, 1989.

[10] D.E. Knuth. *The Art of Computer Programming, Vol.3: Sorting and Searching*. Addison-Wesley Publishing Co., Reading, Mass., 1973.

[11] C. Levcopoulos and O. Petersson. Heapsort — adapted for presorted files. In F. Dehne, J.R. Sack, and N. Santoro, editors, *Proceedings of the Workshop on Algorithms and Data Structures*, pages 499–509. Springer-Verlag Lecture Notes in Computer Science 382, 1989.

[12] C. Levcopoulos and O. Petersson. Splitsort—an adaptive sorting algorithm. In B. Rovan, editor, *Mathematical Foundations of Computer Science*, pages 416–422. Springer-Verlag Lecture Notes in Computer Science 452, 1990.

[13] M. Li and P.M.B. Vitanyi. A theory of learning simple concepts under simple distributions and average case complexity for the universal distribution. In *Proceedings of the 30th IEEE Symposium on Foundations of Computer Science*, pages 34–39, Research Triangle Park, NC., 1989.

[14] H. Mannila. Measures of presortedness and optimal sorting algorithms. *IEEE Transactions on Computers*, C-34:318–325, 1985.

[15] K. Mehlhorn. *Data Structures and Algorithms, Vol 1: Sorting and Searching*. EATCS Monographs on Theoretical Computer Science. Springer-Verlag, Berlin/Heidelberg, 1984.

[16] T. Papadakis, J. I. Munro, and P.V. Poblete. Analysis of the Expected Search Cost in Skip Lists. In J.R. Gilbert and R. Karlsson, editors, *Proceedings of the 2nd Scandinavian Workshop on Algorithm Theory*, pages 160–172, Bergen, Sweden, 1990. Springer-Verlag Lecture Notes in Computer Science 447.

[17] W. Pugh. Skip Lists: A probabilistic alternative to balanced trees. *Communications of the ACM*, 33(6):668–676, 1990.

[18] S.S. Skiena. Encroaching lists as a measure of presortedness. *BIT*, 28:755–784, 1988.

[19] R.L. Wainwright. A class of sorting algorithms based on Quicksort. *Communications of the ACM*, 28:396–402, 85.

[20] A.C. Yao. Probabilistic computations — toward a unified measure of complexity. In *Proceedings of the 18th IEEE Symposium on Foundations of Computer Science*, pages 222–227, 1977.

DATA STRUCTURES AND ACCESS METHODS

FOR READ-ONLY OPTICAL DISKS

Eduardo Fernandes Barbosa[1] and Nivio Ziviani[2]

[1] Departamento de Engenharia Eletrônica
[2] Departamento de Ciência da Computação
Universidade Federal de Minas Gerais
Belo Horizonte, Brazil

ABSTRACT

This paper presents alternatives for efficient file organization and placement on read-only optical disks, known as CD-ROM. We extend an analytical model for retrieval costs found in the literature, adding additional aspects to the model, such as rotational latency and file structure. From CD-ROM standards we derive algorithms for file mapping and access time calculations to build a deterministic model which is used in simulations. Experimental results on different file structures and file sizes show that rotational latency, file size, file structure, and file allocation strongly affects the retrieval performance in CD-ROM disks. A comparative study considering a sequence of accesses to sequential, indexed sequential, B-tree and hashing file structures shows that hashing and indexed sequential are the organizations that presented the smallest total time under the limitations of optical devices. We present an indexed sequential organization for CD-ROM file systems which minimizes disk accesses.

INTRODUCTION

Optical disk technology is currently being used as secondary storage devices with significant advantages over magnetic medium, such as higher storage capacity and lower cost. Read-only compact disks, referred as CD-ROM, is presently being used as storage device for large data base distribution. The growing interest on CD-ROM is due to its large storage capacity (up to 600 megabytes), low cost to the end user and high level of physical and logical integrity. The main differences between CD-ROM and magnetic disks are: (i) CD-ROM is a read-only medium and, as such, the structure of the information is static; (ii) the efficiency of data access is affected by its location on the disk and by the sequence in which it is retrieved. (iii) due to constant linear velocity (CLV) the tracks have variable capacity and rotational latency depends on disk position.

The CD-ROM track has a spiral pattern and an access to distant tracks requires more time due to the need of optical head displacement and changes in disk rotation. The capability of accessing nearby tracks with no displacement of the reading mechanism is called *span* and the number of tracks which can be accessed in this way is called *span size*. In actual CD-ROM drives span size is up to 60 tracks. Accessing data located within span boundaries, seek time takes only 1 millisecond per additional track, which is performed by a single angular laser beam displacement from the current track, which is called *anchor point*. In this situation, seek time is negligible compared to rotational latency. When accessing data located outside span boundaries, seek time requires from 200 to 600 milliseconds due to optical head displacement.

Rotational latency is smaller on inner tracks as a consequence of the constant linear velocity (CLV) scheme adopted in CD-ROM. The smaller rotational latency takes 60 milliseconds and the larger one takes 138 milliseconds. So, file allocation on outer tracks effectively reduces the number of head displacements for any sequence of data accesses because the file occupies a smaller number of tracks (up to 2.3 times smaller), but, conversely, the final cost is charged to larger rotational latencies in this disk area.

For the purposes of this paper, we define an *object* as a record of the data file or the index file. A *qualifying object* is one that should be retrieved to answer a given query. To answer a query it might be necessary to retrieve more than one object. Any object is supposed to be completely contained within a track (called *non-crossing objects*), and the smallest object size that can be retrieved is one sector large (2048 bytes).

Given a sequence of objects to be retrieved, a scheduling algorithm provides an ordered sequence of anchor points that define the head displacements necessary to answer a given query. There are different sets of anchor points and schedules that may answer a query that needs two or more qualifying objects. Tracks within a span may overlap with another span from a neighboring anchor point, that is, there may be a subset of the tracks that belongs to both spans.

Laub (1986) and Zoellick (1986) describe the evolution of optical disks and compare them to magnetic disks. Design considerations can be found in Lambert (1986), Ropiequet (1987) and Sherman (1989). Christodoulakis (1987, 1988 and 1989) presents an analytical model for CD-ROM cost estimation to compute the expected number of optical head displacements needed to answer a query. These papers establish fundamental concepts for CLV optical disk modeling and help to understand the main issues related to CD-ROM logical design. Some early results were presented in Barbosa e Ziviani (1991).

The objective of this paper is to analyze the problem of efficient file organization and placement on CD-ROM disks. We extend the model presented by Christodoulakis by considering file structure and rotational latency for real cost estimation. We present a comparative study for sequential, indexed sequential, B-tree and hashing file structures showing that hashing and indexed sequential are the best choices under the limitations of optical devices. We show how to minimize disk accesses to indexed sequential files by presenting an algorithm and an index structure that uses in full extent the span capability of the CD-ROM drive.

AN EXTENDED ANALYTICAL MODEL FOR CD-ROM

The analytical model proposed by Christodoulakis (1987, 1988, 1989) allows cost measurements by giving the expected number of head displacements that the access mechanism has to perform for the retrieval of a random sequence of objects from CD-ROM disks. The model is developed under a probabilistic approach, taking into account the file size, track capacity and number of objects for retrieval. An important contribution of this model is the definition of an optimal scheduling for retrieving data. These conditions proved to minimize the number of times that the access mechanism is moved, as well as the total distance traveled by the optical head. The theorem for optimal scheduling is stated as: The number of head displacements required to access all qualifying objects in a query is minimized if (a) spans of two consecutive anchor points do not overlap and (b) an anchor point is always positioned on a track with qualifying objects. Moreover, the total distance traveled by the access mechanism is also minimized if the optical head is moved in only one direction during the retrieval of a set of objects (in addition to conditions (a) and (b)). The proof can be found in Christodoulakis (1987).

Although the model gives optimal results with respect to the expected number of head displacements necessary to answer a given query, it ignores the contribution of rotational latency in the retrieval costs. The contribution of rotational latency is ignored by making the assumption that seek time is much larger than rotational latency. We extend this model showing that this assumption is not correct in general, that is, rotational latency plays an important role in many situations.

Following, we present analytical results showing the influence of rotational latency and file structure to estimate the actual cost retrieval, by extending the model presented by Christodoulakis (1987, 1988). The approximated solution for the expected number of optical head displacements H_d to retrieve non-crossing objects with no span overlapping, obtained by Christodoulakis (1987, 1988, p. 290) is

$$H_d = \frac{B}{1 + \frac{Q-1}{N_t-1}(B-1)} \tag{1}$$

where Q represents the span size, N_t represents the number of tracks of the file and B represents the expected number of tracks with objects that qualify a query, which is given by

$$B = N_t \left[1 - \frac{\binom{C \times N_t - C}{n}}{\binom{C \times N_t}{n}} \right] \tag{2}$$

where C is the track capacity, given by the number of objects in each track, and n is the number of objects to be retrieved.

The influence of rotational latency in the retrieval costs can be obtained as follows:

1. Compute the total time spent with head displacements to retrieve n objects;

2. For each retrieved object, add the time due to rotational latency.

We consider also the influence of file structure in the retrieval cost by taking into account l levels of addressing, where l depends on the file structure. Thus, the total access time to retrieve and transfer n objects is given by

$$t_a = H_d \times \overline{t_s} + n(1 + l)(\overline{t_r} + b_{tt}) \tag{3}$$

where $\overline{t_s}$ is the average seek time for each head displacement, t_r is the average rotational latency, b_{tt} is the block transfer time to main memory, and $l = 0$ for direct address files and $l > 0$ for indexed files with l index levels residing on disk.

Table 1. Average access time with and without rotational latency as a function of n

n	H_d Head Displacement		$\bar{t}_a$ (ms) No Latency		$\bar{t}_a$ (ms) With Latency	
	Inner tracks	Outer tracks	Inner tracks	Outer tracks	Inner tracks	Outer tracks
500	257	146	270	160	336	325
1000	346	170	186	99	251	264
1500	391	180	143	73	209	239
2000	418	186	118	60	183	225
2500	435	189	100	51	165	217
3000	448	190	88	45	153	211
3500	457	192	79	41	144	207
4000	464	193	71	38	136	203
4500	470	194	66	35	131	201
5000	475	194	61	33	125	199

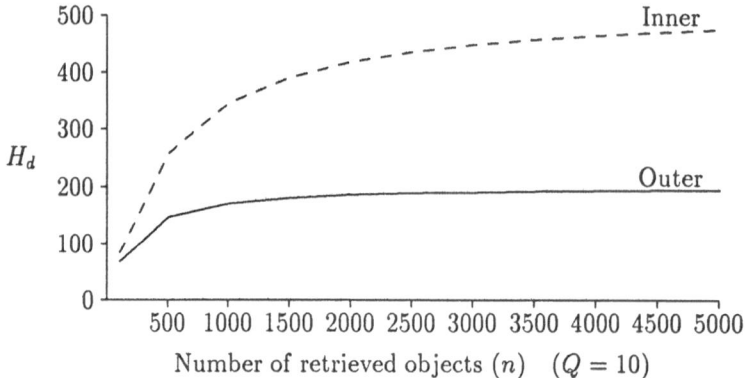

Figure 1. Head displacements according to Table 1

The average time to retrieve one object is given by

$$\overline{t_a} = \frac{t_a}{n} \tag{4}$$

Table 1 presents data related to a file with 45,000 sectors (90 megabytes), using Eq. (1) and Eq. (4), span size $Q = 10$ and the number n of retrieved objects in the range of 500 to 5,000. Notice that a 45,000 sectors file occupy 5,000 internal tracks and 1,956 external tracks. The plot in Figure 1, related to columns two and three of Table 1, illustrates the difference in the number of head displacements H_d for equal sized files allocated on the inner and outer tracks. This is the example used by Christodoulakis (1988, pp. 293–294) to support a general claim that frequently and randomly access files should be allocated on outer tracks. Following, we present a different result for this example by considering the influence of rotational latency.

We extend his example by adding the time due to rotational latency in the last two columns of Table 1. The data related to average access time $\overline{t_a}$ without latency (columns three and four) was obtained from the data presented in columns two and

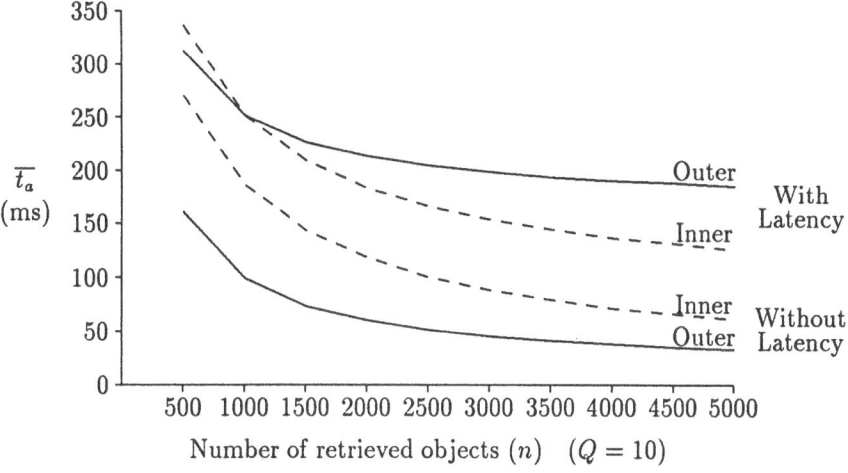

Figure 2. Average access time with and without rotational latency

three by multiplying each value by $\overline{t_s}$ ($\overline{t_s} = 500$ milliseconds), plus the time for one block transfer ($b_{tt} = 13.33$ milliseconds). The data related to average access time $\overline{t_a}$ with latency was obtained by using Eq. (4), considering $\overline{t_r} = 65$ milliseconds for inner tracks, $\overline{t_r} = 153$ milliseconds for outer tracks and $l = 0$ (direct access files).

The plot in Figure 2, related to the last four columns of Table 1, shows that if the time due to rotational latency is considered then the average time to retrieve one object $\overline{t_a}$ is smaller when the file is located on the inner tracks.

The above discussion leads us to the conclusion that frequently and randomly accessed files using the optimal scheduling algorithm should be allocated on inner tracks. Another example that clearly illustrates this conclusion is the following: if a file can be completely contained within span boundaries in any position on disk then retrieval costs will be smaller if this file is located on inner tracks, where rotational latency is smaller.

In practice the objects are not searched according to the optimal scheduling algorithm: the references to objects in the file are done at random. Even in this situation, experimental data presented in Section "Experimental Results" confirm the above results for large and very small files. As we are going to present, there are few exceptions for some small files in the range of 1 to 3 megabytes, which might present smaller average access time when allocated on outer tracks. This is because such file sizes tend to require very few head displacements, when span size is close to the typical value of 60 tracks.

FILE MAPPING AND ACCESS TIME EVALUATION

A deterministic model for file mapping into tracks and sectors is developed from CD-ROM standards. The model is developed from physical and logical characteristics of the disk. The physical characteristics considered were the spiral pitch of the tracks (standard value is 1.6 micrometer), their dimensions, angular velocity, linear velocity (standard value is 1.3 meter/second), sector size and time to read a sector (standard value is 13.33 milliseconds). The logical characteristics considered were sector capacity (2048 bytes), transfer rate (150 kbytes/second), disk capacity, and minimum and maximum track capacity (standard values are 9 and 20 sectors per track, respectively).

The model permits to map files into tracks and sectors, providing exact access time results for any retrieval condition imposed to the reading device. It permits: obtaining the capacity of a given track (in sectors); finding the track corresponding to any given sector address; determining the latency time for any given track; determining initial and final sectors and tracks corresponding to a span size in any disk position; obtaining the number of head displacements necessary to move to the next sector address; and finally, determining the access time to locate sectors and tracks from the drive specifications. This deterministic model was used in a CD-ROM simulator to obtain exact values for access times. The simulator was used to obtain the experimental results presented in Section "Experimental Results."

Disk Mapping

Track Capacity. The capacity for the ith track is given in sectors by

$$C_i = C_1 + (i-1)\,\delta S \tag{5}$$

where C_1 is the track capacity (in sectors) of the first track and δS is the difference between any track and the next. We know that the first track has $C_1 = 9$ sectors and the last has $C_n = 20.6$ sectors. Also, for these boundaries, we know that the number of tracks is $n = 22,500$, and therefore $\delta S = 5.155 \times 10^{-4}$ (sectors). Although the CD-ROM track has a spiral pattern, each complete turn might be approximated by a perfect circle, due to the very small pitch between tracks, and the speed of each track might be also considered as constant.

Track Corresponding to a Given Sector. Firstly, we need the total number of sectors, N_s, from track 1 to track n, obtained from Eq. (5), as follows:

$$N_s = (n \times C_1) + \delta S \sum_{i=1}^{n-1} i \tag{6}$$

The track number corresponding to a given sector address is obtained by solving Eq. (6) for $n = N_t$, as follows:

$$N_t = \frac{\delta S - 2C_1 + \sqrt{(2C_1 - \delta S)^2 + 8N_s\,\delta S}}{2\,\delta S} \tag{7}$$

From the above expression it is possible to compute the track number related to a given sector address, which is necessary to evaluate the seek time. The amount of data contained between two given tracks can also be derived. As an example, the volume of data contained on the 10 outermost tracks is approximately 2.3 times greater than the volume of data that can be contained on the 10 innermost tracks of the CD-ROM. The combination of Eq. (5) and Eq. (7) permits to identify any sector of a given track.

Evaluation of Span Coverage. The volume of data, in kilobytes, contained in a span coverage is given by:

$$BW = \frac{C_i + C_j}{2} \times Q \times 2 \tag{8}$$

where Q is the span size, C_i is the track capacity for track i and C_j is the track capacity for track j, both obtained from Eq. (5), where i and j are the track numbers which

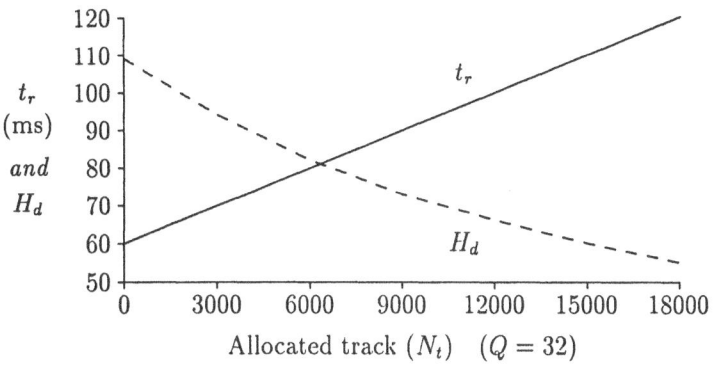

Figure 3. Rotational latency and head displacement as a function of file allocation

bounds a span, that is, $i = a$, the first track of the span with anchor point in track a, and $j = a + Q - 1$, the last track of the same span.

Sector coverage depends not only on the span size, but also on the optical head position over the disk. For inner tracks span coverage is smaller than for outer tracks, as a consequence of differences in track capacity. For a span size $Q = 64$ tracks, the first 64 tracks (inner tracks) are covered from the anchor point allocated in track 1, and the span coverage BW is 1.154 megabytes. The last 64 tracks (outer tracks) are covered from the anchor point allocated in track 22,437. At this location, the span coverage is 2.6346 megabytes. The ratio between these two capacities is 2.3 times. This characteristic demonstrates the importance of file distribution on the disk, since the volume of data covered on the outer tracks is much larger than inner tracks. Conversely, on outer tracks the rotational latency is larger. Thus, the relevant question is: What is the best file placement to minimize access time? In Section "Experimental Results," where real applications are simulated (and so the optimal scheduling algorithm does not apply), it will be shown that the best file placement will depend on the file size and file structure.

Figure 3 shows the number of head displacements H_d needed for retrieve all records of a 12.8 megabytes file (25,600 objects of 512 bytes each), with nonoverlapping spans, as a function of file allocation on disk. In this example, the span size was set to 32 tracks. For comparison purposes, it is also shown the variation of rotational latency as a function of track number.

Access Time Evaluation

The *access time* (t_a) to retrieve an object is given by:

$$t_a = t_s + t_r + t_x \tag{9}$$

where t_s is the *seek time*, t_r is the *rotational latency time*, t_x is the *transfer time* to move data from disk to main memory. We consider that t_s depends on the drive's technology and head displacement, t_r depends on the track radius and t_x depends on the amount of data to be retrieved in each disk access. All the references to data is done on the basis of sector addressing, which can be easily converted from sector number to the format *minute:second:sector*.

If the next track to be accessed is within span boundaries then t_s is computed by considering the displacement of the laser beam at a rate of 1 millisecond per track. This figure is negligible, even when compared with the smallest rotational latency or seek time for tracks allocated outside the span boundaries. If the next track is outside span boundaries, typical values of t_s are between 200 and 600 milliseconds. This time is due to the optical head displacement and its settling in the new position (focusing and tracking adjustments plus rotational stabilization). Seek time for tracks outside span boundaries depends on the distance that must be traveled by the access mechanism. Figure 4 presents typical seek time as function of head displacement magnitude for a reading device with span size of 10 tracks.

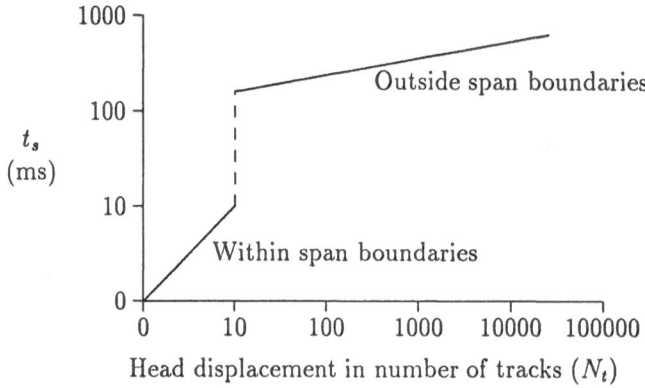

Figure 4. Seek time for a reading device ($Q = 10$)

Computation of rotational latency is done by considering track capacity and the time required to read one sector (which is the same for any track). Thus, $t_r = (C \times b_{tt})/2$, where C is defined by Eq. (5) and b_{tt} is the block transfer time. Typical values of t_r are between 60 and 138 milliseconds.

Transfer time is found by multiplying the number of sectors to be read (block size B) by the block transfer time and so, $t_x = B \times b_{tt}$. Typical transfer rate is 150 Kbytes per second for any position on disk, implying that the time to read one sector is 13.33 milliseconds.

FILE ORGANIZATION AND ACCESS METHODS

In this section, we present a comparative study of data structures and access methods for CD-ROM. The B-tree, sequential, hashing and indexed sequential file organizations are compared considering the restrictions and characteristics of the CD-ROM medium. It is shown that file organizations and algorithms suitable for dynamic applications, usually adequate for traditional magnetic medium, are not necessarily the best choices for read-only disks. We present an indexed sequential organization that minimizes the number of disk accesses, by providing an index structure that enables the reading device to access the maximum number of records within span boundaries.

B-Trees

B-tree structure is very good for dynamic applications, with provision for frequent additions and deletions of records. The expected storage utilization is 69% (Knuth, 1973). Due to the static characteristic of the information stored in CD-ROM media there is no reason to keep empty spaces for future use. Consequently, B-Tree files are not among the best choices for CD-ROM disks.

Sequential Files

If the application accesses data sequentially then the sequential file organization is the most efficient for CD-ROM, both in terms of access time and space utilization. The only existing limitation is the transfer ratio from disk to memory. Some kind of data is always stored and retrieved in sequential form, such as audio and video files.

For small files the sequential organization is also adequate for random access to data. For example, the average access time for a 100 Kbytes file is 330 milliseconds after the access mechanism has been positioned at the beginning of the file.

Hash Files

Hashing file organization is highly efficient since it requires only one disk access for each data retrieval (it requires at most one head displacement and only one rotational latency). Ideally, different keys should map to different addresses, but this is not always possible, and two or more keys may hash to the same address. Such an occurrence, called collision, can be reduced by applying some techniques, such as reducing the storage density, increasing bucket size, and choosing a hash function that evenly spreads all the keys in the available addresses. As a disadvantage, this structure does not allow sequential access to records. When this factor is not important, hashing is the organization method of choice.

Indexed Sequential Files

Indexed sequential files make possible both random and sequential access. The indexed sequential structure is implemented in magnetic disks by keeping a cylinder index in main memory. In this scheme, each data access is done with only one seek, since each cylinder contains a block index with the highest key value on each block in that cylinder index. For dynamic applications this steady state condition can not be kept if a large number of records is added to the file. In the case of CD-ROM, this organization is particularly interesting because of the static nature of the information.

An Efficient Indexed Sequential File for CD-ROM. Indexed sequential structures can be efficiently implemented in CD-ROM, by considering the static nature of the information and the span capabilities of the reading device. The set of tracks covered by a span in a CD-ROM might be compared to the set of tracks belonging to a cylinder in a magnetic disk. We consider each set of tracks bounded by a span as an *optical cylinder*. Two differences between the two media are: the optical cylinders have different capacities (depending on disk position) and a subset of tracks might belong to two or more optical cylinders (span overlapping).

Motivated by this fact and recalling that accessing times depend on disk position we propose an indexed sequential organization for CD-ROM. In this file organization, the reading mechanism will be positioned at pre-selected optical cylinders, avoiding span

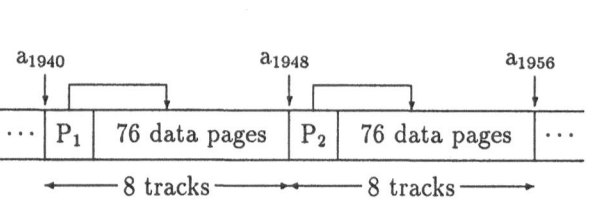

Figure 5. Diagram of the indexed sequential file organization proposed

overlapping. This will be accomplished by designing an index structure so that each index page refer to the largest number of data pages allocated within span boundaries. The diagram in Figure 5 shows this file organization for a 3 megabytes file starting at track number 1940, where each data page is 1 sector long (a span size of 8 tracks starting in track 1940 occupies approximately 78 sectors). To build it we do as follows:

1. Allocate the file on disk by computing initial and final tracks;

2. Compute the total number of optical cylinders needed to cover all file tracks without overlapping, and find their respective anchor points;

3. Build a *Optical Cylinder Index*: It contains the highest key value associated to records stored in the tracks covered by each span (this index should be kept in main memory).

4. Build a *Page Index*: It contains the highest key value associated to records in each data page, comprising the actual span coverage. This page should be stored in the track selected as anchor point, defining an optical cylinder. Due to static characteristic of the information and its regular structure, the explicit addressing might be avoided by computing the address of the next node at lower level from the current node.

Any record is retrieved as follows: given a search key, the corresponding optical cylinder (span) and its anchor point is obtained from the *Optical Cylinder Index*. The reading mechanism is then moved to the selected anchor point (this is the only long seek operation involved). The *Page Index* is then read and the data page containing the given search key is found within the actual span boundaries. This structure were built considering the two conditions for optimal scheduling proposed by Christodoulakis (1987). Here spans of consecutive head displacements do not overlap and the access mechanism is always positioned in an optical cylinder with qualifying objects.

Total access time is given by the sum of the times to find the anchor point, to read the index page and to read the data page, as follows

$$t_a = (t_s + t_r + P_i \times b_{tt}) + (t_r + P_d \times b_{tt}) \tag{10}$$

where P_i is the index page size and P_d is the data page size.

The example shown in Figure 6 illustrates one kind of span overlapping. Let us consider a segment of a file allocated in a disk region where track capacity is 10 sectors and data page and page index are 2 Kbytes (one sector) long. For an index entry of 40 bytes, each page index P_i might refer to $\lfloor 2048/40 \rfloor = 50$ data pages. This corresponds to 50 sectors or 5 tracks in the given conditions. Notice that index pages will always be anchor points and two adjacent anchor points a_i and a_{i+1} will be separated by 5 tracks. If span size is 8 tracks, then we have an overlapping of 3 tracks.

Figure 7 presents a similar problem. If the number of data pages referred to by an index page is larger than the span coverage then there is a chance of having to perform one or more seeks to retrieve a set of records referred to by pointers in the same index page. For a file segment with the same characteristics as the one described in Figure 6 but considering span size $Q = 3$, from an anchor point it is not possible to reach all the objects referred to by the current index page and a new head displacement might be necessary. Moreover, span overlapping also occurs, a worse situation in terms of performance as compared with the example of Figure 6.

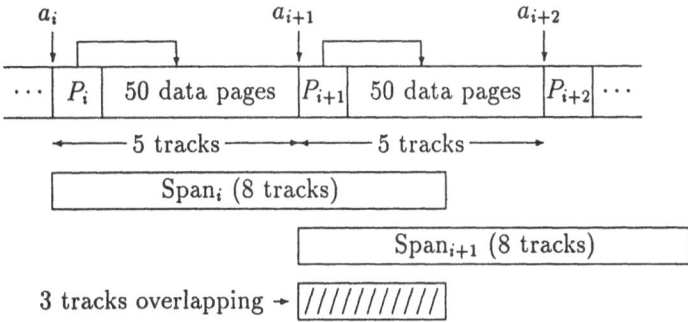

Figure 6. Example of span overlapping in indexed sequential files ($Q = 8$)

The two problems just described can be eliminated by using an page index size so that one page index and all related data pages occupy exactly the number of tracks belonging to the span size Q. This is exactly the indexed sequential structure we have proposed above. In fact, experimental results show that this is the situation when both total access time t_a and number of head displacements H_d present best results. The worst result is obtained when the number of data pages referred to by an index page is larger than the span coverage, as illustrated by Figure 7.

Christodoulakis (1989) has proposed a modified B-Tree structure, named BIM-Tree (Balanced Implicit Multiway Tree). This structure is a perfect balanced m-ary tree, similar to a modified B-Tree in which nodes are completely full. This structure is also similar to the indexed sequential structure proposed above. The main difference is that our algorithm distributes data into pages in a way to fully exploit the span access capability of the optical reading device avoiding span overlapping to obtain reduction of head displacements.

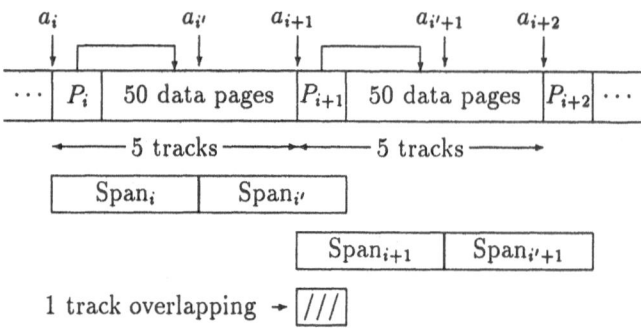

Figure 7. Example of another kind of span overlapping in indexed sequential files ($Q = 3$)

EXPERIMENTAL RESULTS

The CD-ROM simulator based on the deterministic model described in Section "File Mapping and Access Time Evaluation" was used to simulate several files with different structures and sizes. The simulator is informed about file size, block (or page) size, file location, index page size (if applicable), record size, reading device parameters and the number of search keys. It outputs the file mapping, access times for simulated queries and some statistics, such as average, best and worst cases. It also enables the user to perform variations on data file structure and reading device parameters (within boundaries), so that it is possible to examine the influence of these changes on retrieval performance for a given file, using a particular reading device.

The simulator considers actual time characteristics for t_s, as found in actual CD-ROM drives, according to the plot shown in Figure 4. The objects for retrieval may be selected according to the optimal scheduling algorithm (Christodoulakis, 1987) or to a random scheduling algorithm. In a random scheduling each object to be retrieved is selected from a random key generator, each key being converted into sector and track number, depending on the file structure.

Table 2 presents analytical and experimental results for the optimal scheduling algorithm, related to a file with 45,000 sectors (90 megabytes), occupying the 4,500 inner tracks with average track capacity of 10 sectors per track and span size $Q = 10$. This is the same example used in Section "An Extended Analytical Model for CD-ROM" (see Table 1), extracted from Christodoulakis (1988, pp. 293–294), but considering an average track capacity of 10 sectors per track (instead of 9 sectors per track considered by Christodoulakis, which is the capacity of the first track of the file). Obviously, the number of head displacements (H_d) for the optimal scheduling algorithm is smaller than any other algorithm. We can see from Table 2 that for large numbers of objects to be retrieved (n), the number of head displacements for random scheduling increases considerably, mainly due to span overlapping. The simulation results are obtained within 95% confidence interval.

The experimental results presented in the next subsections were obtained using actual CD-ROM drives parameters and random scheduling. Some general conclusions

Table 2. Analytical and experimental results for head displacements (H_d)

n	H_d		
	Optimal Scheduling		Random Scheduling
	Analytical	Experimental	Experimental
100	83	83 ±0.050	100 ±0
500	244	244 ±0.045	499 ±0
1000	322	320 ±0.050	997 ±0
2000	383	380 ±0.050	1996 ±0
3000	408	405 ±0.048	2993 ±0
4000	422	417 ±0.050	3992 ±0
5000	430	426 ±0.038	4985 ±0

for randomly and directly accessed files that maybe derived from this data are:

- Files up to 800 Kbytes can be completely contained within the typical span size of 60 tracks, and so require no head displacements. In that case, retrieval costs will be smaller if the file is allocated on inner tracks, were rotational latency is smaller.

- Very large files (250 megabytes or more) are weakly affected by disk location. Such large files fills up to nearly 50% of the disk, and the number of head displacements needed to retrieve a given number of objects is practically the same in any disk position. Also, average rotational latency is not considerably different for large files when allocated on outer or inner tracks.

- Intermediate sized files (1 to 3 megabytes) present better performance when allocated on outer tracks. Such files, when allocated on inner tracks, overflows the boundaries of span coverage leading to head displacements; when allocated on outer tracks, the files are completely contained within span coverage, leading to no head displacements at all.

In the next subsections we present simulation results for sequential, hashing and indexed sequential files ranging in size from 0.1 to 204.8 megabytes, allocated from the first track to the last one, using different sizes for data and index blocks. During simulations we also considered the influence of different drive parameters, including the span size. Simulation results were presented in terms of best, worst and expected access time and the number of head displacements, as a function of track position and span size. Each result represents the average over 1,000 retrievals. More details can be found in Barbosa (1990).

Sequential Files

The plot in Figure 8 presents simulation results for a 160 Kbytes sequential file with span size $Q = 64$. Some observations are:

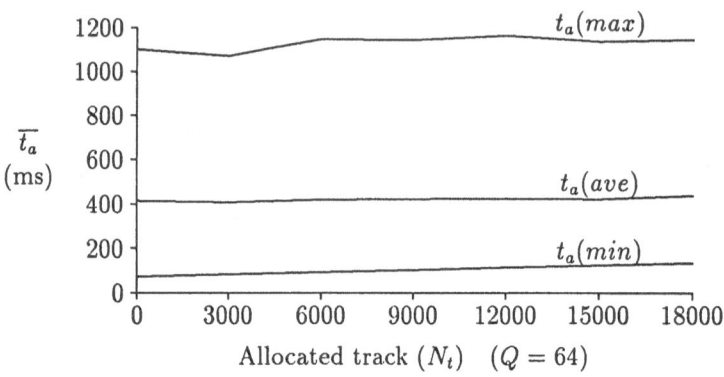

Figure 8. Access time for a sequential file 160 Kbytes large

(a) For minimum access ($t_a(min)$) times there are no head displacements or sequential readings because only the first record of the file is read (only rotational latency and transfer time are involved). In this case, the times are directly proportional to the file position on disk (in Figure 8, for track 1, $t_a = 73$ ms; for track 18,000, $t_a = 135$ ms).

(b) Maximum access times are not affected by file position, because this figure depends only on the time for sequential reading of the file and this time is constant for any position on disk, since the transfer rate is the same for any track. Similarly, expected access times are not affected by file position on disk.

Consequently, sequential file structures are not affected by file position on disk.

Hash Files

The plots in Figures 9, 10 and 11 present simulation results for hash files. Some observations are:

(a) Hash files present the smallest average access times when compared to sequential and indexed sequential, since any object is retrieved with only one disk access and one rotational latency.

(b) The plot in Figure 9 shows that for very small files the best allocation is on inner tracks. Since there is no head displacements for that file size, for the same reasons described in Section "Sequential Files", access times are directly proportional to file position on disk.

(c) The plot in Figure 10 shows results for a representative of intermediate sized files, in the range of 1 to 3 megabytes. It can be seen that they present better performance when allocated on outer tracks, for the reasons presented in Section "Experimental Results". The plot in Figure 11 shows that very large files are weakly affected by file position on disk (variation less than 10%).

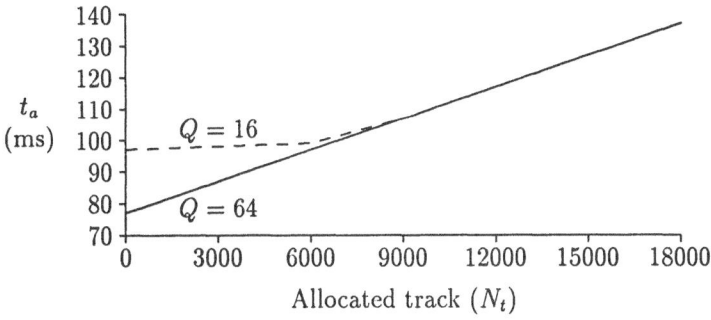

Figure 9. Access time for a 0.2 Mbytes hash file

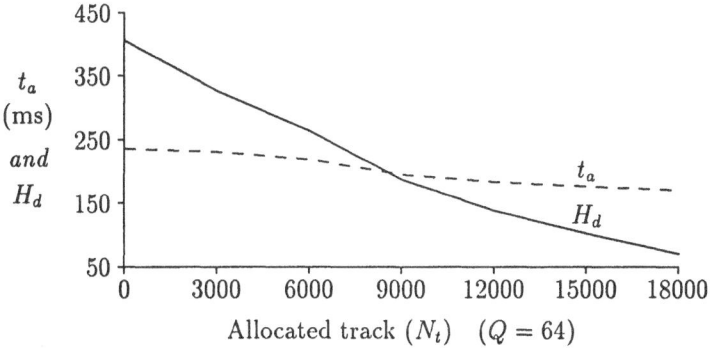

Figure 10. Head displacements and access time for a 1.6 Mbytes hash file

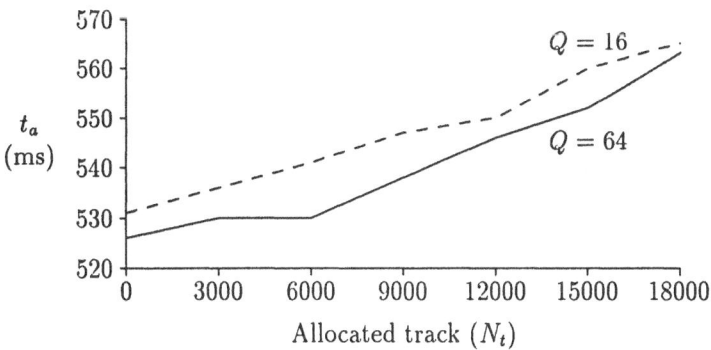

Figure 11. Access time for a 102.4 Mbytes hash file

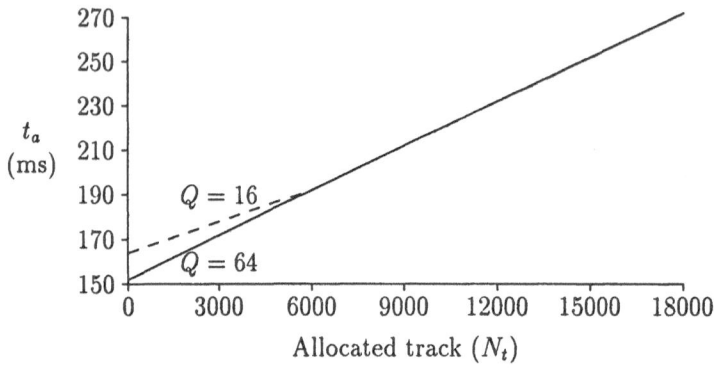

Figure 12. Access time for a 0.2 Mbytes indexed sequential file

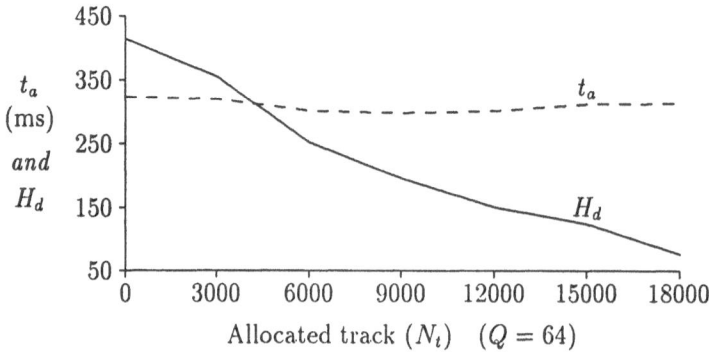

Figure 13. Head displacements and access time for a 1.6 Mbytes indexed sequential file

Indexed Sequential Files

Figures 12, 13, 14, 15 and 16 show simulation results for indexed sequential files. It can be seen the effects of file size, file allocation, and span size on the retrieval performance. Analysis of these results show that:

(a) The plot in Figure 12 shows that for very small files the best allocation position is on inner tracks.

(b) The plot in Figure 13 shows that for intermediate file sizes the number of head displacements decreases as the file is allocated on outer tracks and the smallest access times are obtained when the file is allocated on intermediary tracks. This is because indexed sequential files require at least two rotational latencies, one to retrieve the index page and one to retrieve the data page.

(c) The plot in Figure 14 clearly shows that the best file allocation is on inner tracks. The plot in Figure 15 shows that very large files are weakly affected by file position on disk and also by variations in span size.

(d) The plot in Figure 16 shows that the larger is the span size the least is the influence in retrieval costs.

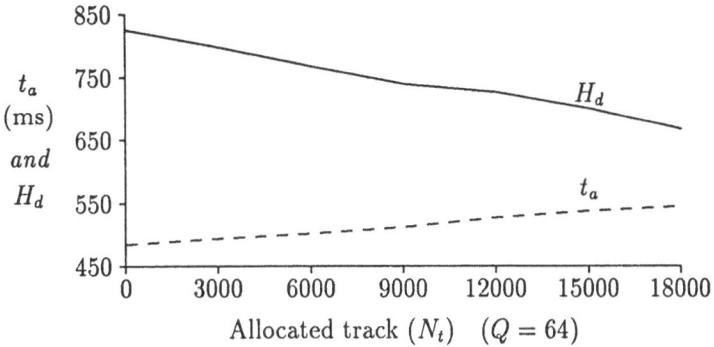

Figure 14. Head displacements and access time for a 6.5 Mbytes indexed sequential file

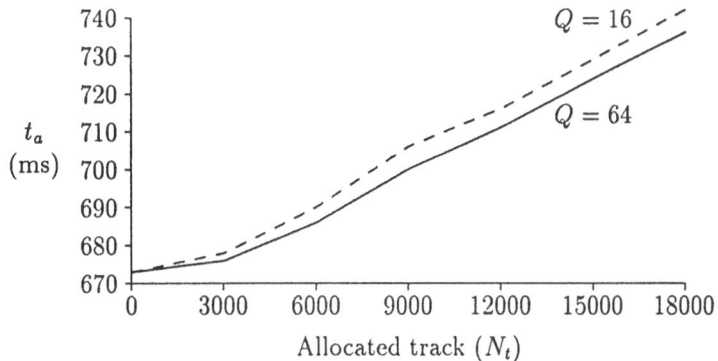

Figure 15. Access time for a 204.8 Mbytes indexed sequential file

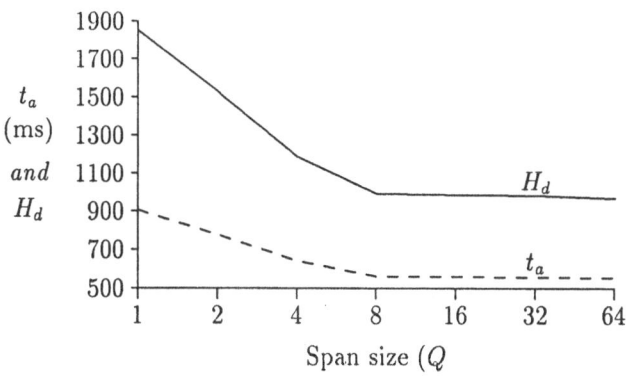

Figure 16. Head displacements and access time for a 26 Mbytes indexed sequential file

SIMULTANEOUS PLACEMENT OF FILES

An interesting optimization problem is the simultaneous placement of files with different sizes and structures. Some files performances are strongly affected by disk position while others are position independent. The problem is to find an optimal placement for all files which minimizes overall retrieval costs.

We propose the following heuristic: Given n files to be allocated on m available tracks ($n \ll m$), for each file we determine the difference between maximum and minimum costs. This difference can be obtained from simulation by varying the file position from the first to the last track. Next, we sort the files by decreasing order of the difference between maximum and minimum costs and allocate them in this order.

This criteria is based on the fact that files with larger differences between maximum and minimum costs will affect more intensily the total retrieval cost and, therefore, they should be the first to be allocated on disk. Consequently, the last files to be allocated will be those with smaller differences in cost for any track. In other words, after having allocated the most critical files, the remaining disk space should be used to allocate files that are weakly affected by disk position, such as sequential files.

CONCLUSIONS

This paper emphasizes the main influence of CD-ROM features in design strategies for organizing and placing files using this technology. We discuss the analytical model proposed by Christodoulakis (1987) and show the importance of rotational latency in considering the computation of retrieval costs. We also show that file size, file structure and file placement on disk have decisive influence on retrieval performance in CD-ROM. A deterministic model was developed from parameters of commercially available CD-ROM drives. This model allows file mapping and the exact computation of access time for various retrieval conditions imposed to the reading device. This enables us to perform a comparative study of B-Tree, sequential, hash and indexed sequential files. Considering specific features and limitations of CD-ROM environment, we concluded that indexed sequential and hash are the best organization choices for register structured files. We present an indexed sequential organization for CD-ROM file systems which minimizes disk accesses. Experimental results obtained from simulation confirm the extended model presented in this paper, leading to basic designing rules on CLV read-only optical disks.

ACKNOWLEDGMENTS

The authors wish to acknowledge the many fruitful discussions with Márcio L. B. de Carvalho. Financial support from the Brazilian CNPq - Conselho Nacional de Desenvolvimento Científico e Tecnológico and IBM do Brasil are also gratefully acknowledged.

REFERENCES

Barbosa, E. F. (1990) "Estruturas de Dados e Alocação de Arquivos em Discos CD-ROM", *Master Thesis*, Departamento de Ciência da Computação, Universidade Federal de Minas Gerais, Brazil.

Barbosa, E. F. and Ziviani, N. (1991) "Estruturas de Dados e Métodos de Acesso para Discos Óticos de Apenas-Leitura", *VI Simpósio Brasileiro de Bancos de Dados*, Manaus, Brazil, 39–58.

Christodoulakis, S. (1987) "Analysis of Retrieval Performance for Records and Objects Using Optical Disk Technology", *ACM Transaction on Database Systems 12* (2), 137–169.

Christodoulakis, S. and Ford, D. A. (1988) "Performance Analysis and Fundamental Performance Trade Offs for CLV Optical Disks", *Proceedings of ACM SIGMOD*, 286–294.

Christodoulakis, S. and Ford, D. A. (1989) "File Organizations and Access Methods for CLV Optical Discs", *ACM SIGIR Forum 23* (1 & 2), 152–159.

Knuth, D.E. (1973) *The Art of Computer Programming; Volume 3: Sorting and Searching.* Addison-Wesley.

Lambert, S. (1986) CD-ROM *The New Papyrus*, Microsoft Press.

Laub, L. (1986) "The Evolution of Mass Storage", *Byte 11* (5), 161–172.

Ropiequet, S. (1987) CD-ROM *Optical Publishing*, Microsoft Press.

Shermann, C. (1989) *The* CD-ROM *Handbook*, McGraw-Hill.

Ziemer, S. M. (1988) "Design Considerations for CD-ROM Retrieval Software", *Journal of The American Society for Information Science 39* (1), 43–46.

Zoellick, B. (1986) "CD-ROM Software Development", *Byte 11* (5), 177–188.

MIXED-RADIX HUFFMAN CODES

Ke-Chiang Chu

John Gill

Advanced Technology Group
Apple Computer, Inc.
20450 Stevens Creek Blvd.
Cupertino, CA 95014

Electrical Engineering Department
115 Durand Building
Stanford University
Stanford, CA 94305

ABSTRACT

A mixed-radix code tree is a tree in which the degree of an internal node may depend on the level of the node. The problem of finding mixed-radix trees with minimum weighted path length is reduced to the construction of optimal alphabetic mixed-radix trees. A dynamic programming algorithm is described whose running time is $O(n^4 \log n)$ and storage requirements are $O(n^3 \log n)$.

1. INTRODUCTION

The main result of this paper is an algorithm for the construction of mixed-radix Huffman codes—optimal variable length prefix codes in which the size of the symbol alphabet may depend on the position within the codeword. Mixed-radix prefix codes are equivalent to mixed-radix trees, where the degrees of internal nodes are functions of the node levels. For a given source probability distribution $\{p_1, p_2, \ldots, p_n\}$, a mixed-radix Huffman code is a code with minimum expected codeword length, and the corresponding mixed-radix tree has mininum weighted path length.

Mixed-radix trees can arise as search trees that occupy several levels in a storage hierarchy. Nodes near the root of the tree, which reside in primary storage, should have small degree. Nodes at a greater depth are located in secondary storage and should therefore have a large degree. Since the cost of accessing the storage block containing a node dominates the time to process the pointers within the node, the node should occupy the entire block. For example, an internal node stored in a 512-byte disk block might contain 128 four-byte pointers to descendant nodes.

Another motivation for mixed-radix codes comes from information theory. Suppose that a single symbol from a large alphabet with probability distribution $\{p_1, p_2, \ldots, p_n\}$ is to be transmitted over a binary communications channel. Further suppose that the symbols can be partitioned into t subsets and that a side channel can be used to send a single number from the set $\{1, 2, \ldots, t\}$ that specifies the subset that contains the symbol to be transmitted. For a given t, how do we choose the partition and the variable-length binary encoding of the symbols within each component of the partition to minimize the communication cost? This is exactly the problem of constructing an optimal mixed-radix code for the radix sequence $\{t, 2, 2, \ldots\}$.

This problem has a simple solution. Use the binary Huffman algorithm (Huffman, 1952) but terminate as soon as the original n symbols have been reduced by pairwise combining to t nodes. The resulting mixed-radix code tree is optimal; it consists of a root of degree t whose subtrees are the t binary trees formed by the incomplete Huffman procedure.

Unfortunately, this simple procedure does not appear to generalize. For example, for the radix sequence $\{t_1, t_2, 2, 2, \ldots\}$, an optimal code tree need not be full at the second level; some of the first level nodes may be terminal. The number of possible level occupation distributions increases rapidly as the radix sequence becomes more complex, and a polynomial time algorithm based on the bottom-up Huffman approach is not apparent.

Instead we use an equivalence between Huffman codes and optimal alphabetic codes to obtain a polynomial time dynamic programming algorithm for constructing optimal mixed-radix codes. We generalize the method of Gilbert and Moore (1959) for finding optimal (minimal weighted path length) alphabetic codes. The original Gilbert and Moore algorithm has running time $O(n^3)$. Knuth (1971) presented a more efficient dynamic programming algorithm for binary alphabetic tree construction, using a monotonicity property, which reduced the running time to $O(n^2)$. Hu and Tucker (1971) discovered a remarkable "bottom-up" algorithm for constructing optimal alphabetic code trees. Their rather complex algorithm can be implemented to run in time $O(n \log n)$. Note that all three algorithms were for binary alphabetic trees. Generalizations to nonbinary code trees and search trees were made by Itai (1976) and Gotlieb (1981).

In Section 2, we define mixed-radix trees and show how the problem of finding optimal mixed-radix trees can be reduced to the problem of finding optimal *alphabetic* mixed-radix trees. In Section 3, we define joint addition chains and cite a useful upper bound on the length of joint addition chains. Finally in Section 4, we develop an algorithm for constructing optimal alphabetic mixed-radix trees as an extension of the methods for contructing optimal binary and t-ary alphabetic code trees.

2. MIXED-RADIX TREES

Definition: A *tree* is a nonempty set of nodes with a designated node called the *root* such that the remaining nodes can be partitioned into $n \geq 0$ disjoints sets $T_1, \ldots, T_n$, where each of these sets is itself a tree. $T_1, \ldots, T_n$ are called the *subtrees* of the root.

Definition: Let $t_1, t_2, \ldots$ be a sequence of integers such that $t_i \geq 2$ for every i. A tree is a *mixed-radix tree* with radix sequence $\{t_1, t_2, \ldots\}$ if the degree of every internal node at level i is at most t_i.

We refer to trees in which the degrees of internal nodes are functions of the node level as mixed-radix trees because each node in such a tree corresponds to a fraction in the unit interval expressed in mixed-radix notation. Using this correspondence, a reasonable notion of mixed-radix entropy can be defined, and many of the expected results from information theory hold. For example, it can be shown that the expected codeword length L for an optimal code satisfies $H_T \leq L < H_T + 1$, where H_T is the entropy of the symbol probability distribution $\{p_1, p_2, \ldots, p_n\}$ in terms of the radix sequence $T = \{t_1, t_2, \ldots\}$.

In the rest of this paper we assume a source alphabet $\{A_1, \ldots, A_n\}$ of n symbols with a probability distribution $\{p_1, \ldots, p_n\}$. Since the actual symbols are irrelevant in determining expected codeword length, we will identify the symbol with its probability. For example, we say that L_i is the length of the codeword for probability p_i rather than the length of the codeword corresponding to the source alphabet symbol A_i.

Definition: A tree is *alphabetic* if the source alphabet symbols $\{A_1, \ldots, A_n\}$ are assigned to the terminal nodes of the tree in left-to-right order.

The following well-known lemma was first pointed out to us by Eugene Lawler (1970).

Lemma 1 *If the weights of the source symbols are in nonincreasing order, then any optimal alphabetic code tree has the same set of path lengths as some Huffman code tree and is therefore optimal.*

Proof: For any Huffman code tree, if $p_i > p_j$ then $L_i \leq L_j$, where L_i and L_j are respectively the lengths of the codewords assigned to p_i and p_j. If instead $p_i > p_j$ and $L_i > L_j$, then by exchanging the codewords assigned to p_i and p_j, we would reduce the expected codeword length, contradicting the assumed optimality of the original code.

Next note that for any code tree, reordering the subtrees at any level does not change the path length of any terminal node. Therefore such a reordering does not change the expected path length and so does not affect the optimality of the code tree.

Now start with any Huffman code tree for the probabilities $p_1 \geq p_2 \geq \cdots \geq p_n$. We can ensure that $L_1 \leq L_2 \leq \cdots \leq L_n$ by reassigning codewords corresponding to symbols of equal probabilities when necessary. Then assign codewords of lengths $L_1, L_2, \ldots, L_n$ in lexicographically increasing order. This alphabetic code tree has the same codeword lengths as the original Huffman code and is therefore also an optimal code tree.

3. ADDITION CHAINS

Itai's method for constructing optimal multi-way search trees uses addition chains to achieve polynomial run time and storage requirements. Similarly, we will use some basic properties of *joint* addition chains to efficiently generate optimal mixed-radix alphabetic code trees. The definitions of addition chains and joint addition chains are taken from Knuth (1969, pp. 402–418).

Definition: An *addition chain* for n is a sequence of integers $a_0, a_1, \ldots, a_r$ with the properties that

1. $a_0 = 1$.

2. $a_r = n$.

3. $a_i = a_j + a_k$, where $0 \leq k \leq j < i$ for all $i = 1, 2, \ldots, r$.

Without loss of generality, we can assume that an addition chain is in increasing order, that is, $1 = a_0 < a_1 < \cdots < a_r = n$. Any addition chain can be replaced by one that satisfies the above requirement by rearranging the sequence into ascending order, then removing repeated terms and terms larger than n. Addition chains satisfying the above conditions are called "ascending" chains. Only ascending chains will be considered in the remainder of this paper.

In general there are many addition chains for n. We let $l(n)$ denote the length of the shortest addition chain for n. Since the algorithms that we describe in the next section do not require optimal addition chains, we use a simple algorithm for constructing nearly optimal addition chains.

This algorithm is the familiar "binary method" for evaluation of powers (Knuth, 1969, p. 399). Write n in the binary number representation with leading zeros suppressed and the leading one bit omitted. Replace each 0 by the letter D and each 1 by the letters DI. The result is a rule for computing the elements of an addition chain for n, where D is interpreted as the operation "double" and I is interpreted as the operation "increment." For example, for $n = 25$, the binary representation is 11001; so we form the sequence $DIDDDI$. This rule states that we should "double, increment, double, double, double, and increment." In other words, starting with $a_0 = 1$, we should successively compute the rest of addition the chain as $2, 3, 6, 12, 24, 25$.

For this method, the largest value of r is $2\lfloor \log_2 n \rfloor$, which occurs when all bits of n are 1. The following lemma gives an upper bound on $l(n)$ for any integer n.

Lemma 2 *The length $l(n)$ of the shortest addition chain for any integer n satisfies*

$$l(n) \leq \lfloor \log_2 n \rfloor + \nu(n) - 1 \,,$$

where $\nu(n)$ is the number of 1's in the binary representation of n.

Note that $\lfloor \log_2 n \rfloor + \nu(n) - 1$ is not in general the optimal value of $l(n)$. For example, the addition chain $1, 2, 3, 6, 12, 15$ shows that $l(15) \leq 5 < 6 = \lfloor \log_2 15 \rfloor + \nu(5) - 1$.

Definition: A *joint addition chain* for s and t is a sequence of integers $a_0, a_1, \ldots, a_r$ with the properties that

1. $a_0 = 1$.

2. $a_i = a_j + a_k$ for all $i \leq r$, where $0 \leq k \leq j < i$.

3. $s = a_{j_s}$ for some $j_s \leq r$.

4. $t = a_{j_t}$ for some $j_t \leq r$.

If $l(s,t)$ denotes the length of the shortest joint addition chain for s and t, then the minimum joint addition chain length has the following obvious properties.

1. $l(s,t) \geq l(s)$ and $l(s,t) \geq l(t)$.

2. $l(s,t) \leq l(s) + l(t)$.

3. $l(s,t) \leq 2 \cdot \max(l(s), l(t))$.

This concept can be extended to joint addition chains for m numbers in the obvious way. If $l(t_1, t_2, \ldots, t_m)$ denotes the length of the shortest joint addition chain for $t_1, t_2, \ldots, t_m$, then

1. $l(t_1, t_2, \ldots, t_m) \geq l(t_s)$ for all $s \leq m$.

2. $l(t_1, t_2, \ldots, t_m) \leq \sum l(t_s)$.

3. $l(t_1, t_2, \ldots, t_m) \leq m \cdot \max(l(t_1), l(t_2), \ldots, l(t_m))$.

Knuth (1969) gives the following upper bound for $l(t_1, t_2, \ldots, t_m)$.

Lemma 3 *Let* $\lambda(n) = \lfloor \log_2 n \rfloor$. *Then* $l(t_1, t_2, \ldots, t_m)$, *the length of the shortest joint addition chain for* $t_1 < t_2 < \cdots < t_m$, *satisfies*

$$l(t_1, t_2, \ldots, t_m) \leq \lambda(t_m) + m\lambda(t_m)/\lambda(\lambda(t_m)) + O(\lambda(t_m)\lambda(\lambda(\lambda(t_m)))/(\lambda(\lambda(t_m)))^2).$$

In the next section we use joint addition chains to generate optimal mixed-radix alphabetic code trees.

4. CONSTRUCTION OF OPTIMAL MIXED-RADIX CODES

In this section we present a dynamic programming algorithm using joint addition chains to construct optimal mixed-radix alphabetic code trees. By Lemma 1, this algorithm therefore constructs mixed-radix Huffman codes. First we review methods for binary and t-ary alphabetic trees.

4.1. Binary Trees

The binary case was first solved by Gilbert and Moore (1959). Their fundamental principle is that all subtrees of an optimal tree are optimal. This principle suggests a computation procedure that systematically looks for larger and larger optimal subtrees.

For $1 \leq i \leq j \leq n$ let $c(i,j)$ be the cost of an optimal alphabetic subtree for the weights $p_i, \ldots, p_j$, and let $w(i,j) = p_i + \cdots + p_j$ be the sum of those weights. Obviously $c(i,i) = 0$ for each i. If $i \leq k < j$ then the minimal cost of a tree for the probabilities $p_i, \ldots, p_j$ that has $k - i + 1$ nodes in the left subtree is

$$w(i,j) + c(i,k) + c(k+1,j).$$

So the best tree for $\{p_i, \ldots, p_j\}$ is found by picking the best value of k:

$$c(i,j) = w(i,j) + \min_{i \leq k < j} (c(i,k) + c(k+1,j)). \tag{1}$$

When $i < j$, we want to find a value of k for which the minimum is achieved, which specifies the root of an optimal subtree. Note that from (1) the optimal cost $c(i,j)$ is determined by $c(i,k)$ and $c(k+1,j)$, where $k - i < j - i$ and $j - (k+1) < j - i$. Using the above relationship, we can evaluate $c(i,j)$, $w(i,j)$, and the corresponding k for which the minimum is achieved, for $j - i = 1, 2, \ldots, n$ and, for each value of $j - i$, for $i = 1, 2, \ldots, n - (j - i)$. The results are stored in a two-dimensional table, which requires space $O(n^2)$.

Once the table has been constructed, we can build the optimal tree. We proceed top-down from the root of the tree. From the entry for $(i,j) = (1,n)$, we find the value $k = k_1$ that specifies the root of the optimal tree; the left subtree consists of the probabilities $\{p_1, \ldots, p_{k_1}\}$. Then at level 2, we find the optimal k for the left subtree in the entry for $(i,j) = (1, k_1)$ and for the right subtree in the entry $(i,j) = (k_1+1, n)$. This process continues recursively until we reach subtrees containing only two probabilities $(j - i = 1)$. Note that the computational effort to build the optimal tree is small compared to the cost of preparing the table.

There are approximately $n^2/2$ entries in the completed table, and the minimization operation is carried out for roughly $n^3/6$ values of k. Therefore an optimal alphabetic tree can be constructed in time $O(n^3)$ and memory $O(n^2)$. (Improved algorithms by Knuth (1971) and Hu and Tucker (1971) have running times $O(n^2)$ and $O(n \log n)$, respectively. We do not consider these algorithms in this paper because they do not generalize to the mixed-radix case.)

4.2. t-ary Trees

Next we consider the construction of optimal t-ary alphabetic code trees. The straightforward extension of the Gilbert-Moore procedure is the following. An optimal subtree for the probabilities $\{p_i, \ldots, p_j\}$ is obtained by the minimization

$$c(i,j) = w(i,j) + \min_{i \le k_1 < \cdots < k_{t-1} < j} (c(i, k_1) + c(k_1 + 1, k_2) + \cdots + c(k_{t-1} + 1, j)),$$

where the costs $c(i, k_1), \ldots, c(k_{t-1} + 1, j)$ have been earlier computed and stored in a table. The storage requirement for this method is still $O(n^2)$, but the running time is $O(n^{t+2})$ because of the minimization over $(t-1)$-tuples $(k_1, \ldots, k_{t-1})$. This running time is excessive for even moderate values of t.

A much faster method is obtained by using larger tables whose entries contain $O(\log t)$ values. The key idea, due to Itai (1976), is to determine optimal *groups* of t-ary alphabetic subtrees for contiguous ranges of the input probabilities.

Definition: An *s-group* of t-ary alphabetic trees for the probabilities $\{p_i, \ldots, p_j\}$ is a set of s trees whose leaves partition the probabilities into s contiguous subsets.

For example, one 3-group of 3-ary trees for the probabilities $\{p_1, \ldots, p_7\}$ consists of trees whose leaves are $\{p_1, p_2\}$, $\{p_3, p_4, p_5\}$, and $\{p_6, p_7\}$. Note that a t-ary tree can be thought of as a 1-group or it can be identified with the t-group consisting of the t subtrees of the root. The following obvious lemma justifies the dynamic programming method below.

Lemma 4 *In any optimal t-ary alphabetic code tree, every s-group is optimal.*

For any $s \leq t$, define $c(i, j, s)$ to be the cost of an optimal s-group of t-ary alphabetic subtrees for the probabilities $p_i, \ldots, p_j$. As above, let $w(i, j) = p_i + \cdots + p_j$.

Clearly $c(i, i, 1) = 0$ for every i. Using the dynamic programming principle, for any s such that $0 < s < t$,

$$c(i, j, t) = \min_{1 \leq h < j} \left(c(i, h, s) + c(h+1, j, t-s) \right), \tag{2}$$

and

$$c(i, j, 1) = c(i, j, t) + w(i, j). \tag{3}$$

Equation (2) states that any optimal t-group of t-ary subtrees can be divided into two groups of subtrees, one group with s subtrees, the other group with $t - s$ subtrees. Any group of subtrees of an optimal tree must be optimal, so for an optimal $c(i, j, t)$, both $c(i, h, s)$ and $c(h+1, j, t-s)$ must be optimal. Equation (3) expresses the optimal cost $c(i, j) = c(i, j, 1)$ of a t-ary tree for the probabilities $p_i, \ldots, p_j$ in terms of the cost of an optimal t-group of subtrees.

If both $c(i, h, s)$ and $c(h+1, j, t-s)$ have been previously computed and stored in the tables for groups of s and $t - s$ optimal subtrees, then $c(i, j, t)$ can be calculated easily, as in the binary case. But the computation for $c(i, h, s)$ will in turn require table entries of the form $c(i, h', s')$ with $i \leq h' < h$ and $0 < s' < s$. By choosing a reasonable number of table entries to compute, we arrive at an efficient procedure.

Let $1 = a_0, a_1, \ldots, a_r = t$ be an addition chain for t. By (2), if $0 < s \leq r$ then

$$c(i, j, a_s) = \min_{i \leq h < j} \left(c(i, h, a_p) + c(h+1, j, a_q) \right), \tag{4}$$

where $a_s = a_p + a_q$ and h is number of nodes in the left group of a_p subtrees. For $s = 0$

$$c(i, j, 1) = c(i, j, t) + w(i, j). \tag{5}$$

The meaning of (4) is simply that an optimum group of a_s t-ary can be partitioned into two groups, one with a_p subtrees, the other with a_q subtrees, and both subgroups must be optimal. That is, in order to achieve the minimal cost $c(i, j, a_s)$, both $c(i, h, a_p)$ and $c(h+1, j, a_q)$ must be minimal. If both $c(i, h, a_p)$ and $c(h+1, j, a_q)$ have already been computed, then $c(i, j, a_s)$ can be calculated by the one-parameter minimization shown in (4).

Note that from (4) the optimal value of $c(i, j, a_s)$ depends on the optimal values $c(i, h, a_p)$ and $c(h+1, j, a_q)$, where $h - i < j - i$, $j - (h+1) < j - i$, $a_p < a_s$, and $a_q < a_s$. Using this fact, we can evaluate $c(i, j, a_s)$, $w(i, j)$, and the corresponding h for which the minimum is achieved in the following order: for $j - i = 1, 2, \ldots, n$; for each value of $j - i$, for $i = 1, 2, \ldots, n - (j - i)$; and for $s = 1, \ldots, r, 0$. The results, $c(i, j, a_s), w(i, j), a_p, h$, are stored in a three-dimensional table, as shown in Figure 1.

Once the table has been constructed, we can build the optimal t-ary tree. We start at the root of the tree. For the entry for $i = 1$, $j = n$, $s = r$, we find the optimal values $h = h_1$, $p = p_1$ to divide n nodes into two groups of t-ary subtrees, one with a_{p_1} subtrees, the other with $t - a_{p_1} = a_{q_1}$ subtrees. Next, in the entries for $i = 1, j = h_1, s = p_1$, and $i = h_1 + 1, j = n, s = q_1$, we can find the points for dividing n nodes into subgroups of optimal t-ary subtrees, where $a_{p_1} + a_{q_1} = t$. This process continues until $p_{x1} = 1$

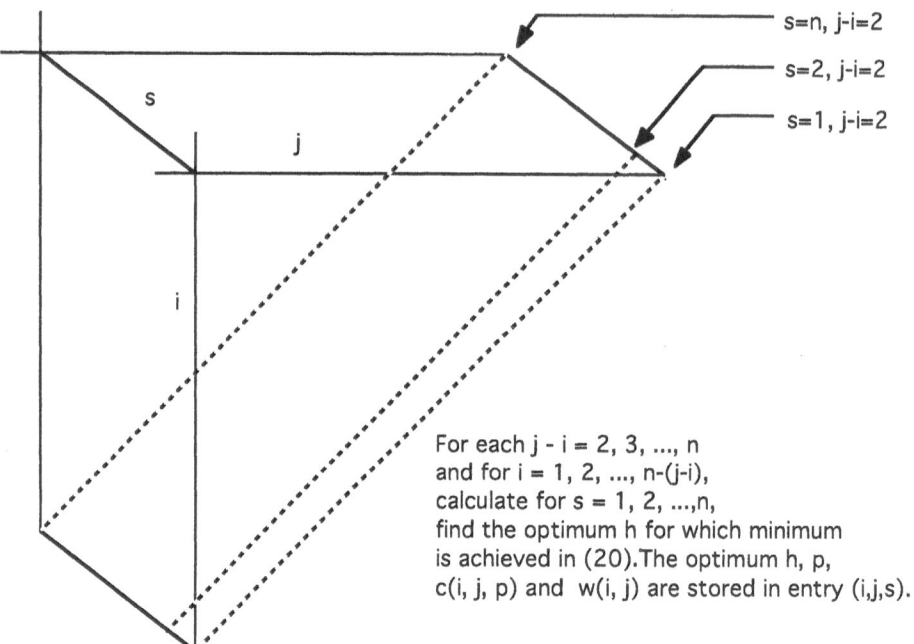

For each j - i = 2, 3, ..., n
and for i = 1, 2, ..., n-(j-i),
calculate for s = 1, 2, ...,n,
find the optimum h for which minimum
is achieved in (20).The optimum h, p,
c(i, j, p) and w(i, j) are stored in entry (i,j,s).

Figure 1. Three-dimensional table for t-ary alphabetic tree construction.

and $q_{y1} = 1$, which indicates that n terminal nodes have been divided into t groups of optimal t-ary subtrees.

At the next level, the tree construction operation is identical to that of the first level, except that we deal with subsets of the original n nodes. The tree construction process is completed when all subtrees reach the bottom of the tree ($j - i < t$).

The overall computation time is $O(r \cdot n^3)$, and the space required is $O(r \cdot n^2)$, where r is the length of the addition chain for t. As noted in the last section, we can choose r so that $r \leq \lambda(t) + \nu(t) - 1 \leq 2\lfloor \log_2 t \rfloor$. Therefore the space requirement is $O(\log_2 t \cdot n^2)$, and the computation time is $O(\log_2 t \cdot n^3)$. Since the optimal code construction problem is trivial when $t \geq n$, we can assume that $t \leq n$, which results in space and time bounds $O(n^2 \log n)$ and $O(n^3 \log n)$, respectively.

4.3. Mixed-Radix Trees

The procedure for constructing optimal mixed-radix alphabetic codes is similar to that for t-ary alphabetic codes. The procedure described in this section is a straightforward extension of the method of Itai (1976).

First we observe that for any tree with out-degree sequence $\mathcal{T}_1 = \{t_1, t_2, \ldots\}$, any subtree whose root is at level ℓ has out-degree sequence $\mathcal{T}_\ell = \{t_\ell, t_{\ell+1}, \ldots\}$. Our goal is to construct an optimal code tree with out-degree sequence $\mathcal{T}_1$, and this will be accomplished by combining optimal subtrees with out-degree sequences $\mathcal{T}_\ell$ for decreasing values of $\ell = n, n - 1, \ldots, 2$.

Let $c(i, j, s, \mathcal{T}_{\ell+1})$ be the cost of an optimal group s subtrees, each with out-degree $\mathcal{T}_{\ell+1}$, for the probabilities $p_i, \ldots, p_j$. Using the dynamic programming principle, if $i < j$

and $0 < s < t_\ell$, and $\ell \geq 1$, then

$$c(i, j, t_\ell, T_{\ell+1}) = \min_{i \leq h < j} \left(c(i, h, s, T_{\ell+1}) + c(h+1, j, t_\ell - s, T_{\ell+1}) \right), \qquad (6)$$

This equation is similar to that of the t-ary case. We divide t_ℓ subtrees with out-degree $T_{\ell+1}$ into two groups, one group with s subtrees, and the other group with $t_\ell - s$ subtrees. Any group of subtrees of an optimal tree must be optimal; in other words, for an optimal $c(i, j, t_\ell, T_{\ell+1})$, both $c(i, h, s, T_{\ell+1})$ and $c(h+1, j, t_\ell - s, T_{\ell+1})$ must be optimal; otherwise, any improvement to either group would improve $c(i, j, t_\ell, T_{\ell+1})$.

We systematically find larger and larger optimal groups of subtrees with out-degree $T_{\ell+1}$ and ultimately determine $c(i, j, t_\ell, T_{\ell+1})$ as follows. Let $1 = a_0, a_1, \ldots, a_r = t_{max} = \max\{t_1, \ldots, t_n\}$ be a joint addition chain for the set of out-degrees $\{t_1, \ldots, t_n\}$. (Since the out-degree at every level is at least 2, the height of an optimal tree is at most $n-1$.) If $0 < s \leq r$ then from (6)

$$c(i, j, a_s, T_{\ell+1}) = \min_{i \leq h < j} \left(c(i, h, a_p, T_{\ell+1}) + c(h+1, j, a_q, T_{\ell+1}) \right), \qquad (7)$$

where $a_s = a_p + a_q$, and

$$c(i, j, 1, T_\ell) = c(i, j, t_\ell, T_{\ell+1}) + w(i, j). \qquad (8)$$

In (7), we try to partition a_s subtrees with out-degree $T_{\ell+1}$ into two groups, one with a_p subtrees, the other with a_q subtrees. In order to achieve the optimal $c(i, j, a_s, T_{\ell+1})$, both $c(i, h, a_p, T_{\ell+1})$ and $c(h+1, j, a_q, T_{\ell+1})$ must be optimal. If both $c(i, h, a_p, T_{\ell+1})$ and $c(h+1, j, a_q, T_{\ell+1})$ have been computed for $i \leq h < j$, then $c(i, j, a_s, T_{\ell+1})$ can be determined by the minimization over h. Equation (8) states that the cost of a single tree is obtained from the cost of the group of its subtrees by adding the costs of the branches that connect the root to its subtrees.

Note that from (7) the optimal value of $c(i, j, a_s, T_\ell)$ depends on the optimal values $c(i, h, a_p, T_\ell)$ and $c(h+1, j, a_q, T_\ell)$, where both $h - i$, and $j - (h+1)$ are less than $j - i$ and both a_p and a_q are less than a_s. For $\ell = n, n-1, \ldots, 1$, we build three-dimensional tables corresponding to each out-degree sequence T_ℓ; for each ℓ, the order of computation is the same as in the algorithm for the t-ary case.

After the table is constructed, we build the optimal mixed-radix tree. We start from the first level of the tree. From the entry for $i = 1$, $j = n$, T_1, and $s = r_{t_1}$ we find the optimal value $h = h_1, p = p_1$ to divide n nodes into two groups, one with a_{p_1} subtrees with out-degree T_2 for the probabilities $\{p_1, \ldots, p_h\}$, the other with $t_1 - a_{p_1}$ subtrees with out-degree T_2 for the probabilities $\{p_{h+1}, \ldots, p_n\}$. Next, in the entries for $i = 1$, $j = h_1$, $s = p_1$, T_1, and $i = h_1 + 1, j = n, s = q_1, T_1$, we can find the points for dividing n nodes into subgroups of optimal subtrees with out-degree T_2, where $a_{p_1} + a_{q_1} = a_{r_{t_1}}$. This process continues until $p_{x1} = 1$ and $q_{y1} = 1$, at which point the n nodes at level 1 have been divided into an optimal group of t_1 subtrees with out-degree T_2.

At levels 2 and greater, the construction is identical to that at the first level, except that we deal with subsets of the original n nodes. The tree construction process is completed when all subtrees reach the bottom of the tree.

Let l be the length of the joint addition chain for $\{t_1, t_2, \ldots, t_n\}$. Then the running time of this algorithm is $O(l \cdot n^3)$ and the space used $O(l \cdot n^2)$. By Lemma 3 of Section 3, l is $O(n \log t_{max})$. Therefore the overall computation time for our construction is $O(n^4 \log t_{max})$ and the memory requirement is $O(n^3 \log t_{max})$. Without loss of generality, we can assume that $t_{max} \leq n$, which yields the time bound $O(n^4 \log n)$ and the space bound $O(n^4 \log n)$.

ACKNOWLEDGMENTS

This research was supported in part by Apple Computer Inc. and by the Defense Advanced Research Projects Administration under contract J-FBI-89-101.

REFERENCES

Gilbert, E.N. and Moore, E.F., Variable-length binary encodings, *Bell System Technical Journal*, vol. 38, no. 4, pp. 933–968 (1959).

Gotlieb, L., Optimal multi-way search trees, *SIAM Journal on Computing*, vol. 10, no. 3, pp. 422–433 (1981).

Hu, T.C. and Tucker, A.C., Optimum computer search trees, *SIAM Journal on Applied Mathematics*, vol. 21, no. 4, pp. 514–532 (1971).

Huffman, D.A., A method for the construction of minimum redundancy codes, *Proceedings of the IRE*, vol. 40, no. 9, pp. 1098–1101 (1952).

Itai, A., Optimal alphabetic trees, *SIAM Journal on Computing*, vol. 5, no. 1, pp. 9–18 (1976).

Knuth, D.E., Optimal binary search trees, *Acta Informatica*, vol. 1, no. 1, pp. 14–25 (1971).

Knuth, D.E., "The Art of Computer Programming," vol. 2, Addison-Wesley, Reading, Massachusetts (1969).

Lawler, E., personal communication (1970).

Object-Oriented Systems

A SCHEMA MANIPULATION MECHANISM FOR AN OODB MODEL

Regina Motz, Raúl Ruggia

Instituto de Computación
Facultad de Ingeniería
E-mail:rmotz@incouy.edu.uy, ruggia@incouy.edu.uy
Universidad de la República
Montevideo - Uruguay

Abstract

A Schema Manipulation Mechanism is proposed in order to enable operations over Database Schemas. The mechanism consists in four main operations and the type consistence is garanted by the definition of invariants. Change propagation over methods and instances is also taken into account. Using the defined operations, problems like schema evolution and integration of different Database Schemas can be resolved.

This mechanism is studied in the context of an Object Oriented Data Model using its standard features, facilitating the use of this mechanism in other OO Data Models.

The effect of the schema operations over the type lattice is formally specified using Modular Z.

INTRODUCTION

The problems of producing reliable software quickly and economically have been widely discussed in recent years, and initial experience has indicated that the use of reusability and modularization can contribute towards a solution.

This is also true in the context of conception and design of database systems. In this area has been proposed a new generation of Data Models and Systems called Object Oriented Database Models and Systems. This new proposal intends to apply the concepts mentioned above to Database Systems [1, 2, 3, 4, 5].

Our work propose a Schema Manipulation Mechanism (SMM) in order to facilitate the resolution of these problems. About the reusability, the schema manipulation mechanism we define allows the design of new DB schemas integrating existing ones. If we consider that the DB schemas encapsulates data and operations associated with a real world situation, it would be interesting to re-use this information to develop applications without breaking their encapsulation. Moreover, with a schema manipulation mechanism we are able to generate partial visions of DB schemas restricting the definitions of a primitive one. Furthermore, this mechanism may assist the DB designer, allowing him to divide a complex application into simple DB schemas and then integrating them. In this way, the schema manipulation mechanism enables to modularize the DB design.

COMPUTER SCIENCE, Edited by R. Baeza-Yates
and U. Manber, Plenum Press, New York, 1992

Besides this, the schema manipulation mechanism offers assistance to resolve the problem of schema evolution (the real world modeled by the DB schema is often very evolutive). In [6], a learning-based approach to evolution is proposed. The framework of this work is an object-oriented database model, consisting in two levels: a kernel and a high level model. Within this model, different kinds of meta-data changes are proposed at both levels. In [7] a tool to aid the database administrator in DB schema transformation and in the DB reorganization is proposed. Further work about schema evolution can be found in [8, 9, 10].

The aim of our work is to define a schema manipulation mechanism with these features to be included into an OODBM. In [11] a structuring mechanism for conceptual modeling is proposed in the context of GALILEO [12]. This mechanism includes schema manipulation operations to resolve the problems mentioned above, but it is rather restrictive in the conditions that impose over the DB schemas in order to apply the operations. In [13] a similar mechanism is proposed in the context of O2 [14] relaxing some restrictions.

An important difference of our approach from those in [11] and [13] is that the SMM enables schema manipulation in two levels. In one of them, the system executes the operations without the assistance of the database designer. In the other, more complex operations can be done but the system acts as an assistance of the database designer.

Other relevant issue of our SMM is the ability to control the modifications performed on the schemas and take into account automatically their impact on the object instances.

In our work, we improve the idea of [13] and develop it in a formal context over the E/D Data Model [15], using the specification language Modular Z [16].

Due to the non existent of any "standard" Object Oriented Database Model (OODBM), we choose the E/D Model because it is formally specified also using Modular Z, and supports all the features currently supported by advanced OODBM. It includes composite objects, multiple inheritance, type lattice and classes.

We believe that the formal specification is an important aspect of the work because supplies a foundation for logical reasoning about the semantics of the data model and the schema manipulation mechanism. Moreover, it supplies a precise, implementation independent, description of the concepts, and gives a basis for reasoning about the correctness of the operations involved. Besides this, the formal specification allows rapid prototyping and documents the design of the model.

The rest of this paper is organized as follows: Section 2 contains a succinctly description of the specification language Modular Z. Section 3 describes the E/D Database Model. In Section 4 is developed our approach of the schema manipulation mechanism. Finally, Section 5 contains some conclusions.

ABOUT THE SPECIFICATION LANGUAGE

The Modular Z notation [16], is a language for expressing mathematical specifications of complex systems. It is based on the Z notation [17], and as well as Z, is based on first order predicate calculus and typed set theory.

Modular Z increases the notion of *schema*, existing in Z, with the notions of *chapters*, *documents* and *library*, which improve its modularity and reusability.

A *schema* is a named piece of mathematical text that introduces some variables, and some predicates which express a constraint relating the possible values of the variables. Schemas are given in the form:

```
> SCHEMA Schema-S;
>     VAR
>     variables;
```

```
> PREDICATE
>       predicates;
> END Schema-S;
```

Schemas can describe operations on data states. Some schemas require input and/or output data. Conventionally we decorate input data with a final query (?), and output data with a final shriek (!).

Although the style in which schemas are used in Modular Z is quite different from that used in Z, both languages have facilities for combining these structural units, and both make some provision for parametrized specification units.

In Z schemas are used for everything whereas in Modular Z there are specific syntactic units for defining functions (DEF), types (TYPE) and algebraic types (ALGTYPE).

A *chapter* clusters types, definitions, schemas and theorems, whereas a *document* groups reference to chapters and represents the whole specification of the system. Documents are given in the form:

```
> DOCUMENT DocName;
>       ChaptersNames;
> END DocName;
```

A *library* contains documents and chapters. Specifications of large systems are built up by specifying smaller sub-systems using chapters, then grouping these chapters into a document. Modular Z allows the importation and exportation of objects[1] among the chapters and the definition of types and local definitions into a schema.

The documentation used is the one known as *literal programming*: lines beginning with the symbol > are lines of specification. The advantage of this type of documentation is that it allows to coexist in a single document the comments and the specification.

AN OVERVIEW OF THE E/D DATABASE MODEL

The E/D Model is an extension of the E-R Model, where structural and behavioral properties are treated explicitly in an integrated way. The E/D Model also possesses features of object-oriented data models: objects (everything instance is an object) , object identity (objects have an unique identifier), types (same as the abstract data type concept in programming languages), classes (gruoping objects) and multiple inheritance.

An *object* is a real-word element or concept which can be distinctly identified. The primary characteristic of an object is that it has an identity which persists through time, however the properties of the object may change. This identity may be considered to be represented by a system generated object identifier (oid). Objects may be explicitly created and destroyed.

Every object is an instance of one or more classes and every class has an associated type. The relation among the types is the common database relation of 'IsA' and the relation among the classes is the 'SubSetOf' relation.

It supports the usual notion of a type lattice, i.e. the possibility of multiple inheritance. The user must resolve conflicts between inherited structures or methods by writing a new structure or method, or explicitly inherit one instance variable or method from among several conflicting ones.

The type of an object may be system-defined or user-defined, and there is no differences between them. The system-defined types are: the atomic types (Integer, Real, String, Bool and Und[2]), the types constructs (Set, List and Record); and the predefined types of the E/D Model (UserType, TypeConstraint, Entity, Relation, Action, Rule, Transaction and MetaRule).

---

[1] In this section, the term *object* is used to reference to types, definitions, schemas and theorems.

[2] UND–The object undefined. This type is obtained every time an operation is not applicable.

```
> ALGTYPE
>       Type :: user UserT          // User defined type
>              | constr TConstr     // Constraint
>              | ent Entity         // Entity
>              | rela Rela          // Relationship
>              | ac Action          // Action
>              | ru Rule            // Rule
>              | tran Trans         // Transaction
>              | metaru MetaRule;   // MetaRule
```

Types have the following common information: a description, its supertypes, the excludents types with it and a set of methods. This information is specified in the following *TypeInf* schema.

```
> SCHEMA TypeInf;
>    VAR
>         description     : Message,
>         supertypes      : SET TypeName,
>         excludent       : SET TypeName,
>         methods         : SET Method; > END TypeInf;
```

The structure of a type is modeled as a parametrized record and it depends of the specific type. The representation of the structure as a record allows us to efficiently manage the multiple inheritance.

```
> TYPE Structure[X] = MAP Label TO X;
```

Scheme and Instance of the E/D Model

The E/D Model consists of two part: the Scheme and the Instance.

Scheme

A **Scheme** contents the information about: Types and Classes.

```
> SCHEMA SchemeE/D;
> VAR
>      tenv    : TypeEnv,
>      classes : Classes;
> END SchemeE/D;
```

The type environment (TypeEnv) associates a type for each type name. It contains all the types defined in an application. Each type in the environment must verify that its supertypes or excludent types also exists in the environment, and that the excludent constraint is not violated.

```
> TYPE TypeEnv = MAP TypeName TO Type
>         | (FORALL Tenv: TypeEnv, t: Type | t IN RNG Tenv •
>              t.supertypes ⊆ DOM Tenv AND
>              t.excludent ⊆ DOM Tenv AND
>              NOT EXIST st:TypeName | st IN t.supertypes •
>              (Tenv st).excludent ∩ t.supertypes <> {});
```

Each class has an associated type (which indicates the type of its objects) and an extension (which groups its objects).

```
> TYPE Classes = MAP ClassName TO ClassBody;
>        ClassBody = (type : NameEntRelaUser,
>                     ext  : SET Oid);
```

⊏Instance⊐

An **Instance** of the E/D Model consists of a partial function (**ObjMem**) which associates an object for each object identifier.

```
> TYPE ObjMem = MAP Oid TO Object;
```

Each object has a state and an associated type which is the most specialized type of it (sp-type). These components of an object must verify an invariant which says that the structure of the state and the type must be in correspondence.

```
> TYPE Object = (sp-type: TypeConstr,
>                state: ObjState);
>   | FORALL obj: Object •
>     (EXIST a: Atom | obj.sp-type = ac (atomname a) •
>      EXIST v: AtomicValue • obj.state = atomic v)
>   AND
>     (EXIST tc: Type-Constr | obj.sp-type = seq-of tc •
>      EXIST s: SEQ Oid • obj.state = sequence s)
> AND
>     (EXIST n: TypeName | obj.sp-type = ac (typename n) •
>      EXIST m: MAP Label TO Oid • obj.state = record m);
```

The structure of the object state (ObjState) shows that all the *type instances* has an uniformity representation as "objects."

```
> ALGTYPE ObjState :: atomic AtomicValue
>                   | set (SET Oid)
>                   | sequence (SEQ Oid)
>                   | record (MAP Label TO Oid);


> ALGTYPE AtomicValue :: integer INT
>                      | real REAL
>                      | string STRING
>                      | bool BOOL
>                      | undef UNDEF;
```

⊏DataBase⊐

A **DataBase** consists of an instance (ObjMem) and a scheme, such that every object of the ObjMem belongs to a unique class of the scheme.

```
> SCHEMA DataBaseE/D;
> INCLUDE SchemeE/D
> VAR
>      objects: ObjMem;
> PREDICATE
>      FORALL id: Oid | id IN DOM objects •
>      UNIQUE c: ClassName | id IN (classes c).ext
> END DataBaseE/D;
```

THE SCHEMA MANIPULATION MECHANISM

The proposed SMM herein offers assistance to resolve the problem of schema evolution. Moreover, this SMM enables to modularize the DB design and allows to design new DB schemas combining existing ones.

The features of the OODM suggests that there are differents groups of database objects that are affected when a schema manipulation is performed, then any solution to the problem of schema manipulation has to include provisions for all these groups: the type lattice, the set of methods and the instances.

Schema generation is controlled using a set of invariants that define the legal configurations of the schema. The notion of schema invariants is discussed first (Section 4.1). The operations allowed are analyzed next (Section 4.2) and their effect over type lattices studied in detail. Propagating the new type definitions obtained by the application of schema operations concerns both the control of their impact on the methods and on the existing object instances. This is discussed in Sections 4.3 and 4.4.

SCHEMA INVARIANTS

A valid or consistent schema is one that verifies the following invariants:

• Strict Inheritance

Strict inheritance must hold both for type structures and for methods. In the case of methods, we consider their signature. Multiple inheritance complicates the name conflict problem. This can be solved by writing a new structure or methods or explicitly inherit one instance variable or method from among several conflicting ones. It would be interesting to re-use a method but the method may be adapted to the new type definitions. This will be discussed later in Section 4.3.

• Structure Correspondence between Objects and Types

The structure of the objects must correspond with their type. This was formally shown in the specification of ObjectState (Section 3). As happened with the methods in the Strict Inheritance, the ObjectState must be adapted to the new type definition. Propagating the type definitions on the object instances is a capability that the SMM supplies (see Section 4.4).

In order to maintain the correspondence between Object and Type "*exception objects*" are added. Exception objects are built from those in the old object memories. Its structure consist of the old oid, old object memory, the present type structure and the object state.

Then, the formal specification of object is now the following:

> ALGTYPE Object :: normal NObject | exception EObject;

Where NObject corresponds to the type Object defined in Section 3 and the EObject corresponds to the following specification:

```
> TYPE EObject = (sp-type: TypeConstr,
>                 oid: Oid,
>                 mem: ObjMem,
>                 state: ObjState);
> | FORALL eobj: EObject •
>     (EXIST a: Atom | eobj.sp-type = ac (atomname a) •
>      EXIST v: AtomicValue • eobj.state = atomic v OR
>        (mem oid).state = atomic v)
>   AND
>     (EXIST tc: Type-Constr | eobj.sp-type = seq-of tc •
>      EXIST s: SEQ Oid • eobj.state = sequence s OR
```

```
>           (mem oid).state = sequence s)
> AND
>     (EXIST n: TypeName | eobj.sp-type = ac (typename n) •
>       EXIST m: MAP Label TO Oid • eobj.state = record m OR
>           (mem oid).state = record m);
```

• Unique Type Name
The type names must be unique in the set of types definitions (this follows from the specification of TypeEnvironment).

• Relation between the pre- and post- Type Hierarchy
Strictly this is not a schema invariant. While the previous schema invariants are static conditions over the schema structure, this "invariant" correspond to dynamic conditions over the operations. It reflects the relation between the orders in the type hierarchies before and after the execution of any SMM operation. This relation must be maintained after the application of the SMM operations, i.e. if two types are in the order A<B (A is subtype of B) in the type hierarchy of some DB Schema, the operations must keep this order in the type hierarchy of the new DB Schema.

The goal of this invariant is to maintain the user vision of the types. This vision is represented by the type hierarchy of the primitive DB Schemas.

For example, if one DB Schema has the type hierarchy shown in Fig. 1a any application of the SMM operations must not generate a DB Schema like that in Fig. 1b.

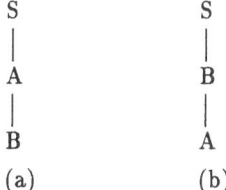

Figure 1. Pre- and Post-Type Hierarchy.

SCHEMA OPERATIONS

As it was mentioned in Section 1, the mechanism can work in two levels: with or without designer supervision. When used at "automatic level" (without designer supervision) the mechanism controls the invariants. When is used as an administrator assistant, the administrator can execute operations (under his control and responsibility) that may arise in invariant violation.

In this section we analyze in detail the SMM Operations at the automatic level over the type lattice.

The mechanism consists in four operations: *Union, Extend, Difference* and *Rename*. All of them take DB schemas and gives a new DB schema.

1. Union

This operation takes two DB schemas and gives a new one which models the real worlds represented by the primitives.

The goal of this operation is to enable the development of applications involving two Data Bases. This implies that the new DB schema has to model, as complete as possible, both worlds. To carry out this goal, the new schema must include all the instances and the union of the types in the initial schemas.

For example, we have the Employees Office DB and the Computer Science Department DB (see Figure 3), and we want the list of Teachers with their address, projects in which they are working and their salary. We need to combine both DB in order to obtain the information. So that we generate a new DB schema (Figure 4) using the Union operation.

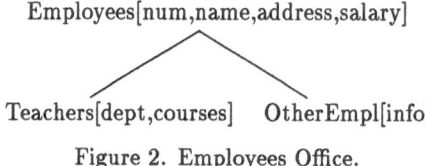

Figure 2. Employees Office.

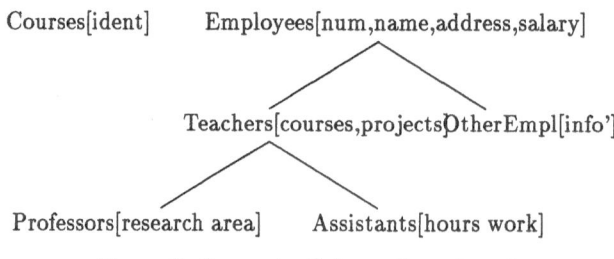

Figure 3. Computer Science Department.

If the type definitions and data are disjoint in the primitive DB schemas, the result is the union of them. For the other situations we study different cases considering types definitions and invariants.

Let be E_1 and E_2 two DB schemas, and E the result of applying the Union operation to E_1 and E_2 ($E = E_1$ U E_2).

For each type A belonging to E_1 or to E_2 can occur:

- **Case 1:** The type A is in only one of the DB schemas
  $\Rightarrow A$ belongs to E with the same type structure and supertypes.

In Figure 4, this rule generates Courses, Professors and Assistants types in the new DB schema.

Sometimes a type A which is only in E_1 can be regarded as subtype of other type B which is in the other DB schema. In this case, working in the automatic level, we avoid to put A as a subtype of B in the final DB schema. The reason is to prevent cases like the following:

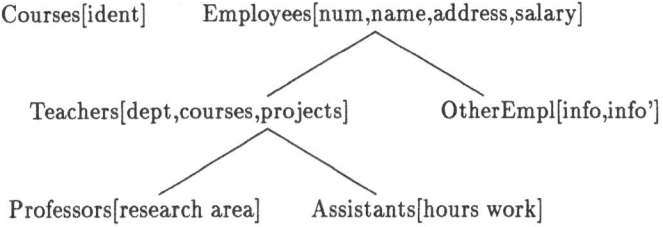

Figure 4. Employees Office **Union** Computer Science Department.

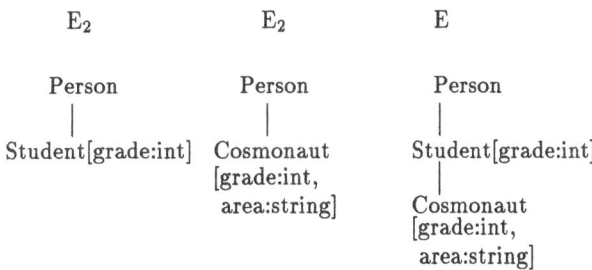

Figure 5. Wrong automatic subtypes.

If we detect that Cosmonaut is a subtype of Student, we may put them in this hierarchy, but this relation may be wrong in some vision of the real world. So the new schema is like in Fig. 6.

Working at assistant level, the designer may choose the first (perhaps not wrong) result.

- **Case 2:** The type **A** is in E_1 and E_2 with the same structure and supertypes
  $\Rightarrow$ **A** belongs to **E** with the same type structure and supertypes.

- **Case 3:** The type **A** is in E_1 and E_2 with different structure but with a common supertype

  - **Case 3.1:** The common supertype part of **A** in E_1 and E_2 are identical, but the additional structure of **A** in E_1 and E_2 are different.

  If there are no conflict between the respectively extra structure, then the type **A** is included in **En** with the union of the structures of **A** in E_1 and **A** in E_2.

  The subtypes of **A** in **E** are the ones in E_1 and E_2 , but propagating over them the new instance variables of A.

  In Figure 4, this rule generates the types Employees, Teachers and Adm. Empl. in the new DB schema.

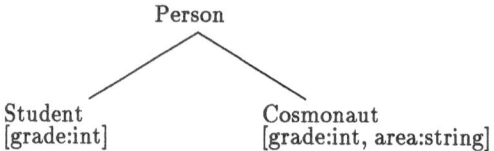

$$E$$

Person

Student
[grade:int]

Cosmonaut
[grade:int, area:string]

Figure 6. Result of the Union.

- **Case 3.2:** The types **A** in E_1 and **A** in E_2 are different refinements of their common supertypes. In other words, the structure of **A** in E_1 and E_2 differs in the common supertype part or in non extra structure. Then the type **A** is included in **E** having the most generic domain types and the disjunction of its constraints.

- **Case 3.3:** The type **A** is a combination of cases 3.1 and 3.2.
  Then, type **A** in **E** has the following structure:
    * the union of extra structure of the types in the primitives environments and
    * the most generic structure of their common supertypes.

In all of these cases (case 1, 2 and 3), the Union operation is successful because there is no supertype of **A** in E_1 which is subtype of **A** in E_2. In general, it can be established the following condition:

The Union can be made iff not exists any type B supertype (subtype) of A in E_1, which is subtype (supertype) of A in E_2.

If this condition does not hold, the operation is rejected. This is to avoid the violation of the Pre- Post- Type Hierarchy invariant.

- **Case 4:** The type **A** is in E_1 and E_2 with different structure and no common supertype (different from the top).

  In this case we consider that types **A** in E_1 and E_2 models objects that are completely different in the real world, so that is not possible to make both definitions compatible. So we reject the operation.

At following we show the specification of the **Union** operation.

> SCHEMA UnionOK = UnionTypeLattice ∪ Re-UsedMethods ∪ UnionInstance;

A successful Union operation implies: the union of type lattices, the possibility of re-use methods and the union of instances.

The specification about the ReUsedMethods and UnionInstances are analized in Sections 4.3 and 4.4 respectively.

```
> SCHEMA UnionTypeLattice;
> VAR
>       envE₁?, envE₂?, newEnv!: TypeEnv;
> PREDICATE
```
The union of types is realized in the cases explained
in this section, cases 1, 2 and 3.
Case 1: The domain of the environments are disjoint,
so that, there are not equal type names.
```
> (DOM envE₁? ∩ DOM envE₂? = {} ⇒ newEnv! = envE₁? + envE₂?) AND
```
Cases 2 and 3: Exists types in the environments with
the same names and the condition of pre- and post- type
hierarchy is verified.
```
> (DOM envE₁? ∩ DOM envE₂? <> {} AND
> FORALL t: TypeName | t IN DOM envE₁? ∩ DOM envE₂? •
> VerifyPre_PostTypeHierarchy t envE₁? envE₂? ⇒
```
The new type lattice of the new environment needs
a build process.
```
> newEnv! = Build_newEnv envE₁? envE₂? (DOM envE₁? ∩ DOM envE₂?));
> END UnionType Lattice;
```

Where the function BuildNewEnv is the following:

```
> DEF BuildNewEnv: TypeEnv → TypeEnv → SET TypeName → TypeEnv;
> FORALL envA,envB: TypeEnv, commontypes: SET TypeName •
> (commontypes = {} ⇒ BuildNewEnv envA envB commontypes = {})
> (commontypes <> {} ⇒ EXIST t: TypeName • t IN commontypes
```
Case 2: The types with the same names that have the same
structure and supertypes
are directly in the union.
```
>       (SameSupertypes t envA envB AND SameStruct t envA envB ⇒
>           BuildNewEnv envA envB commontypes − {t}) AND
```
Case 3.1: The types have a common supertype but differ in some
extra structure then the resulting structure is the structure union.
```
>       (CommonSupertype t envA envB AND DiffExtraStruct t envA envB ⇒
>           BuildNewEnv envA envB commontypes =
>               {t ↦ UnionStruct t envA envB} +
>               BuildNewEnv envA envB commontypes − {t}) AND
```
Case 3.2: The types differ in the refinement of the domains of their
common supertype, then the most generic domain and
the disjunction of the constraints is resulting.
```
>       (CommonSupertype t envA envB AND DiffDomainRef t envA envB ⇒
>       BuildNewEnv envA envB commontypes =
>               {t ↦ GenericConstr t envA envB} +
>               BuildNewEnv envA envB commontypes − {t}) AND
```
Case 3.3: Combination of cases 3.1 and 3.2
```
>       (CommonSupertype t envA envB AND DiffDomainRef t envA envB AND
>           DiffExtraStruct t envA envB ⇒
>           BuildNewEnv envA envB commontypes =
>               {t ↦ UnionStructGenericConstraints t envA envB} +
>               BuildNewEnv envA envB commontypes − {t}) )
> END BuildNewEnv;
```

2. Extend

This operation takes two DB schemas (E_1 and E_2) and gives a new one which contains the type definitions in E_1 and those E_2 which are not in E_1.

The goal of this operation is to extend the definitions of one DB schema with others. This can be useful to enable *schema evolution* or to perform a union maintaining the definitions of one DB schema in the conflictive cases.

In the case of *schema evolution*, the traditional mechanism modifies the schema *type-by-type*. Using this SMM operation, the designer only builds a new DB schema with the changing types.

For example, in the case of Fig. 3, we want to modify CSDep schema, redefining and adding subtypes to type Courses. So we build a DB schema **E** with the types changing:

E

Courses[ident,room]

Laboratory   Theoretical

We perform the operation **CSDeptnew = E ext ECSDept**, and we obtain a DB Schema like in Fig. 7.

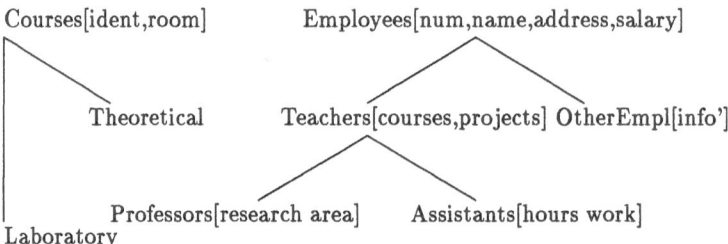

Figure 7. The results of the Extend Operation.

As well as in the Union operation, exists some restrictions in order to maintain the invariants.

For example, a type **A** in Schema E_1 has the B and C subtypes, and type **A** in E_2 has B, C, D and E subtypes. The extend operation between E_1 and E_2 results in the types **A**, **B** and **C** from schema E_1 and the types **D** and **E** from schema E_2. This can be made only when types **D** and **E** are valid subtypes of the type **A** in E_1.

At following we present the specification of this operation.

> SCHEMA ExtendOK = ExtendTypeLattice ∪ ExtendTypeMethods ∪ ExtendInstances;

> SCHEMA ExtendTypeLattice;
> VAR
>   envE$_1$?, envE$_2$?, newEnv!
> PREDICATE
>   *The Extend operation must verify the pre- and post- type hierarchy*
>   *condition and that all the new subtypes in the extension of a type*
>   *may be valid subtypes of it.*
>   ValidExtend envE$_1$?, envE$_2$? AND
>   NewEnv! = envE$_2$? † envE$_1$?;
> END ExtendTypeLattice;

Where ValidExtend is the following function:

> DEF ValidExtend: TypeEnv → TypeEnv → Boolean;
> FORALL envA, envB: TypeEnv •
>   (DOM envA ∩ DOM envB = {} ⇒ ValidExtend envA envB = TRUE) AND
>   (DOM envA ∩ DOM envB <> {} ⇒
>   FORALL t: TypeName • t IN (DOM envA ∩ DOM envB) •
>   VerifyPre-Post-TypeHierarchy t envA envB AND
>   FORALL st:TypeName | st IN Subtypes t envB •
>   ValidSubtype (Inheritance st envB) (Inheritance t envA)
> END ValidExtend;

Where **Inheritance** is a function: Type → TypeEnv → Type, that expands the type with its inherits properties in that environment.

3. Difference

This operation takes two DB schemas **E$_1$** and **E$_2$** and gives a new one **E** with the types in **E$_1$** which are not in **E$_2$**.

The goal of this operation is to enable "Type Deletions" in the type lattice, but doing this in a global (not *type by type*) fashion.

For each type in **E$_2$**, the operation also deletes its subtypes in **E$_1$**, unless they have a supertype which is not in **E$_2$**.

We consider that deleting a type implies deleting all of its properties from the type environment, so we not maintain the deleted type properties into its (not deleted) subtypes.

If there is some property on the subtype which the designer wants to maintain, he can do an Extend operation to redefine this subtype.

The specification of this operation is the following:

> SCHEMA DifferenceOK = DiffTypeLattice ∪ DiffMethods ∪ DiffInstances;

> SCHEMA DiffTypeLattice;
> VAR
>   envE$_1$?, envE$_2$?, newEnv!
> PREDICATE
>   newEnv! = (envE$_1$? ◁ envE$_2$?) ◁ (FreeTypes DOM envE$_2$? DOM envE$_1$?);
> END DiffTypeLattice;

Where FreeTypes is the function: SET TypeName → SET TypeName → SET TypeName; that returns the types in DOM $envE_1$? which have only supertypes in DOM $envE_2$?. This implies that these types must also be deleted.

4. $\boxed{\text{Rename}}$

This operation takes one DB schema, a type name existing in this schema and a new type name. The result is the primitive DB schema, changing the first type name for the second one. The second type name must not exist in the DB schema.

The goal of this operation is to complement the previous operations allowing the designer to change type names in conflictive cases.

At following we present the specification of this operation.

> SCHEMA RenameOK = RenameType ∪ RenameInstances;

> SCHEMA RenameType;
> VAR
>   oldEnv?, newEnv!: TypeEnv;
>   oldTypeName?, NewTypeName?: TypeName;
> PREDICATE
         The oldTypeName is a name of the old environment.
>   oldTypeName? IN DOM oldEnv? AND
         The newTypeName is not a name of the old environment.
>   newTypeName? NOT IN DOM oldEnv? AND
>   EXIST t: Type | t = oldEnv? oldTypeName? •
>   newEnv! = oldEnv? ◁ {oldTypeName? ↦ t} + {newTypeName? ↦ t};
> END RenameType;

SOLUTION FOR INSTANCES

If a type of the new schema corresponds to a changed type of the old schemas (by the addition or deletion of properties) then the instances must be converted to the new definition of the type, in order to maintain the Object-Type Invariant.

This is a common issue in the schema evolution problem. The spectrum of solutions lies between a fully automatic propagation of the changes and a manual one. The first approach is used in GemStone [18] and Orion [19], while the second is used in Encore [9].

An other relevant issue for change propagation is the delay by which the modifications are actually performed on the object instances. Propagation can be immediate or defered.

At immediate propagations, the impact of type modifications is immediately performed on the instances involved. This propagation is adopted in GemStone.

At defered propagation the modifications are propagated only when the instances are accessed. Defered propagations is used in Orion.

In the schema evolution, the first solution emphasizes consistency and informations preservations, but sacrifices performance. The second emphasize performance but requires a permanent propagations mechanism throughout the system's life.

In our case, the propagation of the type changes over the object instances is made by an Initialization process at operation time and the later conversion and copy of the old objects when they are referenced. The initialization process implies the generation of the *exception object* to verify the correspondence object-type, but not implies the copy of the state.

When an exception instance (*except(type,oid,m,state)*) is accessed by the first time, it is "frozen," this means that the old state (which corresponds to the state of the oid in the object memory m) is copied into the new state updating all the old oids with their corresponding ones at the new object memory. Note that this copy only updates the first level of accessed objects. The oid and m information are maintained in order to resolve references to this object.

SOLUTION FOR METHODS

The application of SMM operations affect methods in two aspects. One is about the new signature definition, and the other is about re-using old methods.

If all old types are in the new DB Schema, then there no problem arise with the signature definition. In the case of losing types the method is not longer available.

Our proposal of SMM allows to re-use methods from the old schemas involved in the schema manipulation operations. The re-used methods into a type are restricted to be, for this type, from the same old schema.

This implies that when types of the new schema changed respect to the old ones, the re-used methods may no work on new instance objects.

Types may be changed by the addition or deletion of properties and methods, or by the modification of constraints respect of those at old types. Then, a change in a type definition may affect programs that use objects of the type. Specifically, a program may fail if a property or method is no longer defined or if a value is outside the constraints defined by the old types expected by the program.

A change in the constraints of the type may strengthen a constraint resulting in refinement of a property, or it may relax a constraint resulting in enrichment.

Therefore, an error condition is raised by an object when a program attemps to write a value to the object which is outside the defined domain or no longer defined (*writer's problem*). Or when a program reads an undefined property or operation, or when a constraint is relaxed, the domain becomes wider, and an old method may read an unknown value from an object created with the new type definition (*reader's problem*) [9].

As a solution we propose an **error handling** mechanism for errors occurred in the execution of re-used methods.

This error-handling mechanism supplies the correct type definition corresponding to a specific type from which the method has been re-used.

Error-handlers are systematically associated with the new type definition in order to supply consistent access when an old method is applied for a new instance object.

The error conditions are then *invalid* or *undefined*, and handlers may be included in a type definition for both cases. Handlers may consist on an executable routine or on a complete error diagnostic.

The SMM automatically supplies the "skeleton" of the handlers required, this means the indication of *where* and *why* the handlers are required. The user must write the corresponding actions in every case.

Then type definition must include the error handlers. This implies the addition of handlers into the type definition, as shows the following specification:

```
> SCHEMA NewTypeInf;
> INCLUDE TypeInf,
> VAR
>    errorhandlers: SET EHandler;
> END NewTypeInf;

> TYPE EHandler = (skeleton: HSkeleton, body: Code);
>        HSkeleton = (errortype: ReadWriteUnknownInvalid, instVar: SET Label);
```

Note that objects inherit the behavior defined by their supertypes. Consequently, subtypes either inherit a handler as it is, or may refine it.

In the following, we describe the association of handlers in different cases.

a) Reader's Problem.

An error occurs when an old method tries to read a property which is no in its old DB Schema type. In this case, the SMM supplies a handler associated to the type which has READUNKNOWN error-type and the instance variables which generate the error. The body must be supplied by the user.

A similar error occurs when an old method tries to read a property value which is valid in the new DB SChema but not in the old one. In this case has READINVALID error-type.

b) Writer's Problem.

A similar situation occurs in the Writer's Problem when new DB Schema types have less properties (WRITEUNKNOWN) or more restrictive constraints (WRITEINVALID) than the same type in an old DB Schema.

CONCLUSIONS

We presented a powerful tool for schema manipulation. This mechanism allows to resolve schema evolution problems and enables the reusability and modularization of Database Schemas.

This mechanism includes not only the type lattice generation but also includes the propagation of the changes over the instances and methods.

The mechanism makes use of standard features of the Data Model. In general, it can be used for different DB Models with same standard features and where exception objects and error handlers can be added.

We elaborated a formalization of our mechanism using the specification language Modular Z, which is an adequate tool for the specification, especially by the fact that it supplies a module structure. Formal specifications can be a basis for direct prototyping. In our case, we are working on an object-oriented prototype in Smalltalk/V [20] using the method described in [21]. With the help of this method the development of the prototype becomes fairly easy and allows in some sense the validation of the schema manipulation mechanism and the verification of the formal specification.

Some topics have not been completely covered and are left for future work. One of these is the study of structural type equivalence and synonyms. A solution for this topic implies the study of a type inference mechanism which can detect these equivalences. Once the SMM can detect structural equivalence, it can define synonyms on equivalent types. Other topics are the complete formalization of the handler mechanism and instance management including object identity.

References

[1] M. Atkinson, F. Bancilhon, D. DeWitt, K. Dittrich, D. Maier, and S. Zdonik. The Object-Oriented Database System. Manifesto. In *Proceedings of the 1989.* International Workshop on Object-Oriented Database Systems, 1989.

[2] G. Copeland and J. Stein. Making Smalltalk a Database System. Boston, 1984. ACM - SIGMOD Int. Conf.

[3] D. Fishman, D. Beech, H. Cate, E. Chow, T. Connors, J. Davis, N. Derrett, C. Hoch, W. Kent, P. Lyngbaek, B. Mahbod, M. Neimat, T. Ryan, and M. Shan. Iris: An object-oriented database management system. *ACM Transactions on Office Information Systems*, 5(1), 1987.

[4] C. Lecluse and P. Richard. Modeling complex structures in object-oriented databases. In *ACM PODS conference*, 1989.

[5] Ontologic Publication, Cambridge. *Ontologic Inc.: VBASE for Object Applications*, 1988.

[6] D. McLeod. A learning-based approach to meta-data evolution in an object-oriented database. In *LNCS. Advances in OODB Systems. 1988*, 1988.

[7] A. Habermann B.Staudt. Beyond schema evolution to database reorganization. In *LNCS. Advances in OODB Systems. 1988*, 1990.

[8] J. Barenjee, W. Kim, H. Kim, and H. Korth. Semantics and Implementation of Schema Evolution in OODB. In *Proceedings ACM SIGMOD*, 1987.

[9] A. Skarra and S. Zdonik. The Management of Changing Types in an OODB. In *OOPSLA Proccedings*, 1986.

[10] G. T. Nguyen and D. Rieu. Schema evolution in object-oriented database systems. *Data and Knowledge Engineering.*, 1(4), 1989.

[11] A. Albano, M. Capaccioli, M.Occhiuto, and R.Orsini. A modularization mechanism for conceptual modelling. In *Proceeding VLDB*, 1983.

[12] L. Cardelli A. Albano and R. Orsini. Galileo: a Strongly Typed, Interactive Conceptual Language. *ACM Trans. on Database Systems*, 10(2), 1985.

[13] L. Costa. Manejo de Modulos en Bases de Datos OO. In *Trabajo de Grado. ESLAI*, 1990.

[14] C. Lecluse, P. Richard, and F. Velez. O_2, an object oriented data model. Chicago, 1988. ACM - SIGMOD Int. Conf.

[15] R. Motz. Estudo Formal de um Modelo de Dados Orientado a Objetos. Master's thesis, Universidade Federal de Pernambuco, Recife, 1990.

[16] A. Sampaio and S. Meira. Modular extensions to Z. In *LNCS Proceedings of the VDM'90*, West Germany, 1990. VDM'90: VDM and Z!

[17] B. Sufrin. *The Z Handbook*. Programming Research Group, Oxford, 1986.

[18] D. J. Penney and J. Stein. Class Modification in the GemStone Object-Oriented DBMS. In *Proceeding of OOPSLA'87*, Orlando FL, 1987.

[19] J. Banerjee, W. Kim, J. K. Kim, and H. Korth. Semantics and Implementation of Schema Evolution in Object-Oriented Databases. In *Proceeding ACM SIGMOD Conference*, San Francisco CA, 1987.

[20] A. Goldberg. *Smalltalk-80: The Language and its Implementation*. Addison-Wesley, 1983.

[21] R. Motz, F. Tepedino, and S. Meira. From model based specifications to object-oriented prototypes. In *Anais do X Congresso da SBC*, Vitória, 1990. Sociedade Brasileira de Computação.

VERSIONS IN THE CONTEXT OF
OBJECT-ORIENTED DATABASE SYSTEMS*

Lia Goldstein Golendziner, Clesio Saraiva dos Santos

Universidade Federal do Rio Grande do Sul
Instituto de Informática
Departamento de Informática Aplicada
Caixa Postal 1501
90.001 Porto Alegre RS Brazil
e-mail: lia@vortex.ufrgs.br, clesio@vortex.ufrgs.br

ABSTRACT

This paper proposes an integration of the version concept with the abstraction concepts present in object-oriented database models, considering structural aspects. The possible relationships between objects (and versions) and their ascendents in the class or type hierarchies is discussed and a discipline for version creation is proposed, based on the object constructors used to build the versions.

INTRODUCTION

Object-Oriented Database Systems emerged as a consequence of the requirements imposed by the new computer applications like CAD, CASE and Office Automation. Relevant characteristics of Object-Oriented Data Models are discussed in [Atk 89] and [Bee 89], and we may emphasize the support for complex objects, types or classes and inheritance. When supporting these features, the database model is able to better represent the semantic of applications.

Most of the new applications require the concept of version. Office Automation, for instance, need to represent historic information and data, for statistics and other purposes. Design applications also need to represent previous steps of the projects, for documentation purposes and comparative analysis of the alternatives obtained.

Versions represent design steps or alternatives of primitive or structured objects. A *version* is a description of an object as it exists in a given time and which maintenance is important for the application.

Thus, the support of versions is important together with other object oriented concepts in a database model and the corresponding database system. The combination of versions and the abstraction mechanisms allows the adequate modelling of properties that are common to many versions as well as a better control over their evolution.

Some systems have tried to make the integration of version concept and abstraction mechanisms. The ORION system presents a model of versions of composite objects [Kim 89]. Objects can be versionable, when belonging to a versionable class. The concept

---

* This work has been partly supported by CNPq (Brazilian National Research Council).

of generic object (called a generic instance) is present in the model. However, there is no mention to the behavior of the system when a versionable class belongs to a class hierarchy. In [Ber 88] abstraction concepts are used to model the concept of version. The model allows both type and value inheritance and the concept of generic object does not exist explicitly, but can be modelled through abstract and specialized objects. In both works, rules define versioning possibilities. In none of them, versioned objects structured as sets are considered. In the DAMOKLES system [Dit 87] the concept of generic object exists, but there is no generalization abstraction.

This paper proposes an integration of the version concept with the abstraction concepts present in object-oriented database models, considering structural aspects. A discipline for version creation is proposed, based on the object constructors needed to build the versions.

OBJECT-ORIENTED CONCEPTS

We will comment only those concepts that are essential for the rest of this work.

Object

Any entity of the real world may be considered an object. Objects represented in the database can be either concrete objects, such as a car or a part, or abstract objects, such as numbers. Objects are defined by the user and have properties, described through values. Objects can be atomic or structured. Structured objects are obtained, for example, using set, tuple and list constructors. The set constructor produces a set, representing the collection abstraction, while the tuple constructor represents aggregations [Smi 77]. The list constructor is similar to the set, but it determines an order on its elements.

Type and Class

There is no agreement on whether both concepts are necessary or only one [Atk 89]. Some authors argue that these concepts are used with different purposes and, thus, both are necessary [Alb 85] [Bee 89]. This is also the idea used in this work.

Types denote structure and extension, being the extension the domain of its elements. According to the domain of values, types can be atomic or structured. The extension of a type is the set of all *possible* values having defined characteristics. A class also represents an extension constituted by objects of a given type, explicitly created by the user and actually present in the database. When both concepts are present in a data model, it is possible to define many classes with the same (identified) underlying type, and so semantically compatible with respect to union, intersection and similar operations.

Type, Class Hierarchy and Inheritance

Inheritance is an important characteristic of object oriented data models. It allows making short descriptions of real world objects and factoring out shared specifications and implementations of objects [Atk 89]. Several types of inheritance can be considered. We will consider only those related to a structural model, where there are relationships between types (*type inheritance*) and between classes [Bee 89].

Type inheritance (also called *subtype relationship*) is defined by the structure of the types: t_2 is a subtype of t_1 (or t_1 is a supertype of t_2) in the following situations:

a) t_1 and t_2 are atomic and the domain of t_2 is a subset of the domain of t_1;

b) t_1 and t_2 are tuple types and t_2 has all the attributes of t_1 and possibly more. The type of each attribute of t_2 must be a subtype of the corresponding type in t_1;

c) t_1 and t_2 are set types, say, $t_i = \{s_i\}$ and s_2 is a subtype of s_1.

For tuple types, this relationship can be expressed, for example, by:
t_2 **inherits** t_1 , **add** attribute-list.

Relationships between classes are, usually, subset relationships. A class C_2 can be declared to be a *subclass* of class C_1 (C_1 is considered a *superclass* of C_2).

VERSIONS

To illustrate the concepts presented in the rest of the paper, we will consider some examples from a software engineering environment:

Projects are developed, having a name and a designer associated.
Teams of persons work in projects.
Documents are generated in the environment and are generalizations of *Specifications* and *Manuals*.
Programs are developed and are structured in *Modules*.
Documents and Programs have versions, representing evolution or alternatives for these objects.
Applications that need to represent versions require the possibility of specifying if (and which) objects will present versions.

Versioned Objects

The type concept can be extended to allow "having versions" as a property of the objects of a given type. A versioned object type is, thus, created, in the sense that the objects of this type may have versions. Those types may alternatively define atomic or structured objects.

Subtyping

Considering versioned objects, the subtype definition must be revised in the following way: t_2 is a subtype of t_1 if:

a) t_1 and t_2 satisfy the conditions defined for non-versioned object types [Bee 89] (described in the Object-Oriented Concepts section) and

b) t_1 ad t_2 are both versioned object types or t_2 is a versioned object type and t_1 is not.

Notice that the subtype relationship cannot be established when t_1 is a versioned object type and t_2 is not.

Generic Object

In design applications, it is common to define an object in a top down design process, whose properties are not completely specified. For example, one may want to define a Project, having a name and a designer associated, but the designer is not known yet. However, the project should be created so that it can be used, for example, as a component of another one.

Generic objects have been used to represent one object and its versions [Dit 87] [Kim 89]. We consider a *generic object* as an object that is not completely instantiated yet. It exists in the system with unique identification and can be referenced by other objects. Associated to a generic object, there will be one or more instances to define it, depending of its type. A generic object can be atomic or structured, according to its type. An *atomic generic object* has only one structural property, which is undefined. A *structured generic object* is an object that has, among its properties, at least one which is represented by a generic object. Also according to the type, generic objects can have versions or not. A *generic object without versions* has only one associated instance, while a *generic object with versions* can have several associated instances, which are the versions. Considering the combination of the characteristics **atomic X structured** and **with versions X without versions**, there can be four types of generic objects:

a) atomic generic object without versions
b) atomic generic object with versions
c) structured generic object without versions
d) structured generic object with versions

Figures 1 and 2 show examples of these types that are commented below.

Figure 1(a) shows an atomic generic object Designer without versions, having only one associated instance: **João**. References can be made to the generic object (when there is no associated instance, for example) or directly to the instance.

Version identification is derived from the generic object identification. Figure 1(b) shows an atomic generic object Program_specification with versions. There are three versions of specification, which are organized in a version derivation tree.

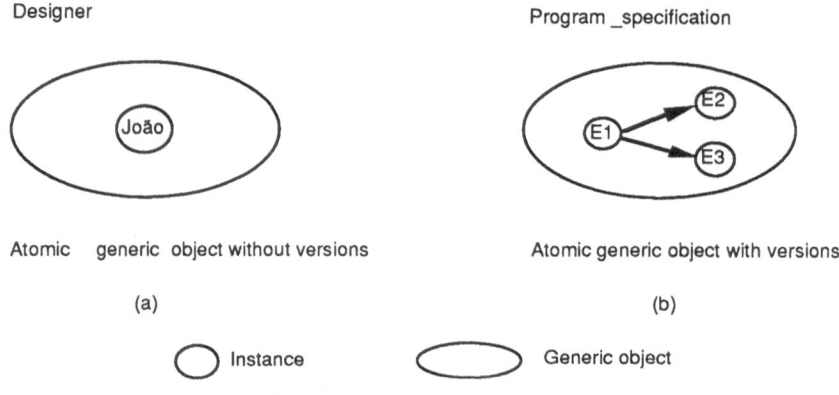

Figure 1. Atomic generic object

A generic object can be used as a component when, for example, the actual component is not known. The solution usually adopted in database systems for unknown information is null values. The following advantages result from using generic objects instead of null values:

- a generic object has already an identification, which will be complemented when the object is substituted by one of its instances;
- several generic objects can coexist without having associated instances. It makes possible, for example, that two new projects be created without previously designated designers, but these must be two different ones. This restriction is not expressible when exclusively using null values.

The set of object versions of a class is partitioned through generic objects. All versions of a class have the same structure, but a group of versions may have other common characteristics that make them interchangeable. This grouping is achieved through generic objects.

It may be convenient to create a structured generic object with some properties already instantiated, which must be maintained in all the associated versions. Thus, versions associated to a generic object inherit both its definition (structure, constraints and operators) and the instances that integrate the composition of the generic object (analogous to value inheritance [Alb 88]). Properties of versions can be changeable or not (the mechanism can be compared to strict and default inheritance [Bor 84]).

Figure 2 shows examples of structured generic objects. The rectangle linked to the ellipse indicates value properties that were defined when the generic object was created, and that will be inherited by the instances.

In figure 2(a) the Design object was partially defined, having a name and a generic object representing the designer. The only associated instance presents properties: **pr1**, project name, inherited from the generic object, and **João**, instance associated to the generic object Designer. Program (figure 2(b)) is a structured generic object with versions, having properties **Pg1**, for description, and a generic object as program_body. Versions of this

242

program inherit its description and present different instances of program_body as components (for this example, suppose program_body is a versioned object).

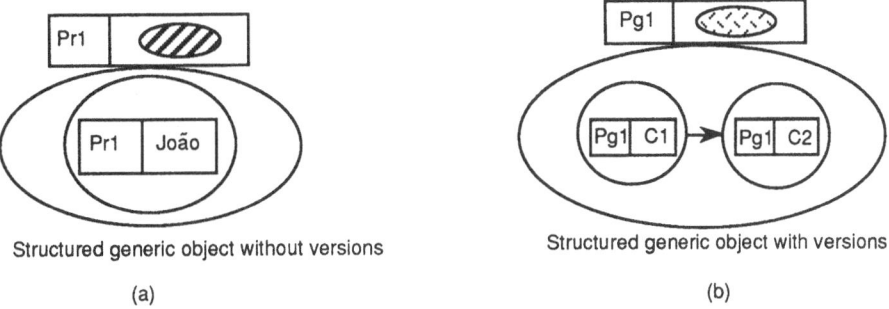

Structured generic object without versions	Structured generic object with versions
(a)	(b)

Figure 2. Structured generic object

VERSIONED CLASSES

We can now define classes, including the concept of generic object and version. A *class* is a collection of generic objects with their associated instances. A class is *versioned* if, for its associated object type, "having versions" is a defined property. Each generic object in the class has a collection of associated instances that constitutes its versions. In a *non versioned class*, each generic object has at most one associated instance (figure 3). Versions associated to a generic object are organized in a version derivation hierarchy, representing its evolution.

Class Hierarchies

In the basic proposed discipline, class hierarchies can be built where the property "has versions", defined for the class object type, is inherited by all types of subclasses. This property can be defined at any level of the hierarchy, not necessarily at the higher one. However, once defined, it cannot be declared again in lower levels, otherwise redundancy or inconsistency in the definition can occur. For example, **PROGRAMS** is a class with versioned objects of type **Program**, defined with properties **programmer_name** and **date**. **C_PROGRAMS** and **PASCAL_PROGRAMS** can be created as subclasses of **PROGRAMS**, and, as such, they have versioned objects and properties **programmer_name** and **date**. Versions of an object can be created in a class and/or in subclasses, and a correspondence must exist between them.

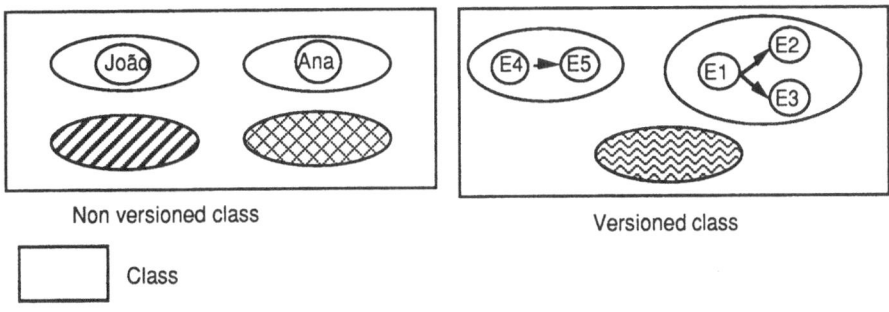

Non versioned class	Versioned class

Class

Figure 3. Versioned and non-versioned classes

Some systems allow redefinition of properties (overriding) in the class hierarchy, what is not incompatible with the proposed discipline.

Relationship between Versions in Classes and in Subclasses

When there is a versioned class and also a versioned subclass (by inheritance), the relationship between versions at both levels can be specified at the subclass definition. Two situations can be identified:

a) Relationship 1:1

In this case, each version present in the subclass must correspond exactly to one version in the superclass (figure 4(a)). For example, each version of C_program must correspond exactly to one version of Program.

b) Relationship 1:N

Several versions in the subclass correspond to only one version in the superclass. This can be the case when, at the subclass level, versions differ from their predecessor in few modifications, keeping inherited properties unchanged (figure 4(b)). For example, **DOCUMENTS** is a class with **SPECIFICATIONS** and **MANUALS** as subclasses. Manuals are Documents when some of its properties are abstracted. Several versions of one manual can be generated, keeping its properties as Document unchanged. So there is a correspondence of one Document version to many Manual versions.

When there is a non-versioned class and a versioned subclass, a relationship is established between a generic object in the class and versions in the subclass.

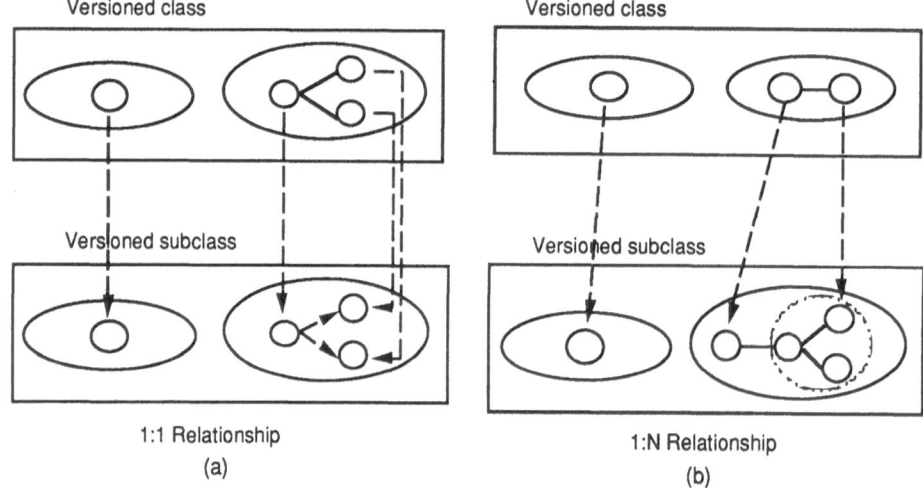

Figure 4. Relationship between versions in classes and subclasses

Relationship between Generic Objects in the Class and Versions in the Subclass

In this case, each generic object in the subclass (with all its versions) correspond exactly to one generic object in the class (figure 5).

OBJECTS FORMED WITH AGGREGATION

Each object in one class can be formed using aggregation, collection or list abstractions. In a design process, it is desirable that object versions keep common characteristics defined by the designer. We will initially consider objets formed with aggregation and analyze constraints applicable to the group of versions of one generic object. Objects formed with collection and list are discussed in the next section.

When defining an aggregate type, each component may be specified indicating the class to which it must belong. For example, the object type **Sort_program** may be defined with components belonging to the classes: **INPUT_MODULE**, **SORT_MODULE** and **OUTPUT_MODULE**. Each Sort_program has component modules that are objects from the component classes. The component object can be a generic object or an instance (in case the component class is non versioned) or a version (in case the component class is versioned).

Versioning Constraints

Restricting the composition of generated versions is desirable for the purpose of ensuring that common characteristics are maintained among them. It may be defined that versions of an aggregate object be composed only of versions of its components , making sure that all of them follow a defined pattern specified by the designer. This option will be called *restricted versioning* (is what is defined in ORION [Kim 89]). We can take the Sort_program example, assuming that the component classes are versioned. With the restricted versioned option defined, versions of a Sort_program should only be constructed with versions of its components modules.

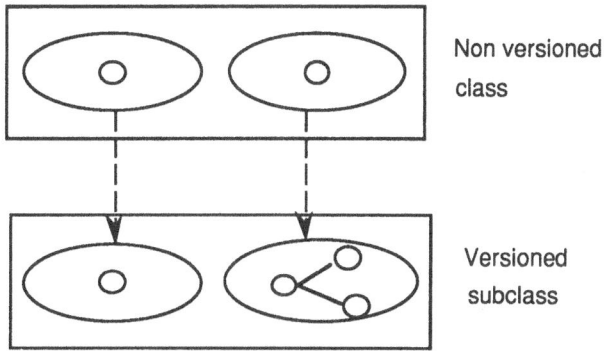

Figure 5. Relationship between generic objects in the class and objects (with versions) in the subclass

Alternatively, it may be defined that the designer can choose other objects/versions from the same component class, instead of being restricted to select only versions of the component object firstly defined. This option will be called *free versioning*. Free versioning allows the substitution of a component to be made not only within the "partition" determined by a generic object (i.e. generic object plus its versions) but within the component class. The decision of whether two objects are versions of the same generic object or are different objects from the same class is subjective, and it is left to the designer.

Table 1 shows versioning possibilities for a structured object (set and list structured objects are explained in section 6) depending on the versioning option (defined for the class to which it belongs) and on the type of component/element it possesses. A version of an aggregate object is also an aggregate, with equal number and type of components, but with different components. The versioning rules define how a new version can be created, either starting from the generic object or deriving from other version, constraining component substitutions that can be made.

Figure 6 shows, for example, three versions of the object Sort_program that have been generated considering free versioning option. If restricted versioning had been considered, the last version would not had been accepted.

Table 1. Versioning restrictions for aggregate/set structured object

Component/element type \ Versioning type	Restricted versioning	Free versioning
1-Generic object without versions	-only associated instance	-only instance -other generic object of the same class
2-Object instance without versions	-cannot be substituted	-generic object from the same class
3-Generic object with versions	-some associated version	-some associated version -other generic object of the same class
4-Version	- other version of the same generic object -correspondent generic object	-other version of the same generic object -generic object from the same class
5-any type (only applicable in case of set structured object)	-same number of elements	-different number of elements

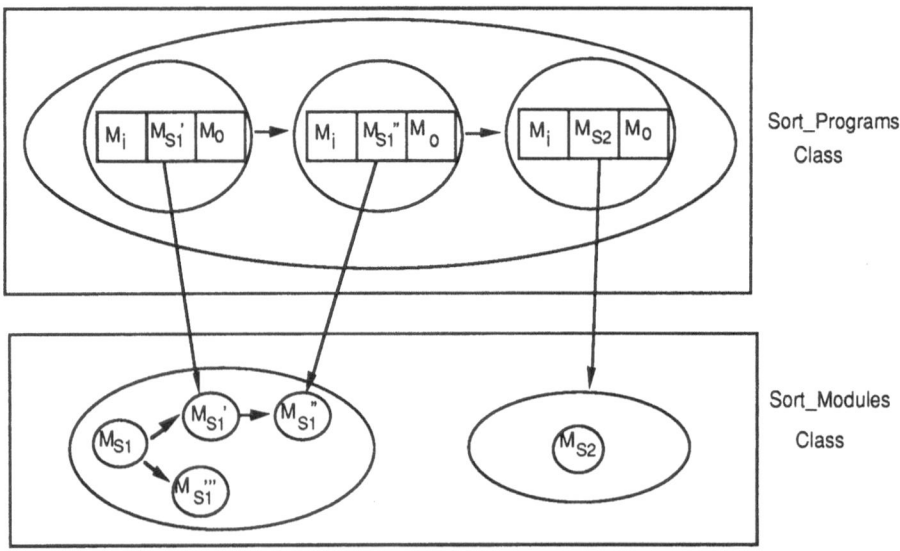

Figure 6. Free versioning for aggregated object

OBJECTS FORMED WITH COLLECTION

A set structured object is defined as a set of objects of one specific class. Elements of a set can be generic objects or instances. Having a generic object as an element means that the element has some already known characteristics but is not completely defined. For example, the class **PROGRAMMERS_TEAM** contains objects of type **Programmer_team = {Programmer}**. When a new project is being defined, the designated team can be created even if not all of its elements are known. Figure 7 shows a generic object Programmer_team with four programmers, where two of them are new ones, represented by different generic objects.

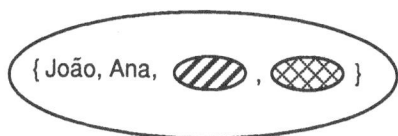

Figure 7. Generic object of set type

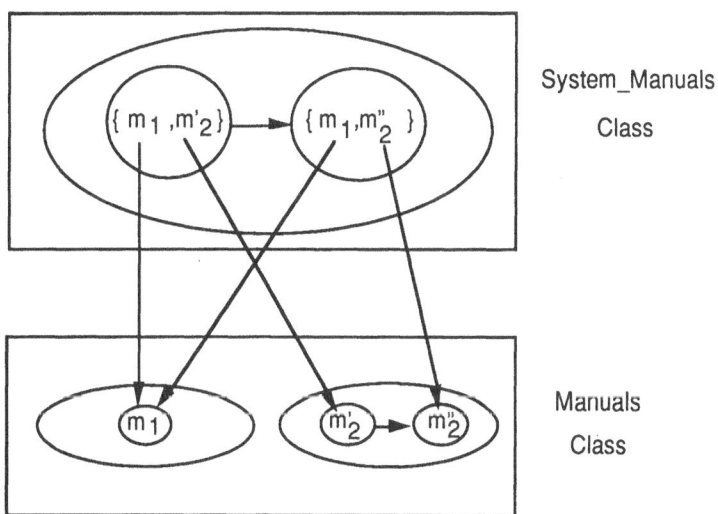

Figure 8. Restricted versioning for set structured object

Objects of set type can be versioned and the system must also manage these generated versions in order to ensure common characteristics to all versions related to a generic object. Value inheritance also occurs from the generic object to its instances.

As with aggregate objects, versioning can be restricted or free. The rules in table 1 define that versions of a set can be build by element substitution (rules 1 to 4) and - only in free versioning - by including or excluding elements (rule 5). Figure 8 shows versions of one System_manuals object (set structured), considering restricted versioning.

List structured objects have analogous rules as those for set structured objects, since the difference is that an order exists among the elements of a list.

CONCLUSIONS

In the present work, an approach to the systematic analysis of the version and the versioning concepts in the context of object orientation was proposed. The main aspects considered were the notion of generic object, relationships between objects (and versions) and their ascendents in the class or type hierarchies, and the process of constructing versions of atomic (primitive) and structured objects.

The concept of generic object was redefined to allow a uniform treatment for objects with or without versions.

Cardinality constraints were defined for the relationship between objects (and their versions) and their ascendents in class or type hierarchies. These constraints are necessary because versions may appear in any level of the hierarchy related with other objects (and versions) appearing in other levels.

It was clear that the versioning process is constrained by the structure and the type of the versions of its components or elements. Objects constructed as an aggregation, a set or a list have similar versioning rules, except by the fact that sets and lists have a variable number of elements, while tuples have a fixed number of components.

The systematic analysis of the version concept in the context of object orientation is required to the comparison of database models and systems. The discipline proposed in the present work attempts to fill the lack of conceptual foundations supporting the version and versioning concepts.

Methods and integrity constraints were not considered in the proposed discipline until the present time.

ACKNOWLEDGEMENTS

We want to thank Isabel H. Manssour, José Valdeni de Lima and Carlos Alberto Heuser for their help in preparing the final version of this paper.

REFERENCES

[Alb 85] Albano, A.; Cardelli,L.; Orsini, R. Galileo: a strongly typed, interactive conceptual language. *ACM Transactions on Database Systems*, 10(2): 230-60, June 1985.

[Alb 88] Albano, A. Comments at the "Workshop on Object-Oriented Database Systems", Bad Münster am Stein-Ebernburg, 1988.

[Atk 89] Atkinson, M.; Bancilhon, F.; DeWitt, D.; Dittrich, K.; Maier, D. & Zdonik, S. *The object-oriented database system - manifesto.* Rapport Technique Altaïr 30-89, 21 août 1989.

[Bee 89] Beeri, C. Formal models for object-oriented databases. *Proc. 1st International Conference on Deductive and Object-Oriented Databases*, Kyoto, December 1989.

[Ber 88] Berkel, T. et al. Modelling CAD-objects by abstraction. Proc. *3rd International Conference on Data and Knowledge Bases*, Jerusalem, Israel, June 28-30, 1988. p. 227-240.

[Bor 84] Borgida, A.; Mylopoulos, J.; Wong, H.K.T. Generalization/specialization as a basis for software specification. In: Brodie, M.L.; Mylopoulos, J.; Schmidt, J.W. (eds.): *On conceptual modelling* (Perspectives from Artificial Inteligence, Databases and Programming Languages), Topics in Information Systems, Springer-Verlag, New York, 1984. p. 87-114.

[Dit 87] Dittrich, K.R.; Gotthard, W.; Lockemann, P.C. DAMOKLES-a database system for software engineering environments. In: Conradi, R.; Didriksen, T.M.; Wanvik (eds.): Advanced Programming Environments. *Lecture Notes in Computer Science* 244, Springer-Verlag, 1987. p. 353-371.

[Kim 87] Kim, W. et al. Composite object support in an object-oriented database system. Proc. *OOPSLA'87*, Orlando, Florida, October 4-8, 1987. p.118-125.

[Kim 89] Kim, W.; Bertino, E.; Garza, J. Composite objects revisited. Proc. *ACM-SIGMOD Conference*, Portland, Oregon, May 31-June 2, 1989. p.337-347.

[Smi 77] Smith, J.M. & Smith, D.C.P. Database abstractions: aggregation and generalization. *ACM Transactions on Database Systems*, 2(2):105-133, June 1977.

DDRAW: AN OBJECT-ORIENTED DESIGN TOOL

M. Glaser

University of Karlsruhe
Institute for Real-Time Control Systems and Robotics
P.O. Box 6980, D-7500 Karlsruhe 1, Germany
Email: glaser@ira.uka.de

ABSTRACT

In general, graphical tools are a powerful approach for engineering activities. During design and analysis they help to model both the problem and potential solutions. During testing or debugging they can provide a quick visual means of generating test cases. And finally, during maintenance, well-executed graphics can guide software engineers in the repair and extension of existing systems.

The philosophy for the development of ddraw was to elaborate a graphical design tool with wide application fields. ddraw allows the construction of hierarchical structures by the use of a small set of graphical elements. A system in ddraw consists of components and relations between those. Components in turn may contain one or more subcomponents. Each component is described by a name, a graphical element, a set of ports and a text field. As graphical objects the user can choose between predefined elements like circles, boxes, rounded boxes and self defined icons. Ports represent the interfaces of components and can be linked to other ports. Additionally, the text field allows the user to attach any semantical meaning to each component.

ddraw has been implemented on top of the X Window System and uses window techniques and pointing devices to make the construction of complex systems manageable. For example, it supports building up and breaking down hierarchies, moving, copying, editing, storing and restoring partial structures, etc. Thus, it is easy to realize top-down, middle-out, or bottom-up design. Furthermore, a survey window facilitates the navigation through the components and their hierarchical levels.

In order to keep ddraw as a general purpose tool, the created structures are stored in an application independent *Model Description Language* (MDL). Structures described in MDL contain the complete information about their topology as well as the graphical and semantical attributes of all components. Thus, systems designed with ddraw can further be used by other tools like code generators, syntax checkers, simulators, etc.

COMPUTER SCIENCE, Edited by R. Baeza-Yates
and U. Manber, Plenum Press, New York, 1992

INTRODUCTION

During all phases of system development, whether in the area of the physical world, economy, or science, it turned out that hierarchical approaches are very sensible and useful for various reasons. At first, hierarchies reproduce the immanent *stratification* of complex systems, and thus provide a very natural means for their development or modeling. System development often evolves in the process of *restructuring* or *redesigning* an existing system to improve its overall functionality or performance. The possibility of completely restructuring or redesigning the total complex in a most rational way is rarely, due to economic, technical, and human constraints. Hierarchical decomposition and modularization supports this process and additionally allows easy *extensions* by the *integration* of well defined subsets of the total complexity. Hierarchical structures overcome potential *limitation* and therefore provides a better *utilization* of resources, which is especially important for large scale systems. Finally, hierarchies improve the *flexibility* and *reliability*. The former, because changes in the decision procedure necessitated by changes in the operation of subsystems can easily be localized and, therefore, accounted for with less cost and in a shorter time, which improves the latter, the reliability [8].

Since the construction of large scale hierarchical systems is a quite complicated job, it is desirable to have a computer guided support. Hierarchical structures present themselves for graphical representation, therefore mainly graphical tools have been provided, especially since powerful graphical workstations have been made available with reasonable costs. Unfortunately, most of these tools are restricted to some special applications or do not provide openended interfaces for further processing.

This paper describes an approach for the development of hierarchical systems called ddraw (design ddraw), an object oriented graphical design tool, that is provided with a well defined, openended user interface, and thus can be employed in wide application fields. The present paper is structured as follows: in the next section, we firstly describe the internal data structure of ddraw. After that, we give a short overview of the graphical user interface. In section 3 we present the external data format, and finally we discuss some aspects of the implementation and our experiences with ddraw.

STRUCTURE AND DESIGN SUPPORT

Each object used in ddraw is derived from the basis class *Element* (see Fig. 1). Each *Element* instantiation contains an unique identifier *Id*, a *Name* and textual (*Text*) as well as graphical (*Graphic*) attributes. *Id* is exclusively used internally in order to keep the consistency of the whole structure and can not be accessed by the user, whereas name and attributes are used by the derived classes.

The classes *Node*, *Port* and *Edge* are derived from the basis class *Element* and have been extended with the necessary information. Thus, *Node* additionally contains pointers to double linked lists of its subnodes and ports, as well as a pointer to its parent node. The class *Port* additionally contains a pointer to the node to which it is attached and its type (input/output). Finally, each *Edge* contains a pointer to the source and destination ports. Due to this class hierarchy all design elements provided by ddraw (nodes, ports, edges) contain a common set of attributes, namely name, text, and graphic, which can be set or changed during the design in different ways. Only ports have fixed graphical attributes.

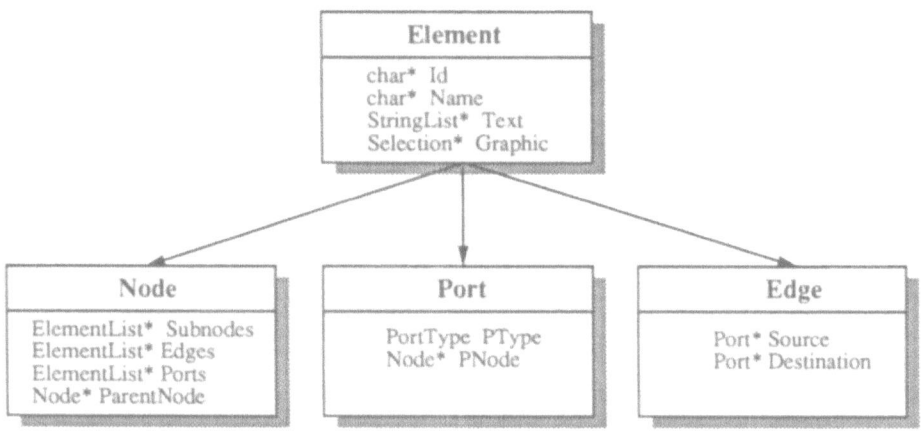

Figure 1. Class hierarchy of ddraw

The user interface of ddraw consists of various means to allow an easy interaction between the user, novice or expert, and ddraw. The user interface of ddraw is composed of four parts, namely: a *status line*, a *tool palette* a *pull-down menu panel* and a *drawing area*. Fig. 2 shows the structure of the ddraw main window.

The **status line** on the top contains fields which give information about some of the current settings. The **tool palette** on the left has several icon fields, which can be selected using a pointing device or the keyboard.

The **drawing area** shows the components of one level in the system hierarchy in a graphical way. Each of these graphical elements are internally represented as abstract objects and thus can be handled separately without interfering with other objects. Therefore, the graphical abilities of the drawing area give ddraw the full expressiveness of an object oriented, general purpose drawing tool.

The user can create new components at the level showed in the drawing area selecting the *Ellipse, Rectangle or Rounded rectangle* icons of the tool palette as in standard drawing programs. After the selection of *Input* or *Output Port* icons, he can attach interaction points or interfaces (ports) to components. Their location is automatically centered to the component's border. Finally, it is possible to link only output ports with input ports using the *DATA* or *CNTRL* modes.

After moving components containing linked ports, all edges will be updated automatically. It is important to mention that the current version of ddraw does not supports automatic layout. For these reason, and in order to allow the user to make his own layout, the edges have been implemented as bsplines with 4 support points, namely one start point, two support points and the end point. Thus, he can adapt the course of the edges considering his preferences.

Following the main requirement imposed to ddraw, i.e. keep the tool as general as possible, the *Inscribe* mode allows to attach a name and textual attributes to each graphical object (component, port, edge). For this purpose the user obtains a new window with a name and text field.

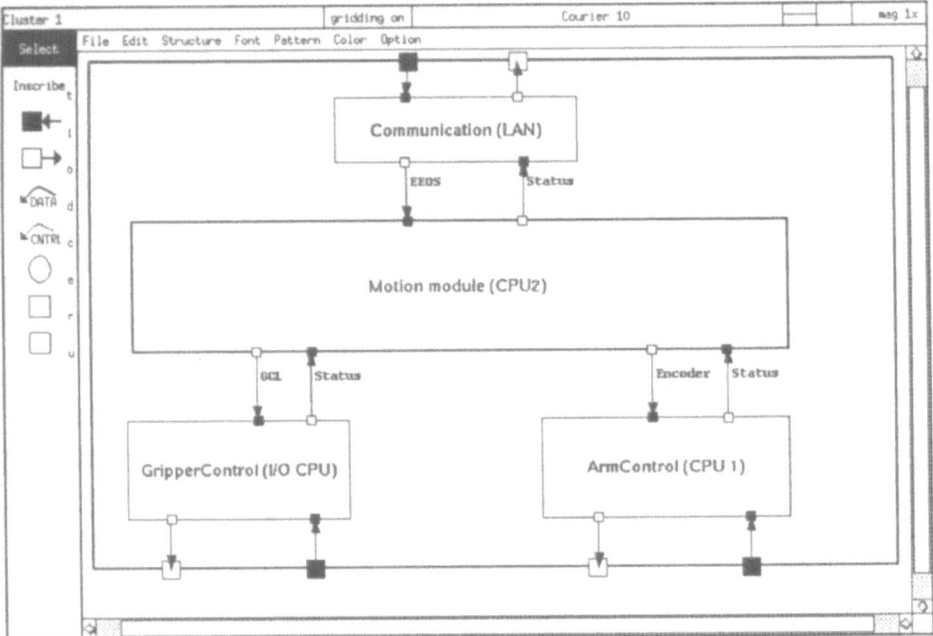

Figure 2. Structure of the **ddraw** window

The *pull-down menu panel* contains menus for setting the component appearance (*Font*, *Pattern* and *Color*), changing some attributes of the drawing field like perspective, grid and others (*Option*). It contains also other menus more related with the system design process.

The *Structure* menu deals with the manipulation of node structures and the navigation through the hierarchical levels. It contains for a example a *Survey* function, which displays in a separate window the complete hierarchy of the system as a tree (see Fig. 3) and highlights the actual node for better orientation. The selection of one node in the survey window allows to change the hierarchy level. Thus, it is very easy to navigate through the structure with the aid of the survey window. Beside this, it is also possible to go one level upper or deeper using the commands *Superstructure* or *Substructure* respectively.

Furthermore, there are two functions which allow to save or load only parts of the whole hierarchical structure (*Read* and *Write*). These two functions are for example very useful during model development by several users. Moreover, they can be used to insert standard parts into new structures, and to create libraries. Finally, with the function *Coarsen* it is possible to group several components into a new one and *Refine* is its reverse function.

EXTERNAL FORMAT: MDL

In general, the information generated by graphical design tools can not further be used by other tools. In some cases it is necessary to add more information in order to get the original structure [12], [9]. In other cases the whole information is kept internally [2], so that the export of the designed structures is not possible. For this reason, and in order to keep the application field of ddraw as general as possible, the structures generated by ddraw are stored in MDL (Model Description Language).

254

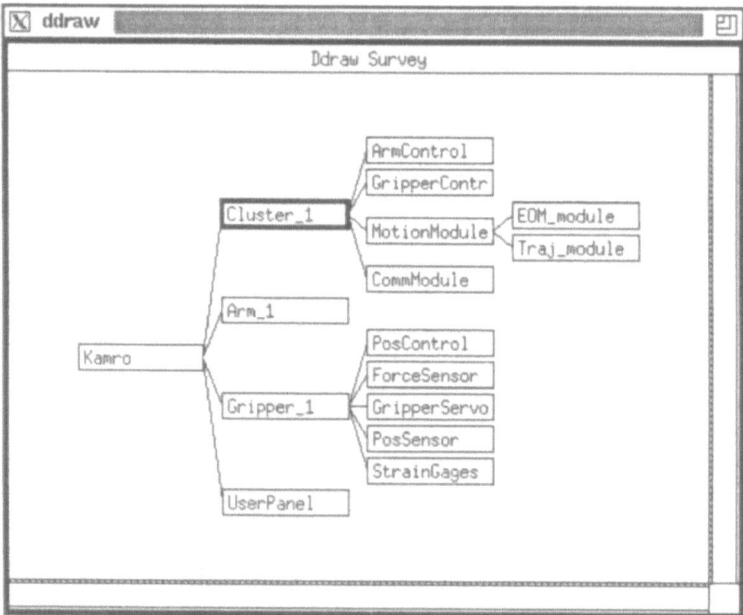

Figure 3. The **ddraw** survey window

MDL has been developed as a language for the representation of any structure (e.g. hierarchical structures) with any number of attributes attached to elements of the structure, and therefore, it is application independent. In **ddraw**, structures described in MDL contain the complete information about their topology as well as the graphical and semantical attributes of all components. MDL only knows *types*, *variables* and *assignments*. There are *basic* and *structured* types. The basic types, expressed in LEX-notation [5] , are the following:

```
NAME            ::= [A-Za-z][A-Za-z0-9_\-]*
DECIMAL         ::= [+-]?[0-9]+ | [+-]?[0-9]*\.[0-9]+
TEXT            ::= \"([^\"]|\\\")*\"
```

and the MDL-grammar can be described in EBNF-notation as follows:

```
start           ::= {[type_decl]|[var_decl] |[var_asignment]}

type_decl       ::= "TYPE"new_type(standard_type| selection_type)
standard_type   ::= old_type|"{"{var_decl}"}"
selection_type  ::= old_type{"|"old_type}

var_decl        ::= old_type(var|var_assignment)
var_assignment  ::= var"="cast_value
cast_value      ::= ["("old_type {["."old_type]}")"]value
value           ::= DECIMAL|TEXT|["*"|"&"]var|list|
                    "{"{var_assignment}"}"
list            ::= "["[cast_value {[","cast_value]}]"]"
```

```
new_type      ::= NAME
old_type      ::= ["LIST OF"]NAME["*"]
var           ::= NAME
```

It is very important to remark that the **ddraw** types expressed in MDL are very similar to the hierarchy class (see Fig. 1). There are only some differences especially due to some graphical representation constraints. In order to give a clear notion how MDL is used by **ddraw** we give in the last part of this section a short example. Fig. 4 shows a system composed of 3 nodes and their interconnections. The file generated by **ddraw** has following form:

```
Node N0 = {                        Port P1 = {
  name = "Proc_1"                    name = ""
  attributes = {                     attributes = {
    text = ""                          text = ""
    graphic = nil                      graphic = PortGraphic
  }                                  }
  position = []                      position = [258,469,8,8]
  parent = nil                       type = In
  subnodes = [&N1,&N2,&N3]           node = N1
  ports = []                         extern_edges = [&E1,&E2]
  edges = [&E1,&E2]                  intern_edges = []
}                                  }
Node N1 = {                        Node Port P2 = {
  name = "Task 1"                    ...
  attributes = {                   }
    text = ""                      Node Port P3 = {
    graphic = StandardGraphic        ...
  }                                }
  position = [192,452,70,42]       Edge E1 = {
  parent = &N0                       name = ""
  subnodes = []                      attributes = {
  ports = [P1]                         text = ""
  edges = []                           graphic = EdgeGraphic
}                                    }
Node N2 = {                          coord = [ 401,473,355,457,
  name = "Task 2"                              308,440,262,473 ]
  ...                                source = P2
}                                    destination = P1
Node N3 = {                        }
  name = "Task 3"                  Edge E2 = {
  ...                                ...
}                                  }
```

IMPLEMENTATION AND CONCLUSIONS

ddraw has been implemented in C++ [13] under the X Window System [10], [4], [11]. We chose C++ because its object-oriented approach is on one hand very useful for the handling with graphical elements and on the other hand very natural for the mapping of hierarchical structures. Furthermore, it is a superset of the language C and allows a clear

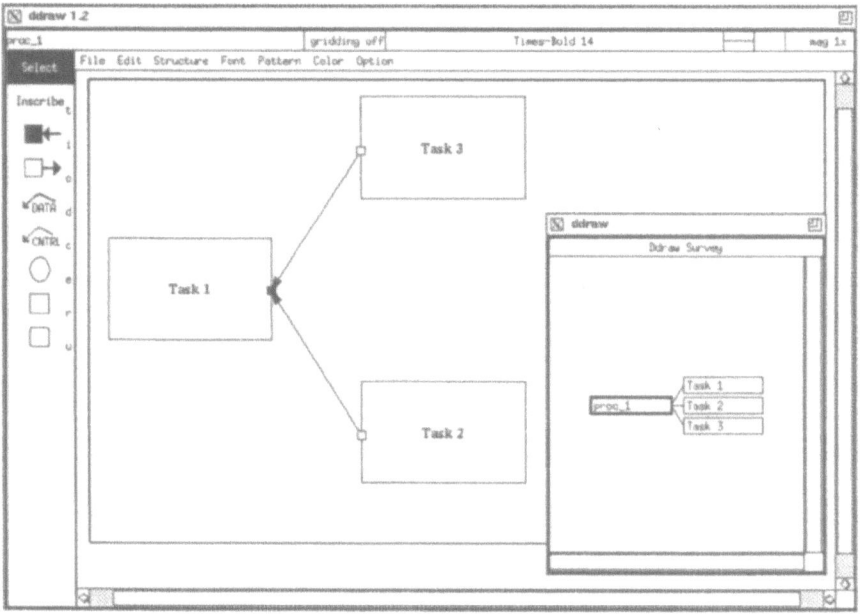

Figure 4. ddraw example

and modular program design. As interface between the X Window System and C++ we used the InterViews Toolkit [1], [7], [6], which is a package that supports the composition of a graphical user interface from a set of interactive objects. The MDL-libraries have been implemented using the UNIX standard packages 'LEX' and 'YACC' [3].

As we showed in the previous sections, ddraw is a graphical design tool with a wide application field and a well-defined interface language which allows the use of designed models as input for other applications. Due to this openness ddraw can be employed in various application areas, like e.g. code generation, simulation, knowledge based systems. One concrete application already uses ddraw-models for the simulation of extended Predicate/Transition nets, and is part of the Esprit Project REX (2080).

Although the current version does not support automatic layout and has some restrictions due to graphical constraints, it is possible to design quite complex systems in short time. During our work with ddraw, we found out that not only the hierarchical structure and the component relations can further be used, but also the graphical information, added by the user during the design phase, can be very useful for applications which show dynamic system behavior (i.e. visualization of the *token game* in Petri nets, monitoring changes in distributed systems during operation, etc.). A first step in this direction has been the development of a visualization tool for ddraw-MDL models, which already uses the complete static information delivered by ddraw.

ACKNOWLEDGMENTS

We would like to acknowledge the advice and expertise of Peter Kneisel for his contribution in the design phase and Stefan Karsten for his contribution in the implementation. We want also gratefully acknowledge the CEC in the Esprit Project REX (2080) for their financial support.

REFERENCES

[1] Computer Systems Laboratory, Stanford University. *InterViews Reference Manual (Version 2.6)*, Nov. 1989.

[2] J. Dähler, P. Gerber, H. Gisiger, and A. Kündig. A Graphical Tool for Design and Prototyping of Distributed System . *ACM SIGSOFT: Software engineering notes*, 12(3):25–36, July 1987.

[3] S. Johnson. Yacc: Yet Another Compiler-Compiler. In *Unix Programmer's Manual*. Bell Laboratories, 1978.

[4] A. Jones. *Introduction to the X Window system*. Prentice-Hall, 1989.

[5] M. Lesk and E. Schmidt. Lex: A Lexical Analyzer Generator. In *Unix Programmer's Manual*. Bell Laboratories, 1978.

[6] M. Linton. Composing User Interfaces with InterViews. *IEEE Computer*, pages 8–22, Feb. 1989.

[7] M. Linton, P. Calder, and J. Vlissides. The Design and Implementation of InterViews. In *Proceedings of the USENIX C++ Workshop, Santa Fe, New Mexico*, Nov. 1987.

[8] M. Mesarovic, D. Macko, and Y. Takahara. *Theory of Hierarchical, Multilevel, Systems*. Academic Press, 1970.

[9] F. Newberry-Paulisch and W. Tichy. EDGE: An Extendible Graph Editor. *Software-Practice and Experience*, 20(S1):63–88, June 1990.

[10] A. Nye and T. O'Reilly. *Volume 3, X Window System User's Guide*. O'Really & Associates, Inc., 1990.

[11] R. Scheifler and J. Gettys. The X Window System. *ACM Transactions on Graphics*, 5(2):79–109, Apr. 1986.

[12] G. Scheschonk. Design/CPN - Ein Werkzeug zur Simulation von hierarchischen CP-Netzen . Technical report, C.I.T. Communication and Information Technology GmbH, Apr. 1989.

[13] B. Stroustrup. *The C++ Programming language*. Addison-Wesley, 1986.

A GRAPHICAL INTERACTIVE OBJECT-ORIENTED

DEVELOPMENT SYSTEM

Michel Adar[1], Eliezer Kantorowitz[1], and Ehud Bar-On[2]

[1]Computer Science Department
[2]Science Education Department
Technion - Israel Institute of Technology
Haifa, Israel

1. Introduction

One of the major obstacles in the construction of large software systems is in the difficulties humans have in understanding the interactions between it's many different parts. Behavioral studies show that humans can only cope with a relatively small amount of elements and relationships at a time. A program development environment should therefore, ideally, only show to the designer the required details and hide all other irrelevant and therefore distracting items. At different stages of the design process different parts of the program and different kinds of relationships between the programs elements are considered. To meet these needs the GOODS (Graphical Object-Oriented Development System) system was developed. GOODS enables the user to get a graphical description (a GOODS diagram) of the the part of the programs that is in her *Focus Of Attention* (FOA) and from the *Point Of View* (POV) that interests her. The POV concept, introduced in this paper, is a specification of the kind of details and relationships that interest the user. Relationships of kinds that are not members of the selected POV will not be shown in the diagram.

GOODS diagrams employ a new graphical language designed to describe the structure of Object-Oriented Programs. It is based on an analysis of current Object-Oriented Programming (OOP) languages and is composed of a small set of element types and the relationships between them. The POV and FOA concepts are precisely defined in terms of the elements and relationships composing the programs structure. This definition permits the automatic production of the diagrams. The heart of the GOODS system is a data base containing the structure of the program being developed. This data base may be updated by editing the graphical representation in the diagrams or by editing the source code. The dual representation of diagrams and code allow the user to switch between the two, any change in one of them will automatically cause the change in the other.

GOODS was implemented in the C++ programming language, using the X-Windows system on a UNIX workstation. All the diagrams contained in this work were produced by this GOODS prototype.

COMPUTER SCIENCE, Edited by R. Baeza-Yates
and U. Manber, Plenum Press, New York, 1992

In the following sections the GOODS graphical language is presented along with it's theoretical foundation, the FOA and POV concepts are precisely defined and finally, an overview of the system that implements the principles of the GOODS language is presented.

2. An overview of the GOODS Language

We define a graphic language that captures the basic components of the object oriented programming paradigm.

After analyzing the concepts employed in most Object-Oriented languages, we concluded that the most important construct of this programming paradigm may be represented by three types of elements, and a set of relationships between them. The elements are:

class
function or method
object

In order to exemplify the strength of the language a simple library containing List manipulation classes will be used as an example.

The graphical representation of these elements are demonstrated in figure 2.1, which shows the definition of the class List. Note that the methods of the class are drawn inside the box of the class. Public members touch the borders but private ones are well inside the box; the member *tail* is a private one. Objects contained in the class are oval and are drawn in the right side of the class box.

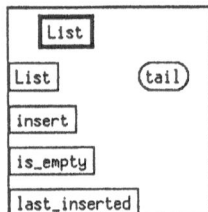

Figure 2.1 - The class List

First order relationships defined

Relationships that connect two elements directly are called first order relationships.

The first order relationships employed in GOODS are:

contains
calls
references
is an instance of
inherits from
returns

There is a graphical representation for each one of the first order relationships. Figure 2.2 shows the class *List_iterator* and all the elements used by it. The arrows mark the *is an instance of* relationship. This class provides the means to iterate over all the elements of a list by using the *more* and *next* methods.

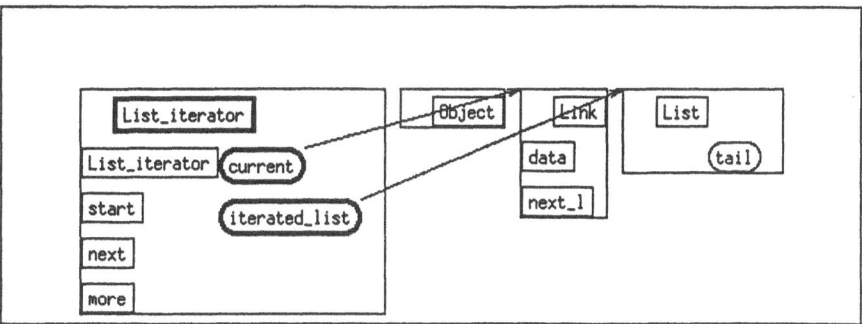

Figure 2.2 - The class *List_iterator* and all the elements used by it

The inheritance relationship

In the literature the inheritance relationship is usually depicted by a tree or DAG (Directed Acyclic Graph). This representation shows only the existence of the inheritance relationship between the classes, but fails to show which elements are inherited. A GOODS diagram shows the elements that are inherited. Inheritance is depicted in GOODS as containment of the parent class inside the child class. This graphical representation is demonstrated in figure 2.3.

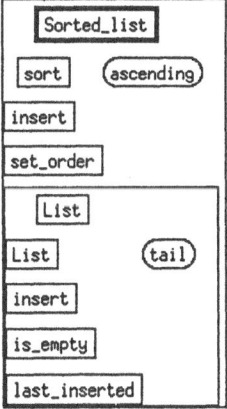

Figure 2.3 - The class *Sorted_list* inherits from the class *List*

The first order relationships may connect any pair of elements. Note however that some programming languages permit only some of these relationships. Pascal, for instance, permits a function being contained in another one, this is however not permitted in C. Figure 2.4 shows the relationships between the elements that are available in languages like C++ and Smalltalk, and which we employ in GOODS.

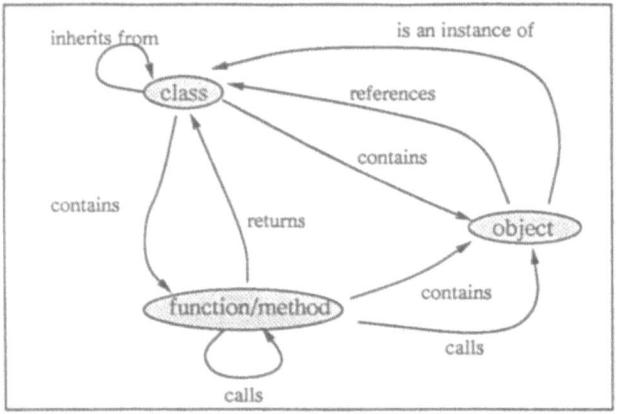

Figure 2.4 - Relationships between the element types

High order relationships defined

Some of the most interesting relationships between program elements are defined by combining first order relationships using the set of operators defined here:

composition – @   *transitive closure* – *   *reverse* – $_R$ *or* – |

Composition

The composition operator concatenates two relationships, for example if we wish to express the relationship between a class and a method called by other methods contained in the class, we may define:

calls$_c$ (calls via contains) ::= contains @ calls

Transitive closure

A class may have many ancestors. In order to represent the relationship between a class and all its ancestors, we define the transitive closure of the *inherits from* relationship by a recursive composition of the *inherits from* relationship with itself, formally:

if *(e$_1$ inherits from e$_2$)* **then** *(e$_1$ inherits from* * *e$_2$)*   (1)

if *(e$_1$ inherits from* * *e$_2$)* **and** *(e$_2$ inherits from e$_3$)* **then** *(e$_1$ inherits from* * *e$_3$)* (2)

Reverse

Relationships are directed, they have an *actor* and a *recipient*. To define a new relationship that inverts the places of the actor and the recipient, we use the reverse operator. For example, we define the relationship that holds between a method and all its callers as:

is called by ::= calls$_R$

Example

The client server relationship between classes may be defined as:

is client of ::= contains @ r @ contains$_R$

where

r ::= calls | references | returns | is an instance of

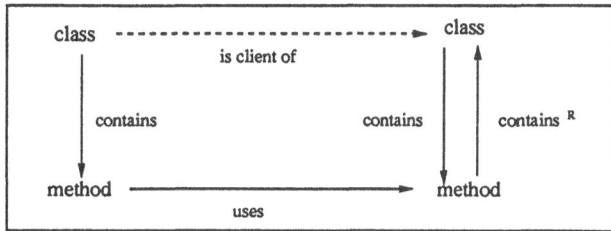

Figure 2.5 - The *is client of* relationship

3. The FOA and POV concepts

As explained in the introduction, one of the main problems in the development of large complex programs are the difficulties that human have in perceiving all the effects of the many kinds of relationships between the different program components. GOODS was therefore designed with the object of giving the maximum support to the humans who try to understand the properties of the program. To achieve this, GOODS enables the user to get whenever required a diagram that shows only the information needed and hides all irrelevant details.

To get such abstraction of the program, the user has only to specify two parameters. The first is called the *Focus Of Attention* (FOA), that is defined as the set of program elements the user wish to study. The second is called the *Point Of View* (POV), that is the set of relationship types to be displayed in the diagram.

The system will display a GOODS diagram comprising of all the members of the FOA. The diagram will furthermore show program elements that are connected to the members of the FOA with relations of the types specified in the POV. A typical diagram will therefore have more components than the FOA, but not cover the entire program (fig. 3.1).

The user can browse through a given program by selecting different FOA. The part of the program selected by the FOA can be studied from different points of view by choosing the corresponding POVs.

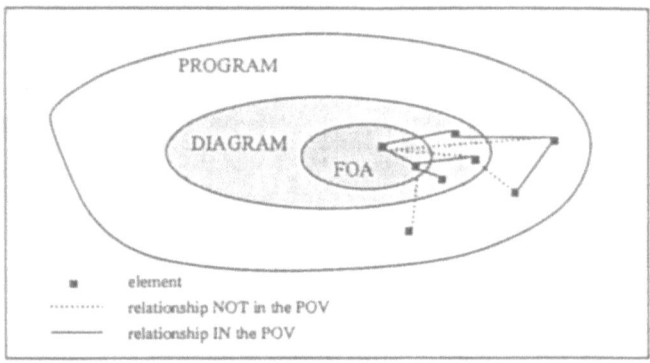

Figure 3.1 - The program, the diagram, the foa

We shall now explain how the system automatically constructs the diagram to be displayed from the user selected FOA and POV. A program can be described by a graph whose edges represent the relationships and the nodes the elements. From the specified FOA and POV, the system automatically determines the nodes and edges of the sub-graph (the GOODS diagram) to be displayed. We shall now explain how the system computes this sub-graph.

Let $D(foa,pov)$ be the GOODS diagram that corresponds to a given FOA, *foa* and a given POV, *pov*. We define:

$$D(foa,pov) = (E,R) \tag{3}$$

where E denotes the set of elements in the diagram, and R denotes the set of relationships in the diagram.

The set E contains all the elements of the FOA and some extra elements that are necessary to understand the FOA. We aim to minimize this set of extra elements so that it includes only elements that are really required. Our premise is that these extra elements are related to the FOA via relationships of the types specified in the POV.

With e, e_1 and e_2 representing elements and r representing relationships, the set E of elements to be displayed is calculated as:

$$E(foa, pov) = \{e \mid (e \in foa) \tag{4a}$$

or

$$(e_1 \in foa) \text{ and } (e_1 \ r \ e \text{ for } type(r) \in pov)\} \tag{4b}$$

We shall now define three POVs, namely, *uses*, *inheritance*, and *servers*.

$$POV_{uses} = \{ contains, inherits\ from^*, uses, contains @ uses, is\ client\ of \} \tag{5}$$

where

$$uses ::= \{ calls, returns, references, is\ an\ instance\ of \}$$

$$POV_{inheritance} = \{ inherits\ from^*, contains, inherits\ from^* \} \tag{6}$$

$$POV_{servers} = \{ is\ client\ of \} \tag{7}$$

Additional types of POVs may be defined to meet needs that arise. To create a new type of POV the user simply defines the set of relationships that connect the elements of interest. If necessary, the user can define new types of relationships, either as a combination of existing ones or as user defined relationships.

4. Using the FOA and POV concepts

We present here several GOODS diagrams that show different views of the example program corresponding to different FOAs and POVs.

Getting an overview

One of the most useful POVs is POV_{uses} because it provides a good overview of the selected class (the class in the FOA).

Figure 4.1 shows the class *Sorted_list* as FOA, displayed with POV_{uses} (this POV is given in definition (6)). The set E of elements to be displayed can be derived from the formulas 4*a* and 4*b* (see section 3). The elements that are displayed as a result of 4*a* are as follows:

- the class *Sorted_list*, because it is in the FOA.

The elements that are displayed as a result of 4*b* are:

- from the *contains* relationship the methods *sort, insert, set_order*

- from the *contains @ uses* relationship the methods *next_l, set_next* from the class Link and the method *is_bigger* from the class *Object*, because they are all called from inside the methods of *Sorted_list*.

- from the *is client of* relationship the classes *Object* and *Link*

- from the *inherits from** relationship the class *List*.

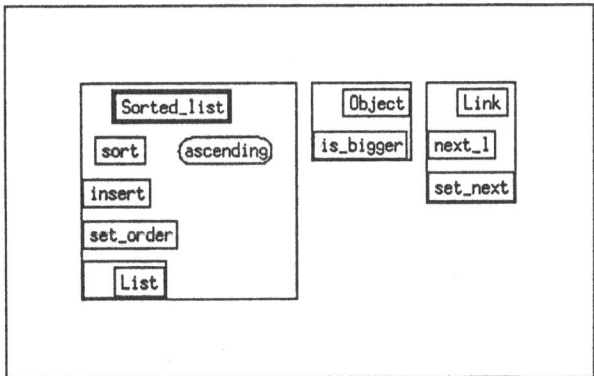

Figure 4.1 - FOA = { *Sorted_list* }, POV_{uses}

In order to examine some other class, for example the class *List*, the user has only to specify FOA = {*List*} and GOODS will generate the diagram shown in Figure 4.2. POV_{uses} remains selected and elements related to the class *List* appear. The *Link* class is shown in greater detail in order to display all the elements used by members of the *List* class.

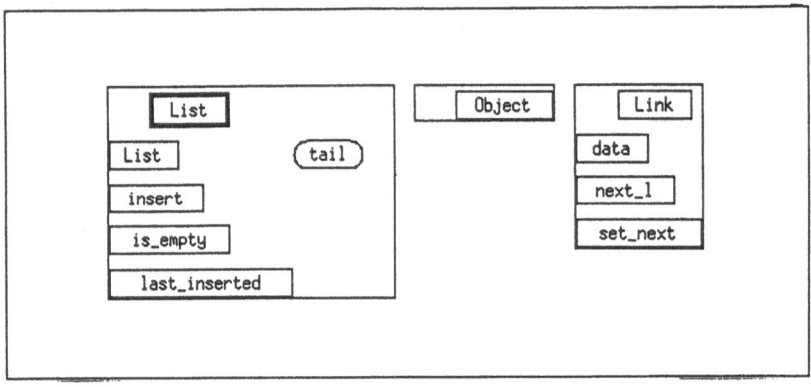

Figure 4.2 - FOA = { *List* }, POV_{uses}

Highlights of the GOODS graphical representation

Some aspects of the GOODS graphical representation are similar to those of the graphical representation of the Ada language by R.J.A Buhr (1984) and G. Booch (1991). GOODS diagrams, however, are more general because they are not related to a specific programming language. They contain constructs that depict the object-oriented aspects of a program, such as inheritance and the public/private mechanism. The GOODS notation for inheritance complements the widely used tree-like notation (this later notation is also available in GOODS). The GOODS notation shows the members available for the class, along with the classes in which those members are defined. When multiple inheritance is used, the following task may be very difficult for the user or the program reader tracing the classes in which the different members are defined and deciding, when a member is defined in more than one of a class's ancestors, which ancestor member will be called for a given invocation. The problem is that different OOP languages use different policies to resolve collisions that result from multiple inheritance. GOODS diagrams address this problem by showing graphically the members of a class and their source, after the multiple inheritance resolution is applied by the system.

In a GOODS diagram, the boundaries of a class box indicate the public/private mechanism. The GOODS system applies the following rule to determine which class members can be accessed:

> A member can be accessed only if an arrow can be
> drawn from the caller to the called element without crossing
> a class boundary from the outside to the inside of the class.

This simple and intuitive rule behaves like the public/private mechanism giving it a graphical representation. To allow conformance with the rule, public class members touch the boundaries of the class box, and private members stay within the limits of the class box.

GOODS is primarily an interactive environment, in which the user can at any point of time specify an FOA and POV and the system will display the corresponding diagram. GOODS also permits the user to assign textual comments to the different program elements being defined, and request that they pop up in special windows. This feature enables GOODS diagrams to serve as a documentation and teaching tool.

5. The GOODS system

The ideas presented in this paper have been implemented in an experimental GOODS system. It was developed on Sun and IBM-RT workstations using the X-Windows system and the C++ language. The system permits the user to browse through the code of a program and edit it. The source code of the program is analyzed and the elements and relationships are recognized and kept in a data base. From this data base GOODS produces the diagram according to the POV and FOA chosen by the user. Figure 5.1 shows a window with the class *Sorted_list* and the method *insert* in the FOA. At the bottom appears the edit window for the characteristics of the *insert* method, this window is opened after the user chose the "edit" option of the method's menu.

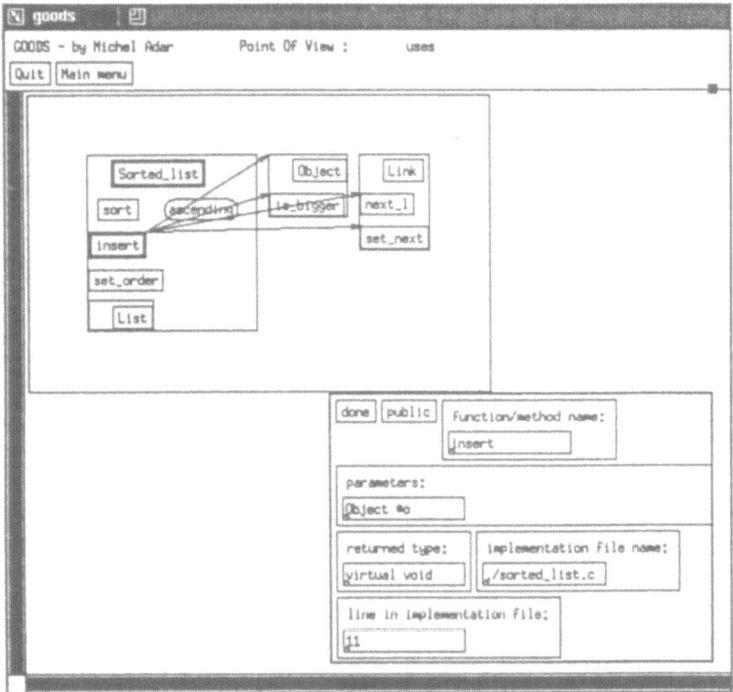

Figure 5.1 - The edit window for the method *insert*

The GOODS data base may be updated in one of two ways, by parsing the files that contain the C++ program listing; or by letting the user edit the elements with the graphical user interface. Figure 5.2 shows the same diagram as in Figure 5.1 along with the file *list.c* being edited in a window that was opened by selecting the "edit implementation" option in the method menu. At the top of this image appears the comment window associated with the *insert* method.

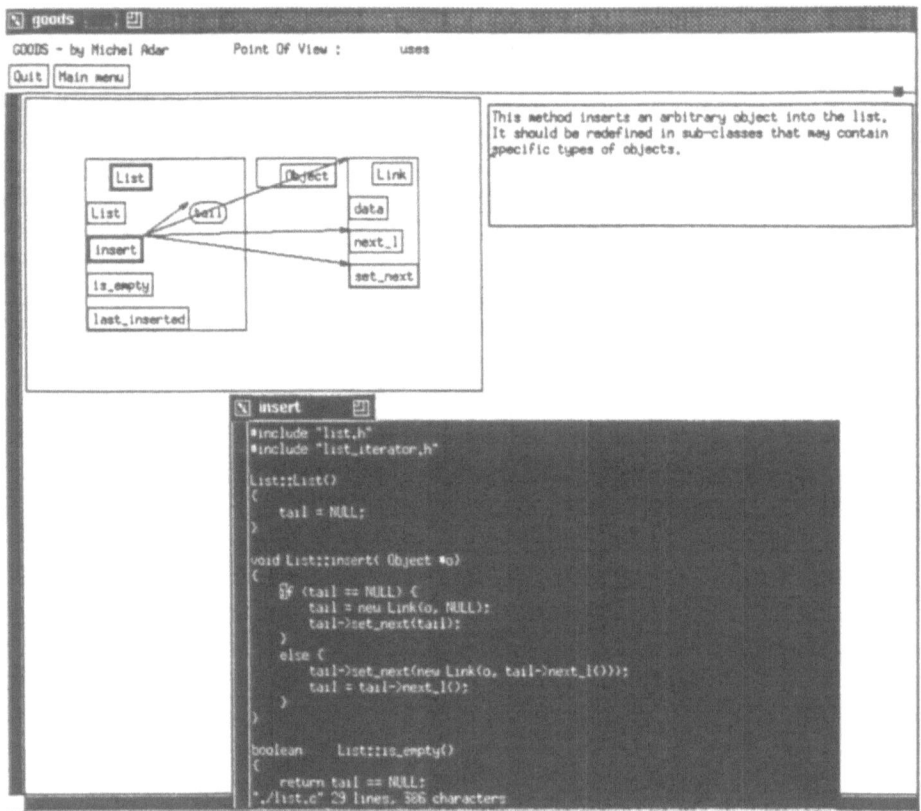

Figure 5.2 - Editing the implementation of a method

6. Experience and Conclusions

This paper describes the GOODS system developed at the Technion. It can at any point of time automatically provide the user a GOODS diagram showing the structure of the part of program (FOA). Showing only the needed details as specified by the selected POV. GOODS is in use in the OOP laboratory in the Technion. The students are exposed to the concepts of the OOP paradigm with the aid of GOODS diagrams even before they learn any OOP language. Afterwards they use GOODS during for the implementation of a management game simulation. Users found the diagrams useful for understanding the structure of the programs and as a development and documentation tool. The integration between the code and the diagrams through a common data base, was helpful in the management of the projects.

REFERENCES

Backus, J., (1978). *Can programming be liberated from the Von Newman style?, A functional style and its algebra of programs.* Communications of the ACM, 21, 8.

Bar-On, E., (1991). *Mental Capacity and Locally Coherent views: Towards a unifying theory.* in preparation.

Beck, K., and Cunningham, W., (1989). *A Laboratory for Teaching Object-Oriented Thinking.* OOPSLA '89 Conference Proceedings, SIGPLAN Notices, Vol. 24, No 10.

Bobrow, D. J., DeMichiel, L. G., Gabriel, R. P., Keene, S. G.,
Kiczales, G., and Moon, N. A., (1988).
Common Lisp Object System Specification. X3J13 document 88-002R.

Booch, G., (1991). *Object Oriented Design with applications*.
The Benjamin/Cummings Publishing Corp. Inc., Redwood City, CA.

Buhr, R.J.A., (1984). *System Design with Ada*. Prentice-
Hall, New Jersey.

Brooks, F., (1987). *No Silver Bullet: Essence and Accidents
of Software Engineering* IEEE Computer, Vol. 20 (4).

Cox, B., (1986). *Object Oriented Programming*,
Addison-Wesley, Reading, MA.

Gibson, E., (1990). *Objects - Born and Bred*.
BYTE October 1990.

Goldberg, A., and Robson, D., (1983). *SMALLTALK-80: the language and
its implementation*. Addison-Wesley, Reading, MA.

Goldberg, A., (1984). *SMALLTALK-80: The interactive Programming
Environment*. Addison-Wesley, Reading, MA.

Hewlett Packard, (1990). *HP C++/SoftBench for HP-UX*. 5952-2933.

Ingalls, D., Wallace, S., Chow, Y., Ludolph, F., Doyle, K., (1988).
Fabrik - A Visual Programming Environment,
OOPSLA '88 Proceedings.

Meyer, B., (1987). *Reusability: The case for Object Oriented Design*,
IEEE Software.

ParcPlace Systems, (1990). *Objectworks release 2*.
Mountain View, CA.

Stroustrup, B., (1987). *The C++ Programming Language*. Addison-Wesley,
Reading, MA.

A CONCURRENT OBJECT-ORIENTED
PARADIGM FOR ATTRIBUTE GRAMMARS

L. Thomas,[1] and S. Cruz-Lara[1]

[1]Centre de Recherche en Informatique de Nancy (CRIN)
Campus Scientifique. Boîte Postale No. 239
54506 Vandœuvre-lès-Nancy. France
thomas@loria.crin.fr, cruzlara@loria.crin.fr

Abstract: *The GEPI system is a programming environment generator. GEPI generates fully-integrated programming environments in which sharing and synchronization between tools, such as language-based editors, static-semantic analyzers, etc., are defined by using attribute grammars. This paper proposes a concurrent object-oriented paradigm for describing and evaluating attribute grammars: an attribute grammar is represented by objects whose persistent memory represents attribute values. Attribute evaluation is performed through asynchronous message passing.*

Keywords: *Programming Environments, Attribute Grammars, Object-Oriented Programming, Concurrency.*

INTRODUCTION

The GEPI system[1] is a programming environment generator. GEPI generates full-integrated programming environments from a language description. An integrated programming environment is formed by a set of software tools that do not work independently: they work simultaneously during program's construction and they collaborate by data exchanges or by sharing and synchronization. In GEPI, collaboration, data sharing and synchronization between tools, are based on attribute grammars[2]. As was first established by Reps and al.[3], attribute grammars (AG) are powerful enough to perform context-dependent analysis in language-based tools. Such tools represent programs as attributed derivation trees. Figure 1 shows the user's interface of a programming environment generated by GEPI. The left-hand-side window is an *Emacs-like* editor: a program is simply considered as a string (i.e. textual representation). The right-hand-side window is a tree-editor: a program is considered as an attributed derivation tree (i.e. syntactic representation). Obviously, a user may build or modify a program by using either its textual or its syntactic representation. Any modification on the textual representation implies a modification on the

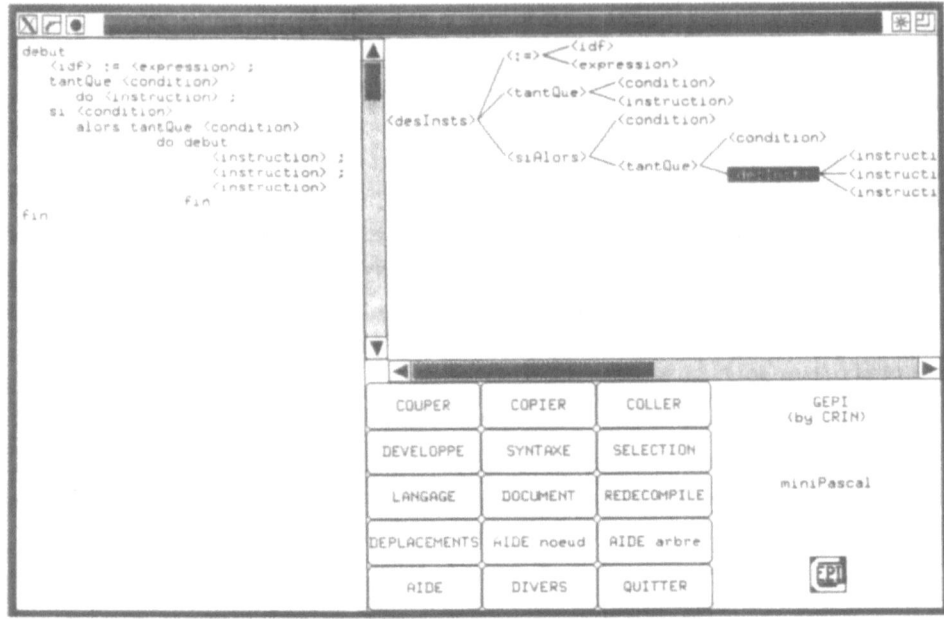

Figure 1. The user's interface of a programming environment generated by GEPI.

syntactic representation and *vice versa*. All tools generated by GEPI work on the abstract tree and their functionalities are described by the attribute evaluation rules associated with each node of the tree. In order to be able to reuse and extend the generative power of GEPI, we used a sequential Object-Oriented representation of the attribute grammars. Our experience with GEPI shows us that we may improve the efficiency of the generated tools in, at least, two ways. We first remark that there was an intra tool source of speedup: it is often possible to compute the attribute values of two sub-trees in parallel and then synchronize their results. Second, there is an inter tools source of speedup: two, or more, tools may use the same node of the abstract tree at the same time to compute unrelated attribute values. We show how to automatically produce an attribute evaluator from an attribute grammar description which will permit multiple threads of control in the abstract tree.

ABCL/1[4] is an object-oriented concurrent language that was designed to help describing concurrency and cooperation between objects. This paper presents an ABCL/1 implementation for describing and evaluating attribute grammars. This implementation has two main properties:

- describing attribute grammars as ABCL/1 objects is straightforward;
- attribute evaluation is realized by asynchronous message passing: it is inferred from the attribute grammar's description, so concurrency and cooperation between attribute occurrences need not be explicitly defined.

USING ATTRIBUTE GRAMMARS IN LANGUAGE-BASED ENVIRONMENTS

An attribute grammar is a context-free grammar extended by attaching attributes to the symbols of the grammar. Associated with each production of the grammar is a set of *semantic equations*; each equation defines one attribute as the value of a *semantic function* applied to other attributes in the production.

A production rule p will be denoted $X_0^p ::= X_1^p X_2^p ... X_{n_p}^p$ where the terminal symbols are omitted (they don't have attributes). A production rule p has an attribute occurrence (a,p,k) if $a \in A(X_k^p)$. The set of attribute occurrences of p is partitioned into two subsets, *DO* for *Defined Occurrences* and *UO* for *Used Occurrences*:

1. $DO(p) = \{(s,p,0)|s \in S(X_0^p)\} \cup \{(i,p,k)|i \in I(X_k^p) \wedge 1 \le k \le n_p\}$
2. $UO(p) = \{(i,p,0)|i \in I(X_0^p)\} \cup \{(s,p,k)|s \in S(X_k^p) \wedge 1 \le k \le n_p\}$

where $I(X_j^p), S(X_j^p)$ are the sets of the inherited and synthesized attributes of the non terminal X_j^p respectively and $A(X_j^p) = S(X_j^p) \cup I(X_j^p)$. Each production rule p has a set of attribute evaluation rules specifying how to compute the values of the attribute occurrences in $DO(p)$. Each attribute evaluation rule has the form

$$(a,p,k) = f((a_1,p,k_1),...,(a_m,p,k_m))$$

where $(a,p,k) \in DO(p)$ and $(a_i,p,k_i) \in UO(p) \wedge 1 \le i \le m$

A derivation tree node labeled X defines a set of *attribute occurrences*, corresponding to the attributes of the syntactic category of X. Because attribute values flow in two directions, bottom-up if synthesized and top-down if inherited, it is necessary to impose conditions to insure that no attribute occurrences are defined *circularly*. Such a restriction may be formalized by using the notion of *dependency graph*, a directed graph that represents functional dependencies among the attribute instances of the tree, and defined as follows:

*   For each attribute occurrence $(a,p,k) \in DO(p)$, the dependency graph contains a vertex labeled a;
*   If an attribute occurrence a' is computed from attribute occurrences a_i', that is, if $(a,p,k) = f(...,(a_i,p,k_i),...)$ and $(a_i,p,k_i) \in UO(p) \wedge 1 \le i \le m$, the dependency graph contains directed edges $a' \leftarrow a_i'$.

An edge from a_i' to a' has the meaning: a_i' is used to determine the value of a'.

Attribute evaluation is a process giving values to all attribute occurrences on a derivation tree. The order in which attribute occurrences are evaluated is arbitrary, subject to the constraint that each semantic function must be evaluated only when all of its argument attribute occurrences are available. It appears that attribute evaluation is a problem related to *topological sorting*. It should be noted that several attribute evaluation algorithms may only evaluate some restricted categories of attribute grammars[5, 6].

Attribute grammars have several desirable qualities as a descriptive notation to specify a language: syntax is defined by a context-free grammar and semantics is defined by attaching semantic equations to each production. Because the arguments to each semantic equation are local to one production, the language's semantics may be defined in a step-by-step modular fashion. Attribute evaluation is not explicitly defined in an attribute grammar, it is implicitly defined by the equations of the grammar and the form of the derivation tree.

This section gives an example of an attribute grammar expressing the relationships a language-based editor needs to provide[7].

Grammar *Example.*

```
1.  Program ::= Block
    (tsym,1,0) = (tsym,1,1)

2.  Block ::= DeclList BEGIN InstList END
    (tsym,2,0) = Verify((decl,2,1),(util,2,2))
    (decl,2,2) = (decl,2,1)

3.  DeclList ::= VAR Ident
    (decl,3,0) = Singleton((value,3,1))
```

```
4.   DeclList ::= VAR Ident DeclList
     (decl,4,0) = Union((decl,4,2),Singleton((value,4,1)))

5.   InstList ::= Instruction
     (decl,5,1) = (decl,5,0)
     (util,5,0) = (util,5,1)

6.   InstList ::= Instruction InstList
     (decl,6,1) = (decl,6,0)
     (decl,6,2) = (decl,6,0)
     (util,6,0) = Union((util,6,1),(util,6,2))

7.   Instruction ::= Ident ':=' Expression
     (util,7,0) = Singleton((value,7,1))

8.   Instruction ::= IF Cond THEN Instruction
     (util,8,0) = (util,8,2)
     (decl,8,2) = (decl,8,0)

9.   Instruction ::= WHILE Cond DO Instruction
     (util,8,0) = (util,8,2)
     (decl,8,2) = (decl,8,0)
```

This simple AG verifies that each declared identifier is used and, that each used identifier has already been defined. *Singleton* constructs a one element set, *Union* returns the union of two sets, and *Verify* tests the equality of two sets.

The following sections will show how to automatically translate an AG like this one into a program that will evaluate any derivation tree allowing as much as concurrency as possible. First we present the computing model supporting concurrency, namely ABCM/1.

THE ABCM/1 MODEL

The information is kept in autonomous entities called *Objects*. By autonomous, we mean that each object has its own processing power and may have its own *persistent* local memory. An object becomes *active** upon receiving a *message*. A message is sent to an object in order to request it to perform some task like updating its local memory. Messages may also be sent as replies to an object. After completion of the task performed in response to an incoming message, the object becomes *dormant* unless there is another message waiting for it to be free. The actions an object can perform are usual symbolic and numerical computation. In addition it can send messages to objects (including itself), create new objects and update its local memory. The way the actions are performed is describe in a *script*.

An object may send a message to an object, called the target, as long as it knows[†] its name. The message passing is point-to-point and asynchronous. Message sends may take place concurrently. However messages arrivals at an object are linearly ordered. The following assumption on message arrival is made:

When two messages are send to an object T by the same object O the temporal ordering of the two messages transmissions (according to O's clock) are preserved in the temporal ordering of the two messages arrivals (according to T's clock).

---

[*]   It is said to be in active mode.

[†]   It is worthwhile to note that the *knows*—relation is dynamic. An object which creates another object knows it. It can send its name to other objects so that the created one becomes known to them.

Suppose a message, say M, arrives at object T whose message queue is empty.

1. If T is in dormant mode, M is checked as to whether or not it is acceptable according to T's script. If acceptable, T becomes active and starts performing his task. If not, M is discarded.
2. If T is in active mode, M is enqueued at the end of the message queue.

The protocols of message passing should provide some way to synchronize the interacting objects. ABCL/1 provides three type of message passing: the *past* type, the *now* type and the *future* type.

In the past type, the sending object does not wait for its message to be received. It just continues its computation after the transmission. This type of message increases the potential concurrency. In the now type, the sending object waits for the receiver to send him back some information. As soon as it receives the reply, it resumes its current computation and works concurrently with the (perhaps still) working receiver. In the future type, the sending object asks the receiver for some value it needs, but not yet. It also specifies in the sending message a special object, called a future, where the receiver must put the value, so later on when it will need that value it will peek it up in the future object.

It should be noted that ABCM/1 is not only a model, but also provides a language, called ABCL/1, which in the current implementation is a superset of Common Lisp. The inter-object message passing relies on the model we described in the previous section, and the representation of the *behavior* (which we called *script* in the model) may contain Common Lisp features.

REPRESENTING ATTRIBUTE GRAMMARS IN ABCL/1

Attribute grammars were first defined by Knuth[2] as a formalism to define context-free languages' semantics. Currently, attribute grammars have became a subject of a very large interest in the scope of modern Computer Science[8].

As it was stated in the introduction, we have used AG in the framework of interactive programming environments. An object-oriented model has allowed us to represent AG in a reusable and extendable manner. However, it doesn't supply any mechanism to describe simultaneous evaluation that may occur in practice. We propose here a method that satisfies our requirements.

The purpose of this paper is to present a method for describing and producing automatically an evaluator which will take advantage of the potential concurrency between attribute evaluation rules. The aim of attribute evaluation is to compute the value of each attribute occurrence of the tree representing the sentence being parsed. Nevertheless, we shall assume, without loss of generality, that the aim of attribute evaluation is to compute the value of some synthesized attribute of the root of the derivation tree. The idea is to represent each rule of the AG by an ABCL/1 object. Moreover, application of the rule defines new dynamically created ABCL/1 objects representing the non-terminal symbols of the rule. Each of these objects will be responsible for asking the values of the attributes it needs and storing them for later use as in incremental evaluation.

The general case. In this section we will present more formally how to translate an AG into ABCL/1 objects.

For each production rule p create an object R_p as follows:

```
[Object Rp
 (script
  (=> [:new xp1 ... xpn_p]
     ![Object
        (state [x1 := xp1] ... [xn_p := xpn_p])
        (script
         ...)])))]
```

Each time the production rule p is used to construct the syntactic tree, object R_p is instantiated with each xp_i bound with the instantiation of the object representing its son X_i^p.

The script of the instance[*] depends on the attribute evaluation rules. Let the arity of f be m

☐ $(a, p, 0) = f(...)$

- $(a, p, 0) = K$ where K is a constant
  Add [a := K] in the state part and (=> [:val-for-a] @ r [r <= [:val-for-a a]]) in the script part

- $(a, p, 0) = f(..., (b, p, 0), ...)$
  For $i \in [1, m]$ add the declaration of the state variables b_i Add also *waiting-for-a* in the state part. In the script part add

```
...
(=> [:val-for-bi v]
    (if (null waiting-for-a) ; don't know where to reply
        ; store the value
        [bi := v]
        ; else we know where to reply
        (if (and b1 . .. bi-1 bi+1 ... bm)
            ; all bj for j ≠ i are received
            [waiting-for-a <= [:val-for-a f(b1,...,bi-1,v,bi+1,...,bm)]]
            ; else just store bi
            [bi := v])))
...
(=> [:val-for-a] @ r
    (if (and b1 .... bm)
        [r <= [:val-for-a f(b1,...,bm)]]
        [waiting-for-a := r]))
```

We add m+1 methods: one for receiving each b_i's value, and one for storing where to reply the value of a. It doesn't matter in which order the messages are sent, because of the persistence permitted by the concept of object. Thanks to it, we don't have to restrict the potential concurrency by choosing a total order on the messages.

- $(a, p, 0) = f(..., (b, p, j), ...) \wedge 1 \leq j \leq n_p$
  Add to the script part

---

[*] There is one such object per application of the rule in the derivation tree. It represents the Left Hand Side of the rule.

```
(=> [:val-for-a] @ r
    (let ((waiting-for-a
           [Object
            (state b_1 ... b_m)
            (script
             ...
             (=> [:val-for-b_j v]
                 (if (and b_1 .. b_{j-1} b_{j+1} ... b_m)
                     ; all b_i are received except for i = j
                     [r <= [:val-for-a f(b_1,...,b_{j-1},v,b_{j+1},...,b_m)]]
                     ; else
                     [b_j := v]))
             ...)])
        ...
        [x_j <= [:val-for-b_j] @ waiting-for-a]
        ...))
```

Note that the ordering of messages sent to an object may be significant : an instance may ask a son for an attribute value while at the same time this one is waiting for an inherited attribute value, so a deadlock situation could occur. To avoid this problem, we create an intermediate object liberating the instance. That is, when receiving a message asking for a's value, create an intermediate object, *waiting-for-a*, and send each son x_j involved in f a message to ask for the particular attribute value it needs. Tell them that the reply destination is *waiting-for-a*. This latter object will collect the responses and forward the final value to the original asker for attribute a's value. Once again we take advantage of OO concepts, namely the dynamic creation of object. Here we use this object to synchronize the responses and to free the creator so he can receive other inquiries while avoiding a potential deadlock.

- $(a, p, 0) = f(..., (b, p, j), ...) \wedge 0 \leq j \leq n_p$
  We just merge the above addings

□ $(a, p, i) = f(...) \wedge 1 \leq i \leq n_p$

- $(a, p, i) = K$ where K is a constant
  Add $[x_i <= [\text{:val-for-a K}]]$

- $(a, p, i) = f(..., (b, p, 0), ...)$
  For $j \in [1, m]$ add the declaration of the state variables b_j in the state part and in the script part add
```
(=> [:val-for-b_j v]
    (if (and b_1 .. b_{j-1} b_{j+1} ... b_m)
        ; all b_i are received except for i = j
        [x_i <= [:val-for-a f(b_1,...,b_{j-1},v,b_{j+1},...,b_m)]]
        ; else just store
        [b_j := v]))
```
  We wait for all the inherited values to arrive before propagating the a's value to the appropriate son.

- $(a, p, i) = f(..., (b, p, j), ...) \wedge 1 \leq j \leq n_p$
  Apply the same rules as in case 1.3 except that
  $$[r <= [\text{:val-for-a } f(b_1,...,b_{j-1},v,b_{j+1},...,b_m)]]$$
  is replaced by
  $$[x_i <= [\text{:val-for-a } f(b_1,...,b_{j-1},v,b_{j+1},...,b_m)]]$$
  and

```
                    (=> [:val-for-a] @ r
      by
                    (=> [:val-for-a]
```

- $(a, p, i) = f(..., (b, p, j), ...) \land 0 \le j \le n_p$
  Merge the two cases above.

Optimizations. The previous method lacks of efficiency in two strongly related ways. First, we may observe that, once computed, an attribute occurrence is sent back to the original asker without being stored into a state variable of the instance which computed it. This value may be needed in a further computation such as comparison in incremental evaluation. We will address this problem in the next paragraph. Second, we may observe that, if needed twice, an attribute occurrence may be computed twice. This is because the instance computing the attribute occurrence may receive other inquiries between the time it receives the first ask for the attribute value and when it receives that value. We will address this second problem in the second paragraph.

The need for storing the attribute value. We must distinguish two cases, depending which object replies the final value. In the first case, the replying object is the one which receives the request (cases 1.2 and 2.2 in the method description). In the second case, the replying object is the one which has been created by the one which receives the request (cases 1.3 and 2.3). The case 1.2 for instance is simply written (with state variable a added to the instance script):

```
(=> [:val-for-bi v]
    [bi := v]
    (if (and b1 . .. bi-1 bi+1 ... bm)
        ; all bj for j ≠ i are received
        (progn
          [a := f(b1,...,bi-1,v,bi+1,...,bm)]
          (if waiting-for-a ; we know where to reply
              ; reply to the original asker
              [waiting-for-a <= [:val-for-a a]])))))
...
(=> [:val-for-a] @ r
    (if (null a)
        [waiting-for-a := r]
        ; else a has been computed so just reply its value
        [r <= [:val-for-a a]))
```

The case 1.3 is now written (where *reply-for-a* has been added to the state variable part):

```
(=> [:val-for-a] @ r
    (if (null a)
        ; not yet computed
        (let ((creator Me))
        (let ((waiting-for-a
              [Object
               (state b1 ... bm)
               (script
                 ...
                 (=> [:val-for-bj v]
                     (if (and b1 .. bj-1 bj+1 ... bm)
                         ; all bi are received except for i = j
                         [creator <= [:val-for-a f(b1,...,bj-1,v,bj+1,...,bm)]]
                         ; else
                         [bj := v])))
```

```
                        ...)])
        ; store where to reply
        [reply-for-a := r]
        ; and ask for the values needed to compute a
        ...
        [$x_j$ <= [:val-for-$b_j$]] @ waiting-for-a]
        ...) ; end of (let ((creator ...
    ; else a has been already computed
    [r <= [:val-for-a a]]))
(=> [:val-for-a v] ; sent by waiting-for-a
    [a := v]
    [reply-for-a <= [:val-for-a a]])
```

Optimality. The solution above stores the value as soon as it is known, so that subsequent ask for it will not cause a complete computation to occur. However, between the time the value is first requested and the time the value is stored, there may be others asks for that value. Those asks must not lead to computation. Instead, they must be enqueued such that, upon receiving the value, the instance replies to all the objects needing it. An attribute value will be computed only once: that's what we meant by optimality. This can be easily done in ABCL/1. Recall that the message passing form is [target <= message]. For now on, *target* has been a single object where the *message* has to be sent. But ABCL/1 permits *target* to be a tree of objects, in which case the *message* is sent in parallel to all the objects in the tree. Thus, suppose attribute occurrence *b* is needed more than once and is computed as in the case 1.3, we simply transform *reply-for-a* to be a list of objects leading to:

```
(=> [:val-for-a] @ r
    (if (null a)
        ; not yet computed
        (if (null reply-for-a)
            ; this the first time the value is needed
            (let ((creator Me))
                ; same as above
                ...
                ...) ; end of (let ((creator...
            ;else just add to the reply destination list
            [reply-for-a := (cons r reply-for-a)])
        ; else a has been already computed
        [r <= [:val-for-a a]]))
(=> [:val-for-a v] ; sent by waiting-for-a
    [a := v]
    ; and broadcast to the reply destinations in the list
    [reply-for-a <= [:val-for-a a]])
```

In the case 1.2:

```
(=> [:val-for-a] @ r
    (if (null a)
        ; add r to the reply destinations list
        [waiting-for-a := (cons r waiting-for-a)]
        ; else a has been computed so just reply its value
        [r <= [:val-for-a a]]))
```

Applying the method to grammar *Example.* The following ABCL/1 code was directly derived from the above rules to implement the object describing the 4th production of grammar *Example*. Object **R4** creates an unnamed object representing the LHS nonterminal instance. The first inquiry for the attribute *decl* creates *waiting-for-decl* which will synchronize the responses needed and send back the value of *decl* to the unnamed object. The latter is free to accept other inquiry, in which case it simply stores where to reply.

Once it has received the value from *waiting-for-decl*, it stores it, so that later inquiry will be responded immediately, and sends the value to all the requestors he knows so far.

```
[Object R4
 (script
  (=> [:new Ident DeclList]
   ![Object
     (state decl reply-for-decl)
     (script
      (=> [:val-for-decl] @ r
        (if (null decl)
         (if (null reply-for-decl)
          (let ((creator Me))
           (let ((waiting-for-decl
                  [Object
                   (state decl value)
                   (script
                    (=> [:val-for-decl v]
                      (if value
                          [creator <= [:val-for-decl
                                        (union v (singleton value))]]
                          [decl := v]))
                    (=> [:val-for-value v]
                      (if decl
                          [creator <= [:val-for-decl
                                        (union decl (singleton v))]]
                          [value := v])))]-]))
                 [reply-for-decl := r]
                 [Ident <= [:val-for-value] @ waiting-for-decl]
                 [DeclList <= [:val-for-decl] @ waiting-for-decl]))
          [reply-for-decl := (cons reply-for-decl r)])
         [r <= [:val-for-decl decl]]))
      (=> [:val-for-decl v]
       [decl := v]
       [reply-for-decl <= [:val-for-decl decl]])))])]
```

CONCLUSION

In the framework of programming environments generators, we first used attribute grammars as a common formalism to describe the syntax of context-free languages, and to specify collaboration, data sharing and synchronization between tools of the generated environments[9, 1].

Describing this formalism by using OO concepts, gave us invaluable insights. However it quickly appeared that to generate really efficient environments, we needed an efficient and dynamic AG evaluator. We show in this paper how OO helps us in designing a concurrent attribute evaluator. Attribute grammars are statically described by a list of objects and attribute evaluation is inferred from this static description. Thus, attribute evaluation is realized through message passing, so concurrency and cooperation between objects need not be explicitly defined.

Because of the OO concepts as persistence, dynamic instance creation, etc., there is no need to construct a dependency graph before each evaluation. An evaluation ordering between attribute occurrences will be found automatically at execution time.

The idea of translating AG into procedures for evaluation is not new [10, 11]. The object-oriented approach has been tackled in [9, 12].

Our method is based on translation of productions into objects whose scripts create new objects — that we called *instances* — representing the production's left hand side.

The script of these instances is derived from the attribute computation rules. The ABCM/1 model is well-suited for AG translation because

— it is **object-oriented**.

Each non-terminal symbol is represented by an object whose state variables are persistent. This allows attribute occurrences to be computed only once. In addition, dynamic binding permits independent descriptions of each rule and dynamic object creation allows synchronization schemes to be done during attribute evaluation. This last advantage is enforced by the next point.

— it is a **concurrent** model.

As in FOLDS[13] attribute values are computed in parallel. However, our method frees implementers to explicitly define simultaneous evaluation of attribute occurrences and from the need to know the attribute dependencies. The values needed at one non-terminal may be asked in any order (or even in parallel) and one (or more) object(s) are dynamically created to receive the value.

The grammar in Appendix A is a good example: the ordering evaluation is statically ordered by the rules, but there is no need for the implementer to worry about it. This ordering will be *discovered* by the program during the evaluation phase.

Obviously, our method is not intended for circular grammars, but we claim that our method can evaluate any non circular AG.. Intuitively, as no static analysis is performed, we have no over-pessimistic dependencies that no subtree could exhibit [5].

In the framework of attribute evaluation, our method allows to compute all attribute occurrences on an attributed derivation tree, even those which values are not strictly necessary to obtain the values of the synthesized attributes of the axiom. We can also retrieve any attribute occurrence, if its value has already been computed, even if the whole evaluation process has not been completed yet.

Appendix A AN EXAMPLE

The attribute grammar is taken from Katayama[10].

$$R_1 : \begin{cases} S ::= & A \\ (k,1,0) = & (k,1,1) \\ (h,1,1) = & (g,1,1) \\ (f,1,1) = & 0 \end{cases}$$

$$R_2 : \begin{cases} A ::= & aA \\ (f,2,1) = & (f,2,0)+1 \\ (h,2,1) = & (h,2,0)+1 \\ (g,2,0) = & (g,2,1)+1 \\ (k,2,0) = & (k,2,1)+1 \end{cases}$$

$$R_3 : \begin{cases} A ::= & a \\ (g,3,0) = & (f,3,0) \\ (k,3,0) = & (h,3,0) \end{cases}$$

```
[Object R3
 (script
  (=> [:new]
   ![Object
     (state waiting-for-g waiting-for-k
            f h )
     (script
      (=> [:val-for-g] @ r
       (if (null f)
           [waiting-for-g := r]
           [r <= [:val-for-g f]]))
      (=> [:val-for-k] @ r
       (if (null h)
           [waiting-for-k := r]
           [r <= [:val-for-k h]]))
      (=> [:val-for-f v]
       (if (null waiting-for-g)
           [f := v]
           [waiting-for-g
                 <= [:val-for-g v]]))
      (=> [:val-for-h v]
       (if (null waiting-for-k)
           [h := v]
           [waiting-for-k
                 <= [:val-for-k v]])
   )])])]
```

```
[ aaaa := [R1 <== [:new
            [R2 <== [:new
             [R2 <== [:new
              [R2 <== [:new
               [R3 <== [:new]]]]]]]]]]]
(progn
 [aaaa <= [:val-for-k] @ printer]
 [aaaa <= [:val-for-h]]
 [aaaa <= [:val-for-f]])
```

```
[Object R2
 (script
  (=> [:new ah]
   ![Object
     (state [a := ah])
     (script
      (=> [:val-for-k] @ r
       (let
        ((wait-for-k
          [Object
           (script
            (=> [:val-for-k v]
             [r <=
                [:val-for-k (1+ v)]])])))
        [a <= [:val-for-k] @ wait-for-k]))
      (=> [:val-for-g] @ r
       (let
        ((wait-for-g
          [Object
           (script
            (=> [:val-for-g v]
             [r <=
                [:val-for-g (1+ v)]])])))
        [a <= [:val-for-g] @ wait-for-g]))
      (=> [:val-for-f v]
       [a <= [:val-for-f (1+ v)]])
      (=> [:val-for-h v]
       [a <= [:val-for-h (1+ v)]])])))]
```

```
[Object R1
 (script
  (=> [:new ah]
   ![Object
     (state [a := ah] [f := 0])
     (script
      (=> [:val-for-k] @ r
       (let
        ((wait-for-k
          [Object
           (script
            (=> [:val-for-k v]
             [r <= v])])))
        [a <= [:val-for-k] @ wait-for-k]))
      (=> [:val-for-h]
       (let
        ((wait-for-g
          [Object
           (script
            (=> [:val-for-g v]
             [a <= [:val-for-h v]])])))
        [a <= [:val-for-g] @ wait-for-g]))
      (=> [:val-for-f]
       [a <= [:val-for-f f]])))))]
```

Appendix B A QUICK OVERVIEW OF ABCL/1 SYNTAX

A full description of the model and its language may be found in [14]. An ABCL/1 program is a collection of object definitions. Each object has an optional *state* part to store its persistent kwnoledge, and a *script* describing the messages it accepts and how those messages are answered. The body of the message handlers are written in a superset of Comon Lisp, introducing message sending forms and assignment form.

1. An Object is defined by [**Object** Name (**state** ...) (**script** ...)],
2. the state part declares and assigns initial values to variables representing the persistent memory of the object. The default value is *nil*,
3. the script part is a collection of tuples (pattern, body). The object tries to match the pattern with the incoming message, in which case the body is evaluated. Pattern keywords, as in Common Lisp, begin with a semi-colon. The message pattern may specify the object where to reply by appending @ `reply-object` to the pattern,
4. besides the Common Lisp forms, a body may use the following forms :

   a. a past sending form (asynchronous message passing) : [an-object **<=** a-message],
   b. an assigment form : [a-variable **:=** a-value], wich binds *a-value* to *a-variable*,
   c. a reply form, !a-form, which sends back the result of the evaluation *a-form*. This form allows dynamic object creation as the evaluated form may be an object definition,
   d. many others we don't use in this paper.

Appendix C BIBLIOGRAPHY

1. G. Canals, D. Colnet, S. Cruz-Lara, and J. C. Derniame. GEPI : un Générateur d'Environnements de Programmation Intégrés. In *Le genie logiciel et ses applications*, pages 406–421, Toulouse, 1988.

2. D.E. Knuth. Semantics of context-free languages. *Math. Syst. Theory*, 2(2):127–145, 1968.

3. T. Reps, T. Teitelbaum, and A. Demers. Incremental Context-Dependent Analysis for Languages-Based Editors. *ACM Transactions on Programming Languages and Systems*, 5(3):449–477, 1983.

4. A. Yonezawa, H. Matsuda, and E. Shibayama. An Approach to Object Oriented Concurrent Programming, A Language ABCL. In *Actes des 3èmes JLOO, Bigre+Globule No. 48*, pages 125–134, Paris, 1986.

5. K. Kennedy and S.K. Warren. Automatic Generation of Efficient Evaluators for Attribute Grammars. In *Conference Record of the 3rd Symposium on Principles of Programming Languages*, pages 32–49, Atlanta, Ga, 1976.

6. U. Kastens. Ordered attribute grammars. *Acta Informatica*, 13(3):229–256, 1980.

7. T. Reps. *Generating Language-Based Environments*. PhD thesis, Cornell University, 1983.

8. P. Deransart, M. Jourdan, and B. Lorho. *Attribute Grammars*. Lecture Notes in Computer Science, Volume 323. Springer-Verlag, Berlin, 1988.

9. S. Cruz-Lara. *GEODE : un système pour la génération d'environnements de programmation intégrés*. Thèse, Institut National Polytechnique de Lorraine, 1988.

10. T. Katayama. Translation of Attribute Grammars into Procedures. *ACM Transactions on Programming Languages and Systems*, 6(3):345–369, 1984.

11. M. Jourdan. An Optimal-time Recursive Evaluator for Attribute Grammars. In *Lecture Notes in Computer Science, Volume 167*. Springer-Verlag, Berlin, 1984.

12. G. Hedin. An Object-Oriented Notation for Attribute Grammars. In *Proceedings of the Third European Conference on Object Oriented Programming (ECOOP'89)*, 1989.

13. I. Fang. FOLDS, A Declarative Format Language Definition System. In *Structure et Programmation des calculateurs*, pages 275–290, Rocquencourt, France, 1973.

14. A. Yonezawa, editor. *ABCL: An Object-Oriented Concurrent System.* Massachusetts Institute of Technology, Cambridge, Massasuchetts, 1990.

Distributed Systems

PRESERVING DISTRIBUTED DATA COHERENCE
USING ASYNCHRONOUS BROADCASTS

José M. Piquer

Depto. Ciencias de la Computación
Universidad de Chile
Santiago
Chile
email: jpiquer@dcc.uchile.cl

Abstract

In distributed systems, data replication is often necessary to ensure availability and reliability. Updating replicated data is a hard problem with many different solutions, depending on the restrictions imposed on the base communication system.

This paper presents a new update algorithm for replicated data (using a copy invalidation protocol), based on an asynchronous global broadcast, respecting a relaxed causal ordering. Very weak order conditions are imposed on broadcast and message deliveries, but a reliable message-passing system is supposed.

The algorithm is intended to run on medium-size systems, sharing fine-grain data elements. As the communication protocol is asynchronous, updates can be performed without the overhead of blocking, waiting for the replies.

The update algorithm has been implemented and tested as the base of a distributed Lisp system called TransPive[Piqu 90], running on a network of Transputer[1] processors (without a global broadcast bus).

1 Introduction

When distributed systems are used to solve problems in a coordinated way, some information must be shared between processors. In general, sharing data structures on distributed systems is an interesting tool for solving distributed problems (even if it is almost a contradiction to use shared structures in distributed systems). Sometimes, this shared information must be replicated on multiple sites to ensure fast local read accesses (the local copy acting as a cache), high availability or to meet some fault-tolerance requirements. However, if the shared data can be modified, the system must provide a consistency protocol to ensure that different copies of the same data do not contain contradictory values.

---

[1]Transputer is a trademark of INMOS Ltd.

Many consistency protocols exist for cache consistency on shared-memory parallel machines, and some other protocols have been designed for distributed systems, depending on the data granularity (virtual memory pages, file records, objects or data structures), the underlying communication system (unreliable, faulty, etc.), the strength of the provided consistency (strong, weak)[Dubo 86] and the read/write access protocol (multiple copies, invalidation, in-situ updates).

This paper presents a very simple and efficient update algorithm, designed for a medium-size reliable distributed system. The algorithm provides replica consistency using relaxed causal asynchronous broadcasts and implementing an invalidation protocol, guaranteeing order preservation between synchronization points and data updates. This algorithm was designed for a distributed Lisp system, where data update is not a frequent operation.

The basic motivation for the algorithm is to avoid synchronism in the communication primitives as much as possible. The idea behind this is the observation that the sending of a message is an expensive operation, but the sending of a message plus the time lost waiting for a reply is more than four times more expensive because it involves numerous operations (send, in transit, reception, treatment, send, in transit, reception). This is even more important when using global broadcasts[2] because the number of replies to wait for can be very large.

The organization of the paper is as follows: section 2 describes the problem and the environment considered in the design of the solution, given the order restrictions imposed on the broadcast primitives. Section 3 explains the invalidation algorithm, and the restrictions imposed on the replication protocol. Section 4 studies related work done by other people and section 5 presents the conclusions.

2 Message Ordering

Many solutions to the consistency protocol impose a synchronous behaviour on modifications. This means that a *write* operation does not return until *every* distant copy of the object has been modified, providing what is called *strong coherency*, and also *sequential consistency*. Normally, this implies a heavy protocol because the modifier site must wait for every reply before resuming the *write* operation. (This synchronism can be imposed by a synchronous broadcast protocol). However, this strong synchronism can be eliminated without changing the expected order of events. When the *write* operation returns without waiting for every copy to be updated, we provide a weak coherency (a read operation may return an "old" value).

However, in a distributed system, the only order between events is the order imposed by the "happened before" ($\rightarrow$) relation[Lamp 78]. This relation is defined by:

1. if a and b are two events at the same site and a occurred before b, then $a \rightarrow b$.

2. if m is a message, and $sending(m)$ denotes the event of emitting m at the sender site, and $deliver(m)$ the reception at the destination site, then $sending(m) \rightarrow receiving(m)$.

3. if $a \rightarrow b$ and $b \rightarrow c$ then $a \rightarrow c$.

---

[2]Global broadcast means that a message is sent to *every* site of the distributed system. Reduced broadcast (often called multicast) could be considered also, but this paper will only talk about global broadcasts because it greatly simplifies the discussion.

```
shared int a = 0;

Site1:
        a = 1;
        send(OK, Site2);

Site2:
        receive(OK, Site1);
        /* here we expect that a == 1 !!! */

        send(OK, Site3);

Site3:
        receive(OK, Site2);
        /* again, a == 1 !! */
```

Figure 1. Shared variables and synchronization.

This order is not enough to provide memory coherence. For example, if a process changes a shared data item and then synchronizes with another site, we expect the data (after the synchronization) to have the same value in both sites (see Figure 1).

The use of asynchronous messages can violate this, because messages can follow different paths and arrive in a different order from that in which they were sent. Supposing a protocol that sends asynchronous update messages, we can have the situation shown in Figure 2, leading to unexpected results.

Obviously, we can use synchronous messages, but the idea is to avoid the blocking delay inherent in synchronous solutions. Another solution is to provide a stricter order between messages. For this, the system should provide an order preserving the *causal* ordering. This necessitates adding only one rule:

- if m_1 and m_2 are two messages with the same destination and $sending(m_1) \rightarrow sending(m_2)$, then $deliver(m_1) \rightarrow deliver(m_2)$.

This order is very attractive, because it is the natural extension from synchronous (or shared-memory order) to distributed systems. The problem is how to implement it without a big overhead. Some interesting implementations do exist for messages [Rayn 89, Schi 89], and for broadcasts [Birm 87, Peter 89], but they remain difficult to implement efficiently on generic networks. If messages are not restricted to some given paths, messages have to be timestamped with timestamps of size n^2, where n is the number of hosts in the network.

We will suppose the existence of a reliable global broadcast primitive, with relaxed causal order restrictions. Instead of the strict causal ordering above, we divide the world between broadcasts (messages sent to every site) and simple messages (with only one destination). Broadcasts impose a relaxed causal order on messages. We replace the extra causal rule by two new rules. Denoting $bcast(a)$ the initiation of broadcast a, the new ordering rules are:

1. if $bcast(a) \rightarrow sending(m)$ then $deliver(a) \rightarrow deliver(m)$ at the destination site of m.

initially a = 0

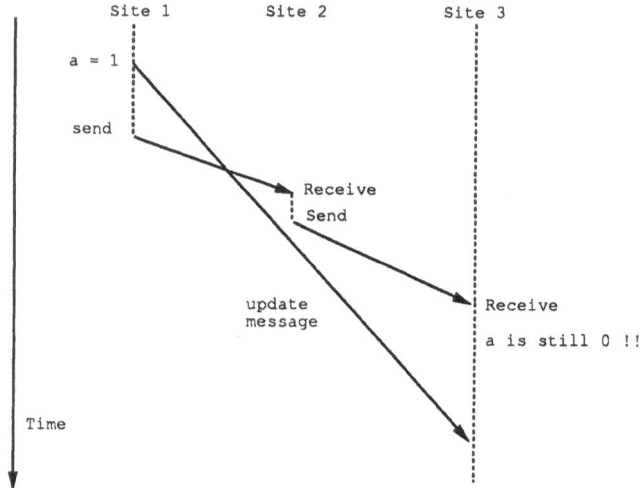

Figure 2. An Invalid Message Order

2. if $sending(m) \rightarrow bcast(a)$ and both are emitted from the *same* originator site, then
$deliver(m) \rightarrow deliver(a)$ at the destination site of m.[3]

Two broadcasts can arrive in different order at different sites. A message that causally precedes a broadcast can arrive after it, if they do not originate at the same site.

These are important relaxations of the strict causal order rules, and they allow us to construct a very efficient asynchronous diffusion broadcast primitive on top of any network with or without hardware support for broadcasts (as point-to-point connected networks, and bus-based networks).

In particular, the broadcast-to-message causality, Rule 1, can be implemented with timestamps of size n (also known as vector clocks[Fidg 88, Matt 89], where n is the number of hosts in the network), or timestamps of size one and a broadcast manager[Piqu 90], while Rule 2 comes naturally from the FIFO property of communication channels.

If every communication uses a broadcast medium, such as a bus, these order restrictions are easy to satisfy. (However, it can be difficult to satisfy Rule 2 on a mixed machine where messages use links and broadcasts use a special bus.)

3   The Coherence Algorithm

The algorithm is based on the classic weak coherence invalidation algorithms, but it supports the weaker causal ordering of the broadcast explained in the preceding section. As we are going to use a global broadcast to invalidate the copies, we do not

---

[3]This rule should be: if $sending(m) \rightarrow bcast(a)$ then $deliver(m) \rightarrow deliver(a)$ at the destination site of m (independent from the originator). However, this is almost as difficult to implement as full causality. Restricting it to the local case is enough for our application.

need to maintain the list of sites sharing an object (which is very important when managing small objects).

By definition, every shared object must have a site which is its *owner*. Only the *owner* of an object has the right to send *copies* of it to the rest of the system, and it is the only site with the right to perform modifications to its value. The other sites holding a copy of the object can only read it and send references to it (a reference includes the current *owner* for this object). To update it, they must become the *owner* first.

When the *owner* is going to modify an object, it broadcasts an *INVALIDATION* message and then it performs the modification. As broadcasts are asynchronous, there is no important delay for this operation.

When a site, holding a copy or a reference to an object (but not being the *owner*) wants to perform a modification, it must first become the *owner*, asking the permission of the current *owner*. Upon reception of a *PERMISSION* message, the *owner* performs a broadcast of a *MIGRATION* message, notifying the new object *owner* and invalidating every object copy at the same time. After this, the *owner* replies the *PERMISSION* message, giving up the object ownership. An example of the migration protocol can be seen in Figure 3.

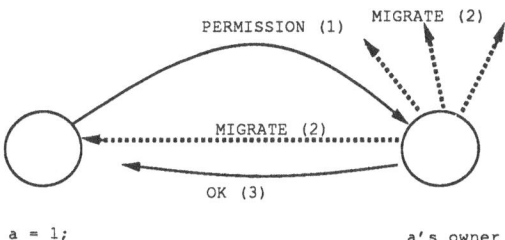

Figure 3. The migration protocol.

Note that the migration protocol includes an invalidation, plus the *owner* change. In fact, this algorithm performs the classic shared token algorithm[Birm 89] using only two messages and one asynchronous broadcast.

The ordering rules are important because we must preserve the causality of modifications. Ordering Rule 1 guarantees that any message depending on a previous modification (as in the example shown in Figure 1) will always be received after the modification. Rule 2 is important to guarantee that every existing copy will be invalidated, including every copy in transit in the network. As the *owner* is the only site that is allowed to send copies, and also the site that performs the broadcast, Rule 2 assures that the copy is received before the *INVALIDATION* message. (If we had full causality, copies could be sent from any host holding one in the network.)

Two broadcasts can arrive in different order at different sites, so we must support incorrect *owner* fields in the remote references. This would be true even if broadcasts were causally ordered because copy holders (not *owners*) can send *references* to a distant object, which include the current *owner* value for this object. If a *MIGRATION* message is broadcasted while the message is still in transit, the *owner* value will be invalid upon reception, and it is hard to detect this at the receiving site. We will tolerate this behaviour, and we will force the read protocol to correct the *owner* of an object upon access.

This problem arises only with the distant references, not with the remote copies, because the order is unimportant for the *INVALIDATION* messages (as they always invalidate the copy) and because every copy sent will arrive before the *INVALIDA-TION* or *MIGRATION* message corresponding to it (Rule 2).

The algorithm is very efficient because it allows a great degree of asynchronism, based on the relaxed causality rules. Every modification done by the *owner* implies only one asynchronous broadcast. Every migration (to perform a modification at a non-owner site) implies one synchronous communication with the *owner* and one asynchronous broadcast.

It is very simple to add a tag to the objects to avoid the broadcasting of *INVALIDATION* messages when the *owner* is going to update a shared object without any distant copy. After broadcasting an *INVALIDATION* message, the *owner* knows that there is no valid distant copy. So, every subsequent modification can be performed locally without any communication. The tag can be changed when a copy is sent (which is also done by the *owner*) to mark it as shared.

However, each modification generates a global broadcast, that must be handled by every site, even if the object is shared by only a couple of sites.

4 Related Work

A number of papers have been published in the literature, but we are going to compare our work with those most related to distributed language implementation and data coherency.

Kai Li and Paul Hudak[Li 86] propose a shared virtual memory for distributed systems, implemented using pages and a protocol to invalidate distant copies of a modified page. They propose several algorithms to maintain the *owner* field for a page, but the invalidation messages are synchronous. It is not explicitly stated in the paper, but the protocol does not respect the order restrictions if the invalidation messages are not acknowledged.

Henry Bal and Andrew Tanenbaum[Bal 88] present a distributed language called Orca that supports replicated objects. The coherency protocol is an update protocol, which makes things more complicated, and they enforce atomic and mutually exclusive access to the object. They do not consider objects in transit in the network during updates, and they keep a local list with the sites holding copies in order to use reduced broadcasts (or multicasts). They propose different implementations for different hardware, using point-to-point messages or system provided multicast. The point-to-point version uses a heavy protocol, with $3n$ messages for n copies of the object. The protocol is synchronous. When using a multicast primitive, they impose an atomicity restriction over the multicast primitive (every site receives multicasts in the same order), which is very expensive.

Thomas Joseph and Kenneth Birman[Jose 86] propose an update algorithm based on broadcasts, and using piggy-backed messages to improve the performance. Their main interest is to provide a fault-tolerant replication algorithm, so it is hard to compare it with ours. The order restrictions they impose on broadcasts are very close to the causal order, and theirs are more strict than ours. In a newer version[Birm 90], they use vector clocks to provide causal broadcasts (CBCASTS), and to provide group multicast they use n^2 timestamps (some optimizations can be applied if the network topology is known). They treat point-to-point messages as broadcasts to a group of size one, imposing a heavy order restriction.

David Chaiken *et al.*[Chaik 90] propose a directory-based copy consistency protocol using invalidation. The directory keeps the set of sites holding copies of an object, and they distribute this directory as a linked list of all the sites involved. Instead of a broadcast, they send the INVALIDATION messages along the chained list, and wait for an acknowledgement from the last site. Even if the number of messages is fewer, this protocol is synchronous and a write operation must be blocked until every copy has been invalidated, providing a strong coherency algorithm.

5   Conclusions

We have presented a new coherency algorithm, based on global broadcasts, well-suited for small and reliable multi-computer networks, such as a net of Transputer processors. The algorithm needs only a relaxed causal order between broadcasts and messages, which is very cheap to implement in point-to-point connected networks using diffusion broadcasts.

The algorithm is very efficient, using only two messages and one global broadcast which is asynchronous, so there is no important delay in its use. However, we are paying the price of handling extra broadcast messages, at sites which had no references to the modified object.

The algorithm is not fair, because the *PERMISSION* message must be re-sent to the new owner, without any knowledge of the previous history. Fairness can be introduced, at an extra cost, using a broadcast for the *PERMISSION* operation.

The same idea could be extended to design an update algorithm (changing the copies instead of just invalidating them), but the order restrictions should also be extended. In particular, broadcasts should be causally ordered, and it can be done without additional cost. Furthermore, there is no need for an atomic broadcast (imposing a total ordering) because the uniqueness of the *owner* for a given object ensures that it is impossible to have two independent broadcasts (not related by the "happened before" relation) for the same object. There is no need to have causally ordered messages either.

The relaxed causal order can be implemented more efficiently than the strict causal order on top of many architectures, except for networks using point-to-point links for messages and a bus for broadcasts.

References

[Bal 88]   H. E. Bal, A. S. Tanenbaum, *Distributed Programming with Shared Data*, Proc. of the IEEE CS 1988 International Conference on Computer Languages, Miami, Fla. October 9-13, 1988.

[Birm 87]   K. P. Birman, T. A. Joseph, *Reliable Communication on the Presence of Failures*, ACM Trans. on Computer Systems, Vol. 5, N. 1, pp. 47-76, Feb. 1987.

[Birm 89]   K. P. Birman, T. A. Joseph, *Exploiting Replication in Distributed Systems*, in 'Distributed Systems', edited by S. Mullender, ACM Press, N.Y., 1989.

[Birm 90]   K. P. Birman, A. Schiper, P. Stephenson, *Fast Causal Multicast*, Technical Report TR-90-1105, Cornell University Computer Science Department, Ithaca, NY, April 1990.

[Chaik 90] D. Chaiken, C. Fields, K. Kurihara and A. Agarwal, *Directory-Based Cache Coherence in Large-Scale Multiprocessor*, IEEE Computer, June 1990.

[Dubo 86] M. Dubois, C. Scheurich, F. Briggs, *Memory Access Buffering in Multiprocessors*, 13th ISCA, pp. 434-442, IEEE, June 1986.

[Fidg 88] C. Fidge, *Timestamps in Message-Passing Systems that Preserve the Partial Ordering*, Proc. 11th Australian Computer Science Conference, 1988.

[Jose 86] T. A. Joseph, K. P. Birman, *Low Cost Management of Replicated Data in Fault-Tolerant Distributed Systems*, ACM Trans. on Computer Systems, Vol. 4, N. 5, pp. 54-70, Feb. 1986.

[Lamp 78] L. Lamport, *Time, Clocks, and the Ordering of Events in a Distributed System*, Comm. ACM, Vol. 21, No. 7, pp. 558-565, July 1978.

[Li 86] K. Li, P. Hudak, *Memory Coherence in Shared Virtual Memory Systems*, Proc. of the 5th annual ACM Symp. on Principles of Distributed Computing, Calgary, Canada, Aug. 13-18, 1986.

[Matt 89] F. Mattern, *Time and Global States in Distributed Systems*, Proc. of the International Workshop on Parallel and Distributed Algorithms. North-Holland, 1989.

[Peter 89] L. L. Peterson, N. C. Bucholz, R. D. Schlichting, *Preserving and Using Context Information in Interprocess Communication*, ACM Trans. on Computer Systems, Vol. 7, N. 3, pp. 217-246, Aug. 1989.

[Piqu 90] J. M. Piquer, *Sharing Data Structures in a Distributed Lisp*, High Performance and Parallel Computing in Lisp, Twickenham, UK, Nov. 1990.

[Rayn 89] M. Raynal, A. Schiper, S. Toueg, *The Causal Ordering Abstraction and a Simple Way to Implement It*, INRIA Research Report 1132, Dec. 1989.

[Schi 89] A. Schiper, A. Sandoz, J. Eggli, *A New Algorithm to Implement Causal Ordering*, 3rd. Workshop om Distributed Algorithms, LNCS 392, pp. 219-232, 1989.

AN IMPLEMENTATION OF SERVICE REBALANCING

Eric H. Herrin II and Raphael A. Finkel

Department of Computer Science
University of Kentucky
Lexington, Kentucky 40506

Abstract

Service rebalancing is a method for designing programs that adhere to the client/server model. Decisions about the division of labor between client and server are made dynamically at runtime rather than at design time. Service rebalancing may improve performance, because the division of effort is based upon an evaluation of the current environment. Other benefits of service rebalancing include on-the-fly updating of modules, a degree of load balancing, sharing of code common to several clients, encouragement of neatly modularized programs, and the elimination of an absolute division of effort between client and server. In this paper we discuss the benefits, problems and issues of service rebalancing. Our implementation, Equanimity, is described in some detail. Finally, we compare service rebalancing with previous work and discuss future plans.

1   INTRODUCTION

This paper discusses dynamic distribution of effort between client and server processes. A **server** process abstracts resources and provides entry points that clients can invoke to use the abstraction. A **client** is a process that needs a particular resource. Each client makes requests of servers, and the servers reply with the status of the request. Communication between client and server is generally accomplished via remote procedure call [13] or message passing.

Although the client/server model is quite productive in practice, practitioners often find that the model leads to code that is difficult to build, optimize and modify. It is not easy to find the division between client and server that gives the best performance. A chosen division may be more or less appropriate over time as conditions with respect to network and machine load change. Redefining the client/server interface is usually quite difficult after the initial design, since each client must be changed to accommodate the new interface.

Service rebalancing means dynamically modifying or augmenting the interface between client and server. In particular, we restrict ourselves to migration of modules between processes. A **module** is a self-contained collection of subroutines and their data structures. A module that originates on a machine is **native** to that machine; all migrated modules are **guests**. Some interesting features of service rebalancing include:

1. A client/server pair can change the interface between them as conditions change. The faster machine can perform the more complicated tasks. Modules may migrate from client to server or server to client; the decision to migrate from server to client may be specific to a particular client.

2. Modules migrated from a client to a server can be shared by the other clients of that server, although they are not forced to use the migrated module.

3. Communication costs may be reduced after a module is migrated, depending on how much data needs to cross the new interface between client and server.

4. Intermediate processes may be introduced to host modules between the client and server. Such processes increase communication costs but reduce the load on the client and server machines.

5. Servers may dynamically load new versions of services, keeping old versions intact and old clients running.

The following sections address the issues raised by service rebalancing. First, we provide an example of two clients that share and migrate code using a single service. Next, we will discuss the problems and solutions associated with implementing service rebalancing. Our implementation of service rebalancing, `Equanimity`, will then be described in detail. Finally, we will review research in related areas and discuss our results.

2 AN EXAMPLE

This section will describe a pair of simple clients and a server that can share code through service rebalancing. These processes are described only deeply enough to motivate the example and are not intended to represent a complete (or even high-quality) design. The clients make use of a single server called the **graphics server**. The graphics server exports basic pixel manipulation routines, and the clients build useful layers of software upon the server's exported procedures.

2.1 The Graphics Server

The graphics server provides only basic pixel oriented routines and mouse/keyboard input. A client can call the following procedures.

> `DoPixelOps`: This procedure performs operations on individual pixels. The parameters are the pixel coordinates and the desired operation.

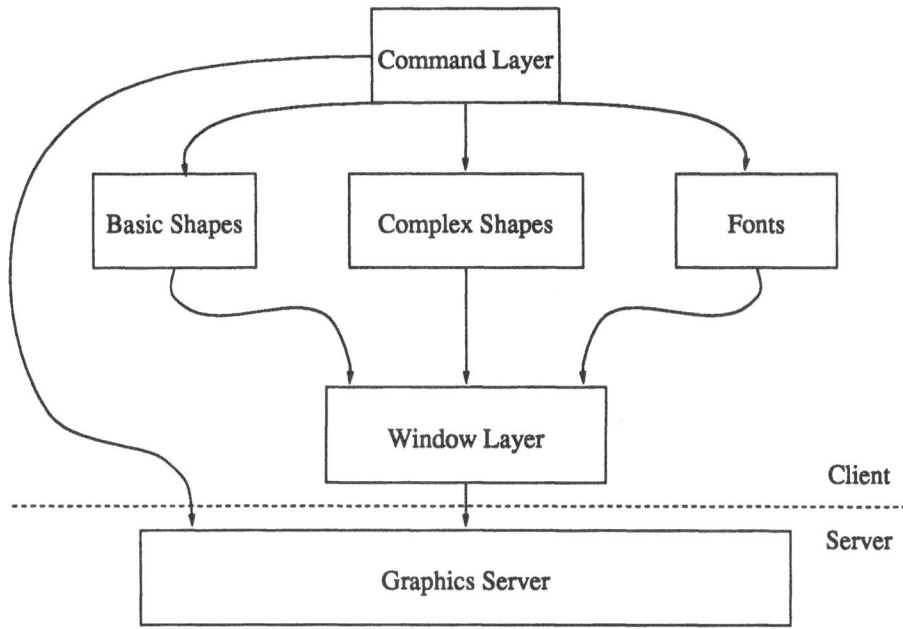

Figure 1. The layers of the drawing client

GetCharacteristics: This function returns the size of the video screen and other characteristics necessary to properly draw on the screen.

GetNextEvent: This function returns the next device event from the keyboard or mouse.

Higher layers of software are expected to manage the screen; when the server starts, its only function is to draw pixels and retain screen information.

2.2 The Drawing Client

The drawing client allows a user to draw pictures interactively in a window. The layers of software necessary to perform this function are:

Command layer: Command interpretation using GetNextEvent.

Window layer: Window setup using DoPixelOps. This layer provides a routine called **RelativeDoPixelOps** that translates pixel coordinates within a window into pixel coordinates on the screen.

Basic shape-drawing layer: using RelativeDoPixelOps.

Font-drawing layer: using RelativeDoPixelOps.

Complex shape-drawing layer: using RelativeDoPixelOps.

Figure 1 depicts the relationship of these software layers.

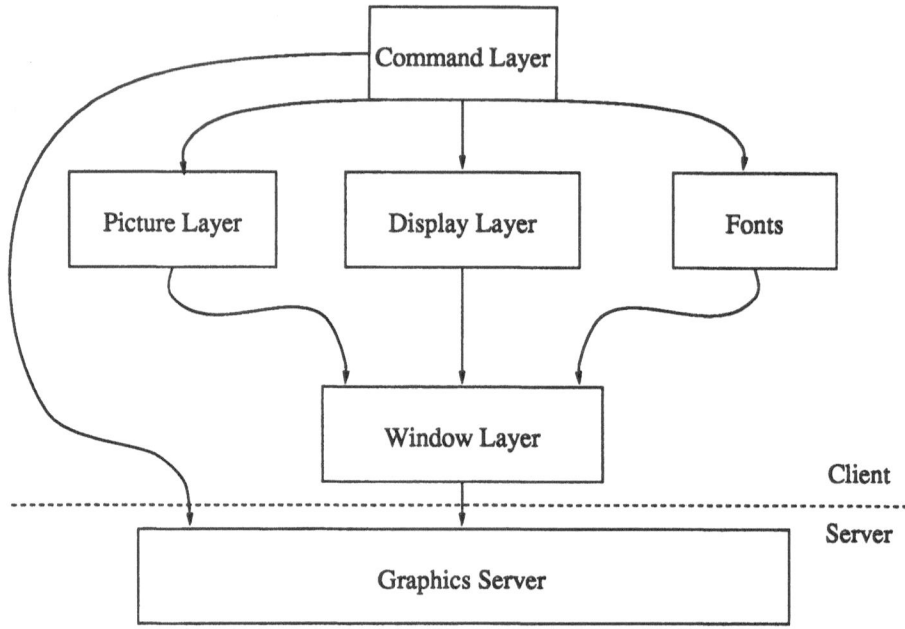

Figure 2. The layers of the text client

2.3 The Text-previewer Client

The text-previewer client displays text from a data file within a window. Pictures may be embedded in the text, and various commands are available to control the portion of the text displayed at a given time. The necessary software layers are:

Command layer: Command interpretation using GetNextEvent.

Window layer: Same as the drawing client.

Font-drawing layer: Same as the drawing client.

Picture layer: Translates a bitmap into window coordinates that the window layer can use. Calls the window layer to display the picture.

Display layer: Formats the page (or portion of a page) so that it fits in a window.

Figure 2 shows the relationship of these layers.

2.4 An Example of Service Rebalancing

Figures 1 and 2 show that both clients use the window layer and the font layer. The font layer depends on the window layer, and the window layer communicates directly with the graphics server. It is easy to see that the number of remote calls to the server will be reduced if these layers are moved from the clients to the server. Figure 3 shows a possible new structure of the drawing client/server after rebalancing.

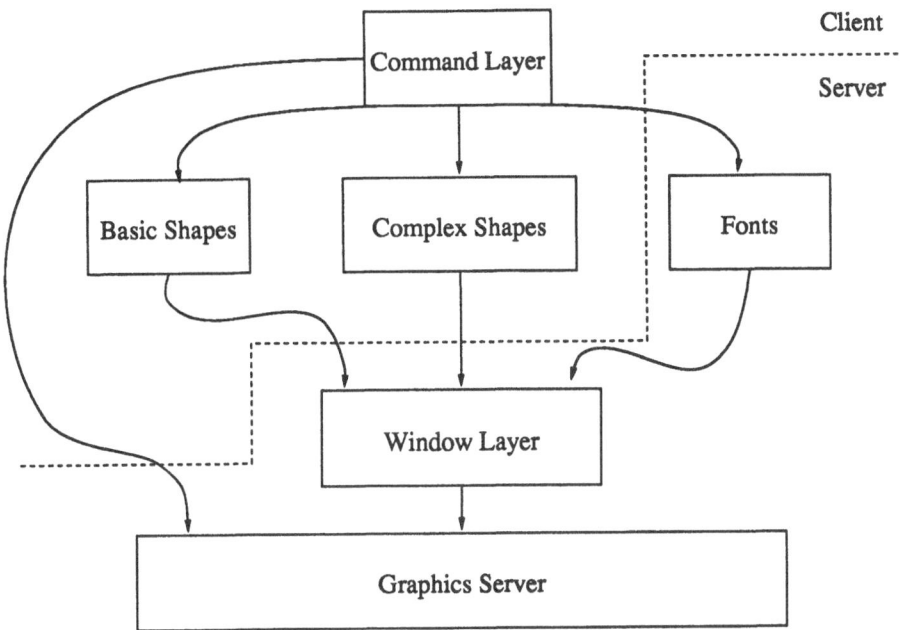

Figure 3. The layers of the drawing client after rebalancing

Migrating the font and window layers to the server is only useful if we are concerned with the number of remote calls to the server. Another relevant factor is the speed of the machines running the client and server programs. If the client machine is an order of magnitude faster than the server, it may be reasonable to let the client perform complex drawing computations. If both the client and server are slow, calculations can be performed on a fast intermediate machine where the computation can be performed much more quickly. Rebalancing can therefore improve performance without manually changing the client or the server.

3   PROBLEMS AND ISSUES IN SERVICE REBALANCING

Several problems need to be addressed in the design of a service-rebalancing facility. First, standard process-migration policy choices apply to service rebalancing, including

- Selection: Which modules should migrate and when?

- Calculation: How does the policy know that its choice will improve performance? What measurements does it use in its calculations?

- Leadership: Who makes these important decisions?

This paper does not deal further with policy.

Next, mechanism problems must be addressed, such as client and server authentication, privacy, safety, availability, version control, failure semantics, and communication. We will discuss each mechanism problem in turn.

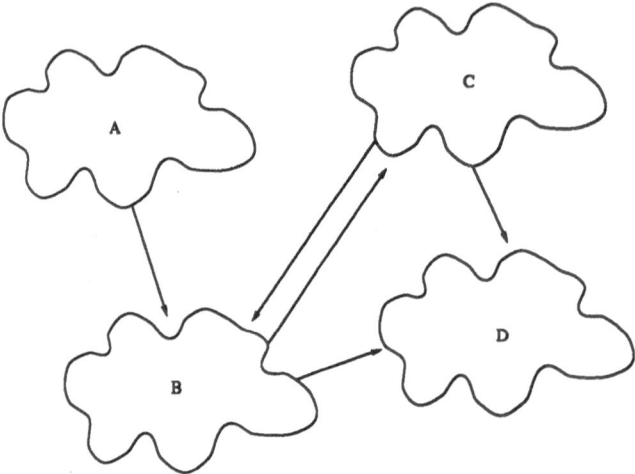

Figure 4. Address-space relationships

3.1 Client and Server Authentication

Authentication is the technique by which the client and server determine the other's identity. They need to know not only that the other has the right program (that is, a client that wishes to speak to a file server would be confused if it found itself dealing with a name server), but also on behalf of what user the other process is running (the file server is willing to undertake some accesses but not others, depending on the user). Inadequate authentication is often unacceptable for security reasons; thus, protocols to insure correct authentication must be developed.

Client/server authentication is a well-known problem and can be solved using protocols developed for RPC [1]. Service rebalancing requires that both the client and server be authenticated since modules can migrate in either direction.

3.2 Privacy

Privacy of internal data structures can be important when clients or servers manipulate sensitive data. Modules should not be able to directly access data stored in the address space to which they are migrated; likewise, the address space of migrated modules should be hidden from their new hosts.

One solution to this problem is to use only architectures that support access to multiple address spaces, possibly using capabilities. Each module has its own protection domain, which allows it to access its data and entry points into other modules. A capability-based architecture could temporarily give procedures a capability to access parameters passed by reference. Invocation of other modules switches protection domains. Figure 4 shows a graph where nodes denote protection domains and arcs denote which domains are accessible from a node.

Since machines that allow this type of access to multiple address spaces are not readily available, another solution is to switch between address spaces whenever an access is made into a new area of memory. The kernel performs the switch whenever an invalid-memory trap occurs for a valid entry point into a new module. Although this method is expensive, it does produce the same effect. Operating system support is needed that would have to be implemented in the kernel.

3.3 Safety

Services should be migrated without the possibility of introducing bugs into the server or client. Any migrated module that causes a server or client to fail is unacceptable. Malfunctions can be caused by misleading or malfunctioning code.

`Misleading` code does not live up to a caller's or a callee's expectations. A caller can mislead a callee by providing bad arguments. A callee can mislead a caller by producing bad results, destroying arguments passed by reference, or by failing to terminate loops. These problems are dealt with conventionally by performing sanity checks on all arguments, parameters and return values. Non-terminated loops must be dealt with by timeouts. The decision as to whether these safeguards are used when modules migrate should be left up to the programmer, based on the degree of trust the programmer has for the module in question.

Protection against malfunction of a migrated module requires the same solutions as the privacy problem. The solutions of the privacy problem will protect a client or server from faulty memory accesses outside the address space of the guest, but not from faulty memory accesses within the module. The problem of guarding against malfunction of a guest is equivalent to the problem of guarding against malfunction in a normal program. We do not see a good solution to this problem and suggest that any safeguard would be too weak to solve it completely. No safeguard can replace careful programming, and we believe modules should be carefully debugged before a programmer allows them to become migratable.

3.4 Availability

Service availability, either of the server or the client, is an important problem with service rebalancing. A server that does not implement service rebalancing need not worry about non-terminating loops, deadlocks and very long running routines because the implementor of the server will discover and correct these errors during implementation. A process that allows modules to migrate in, however, must guard against such malicious or negligent routines. Timeouts, preemptive lightweight threads, or separate processes could be used to prevent interruption of service to clients caused by guest modules.

3.5 Version Control

Clients should be able to share migrated modules in the midst of versions and revisions. We define a **version** to be a change in a module's interface or function, while a **revision** is an internal change to the module that does not affect calling modules. Versions or revisions should be able to migrate to the server even though some clients are using older versions or revisions. Old guests must be maintained as long as any client needs them; a reference count can provide for eventual reclamation when all clients are done.

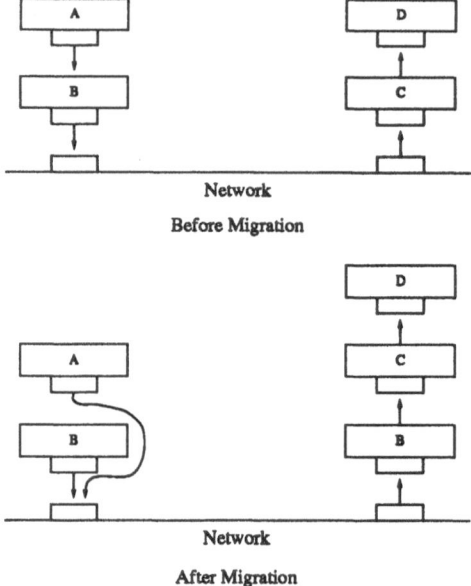

Before Migration

After Migration

Figure 5. Rebalancing a module

A server must manage client-specific data whenever multiple clients share a module. A module that cannot handle multiple clients must be duplicated for each client. The methods used to control versions or revisions of a module may also be used to multiplex modules that require client-specific data.

3.6 Communication

Communication between modules is typically by messages, often with a procedure call software layer above the bare messages. We prefer the procedure call interface because we feel it is a more natural way for program modules to communicate. Regardless of the communication method, we must make calling modules oblivious to the physical location of called modules, because the location may change while either module is running.

We suggest that a switch be inserted between all migratable modules in a client or server; we call this switch an LR switch, or local-remote switch. The LR switch is a stub that transfers control of a procedure call either to a local or remote copy of the module. After a rebalancing occurs, the switch is toggled, and all subsequent calls to the migrated module are directed to the appropriate location. Figure 5 shows a client/server before, during and after a rebalancing.

4 EQUANIMITY: AN IMPLEMENTATION OF SERVICE REBALANCING

Equanimity is a software package for building client/server programs with service rebalancing. It has the following features:

- Loading of relocatable modules into the address space of running programs.

- Dynamic runtime binding of modules.

- Migration of modules between processes.

This section details some of the features of Equanimity and discusses the problems of implementing service rebalancing.

4.1 Dynamic loading and runtime binding

Equanimity's dynamic loading facility, dload, allows a running program to load a relocatable module into its address space. Once loaded, modules may be bound together in any of the following ways:

1. A module may be bound to a shared library.

2. A module may be bound to another module.

3. A module may be bound to an LR switch for remote procedure call.

When dload reads an object module into an executing process, it loads all data and code sections into the virtual space of that process. Relocatable addresses that are within the module are resolved immediately. Undefined references are resolved when the module is explicitly bound to other modules.

Dload keeps information about each module as it loads and binds it. This information is critical to the migration of the module, since the module must be reloaded and rebound whenever a module migrates away from its original host.

The implementation of dload is machine and operating-system dependent. It must be reimplemented for each new architecture, and many changes have to be made when porting to different operating systems. Although reimplementation appears to be a considerable amount of work, the code should not be difficult to write for an experienced systems programmer. The interface is well defined, and all code using dload is completely portable. We equate the difficulty of reimplementing dload to that of writing a simple device driver.

4.1.1 The local-remote switch

The local-remote switch, or LR switch, is a stub specifically designed to facilitate the migration of modules between client and server. It relieves dload of recording binding operations and speeds the migration process considerably. When a calling module **A** is bound to a called module **B**, an LR switch is placed between the two modules. The switch is logically associated with the module **B**, so all calling modules that are subsequently bound to **B** are actually bound to the switch.

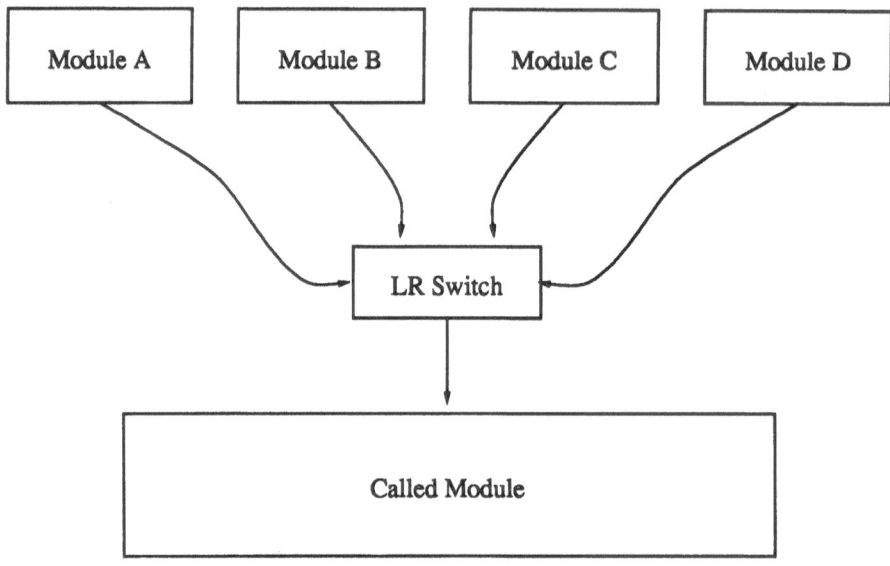

Figure 6. Several modules bound to an LR switch

A diagram of an LR switch used by several calling modules is shown in figure 6. The calling modules are actually bound to the switch, not to module **B**. When **B** migrates to a remote host, a bit is toggled in the data space of the switch, and all subsequent calls to **B** are translated into remote procedure calls.

The structure of an LR switch is extremely simple and easy to generate. Figure 7 shows a simple switch and its corresponding module. The switch is divided into two levels to avoid linking problems that would prevent us from transparently inserting switches between modules. For example, if the switch contains a label **f:** which contains a jump to another label **f:** in its associated module, the assembler generally assumes that the jump is local (that is, a short jump) and generates a local relative address. In this case, we want the assembler to generate a relocatable address so that we can bind the switch to the module when the it is dynamically loaded. The two-level LR switch forces the assembler to generate the instructions we desire. The calling module is bound to the level-one LR switch, which in turn is bound to the level-two LR switch. The level-two LR switch is bound to the called module. When function **f:** is called, a jump to the label **_f:** in the second-level LR switch occurs (if the switch is zero). The second-level LR switch will then jump to the label **f:** in the module to which it is bound.

4.2   Remote procedure call

Equanimity uses remote procedure call (RPC) to communicate between client and server. We made this decision due to the availability of a standard RPC package [18] and the similarity of RPC semantics to those in standard programming languages. This choice is purely an implementation decision; we could use message passing just as easily. Parameters to remote modules are marshaled using stub routines built upon the external data representation standard (XDR) [17]. We currently build the stubs that invoke these routines manually; we will soon have a semi-automatic mechanism.

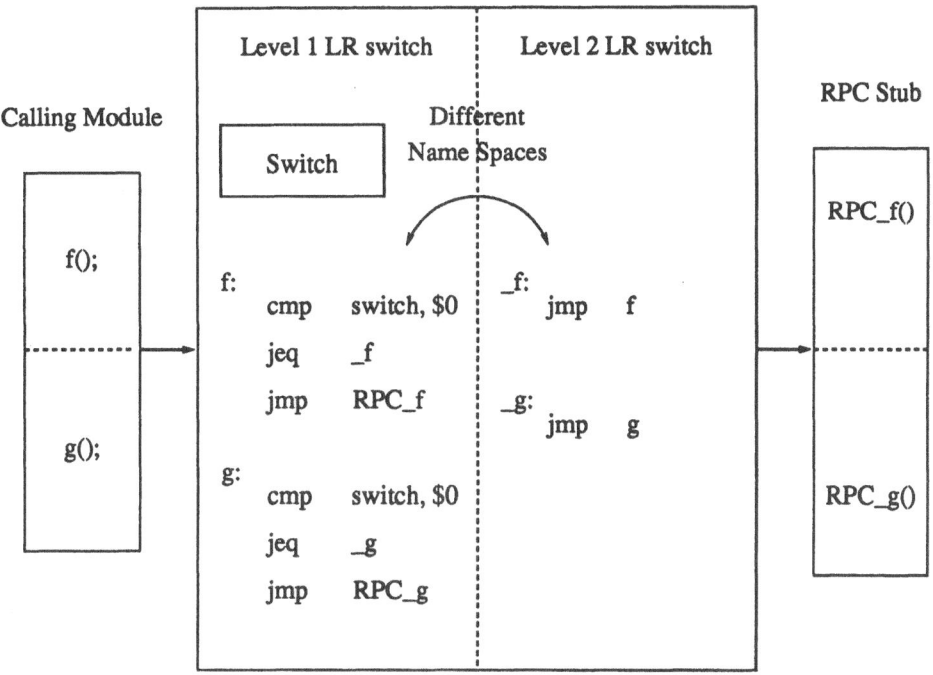

Figure 7. An LR switch in detail

4.3 Module migration

The migration of modules between client and server relies on the features of dload. The dynamic loading and binding of modules, the LR switch, and the standard RPC package collectively allow module migration to take place. Only one other feature is needed to implement basic module migration: a transfer protocol.

There are many ways to transfer a module between client and server. We decided to initially use existing remote file systems (NFS [19]) and stream protocols (TCP/IP). The module to be migrated is written by the source module to a file, and then a message is sent via stream protocols to the destination module. The destination module finds that file via NFS. Future versions of the migration facilities will use only stream protocols.

4.4 Status

Equanimity is currently running under UNIX^{tm} System V/386 Release 4.0 on a variety of machines. All dynamic loading, binding, and migration utilities exist and are in use. Modules may migrate between processes on different machines. Many useful features are still missing. In particular, we have not addressed policy issues yet (migration is manual), nor is our implementation fault tolerant. We plan to demonstrate Equanimity by modularizing the X Window System [15], a popular networked windowing system, in the near future.

4.5 Implementation of a file server with Equanimity

Our preliminary impression is quite positive. Our first use of Equanimity was in the implementation of a file server and client. The original program, designed as an example for an operating systems course, constructs a UNIX^{tm}-like file system within a UNIX^{tm} file. It is fairly well-layered (since it is an example for students), and is large enough to provide some preliminary timing results.

We split the program into three distinct modules: the application module, the file/byte/cache module, and the block module. The client initially contains the application and file/byte/cache modules, and the server initially contains the block module. The function of each module is as follows:

- `application module`: translates user commands into subroutine calls to lower layers.

- `file/byte/cache module`: provides a file interface with the usual *open*, *close*, *read*, *write*, *seek*, *delete*, and various directory-manipulation routines.

- `block module`: provides a raw block interface to the pseudo-disk (the UNIX^{tm} file).

The application and block modules are resident to the client and server respectively. The only module that can migrate is the file/byte/cache module.

We ran the program using a consistent set of input: calls that deal with files use an identical 10KB file, and calls that deal with directories use a single empty directory. We obtained the timings shown in Table 1.

It requires approximately 200 milliseconds to migrate the module in either direction. The user may migrate the module back and forth at any time that it is not active, that is, when none of its procedures are currently invoked.

When the file/byte/cache module is local to the client process, all function calls that do not require communication with the block layer are considerably faster than when the file/byte/cache module is located at the server. Functions that require communication with the block layer are considerably faster when the module is located at the server. Clients that heavily use *open* calls and *read* many random locations in files would benefit by migrating the module to the server. Clients that read and write the same location many times would benefit by keeping the module in the client, since the cache reduces the number of calls to the server.

5   RELATED WORK

Many ideas from other research in operating systems and distributed systems influenced our work with service rebalancing. We will discuss only research that we believe affected our current results: remote evaluation, upcalls and distributed upcalls (CLAM), dynamic modification of code, network shared libraries, and process migration.

Table 1. Timings for the file server

Function call time in milliseconds		
Function	file/byte/cache at client	file/byte/cache at server
Create file	170	130
Open file	260	120
Read 1000 bytes	300 (40-80 if cached)	170
Write 10000 bytes	910	560
Seek in file	10	130
Close file	10	120
Delete file	180	120
Create directory	10	120
Delete directory	10	130
List directory	200	120

5.1 Remote Evaluation

Remote procedure call (RPC) [2] is our chosen interface for service rebalancing. Although message passing may be used, we feel that the procedure call is a more natural way for our migrating modules to communicate. Remote evaluation (REV) [9, 10] is similar to RPC in that a set of remote procedures are exported by a server for use by a client. The client passes an entire procedure as an argument to the server for execution. The server attempts to execute the procedure after binding it with the set of exported procedures. The procedure may also require binding with the exported procedures of other servers. When the server has completed the procedure, the result (if any) is returned and the procedure is discarded.

Both remote evaluation and service rebalancing send code to the server for execution, but service rebalancing changes the client/server interface. When a client migrates a module to the server, the module remains at the server until either the server dies or the module is removed. An REV request, on the other hand, sends the module each time it wishes to use it.

REV and service rebalancing share some of the same problems due to their similarities. Protection of the server is of major concern, and the problems of secrecy and integrity are addressed by Stamos and Gifford [9]. The solutions presented there are:

1. Use separate address spaces and authorization checks. For example, IBM's MVS system runs on a proprietary IBM machine that allows efficient access of multiple address spaces by authorized programs.

2. Use interpreted code that can be checked at runtime. (SunOS uses this approach with their NIT interface [16].)

3. Develop an acceptance algorithm to examine REV requests at compile time.

Still other problems include authentication and starvation caused by non-terminating loops in procedures sent to the server.

5.2 Distributed Upcalls and CLAM

Upcalls were introduced to avoid the inefficiencies of asynchronous software signals, especially excess data buffering [5]. An upcall typically consists of an arming stage, when a higher layer registers intent to be called on an event, and a firing stage, when the event occurs.

CLAM [3] is an open system for graphical user interfaces. The features of CLAM most interesting to us are distributed upcalls and the dynamic loading of services. Distributed upcalls were designed with an intent similar to upcalls, except the upcalls can cross machine boundaries. Dynamically loaded services are loaded into the server on demand by a client, and CLAM supports multiple versions and revisions of the same service. The services are loaded only once, even when multiple clients need to access the same service.

Dynamic loading of services helps a programmer find a good division of client and server by experimentation. The division, once found, is static in CLAM, and the programs are changed to change the division. It seems possible to build clients and servers in CLAM that dynamically change the interface by loading different services under different load conditions, but no mention of this is given in the literature.

5.3 Dynamic Modification of Code

Research on programs that dynamically modify running code seems to date back to Fabry's early work [7]. Fabry uses indirect jump statements that can be atomically changed so that subsequent invocations of a service use the new version. Goullon [8] describes an operating system called DAS (dynamically alterable system) that allows dynamic modifications anywhere except the kernel. DAS uses virtual memory for dynamic modification. Each time a process calls upon a module to perform some work, DAS replaces part of the process' virtual address space with the contents of the latest version of the module. Modules cannot be added, deleted or changed in a way that makes the module's specification different from the original. Lee [11] designed a complete environment for the dynamic modification of StarMod [6] programs. Programmers can modify modules to nearly any extent. The specification of a module can be changed if modules that depend upon the changed module are modified appropriately.

5.4 Network Shared Libraries

Network shared libraries [20] are designed for the sharing of common library routines across a network. RPC is used to communicate with the remote machine that runs a library server. The main benefit of network shared libraries is a tremendous savings in both main-memory and file space. Very large libraries do not need to be resident on every machine on a network; instead, they can reside on a few very large, fast machines. Performance does not seem to degrade appreciably when the services are reasonably complex and will actually improve when the client machine is slow or overloaded.

Implementation of network shared libraries requires that a stub generator replace all calls to local library procedures with calls to remote procedures. A library server program must handle the requests. The implementation of Equanimity is considerably more complex. Instead of always introducing an intermediate library server, we allow the remote server to upgrade its level of service by dynamically loading and binding the library.

5.5 Process Migration

Process migration is designed to balance the overall load of a collection of machines. Processes move from one machine to another, usually using some heuristic algorithm, with the hope that overall performance will benefit.

There have been many investigations of process migration, most of which are implemented on message-based operating systems (V is a notable example [4]). Message-based operating systems can easily redirect messages so that migration is mostly transparent. Other traditional-style operating systems, for example Sprite [14], encounter numerous problems associated with the migration of local resources such as open file descriptors and the redirection of connections based upon the original address of the process.

6 PLANS

The current implementation of Equanimity is useful, but not complete. We plan to add the following features to Equanimity in the near future.

- An implementation of distributed upcalls (useful when a client is not strictly layered, or when a module in one layer needs to invoke a module at a higher layer).

- An RPC stub and LR switch generator. Currently, we build RPC stubs and LR switches manually.

- A mechanism that allows a module to remotely access global data located in other modules. We will use a method based on the work of Kai Li [12].

- Policies to migrate modules automatically, using a heuristic algorithm based upon the environment of the client and server.

- A mechanism and associated policies to introduce intermediate servers when appropriate.

We will also investigate the policy questions of service rebalancing presented in Section 3. Finally, we will implement several major applications involving service rebalancing to gain a better quantitative understanding of its advantages and disadvantages.

7 SUMMARY

We have presented service rebalancing by describing the benefits, problems, issues, and our current implementation, Equanimity. We have also shown the similarities and differences between our work and others. Finally, we presented our plans for service rebalancing and described the types of applications that we believe would benefit from it. Only through experience with service rebalancing will we be able to determine its practicality. Thus far, we believe it is both practical and beneficial to a wide class of client-server interactions.

References

[1] Andrew D. Birrell. Secure communication using remote procedure calls. *ACM Transactions on Computing Systems*, 3(1):1–14, February 1985.

[2] Andrew D. Birrell and Bruce Jay Nelson. Implementing remote procedure calls. *ACM Transactions on Computer Systems*, 2(1):39–59, February 1984.

[3] Lisa A. Call, David L. Cohrs, and Barton P. Miller. Clam - an open system for graphical user interfaces. In Norman Meyrowitz, editor, *Object-oriented Programming Systems, Languages and Applications Conference Proceedings*, pages 277–286, Orlando, FL, October 1987. Association for Computing Machinery. Also printed as SIGPLAN Notices, Volume 22, Number 12, December 1987.

[4] David R. Cheriton. The v distributed system. *Communications of the ACM*, 31(3):314–333, March 1988.

[5] David D. Clark. The structuring of systems using upcalls. In *Proceedings of the Tenth ACM Symposium on Operating Systems Principles*, pages 171–180, Orcas Island, Washington, December 1985. Association for Computing Machinery. Also Operating Systems Review, Volume 19, Number 5.

[6] R. P. Cook. *mod–a language for distributed programming. *IEEE Transactions on Software Engineering*, 6(6):563–571, November 1980.

[7] R. S. Fabry. How to design a system in which modules can be changed on the fly. In *Proceedings of the 2nd International Conference on Software Engineering*, pages 470–477, San Francisco, California, October 1976.

[8] Hannes Goullon, Rainer Isle, and Klaus-Peter Löhr. Dynamic restructuring in an experimental operating system. *IEEE Transactions on Software Engineering*, 4(4):298–307, July 1978.

[9] James W. Stamos and David K. Gifford. Remote evaluation. *ACM Transactions on Programming Languages and Systems*, 12(4):537–565, October 1990.

[10] James W. Stamos and David K. Gifford. Implementing remote evaluation. *IEEE Transactions on Software Engineering*, 16(7):710–722, July 1990.

[11] Insup Lee. *DYMOS: A Dynamic Modification System*. PhD thesis, University of Wisconsin-Madison, Madison, Wisconsin, May 1983.

[12] Kai Li and Paul Hudak. Memory coherence in shared virtual memory systems. In *Proc. 5th Annual ACM Symposium on Principles of Distributed Computing*, pages 229–239, August 1986.

[13] Bruce Jay Nelson. *Remote Procedure Call*. PhD thesis, Carnegie-Mellon University, Pittsburgh, Pa., May 1981. (Also available as Xerox PARC Technical Report CSL-81-9, Xerox Palo Alto Research Center, Palo Alto, California, 1981.).

[14] John Ousterhout, Andrew Cherenson, Fred Douglis, Michael Nelson, and Brent Welch. The sprite network operating system. Technical Report UCB/CSD 87/359, University of California, Berkeley, June 1987.

[15] R. W. Scheifler and J. Gettys. The x window system. *ACM Transactions on Graphics*, 5(2), April 1986.

[16] Sun Microsystems. *SunOS Programmer's Reference Manual*, release 4.1 edition, 1990.

[17] Sun Microsystems, Inc. Xdr: External data representation standard. Internet Request for Comments: RFC1014, June 1987.

[18] Sun Microsystems, Inc. Rpc: Remote procedure call protocol specification version 2. Internet Request for Comments: RFC1057, June 1988.

[19] Sun Microsystems, Inc. Nfs: Network file system protocol specification. Internet Request for Comments: RFC1094, March 1989.

[20] V. S. Sunderam. An experiment with network shared libraries. In *USENIX Conference Proceedings*, pages 39–49, Baltimore, Maryland, June 1989. USENIX.

BIT OPTIMAL DISTRIBUTED CONSENSUS

Piotr Berman,[1] Juan A. Garay,[2] and Kenneth J. Perry[2]

[1] Department of Computer Science
The Pennsylvania State University
University Park, PA 16802
[2] I.B.M. T.J. Watson Research Center
P.O. Box 704
Yorktown Heights, New York 10598

ABSTRACT

The *Distributed Consensus* problem involves n processors each of which holds an initial binary value. At most t processors may be faulty and ignore any protocol (even behaving maliciously), yet it is required that non-faulty processors eventually agree on a common value that was initially held by one of them. The quality of a consensus protocol is measured using the following parameters: the number of processors n, the number of rounds of message exchange r and the total number of bits transmitted B. The known lower bounds are respectively $3t + 1$, $t + 1$ and $\Omega(nt)$.

While no known protocol is optimal in all three aspects simultaneously, the protocol presented in this paper takes further steps in this direction: it achieves for the first time asymptotically optimal bit transfer $(B = O(nt))$, together with optimal number of processors n and nearly optimal r. Previously existing consensus protocols required $B = \Omega(n^2 t)$, regardless of the other parameters' values.

INTRODUCTION AND PROBLEM STATEMENT

The *Distributed Consensus* problem is one of the central topics in the theory of reliable distributed systems. Given a set P of processors, we are told that some unknown subset T of size no more than t are faulty. The goal of the Consensus problem is to cause the *correct* processors (i.e., those in $P - T$) to agree on an outcome regardless of the behavior of the *faulty* processors (i.e., those in T). Motivated by practical concerns, a recent focus of research has been on the efficiency of protocols that solve the problem.

The standard model used in studying this problem is of a network of n synchronous processors numbered from 1 to n. The computation performed by the network evolves as a series of *rounds*.[1] In each round, the correct processors exchange messages over reliable network links and perform local computations according to the protocol. In contrast, the faulty processors may exhibit arbitrary (*Byzantine*) behavior, even appearing to act in concert maliciously. Each processor p starts with a binary value stored in local variable V_p. A protocol solves the binary Distributed Consensus problem if it always terminates and satisfies the following two conditions:

- *Agreement*: at termination $V_p = V_q$ for all $p, q \in P - T$.

- *Validity*: if $V_p = v$ for every $p \in P - T$ is true at the beginning of the computation, then it is also true at the end.

This is a variant of the *Byzantine Agreement* problem in which the processors are required to agree on a value sent to them by one of the processors (called the *general*) in an initial round [LSP].

There are several parameters that characterize the quality of a protocol that solves this problem. These parameters (with their optimal values indicated in parentheses) are:

- the number of processors n as a function of the maximum number of faulty processors t allowed ($n \geq 3t + 1$ [LSP]);

- the number of communication rounds r ($r \geq t + 1$ [DS]);

- the communication costs, alternatively given by the maximum message size m ($m \geq 1$, obvious), or the total number of transmitted bits B ($B \geq (n - t)(t + 1)/4$ [DR]).

Convinced that communication costs are one of the dominant factors in a protocol's performance [G], in this paper we focus on optimizing these costs, in particular B, the total bit transfer. Recent work by Hadzilacos and Halpern [HH] also addresses this concern by studying the message and bit complexity of runs that are failure-free.

All previous protocols (e.g., [BD, BDDS, BG1, BGP, LSP, MW]) require $B = \Omega(n^2 t)$, regardless of the value of the other parameters. The contribution of this paper is the first consensus protocol that achieves asymptotically optimal bit transfer (i.e., $B = O(nt)$) using the optimal number of processors ($n > 3t$) and nearly optimal number of rounds ($r = t + o(t)$). A similar result has been concurrently and independently obtained by Coan and Welch [CW1].

The remainder of the paper is organized as follows. The first section describes the *Phase King* protocol of [BGP], a consensus protocol that is optimal in n and asymptotically optimal in r and m. The following section shows that the number of rounds required to run *Phase King* may be reduced by applying the *committee* technique of [BG1]. In the subsequent section, we further transform *Phase King*, resulting in a protocol that is optimal in total bit transfer. The resulting protocol uses the committee technique and consists of just two phases; in each phase the committee recursively runs

---

[1]A certain level of synchrony is necessary to obtain distributed consensus (see [FLP]). Thus every known protocol either assumes perfect synchrony, as here, or at least bounds the number of steps that a correct processor may execute before receiving a reply from another correct processor. Interesting new results in this model were obtained recently by Attiya *et al.* [ADLS].

```
for k := 1 to t + 1 do begin
                    (* universal exchange 1 *)
        send(V)
        for j := 0 to 1 do
                    C[j] := the number of received j's;

                    (* universal exchange 2 *)
        for j := 0 to 1 do
                    send(C[j] ≥ n − t)
                    D[j] := the number of received 1's;
        V := D[1] > t;

                    (* king's broadcast *)
        if k = p then send(V);
        if D[V] < n − t then
                    V := the message received from k;
    end;
```

Figure 1. Protocol *Phase King*, code for processor p.

the same protocol. We conclude with a discussion of recent developments and open problems.

CONSTANT MESSAGE SIZE WITH OPTIMAL RESILIENCY

The *Phase King* protocol of [BGP], shown in Figure 1, is asymptotically optimal with respect to r and m and is exactly optimal in the number of processors (i.e., $n > 3t$). The protocol uses messages of constant size (2 bits) and runs in $t + 1$ phases, each consisting of three exchange rounds: two universal exchanges and the king's broadcast. A universal exchange ensures that a processor will hold a value in local variable V only if enough processors claim to hold that value; the arrays C and D record the number of processors claiming to hold each value prior to the two universal exchanges. During the king's broadcast, the processor designated as king of the phase broadcasts its V and each processor replaces its own value of V with the king's unless it is certain that all correct processors computed the same majority. We will show that a processor can conclude the latter if its own majority exceeds the required threshold by t. The protocol gets its name since a different processor is designated as king in each phase.

Theorem 1: Phase King *solves the Distributed Consensus problem using $3(t+1)$ exchange rounds and two-bit messages (or $4(t + 1)$ rounds and single-bit messages), provided $n > 3t$.*

Proof: Observe that the second universal exchange can be implemented either as a single round with two-bit messages or two rounds with single-bit messages. A simple inspection of the code confirms the respective round and message size complexities obtained for each alternative. Correctness will be established using the following preliminary result. Throughout the paper X_p denotes the value of local variable X for processor p.

Persistency. If for all $p \in P − T$, $V_p = v$ is true at the start of a phase, it remains true at the end of the phase.

To see this, observe that after the first universal exchange each correct processor p has $C[v]_p \geq n - t > 2t$ and $C[\bar{v}]_p \leq t$. Consequently, in the second universal exchange, each correct processor sends 1 for v and 0 for $\bar{v}$, resulting in each correct processor p ignoring the king's broadcast since $D[v]_p \geq n - t$ and $D[\bar{v}]_p \leq t$. Thus $V_p = v$ for each correct processor p.

Now we can address the correctness of the protocol.

Agreement. Since the number of phases $(t + 1)$ exceeds the number of faulty processors (t), there is some first phase g with a non-faulty king. At the end of phase g one of the following cases holds:

1. $D[V]_p < n - t$ for each $p \in P - T$. Then every correct processor assigns V_g to V during king g's broadcast.

2. $D[V]_p \geq n - t$ for some $p \in P - T$. Note that since there are no more than t faulty processors, $|C[b]_q - C[b]_s| \leq t$ and $|D[b]_q - D[b]_s| \leq t$, for every $q, s \in P - T$ and $b \in \{0, 1\}$. Therefore if some correct processor q sends 1 for b in the second universal exchange, then no correct processor s can send 1 for $\bar{b}$ (since $C[b]_q \geq n - t$ implies $C[b]_s \geq n - 2t$, $C[\bar{b}]_s$ must be at most $2t < n - t$). Let $V_p = v$. By the same logic, $D[V]_p \geq n - t$ implies that phase g's king (g) broadcasts v, since $D[V]_g \geq n - 2t > t$. Therefore each correct processor q sets V to v, either because $D[V]_q \geq n - t$ or by receiving King g's broadcast.

Persistency assures that no correct processor subsequently alters V.

Validity. Follows trivially from Persistency. ∎

REDUCING THE NUMBER OF ROUNDS WITH COMMITTEES

While the consensus protocol presented in the previous section is processor-optimal and has a very small message size (1 or 2 bits), its round complexity is at least three times optimal. In this section we show how the committee technique of Berman and Garay [BG1] can be used to improve the round complexity to $t(1 + 1/d)$ rounds for every constant d, while maintaining the same number of processors and messages of constant size.

The idea is as follows. Correctness of the *Phase King* protocol depends on the existence of a phase in which the king is non-faulty; running for $(t + 1)$ phases assures this. We can instead partition the processors into R disjoint committees, replace the king of phase k by committee Q_k, and run for R phases. By carefully choosing R, the committee size, and the intra-committee protocol, we can assure that the committees are valid substitutes for the phase kings, that a correct committee will occur, and that R is small. The tradeoff is that each phase requires multiple rounds for the intra-committee protocol to run so that the total number of phases is some constant times R.

To implement this idea, we modify the *Phase King* protocol to that shown in Figure 2. We change the number of phases in Fig. 1 from $t + 1$ to R (where R will be established later) and replace the king's code by committee Q_k's code. Intra-committee the processors run protocol DCP, where DCP is any round-optimal distributed consensus protocol that satisfies the following properties:

1. in each round a correct processor sends the same message to all other processors;

```
for k := 1 to R do begin
                (* universal exchange 1 *)
        send(V);
        for j := 0 to 1 do
                C[j] := the number of received j's;

                (* universal exchange 2 *)
        for j := 0 to 1 do
                send(C[j] ≥ n − t)
                D[j] := the number of received 1's;
        V := D[1] > t;

                (* committee's broadcast *)
        if p ∈ Q_k then
                run DCP within Q_k using V as the initial
                value and sending the messages required by this
                protocol to all processors;
        if D[V] < n − t then
                V := the consensus value of Q_k;
end;
```

Figure 2. Reducing the round complexity of *Phase King*, code for processor p.

2. a recipient of these messages that is not a committee member can compute the consensus value; and

3. fewer than 1/3 of the processors may be faulty.

All published deterministic round- and processor-optimal protocols satisfy these properties [BDDS, BG2, LSP]. A round-optimal protocol is used intra-committee to accelerate consensus yet messages of only moderate size result because committees contain few processors.

Correctness of this idea will follow from *Phase King*'s correctness once we show that R committees can be chosen so as to guarantee the existence of one in which correct processors dominate. Let t_k denote the maximum number of faulty processors that can be tolerated by the DCP of the kth committee Q_k. By choosing an R that satisfies $\sum_{k=1}^{R}(t_k + 1) = t + 1$, it is possible to partition the n processors into R committees such that $|Q_k| = 3t_k + 1$ since

$$\sum_{k=1}^{R}(3t_k + 1) = 3\sum_{k=1}^{R}(t_k + 1) - 2R = 3(t + 1) - 2R = 3t + 1 - 2(R - 1) \leq n.$$

By the pigeonhole principle there is at least one committee Q_k with no more than t_k faulty members. The DCP run by this Q_k succeeds in broadcasting the correct members' consensus to all correct processors and thus the members collectively serve the role of the non-faulty king required in *Phase King*'s correctness proof.

Now we can analyze the number of rounds of the resulting protocol. Phase k requires two universal exchanges plus the number of rounds necessary for the DCP Q_k, which is $t_k + 1$ since DCP is round optimal. Thus, the entire protocol uses $r = \sum_{k=1}^{R}(t_k + 1 + 2) = t + 1 + 2R$ rounds. This allows us to prove

Theorem 2: *For each $d > 1$ there exist a constant m_0 and a Distributed Consensus protocol that uses $n > 3t$ processors, $r \leq t(1 + 1/d) + 3$ rounds and messages of size m_0.*

Proof: The required protocol is an instance of the protocol in Figure 2. Our choice for DCP is any processor- and round-optimal consensus protocol satisfying the three conditions specified above (e.g. [BG2]); we simply argue that for a bounded committee size any DCP will yield bounded message size. We need to assure $t_k < 2d$, which is achieved as follows: choose $R = \lceil (t+1)/2d \rceil$, $t_k = 2d - 1$ for $1 \leq k \leq (R-1)/d$, and $t_R = \lceil (t+1) \bmod 2d \rceil - 1$. The resulting number of rounds is $t + 1 + 2R = t + 1 + 2\lceil (t+1)/2d \rceil < t(1 + 1/d) + 3$. ∎

Remark: The size of the constant in Theorem 2 depends on the choice of a protocol which is optimal in both r and n. The classic protocol of Lamport *et al.* yields $m_0 = d^{O(d)}$ [LSP]. In [BG2] Berman and Garay describe protocol $ESDM$ with messages of size $O(1.5^t)$, yielding $m_0 = O(1.5^d)$. Admittedly, the existing round- and processor-optimal protocols make Theorem 2 practical only for small values of d.

CONSENSUS WITH OPTIMAL BIT TRANSFER

In this section we show that it is possible to reach consensus with asymptotically optimal bit transfer (i.e. $B = O(nt)$). The resulting protocol also achieves processor optimality and near round optimality. In order to obtain this result we apply the method of the previous section in the extreme: the processors are split into two committees, each acting the role of king in one of two phases of the *Phase King* protocol. Intra-committee, the processors reach consensus by recursively applying the technique until the committee size becomes small, in which case they use the $ESDM$ protocol of [BG2]. This results in only 6 exchange rounds involving all n processors, 12 rounds involving about $n/2$ processors, 24 rounds involving $n/4$ processors, etc. Thus, the total bit transfer is $cn^2(1 + 1/2 + 1/4 + ...)$. The choice of $ESDM$ as the basis results in near round optimality, as we shall demonstrate.

To describe the technique in detail, let Q_1 be equal to P, the set of all processors. Q_w is recursively partitioned into two committees Q_{2w} and Q_{2w+1} of balanced size. We call the resulting protocol *Recursive Phase King* (see Figure 3). At the top level, the processors execute $RPK(1, V)$, where V contains the processor's initial binary value. The value of parameter M, which appears in the protocol, will be computed later.

Theorem 3: Recursive Phase King *solves the Distributed Consensus problem using optimal number of processors ($n > 3t$), $r = t + o(t)$ communication rounds, and total bit transfer $B = O(nt)$.*

Proof: *Correctness.* If $|Q_w| > 3|Q_w \cap T|$ then in the call to $RPK(w, V)$ the values of V of the processors from $Q_w - T$ satisfy the *Validity* and *Agreement* conditions. In the case when $|Q_w| \leq M$, the claim follows from the correctness of $ESDM$. In the other case, note that either $|Q_{2w}| > 3 \cdot |Q_{2w} \cap T|$, or $|Q_{2w+1}| > 3 \cdot |Q_{2w+1} \cap T|$. The subcommittee with the favorable ratio plays the role of the honest king in *Phase King*, and its proof of correctness applies (Theorem 1).

Number of rounds. The number of rounds required by RPK can be expressed as the following recurrence (where $|Q_w| = s$):

```
procedure RPK(w: integer; var V: {0,1});
var C, D: array[0..2] of integer;
    U: {0,1}; t_w: integer;
begin
    t_w := (|Q_w| - 1) div 3;
    if |Q_w| ≤ M then
        ESDM(w, V)
    else for k := 0 to 1 do begin
        perform universal exchanges of Phase King within Q_w,
        which causes arrays C, D and possibly variable V to be set;
        if p ∈ Q_{2w+k} then begin
            U := V;
            RPK(2w + k, U);
            send U to Q_{2w+(1-k)}
        end;
        if p ∈ Q_{2w+(1-k)} then
            U := the most frequent value received
            from members of Q_{2w+k};
        if D[V] < |Q_w| - t_w then
            V := U;
    end
end;
```

Figure 3. Recursive Phase King, code for processor p.

$$r(s) = \begin{cases} \lfloor s/3 \rfloor + 1 & \text{if } s \le M \\ r(\lfloor s/2 \rfloor) + r(\lceil s/2 \rceil) + 6 & \text{otherwise} \end{cases}$$

For example, for $s = 2^k M$ processors this recurrence yields $r(s) = (2^k - 1)6 + 2^k(\lfloor M/3 \rfloor + 1) < 2^k(\lfloor M/3 \rfloor + 7) \le \frac{s}{3}(1 + \frac{21}{M})$. In general, $r(3t + 1) = t + o(t)$, provided $M = \omega(1)$.

Total bit transfer. From Fig. 3, the total number of bits communicated can be expressed by the recurrence:

$$B(s) = \begin{cases} c2' & \text{if } s < M \\ B(\lfloor s/2 \rfloor) + B(\lceil s/2 \rceil) + 6.5s^2 & \text{otherwise} \end{cases}$$

For $s = n = 2^k M$ processors this recurrence yields $6.5M^2(2^{2k} + 2^{2k-1} + \cdots + 2^k) + c2^k 2^M \le 13(2^k M)^2 + 2^k M \frac{c2^M}{M} \le 14(2^k M)^2 = 14n^2$, provided $\frac{c2^M}{M} \le n$.

The latter is true for $M < \alpha \log n$, where α is a suitable constant. ∎

CONCLUSIONS AND OPEN PROBLEMS

In this paper we have presented a simple Distributed Consensus protocol that achieves asymptotically optimal bit transfer ($B = O(nt)$), together with the optimal number of processors and nearly optimal number of communication rounds. Previous consensus protocols required $\Omega(n^2 t)$ bit transfer, regardless of the other parameters' values. The same result was independently and concurrently obtained by Coan and Welch [CW1].

The starting building block for our result is the *Phase King* protocol of [BGP]. This simple protocol has proven useful in other directions as well: An "early-stopping" version of the protocol has been recently used by Bar-Noy *et al.* [BDGK] to achieve optimal consensus in the *amortized* sense. Namely, they look at the cost of consensus when it is repeatedly needed, showing in particular that consensus is possible in *constant* amortized number of rounds.

In an interesting new development, Coan and Welch show how to achieve consensus with basically the same parameters as in this paper, but with 1-bit messages [CW2]. Finally, it remains open whether Distributed Consensus is achievable in the optimal number of rounds, using the optimal number of processors and polynomial communication. The best known algorithm so far is that of [BG2], which achieves consensus in the optimal number of rounds, with $n = (3 + \varepsilon)t$ processors and messages of size $O(2^{1/\varepsilon}\mathrm{poly}(t))$ (i.e., polynomial communication for $\varepsilon \geq 1/\log t$).

References

[ADLS] H. Attiya, C. Dwork, N. Lynch and L. Stockmeyer, "Bounds on the time to reach agreement in the presence of timing uncertainty," *Proc. 23rd STOC*, pp. 359-369, May 1991.

[BD] A. Bar-Noy and D. Dolev, "Families of Consensus Algorithms," *Proc. 3rd Aegean Workshop on Computing*, pp. 380-390, June/July 1988.

[BDDS] A. Bar-Noy, D. Dolev, C. Dwork and H.R. Strong, "Shifting gears: changing algorithms on the fly to expedite Byzantine Agreement," *Proc. 6th PODC*, pp. 42-51, August 1987.

[BDGK] A. Bar-Noy, X. Deng, J. Garay and T. Kameda, "Optimal Amortized Distributed Consensus," to appear in *Proc. 5th International Workshop on Distributed Algorithms (LNCS)*, Delphi, Greece, October 1991.

[BG1] P. Berman and J.A. Garay, "Asymptotically Optimal Distributed Consensus," *Proc. ICALP 89*, LNCS Vol. 372, pp. 80-94, July 1989.

[BG2] P. Berman and J.A. Garay, "Efficient Distributed Consensus with $n = (3+\varepsilon)t$ Processors," to appear in *Proc. 5th International Workshop on Distributed Algorithms (LNCS)*, Delphi, Greece, October 1991.

[BGP] P. Berman, J.A. Garay and K.J. Perry, "Towards Optimal Distributed Consensus," *Proc. 30th FOCS*, pp. 410-415, October/November 1989.

[CW1] B.A. Coan and J.L. Welch, "Modular Construction of a Byzantine Agreement Protocol with Optimal Message Bit Complexity," *Proc. 27th Allerton Conference on Communication, Control, and Computing*, pp. 1062-1071, 1989. To appear in *Information and Computation*.

[CW2] B.A. Coan and J.L. Welch, "Modular Construction of an Efficient 1-Bit Byzantine Agreement Protocol," personal communication. To appear in *Mathematical Systems Theory*, special issue dedicated to Distributed Agreement.

[DR] D. Dolev and R. Reischuk, "Bounds of Information Exchange for Byzantine Agreement," *JACM*, Vol. 32, No. 1, pp. 191-204, 1985.

[DS]   D. Dolev and H.R. Strong, "Polynomial Algorithms for Multiple Processor Agreement," *Proc. 14th STOC*, pp. 401-407, May 1982.

[FLP]   M. Fisher, N. Lynch and M. Paterson, "Impossibility of Distributed Consensus with one faulty process," *JACM*, Vol. 32, No. 2 (1985), pp. 374-382.

[G]   J. Gray, "The Cost of Messages," *Proc. 7th PODC*, pp. 1-7, August 1988.

[HH]   V. Hadzilacos and J. Halpern, "Message-Optimal Protocols for Byzantine Agreement," *Proc. 10th PODC*, pp. 309-324, August 1991..

[LSP]   L. Lamport, R.E. Shostak and M. Pease, "The Byzantine Generals Problem," *ACM ToPLaS*, Vol. 4, No. 3, pp. 382-401, July 1982.

[MW]   Y. Moses and O. Waarts, "Coordinated Traversal: $(t+1)$-Round Byzantine Agreement in Polynomial Time," *Proc. 29th FOCS*, pp. 246-255, October 1988.

AN EFFICIENT DISTRIBUTED TERMINATION

Eliezer L. Lozinskii

Institute of Mathematics and Computer Science
The Hebrew University of Jerusalem, Israel

ABSTRACT

Detecting termination of a program is an important task in distributed computing systems. We describe a method for detecting distributed termination, called $SP - termination$, which has certain advantages over the known methods: shorter time delays, better distribution of control messages over the communication network, suitability for concurrent job processing, higher reliability. This approach provides also an improvement for dynamic distributed systems.

1. INTRODUCTION

The recent progress in VLSI technology and development of multiprocessor systems has given rise to intensive research in distributed execution of concurrent programs. One of the problems arising in this field and stimulating a considerable amount of work is the *Distributed termination problem* (Apt, 1986; Cohen and Lehmann, 1982; Dijkstra et al., 1983; Francez, 1980; Francez and Rodeh, 1982; Misra, 1983; Rana, 1983; Richier, 1984; Topor, 1984).

Consider the computational model of *Communicating Sequential Processes, CSP* (Hoare, 1978), according to which a program, P, consists of a set of *processes*, $\{P_1, P_2, \ldots, P_n\}$, such that the processes share no common variables, and communicate only by exchanging messages through communication channels (either real or virtual). Each process, P_i, is associated with a local predicate, B_i, which is true iff P_i has completed its processing, and is ready to terminate unless some other process of P will communicate with it. So, P_i will terminate when all B_i, $1 \leq i \leq n$, are true simultaneously. And this is a necessary and sufficient condition for termination of the whole program P. Checking this global condition and detecting its satisfaction constitute the *Distributed termination problem (DTP)*, introduced by Francez (1980).

A number of solutions to DTP has been given recently.

Francez (1980) came up with DTP, and defined for a program, P, a *communication graph*, G_p, containing one node for each P_i and an arc (P_i, P_j) for each P_i sending a message to P_j. Then a spanning tree, T_p, in the undirected graph underlying G_p is used as a *control pattern* for detecting termination of P by means of a special algorithm in such a way that each node notifies its parent in T_p whether all nodes in its subtree have satisfied their local termination predicates, and when the root of T_p is informed that all the B_i's are true, it initiates a *termination wave* that reaches all P_i's. In general, the *Distributed termination pattern theorem* (Francez, 1980) proves that P terminates only if the control pattern reflecting all termination dependencies among the processes of P is acyclic.

Cohen and Lehmann (1982) have analyzed a dynamic distributed system in which any process can initiate some new processes and become *responsible* for them. A program execution begins with one *root-process*. At any moment each process has only a single parent-process responsible for it, hence initiation of processes generates a *responsibility tree*. If a leaf of the tree satisfies its local termination condition it drops out of the tree. When the tree becomes empty, then the program terminates (see also section 5).

A number of known methods for solving DTP are based on a cycle in G_p that includes all the vertices of G_p (Apt, 1986; Dijkstra et al., 1983; Rana, 1983; Richier, 1984) or even all the edges of G_p (Misra, 1983). A process sends a special control message along this cycle, and when after visiting all the vertices (or after passing all the edges) the message returns to the sender, the latter can check whether or not the condition of global termination has been fulfilled.

Known solutions of DTP have some drawbacks or, at least, some properties that require improvement.

(i) Let dd denote *detection delay*, i.e., the period of time between the fulfillment of the global termination condition for a program, P, and the moment when this fact has been detected by a process of P, and td stand for a *termination delay*, which is the period of time between a detection of termination of P by a process and the moment when all the processes of P have been informed about this fact (in order not to keep any longer any information relevant to P). Let n denote the number of processes in P. Then for cycle-based methods in all cases $dd = O(n)$, and in the worst case of the method by Misra (1983) $dd = O(n^2)$. Even for tree-based methods (Cohen and Lehmann, 1982; Francez, 1980; Francez and Rodeh, 1982; Topor, 1984) in the worst case $dd = O(n)$, because no restriction is imposed on T_p, and the responsibility tree is built up in the order of message exchange among the processes in the course of execution of P, while no care is taken of the depth of the tree. The termination delay is determined by the time required for broadcasting a signal to all processes of P, so in the worst case $td = O(n)$.

One may wish to devise a DTP solution with much shorter delays.

(ii) Consider a program $P = \{P_1, P_2, \ldots, P_n\}$. Each particular execution of the program may involve processes of a (probably small) subset, S, of P. (This feature

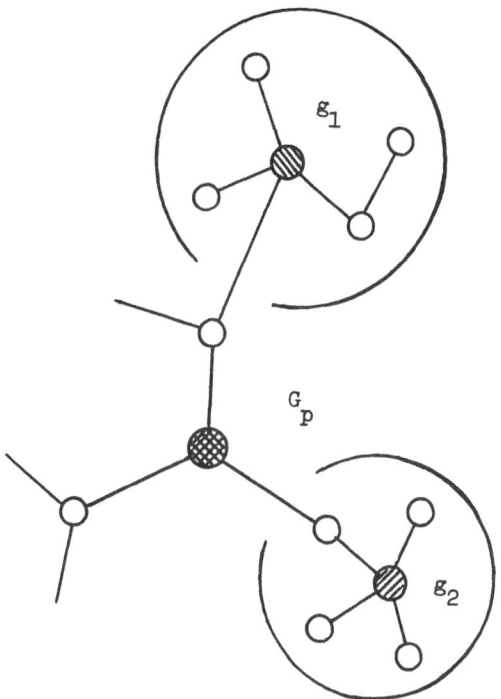

Figure 1. Control patterns: global G_p and local g_1, g_2.

is characteristic of branching programs.) Let these subsets, S_i, corresponding to different executions of P, be represented by subgraphs, g_i, of G_p (e.g., g_1, g_2 in Fig.1). The known methods for DTP use the same global control pattern (e.g., the one depicted in Fig. 1) for all executions of P regardless of the actual cardinality of S and the local structure of g.

One may try to work out a method that takes advantage of the relatively small dimensions of g.

(iii) Let us say that each execution of P is performed for a certain *query, q*. If there is a path in G_p from P_i to P_k (see Fig. 2, displaying a fragment of G_p), then P_i is called a *predecessor* of P_k, and P_k a *successor* of P_i. Consider a set, S_1, of *independent* processes such that no two of them are predecessors of one another, and hence receive no messages from one another (e.g., $S_1 = \{\ldots, P_i, P_j, P_n, \ldots\}$ in Fig. 2(a)). Processes of S_1 can work concurrently either for the same query or for different queries. Consider another set, S_2, consisting of processes which are pairwise predecessors of one another (e.g., $S_2 = \{\ldots, P_j, P_k, P_l, \ldots\}$ in Fig. 2(a)). Processes of S_2 constitute a *pipeline* such that they can work concurrently for different queries. Thus, a set of queries, Q, can be processed concurrently by P. If the same control pattern, C (e.g., displayed by broken lines in Fig. 2(a)), with the same root-process, P_r, is used for detecting of termination of all queries of Q, then the channels of C and the process P_r are heavily overloaded, which may cause additional delays.

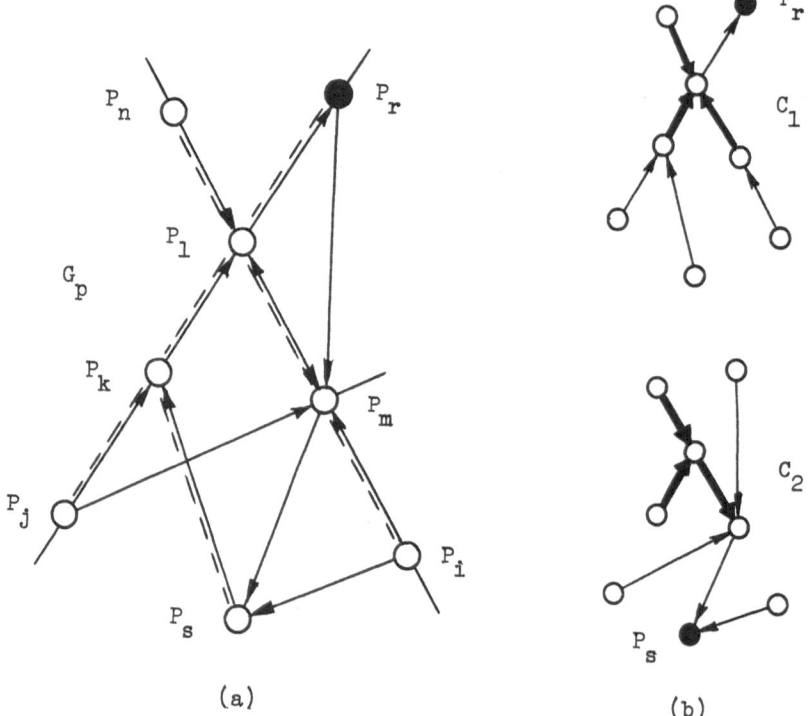

Figure 2. Sharing control load.

One may attempt to find a DTP solution which distributes control messages for different concurrent queries among different processes of P and subgraphs of G_p. For example, Fig. 2(b) shows two subgraphs, C_1, C_2, of the G_p displayed in Fig. 2(a), which have only a part of the arcs in common (drawn in bold lines). C_1 and C_2 have different root-processes, P_r, P_s, and can be used as control patterns for different concurrent queries.

In what follows we describe a method called *SP-termination,* which is advantageous from the aforesaid points of view.

2. SP - TERMINATION

Let P_i denote both a process and the node representing it in G_p, and $SP(P_i, P_j)$ be a particular shortest path from P_i to P_j. We call *activate-successors of P_i towards P_j* all nodes belonging to $SP(P_i, P_j)$, and *activate-predecessors of P_i towards P_j* all nodes P_k such that P_i belongs to $SP(P_k, P_j)$. For each query, q, there is a process called the *target-process of q* (denoted *targ(q)*), which is intended for detecting the termination of q.

Each process P_i has *input ports* corresponding to every incoming arc of the node that represents P_i in G_p. With respect to a query, q, a port, p, may be in one of the two states: $on(p, q)$, $off(p, q)$.

Each process, P_i, may assume one of the following three main states with regard to a query q:

$active(P_i, q)$, this means that P_i itself or some of its activate-predecessors towards $targ(q)$ is executing a processing for q; in the latter case there exists an input port, p, of P_i in the state $on(p, q)$;

$passive(P_i, q)$, this means that neither P_i nor any of its activate-predecessors towards $targ(q)$ is $active(q)$, but there still takes place some processing for q in P, and therefore P_i may resume its processing for q; so P_i keeps certain information pertinent to q;

indifferent (P_i, q), means that P_i has nothing to do with q.

When a program, P, is being executed for a query, q, then the processes involved in the execution exchange messages, $m(q)$, that constitute a *basic communication*. In addition, a *control communication* takes place among the processes: they send and receive signals intended for detecting the query termination. These signals, $activate(q)$, $passive(q)$, $delete(q)$, mean that the sending process is changing its state, respectively, to $active(q)$, $passive(q)$, $indifferent(q)$.

The following rules determine the control operation and communication of processes:

(1) A processing of a query, q, begins with sending of an initiating message, $m(q)$.

(2) When a process, P_i, receives a basic message $m(q)$ or a control signal $activate(q)$ at a port, p, then if P_i is not $active(q)$, it sends $activate(q)$ to its immediate activate-successor towards $targ(q)$, and sets $active(P_i, q)$. In addition, if $activate(q)$ arrives at a port, p, then the process sets $on(p, q)$. So, $activate(q)$ signals are sent to the target-process of q from all processes involved in evaluating q, along shortest paths from these processes to the target. Although there can be a number of different shortest paths from a process P_i to the $targ(q)$, only one of these shortest paths is chosen for transmitting $activate(q)$ signals to the target. Thus, the control pattern for q is a spanning tree of G_p such that it is a union of particular shortest paths from the involved processes to the target of q.

(3) When *passivate* (q) arrives at p, it sets *off* (p,q).

(4) If P_i has completed its local computation for q and all input ports of P_i are $off(q)$ then the local predicate $B_i(q)$ is true.

(5) When $B_i(q)$ becomes true, then P_i sends $passivate(q)$ to its immediate activate-successor towards $targ(q)$, and sets $passive(P_i, q)$. $Passivate(q)$ and $activate(q)$ signals are sent to the target-process of q along the same shortest paths.

(6) When P_i receives $delete(q)$ then it transfers this signal to all its immediate predecessors and sets $indifferent(P_i, q)$.

(7) A target-process operation differs from that of a non-target one in two aspects: it does not send $activate(\dots)$ or $passivate(\dots)$ signals, and -- this is even more significant -- it detects the global termination of the corresponding query. It is shown in section

3 that if a target T of q at some moment becomes *passive*(T, q), and remains in this state for a certain period of time, $\tau(T)$, then this indicates that the processing of q is terminated. Thus, when T becomes *passive*(T, q), it starts counting time for q (after setting the counter to zero). Becoming *active*(T, q) it stops counting. When the counter reaches the value of $\tau(T)$ then the result of q is displayed, T sends *delete*(q) to all its immediate predecessors, and sets *indifferent*(q). As a result, the query is deleted all over the system.

(8) A communication channel must not change the time sequence of the signals and messages transmitted through it. This means that if, for example, *activate*(q), $m(q)$, *passivate*(q), were sent in a certain time sequence from a process P_i to P_j, then they must arrive at a port, p, of P_j in the same sequence (although, time intervals between messages may change, and their time stamps are only relative, because each process may run asynchronously its own local time). Every P_j must process messages arriving at each of its ports according to the time sequence of their arrivals at this particular port. Thus, processes maintain input queues of messages for each of input ports. Messages appearing at different input ports are processed in the following order of decreasing priority: *activate*(q), $m(q)$, *passivate*(q), *delete*(q).

(9) For a proper routing of control signals each process keeps pointers to its immediate predecessors, and a pointer to its immediate activate-successor towards every $P_i \in P$. Pointers to the immediate activate-successors define a unique control tree for every process, P_i, of P in case that P_i becomes the target process for a query. These control patterns (consisting of shortest paths among processes) are precomputed at a compile-time of P.

The SP-termination algorithm can be expressed conveniently in terms of CSP (Hoare, 1978) as follows ("*message* at p" means that the *message* is the first one to be served in the input queue of port p; a number in the parenthesis preceding a command corresponds to the priority of the latter relatively to other commands that are ready for execution; 0 denotes the highest priority).

For a non-target process:
{
1.1: (0) *activate*(q) at p $\rightarrow$
      if not *active*(q) then send *activate*(q) and set *active*(q);
      set *on*(p, q).
1.2: (1) $m(q)$ at p and not *active*(q) $\rightarrow$
      send *activate*(q); set *active*(q).
1.3: (2) *passivate*(q) at p $\rightarrow$
      set *off*(p, q).
1.4: (2) local computations for q are completed and all input ports $\supseteq$
      are *off*(ip, q) $\rightarrow$
      if *active*(q) then send *passivate*(q) and set *passive*(q).
1.5: (3) *delete*(q) at p $\rightarrow$
      if not *indifferent*(q) then send *delete*(q) and set *indifferent*(q).
}

For a target process, $targ(q)$:

2.1: (3) initialize q, i.e., send $m(q)$;
2.2: (3) set $passive(q)$;
2.3: (3) start $count(q)$;
{
2.4: (0) $activate(q)$ at p $\rightarrow$
    stop $count(q)$; set $active(q)$; set $on(p, q)$.
2.5: (2) $passivate(q)$ at p $\rightarrow$
    set $off(p, q)$.
2.6: (2) local computations for q are completed and all input ports inp
    are $off(inp, q)$ $\rightarrow$
    if $active(q)$ then set $passive(q)$ and start $count(q)$.
2.7: (3) $end - count(q)$ $\rightarrow$
    display results of q; send $delete(q)$; set $indifferent(q)$.
}

3. CORRECTNESS OF SP-TERMINATION

We say that a process is *activated* or *passivated* when its state changes to $active(q)$ or $passive(q)$, respectively. If a process is activated at a time t_1 (see paragraph (2), section 2), it sends $activate(q)$ to its immediate activate-successor, and the latter receives this signal at a time t_2, after a short delay, $\alpha = t_2 - t_1$. Because of the highest priority of $activate(q)$ all other signals and messages have delays equal or greater than α. Let β denote the delay of $passivate(q)$, $\beta \geq \alpha$.

Consider a query, q, which is being processed at some time t_0, i.e. at t_0 there is a process $active(q)$. Suppose that at a time t_1 there is no process $active(q)$, but there might be signals of q delayed in the communication network which might activate a process at some time $t_2 > t_1$. Let γ be the maximum communication delay of a signal. So, if during the period of time from t_1 till $t_1 + \gamma$ there was no process $active(q)$, then no process will become $active(q)$ at any time $t_3 > t_1 + \gamma$, and hence at t_1 the query q has been *terminated*.

Let T be the target-process of q such that there is a path to T from every process of P involved in executing q, and $L(T)$ denote the maximum length (measured in number of arcs) of a shortest path to T from its predecessors. The following propositions establish correctness of SP-termination.

Proposition 1. A query, q, is terminated at a time, t, if the target, T, of q is $passive(q)$ for a period of time from t till $t + \gamma + \alpha \cdot L(T)$.

Proof. Assume that T is $passive(q)$ from t till $t + \gamma + \alpha \cdot L(T)$, but there is a predecessor, P_i, of T which is $active(q)$ at some time, t_1, such that $t \leq t_1 \leq t + \gamma$. Consider the shortest path from P_i to T, of length $k \leq L(T)$, and let $SP(P_i, T) = \{P_i, P_{j_1}, P_{j_2}, \ldots, P_{j_{k-1}}, T\}$. If P_i is $active(q)$ at t_1, this means that P_i has been activated at some time $t' < t_1$ and will not be passivated until $t'' > t_1$. Hence

329

P_{j_1} has received $activate(q)$ from P_i at t_2, $t_2 = t' + \alpha < t_1 + \alpha$, and will not be passivated until $t_3^{\sim}$, $t_3 = t'' + \beta > t_1 + \alpha$. Therefore P_{j_1} is $active(q)$ at the time $t_1 + \alpha$. By induction on activate-successors of P_i towards T one concludes that T must be $active(q)$ at $t_4 = t_1 + \alpha k$. Since $t < t_4 \leq t + \gamma + \alpha \cdot L(T)$, this contradicts the assumption. Q.E.D.

Proposition 2. If a query, q, is terminated at a time, t, then its target-process, T, must be $passive(q)$ at the time $t + \beta \cdot L(T)$, and will not get $active(q)$ afterwards.

Proof. If q is terminated at t then before t every process has completed its local computation for q and sent its last activating signal. Let P_k be a remotest predecessor of T, at the distance $L(T)$ from T. P_k has no activate-predecessors towards T, therefore P_k has not received any $activate(q)$ signal in the course of processing q, and so all its input ports are $off(p, q)$. Hence, as soon as P_k has completed all its local computations for q, it has sent $passivate(q)$ to its immediate activate-successor, P' (see paragraphs (4),(5), section 2), and this must have happened at a time $t_k \leq t$. Process P' must receive $passivate(q)$ from P_k at a time t', such that $t' \leq t_k + \beta \leq t + \beta$. So, every process at the distance $L(T) - 1$ from T must receive $passivate(q)$ from all its activate-predecessors not later than $t + \beta$. These signals set all input ports of the process to $off(p, q)$, while, by the assumption, all its local computations for q have already been completed since the time t. Hence, at this moment each process at the distance $L(T) - 1$ from T must send $passivate(q)$ to its immediate activate-successor, and the latter must receive this signal not later than $t + 2\beta$. By induction on shortest paths to T one concludes that not later than $t + \beta \cdot L(T)$ the target T receives $passivate(q)$ from all its predecessors, becomes $passive(T, q)$, and will not get $active(q)$ afterwards because since t there were no activating signals of q in the network. Q.E.D.

Propositions 1, 2 imply the following result.
Proposition 3. The detection delay of SP-termination is at most

$$(\alpha + \beta) \cdot L(T) + \gamma.$$

4. RELIABILITY OF SP-TERMINATION

All known methods for detecting of distributed termination are sensitive to losses of control signals in the sense that if a control signal does not reach its destination (say, because of a communication failure), then the program termination can not be detected. As a result, the program will not be completed correctly, and, that is even more harmful, this may cause a deadlock, because the system will wait infinitely long for the lost signal, and the information relevant to the locked program will stay in the system memory. The following fairly general way of recovery can be utilized in this case: if there is an estimate of a maximum (or reasonable) duration of a query processing, then after a corresponding period of idling (or waiting for a signal) the query termination may be forced by the system.

So, it looks quite natural that SP-termination method assumes the knowledge of maximum delays of control signals, α, β, γ, which are parameters of the system, and do not depend on queries. This knowledge provides SP-termination with certain error-tolerance, such that any loss of an $activate(q)$ does not prevent detecting of the termination of q, although this loss may impair correct evaluation of the query. Indeed, if an $activate(q)$ signal, s_1, is lost while the target process, $targ(q)$, is $active(q)$, this means that the $targ(q)$ was activated by another $activate(q)$ signal, s_2 (see command 2.4, section 2), and will be passivated by the corresponding $passivate(q)$ signal which follows s_2 (so, the system behaves as if the lost $activate(q)$ was never sent); if an $activate(q)$ is lost while the $targ(q)$ is $passive(q)$ (cf. paragraph (7), section 2), then the latter will keep counting time, and after the period of $\gamma + \alpha \cdot L(T)$ it will detect the imaginary termination of q (perhaps, prematurely), display its (partial) results, and delete q.

However, if a $passivate(q)$ signal is lost while the $targ(q)$ is $active(q)$, then the $targ(q)$ will not be able to detect the termination of q. The general way of recovery mentioned at the beginning of this section takes into account the maximum execution time of a process, but this time depends on the query (in contrast to α, β, γ), and varies in a wide range, so its estimate is inevitably rough and exaggerated. Fortunately, SP-termination offers another remedy: assign to q a second target node randomly.

Thus, suppose that a query, q, is assigned randomly two target nodes, T_1 and T_2, both belonging to the subgraph g of G_p corresponding to q (see (ii), section 1). T_1 and T_2 determine two control patterns, C_1 and C_2. Each control pattern is a spanning tree of g, and contains at most $n - 1$ arcs (if n is the number of nodes of G_p). A realistic assumption is that the main reason of signal losses are failures of communication links. Let p be the probability that a particular link fails in transmitting of a signal, while $F(C_1)$ stands for the probability that a control pattern C_1 fails (the latter means that there is a link of C_1 which fails):

$$F(C_1) = 1 - (1 - p)^{n-1} \approx (n - 1)p.$$

Let C_0 be the set of common arcs of C_1 and C_2, while ΔC_1, ΔC_2 denote, respectively, the sets of arcs of C_1, C_2 that are not in common. Then the probability that both C_1 and C_2 fail is as follows:

$$F(C_1 \ and \ C_2) = F(C_0) + (1 - F(C_0)) \cdot F(\Delta C_1) \cdot F(\Delta C_2)$$

$$< F(C_0) + F^2(C_1).$$

So, $F(C_1 \ and \ C_2)$ is determined by $F(C_0)$. Let C_0 contain k arcs, then

$$F(C_0) = 1 - (1 - p)^k \approx kp.$$

Each node within a control tree has exactly one outgoing arc. Consider a node, i, of G_p that has an outgoing degree d_i, and let a_i be the outgoing arc of node i in C_1. Because C_2 has been chosen randomly, the probability that the same arc, a_i, is the outgoing arc of i in both C_1 and C_2, is $1/d_i$. Therefore the mean number of arcs common to C_1 and C_2 is

$$\bar{k} \le \sum_{i=1}^{n-1} 1/d_i.$$

Hence, the more complex is the program P, and more arcs contains G_p, the larger are outdegrees of nodes, smaller is $F(C_1 \text{ and } C_2)$ comparing to $F(C_1)$, and therefore higher is the probability that when one of the two control patterns, C_1 or C_2, fails, then the other one will still correctly detect the query termination. Thus, the reliability of SP-termination can be increased by assigning of additional target nodes to queries.

5. AN IMPROVEMENT FOR DYNAMIC SYSTEMS

A concurrent program P in the model of CSP (Hoare, 1978) is static in the sense that all processes of P and their communication are defined and initiated in the very beginning of each execution of P. Cohen and Lehmann (1982) describe a dynamic distributed system (see also section 1) where new processes are added at execution time, and their number can be infinitely large. The control pattern is a *responsibility tree* which contains all *non-sleeping* processes, i.e. the ones that actively take part in the processing at the moment. A program execution starts with a single *root-process* which detects later on the distributed termination of the program. If a non-sleeping process, P_i, communicates with a *sleeping* one, P_j (i.e., the one that does not yet take an active part in the processing), then P_j joins the responsibility tree as a son of P_i. If two non-sleeping processes communicate, then their locations in the tree do not change.

Such a dynamic system can be improved by applying the idea of SP-termination in the following way. Each process, P_i, keeps its distance, δ_i, from the root-process. When two non-sleeping processes, P_i and P_j, communicate, then their locations remain unchanged only if $|\delta_i - \delta_j| \leq 1$, else suppose (without loss of generality) that $\delta_i > \delta_j + 1$, then P_i becomes a son of P_j. Now δ_i becomes $\delta_j + 1$, which means that P_i has moved towards the root. This approach places the processes as close as possible to the root of the responsibility tree, and therefore shortens detection and termination delays in the system.

6. SUMMARY

SP-termination has certain properties advantageous over the known DTP solutions.

(a) Because control signals are sent along shortest paths in G_p, both detection and termination delays are proportional to the *diameter* (the longest shortest path) of G_p, and hence are shorter than the delays of the best known methods (cf. (i), section 1).

(b) Local terminations are reported *immediately* (not in responce to a special examining message) to the target of the query by means of *passivate(q)* signals (cf. paragraph (5) and command 1.4 of section 2). This together with property (a) implies that SP-termination provides the shortest time delays for a given communication graph.

(c) The acyclic control pattern for a query, q, used by the proposed method is the union of shortest paths from all processes involved in q to its target. All shortest paths in G_p are preprocessed, and pointers to the corresponding activate-successors kept by processes. Then assigning a target to a query determines uniquely its control pattern. Thus, assigning different targets to different concurrent queries enables distribution of control messages all over G_p (cf. (iii), section 1). If the target of q belongs to the subgraph, g, of G_p involved in processing q (see (ii), section 1), then all control messages for q are limited to g, and do not overload extra processes beyond it. This approach is well suited for a variety of programs, e.g. inferential database systems (Gallaire et al., 1984; lozinskii, 1986), where different queries activate different relations in a very natural way.

(d) SP-termination is partially error-tolerant (insensitive to losses of $activate(q)$ signals). Its reliability can be further increased by assigning additional targets to a given query.

References

Apt, K.R., 1986, Corectness proofs of distributed termination algorithms, *ACM TOPLAS* **8**: 388-405.

Cohen, S., and Lehmann, D., 1982, Dynamic systems and their distributed termination, *Proc. ACM SIGACT-SIGOPS Symp. on Principles of Distributed Computing*, Ottawa, 29-33.

Dijkstra, E.W., Feijen, W.H.J., and van Gasteren, A.J.M., 1983, Derivation of a termination detection algorithm for distributed computations, *Information Processing Letters* **16**: 217-219.

Francez, N., 1980, Distributed termination, *ACM TOPLAS* **2**: 42-55.

Francez, N., and Rodeh, M., 1982, Achieving distributed termination without freezing, *IEEE Trans. on Software Engineering*, **SE-8**: 287-292.

Gallaire, H., Minker, J., and Nicolas, J.-M., 1984, Logic and databases: a deductive approach, *ACM Computing Surveys*, **16**: 153-186.

Hoare, C.A.R., 1978, Communicating sequential processes, *Comm. ACM* **21**: 666-677.

Lozinskii, E.L., 1986, A problem-oriented inferential database system, *ACM TODS* **11**: 323-356.

Misra, J., 1983, Detecting termination of distributed computations using markers, *Proc. 2nd Annual ACM Symp. on Principles of Distributed Computing*, Montreal, 290-294.

Rana, S.P., 1983, A distributed solution of the distributed termination problem, *Information Processing Letters* **17**: 43-46.

Richier, J.L., 1984, Distributed termination in CSP: symmetric solutions with minimal storage, *TR 84-49*, Universite P. et M. Curie, Paris.

Topor, R.W., 1984, Termination detection for distributed computations, *Information Processing Letters*, **18**: 33-36.

ALLOCATING MODULES TO PROCESSORS IN A DISTRIBUTED SYSTEM WITH LIMITED MEMORY

David Fernández-Baca[1] and Anand Medepalli[1] [2]

[1]Department of Computer Science
[2]Department of Mathematics
Iowa State University
Ames, Iowa 50011

Abstract

We consider the problem of finding a minimum-cost assignment of program modules to processors in a distributed system where one of the processors has limited memory. This problem is NP-hard, even if the communication graph is a tree. We show that a fully polynomial-time approximation scheme exists for the case where the communication graph is a partial k-tree. A faster approximation scheme is presented for the case of trees with uniform costs. Both schemes are derived from algorithms for the allocation problem without memory constraints. We also show that, if the communication graph is unrestricted, there is no fully polynomial-time approximation scheme for the memory-constrained problem unless $P = NP$.

Keywords: Computer networks, distributed systems, dynamic programming, knapsack problems, scheduling, task allocation.

1 Introduction

The problem of assigning program modules to processors in a distributed system has received considerable attention in the literature [26, 27, 22, 7, 25, 20, 14, 11, 4, 12]. Formally, we can state the problem as follows. We are given a program with n modules, each of which must be assigned to one of p processors, and an undirected, connected graph G, called the *communication graph* of the system, whose vertices are the modules of the program and such that there is an edge between two vertices if the corresponding

COMPUTER SCIENCE, Edited by R. Baeza-Yates
and U. Manber, Plenum Press, New York, 1992

modules communicate. We assume that modules are numbered from 1 to n and processors are numbered from 1 to p. An assignment of modules to processors is represented by a vector $X = (x_1, \ldots, x_n) \in \{1, \ldots, p\}^n$, where $x_i = a$ if module i is assigned to processor a. The cost of executing module i on processor x_i is denoted by $e_i(x_i)$. If modules i and j communicate, then $c_{i,j}(x_i, x_j)$ denotes the communication cost between modules i and j when i is assigned to processor x_i and j is assigned to processor x_j. The *module allocation problem* (MAP) is to find an assignment X that minimizes [1]

$$C(X) = \sum_{i \in V(G)} e_i(x_i) + \sum_{(i,j) \in E(G)} c_{i,j}(x_i, x_j). \tag{1}$$

Module allocation is an important aspect of all phases of the development of a distributed system. Algorithms for the problem are useful during the design stage, where they can aid in determining a configuration that achieves a certain performance level; during the operational stage, where they can provide a strategy for optimum use of the available resources; and during reconfiguration, where tasks may have to be reassigned due to changes in the system [7].

MAP is known to be NP-hard in general [7]. Communication costs are said to be *uniform* when the communication cost between any two modules is equal to zero if the modules are coresident and, if modules are assigned to different processors, is not a function of the processors to which they are assigned (i.e. $c_{ij}(a, b)$, $a \neq b$, is independent of a and b). For $p = 2$ and arbitrary G, MAP with uniform costs can be solved in polynomial time using maximum-flow algorithms [26]. Tamir [28] has noted that results by Dalhaus et al. [9] imply that MAP with uniform costs is NP-complete for $p \geq 3$. In [11] we showed that, unless P = NP, there exists no polynomial-time approximation algorithm with relative error at most ϵ for non-uniform MAP, even if $p = 3$ and the underlying graph is planar and bipartite. (Definitions regarding approximation algorithms shall be given in section 2). In the same paper, earlier algorithms for trees and series-parallel graphs were generalized to obtain a $O(np^{k+1})$ algorithm when G is a *partial k-tree* (see section 2) and a $O(np^{\lceil k/2 \rceil + 2})$ algorithm when G is an *almost tree* with parameter k (see [16] for a definition of this concept). These methods apply even if costs are not uniform. Billionet [4] improved the bound for trees to $O(np)$ for the case where costs are uniform.

Here we study a version of the allocation problem where one of the processors, for convenience assumed to be processor 1, has limited memory, while the remaining processors have unlimited memory. Let $M \in Z_0^+$ denote the memory capacity of processor 1, and for $i \in \{1, \ldots, n\}$, let $m_i \in Z_0^+$ denote the memory requirement of module i. An assignment X is *feasible* if it satisfies $\sum\{m_i : x_i = 1\} \leq M$. The *memory-constrained module allocation problem* (CMAP) is to determine a feasible assignment that minimizes (1). This problem was originally studied by Rao et al. [22], who were motivated by the situation that arises when a host computer with large memory shares its load with a smaller, more specialized processor with limited memory capacity. It was observed in [22] that the knapsack problem is polynomially reducible to CMAP, and thus, the latter problem is NP-hard. Indeed, it is not difficult to prove that the problem remains NP-hard even if the communication graph is a tree. This is not altogether discouraging. Johnson and Niemi in [17] have presented approximation schemes for two other knapsack-like problems on trees, which leads one to ask whether similar algorithms exist for CMAP.

We shall present an exact $O(n(pC^*)^{k+1})$ algorithm for CMAP when the underlying graph is a partial k-tree. Here C^* denotes the cost of an optimum assignment. This

---

[1]Throughout this paper $V(G)$ and $E(G)$ denote, respectively, the vertex and edge sets of graph G. Z_0^+ is the set of nonnegative integers. All costs are assumed to be in Z_0^+.

algorithm is practical if k, p, and C^* are small. We use this procedure to produce an approximation scheme for CMAP when the communication graph is a partial k-tree. Given any $\epsilon > 0$, this scheme will compute a solution whose cost is no more than $(1 + \epsilon)C^*$ in $O(n^{k+2}p^{k+1}(1/\epsilon^{k+1} + \log C^*))$ time. For the case where G is an almost tree with parameter r, we obtain a $O(n(pC^*)^{\lceil r/2 \rceil + 2})$ exact algorithm and a $O(n^{\lceil r/2 \rceil + 3}p^{\lceil r/2 \rceil + 2})(1/\epsilon^{\lceil r/2 \rceil + 2} + \log C^*)$ approximation scheme for CMAP. When G is a tree and costs are uniform, we can exploit the ideas of [4] to obtain a $O(np(C^*)^2)$ algorithm to find the optimum feasible assignment, which leads to a $O(n^3p(1/\epsilon^2 + \log C^*))$ time approximation scheme for this case. Note that the running times of the exact algorithms are polynomial in C^*, and hence are *pseudopolynomial* in the input size [15]. Thus, while these algorithms are exponential in the worst case, they may be reasonable if k and C^* are small. Since the approximation schemes are polynomial in $\log C^*$ and $1/\epsilon$, they are *fully polynomial approximation schemes* (see section 2). Finally, we prove that, if we allow arbitrary communication graphs, no fully polynomial-time approximation scheme exists unless P = NP.

Organization of the paper. Basic definitions on approximation schemes and partial k-trees are given in section 2. In section 3 we review the algorithms for unconstrained module allocation on k-trees and on trees with uniform costs presented in [11] and [4], respectively. We then show how to extend them to handle memory constraints. These results are applied in section 4 to obtain fully polynomial-time approximation schemes for CMAP. In section 5, we present further results, including a proof of the non-existence of approximation schemes if the communication graph is arbitrary and an approximation scheme for almost trees, and present some conclusions.

2   Preliminaries

Fully polynomial-time approximation schemes. Let C^* be the cost of an optimum solution to a minimization problem Π. An ϵ-*approximate algorithm* for Π is an algorithm that produces a feasible solution of cost C such that $C \leq (1 + \epsilon)C^*$. An *approximation scheme* for Π is a family of algorithms $\{A_\epsilon\}$ such that for each $\epsilon > 0$, A_ϵ is an ϵ-approximate algorithm for Π. We say that an approximation scheme is a *polynomial-time approximation scheme* if, for any fixed $\epsilon > 0$, A_ϵ runs in time polynomial in the size of its input. The scheme is a *fully polynomial-time approximation scheme* (FPTAS) if its running time is polynomial both in $1/\epsilon$ and the input size.

Partial k-trees. A k-*clique* is a set of k pairwise adjacent vertices. A k-*leaf* is a vertex of degree k such that its neighbors form a k-clique. A graph is a k-*tree* if and only if

1. it is K_k, the complete graph on k vertices, or

2. it has a k-leaf v such that the graph obtained by removing v together with its incident edges is a k-tree.

It follows from the above definition that an n-vertex k-tree has $k(n - k) + k(k - 1)/2$ edges and $k(n - k) + 1$ k-cliques.

A *partial k-tree* is a subgraph of a k-tree. If G is a partial k-tree, there exists a k-tree H, called an *embedding k-tree* of G, such that $V(G) = V(H)$ and $E(G) \subseteq E(H)$ [2]. Partial k-trees are precisely the graphs of *treewidth* k studied by Robertson and Seymour [23]. Trees and series-parallel graphs are partial k-trees with $k = 1$ and $k = 2$.

Halin graphs are partial 3-trees [6], Δ-*Y-reducible* graphs are partial 4-trees [10], almost trees with parameter r are partial $(r+1)$-trees [5], *bandwidth-r* graphs are partial r-trees [5], and *r-outerplanar* graphs are partial $(3r-1)$-trees [6].

The problem of determining whether a graph is a partial k-tree has been attacked by several researchers, starting with Arnborg et al. [2] and Robertson and Seymour [24]. Let G be an n-vertex graph. It is NP-hard to find the smallest k such that there exists an embedding k-tree for G [2]. On the positive side, for $k = 1, 2, 3$ it is possible to determine if a graph G is a partial k-tree, and, if so, to construct an embedding k-tree in $O(n)$ time [3, 21]. Furthermore, Lagergren [18] has shown that, for any fixed k, it is possible to determine in $O(n \log^2 n)$ time whether G is a partial k-tree.

Consider an instance of MAP on a partial k-tree G. This can be converted into an equivalent k-tree problem by first finding an embedding k-tree H and then creating a new instance of the allocation problem with the same execution costs and where the communication cost between modules i and j, $(i,j) \in E(H)$, is the same as in the original problem if $(i,j) \in E(G)$, and equal to zero, regardless of the assignments for i and j, if $(i,j) \notin E(G)$. Clearly, the optima for both problems are the same. In subsequent discussions we therefore always assume that the input graph is a k-tree.

It follows from earlier definitions that if G is a k-tree it has a vertex elimination ordering that allows it to be reduced to a single k-clique such that, at the time when a vertex is eliminated, it is a k-leaf. We shall henceforth assume that the vertices of a k-tree are numbered according to such an ordering. The k-clique left after $n-k$ vertices are eliminated shall be called the *root clique*. All the algorithms presented here are based on using the elimination ordering to reduce the original problem on a communication graph G to a problem on the root clique of G. This technique yields a sequence of graphs $G_0, \ldots, G_{n-k}$ where $G_0 = G$ and, for $l \in \{1, \ldots, n-k\}$, $G_l = G - \{1, \ldots, l\}$. Associated with the l-th vertex in the elimination ordering for a k-tree, let $K(l)$ be the k-clique that contains the neighbors of l at the time it is removed. Thus, $K(n-k)$ is the root clique. For each vertex $j \in K(l)$ there is a k-clique $K_j(l)$ induced by the vertices in $(K(l) - \{j\}) \cup \{l\}$.

3 Exact Algorithms

We now present two dynamic programming algorithms for CMAP, one for k-trees and arbitrary communication costs and one for trees with uniform costs. They are based on methods for the unconstrained problem presented in [11] and [4], and rely on the variable elimination technique of *nonserial dynamic programming* [8] (see also [1]). We shall first review these approaches. Our algorithms perform reasonably well as long as costs are not too large. Furthermore, they are the basis for the fully polynomial-time approximation schemes to be presented in section 4.

3.1 Unconstrained Module Allocation

3.1.1 k-Trees with Arbitrary Costs

To each k-clique K in G we associate a function $h_K(X_K)$, where $X_K = \{x_i : i \in K\}$. The algorithm carries out $n-k$ iterations, at the lth of which vertex l is removed from the graph and the corresponding variable, x_l, is eliminated from the objective function. The information about the eliminated variable is retained by updating $h_{K(l)}(X_{K(l)})$.

The details of the algorithm are given below. For convenience, we write

$$D_l(x_{l+1}, \ldots, x_n) = \sum_{i=l+1}^{n} e_i(x_i) + \sum_{(i,j) \in E(G_l)} c_{i,j}(x_i, x_j)$$

and use "$K \in G$" as shorthand for "K is a k-clique in G". Note that $D_0 = C$.

Algorithm MA;
begin
1      $G_0 \leftarrow G$;
2   **forall** $K \in G$ and $X_K \in \{1, \ldots, p\}^k$ **do**
3         $h_K(X_K) \leftarrow 0$;
4   **for** $l \leftarrow 1$ to $n - k$ **do begin**
5   **forall** $(x_l, X_{K(l)}) \in \{1, \ldots, p\}^{k+1}$ **do**
6           $g_l(x_l, X_{K(l)}) \leftarrow e_l(x_l) + \sum_{j \in K(l)} c_{l,j}(x_l, x_j)$
                              $+ h_{K(l)}(X_{K(l)}) + \sum_{j \in K(l)} h_{K_j(l)}(X_{K_j(l)})$;
7   **forall** $X_{K(l)} \in \{1, \ldots p\}^k$ **do**
8           $h_{K(l)}(X_{K(l)}) \leftarrow \min_{x_l} g_l(x_l, X_{K(l)})$;
9         $G_l \leftarrow G_{l-1} - \{l\}$;
     end;
10   **return** $\min_{X_{K(n-k)}}\{D_{n-k}(X_{K(n-k)}) + h_{K(n-k)}(X_{K(n-k)})\}$
end

Let h_K^0 denote h_K immediately before statement 4 and let h_K^j denote h_K at the end of the jth iteration of the loop beginning at statement 4. For $l \in \{0, \ldots, n-k\}$ define

$$C_l(x_{l+1}, \ldots, x_n) = D_l(x_{l+1}, \ldots, x_n) + \sum_{K \in G_l} h_K^l(X_K),$$

Thus, $C_0 = C$. To eliminate x_l for $l = 1, \ldots, n - k$, MA collects all terms that are functions of x_l by constructing $g_l(x_l, X_{K(l)})$ in statements 5–6. The information about x_l that is needed for minimization is retained by updating $h_{K(l)}$ in steps 7–8. In [11], it is shown that

$$\min_{x_{l+1}, \ldots, x_n} C_l(x_{l+1}, \ldots, x_n) = \min_{x_l, \ldots, x_n} C_{l-1}(x_l, \ldots, x_n).$$

Since step 10 returns $\min_{X_{K(n-k)}} C_{n-k}(X_{K(n-k)})$, we conclude that MA delivers the cost of an optimum assignment. It can be shown (see [11]) that the total running time of MA is $O(np^{k+1})$.

3.1.2   Trees with Uniform Costs

The k-tree algorithm specializes to a $O(np^2)$ algorithm for trees. Billionet [4] has presented a simple approach to improve this to $O(np)$ if costs are uniform.

For uniform costs, we have

$$c_{ij}(x_i, x_j) = \begin{cases} 0 & \text{if } x_i = x_j \\ r_{ij} & \text{otherwise.} \end{cases}$$

Billionet's algorithm carries out a series of vertex eliminations until a single vertex is left. Unlike MA, the procedure does not require special functions associated with cliques.

```
        Algorithm UTMA
        begin
1           while |V(G)| > 1 do begin
2               Choose any leaf (vertex of degree one) i ∈ G;
3               Let j be the neighbor of i in G;
4               q ← min_{a∈{1,...,p}} e_i(a);
5               forall b ∈ {1,...,p} do
6                   e_j(b) ← e_j(b) + min{e_i(b), q + r_{ij}};
7               G ← G - {i};
            end;
8           Let s be the remaining vertex of G;
9           return min_{a∈{1,...,p}} e_s(a)
        end
```

Every time a leaf i is eliminated, the information about it is stored in the neighbor of i in the tree. At the end, all the information about the eliminated vertices needed for minimization is stored in the remaining vertex s. For a full proof of correctness, see [4]. Each iteration of the **while** loop clearly takes $O(p)$ time, yielding an overall time bound of $O(np)$.

3.2 Constrained Module Allocation

The algorithms described in the previous section do not solve CMAP, since during their variable elimination steps they only retain the smallest-cost partial solution. In the presence of a memory constraint, it will be necessary to retain solutions of larger cost, but smaller memory requirement, as one of these might lead to an optimum assignment. For this reason, our algorithms associate to each possible assignment to the variables in a k-clique a *list* of ordered pairs (c, b), where c and b are the cost and total memory requirement of some partial assignment.

Definition 1 Given two lists L_1, L_2 of pairs, $L_1 \oplus L_2$ is the list of all pairs (c, b) where $c = c_1 + c_2$, $b = b_1 + b_2$, for some $(c_1, b_1) \in L_1$ and $(c_2, b_2) \in L_2$.

Definition 2 Given two pairs $p_1 = (c_1, b_1)$ and $p_2 = (c_2, b_2)$ where $c_1 = c_2$, p_1 *dominates* p_2 if $b_1 \leq b_2$.

As in the unconstrained problem, we work by successive elimination of variables. The input is an instance $\mathcal{M}$ of the problem (with the associated execution and communication costs and a memory constraint M) and an integer U. The result delivered by both of our algorithms will be the cost of the optimum feasible assignment and whose cost does not exceed U. If no such assignment exists, the procedure returns ∞. We shall show how these algorithms, when combined with a simple search procedure, can be used to obtain an optimum assignment.

Let M and U be as above and let L denote a list of pairs. Our algorithms use the following operations.

OPT(L): Return $\min(\{\infty\} \cup \{c : (c, b) \in L, c \leq U, b \leq M\})$.

REDUCE(L): Return a maximal sublist L' of L such that (i) for all $(c, b) \in L'$, $c \leq U$ and $b \leq M$, and (ii) for any two pairs $p_1, p_2 \in L'$, p_1 does not dominate p_2.

We define the function $w : \{1, \ldots, p\} \to Z_0^+$ where

$$w(a) = \begin{cases} m_i & \text{if } a = 1 \\ 0 & \text{otherwise.} \end{cases}$$

3.2.1 k-Trees with Arbitrary Costs

Define $w(x_{l+1}, \ldots, x_n) = \sum_{i=l+1}^{n} w(x_i)$. The following modification of MA solves CMAP.

Algorithm CMA$(\mathcal{M}, U)$;
begin
1      $G_0 \leftarrow G$;
2   **forall** $K \in G$ and $X_K \in \{1, \ldots, p\}^k$ **do**
3          $\mathcal{H}_K(X_K) \leftarrow \langle (0,0) \rangle$;
4   **for** $l \leftarrow 1$ **to** $n - k$ **do begin**
5   **forall** $(x_l, X_{K(l)}) \in \{1, \ldots, p\}^{k+1}$ **do begin**
6              $\mathcal{G}_l(x_l, X_{K(l)}) \leftarrow \langle (e_l(x_l) + \sum_{j \in K(l)} c_{l,j}(x_l, x_j), w(x_l)) \rangle$
                          $\oplus \mathcal{H}_{K(l)}(X_{K(l)}) \oplus \left(\bigoplus_{j \in K(l)} \mathcal{H}_{K_j(l)}(X_{K_j(l)}) \right)$;
7              $\mathcal{G}_l(x_l, X_{K(l)}) \leftarrow \text{REDUCE}(\mathcal{G}_l(x_l, X_{K(l)}))$
         end;
8   **forall** $X_{K(l)} \in \{1, \ldots p\}^k$ **do begin**
9              $\mathcal{H}_{K(l)}(X_{K(l)}) \leftarrow \bigcup_{x_l = 1}^{p} \mathcal{G}_l(x_l, X_{K(l)})$;
10         $\mathcal{H}_{K(l)}(X_{K(l)}) \leftarrow \text{REDUCE}(\mathcal{H}_{K(l)}(X_{K(l)}))$
         end;
11      $G_l \leftarrow G_{l-1} - \{l\}$
     end;
12   **return**
         $\min_{X_{K(n-k)}} \{ \text{OPT}(\langle (D_{n-k}(X_{K(n-k)}), w(X_{K(n-k)})) \rangle) \oplus \mathcal{H}_{K(n-k)}(X_{K(n-k)})) \}$
end

To prove the correctness of CMA, we define a sequence of functions $\mathcal{C}_0, \ldots, \mathcal{C}_{n-k}$. Let $\mathcal{H}_K^0$ denote the function $\mathcal{H}_K$ immediately before statement 4 and let $\mathcal{H}_K^j$ denote the function $\mathcal{H}_K$ at the end of the jth iteration of the loop in statements 4–10. For $l \in \{0, \ldots, n - k\}$, let

$$\mathcal{C}_l(x_{l+1}, \ldots, x_n) = \langle (D_l(x_{l+1}, \ldots, x_n), w(x_{l+1}, \ldots, x_n)) \rangle \oplus \bigoplus_{K \in G_l} \mathcal{H}_K^l(X_K).$$

Lemma 3.1 *For* $l \in \{1, \ldots, n - k\}$,

$$\min_{x_{l+1}, \ldots, x_n} (\text{OPT}(\mathcal{C}_l(x_{l+1}, \ldots, x_n))) = \min_{x_l, \ldots, x_n} (\text{OPT}(\mathcal{C}_{l-1}(x_l, \ldots, x_n))).$$

Proof It suffices to show that, for any $(x_{l+1}, \ldots, x_n) \in \{1, \ldots, p\}^{n-l}$,

$$\text{OPT}(\mathcal{C}_l(x_{l+1}, \ldots, x_n)) = \min_{x_l}(\text{OPT}(\mathcal{C}_{l-1}(x_l, \ldots, x_n))). \qquad (2)$$

For this, consider the lth iteration of CMA. Let

$$\mathcal{S}(x_{l+1}, \ldots, x_n) = \bigcup_{x_l = 1}^{p} \mathcal{C}_{l-1}(x_l, \ldots, x_n).$$

By construction, $\mathcal{C}_l(x_{l+1}, \ldots, x_n) \subseteq \mathcal{S}(x_{l+1}, \ldots, x_n)$. It is straightforward, but tedious, to prove that, in the absence of the REDUCE operations of steps 7 and 10, $\mathcal{C}_l(x_{l+1}, \ldots, x_n) = \mathcal{S}(x_{l+1}, \ldots, x_n)$, and equation 2 follows. It can be verified that, if the REDUCE operations are carried out, a pair $(c, b) \in \mathcal{S}(x_{l+1}, \ldots, x_n)$ will not be in $\mathcal{H}_l(x_{l+1}, \ldots, x_n)$ only if either (i) $c > U$, or (ii) $b > M$, or (iii) there exists another pair $(c', b') \in \mathcal{S}(x_{l+1}, \ldots, x_n)$ such that (c', b') dominates (c, b). $\square$

Theorem 3.1 CMA *correctly computes the minimum-cost feasible assignment of cost not exceeding* U *in* $O(n(pU)^{k+1})$ *time.*

Proof We first argue the correctness of CMA. Note that for every $(x_1, \ldots, x_n) \in \{1, \ldots, p\}^n$, $\mathcal{C}_0(x_1, \ldots, x_n)$ consists solely of the pair $(D_0(x_1, \ldots, x_n), w(x_1, \ldots, x_n))$ if $D_0(x_1, \ldots, x_n) \leq U$ and $w(x_1, \ldots, x_n) \leq M$; otherwise, it is the empty list. Thus, since $D_0 = C$, $\min_{x_1, \ldots, x_n} \text{OPT}(\mathcal{C}_0(x_1, \ldots, x_n))$ is the cost of the optimum assignment whose cost does not exceed U. Since CMA returns

$$\min_{X_{K(n-k)}} \text{OPT}(\mathcal{C}_{n-k}(X_{K(n-k)})),$$

an inductive proof of the correctness of CMA using Lemma 3.1 is obtained. We omit the details.

We now analyze the running time of CMA. Steps 1-3 can be implemented in $O(np^k)$ time. Note that for $j \in \{0, \ldots, n-k\}$, $|\mathcal{H}_K^j(X_K)| \leq U$ for all $X_K \in \{1, \ldots, p\}^k$. This is obviously true for $j = 0$ and remains true for $j > 0$, since the application of REDUCE in step 10 ensures that the elements of $\mathcal{H}_K(X_K)$ have distinct costs. Thus, in step 6, $\mathcal{G}_l(x_l, X_{K(l)})$ will have at most $(U+1)^{k+1}$ elements and can be computed in $O(U^{k+1})$ time for every $(x_l, X_{K(l)}) \in \{1, \ldots, p\}^{k+1}$. This implies the same time bound for step 7. Thus, the loop starting at 5 can be executed in $O(p^{k+1}U^{k+1})$ time. After step 7, $\mathcal{G}_l(x_l, X_{K(l)})$ will have $O(U)$ elements. Because of this, steps 9 and 10 can be combined to produce $\mathcal{H}_{K(l)}(X_{K(l)})$ in $O(pU)$ time for every $X_{K(l)} \in \{1, \ldots, p\}^k$, Thus, the loop starting at step 8 can be done in $O(p^{k+1}U)$ time. Statement 12 can be implemented by exhaustive enumeration in $O(p^k U)$ time. Since the main **for** loop is iterated $n-k$ times, the running time is $O(n(pU)^{k+1})$ as claimed. $\square$

We can compute the cost C^* of an optimum assignment by repeated invocations of CMA$(\mathcal{M}, U)$, starting with $U = 1$. Each time, if the answer returned is ∞, we double the value of U and call CMA again, otherwise, we stop. When this process terminates, we must have $U \leq 2C^*$. By Theorem 3.1, the total execution time of this procedure will be $O(n(pC^*)^{k+1})$. We thus have

Theorem 3.2 *An optimum feasible assignment for CMAP on a k-tree can be found in* $O(n(pC^*)^{k+1})$ *time.*

As discussed above, for each $K \in G$ and each $X_K \in \{1, \ldots, p\}^k$, $\mathcal{H}_K(X_K)$ will have $O(C^*)$ elements. Since G has $k(n-k)+1$ k-cliques, the total memory requirement is $O(np^k C^*)$. It should be noted that both the time and memory bounds are overestimates, and that we would expect the actual figures to be much lower in practice.

We have omitted the details of how to construct the optimum assignment after CMA is executed. For this we can use standard "back pointer" techniques from dynamic programming (see, for instance, [19]). Each pair generated in step 6 is the sum of $k+2$ pairs, k of which come from cliques $K_j(l)$, $j \in K(l)$ that are disappearing as a consequence of the elimination of vertex l. For each such newly-generated pair, we maintain a pointer to the k pairs associated with the disappearing cliques. With this structure, it is possible to reconstruct the optimum solution in $O(n)$ time, once CMA is done, by tracing back following the pointers.

3.2.2 Trees with Uniform Costs

If the communication graph is a tree, CMA will run in $O(n(pU)^2)$ time, leading to a $O(n(pC^*)^2)$ algorithm to determine the optimum assignment. We can improve this to $O(np(C^*)^2)$ by modifying Billionet's approach (see section 3.1.2).

As before, we use lists of cost-memory pairs (c, b). This time, to each vertex $i \in G$ we associate a list function $\mathcal{E}_i(x_i)$. The algorithm we propose, which we call UTCMA, will return the cost of an optimum feasible assignment of cost not exceeding U. If no such assignment exists, it returns ∞. Our notation is the same as in algorithm CMA.

Algorithm UTCMA($\mathcal{M}, U$)
begin
1   **forall** $i \in G$ and $a \in \{1, \ldots, p\}$ **do**
2         $\mathcal{E}_i(a) \leftarrow \langle(e_i(a), w(a))\rangle$;
3   **while** $|V(G)| > 1$ **do begin**
4   Choose any leaf $i \in G$;
5   Let j be the neighbor of i in G;
6         $\mathcal{Q} \leftarrow \bigcup_{a \in \{1, \ldots, p\}} \mathcal{E}_i(a)$;
7         $\mathcal{Q} \leftarrow$ REDUCE($\mathcal{Q}$);
8   **forall** $b \in \{1, \ldots, p\}$ **do begin**
9            $\mathcal{E}_j(b) \leftarrow \mathcal{E}_j(b) \oplus (\mathcal{E}_i(b) \cup (\mathcal{Q} \oplus \langle(r_{ij}, 0)\rangle))$;
10        $\mathcal{E}_j(b) \leftarrow$ REDUCE($\mathcal{E}_j(b)$)
         end;
11        $G \leftarrow G - \{i\}$
      end;
12   Let s be the remaining vertex of G;
13   **return** $\min_{a \in \{1, \ldots, p\}}$ OPT($\mathcal{E}_s(a)$)
end

The correctness of this approach follows from the correctness of Billionet's algorithm and arguments similar to those used for CMA. We leave the details to the reader.

Steps 1–2 of UTCMA take $O(np)$ time. The **while** loop beginning at step 3 is carried out $n - 1$ times. The initialization of the $\mathcal{E}_i$'s and the application of REDUCE in step 10 ensure that, immediately before and after every execution of the **while** loop, $|\mathcal{E}_i(a)| \leq U + 1$, for all $i \in V(G)$ and all $a \in \{1, \ldots, p\}$. Thus, steps 6 and 7 can be implemented in $O(pU)$ time. Since, after step 7, $|\mathcal{Q}| \leq U + 1$, steps 8–10 take $O(pU^2)$ time. After the **while** loop is exited, we will have $|\mathcal{E}_s(a)| \leq U + 1$ for all $a \in \{1, \ldots, p\}$ in lines 12 and 13. Thus, the cost of an optimum feasible assignment of cost not exceeding U can be computed in $O(npU^2)$ time. Exactly the same search procedure as that applied for k-trees can now be used to obtain the following result.

Theorem 3.3 *If G is a tree and costs are uniform, an optimum feasible assignment can be computed in $O(npC^*)$ time where C^* is the cost of this assignment.*

We leave it to the reader to verify that the space requirement of this algorithm is $O(nC^*)$. Back pointers can be used to reconstruct the optimum solution in $O(n)$ time.

4 Approximation Schemes

We can use the algorithms from the previous section together with well-known scaling techniques [17, 19] to obtain FPTAS's for CMAP. The schemes rely on the following procedure.

APPROX-CMA($\mathcal{M}, U_1, U_2, \epsilon$): $\mathcal{M}$ is an instance whose optimum solution has cost C^*, U_1, U_2, are positive integers, where $U_1 \leq C^*$ and $U_2 \geq U_1$, and $\epsilon > 0$ is the allowed relative error. Return the cost C' of a feasible solution to $\mathcal{M}$ such that $C' - C^* \leq \epsilon C^*$ and $C' \leq U_2$. If no such solution exists, return ∞.

We implement APPROX-CMA as follows. Let $J = \lfloor U_1\epsilon/(2nk)\rfloor$. Given an instance $\mathcal{M}$, we construct another instance $\mathcal{M}'$ with the same graph, memory requirements, and memory constraint, but where the execution and communication costs are $e_i' = \lceil e_i/J\rceil$ for all $i \in V(G)$ and $c_{ij}' = \lceil c_{ij}/J\rceil$ for all $(i,j) \in E(G)$. APPROX-CMA returns $J \cdot C'$, where $C' = \text{XCMA}(\mathcal{M}', U_2/J)$. XCMA will be either CMA or UTCMA, depending on whether we are dealing with k-trees or with trees with uniform costs. We need to verify that $J \cdot C'$ fulfills the necessary requirements. It is not hard to show that, if $C' < \infty$,

$$J \cdot C' - C^* \leq J(|V(G)| + |E(G)|),$$

which implies that, since $|V(G)| = n$ and, for a k-tree, $|E(G)| = k(n-k) + k(k-1)/2$,

$$J \cdot C' - C^* \leq \epsilon C^*.$$

Thus, $J \cdot C'$ is the desired ϵ-approximate solution. On the other hand, if $C' = \infty$, it must be because $U_2 < (1 + \epsilon)C^*$. Therefore APPROX-CMA produces the required output. If CMA is being used, the running time of APPROX-CMA is $O(n(pU_2/J)^{k+1})$, which, for fixed k, is

$$O\left(n^{k+2}\left(\frac{p}{\epsilon}\right)^{k+1}\left(\frac{U_2}{U_1}\right)^{k+1}\right)$$

If UTCMA is being used, the running time of APPROX-CMA is $O(npU_2/J)$, which is

$$O\left(n^2\left(\frac{pU_2}{\epsilon U_1}\right)\right)$$

Now, using a technique due to Johnson and Niemi [17], we can apply APPROX-CMA to obtain a FPTAS for CMAP. The procedure consists of two phases. In the first, using the following procedure, we find values U_1, and U_2 such that $U_1 \leq C^* \leq U_2$ and $U_2/U_1 \leq 2$.

1   $U_1 \leftarrow 1$
2   $U_2 \leftarrow 4U_1$
3   $C' \leftarrow \text{APPROX-CMA}(\mathcal{M}, U_1, U_2, 1)$
4   if $C' < \infty$ then return $U_1 = \lceil C'/2\rceil$ and $U_2 = C'$
5   else $U_1 \leftarrow 2U_1$; goto 2

A proof of correctness can be found in [17]. Since $\epsilon = 1$ and $U_2 = 4U_1$ at step 3, the time time taken by this search will be $O(n^{k+2}p^{k+1}\log C^*)$ if CMA is being used and $O(n^3 p\log C^*)$ if UTCMA is being used.

In the second phase, we use the above values of U_1 and U_2 and our desired error ratio to call APPROX-CMA$(\mathcal{M}, U_1, U_2, \epsilon)$. Since at this point $U_2/U_1 \leq 2$, this will take $O(n^{k+2}p^{k+1}(1/\epsilon^{k+1}))$ time for k-trees and $O(n^3 p(1/\epsilon^2))$ time for trees with uniform costs. The total running time is therefore $O(n^{k+2}p^{k+1}(1/\epsilon^{k+1} + \log C^*))$ for k-trees, and $O(n^3 p(1/\epsilon^2 + \log C^*))$ for trees with uniform costs.

5   Discussion

It is natural to ask whether a FPTAS is possible when the communication graph is unrestricted. We shall show that such a scheme can not exist unless P $=$ NP. The proof uses the notion of strong NP-completeness. A decision problem on graphs is *strongly NP-complete* if there exists a polynomial p such that the problem remains NP-complete even when restricted to the case where no cost exceeds $p(n)$, where n is the number of vertices. (For simplicity, we shall restrict the subsequent discussion to graph problems. A full discussion on strong NP-completeness can be found in [15].) We have the following Lemma, taken from [15], pp. 140–141.

Lemma 5.1 *Suppose that an optimization problem A on graphs has the properties that (a) its decision version is strongly NP-complete, and (b) for any instance I of A, the optimal cost is polynomially bounded in n and in the size of the largest cost appearing in I. Then there exists no FPTAS for A, unless P = NP.*

The decision version of MAP is: Given an instance of MAP and an integer T, determine whether there exists an assignment of cost at most T.

Lemma 5.2 *MAP is strongly NP-complete for $p \geq 2$ even if G is planar.*

Proof The vertex cover problem is to determine whether, given a graph G and an integer $K < |V(G)|$, whether there exists a $B \subseteq V(G)$ such that for all $(u, v) \in E(G)$, $\{u, v\} \cap B \neq \emptyset$, and $|B| \leq K$. This problem is strongly NP-complete even for planar graphs [15]. Vertex cover can be reduced to an instance of MAP with communication graph G, $p = 2$, and $T = K$ where costs are as follows. For all $i \in V(G)$, $e_i(1) = 0$, $e_i(2) = 1$. For all $(i, j) \in E(G)$, $c_{ij}(a, b) = n + 1$ if $a = b = 1$, and $c_{ij}(a, b) = 0$ otherwise. Intuitively, $x_i = 1$ will mean that $i \notin B$, and $x_i = 2$ will mean that $i \in B$. Obviously, all costs are polynomially bounded in n. $\square$

We use these facts to prove:

Theorem 5.1 *Unless P = NP there exists no FPTAS for CMAP, even if the communication graph is planar.*

Proof The decision version of CMAP is to determine whether there exists a feasible assignment of total cost at most U. This problem contains MAP as a special case. Therefore, from Lemma 5.2 it follows that CMAP strongly NP-complete. This fact, together with Lemma 5.1, implies the Theorem. $\square$

Thus, unless P = NP, we can only expect to obtain FPTAS's for special cases. The theorem also implies that (again, unless P = NP) an exponential dependence on k is unavoidable. Of course, faster approximation schemes for CMAP on partial k-trees may exist for special cases. We encountered one such situation when the communication graph was a tree and costs were uniform.

It is interesting to note that we constructed CMA and UTCMA starting from their respective counterparts for the unconstrained case using essentially the same methods. Instead of working with integer-valued functions, we worked with list functions; instead of doing ordinary addition, we did list sum; instead of the "min" operation, we used list union; and, to keep list sizes small, we used REDUCE, which exploits dominance relations. Not surprisingly then, we observe that the $O(np^{\lceil r/2 \rceil + 2})$ algorithm of [11] for almost trees with parameter r can be converted into a $O(n(pC^*)^{\lceil r/2 \rceil + 2})$ exact algorithm and a $O(n^{\lceil r/2 \rceil + 3} p^{\lceil r/2 \rceil + 2})(1/\epsilon^{\lceil r/2 \rceil + 2} + \log C^*))$ FPTAS for the constrained problem. The transformation is along the lines of those in sections 3 and 4. For conciseness, we omit the details and, instead, refer the reader to section VII of [11]. This algorithm has the advantage of not requiring an embedding k-tree.

Our algorithms require a lot of memory. It seems worthwhile to see if variants of the memory-saving techniques of [17] are applicable to our problem. We note that improving the running time of our FPTAS for partial k-trees appears to require a more clever exact algorithm, which in turn would require a more clever algorithm for the unconstrained problem. It is natural to ask (as Billionet does in [4]) whether such an algorithm exists for the uniform cost case on k-trees.

Several variants of the assignment problem remain to be studied. One question is whether there exist approximation schemes for the problem where there are memory constraints on more than one processor. Recently, we have obtained results on the problem of finding an assignment that minimizes the maximum processor load. This work is reported in [13].

Acknowledgement

This work was supported in part by the National Science Foundation under grant No. CCR-8909626.

References

[1] S. Arnborg and A. Proskurowski. Linear time algorithms for NP-hard problems restricted to partial k-trees. *Discr. Appl. Math.* 23:11–24 (1989).

[2] S. Arnborg, D.G. Corneil, and A. Proskurowski. Complexity of finding embeddings in a k-tree. *SIAM J. Alg. Discr. Methods* 8(2):277–284 (1987).

[3] S. Arnborg and A. Proskurowski. Characterization and recognition of partial 3-trees. *SIAM J. Alg. Discr. Methods* **7** (1986), 305-314.

[4] A. Billionet. Allocating tree-structured programs in a distributed system with uniform communication costs. *Manuscript.*

[5] H.L. Bodlaender. Classes of graphs with bounded tree-width. Technical Report RUU-CS-86-22, Department of Computer Science, University of Utrecht, The Netherlands (December 1986).

[6] H.L. Bodlaender. Some classes of graphs with bounded tree-width. *Bulletin of the EATCS*, **36** (1988), 116-126.

[7] S. Bokhari. *Assignment Problems in Parallel and Distributed Computing.* Kluwer Academic Publishers, Boston 1987.

[8] U. Bertelè and F. Brioschi. *Nonserial Dynamic Programming.* Academic Press, New York, 1972.

[9] E. Dalhaus, D.S. Johnson, C.H. Papadimitriou, P. Seymour, and M. Yannakakis. The complexity of multiway cuts. Unpublished Report, 1983 (cited in [28]).

[10] E.S. Elmallah and C.J. Colbourn. Reliability of Δ-Y networks. *Congressus Numerantium* **48** (1985), 49-54.

[11] D. Fernández-Baca. Allocating modules to processors in a distributed system. *IEEE Trans. Software Eng.*, SE-15(11):1427–1436 (1989).

[12] D. Fernández-Baca and A. Medepalli. Parametric module allocation on partial k-trees. Technical Report 90-25, Department of Computer Science, Iowa State University (1990).

[13] D. Fernández-Baca and A. Medepalli. Approximation algorithms for certain assignment problems in distributed systems. Technical Report 91-17, Department of Computer Science, Iowa State University (1991).

[14] D. Fernández-Baca and G. Slutzki. Solving parametric problems on trees. *J. Algorithms* 10:381–402 (1989).

[15] M. Garey and D. Johnson. *Computers and Intractability: A Guide to the theory of NP-Completeness.* Freeman, San Francisco, 1979.

[16] Y. Gurevich, L. Stockmeyer, and U. Vishkin. Solving NP-hard problems on graphs that are almost trees and an application to facility location problems. *JACM* 31(3):459–473, 1984.

[17] D.S. Johnson and K.A. Niemi. On knapsacks, partitions, and a new dynamic programming technique for trees. *Math. Oper. Res.* 8(1):1–14 (1983).

[18] J. Lagergren. Efficient parallel algorithms for tree-decomposition and related problems. In *Proceedings of 31st Annual Symposium on Foundations of Computer Science*, pp. 173–182 (1990).

[19] E. L. Lawler. Fast approximation algorithms for knapsack problems. *Math. Oper. Res.* 4(4):339–356, 1979.

[20] V.M. Lo. Heuristic algorithms for task assignment in distributed systems. *IEEE Trans. Comput.* C-37(11):1384-1397, 1988.

[21] J. Matoušek and R. Thomas. Algorithms finding tree-decompositions of graphs. *J. Algorithms* 12:1–22, 1991.

[22] G.S. Rao, H.S. Stone, and T.C. Hu. Assignment of tasks in a distributed processor system with limited memory. *IEEE Trans. Computers* C-28(4):291–299, 1979.

[23] N. Robertson and P.D. Seymour. Graph minors II: Algorithmic aspects of treewidth. *J. Algorithms* 7:309–322, 1986.

[24] N. Robertson and P.D. Seymour. Graph minors XIII: The disjoint paths problem. *Manuscript*, September 1986.

[25] J.B. Sinclair. Efficient computation of optimal assignments for distributed tasks. *Journal of Parallel and Distributed Computing* 4(4):342–362, 1987.

[26] H. Stone. Multiprocessor scheduling with the aid of network flow algorithms. *IEEE Trans. Software Eng.* SE-3:85–94, 1977.

[27] H. Stone. Critical load factors in two-processor distributed systems. *IEEE Trans. Software Eng.* SE-4:254-258, 1978.

[28] A. Tamir. Personal communication.

Complexity and
Parallel Algorithms

THE COMPLEXITY OF ALGORITHMIC PROBLEMS
ON SUCCINCT INSTANCES*

José L. Balcázar, Antoni Lozano, and Jacobo Torán

Dep. Llenguatges i Sistemes Informàtics
Univ. Politècnica de Catalunya (ed. FIB)
08028 Barcelona, Spain

balqui@lsi.upc.es, lozano@lsi.upc.es, jacobo@lsi.upc.es

Abstract: Highly regular combinatorial objects can be represented advantageously by some kind of description shorter than their full standard encoding. For instance, graphs exhibiting enough regularities can be described using encodings substantially shorter than the full adjacency matrix. A natural scheme for such succinct representations is by means of boolean circuits computing, as a boolean function, the values of individual bits of the binary encoding of the object. The complexity of many algorithmic problems changes drastically when this succinct representation is used to present the input. Two powerful lemmas quantifying exactly this increase of complexity are presented. These are applied to show that previous results in the area can be interpreted as sufficient conditions for completeness in the logarithmic time and polynomial time counting hierarchies.

1. INTRODUCTION

One of the main goals of complexity theory is the classification of computational problems in complexity classes according to the amount of resources needed to solve them. Inputs to the algorithms are usually binary encodings of certain combinatorial objects, such as graphs. Actually, in order to use efficient combinatorial algorithms to solve problems by computer, such combinatorial structures must be found or imposed on the data to the programs.

---

* This research was partially supported by the ESPRIT-II Basic Research Actions Program of the European Community under contract no. 3075 (project ALCOM).

Consider combinatorial objects to be treated by computer programs. The case may arise that these objects turn out to be highly regular. Representing such regular objects by means of data structures that take advantage of these regularities is a very natural idea, since memory space in computers should be employed efficiently and therefore it is good to encode the objects in a more succinct way.

For instance, data structures for sparse matrices, with a small number of nonzero entries, have been studied since long time. Actually, such data matrices appear in many applications of combinatorial optimization problems. Several other possibilities have been proposed to obtain representations of regular graphs smaller than the adjacency matrix ([6], [28], [29]).

Here we continue a study initiated in [6], where the adjacency matrix of a graph is represented by a hopefully small boolean circuit which, on input the binary representations of i and j, computes the (i,j) entry of the adjacency matrix. We will study problems not only on graphs, but also on numbers, strings, sets, and boolean functions. We are interested in using boolean circuits to describe the inputs to algorithms for various decisional problems. On the one hand, since the size of the input may be much smaller, the complexity of the algorithms must be expected to grow. On the other hand, since only very regular objects can be described by circuits with substantial degree of succinctness, one might hope that some trade-off exists, making the problem easier for compactly described instances due to the regularity of the represented object.

In [6] and subsequently in [20] these hopes are destroyed for many graph problems. Indeed, it is shown in [6] that checking quite simple graph properties, such as nonemptiness of the set of edges, become NP-hard if the input is given by a circuit. A sufficient condition for NP-hardness of succinct versions of problems is given; we will discuss this further later on. Many more complex problems jump to much higher complexity classes. This work was extended in [20] by proving that sets that are NP-complete for certain reducibility (known as "projection") become $NEXPTIME$-complete when the input is given by a circuit representation. This last reference states that similar techniques can be applied to projection-complete sets in other complexity classes, such as P or NL, and asserts that from such a construction for NL other lower bounds of [6] can be improved to optimal.

Our aim in this paper is to show how to distill from the proof of the main result of [20] some uniform, powerful lemmas, with simpler proofs, which can be used to, first, obtain uniformly all the results known about the complexity of succinct versions of particular problems; second, to add many more to the list, and third, to show how the sufficient condition for NP-hardness of the succinct version of a problem, given in [6], is essentially a sufficient condition for the hardness of the standard problem with respect to a much less powerful class. To do this, we will introduce a form of reducibility more general than that of [20], and will show that their use of Cook's formula, restricted to a case of low Kolmogorov complexity, is actually unnecesary and can be replaced by a simpler encoding characterized also by its low information contents.

Our main lemma is completely independent of the class on which the computational problems lie, since its statement regards just decisional problems and their succinct versions. This presentation is both easier and better, since the independence of complexity classes allows us to carry over the result to classes with surprisingly low computational power.

Actually, our results can be applied to find complete sets for the lower classes of the logarithmic time and the polynomial time counting hierarchies, as well as for arbitrary levels of some subhierarchies. In this way we obtain precise classifications of the complexity of many problems about finite functions, both under the standard and under the succinct encoding.

In [20] it is pointed out that a proof similar to the one they give applies to problems on directed graphs such as accesibility. However, to apply it to undirected accessibility, or to other problems on undirected graphs such as connectivity, bipartiteness, or acyclicity, some difficult results must be used which prove that acceptance of deterministic logarithmic space machines can be reduced to undirected accessibility [16], by means of the class SL (symmetric logarithmic space). We give here a different proof of these results, which we consider very instructive since it pushes further a technique of [6] which the authors did not expect to work. We apply it also to other problems, namely planarity, and using results of Reif [21] we settle the particular case of bounded degree graphs.

This paper includes and extends results announced in [18] and [26], which in turn were based on parts of the M. Sc. Thesis of the second author and the Ph. D. dissertation of the third, both under the advice of the first.

2. COMPLEXITY CLASSES AND REDUCIBILITIES

We consider inputs to decisional problems encoded as words over the two letter alphabet $\Gamma = \{0,1\}$. In particular the standard encoding of a binary string is itself; the standard encoding of a positive integer is its binary description, in principle with no leading zeros (although leading zeros may be accepted for padding purposes); that of a finite set, its characteristic function, usually as a subset of Γ^n; that of a directed graph, its adjacency matrix; and that of a boolean function, its truth table (generalized to multiple outputs if necessary). Observe that all those encodings can be seen simply as binary words.

Regarding undirected graphs, for technical reasons we allow as encoding of an undirected graph the encoding of any of the directed graphs that can be obtained from it by directing the edges. Thus, edge (i, j) is in an undirected graph if and only if either of the entries (i, j) or (j, i) (or both) are 1 in the adjacency matrix. The property we need of this representation is that adding an edge can be done by changing a single bit of the encoding.

Given a binary string x, we denote by $[x]$ the integer represented in binary by x; sometimes we will explicitly prefix x with a 1 beforehand to avoid problems with leading zeros. The length (i.e. number of bits) of a binary string x is denoted $|x|$, and the i-th bit of x is denoted x_i. The cardinality of a finite set B is denoted $||B||$. We identify each decisional problem with the set of encodings of inputs on which the answer is YES.

We mention in the text several complexity classes, i.e. classes of sets that can be decided within a given resource bound by a sequential computation model such as, e.g., multitape Turing machines. Results regarding complexity classes may be found, among others, in [1] and [7]. These complexity classes are: deterministic logarithmic space, denoted L, nondeterministic logarithmic space, denoted NL, deterministic polynomial time, denoted P, nondeterministic polynomial time, denoted NP, polynomial space, for which deterministic and nondeterministic classes coincide and therefore is denoted just $PSPACE$, deterministic exponential (i.e. $O(2^{n^k})$ for constant k) time, denoted $EXPTIME$, and nondeterministic exponential time, denoted $NEXPTIME$. We denote by FP the set of functions computable in polynomial time.

We will work also with some complexity classes of very low computational power, defined by machines working in logarithmic time. The device for reading the input usually provided to a standard Turing machine is sequential: in logarithmic time, only the first $O(\log n)$ bits of the input could be read. In order that all bits of the input be equally relevant, we will use a known variant of Turing machine with direct access to the bits of the input. The machine will include the following elements:

- an input tape;
- a fixed number of standard work tapes;
- a special tape to point to a bit of the input, which may be subsequently read in;
- a special tape on which the symbol just read from the input appears written;
- a "read" state.

The machine is otherwise standard. It reads its input in the following way: the machine can write on the pointer tape the number of a position i of the input tape; whenever the "read" state is entered, in one computation step, the machine gets in the second special tape the contents of the i-th position of the input tape. If the input has length less than i, then the machine does not get anything. The previous contents of the second special tape is overwritten, but the contents of the pointer tape and the position of its head remain untouched.

Under a linear or larger than linear time bound, these machines can be simulated by standard Turing machines within roughly the same resource bounds. The interest of indirect access machines arises when we consider sublinear time bounds. In particular, we will consider indirect access machines with computation time bounded by $O(\log n)$.

1. *Example.* Let us show how an indirect access machine working in $O(\log n)$ steps can compute the length of its input; this fact will be used later on. This is done by using the following binary search technique: first, probe positions 2^i of the input tape, increasingly, until the first empty cell is found; every probe can be done in constant time since in order to change the contents of the pointer tape from 2^i to 2^{i+1} only one (or two) bits must change. Once an integer k is found such that $2^k \leq |x| < 2^{k+1}$, perform a binary search to find the last input position; again each probe requires only constant time since at most one bit of the pointer tape has to change. The whole procedure requires a logarithmic number of steps.

We will denote by LT the class of languages accepted by deterministic indirect access Turing machines within a computation time bounded by $O(\log n)$, and similarly we denote FLT the class of functions computable by such machines in $O(\log n)$ time.

The concept allowing us to compare the difficulty of different problems is reducibility. Intuitively, a problem A is reducible to a problem B if an efficient algorithm for solving B can be transformed into an efficient algorithm for solving A.

We will use two reducibilities. The first is the standard polynomial time m-reducibility, defined as follows: problem A is polynomial time m-reducible to problem

B, denoted $A \leq_m^P B$, if and only if there is a polynomial-time computable function f such that $x \in A \iff f(x) \in B$ for every string x. We will call this simply m-reducibility, omitting "polynomial time."

The second reducibility is similar, but under a more strict resource bound: logarithmic time m-reducibility, which we will abbreviate to LT-reducibility and denote as $\leq_m^{LT}$. We will need such a fine reducibility to work at the level of the logarithmic-time counting hierarchy. The first approximation is that $A \leq_m^{LT} B$ if and only if there is a logarithmic-time computable function f such that $x \in A \iff f(x) \in B$ for every x. However, this is inappropriate since in logarithmic time big problem instances could only be reduced to small problem instances. We avoid these problems by using a definition of reducibility which translates "locally" parts of problem instances in logarithmic time.

Thus, our condition on the reduction function f for the definition of LT-reducibility will be that the following function φ be computable in logarithmic time: for $x \in \Gamma^\star$ and $i \in \mathbb{N}$, $\varphi(x, i)$ is $f(x)_i$ (the i-th bit of $f(x)$) if $i \leq |f(x)|$, and is undefined otherwise.

Previous work on succinct instances used projection reducibility [20], [18]. This is a very weak reducibility, a version of the nonuniform projection reducibility of [23], and is characterized by the fact that each nonconstant bit of the output coincides with a bit of the input (or its negation), found in a fixed position which depends only on the given position in the output. We will not use this reducibility here.

Given a reducibility and a complexity class, a problem is *hard* for the class under the reducibility if every problem in the class is reducible to it, and is *complete* for the class if it is hard for it and also belongs to it.

3. SUCCINCT INSTANCES AND THE CONVERSION LEMMA

This section proposes a different, simpler and more general way of presenting some of the arguments of [20], so that the results there, previous ones from [6] and [29], and many others then follow immediately in a unified fashion.

A succinct representation of a binary word x is a boolean circuit that on input (the binary representation of) i outputs two boolean values, one indicating whether $i \leq |x|$ and another one indicating, in that case, the i-th bit of x. The same criteria can be used to define succinct representations of integers, finite sets, graphs, or boolean functions. For instance, in the case of graphs, a succinct representation is a boolean circuit which, on input the binary representations of i and j, computes the entry (i, j) of the adjacency matrix.

The succinct version sA of any decisional problem A is: given a boolean circuit describing a word x, decide whether $x \in A$.

The succinctly represented problem is at most exponentially more difficult than the problem on standard encodings. The following observation is proved for graphs in [6], and can be stated similarly for any binary encoding.

2. *Lemma.* Let $f(n) \geq \log n$ be a nondecreasing bound, and let A be a decisional problem. Assume that $A \in DTIME(f(n))$. Then, for the succinct version sA of A, we have $sA \in DTIME(f(2^n)n^2)$.

The same holds for *NTIME*, and similarly for *DSPACE* or *NSPACE*, in which case the new space bound is simply $f(2^n)$. A later lemma will state similar facts for complexity classes in the counting hierarchies.

The same reference proves a sufficient condition for *NP*-hardness of succinct problems: if certain "critical" graphs exist for a graph property, then testing this property on succinctly represented graphs is *NP*-hard. Actually, the form in which this condition is stated in [6] is too weak for the proof to be correct: the interested reader can find in [17] counterexamples not only to the proof, but (assuming $P \neq NP$) to the statement itself. The expert in structural complexity notions will enjoy the constructions, based on the concept of bi-immunity. The corrected statement of the sufficient condition for *NP*-hardness is also given in [17].

We will see in this paper that this kind of sufficient condition, seemingly tailored to succinct representations, actually can be applied to standard encodings, as soon as the logarithmic-time complexity classes are available (theorem 11 below). Then, the results of [6] follow by combining the criticality argument with the precise relationships between standard and succinct encodings that follow from the next two lemmas.

The following lemma, which we name *Conversion Lemma*, shows how to obtain m-reducibilities among succinctly represented problems from LT-reducibilities among the standard problems. Some ideas of its proof are based on a fragment of the proof of the main theorem of [20]. The advantages are, first, that a more flexible and useful form of reducibility among the standard problems is used here (at the price of a technical complication in the proof), and second, that it is now independent of the fact that the problems belong to any particular complexity class.

3. *Lemma.* (*Conversion Lemma*) If $A \leq_m^{LT} B$ then $sA \leq_m^P sB$.

Proof. Let w be an instance of A. Assume as input an instance of sA, given by a boolean circuit C_w describing w. Observe that the size of C_w is at least $\log |w|$, which is the number of inputs, and therefore $|w| \leq 2^{|C_w|}$.

Let f be the reduction function: for all w, $w \in A \iff f(w) \in B$; and let M be the machine that, on input $\langle w, i \rangle$, computes the i-th bit of $f(w)$ in logarithmic time. There is a standard translation of Turing machines into circuits (see [1], section 5.4), appropriate for Turing machines that read directly their input tapes, yielding a circuit of size quadratic in the running time of the machine computing the same output. Each level of the circuit simulates one step of the machine.

Now if the Turing machine has indirect access, the mechanism to supply the input bits in the standard simulation does not work. Fortunately, by hypothesis we have now a circuit C_w supplying individual bits of the input w. Assume that the machine starts by reading in sequentially and storing on worktape the second argument i. This part is simulated by the circuit in the straightforward way since i is read sequentially. For the remaining part of the computation, where bits of w must be read, we can insert one copy of the circuit C_w at each level, fed by the bits in the pointer tape (which are computed by other gates of that level), so that the requested input bit is available at the output of C_w. This extended circuit C' (which is now of size at most cubic on $|C_w|$) does not need w as input anymore: simply, on input i, it produces the i-th bit of $f(w)$.

Therefore, this circuit C' is precisely what we need: a succinct description of $f(w)$, the image of w under the LT-reduction. Indeed, now C_w is in sA if and only if

w is in A, if and only if $f(w)$ is in B, if and only if C' is in sB. It is easy to see that C' can be computed in time polynomial in the size of C_w. ∎

In order to prove completeness of a succinctly represented problem sA in a complexity class, we need a way of translating arbitrary problems in the class into a region where we can use a hypothesis about A, which is exponentially below. (Actually, we are addressing now the problem solved in a more complex way in another fragment of the main proof of [20]).

A possibility could be using tally encodings, which will be of much lower complexity due to the exponential blow-up of the input size; but this requires to check that all bits are equal, and this cannot be done in logarithmic time. Yet we will encode problems in a form similar to tally sets, and with similar properties. For a problem A, define long(A) as follows: $x \in$ long(A) if and only if the binary expression of the length of x is in $1A$. (The 1 prefixing all words here avoids the technical difficulty of the leading zeros.) Thus, for each length n, either all the words of that length are in long(A), if the binary expression of n is in $1A$, or all the words of that length are out of long(A), otherwise. Observe that

$$A \in DTIME(f(2^n)) \iff \text{long}(A) \in DTIME(f(n))$$

and similarly for other complexity classes. We prove next that the succinct version of long(A) jumps up again at least to the difficulty of A.

4. *Lemma.* For every A, $A \leq_m^P s(\text{long}(A))$.

Proof. Since A trivially reduces to $1A$ and the reducibility is transitive, we exhibit a reduction from $1A$ to $s(\text{long}(A))$. Recall that $[x]$ is the integer denoted by x in binary notation. Given x starting with 1, construct a circuit C representing the word $0^{[x]}$, which outputs zero for all inputs up to $[x]$. The time required to construct this circuit is easily seen to be polynomial in $|x|$, and by the definitions we have $x \in 1A \iff 0^{[x]} \in \text{long}(A) \iff C \in s(\text{long}(A))$. ∎

Now we can state and easily prove the following result, which will be readily applied. The proof is simple since the essence of it has been captured by the Conversion Lemma.

5. *Theorem.* Let C_1 and C_2 be arbitrary complexity classes such that for every $A \in C_1$, long(A) $\in C_2$. Then, for every B, if B is hard for C_2 under LT-reducibility, then sB is hard for C_1 under m-reducibility.

Proof. Assume that B is hard for C_2 under LT-reducibility, and let A be an arbitrary set $A \in C_1$. The hypothesis imply long(A) $\in C_2$ and therefore long(A) $\leq_m^{LT} B$. By the Conversion Lemma, $s(\text{long}(A)) \leq_m^P sB$. Since by lemma 4 $A \leq_m^P s(\text{long}(A))$, by transitivity, $A \leq_m^P sB$ and thus sB is m-hard for C_1. ∎

As an example of application, let us prove now that the results fully proved in [20] can be obtained as immediate corollary: since Hamiltonian path, k-colorability, and many other NP-complete sets can be proved complete via LT-reductions [7], we have:

6. Corollary. The succinct versions of Hamiltonian path, k-colorability, etc. are m-complete in $NEXPTIME$.

Proof. Membership follows from lemma 4, and hardness from theorem 5. ∎

Subsequent sections will describe further applications of this set of lemmas, capturing in very clear ways the essentials of the optimal results about NP-completeness from [6] and many other results.

4. THE COUNTING HIERARCHIES

Probably the best known complexity classes are P and NP. Also well-known is the polynomial-time hierarchy PH [24], a natural generalization of the class NP. Nevertheless there are many natural computational problems whose complexity cannot be modelized in terms of existential or universal quantifiers; sometimes this complexity is captured by other complexity classes, more adapted to the idea of *counting*.

Wagner [29] defines the counting hierarchy CH in a similar way as the polynomial-time hierarchy. The counting hierarchy turns out to be a very useful tool to express the complexity of many natural problems. It contains the polynomial-time hierarchy and is included in $PSPACE$. Wagner shows that every level of CH has complete problems and proves some other properties.

In this section we will define the polynomial-time counting hierarchy CH and the logarithmic-time counting hierarchy LCH. The classes in these hierarchies are characterized by polynomially bounded quantification, resp. logarithmically bounded quantification, over a predicate computed in polynomial, resp. logarithmic time.

The polynomial counting quantifier $\mathbf{C}$ is defined in the following way: for a function $f : \Gamma^* \mapsto \mathbb{N}$, $f \in FP$, a polynomial p and a binary predicate P,

$$\mathbf{C}^p_{f(x)} y : P(x,y) \iff ||\{y : |y| \leq p(|x|) \text{ and } P(x,y)\}|| \geq f(x).$$

If K is a language class, for any set A, $A \in \mathbf{C}K$ if there is a function f in FP, a polynomial p, and a language $B \in K$ such that for any $x \in \Gamma^*$

$$x \in A \iff \mathbf{C}^p_{f(x)} y : \langle x,y \rangle \in B$$

The polynomial counting hierarchy CH is the smallest family of language classes satisfying:

i/ $P \in CH$;

ii/ if $K \in CH$ then $\exists^p K$, $\forall^p K$ and $\mathbf{C}^p K$ belong to CH.

For simplicity, $\mathbf{C}$ will denote the class $\mathbf{C}P$, and the context will make clear when we talk about a quantifier and when about a language class. Also, we will drop the superscript p from all the quantifiers.

We should point out here the following properties:

7. *Proposition.*

a/ $CH \subseteq PSPACE$

b/ $PH \subseteq CH$

c/ For every class K in CH, $\exists K \cup \forall K \subseteq \mathbf{C}K \subseteq \exists \mathbf{C}K \cap \forall \mathbf{C}K$.

d/ Every class in CH is closed under m-reducibility.

e/ Every class in CH has complete problems with respect to the m-reducibility.

Similarly, we define now the logarithmic-time counting hierarchy. The logarithmic existential, universal, and counting quantifiers are defined in the following way: for a function $f : \Gamma^* \mapsto \mathbb{N}$ computable in logarithmic time, a constant c and a binary predicate P,

$$\exists^{lc} y : P(x,y) \iff \bigvee_y |y| \leq c \lceil \log |x| \rceil \text{ and } P(x,y)$$

$$\forall^{lc} y : P(x,y) \iff \bigwedge_y |y| \leq c \lceil \log |x| \rceil \text{ and } P(x,y)$$

$$\mathbf{C}_{f(x)}^{lc} y : P(x,y) \iff \|\{y : |y| \leq c \lceil \log |x| \rceil \text{ and } P(x,y)\}\| \geq f(x)$$

If K is a language class, for any set A, $A \in \exists^l K$ if there is a language $B \in K$ and a constant c such that for any $x \in \Gamma^*$

$$x \in A \iff \exists^{lc} y : \langle x,y \rangle \in B$$

and analogously for $A \in \forall^l K$. $A \in \mathbf{C}^l K$ if there is a language $B \in K$, a constant c and a function f computable in logarithmic time such that for any $x \in \Gamma^*$

$$x \in A \iff \mathbf{C}_{f(x)}^{lc} y : \langle x,y \rangle \in B$$

The logarithmic-time counting hierarchy LCH is the smallest family of language classes satisfying

i/ $LT \in LCH$;

ii/ if $K \in LCH$ then $\exists^l K, \forall^l K$ and $\mathbf{C}^l K$ belong to LCH.

In [2], the alternating log-time hierarchy LH is defined using log-time indirect access Turing machines that alternate between existential and universal states. This hierarchy coincides with the subfamily of LCH defined using only $\exists^l$ and $\forall^l$ quantifiers, and is known to be proper [22]. Additionally, in [5] it is shown that $\mathbf{C}^l LT$ is not included in LH, and in [27] it is proved that the inclusions $\mathbf{C}^l LT \subset \exists^l \mathbf{C}^l LT$ and $\mathbf{C}^l LT \subset \forall^l \mathbf{C}^l LT$ are strict.

By analogy with the polynomial-time hierarchy, and following common usage, we will call $\Sigma_k^l = \exists^l \forall^l \exists^l \ldots Q^l LT$, the class defined by $k-1$ alternations of logarithmically bounded quantifiers $\exists$ and $\forall$, being $Q^l = \forall^l$ if k is even and $\exists^l$ if k is odd; also we will use the notation $\mathbf{C}_k^l = \mathbf{C}^l \mathbf{C}^l \ldots \mathbf{C}^l LT$ for the class defined by k logarithmically bounded counting quantifiers. We will denote sometimes $NLT = \exists^l LT$ since it corresponds to nondeterministic logarithmic time.

Several properties and inclusions of CH translate directly to LCH. Let us point out just three properties.

8. *Proposition.*

a/ $LCH \subseteq L$.

b/ For every class K in LCH, $\exists^l K \cup \forall^l K \subseteq \mathbf{C}^l K \subseteq \exists^l K \cap \forall^l K$.

c/ If two classes of the LCH coincide, so do their corresponding classes of CH.

The next decision problems are complete in $\exists^l LT$ and in $\mathbf{C}^l LT$ respectively.

9. *Example.* Nonzero string.

Let $L_1 = \{w \in \Gamma^* : w \text{ has at least one 1}\}$.

L_1 is $\exists^l LT$-complete. Let us prove it.

$L_1 \in \exists^l LT$. Consider the language L_0 accepted by a deterministic indirect access log-time machine M that on input $\langle x, i \rangle$, $|i| = \lceil \log |x| \rceil$, accepts if and only if the i-th bit of x is a 1. It is clear that $L_0 \in LT$ and that for all $x \in \Gamma^*$,

$$x \in L_1 \iff \bigvee_i |i| \leq \lceil \log |x| \rceil \langle x, i \rangle \in L_0$$

L_1 is hard for $\exists^l LT$ with respect to the LT-reducibility. Let $L \in \exists^l LT$

$$x \in L \iff \bigvee_i |i| \leq c \lceil \log |x| \rceil P(x, i)$$

being $P(x, i)$ a predicate in LT. Consider the function g and a logarithmic-time computable function φ computing the bits of $g(x)$ as follows: $g(x)$ will have a "1" in position i if the i-th string of length $\leq c \lceil \log |x| \rceil$ is a witness of $x \in L$, and it will have a "0" in this position otherwise. For a given x, let $n = c \lceil \log |x| \rceil$. Then for $|i| \leq n$,

$$\varphi(x, i) = \begin{cases} 1 & \text{if } P(x, i) \\ 0 & \text{if } \neg P(x, i) \end{cases}$$

The function φ can be computed in log-time since $P(x, i)$ is a log-time predicate, and $n = c \lceil \log |x| \rceil$ can be calculated by first computing $l = |x|$, as described in example 1, then computing the length of l, which is $\lceil \log |x| \rceil$, and multiplying by the constant c. It is clear that $x \in L \iff g(x) \in L_1$.

10. *Example.* Majority.

Let $L_2 = \{w \in \Gamma^* : w \text{ has more 1's than 0's}\}$.

Let us prove that L_2 is $\mathbf{C}^l LT$-complete. Observe that $w \in L_2$ if and only if more than half of the bits of w are 1.

$L_2 \in \mathbf{C}^l LT$. Consider the LT language L_0 of the previous example. For all $x \in \Gamma^*$

$$x \in L_2 \iff ||\{i : |i| \leq \lceil \log |x| \rceil \langle x, i \rangle \in L_0\}|| \geq \left\lfloor \frac{|x|}{2} \right\rfloor + 1$$

and this bounding function is log-time computable.

L_2 is hard for $\mathbf{C}^l LT$ with respect to LT-reducibility. Let $L \in \mathbf{C}^l LT$

$$x \in L \iff ||\{i : |i| \leq c\lceil \log|x|\rceil P(x,i)\}|| \geq f(x)$$

being $P(x,i)$ a predicate in LT and f a function in FLT. Consider again functions g and φ like in the previous example, the difference lying in that now we have to create a certain amount of 1's to change the bound f into one half. Once more, for a given x, let $n = \lceil c \log|x|\rceil$.

$$\varphi(x,i) = \begin{cases} 1 & \text{if } |i| \leq n \text{ and } P(x,i) \\ 0 & \text{if } |i| \leq n \text{ and } \neg P(x,i) \\ 0 & \text{if } n < |i| \leq n + f(x) - 1 \\ 1 & \text{if } n + f(x) - 1 < |i| \leq 2n \end{cases}$$

By the same arguments as for the reduction to L_1, φ can be computed in log-time. Observe that here the valued mapped to by the reduction contains in its second part $n - f(x) + 1$ ones, so that $g(x) \in L_2$ if and only if in the first part there are at least $f(x)$ ones. This technique can be applied in many other contexts, and transforms an arbitrary counting quantifier into one whose threshold is exactly $1/2$. Thus we will assume, whenever needed, that our counting quantifiers have threshold $1/2$, by appealing to this construction.

5. SUFFICIENT CONDITIONS FOR HARDNESS

The purpose of this section is to present a general tool for proving LT-hardness results for some classes of the logarithmic-time counting hierarchy. Essentially, such ideas appear in [6], where they are presented as sufficient conditions for succinct versions of problems being NP-hard or Σ_2-hard. As can be seen from our results in this section, their NP-hardness results can be strengthened substantially with the help of the Conversion Lemma and the logarithmic-time counting hierarchy: we will show a similar but more general sufficient condition for problems being NLT-hard, and several applications; then, in the next section, the Conversion Lemma will apply to show immediately that the corresponding succinct versions are NP-hard, encompassing all NP-completeness or co-NP-completeness results of [6] and [29] and many more cases. More importantly, in this way an explanation is found for the fact that many succinct problems are NP-complete.

As a general setting, we study the complexity of problems stated on boolean functions of finite domain, always of the form $f : \Gamma^n \mapsto \Gamma^m$. From now on we call these objects "finite functions". The encoding of such a function f is by 2^n blocks of m bits, starting each one of them by the special separator symbol #, and the i-th block being the image of the i-th word of Γ^n. In the special case in which $m = 1$, i.e. when f is a boolean function, it is not necessary to use the separators and the i-th bit will represent the image of the i-th word of Γ^n. In the case when $m > 1$ it is not hard to see that the problem of whether a given input is a correct encoding of a function is in $\forall^l LT$.

We will interpret the blocks in the encoding of the function as integers sometimes. For instance, the "non-zero string" problem of example 9 can be reworded in this setting as "not identically zero function" from Γ^n to Γ for some n. Given a (finite or infinite) function f and a finite set A, we denote $f|_A$ the restriction of f to A; this set A will usually be of the form Γ^n.

The next theorems give sufficient conditions for a problem on finite functions to be hard for $NLT = \exists^l LT$ and $\mathbf{C}^l LT$. These conditions will be given by the existence of "$\exists$-critical" (resp. "C-critical") functions. We need some definitions.

Let Q be a property on finite functions, and let f and g be two linear-time computable functions, $f, g : \Gamma^\star \mapsto \Gamma^\star$, such that for every n and for every $z \in \Gamma^n$, $|g(z)| = |f(z)| = m$ where m is a power of 2 that only depends on n. We will say that the pair (f, g) is $\exists$-critical for Q if for every $n \in \mathrm{IN}$ the following conditions hold:

i/ the restriction $f|_{\Gamma^n} \notin Q$;

ii/ for every nonempty set $B \subseteq 0\Gamma^{n-1}$, that is, every nonempty set of words of length n beginning with 0, the function $h_B|_{\Gamma^n} \in Q$, where

$$h_B(z) = \begin{cases} f(z) & \text{if } z \notin B \\ g(z) & \text{if } z \in B \end{cases}$$

Most applications will take $m = 1$. We will identify each property Q with the decisional problem of deciding whether the input has the property Q. Now the following powerful theorem yields easily many complete problems for $\exists^l LT$.

11. **Theorem.** Let Q be a property of finite functions. If there exists a $\exists$-critical pair (f, g) of functions for Q, then Q is $\exists^l LT$-hard for the LT-reducibility.

Proof. We show how to reduce L_1 to Q. Given x, we must indicate a value y such that $x \in L_1 \iff y \in Q$, and explain how to compute in logarithmic time the function φ that finds the bits of y.

We use the following notation. Let n be the minimum integer such that $|x| \leq 2^{n-1}$, so that $n < \log|x| + 2$; it can be computed as in example 1. Let the length of the values of f and g on inputs of length n be m, a power of 2. Observe that divisions by m are mere shifts, and thus can be easily computed. The value m itself is computable by evaluating f on 0^n, in time linear in n and thus logarithmic on $|x|$.

The value y is to be interpreted as a finite function from Γ^n to Γ^m, interleaving values of f and values of g. Its length will be $|y| = m2^n$: a total of 2^n blocks of m bits, each corresponding to a value of f or g.

For the first $|x|$ blocks (less than half the blocks), the corresponding bit of x determines whether the block comes from f or from g: if the k-th bit of x is $x_k = 1$, then y will have a value of g as k-th block; otherwise it will have a value of f. The remaining blocks are extra values of f, added in order to complete y.

Thus the i-th bit of y is computed by finding out the block r on which it falls, and its relative position j within the block: those are quotient and remainder of i divided by m; then, checking x_r to see if f or g is being used for that block (for the first $|x|$ blocks only), and extracting the j-th bit of the value of f or g corresponding to the block.

The complete description of φ is as follows. Bits of words (and also blocks) are assumed to be numbered starting from zero to simplify the arithmetics.

$$\varphi(x,i) = \begin{cases} g(r)_j & \text{if } r = \lfloor \frac{i}{m} \rfloor \text{ and } j = i \bmod m \\ & \text{and } i < m|x| \text{ and } x_r = 1 \\[2ex] f(r)_j & \text{if } r = \lfloor \frac{i}{m} \rfloor \text{ and } j = i \bmod m \\ & \text{and } i < m|x| \text{ and } x_r = 0 \\[2ex] f(r)_j & \text{if } r = \lfloor \frac{i}{m} \rfloor \text{ and } j = i \bmod m \\ & \text{and } m|x| \le i < m2^{n-1} \\[2ex] f(r)_j & \text{if } r = \lfloor \frac{i}{m} \rfloor \text{ and } j = i \bmod m \\ & \text{and } m2^{n-1} \le i < m2^n \end{cases}$$

Here $f(r)$ is interpreted as writing r in binary, padding with leading zeros up to length n if necessary, and applying f, and similarly for $g(r)$. Computing either f or g takes time linear on $|r| < \log|x| + 2$. Observe that the last line covers exactly those blocks for which r begins with a 1, i.e. half of them.

Let us see that this is a reduction. If $x \in L_1$ then there is at least a 1 in some position of x, and then the list of the function values will have one value of g for an argument beginning with 0. By condition ii/ in the definition of criticality, it follows that the function represented by y belongs to Q. Conversely, if $x \notin L_1$, then y will be exactly the encoding of $f|_{\Gamma^n}$, and by condition i/ in the definition of criticality, y is not in Q. ∎

12. **Remark.** The fact that the value m is a power of 2 is not essential, since the fact that the divisions are shifts may be guaranteed in other ways. For instance, if for all z the critical pair fulfills $|f(z)| = |g(z)| = |z|$ instead, we would get $m = n$; in the reduction we let n be the minimum integer such that $|x| \le 2^{n-1}$ and n is a power of 2. It can be computed in the following way: first, as in example 1, find the minimum integer k such that $|x| \le 2^k$; then n is the string $10^{|k|}$ of a single one followed by $|k|$ zeros. The bound on $n = |r|$ would be $2\log|x| + 2$. The proof goes through.

13. **Remark.** Similarly, the fact that the ratio of actual bits affected by the reduction is one half, as implied by $B \subseteq 0\Gamma^{n-1}$, is not crucial either. The reader can check that we could have taken, for instance, $B \subseteq 0^{3n/4}\Gamma^{n/4}$. Of course $|x|$ must be less than the size of the part of the output indexed by B; in this case, for instance, taking n so that $2^{n/8} \le |x| < 2^{n/4}$ works. The bound on $|r|$ is still linear on $\log|x|$.

We will use theorem 11 for classifying the next problems. Observe that in order to show that a problem is $\exists^l LT$-hard, we only need to give a pair of $\exists$-critical functions (f,g) for the problem. Similarly, it can be proved that a problem is $\forall^l LT$-hard by showing that its complement is $\exists^l LT$-hard. The following four problems are $\forall^l LT$-complete: we give an $\exists$-critical pair for the complement. It is left to the reader to prove that these problems are in $\forall^l LT$ and that the pairs are actually $\exists$-critical for their complements.

14. **Example.** Constant function.

$L_3 = \{\xi : \Gamma^n \mapsto \Gamma^m \text{ such that } \xi \text{ is a constant function } \}$

$\exists$-critical functions for the complement: $f(z) = 0$, $g(z) = 1$.

15. *Example*. Injectiveness.

$L_4 = \{\xi : \Gamma^n \mapsto \Gamma^n$ such that ξ is an injective function $\}$

$\exists$-critical functions for the complement: $f(z) = z$, $g(z) = 1^{|z|}$. Here we use the condition in the definition of $\exists$-critical that words of B begin with 0 and remark 12.

16. *Example*. Increasing function.

$L_5 = \{\xi : \Gamma^n \mapsto \Gamma^n$ such that ξ is strictly increasing $\}$

$\exists$-critical functions for the complement: $f(z) = z$, $g(z) = 1^{|z|}$.

17. *Example*. Conservation of parity.

$L_6 = \{\xi : \Gamma^n \mapsto \Gamma^m$ such that for every $z \in \Gamma^n$, $lb(z) = lb(\xi(z))\}$

where we denote by $lb(z)$ the last bit of z. $\exists$-critical functions for the complement: $f(z) = lb(z)$, $g(z) = 1 - lb(z)$.

The following examples are taken from [6], where actually only succinct versions are considered. We will consider standard problems here, and obtain the results of [6] in the next section as applications of the Conversion Lemma. It should be observed that the problem "nonemptiness" of [6], under our encoding of undirected graphs, is exactly the "nonzero string" problem L_0. In the next examples the functions ξ are identified with the adjacency matrix of a graph on $n = 2^k$ vertices; each potential edge is thus identified by exactly $2k$ bits, k for each endpoint (padding with leading zeros if necessary).

18. *Example*. Triangle.

$L_7 = \{\xi : \Gamma^{2k} \mapsto \Gamma$ has a triangle $\}$

$\exists$-critical functions:

$$f(z_1 z_2) = \begin{cases} 1 & \text{if } z_1 = n/2 = 2^{k-1}, \text{ i.e. } z_1 \text{ is a one and } k-1 \text{ zeros} \\ 0 & \text{otherwise} \end{cases}$$

representing a "star" graph in which vertex 2^{k-1} is connected to all other vertices and no other edge exists, and $g(z_1 z_2) = 1$. A value taken from g for an argument beginning with 0 corresponds to adding an edge between two vertices different from (smaller than) 2^{k-1}. Since both are connected to it, a triangle appears. We accept as a triangle here a trivial one formed by an edge and a self-loop.

19. *Example*. k-path.

$L_8 = \{\xi : \Gamma^{2k} \mapsto \Gamma$ has a k-path $\}$

We use remark 13 to assume that $B \subseteq 0^{3k/2}\Gamma^{k/2}$. The function f will represent a graph with $k-1$ consecutive edges, with an endpoint at vertex 0 and all other vertices past $n/2$. As soon as an edge is added from vertex 0 to any vertex strictly between 0 and $n/2$, a k-path appears.

The $\exists$-critical functions are: $f(z_1 z_2) = 1$ if $z_1 = 0$ and $z_2 = n/2$, or if z_1 and z_2 are consecutive and strictly between $n/2$ and $n/2 + k - 2$, and 0 otherwise; and $g(z_1 z_2) = 1$. Similarly, for the problem k-cycle, it is enough that in the graph defined by f an edge is added connecting 0 to the last vertex in the path.

20. *Example.* Maximum degree $\Delta \geq k$

$L_9 = \{\xi : \Gamma^{2k} \mapsto \Gamma \text{ with } \Delta(\xi) \geq k\}$

We interpret the degree of ξ at $z \in \Gamma^k$ as the number of ones in the column $\{f(z'z) : z' \in \Gamma^k\}$. The maximum degree of ξ, $\Delta(\xi)$, is the maximum of the degrees of ξ at any z. The correspondence with the graph-theoretic notion is apparent.

$\exists$-critical functions: $f(z_1 z_2) = 1$ if and only if $z_1 > n - k + 1$, and $g(z) = 1$.

Now we present some examples taken from [29], concerning problems on finite sets of integers. We represent the sets by their characteristic functions as subsets of Γ^n, where n is large enough to write any integer from the set with exactly n bits (again using leading zeros as padding). In [29], succinct versions were considered, actually in terms of various compact description languages. Again we will consider standard problems here, and leave the results on succinct versions to the next section as applications of the Conversion Lemma. Again the "nonemptiness" problem for sets is L_0. For those problems involving two sets, we encode both in the same function: the restriction of the function to $0\Gamma^{n-1}$ will encode the first and the restriction to $1\Gamma^{n-1}$ the second. Sometimes single elements appear as data in [29]: we fix their value to appropriate constants without loss of generality.

21. *Example.* Critical element.

An element a is critical for a set if a not being in the set implies that it is empty [29].

$L_{10} = \{\xi : \Gamma^n \mapsto \Gamma \text{ s.t. } 2^n \text{ is critical }\}$

$\exists$-critical functions for the complement: $f(z) = 0$ and $g(z) = 1$.

22. *Nonempty intersection.*

$L_{11} = \{\xi : \Gamma^n \mapsto \Gamma \text{ s.t. } \exists z f(0z) = f(1z) = 1\}$
$\exists$-critical functions: $f(0z) = 0$, $f(1z) = 1$; $g(z) = 1$.

23. *Example.* Maximum below a boundary.

Is a the maximum element in the set smaller than b?

$L_{12} = \{\xi : \Gamma^n \mapsto \Gamma \text{ s.t. } 0 \text{ is the maximum argument } z \text{ smaller than or equal to } 2^n \text{ for which } \xi(z) = 1\}$

$\exists$-critical functions for the complement: $f(0) = 1$, $f(z) = 0$ for $z > 0$, $g(0) = 0$, $g(z) = 1$ for $z > 0$.

24. *Example.* Subset.

$L_{13} = \{\xi : \Gamma^n \mapsto \Gamma \text{ s.t. } \forall z f(0z) \leq f(1z)\}$

$\exists$-critical functions for the complement: $f(z) = 0$ and $g(z) = 1$.

25. *Example.* Equality.

$L_{14} = \{\xi : \Gamma^n \mapsto \Gamma \text{ s.t. } \forall z f(0z) = f(1z)\}$

$\exists$-critical functions for the complement: $f(z) = 0$ and $g(z) = 1$.

26. *Example.* Set connectedness.

The set represented by ξ is connected if $\forall x, y, z$ with $x < y < z$,

$$\xi(x) = 1 \wedge \xi(z) = 1 \Rightarrow \xi(y) = 1.$$

$L_{15} = \{\xi : \Gamma^n \mapsto \Gamma \text{ is connected }\}$

$\exists$-critical functions for the complement: $f(z) = 1$ if and only if $z_1 > 2^{n-1}$; and $g(z) = 1$.

We move now to a similar sufficient condition for $\mathbf{C}^l LT$ completeness, as announced before. It has a similar structure to that of theorem 11. The analogous condition is as follows.

Let Q be a property on finite functions, and let f and g be two linear-time computable functions, $f, g : \Gamma^\star \mapsto \Gamma^\star$, such that for every $x \in \Gamma^n$, $|g(x)| = |f(x)| = m$ where m is a power of 2 that depends only on n. We will say that the pair (f, g) is C-critical for Q if the following condition holds:

For every nonempty set $B \subseteq \Gamma^n$, the function $h_B|_{\Gamma^n} \in Q$ if and only if $\|B\| > 2^{n-1}$, where as before

$$h_B(x) = \begin{cases} f(x) & \text{if } x \notin B \\ g(x) & \text{if } x \in B \end{cases}$$

27. *Theorem.* Let Q be a property of finite functions. If there exists a C-critical pair (f, g) of functions for Q, then Q is $\mathbf{C}^l LT$-hard for the LT-reducibility.

Proof. The proof is analogous to that of theorem 11, reducing instead problem L_2 to Q. This function φ that computes the bits of the image y is quite similar to that of theorem 11. Essentially, for a given string x, here we have to produce a list having as many values of f as 0's in x, and as many values of g as 1's in x. We must be careful also that in the part that pads up y to complete a finite function we put as many values of f as values of g. The resulting word y coding the resulting finite function will have size $m2^n$, where n is the smallest integer such that $|x| \leq 2^n$ and $m = |f(0^n)|$, m a power of 2. Instead of describing the function in detail as we did for theorem 11, we just give the definition:

$$\varphi(x, i) = \begin{cases} g(r)_j & \text{if } r = \lfloor \frac{i}{m} \rfloor \text{ and } (i \bmod m) = j \\ & \text{and } ((i < m|x| \text{ and } x_r = 1) \text{ or } (m|x| \leq i < m2^n \text{ and } r \text{ odd})) \\[2ex] f(r)_j & \text{if } r = \lfloor \frac{i}{m} \rfloor \text{ and } (i \bmod m) = j \\ & \text{and } ((i < m|x| \text{ and } x_r = 0) \text{ or } (m|x| \leq i < m2^n \text{ and } r \text{ even})) \end{cases}$$

For a given x, x has more 1's than 0's if and only if y encodes a function with the values of g arising more frequently than the values of f, which by the condition in the definition of C-critical function implies that $y \in Q$. ∎

28. *Remark.* Again there is no mystery about the lower bound 2^{n-1} on $\|B\|$. By adjusting the ratio of f's and g's in the section between $m|x|$ and $m2^n$, other thresholds can be used in the same simple manner.

This theorem can be easily applied to a number of problems in the straightforward way. The reader can probably suggest several natural examples along the lines of the previously presented ones. In particular, interesting examples are the cardinality problem and the number of components problem, defined in [29], where it is proved that in succinct form they are complete for $\mathbf{C}^p P$. Here we infer easily from theorem 27 that their standard forms are complete for $\mathbf{C}^l LT$.

In the next section we will discuss what happens to the succinct versions of all the problems studied here: all of them will increase in complexity by exactly one exponential, and this will follow from the Conversion Lemma.

6. COMPLETE SETS AT HIGHER LEVELS

We give now some more examples of function problems that are complete in some other levels of LCH, sketching the proof of their completeness. We treat some classes at what could be called the second level of the hierarchy, and then discuss complete problems in any of the classes of some subhierarchies of LCH. Relaxing certain bounds, we will obtain P-complete problems. Finally, we apply the Conversion Lemma to translate complete sets for LCH into succinct versions that turn out to be complete for CH.

The Second Level

We understand by "the second level" those classes that can be defined using two quantifiers. We give some problems whose complexity corresponds to this level.

29. *Example.* Surjective function.

$$L_{16} = \{\xi : \Gamma^{2n} \mapsto \Gamma^{2n} \text{ such that } \xi \text{ is surjective on } 0^n \Gamma^n\}$$

First we prove that $L_{16} \in \forall^l \exists^l LT$. For a given $w \in \Gamma^\star$, $|w| = 2n \cdot 2^{2n}$, it has to be checked that every value of the form $0^n w$ appears in the given string and starting in a correct position. This can be expressed using quantifiers, in the following way:

$$w \in L_{16} \iff w \text{ is correct encoding of a function } \xi : \Gamma^{2n} \mapsto \Gamma^{2n} \text{ and}$$
$$\forall y(|y| = n) : \exists i : w_i = \#, \text{ and } w_{i+1} \cdots w_{i+2n} = 0^n y$$

Let us see that L_{16} is hard for $\forall^l \exists^l LT$. Let $L \in \forall^l \exists^l LT$. There is a constant c and a LT-predicate P such that for every $x \in \Gamma^\star$,

$$x \in L \iff \forall^{lc} y : \exists^{lc} z : P(x, y, z)$$

We give a reduction from L to L_{16}. For a given x, let n be the smallest power of 2 greater than or equal to $c\lceil \log |x| \rceil$. The image $g(x)$ will have size $2n \cdot 2^{2n}$. The idea is that in this image, for every y, we will make the substring $0^n y$ to appear if there is a z such that $P(x, y, z)$, constructing the substring 1^{2n} otherwise. Giving the function φ bit by bit as we did in the previous examples makes it difficult to understand it;

therefore we give it in "pieces" of length $2n$. Recall from the preliminaries that we denote by $[w]$ the integer whose binary expansion, padded up to length $2n$, is w.

$$\varphi(x, [yz] \cdot 2n + 1) \cdots \varphi(x, ([yz] + 1) \cdot 2n) = \begin{cases} 0^n y & \text{if } |y| = |z| = n \text{ and } P(x, y, z) \\ 1^{2n} & \text{if } |y| = |z| = n \text{ and } \neg P(x, y, z) \end{cases}$$

Observe that again we need the fact that n is a power of 2, since by giving function φ in pieces of length $2n$, we are actually hiding a division by $2n$. The transformation from an integer i into the corresponding string is trivial since one just has to add 0's to the left until the string has length $2n$.

30. *Example.* Minimum degree $\delta \geq k$

$$L_{17} = \{\xi : \Gamma^{2k} \mapsto \Gamma \text{ with } \delta(\xi) \geq k\}$$

The degree of ξ at $z \in \Gamma^k$ was defined in the example 20. The minimum degree of ξ, $\delta(\xi)$, is the minimum of the degrees of ξ at any z. Again there is a correspondence with the graph-theoretic notion. This problem is complete for Π_2-alternating logarithmic time. We omit the proof: it is similar to the previous one.

31. *Example.* Large injective restriction.

$$L_{18} = \{\xi : \Gamma^{2n} \mapsto \Gamma^{2n} \text{ s.t. there is an injective restriction of } \xi \text{ of size } \geq 2^n\}$$

L_{18} is complete in $C^l \exists^l LT$. The proof follows again guidelines similar to the previous ones.

Complete Problems for Σ_k^l: a Tiling Game

We will consider a finite set of strings $T \subseteq \Gamma^{2s}$ as the set of tiles of a one-dimensional domino game. Given a string $x \in T$, a second string $y \in T$ will match with x if the last s digits of x coincide with the first s digits of y. We will also consider a number $m \in \mathbb{N}$ and two players, Constructeur and Saboteur as in [4], building a tiled row of dominoes. Given a starting tile, alternately, each of the two players selects a domino that matches with the right part of the last selected tile, and adds it to the row. The aim of Constructeur is to build a tiled row of $m + 1$ tiles, while the aim of Saboteur is to prevent Constructeur from reaching his aim. We investigate different versions of this tiling game. Similar tiling games have been independently defined by Grädel in [9], where they are used as tool to study the complexity of boolean algebras. For each odd m we define the following problem:

$R(m)$: *Tiling game of length m* ($m > 1$ and odd). Consider a tiling game of 2^{mn} tiles of length $2mn$ given one after another in a string and separated by the marker $\#$. The starting tile is given by the first $2mn$ digits of the string. If Constructeur starts the game, can he complete a tiled row of $m + 1$ tiles?

32. *Proposition.* $R(m)$ is Σ_m^l-complete.

Proof. We prove first that $R(m) \in \Sigma_m^l$. Given $w \in \Gamma^\star$, $|w| = 2mn \cdot 2^{mn}$, we can write the decision problem as a string of m quantifiers followed by a log-time predicate, so that the meaning of the expression is that Constructeur has a way to select tiles in which Saboteur either plays unfair (placing tiles that do not match) or cannot prevent Constructeur from making the tiled row:

$w \in R(m) \iff w$ has the correct encoding and $\exists i_1 \forall i_2 \ldots \exists i_m$:

$$w_{i_1} = w_{i_2} = \ldots = w_{i_m} = \# \text{ and}$$

$$w_{i_1+1} \ldots w_{i_1+2mn} w_{i_2+1} \ldots w_{i_2+2mn} \ldots w_{i_m+1} \ldots w_{i_m+2mn}$$

is a correct row of the domino game, or for some even j

$$w_{i_j+1} \ldots w_{i_j+2mn} \text{ does not match with } w_{i_{j-1}+1} \ldots w_{i_{j-1}+2mn}.$$

To prove that $R(m)$ is hard for Σ_m^l (m odd), let L be a language in Σ_m^l. For a certain constant c and a log-time predicate P, and for every $x \in \Gamma^*$,

$$x \in L \iff \exists^{lc} u_1 \forall^{lc} u_2 \ldots \exists^{lc} u_m : P(x, u_1, \ldots, u_n)$$

Let n be the smallest power of two greater than or equal to $c\lceil \log |x| \rceil$; for any $k < 2^n$, represent by $(k)_n$ the binary expansion of length n of k. We will reduce L to $R(m)$. For this we will construct a domino game of $2^{2(m+1)n}$ tiles of size $2(m+1)n$ in such a way that in any row, the first m tiles can always be placed. The tile $m+1$, corresponding to Constructeur, is related to the predicate P and to the tiles placed before, and if both players have played right, it can only be placed if $x \in L$. This will be argued after the definition of the function φ. Again, for clarification, we will describe the function in pieces, each piece corresponding to a tile of the domino game in the reduction. Again $[\cdot]$ represents the standard mapping from strings in $\Gamma^{2(m+1)n}$ into integers.

$$\varphi(x, [u_1 u_2 \ldots u_m u_{m+1}] \cdot 2(m+1)n + 1) \ldots \varphi(x, ([u_1 u_2 \ldots u_m u_{m+1}] + 1) \cdot 2(m+1)n) =$$

$$= \begin{cases}
\overline{|(m)_n 0^n 0^n \ldots 0^n|(0)_n 0^n 0^n \ldots 0^n|} & \text{if } u_j = (0)_n \text{ for } j \in \{1 \ldots m+1\} \\[2mm]
\overline{|(0)_n 0^n 0^n \ldots 0^n|(1)_n u_1 0^n \ldots 0^n|} & \text{if } u_j = (1)_n \text{ for } j \in \{2 \ldots m+1\} \\[2mm]
\overline{|(1)_n u_1 0^n \ldots 0^n|(2)_n u_1 u_2 0^n \ldots 0^n|} & \text{if } u_j = (2)_n \text{ for } j \in \{3 \ldots m+1\} \\[2mm]
\overline{|(2)_n u_1 u_2 0^n \ldots 0^n|(3)_n u_1 u_2 u_3 0^n \ldots 0^n|} & \text{if } u_j = (3)_n \text{ for } j \in \{4 \ldots m+1\} \\[2mm]
\ldots \\
\ldots \\
\overline{|(m-2)_n u_1 u_2 \ldots u_{m-2} 0^n 0^n|(m-1)_n u_1 \ldots u_{m-2} u_{m-1} 0^n|} & \\
\qquad\qquad \text{if } u_j = (m-1)_n \text{ for } j \in \{m, m+1\} \\[2mm]
\overline{|(m-1)_n u_1 u_2 \ldots u_{m-2} u_{m-1} 0^n|(m)_n u_m 0^n \ldots 0^n|} & \\
\qquad\qquad \text{if } u_{m+1} = (m)_n \text{ and } P(x, u_1, u_2 \ldots u_m) \\[2mm]
\overline{|(m)_n 0^n \ldots 0^n|(0)_n 0^n \ldots 0^n|} & \text{otherwise}
\end{cases}$$

We will see that Constructeur can build a tiled row of $m+1$ tiles if and only if $x \in L$. Observe that the only tiles that depend in the predicate P have the form $\overline{|(m-1)_n u_1 \ldots u_{m-1} 0^n|(m)_n u_m 0^n \ldots 0^n|}$. In these tiles is encoded the whole history of the game, i.e., the $u's$ will correspond to the quantified variables is the definition of L. The remaining tiles will always be in our set of dominoes; this means that the tiled row constructed in the game will always have length at least m. The string of length n written at the left of every tile guarantees that the j-th tile in the row encodes an election u_{j-1} for the quantifier $j-1$. It will be possible to place the tile $m+1$ if and only if there is a choice of u_m such that $P(x, u_1, \ldots u_m)$. If $x \in L$ then $\exists u_1 : \forall u_2 \ldots \exists u_m : P(x, u_1, \ldots u_m)$. Considering Saboteur's selections, Constructeur only needs to select the tiles that codify the values corresponding to the existential quantifiers in the formula. Conversely, if $\forall u_1 : \exists u_2 \ldots \forall u_m : \neg P(x, u_1 \ldots u_m)$, then Saboteur can select tiles so that the m-th domino in the row is $\overline{|(m-2)_n u_1 \ldots u_{m-2} 0^n 0^n|(m-1)_n u_1 \ldots u_{m-2} u_{m-1} 0^n|}$ and for any u_m the tile $\overline{|(m-1)_n u_1 \ldots u_{m-2} u_{m-1} 0^n|(m)_n u_m 0^n \ldots 0^n|}$ is not in our set of dominoes. It follows that Constructeur cannot finish the row. ∎

We require the game to have an odd number of moves since we want Constructeur to start and finish the game. This is why the related problem lies in an odd level of the logarithmic time hierarchy. Analogous games could be defined for the even levels.

Complete Problems for $\mathbf{C}_k^l$: the Green Tree

Consider a tree whose leaves can be labeled with either a 1 (the leaf is green) or a 0 (the leaf is brown). We will say that an interior node of the tree is green if more than half of its direct descendants are green. A tree is green if its root is green. We will restrict ourselves to complete trees having degree 2^n, $n \in \mathbb{N}$ i.e. each interior node has 2^n direct descendants. A complete tree with its leaves labeled, having k levels and with every node having 2^n direct descendants will be represented by a list of 2^{kn} bits, each representing the label of one of the leaves. The problem is as follows:

$T(k)$: *Green tree of height k.* Given a list of 2^{kn} bits, does it encode a green tree of k levels?

33. *Proposition.* $T(k)$ is $\mathbf{C}_k^l$ complete.

Proof. We prove that $T(k) \in \mathbf{C}_k^l$. Given $w \in \Gamma^\star$, the length of w can be checked using standard techniques. Suppose $|w| = 2^{kn}$, $n \in \mathbb{N}$.

$$w \in T(k) \iff \mathbf{C}i_1(|i_1| = n) : \mathbf{C}i_2(|i_2| = n) \cdots \mathbf{C}i_k(|i_k| = n) : w_{(i_1 i_2 \ldots i_k)} = 1$$

To see that $T(k)$ is hard for $\mathbf{C}_k^l$, let $L \in \mathbf{C}_k^l$. There is a constant c and a polynomial-time predicate P such that for every $x \in \Gamma^\star$,

$$x \in L \iff \mathbf{C}^{lc} u_1 : \mathbf{C}^{lc} u_2 \cdots \mathbf{C}^{lc} u_k : P(u_1 \ldots u_k)$$

where without loss of generality we assume all thresholds to be $1/2$. We give the reduction from L to $T(k)$. Let n be the smallest power of 2 greater than or equal to $c\lceil \log |x| \rceil$. The image $g(x)$ will have size 2^{kn}, and the function φ defining its bits is simply

$$\varphi(x, (u_1 u_2 \ldots u_k)) = \begin{cases} 1 & \text{if } P(u_1 u_2 \ldots u_k) \\ 0 & \text{if } \neg P(u_1 u_2 \ldots u_k) \end{cases}$$

Unbounded Versions of the Tiling Game and the Green Tree

This subsection is an aside with little relation with the rest of the paper. Observe that the last two problems studied are "bounded" in the sense that we only allow a tiling game to have a constant number of moves, or a tree to have a constant depth. What happens if we do not enforce these limitations? We show that in this case the problems are complete for P.

R': Given a set of tiles of length k, a starting tile t_1 and an ending tile t_2, can Constructeur finish a tiled row from t_1 to t_2, with Saboteur trying to prevent him from reaching his aim, and moving alternatively?

$$T' = \{k \# w : k \in \mathbb{N}, w \in \Gamma^{2^{kn}} \text{ s.t. } w \in T(k)\}$$

34. Proposition. R' and T' are LT-complete for P.

Proof. We see the proof for T'; the one for R' is easier.

To see that $T' \in P$, given $k \# w$, first check $|w| = 2^{kn}$ for a certain $n \in \mathbb{N}$. Then write a string of size $2^{k(n-1)}$ with a labeled list of the nodes at distance 1 from the leaves (encoding them by a 1 if they are green or by a 0 if they are brown), and iterate k times the process until the root is reached. Since $|w| = 2^{kn}$ the process is polynomial with respect to $|w|$.

To see that T' is hard for P, we reduce to T' the problem G described below. G is a simplified version of the problem "Game" which is shown to be complete in P in [12]. The completeness of G for the class P can be proved using the characterization of P in terms of alternating log-space machines [2].

G: Given a two-player game, encoded by a complete tree with every node having exactly n direct descendants and with its leaves labeled 0 (losing position for the first player) or 1 (winning position for the first player), the two players select alternatively a path going from the standing node to one of its descendants. Does the first player have a winning strategy that takes him from the root to a leaf labeled 1?

To reduce G to T', we use a trick similar to the one used by Gill [8] to show that $NP \subseteq PP$. Given a complete tree t with k levels and with each node having exactly n direct descendants (t can be encoded with 2^{kn} bits), we can construct a new tree t', with every node having $2n$ direct descendants. For l equals 1 to k, connect every node of level l in t, with n new trees of $l - 1$ levels, being all the new trees green if l corresponds to a level in which the first player moves, and all ot them brown if l corresponds to a move of the second player. The resulting tree t', that can be encoded with 2^{2kn} bits, is green if an only if in t the first player has a winning strategy. ∎

Succinct Representations

We have fruitfully discussed completeness for many classes of LCH. Let us consider now succinct versions of these problems. As before, the succinct version sA of a problem A on finite functions gets as input a boolean circuit computing a function from Γ^n to Γ^m, and consists of solving the standard problem for the finite function computed by the circuit.

Let us first prove a simple extension of lemma 2 to the classes defined by means of alternating quantifiers.

35. Lemma. If L is a problem in K, $K \in LCH$, then the succinct version of L, sL, is in K', being K' the corresponding exponentially larger class in CH.

Proof. Let $K \in LCH$ and $L \in K$. By definition, for a certain $k \in \mathbb{N}$, a constant c_1, and a log-time predicate P, and for any $x \in \Gamma^*$,

$$x \in L \iff Q_1^{lc_1} i_1 : Q_2^{lc_1} i_2 \cdots Q_k^{lc_1} i_k : P(x, i_1, i_2 \ldots i_k)$$

where each Q_i is an existential, universal, or counting quantifier. Let sL the succinct version of L, and C_x the boolean circuit representation of an instance x. Suppose that C_x receives n bits as input, and produces m bits as output. C_x encodes then a string x of $m2^n$ bits, and since $m + n \leq |C_x|$, we have $2^{|C_x|} \geq |x|$. It follows that for some polynomial p

$$C_x \in sL \iff Q_1^p i_1 : Q_2^p i_2 \cdots Q_k^p i_k : P'(x, i_1, i_2 \ldots i_k)$$

being P' a polynomial-time predicate (respect to C_x) working like P, except that when P queries a bit in a position i of x, P' queries the bit indirectly from C_x using the following process: compute $r = \lfloor \frac{i}{m} \rfloor$, the input that produces the part of x that contains its i-th bit; then feed into the circuit the r-th string of length n in lexicographical order, evaluate it, and select from the output the bit in position $i \bmod m$. This is the i-th bit of x. This simulation process can be done in polynomial time with respect to C_x. It follows that $sL \in K'$. ∎

As a consequence of lemma 35 and theorem 5 (essentially, the Conversion Lemma), the succinct versions of the problems that we have shown to be complete in different classes of LCH are complete in the corresponding classes of CH with respect to the m-reducibility. This includes all the NP-completeness and co-NP-completeness results of [6] and [29] and most of their other results for other classes. The remaining ones are settled in the next section.

36. *Corollary.* The succinct versions of the problems $L_1 \ldots L_{18}$, $R(m)$, and $T(k)$ are complete in the corresponding classes of CH with respect to the m-reducibility.

7. UNDIRECTED ACCESSIBILITY AND RELATED PROBLEMS

The main result in this section is a construction of a graph associated to a given quantified boolean formula, which has the following property: for two selected nodes in the graph, there is a path joining them if and only if the quantified boolean formula is true. Although the size of the graph is exponential in the formula, we will see that it can be described by a considerably shorter boolean circuit which can be constructed from the formula in polynomial time.

We employ this construction to present an ad-hoc proof of the $PSPACE$-hardness of the succinct version of undirected accessibility. From it, combining the Conversion Lemma with known LT-reducibilities among graph problems, we will obtain further classifications of succinct versions of graph problems, including planarity, bipartiteness, connectivity, acyclicity, Eulerian path, and perfect matchings in bipartite graphs. We end the section by discussing the interesting particular case of bounded degree planarity.

The result regarding undirected accessibility can be inferred from the work of [16] on symmetric computation, since they prove that this problem is complete for the class SL of symmetric logarithmic space, and that this class includes L. Therefore, by the Conversion Lemma, the succinct version is $PSPACE$-complete. The interest of the proof we present here is: first, that it is very intuitive and clear, independent of the complex simulations of [16]; second, that it is essentially a natural (albeit nontrivial) extension of a technique of [6] which the authors did not expect to reach any further, as mentioned in their conclusions; third, that it can be immediately seen to apply to planarity for bounded degree graphs, a case for which we are able to completely settle the problem.

Before presenting the construction, let us define *quantified boolean formulas*. A boolean formula is either a boolean variable, its negation, a boolean constant "true" or "false," the conjunction of two boolean formulas, or the disjunction of two boolean formulas. An assignment of boolean values to the variables *satisfies* the formula if and only if once the substitution is made, the formula evaluates to "true." Quantified boolean formulas are boolean formulas preceded by a string of quantifiers (prenex form), each refering to one of the variables of the formula, so that no free variables remain. The allowed quantifiers are $\forall$ and $\exists$. Such a formula is evaluated as follows: $\forall v\, F$ is true if, when substituting "true" and "false" for v, both resulting formulas are true; and $\exists v\, F$ is true if, when substituting "true" and "false" for v, at least one of the resulting formulas is true. Otherwise, the formula evaluates to "false."

The problem QBF is the following: given a quantified boolean formula, decide whether it evaluates to "true." More information about quantified boolean formulas and the problem QBF can be found in [1], including the following fact.

37. *Theorem.* QBF is *PSPACE*-complete.

We present now the construction announced above. We describe it inductively on the form of the formula, by induction on the number of quantifiers. The nodes are identified by sequences of binary numbers. Without loss of generality, we assume that the variables are numbered according to their position in the quantifier string, the innermost being smallest.

Induction Basis. The formula has no quantifiers. Since no free variables are allowed, it evaluates either to "true" or to "false." The associated graph consists of two vertices, labeled 0 and 1, joined by an edge in case the fromula is true, or disconnected if the formula is false. Arbitrarily declare *source node* the node 0 and *target node* the node 1.

Induction Step. We have two cases depending on the outermost quantifier. Let F be the given formula, and assume first that F is $\exists v_i\, F'$. Construct F_0 and F_1 substituting "false" and "true," respectively, for v_i, and inductively consider the graphs associated to them, G_0 and G_1. Re-label all nodes in these graphs by concatenating "$i00;$" and "$i10;$" respectively to their labels. Create two more vertices with labels $i01$ and $i11$. Declare the first *source node* and join it to the source nodes of G_0 and G_1. Declare the other *target node* and join it to the target nodes of G_0 and G_1. The case of F being $\forall v_i\, F'$ is similar, but the graphs are connected in series instead of in parallel, i.e. the new source node is linked to the source of G_0, the target of G_0 is linked to the source of G_1, and the target of G_1 is linked to the new target node.

It is easy to see by induction that the source and target nodes of the obtained graph are connected if and only if the formula evaluates to true. The graph requires exponential time to be constructed, and is itself of size exponential in the size of the formula. However, given the formula, it is possible to decide whether an edge exists between two nodes in time polynomial on the labels of the nodes. Assume that the formula has n variables. If both labels consist of n numbers then the edge corresponds to a nonquantified formula, and the labels provide the value of each variable, so that it only remains to evaluate the formula. This can be done in polynomial time [19].

Else, only sources and targets of the same stage or two consecutive stages can be linked, and this is easy to check by looking at one of the quantifiers in the prefix of the formula.

This algorithm for checking whether an edge exists can be presented by a boolean circuit depending only on the formula F, and the circuit can be constructed in polynomial time from F using the techniques of [15] (see also [1], section 5.4). Thus, we have a circuit C_F which can be constructed in time polynomial in the size of F, which represents a graph in which a source and a target node are selected, such that F evaluates to true if and only if there is a path from the source node to the target node in the graph. This is a polynomial time m-reducibility from QBF to the succinct version of undirected graph accessibility, and therefore we obtain the following theorem:

38. *Theorem.* The succinct version of the graph accessibility problem for undirected graphs is *PSPACE*-hard for the m-reducibility.

A similar reduction works for planarity testing:

39. *Theorem.* The succinct version of the planarity problem for undirected graphs is *PSPACE*-hard for the m-reducibility, even when restricted to graphs of bounded degree.

Proof. Given F, construct a circuit describing a complete graph with five nodes, and then substitute the previously constructed graph for one of the edges, identifying the endpoints with the selected source and target nodes. The resulting graph is nonplanar if and only if there is a path between the source and target nodes, if and only if the formula evaluates to true. Observe that the degree of the graph is bounded. ∎

Some more results will be derived from known relationships between graph problems. In [3] many problems are compared according to projection and constant depth reducibility. Although their projections are reducibilities different from the ones employed here, it is easily seen that all the reductions that we need are actually LT-reductions. We will use also a reduction from [13], where it is stated for logarithmic space reducibility; from the proof it is easily seen that it is also a LT-reduction.

40. *Theorem.* [13] The undirected graph accessibility problem is LT-reducible to the problem of deciding whether an undirected graph is bipartite.

41. *Theorem.* [3] The undirected graph accessibility problem is LT-reducible to the following problems on undirected graphs: connectivity, having a cycle, having an Eulerian path, and having a perfect matching (the last, for bipartite graphs).

In fact, that reference shows that all these problems except perfect matching are equivalent under appropriate reducibilities. From these two results and the Conversion Lemma, for the hardness part, and lemma 2 for the membership part, and using the facts that acyclicity is in L [10], and connectivity, Eulerian path [3], and bipartiteness [13] are in NL, we obtain:

42. *Theorem.* The succinct versions of acyclicity, connectivity, bipartiteness, and Eulerian path are *PSPACE*-complete.

For perfect matching we are left with:

43. *Theorem.* The succinct version of perfect matching is *PSPACE*-hard.

Since perfect matching and planarity are in P, their succinct versions are in *EXPTIME*, and therefore are the only ones left in which the upper and lower bounds are still far apart: we only know their *PSPACE*-hardness. However, we can show that a combination of known results proves that planarity of succinctly represented graphs of bounded degree is in *PSPACE*, and therefore *PSPACE*-complete by theorem 39.

44. *Theorem.* Testing planarity of bounded degree graphs is in *NL*, and therefore its succinct version is *PSPACE*-complete.

Proof. In [21] it is shown that this problem is in the third level of the symmetric complementation logarithmic space hierarchy, which is included by definition in the logarithmic space hierarchy. However, Immerman [11] and Szelepcsényi [25] have shown that *NL* is closed under complementation, and therefore the logarithmic space hierarchy coincides with *NL*. Thus, planarity of bounded degree graphs is in *NL*. ∎

8. DISCUSSION

We have considered decisional problems in which the input is represented in a non-standard form. All combinatorial objects can be naturally encoded as binary words, the adjacency matrix of directed graphs being a prime example. Since such encodings can be viewed as boolean functions, they can be represented by a possibly small boolean circuit. In case the objects are particularly regular, such a representation is shorter than the full standard encoding. Following the research initiated in [6], we have studied how this change in the presentation of the input affects the complexity of the decisional problems.

It was known that the succinctly represented problem is at most exponentially harder than the problem on standard encodings. In [6] it was shown that quite simple succinct graph problems are already *NP*-hard; in [20] it was shown that *NP*-complete standard problems (for projection reducibility) become *NEXPTIME*-complete for succinct inputs, and such an exponential blow-up for problems in P was stated.

By introducing logarithmic-time reducibility and two counting hierarchies corresponding to logarithmic time and polynomial time, we have been able to find a generalization that carries over to other, computationally much weaker classes and yields in a uniform manner all the known lower bounds and many others.

More precisely, our Conversion Lemma shows that LT-reducibilities among the standard problems translate into m-reducibilities among succinctly represented problems, independently of any membership or completeness property of the sets in any particular complexity class. Together with known upper bounds, we get precise classifications of problems in *LCH* and *CH*.

As can be expected, research relating two subjects sheds light on both. In this case, not only we have now a better understanding of the phenomenon of succinct descriptions via boolean circuits, but also we have gained knowledge about the logarithmic-time counting hierarchy, providing very natural complete problems and powerful sufficient conditions to find new ones, and giving precise classifications for problems about finite functions in *LCH* and in *CH* for their succinct version. The logarithmic-time counting hierarchy deserves deeper study, since the union of its classes is precisely the class TC_0 of problems solved by constant depth threshold circuits, which characterizes certain neural computation patterns and other models of fast parallel computation; moreover, this hierarchy is the only one where actual separation results are known between infinitely many classes.

Natural continuations of this work would consist of the study of other languages for the representation of succinct instances, such as those introduced in [28], [29], and [14], where also comparisons between the descriptive power of those languages are made. Is it possible to characterize the complexity jump derived from the use of these languages in such an exact way as for the boolean circuit model?

9. REFERENCES

[1] J.L. Balcázar, J. Díaz, J. Gabarró: *Structural Complexity I*. EATCS Monographs on Theoretical Computer Science, vol. 11, Springer-Verlag (1988).

[2] A. Chandra, D. Kozen, L. Stockmeyer: "Alternation". *Journal ACM* **28** (1981), 114–133.

[3] A. Chandra, L. Stockmeyer, U. Vishkin: "Constant depth reducibility". *SIAM Journal on Computing* **13** (1984), 423–439.

[4] B.S. Chlebus: "Domino-Tiling games". *Journal of Computer and System Sciences* **32** (1986), 374–392.

[5] M. Furst, J.B. Saxe, M. Sipser: "Parity, circuits, and the polynomial-time hierarchy". *Mathematical Systems Theory* **17** (1984), 13–27.

[6] H. Galperin, A. Wigderson: "Succinct representations of graphs". *Information and Control* **56** (1983), 183–198.

[7] M. Garey, D. Johnson: *Computers and Intractability: A Guide to the Theory of NP-completeness*. Freeman (1978).

[8] J. Gill: "Computational complexity of probabilistic Turing machines". *SIAM Journal on Computing* **6** (1977), 675–695.

[9] E. Grädel: "Domino games with an application to the complexity of boolean algebras with bounded quantifier alternation". Proc. 5th Symp. Theor. Aspects of Comp. Sci. LNCS 294, Springer-Verlag (1988), 98–107.

[10] J. Hong: "On some deterministic space complexity problems". *SIAM Journal on Computing* **11** (1982), 591–601.

[11] N. Immerman: "Nondeterministic space is closed under complementation". *SIAM Journal on Computing* **17** (1988), 935–938.

[12] N. Jones, W. Laaser: "Complete problems for deterministic polynomial time". *Theoretical Computer Science* **3** (1977), 105–117.

[13] N.D. Jones, E. Lien, W.T. Laaser: "New problems complete for nondeterministic log space". *Mathematical Systems Theory* **10** (1976), 1–17.

[14] M. Kowaluk, K. Wagner: "Vector language: simple description of hard instances". Proc. Math. Found. of Comp. Sci. LNCS 452, Springer-Verlag (1990), 378–384.

[15] R.E. Ladner: "The circuit value problem is log space complete for *P*". *SIGACT News* **7** (1975), 18–20.

[16] H.R. Lewis, Ch. Papadimitriou: "Symmetric space-bounded computation". *Theoretical Computer Science* **19** (1982), 161–187.

[17] A. Lozano: "*NP*-hardness on succinct representations of graphs". *Bulletin of the EATCS* **35** (1988), 158–163.

[18] A. Lozano, J.L. Balcázar: "The complexity of graph problems for succinctly represented graphs". Proc. Graph-Theoretic Concepts in Comp. Sci. LNCS 411, Springer-Verlag (1989), 277–285.

[19] N. Lynch: "Logspace recognition and translation of parenthesis languages". *Journal ACM* **24** (1977), 583–590.

[20] C.H. Papadimitriou, M. Yannakakis: "A note on succinct representations of graphs". *Information and Control* **71** (1986), 181–185.

[21] J.H. Reif: "Symmetric complementation". *Journal ACM* **31** (1984), 401–421.

[22] M. Sipser: "Borel sets and circuit complexity". Proc. 15th Symp. Theory of Comp. (1983), 61–69.

[23] S. Skyum, L.G. Valiant: "A complexity theory based on boolean algebra". *Journal ACM* **32** (1985), 484–502.

[24] L.J. Stockmeyer: "The polynomial time hierarchy". *Theoretical Computer Science* **3** (1977), 1–22.

[25] R. Szelepcsényi: "The method of forced enumeration for nondeterministic automata". *Acta Informatica* **26** (1988), 279–284.

[26] J. Torán: "Succinct representations of counting problems". 6th Int. Conference on Applied Algebra, Algebraic Algorithms, and Error Correcting Codes LNCS 357, Springer-Verlag (1988), 415–426.

[27] J. Torán: "Complexity classes defined by counting quantifiers". *Journal ACM* **38**, 753–774.

[28] K. Wagner: "The complexity of problems concerning graphs with regularities". Proc. Math. Found. of Comp. Sci. LNCS 176, Springer-Verlag (1984), 544–552.

[29] K. Wagner: "The complexity of combinatorial problems with succinct input representation". *Acta Informatica* **23** (1986), 325–356.

PARALLEL ALGORITHMS FOR NP-COMPLETE PROBLEMS

J. M. Robson

Australian National University
GPO Box 4
Canberra, ACT 2601
Australia

INTRODUCTION

The discovery of the NP-Complete problems has created a vigorous industry producing proofs of NP-Completeness. But does NP-Completeness really imply intractability of interesting instances? This question seems to divide the Computer Science community into two camps, the pessimists who believe that NP-Complete problems require exponential resources and are therefore intractable and the optimists who expect a subexponential algorithm to emerge eventually. There is however a viable third belief, namely that the resources required do rise exponentially but slowly enough for large practical problems to be tractable. A number of algorithms have been reported, using an approach more sophisticated than the obvious search of all possible solutions to achieve run times significantly less than the naive approach would suggest (Iwama, 1987; Schroeppel and Shamir, 1981; Stearns and Hunt, 1990; Tanaka, 1991) but on a sequential machine these do not yet seem to solve real large problems in reasonable time. On the other hand the naive approach to most NP-Complete problems parallelises easily but yields an algorithm which is too slow even on large parallel machines. However, where the sophisticated algorithms can be parallelised, the result may well be that very large problems which have appeared intractable can be solved quite easily with machines which exist today and will be cheap tomorrow. One interesting development in this direction is described by Ferreira (this volume).

RANDOM INSTANCES OF SAT

We will illustrate another approach by describing an algorithm for resolving instances of CNF satisfiability. The algorithm performs well on average for moderate sized problems and we are currently engaged in implementing it for a parallel machine with a speed up which is less than optimal only by a factor depending on the efficiency of sorting.

The claim of reasonable average case behaviour depends heavily on the model of random instances. We have chosen the one favoured by other writers on this subject, namely that of a determined number of clauses over a determined number of variables where each literal (a variable or its negation) occurs in each clause with a probability p independent of other clauses and other literals. We restrict our attention to instances where the number of clauses is polynomial in the number v of variables since, otherwise, brute force search has a run time fairly small as a function of the input length n, namely $o(2^{n^{1/k}})$ for any k.

Outside a fairly narrow range of values of p the instances produced in this way are somewhat uninteresting because a trivial algorithm will settle a typical case. On the one hand, if p is large, say $\Omega(v^{-1+\alpha})$ for positive α, the number of literals in an average clause is large and the proportion of assignments of values to the variables which fail to satisfy the clause is very small; thus a super-polynomial length expression is required before the clause might possibly not be satisfiable. On the other hand, if p is small, say $O(v^{-1})$, the average number of literals is bounded as v increases so that there is a probability bounded away from zero of any clause containing zero literals and so being unsatisfiable. Thus as v and the number of clauses increase, the probability of an expression not being trivially unsatisfiable decreases towards zero. It is interesting (and somewhat disappointing) to note that the claims of polynomial average behaviour (Iwama, (1989); Purdom and Brown, (1985, 1987); have concerned values of p which suffer from one or other of these problems. To avoid the two extremes of almost certain satisfiability and almost certain unsatisfiability, we choose to deal with those values of p which give a probability of satisfiability close to ½. It is not obvious what values of p will achieve this but, in practice, values of p close to $\ln v / v$ and expressions of v clauses seem to come close to it. Another reasonable approach would be to fix the number of literals in each clause, for instance to three; the method reported here would still be viable in that case but no analysis has yet been done of its performance.

SOLUTION BY COUNTING

The basis of our method is the idea, apparently first published by Iwama (1987, 1989), of determining satisfiability by counting the number of non-satisfying assignments. The number of assignments failing to satisfy a given non-tautologous clause is easily seen to be $2^{number\ of\ variables\ not\ occurring\ in\ the\ clause}$ and the number simultaneously failing to satisfy all of a set of clauses is similarly $2^{number\ of\ variables\ not\ occurring\ in\ the\ set}$ unless some variable occurs both positively and negatively in the set in which case it is zero. Now counting the number of clauses failing to satisfy at least one clause is achieved by a standard inclusion/exclusion counting process. This inclusion/exclusion process has a very regular structure and is easily parallelisable. The clue to efficient use of this principle in the range of values of interest lies in drastically reducing the number of sets of clauses considered while retaining the parallelisable structure.

The process can be visualised as the construction of a tree whose nodes correspond to those sets of clauses which do not contain any two complementary literals. Starting with a single node which represents the empty set of clauses (having first discarded any tautologous clauses), we repeatedly add a new layer of nodes to the tree where a node in the i th layer is obtained by adding clause number i to each existing node in the tree except those which contain a literal complementary to one in clause i. Each node has a weight of $2^{number\ of\ variables\ occurring\ in\ none\ of\ the\ clauses} \times (-1)^{number\ of\ clauses\ -\ 1}$ and the required number of non-satisfying assignments is simply the sum of the weights of the nodes other than the initial node.

FROM TREES TO GRAPHS

Once the construction is complete as far as a certain layer, the sum of the weights of the remaining nodes can be expressed as a linear function of the weights of existing nodes. This suggests that two nodes can be amalgamated if they have equal coefficients in this linear function. Unfortunately the coefficients are not known until the construction is complete. The improvements made to the algorithm consist of locating pairs of nodes whose coefficients are obviously going to turn out to be equal.

The first modification to the process is to identify any two or more nodes on the same layer whose clauses contain identical sets of literals. This modification turns the tree into a directed acyclic graph and means that the weight of a node is to be computed as a sum of contributions from its immediate predecessors, each contribution being $-\ weight\ of\ predecessor \times 2^{-\ number\ of\ new\ variables\ introduced}$ but otherwise the process remains the same. A sorting step can be used at each layer to locate and amalgamate sets of identified nodes. It is even possible to identify nodes on different layers though this complicates the program, as a node can now be its own successor violating the dag structure. This apparently simple modification reduces the number of nodes to be considered to a reasonable level even for very large problems. We can derive an expression for the expected number of nodes in the graph for given numbers of variables and clauses and probability $(v, c$ and $p)$, namely $\sum_{s=1}^{v} 2^s \binom{v}{s} \sum_{i=1}^{c} (1-(1-p)^i)^s x^i (1-x)^{c-i} \binom{c}{i}$ where $x = (1-p)^{2v-s}$ is the probability that a given clause contains no literals other than those in a given set of s literals. If we fix p as $\ln v / v$ and consider expressions with v clauses, then the expected number of nodes is 6.815×10^{12} for $v = 200$ and appears to be rising roughly proportionally to $2^{v/6}$. Since the time complexity of the algorithm is bounded by this number of nodes $\times v \times c$, this shows that apparently enormous problems can possibly be resolved. For the case $p = (\ln v / v)^{1/2}$ considered in Iwama (1989) and proved solvable in expected polynomial time, the expected number of nodes turns out to be less than 2, reflecting the fact that it is unlikely that any non-tautologous clauses exist.

A further improvement comes from the observation that the information kept about each node (apart from its weight) can be reduced to two sets, firstly the set of later clauses with which the node is "compatible" (i.e. the literals making up the node contain no literals complementary with a literal of the later clause), to determine the graph structure, and secondly the set of literals from those later clauses which already occur at the node, (needed to compute the weights of new nodes). Once a node is represented by these two sets, it becomes apparent that any two or more nodes for which the two sets are identical can be identified (and their weights added). Again this simple modification reduces the number of nodes enormously though we no longer know how to compute exactly the expected number of nodes for given parameters. However we can compute an upper bound since, given the number of clauses in a potential compatible set S and given the number of variables present in that set and how many of them are present in their positive and negative forms, we can compute the probability that this set and a given subset L of its literals is the (compatibility set, literal set) pair of a set of a given number of earlier clauses; these probabilities are far from independent but we can bound the probability that (S, L) is the (compatibility set, literal set) pair of some earlier set of clauses by the minimum of 1 and the sum of all the probabilities involving S and L. As an example of the reduction obtained, the expected number of nodes for the parameters (50, 50, 0.04) after the first improvement was 3.0×10^7; the upper bound after the second improvement gives 4.0×10^5.

FURTHER WORK

The considerable success of these two fairly minor modifications to Iwama's algorithm can be explained by the preponderance of nodes which can be identified near the fringe of the tree. In these parts of the tree, where nodes already represent large sets of literals which will be compatible with very few remaining clauses, the number of nodes collapses dramatically as a result of our two stages of identification. But the trees in question, being fairly "bushy", have most of their nodes near the leaves so that collapsing these nodes is enough to reduce the overall number of nodes enormously.

A sequential version of the algorithm has been tested so far with encouraging results. It processed 100 expressions each of 50 clauses in 50 variables with $p = 0.04$ in four hours (on a SUN 3). It turned out that 75 of these randomly generated expressions were satisfiable showing that the choice of p came close to the desired value which would make half of all clauses generated satisfiable. The greatest number of nodes in the dag was 142906 compared with the computed upper bound on the average mentioned above of 4.0×10^5. These results suggest that when the parallel version is completed it will be able to handle hard instances with up to about 100 clauses in 100 variables in a reasonable time. (The upper bound, which we have seen to be fairly pessimistic gives 4.2×10^9 for 96 clauses on 96 variables with p equal to 0.025.) The limitation seems to be more in the space required for storing the nodes of the dag (edges need no explicit representation) than in the time. It has been noted that sorting can be used to locate pairs of nodes to be identified. The sequential version of the algorithm does not do this but uses a hash table instead. In the parallel version, sorting is essential to get a constructed node to the appropriate processor to handle it but it is not obvious if nodes should be sorted on the bit pattern representing the information describing the node (compatibility set, literal set) or on a hash function of this information: with the first method constructed nodes will tend to be roughly in sorted order reducing the time spent sorting; with the second method good load balancing between processors will be obtained automatically by taking certain bits of the hash function as the processor number.

Once the parallel implementation (on a Connection Machine) is complete, it will be used to gather information about the differences between the random distribution considered so far and possibly more realistic distributions such as the distribution obtained by fixing the number of literals per clause and randomly choosing a set of literals of exactly that size (with or without a prohibition of complementary pairs of literals).

The observation that space is more important than time suggests that it will be worthwhile doing more work on each node to reduce the number of nodes constructed. Two ways of doing this seem worth investigation. The first is to update the information held at each node on which later clauses are compatible, removing mention of a clause as soon as its corresponding layer has been constructed. This will imply also updating the information about variables in the node which occur in these compatible clauses. If these updates are made, pairs of nodes may be identified later in the process which were distinct earlier and nodes constructed later are more likely to be identified with ones from earlier layers; this suggestion will not change the total number of nodes in the graph but it will reduce the number active at a given stage of the computation and so the critical space requirement. The second approach is to note that two nodes with the same compatibility sets but different literal sets may be identified if, for instance, the two literal sets can be transformed one into the other by exchanging pairs of literals which are equivalent with respect to the clauses in the compatibility set; (where two literals are equivalent with respect to a set of clauses if they each occur in the same subset of the clauses). The amount of work which it will be worthwhile to expend on this type of analysis will depend critically on the ratio of computation speed to communication speed and so can only be determined by experimentation.

REFERENCES

1. A. Ferreira, Parallel search in sorted multisets, and applications to NP-Complete problems, this volume.
2. K. Iwama, Complementary approaches to CNF Boolean equations, *in* "Discrete Algorithms and Complexity", Academic Press, New York, (1987), pp223-236.
3. K. Iwama, CNF satisfiability test by counting and average polynomial time, *SIAM J. Comput.* 18 (1989), pp385-391.
4. P. Purdom and C. Brown, The pure literal rule and polynomial average time, *SIAM J. Comput.* 14 (1985), pp943-953.
5. P. Purdom and C. Brown, Polynomial-average-time satisfiability problems, *Inform. Sci.* 41 (1987), pp23-42.
6. R. Schroeppel and A. S. Shamir, A $T=O(2^{n/2})$, $S=O(2^{n/4})$ algorithm for certain NP-Complete problems, *SIAM J. Comput.* 10 (1981), pp 456-464.
7. R. E. Stearns and H. B. Hunt III, Power Indices and Easier Hard Problems, *Mathematical Systems Theory* 23 (1990), pp209-225.
8. Y. Tanaka, A dual algorithm for the satisfiability problem, *IPL* 37 (1991), pp85-89.

PARALLEL SEARCH IN SORTED MULTISETS, AND NP–COMPLETE PROBLEMS

Afonso G. Ferreira[1]

CNRS - LIP/IMAG
Ecole Normale Supérieure de Lyon
69364 Lyon Cédex 07
France
ferreira@lip.ens-lyon.fr

INTRODUCTION

The quest for effective resolutions of NP-Complete problems has helped to develop a number of techniques for algorithm design, usually related to the proposition of subexponential algorithms that use properties of special data structures to allow the treatment of larger instances. While many results exist for solving NP-Complete problems in a sequential model [Gar79,...], one attempt to *exactly* solve an NP-Complete problem (the subset sum problem) in parallel has been reported in [Kar84], where the parallel time complexity was the same as the time of the initial sequential algorithm. Only the space complexity was improved. On the other hand, the solution of extremely large subset sum problems can be *approximated* in parallel, with the help of some random branching techniques [Fe89] that do not terminate if there is no solution to the problem. Such an approach is theoretically justified since it has been shown that the probability that the subset sum problem has a solution (under some restrictions on the input) tends to one with the size of the problem [Ka86].

In this paper, we use the theory of partial ordered sets to show how parallel machines can bring very large instances of some NP-Complete problems under the reach of an *exact* solution. Clearly, parallelism cannot change the exponential complexity of such problems. However, up to our knowledge, the parallel algorithm we present in this paper is the first to require a feasible amount of memory space per processor, still yielding an optimal speedup over the sequential subexponential time complexity. This algorithm was initially designed to search in a special data structure called sorted multisets, which is closely related to a certain class of NP-Complete problems. Since no parallel algorithm existed to search such a structure, this paper can be viewed either as new results in the theory of partial ordered sets or as an attempt to seek for effective means to solve large NP-Complete problems. We also propose new sequential algorithms for searching and selecting special subsets of the set formed by the Cartesian sum of two sorted vectors of cardinality n (i.e., sorted X+Y).

Sorted multisets are important data structures that can be applied, for instance, in statistics, partially ordered sets or VLSI design [Har75,Fre82,Mir84,Fre84,Lin85]. An nxn matrix is said to have sorted rows (columns) if each of its rows (columns) respects some total order. When its rows and columns are ordered a matrix is called sorted. A particular case of the class of sorted matrices occurs when a matrix A can be defined as the cartesian

---

[1] On leave from the University of Sao Paulo, Brazil. Member of the BID/USP project.

sum of two sorted n-vectors X and Y: A=X+Y, i.e., $a_{ij}=x_i+y_j$. Finally, we call sorted multiset the summation $\sum X_i$, where all the vectors X_i are sorted.

Search, selection and sorting in sorted matrices and X+Y have received considerable attention in the literature. Searching sorted X+Y and sorted matrices for a given element has been proved to have complexity $\Theta(n)$ [Cos89b].

The existing order of the rows and columns of a sorted matrix was proved not to help the task of sorting its elements, i.e., the complexity of the sorting problem in sorted matrices is $\Theta(n^2 \log n)$. On the other hand, a non constructive proof was given in [Fr75] for an upper bound on $O(n^2)$ for the number of comparisons required for sorting the elements of sorted X+Y, and an $O(n^2 \log n)$ time, $O(n^2)$ comparison algorithm was proposed in [Lam90].

Finally, the complexity of selecting the k-th smallest element in sorted matrices [Fre84] and in sorted X+Y [Cos89c] was proved to be $\Theta(\sqrt{k})$. In X+Y other cases have been studied, depending on whether the vectors are sorted or not [Joh78a,Joh78b,Fre82].

Most of the results described above could be extended to arbitrary dimensions. For instance, sorted m-cubes - the generalization of sorted matrices, from dimension 2 to dimension m -, cannot be searched in less than $\Omega(n^{m-1})$ and this bound is tight [Lin85]. However, studying the complexity of the search problem in sorted multisets ($\sum X_i$, X_i sorted) appeared more complex than a natural generalization of the bounds obtained for the dimension 2. For instance, search in sorted X+Y+R+S can be performed in $O(n^2)$ time (i.e., $\Omega(n^3)$ is not a lower bound !) with $O(n^2)$ storage requirements. Surprisingly, if only $O(n)$ memory space is available then it is still possible to efficiently solve this problem in time $O(n^2 \log n)$. On the other hand, some apparently simple problems remain open. Take for instance the case where m=3: search in sorted X+Y+Z with only $O(n)$ memory space has a trivial lower bound for the running time on $\Omega(n)$ but no better algorithm known than in time $O(n^2)$ [Cos89b].

Parallel algorithms were proposed for searching in sorted matrices and in sorted X+Y, with the aim of trading off model of computation (shared or distributed memory), number of processors and time/space requirements [Cos89a]. Due to its applications to the resolution of NP-Complete problems, an important question concerns the existence of a parallel algorithm to search in X+Y+R+S with the restriction that only $O(n)$ memory space is allowed.

In this paper, we show an algorithm to solve the problem of searching sorted X+Y+R+S for a given element, on a distributed memory machine (D-RAM) with $O(n)$ memory space per processor. If the number of processors is less than the number of elements in each vector, then the algorithm is cost optimal, i.e., it yields an optimal speedup. In particular, with the use of such an algorithm large instances of some NP-Complete problems (100 or more variables) would be within reach of feasible parallel systems, depending on the constants involved. Solving such a problem with only $O(n)$ total storage requirements on a D-RAM is still open.

This paper is organized as follows. In the next section we recall some concepts of the theory of sorted matrices and sorted multisets, and also show how to use such data structures to solve some NP-Complete problems. In Section 3 some properties of searching in sorted X+Y are adressed and in section 4 new algorithms are introduced. The parallel algorithm for searching in sorted X+Y+R+S with only $O(n)$ space per processor is given in section 5 and its time complexity proved. We conclude by discussing some open problems and directions for further research.

PRELIMINARIES

Model of Computation

We suppose that we are given p processing elements PE_i, $1 \leq i \leq p < n$, connected through an interconnection network. Each PE_i has $O(n)$ local memory space and communicates with its neighbors through the interconnection network links. The cost of an elementary operation inside a processor is $O(1)$, and sending/receiving a constant piece of data to/from a neighbor costs also $O(1)$.

Sorted Matrices and Multisets

An nxn matrix is called a sorted matrix if its rows and columns are ordered. Without loss of generality, suppose that a matrix is sorted if each row and each column is sorted in increasing order. A particular case of sorted matrices are the matrices defined as the cartesian sum of two sorted n-vectors, i.e., there exist two sorted vectors of cardinality n, X and Y, such that each element of a matrix $A=X+Y$ ($a_{ij}=x_i+y_j$) can be obtained in constant time from X and Y. One of the main advantages of the $X+Y$ data structure is that it contains $O(n^2)$ elements that can be stored with only $O(n)$ memory space.

The generalization of this definition to higher dimensions is straightforward. A sorted cube A on $\{1,...,n\}^m$ is composed of m dimensions with n elements each, for a total of n^m elements. Furthermore, the elements in each dimension are sorted (in an increasing order). A sorted multiset is a sorted cube A defined as the sum of m sorted vectors of cardinality n: $A=\sum X_i$, $1 \leq i \leq m$, where $A[i_1,...,i_m] = X_1[i_1] + ... + X_m[i_m]$.

We are particularly interested in searching sorted multisets where m=4. Throughout this paper we shall refer to this special case as search in sorted $X+Y+R+S$.

Sorted Multisets and NP-Complete Problems

Schroeppel and Shamir defined the class of NP-Complete problems that are *polynomially enumerable* (whose input size is n') that could be solved in time $O(n' 2^{n'/2})$ and space $O(2^{n'/4})$ [Sch81] (*cf.* Appendix A). Their algorithm, known as the two-list four-table algorithm is essentially based on the two-list algorithm, introduced by Horowitz and Sahni, which was used to solve the knapsack problem in time $O(n' 2^{n'/2})$ and space $O(2^{n'/2})$ [Hor74]. (It is important to notice, however, that the two-list four-table algorithm had been first proposed in [Ahr75].)

An instance of the knapsack problem (also known as the subset sum problem) consists of a n' weights and a target value M, the knapsack capacity. The goal is then to find a combination of the weights whose sum is exactly M. Suppose that the weights are divided into two sub-vectors of cardinality n'/2. In its first step the two-list algorithm generates, two increasingly sorted lists A and B, of $2^{n'/2}$ elements each, with all the subset sums of each sub-vector. Since the solution of the knapsack problem, becomes a composition of an element of list A with an element of list B, then the two-list algorithm proceeds as follows: the starting element (a_i+b_j) to be compared to M is formed by the sum of the smallest element of A with the largest element of B ($a_1+b_{2^{n'/2}}$). The following is then repeated until a solution is found or one of the lists becomes empty: if the sum (a_i+b_j) adds to M then a solution has been found. Otherwise, because the two lists are sorted in an increasing order, if the sum (a_i+b_j) is smaller than M then i becomes i+1, else j becomes j-1.

Notice that such a procedure is the same as searching a structure of the type sorted $X+Y$ for a given element (M, in this case). The two-list four-table algorithm from [Sch81] uses exactly the same method, with only one difference, that the elements of the lists A and B, above, shall be generated upon request, with the help of two priority queues (heaps) holding $O(2^{n'/4})$ elements each. Thus, each of the lists A and B is in its turn of the type sorted $X+Y$, being formed by the cartesian sum of two other sorted tables. (Notice that this is the same as search in sorted $X+Y+R+S$ under the strict parenthesization $(X+Y) + (R+S)$). The time complexity of the two-list four-table algorithm is the same as the two-list algorithm, since at most $2.2^{n'/2}$ elements are generated, at the cost of updating the heaps for each element, that is, in total time $O(n' 2^{n'/2})$. On the other hand the space complexity was reduced to $O(2^{n'/4})$ (*cf.* [Sch81] for details).

The same technique summarized above can be used to solve a larger class of NP-Complete problems, by simply changing the definition of the usual operator "+" to some other composition operators. The definitions from [Sch81] that characterize the class of polynomially enumerable NP-Complete problems which can be solved by the two-list four-table algorithm, are shown in Appendix A. Satisfiability, exact satisfiability and knapsack are examples of such problems ([Sch81]).

We remark that an instance of a polynomially enumerable problem can be solved through search in sorted multisets. The explicit generation of the sorted sets can be considered as a preprocessing phase. The overall time complexity is then the maximum between the time taken by the preprocessing and the search phases.

SEARCH AND SELECTION IN X+Y

Before introducing the main result of this paper, i.e., a parallel algorithm to search sorted X+Y+R+S, we need some techniques used for search and selection in sorted X+Y.

Search

We have indicated in the Introduction that the complexity of searching sorted X+Y for a given element z is $\Theta(n)$. An optimal sequential algorithm to solve this problem is as follows [Cos89b]:

Algorithm find(X,Y,z);

> i:=n ; j:=1 ;
> **While** ((i≥1) **and** (j≤n)) **do**
> > **If** ($x_i + y_j = z$) **then** return (i,j) ;
> > **If** ($x_i + y_j > z$) **then** i:=i-1 **else** j:=j+1 ;
> **end-while.**

Figure 1. Algorithm find.

Search in sorted X+Y+R+S

For the sake of clarity we recall from [Cos89b] an algorithm to search sorted X+Y+R+S for a given element z. We suppose that in a preprocessing phase two heaps H and H' were initialized with $\{x_n + y_t \mid 1 \le t \le n\}$ and $\{r_1 + s_q \mid 1 \le q \le n\}$, respectively. I.e., H contains all the elements of the last row of X+Y, while H' holds the first row of R+S. This is so because H will be a max-heap and H' a min-heap.

The idea is to successively generate the elements of X+Y (and R+S) in sorted order. The elements of X+Y are generated in a decreasing order, while the elements of R+S are generated in an increasing order. Hence, starting from the very first element of X+Y and the very last element of R+S), a simulation of algorithm *find* that searches in ((X+Y) + (R+S)) is obtained.

This algorithm requires O(n) auxiliary storage to store the heaps H and H'. Its time complexity is the same as for algorithm *find*, where each vector is of cardinality n^2, except for updating the heaps at each step. It takes then $O(n^2 \log n)$ time to search in X+Y+R+S.

Algorithm findfour(z,X,Y,R,S,H,H',M)

> i:=M ; j:=1 ;
> (a_1,b_1) := pair with the largest sum in H ; /* the root of H */
> (a_2,b_2) := pair with the smallest sum in H' ; /* the root of H' */
> **While** ((i≥1) **and** (j≤M)) **do**
> > **If** (($a_1 + b_1$) + ($a_2 + b_2$) = z) **then** halt ; /*the search is successful */
> > **If** (($a_1 + b_1$) + ($a_2 + b_2$) > z)
> > > **then** delete (a_1,b_1) from H ; i:=i-1 ;
> > > > **if** {the predecessor a'_1 of a_1 in X is defined}
> > > > > **then** insert (a'_1,b_1) into H ;
> > > **else** delete (a_2,b_2) from H' ; j:=j+1 ;
> > > > **if** {the successor a'_2 of a_2 in R is defined}
> > > > > **then** insert (a'_2,b_2) into H ;
> > **end-if** ;
> **end-while.**

Figure 2. Algorithm findfour.

Selection

In the next section we will also require a procedure that selects, for a given k, the k-th smallest element of sorted X+Y. We saw in the Introduction that this can be done in time $\Theta(\sqrt{k})$. We shall refer to such an algorithm as algorithm *select*(k,X,Y) [Fre84].

NEW ALGORITHMS IN X+Y

In this section, we introduce some new results that will be used in the next section. The sequential algorithms that follow are essential to the development of our solution.

Let q be a divisor of n. Let the vectors X and Y be divided into q blocks each, BX_i and BY_i, $1 \leq i \leq q$, with n/q successive elements per block. Notice that algorithm *find* (figure 1) defines a path on the X+Y matrix. Furthermore, such a path defines all the BX_i+BY_j matrices, $1 \leq i,j \leq q$, that could contain z, and we can show that the number of such matrices is restricted.

Lemma 1.   *Let nsm be the number of submatrices BX_i+BY_j, $1 \leq i,j \leq q$, that can contain z in the structure defined above. Then nsm < 2q.*

Proof:
Let LBX and LBY be two lists formed by the last element of each block BX and BY, respectively. Consider LBX in a decreasing order and LBY in an increasing order.

Let the elements of LBX and LBY be indexed from 1 to q. Let r_i, $1 \leq r_i \leq q$, be the position resulting from the search of lbx_i into LBY:
$$LBY[r_i] > z-lbx_i > LBY[r_i+1].$$

Therefore, regarding BX_1, z can belong to the submatrices generated by the cartesian sum of BX_1 and (r_1+1) blocks of Y, namely $BY_1, ..., BY_{r_1}$, and BY_{r_1+1}. Regarding BX_2, z can belong to the submatrices generated by the cartesian sum of BX_1 and $BY_{r_1+1}, ..., BY_{r_2}$, and BY_{r_2+1}. In general, the submatrices that can contain z are formed by the cartesian sum of BX_i and $BY_{r_{i-1}+1}, ..., BY_{r_i+1}$.

It is easy to see that for each BX_i the number of submatrices to search is $(r_i - r_{i-1} + 1)$. Hence,

$$nsm = r_1+1+\sum_{2}^{q} (r_i-r_{i-1}+1) = q+r_q \leq 2q.$$

In order to have *nsm*=2q it should hold that $r_q=q$. In this case, however, since $LBY[r_q]$ is the last element of LBY, the number of submatrices generated by the block BX_q is r_q-r_{q-1} and no longer $1+r_q-r_{q-1}$. Thus nsm < 2q. []

Lemma 2. *Let $z=x_u+y_v$, an element of sorted X+Y, be given. Then the successive generation of z and its immediate q successors in an increasing or a decreasing order can be done in O(q log n) sequential time, with O(n) preprocessing time and O(n) space.*

Proof:
Suppose that we want to successively generate z and its immediate q successors in an *increasing* order. Since X is sorted, it is sufficient to distinguish a set containing, for each column, the smallest element that is larger than z. Such a set surely contains the successor of z in the total order over X+Y. Furthermore the successor of z is the minimum element of this set. Therefore, we build a min-heap from this set and each time an element is chosen as the next element in the sorted order, it is substituted by its successor in its column and the heap updated.

To generate the successors of z in a *decreasing* order is analogous, this time with the help of a max-heap.

In order to efficiently generate such heaps we first apply algorithm *selectnextset*, introduced below, to determine the set of elements to initialize the heap. Secondly, any linear algorithm for constructing a heap H from a set L (say, algorithm *buildheap*(H,L,order), where order indicates whether the heap is to be built in an increasing or decreasing partial order) can be used [Gon86,Mcd89], enabling us to generate as many successors of z, in sorted order, as requested.

Algorithm selectnextset(X,Y,z,nextset,ord);

```
If ord='incr'
    then        i:=1 ; j:=n ;
                While ((i≤n) and (j≥1)) do
                    If (x_i+y_j < z)
                            then        i:=i+1
                            else
                                        {insert x_i+y_j into nextset};
                                        j:=j-1;
                    end-if;
                end-while
    else        i:=n ; j:=1 ;
                While ((i≥1) and (j≤n)) do
                    If (x_i+y_j > z)
                            then        i:=i-1
                            else
                                        {insert x_i+y_j into nextset};
                                        j:=j+1;
                    end-if;
                end-while ;
end-if.
```

Figure 3. Algorithm selectnextset.

Proposition 1. The time complexity of algorithm selectnext is O(n).

Proof:

An execution of the algorithm *selectnext* is composed by a single while loop. []

Once the set of candidates has been selected, algorithm *generateheap* introduced below initializes a priority queue to further utilisation.

Algorithm generateheap(X,Y,z,H,order);

```
selectnextset(X,Y,z,nextset,order);
buildheap(H,nextset,order).
```

Figure 4. Algorithm generateheap.

Proposition 2. The time complexity of algorithm generateheap is O(n).

Proof:
It stems from proposition 1 and [Gon86,Mcd89]. []

At this point, the heap is initialized with all the candidates in X+Y to be the successor of z. To generate the q successors of z, every time an element of X+Y, say x_u+y_v, is chosen from the priority queue, then the data structure is updated in such a way that it contains **next**(x_u+y_v), the successor of x_u+y_v.

Algorithm generate-q-successors(X,Y,z,order,q);

generateheap(X,Y,z,H,order);
i:=1 ;
While ((i≤q) **and** (H is not empty)) **do**
 (a,b) := pair with the smallest sum in H' ; /* the root of H' */
 return(a,b) ;
 i:=i+1 ;
 delete (a,b) from H ;
 if {the predecessor a' of a in X is defined}
  then insert (a',b) into H ;
end-while.

Figure 5. Algorithm generate-q-successors.

Proposition 3. *The time complexity of algorithm generate-q-successors is $O(n + q \log n)$.*

Proof:
 The call to generateheap costs $O(n)$, and at most q elements are generated, costing $O(\log n)$ time each for updating the heap. []

Since only the input vectors and a heap of n elements are used, the space complexity is $O(n)$. This completes the proof of the lemma. []

THE PARALLEL SEARCH ALGORITHM

We suppose that at the beginning of the algorithm the four sorted vectors are stored in the local memory of each PE_i, $1 \le i \le p < n$. The correctness of our parallel search algorithm stems from algorithm *findfour* (figure 2) along with lemma 1. Below we first discuss its basic steps and then show how they can be implemented in a distributed environment in the claimed time complexity. The number p of processors is restricted to be strictly smaller than the cardinality of the vectors ; otherwise the total *memory* available on the system would be at least $O(n^2)$ and the problem could achieve a p-fold speedup (for some range values of p) by simply generating (X+Y) and (R+S), and sorting them together [Fer89].
The main result we prove is :

Theorem 1. *Let $p < n$ processors be coupled in parallel, each with $O(n)$ memory space. Let each processor have a copy of four vectors of cardinality n: X, Y, R, and S. Then the problem of parallel search in sorted X+Y+R+S can be solved in time $O((n^2 \log n)/p)$, which is optimal.*

Proof:
 Let A=X+Y and B=R+S be two virtual tables of size $N=n^2$. We mean by virtual that they are never really generated; we refer to an element a_i (b_i) but it is actually defined by the sum of an element in X and an element in Y (R and S, respectively).
 From lemma 1 we know that search in A+B can be reduced to search in at most 2p submatrices of A+B, if a preprocessing is done in two sublists from A and B. These sublists - called LBA and LBB - are such that $LBA=\{A_{N/p}, A_{2N/p}, \ldots, A_N\}$ and $LBB=\{B_N, B_{(p-1)N/p}, \ldots, B_{N/p}\}$ and can be obtained by p selections in X+Y and p selections in R+S. Notice that LBA is in an increasing order, while LBB is in a decreasing order.
 Following the steps described at lemma 1, once both sublists have been generated, we should find, for each lba_i, its respective r_i. An efficient way is to perform a merge between LBA and LBB', where $lbb'_i = z - lbb_i$. At the end of this merge, the submatrices $(BA_i + BB_j)$ to be searched have been determined.

The main problem is then how to search such submatrices. Search in the cartesian sum of two sorted vectors cannot be used as is, because the blocks BA_i and BB_j are virtual, and we only know the first element of each one. Similarly, since each block is itself a subset of the cartesian sum of two sorted vectors, one would be inclined to apply search in sorted multisets to perform the search operation. Unfortunately, however, each block BA_i is not formed by the cartesian sum of *contiguous* elements of X with *contiguous* elements of Y. Actually they contain a first element - which is known -, from LBA, and its N/p successors in the *total order* over X+Y, which are not known. It is analogous for the blocks BB_j.

Therefore, we need to successively generate, in sorted order, a number of elements of the table A (respectively, B), starting from the very first element of BA_i (resp., BB_j). This can be done by a technique similar to the one described in Lemma 2. Two heaps are initialized with the candidates in X+Y (resp., R+S) to be the successor of the first element of BA_i (resp., BB_j). Then these heaps are made input to a call to algorithm *findfour*, described at section 3, that performs the search.

Summarizing, given a sorted multiset composed by the cartesian sum of four sorted vectors to search for a given element z, the steps to follow are:

1. Generation of lists LBA and LBB;
2. Selection of the submatrices $(BA_i + BB_j)$, $1 \leq i, j \leq p$, to search;
3. Generation of heaps for all selected BA_i and BB_j;
4. Search all selected $BA_i + BB_j$.

Below we give the description of a parallel algorithm that implements such four basic steps in a general distributed environment.

Algorithm Distributedfindfour(X,Y,R,S,z) ;

1.	Each PE_i:	Select(p.i,X,Y);
		Select(p.i,R,S);
2.	All PE_i:	Concentrate lists LBA and LBB into PE_0;
	PE_0:	Merge(LBA,z-LBB);
		find r_i for each lba_i;
		select submatrices $(BA_i + BB_j)$ to search;
		count such submatrices;
2'.	All PE_i:	Task allocation among the PE's;
3.	Each PE_i:	Generateheap(X,Y,lba_i,H_i,incr);
		Generateheap(R,S,lbb_j,H'_i,decr);
4.	Each PE_i:	Findfour(N/p,H_i,H'_i,X,Y,R,S).

Figure 6. Distributedfindfour.

Proposition 4 . *If p<n, then the total time complexity of Distributedfindfour is $O((n^2 \log n)/p)$, which is optimal.*

Proof:

Step 1 is constituted by two calls of function *select*, which cost O(n). Concentrating the lists in step 2 can be implemented by a well known all-to-one procedure, with only a constant amount of information exchanged between any two processors within a time step. Also, the procedures executed by PE_0 have all time proportional to the length of lists LBA and LBB, i.e., O(p). Finally, as seen in Lemma 2, procedure *generateheap* has time complexity O(n), while algorithm *findfour* takes $O((n^2 \log n)/p)$ time.

A task allocation among the processors must be performed between steps 2 and 3. Often such a consideration is neglected, but it can have a severe impact on the time complexity. In our case, since PE_0 knows the number of blocks to be searched, some procedures like Concentrate, Partial Sum, Generalize and others [Nas81] can be used to implement a load balancing in $O(\log p)$ in hypercubes and perfect shuffles, for instance. Actually, the time complexity of this step is proportional to the diameter of the interconnection network, being bounded below by $\Omega(\log p)$. []

With this the proof of the theorem is complete. []

Corollary: *Let P be a polynomially enumerable problem, of size n'. Then, p processors can solve P in time $O(n'\, 2^{n'/2}/p)$ with $O(2^{n'/4})$ memory space per processor.*

CONCLUSION

We showed how to search a data structure of the type sorted X+Y+R+S for a given element, on a distributed memory machine with a processor memory space proportional to the cardinality of each vector. If the number of processors is less than the number of elements in each vector, then the algorithm is cost optimal, i.e., it yields an optimal speedup over the best known sequential algorithm.

The same algorithm can be used to solve a certain class of NP-Complete problems in parallel. Depending on the constants involved, very large instances of such NP-Complete problems could be solved with the help of parallel systems.

Although the description of the algorithm Distributedfindfour proposed in section 4 leads to an optimal speedup, if one is interested in an effective implementation then an improvement can be made concerning the communication procedures, depending on the topology of the interconnection network. For instance, the selection of the submatrices to search (Step 2) can be done through a distributed merging, costing $O(\log p)$ in machines connected as hypercubes.

Among open questions and directions for further research, we can refer to some problems on searching in sorted multisets. Notice that the algorithm we proposed in this paper could be used to solve real huge problems. Solving a 100-variable knapsack problem, for instance, can be done with the help of approximately one thousand processors holding some 32 Mbytes of *local memory*, for a reasonable amount of running time. Although such a parallel system is not excluded by current technology, it is a fact that no such systems really exist. On the other hand existing Transputer based machines couple such a number of processors for a *total memory* of more than 1 Gbyte. Therefore, a parallel algorithm to search sorted X+Y+R+S, and consequently solve some NP-Complete problems, with only $O(n)$ total memory space, would be a major issue in this field. It is worth mentioning that such an algorithm has been implemented on a T-Node machine with 32 processors. Experimental data should be available soon.

Still in connection with sorted multisets, Linial and Saks [Lin85] proved that for sorted matrices of dimension m, the complexity of searching is $\Theta(n^{m-1})$. For sorted multisets the complexity is the same for m=2. For the case where m=4, we saw that searching can be done in $O(n^2\log n)$, but no lower bound better than $\Omega(n)$ exists. The case where m=3 is even worse. The best known algorithm is trivially calling n times the case m=2 and takes $O(n^2)$, for the same lower bound of $\Omega(n)$. Besides being very interesting *per se* and in partial order theory, narrowing these gaps could yield some insights on the different complexity classes inside NP.

ACKNOWLEDGMENTS

The author is grateful to L. Bouge and M. Cosnard for their helpful comments on the presentation of this paper, and to the anonymous referee for the careful reading of the manuscript.

REFERENCES

[Ahr75] : J.H.Ahrens and G.Finke, "Merging and sorting applied to the zero-one knapsack problem", *Operations Research*, vol. 23, No. 6 (1975), pp 1099-1109

[Akl85] : S.G.Akl, *Parallel Sorting Algorithms*, Academic Press, Inc. (1985)

[Cos89a] : M.Cosnard and A.G.Ferreira, "Parallel algorithms for searching in X + Y", in *Proceedings of the International Conference on Parallel Processing 89*, Vol. 3 - Algorithms & Applications, F.Ris and P.M.Kogge (Eds.), Penn State University Press, pp 16-19

[Cos89b] : M.Cosnard, J.Duprat and A.G.Ferreira, "The complexity of searching in X + Y and other multisets", *Information Processing Letters*, 34 (1990) 103-109

[Cos89c] : M.Cosnard, J.Duprat and A.G.Ferreira, "Known and new results on selection, sorting and searching in X + Y and sorted matrices", *Research Report RR 89-9*, Septembre 1989, LIP-IMAG, Lyon (France)

[Fe89] : M.C.Ferris, "Parallel solution of extremely large knapsack problems", *Research Report 842*, April 1989, CSD - University of Wisconsin-Madison

[Fer89] : A.G.Ferreira, "The knapsack problem on parallel architectures", *Parallel & Distributed Algorithms*, Proceedings of the International Workshop on Parallel & Distributed Algorithms, Gers, France, October 1988, M. Cosnard et al. (Eds.), North-Holland, pp 145-152

[Fr75] : M.L.Fredman, "Two applications of a probabilistic search technique : sorting X + Y and building balanced search trees", in *Proc. 7-th Annual ACM Symp. on Theory of Computing*, (May 1975), ACM, 1975, pp 240-244

[Fre82] : G.N.Frederickson and D.B.Johnson, "The complexity of selection and ranking in X + Y and matrices with sorted columns", *JCSS* 24 (1982), pp 197-208

[Fre84] : G.N.Frederickson and D.B.Johnson, "Generalized selection and ranking : sorted matrices", *SIAM J. Comput.* 13 (1), Fevrier 1984, pp 14-30

[Gar79] : M.R.Garey and D.S.Johnson, *Computers and Intractability : A Guide to the Theory of NP-Completeness*, W.H.Freeman (1979)

[Gon86] : G.H.Gonnet and J.I.Munro, "Heaps on heaps", *SIAM J. Comput.* 15 (4) (1986), pp 964-971

[Har75] : L.H.Harper, T.H.Payne, J.E.Savage and E.Straus, "Sorting X+Y", *Comm. ACM* 18 (6) (1975), pp 347-349

[Hor74] : E.Horowitz and S.Sahni, "Computing partitions with applications to the knapsack problem", *J. of the ACM*, vol 21, n° 2, April 1974, pp 277-292

[Joh78a] : D.B.Johnson and S.D.Kashdan, "Lower bounds for selection in X+Y and other multisets", *J. ACM* 25 (5) (1978), pp 556-570

[Joh78b] : D.B.Johnson and T.Mizoguchi, "Selecting the k-th element in X+Y and $X_1+X_2+...+X_m$", *SIAM J. Comput.* 7 (2) (1978), pp 147-153

[Ka86] : N.Karmarkar, R.M.Karp, G.S.Lueker, and A.M.Odlysko, "Probabilistic analysis of optimum partitioning, *Journal of Applied Probability*, 23:626-645, 1986

[Kar84] : E.D.Karnin, "A parallel algorithm for the knapsack problem", *IEEE Transactions on Computers*, vol c-33, n° 5, May 1984, pp 404-408

[Lam90] : J.L.Lambert, Sorting the elements of X+Y with $O(n^2)$ comparisons, in *Proceedings of STACS 90*, Feb. 1990, Rouens, France

[Lin85] : N.Linial and M.Saks, "Searching ordered structures", *Journal of Algorithms* 6 (1985), pp 86-103

[Mcd89] :C.J.H.McDiarmid, B.A.Reed, "Building heaps fast", *J. Algorithms* 10 (1989), pp 352-365

[Mir84] : A.Mirzaian, "Channel routing in VLSI", in *Proceedings of the 16-th Annual ACM Symposium on Theory of Computing*, Washington D.C. (USA), April 1984, pp 101-107

[Nas81] : D.Nassimi and S.Sahni, "Data broadcasting in SIMD computers", *IEEE Trans. on Comp.*, Vol. c-30, n° 2, 1981, pp 101-106

[Sch81] : R.Schroeppel and A.S.Shamir, "A $T=O(2^{n/2})$, $S=O(2^{n/4})$ algorithm for certain NP-Complete problems", *SIAM J. Comput.*, 10 (3), 1981, pp 456-464

APPENDIX A : CHARACTERIZATION OF POLYNOMIALLY ENUMERABLE NP-COMPLETE PROBLEMS

Definition 1. A problem of size n' is a predicate P over n'-bit binary strings. A string x is a solution of the problem if P(x) is true. The goal is to find one such x, if it exists. The size of a problem P is denoted |P|.

Definition 2. A binary operator $\oplus$ on problems is a composition operator if

(i) it is additive: for all P' and P", |P'$\oplus$ P"| = |P'| + |P"|;

(ii) it is sound: for any two solutions x' of P' and x" of P", the string concatenation (or any other simple operation which is length-additive) x'x" is a solution of P'$\oplus$ P";

(iii) it is complete: for any solution x of P and for any representation of x as x=x'x", there are problems P' and P" such that x' solves P', x" solves P", and P=P'$\oplus$ P";

(iv) it is polynomial: the problem P'$\oplus$ P" can be calculated in time which is polynomial in the sizes of P' and P".

Definition 3. A composition operator is monotonic if the problems of each size can be totally ordered in such a way that it behaves monotonically: |P'|=|P"| and P'<P" imply that P'$\oplus$ P < P"$\oplus$ P and P$\oplus$ P' < P$\oplus$ P".

Definition 4. A set of problems is polynomially enumerable if there is a polynomial time algorithm which finds for each bit string x the subset of problems which are solved by x.

Theorem [Sch81]. If a set of problems is polynomially enumerable and has a monotonic composition operator, then its instances of size n' can be solved in time $T = O(n' 2^{n'/2})$ and space $S = O(2^{n'/4})$.

TOWARDS UNDERSTANDING THE EFFECTIVE
PARALLELIZATION OF SEQUENTIAL ALGORITHMS

Raymond Greenlaw

Department of Computer Science
University of New Hampshire
Durham, New Hampshire 03824

Abstract

There are very few parallel programming paradigms that consistently produce fast parallel algorithms. Divide-and-conquer is the one notable exception. The most common approach to parallel algorithm development is to try and parallelize existing sequential algorithms. The goal of this paper is to further our understanding about why some sequential algorithms parallelize better than others. We study the maximum acyclic subgraph problem and several closely related sequential approximation algorithms for it. The standard parallelization approach is applied to the sequential algorithms and vastly different parallel complexities are obtained for the resultant algorithms. That is, some of our parallel algorithms run in $\mathcal{NC}$, whereas decisions problems based on others turn out to be $\mathcal{P}$-complete. We find the contrasting nature of these results interesting.

INTRODUCTION

There are very few parallel programming paradigms that consistently produce extremely fast parallel algorithms ($\mathcal{NC}$ algorithms). Divide-and-conquer is the notable exception. The most common approach to parallel algorithm development is to try and parallelize existing sequential algorithms. Although such approaches are occasionally successful, many of them fall short of their objectives. The main goal of this research is to gain additional understanding as to why some sequential algorithms parallelize better than others. It would be very interesting and useful to develop a method to evaluate the parallelization potential of a sequential algorithm. Such a procedure when given a sequential algorithm would indicate whether or not the algorithm could be parallelized effectively. For example, given a sequential algorithm can it be directly parallelized or does a new strategy need to be formulated in order to develop a good parallel algorithm. The results we present in this paper are the first steps toward developing such a methodology.

There are three basic parts to our overall approach. We describe each part briefly and then more fully below. The first step is to find a set of related sequential algorithms for an interesting problem. The second is to try and parallelize each of the sequential algorithms. The third component is to classify the algorithms according to the complexity of the resulting parallel algorithms.

In order to make the approach as meaningful as possible we found a well-studied problem that development of parallel algorithms for is important. In addition, it seemed desirable to have the sequential algorithms for the problem as closely related as possible. Recently, there has been a strong interest in developing $\mathcal{NC}$ approximation algorithms for problems that are either $\mathcal{P}$-complete or $\mathcal{NP}$-complete. Because of the great interest in parallelizing approximation algorithms, we focused attention on sequential approximation algorithms for a well-known $\mathcal{NP}$-complete problem. We selected the *maximum acyclic subgraph problem* to study because we found several classes of well-known sequential approximation algorithms for the problem.

The approximation algorithms we examine are all similar. The quality of approximations these algorithms produce has been well studied [2]. Our focus is on understanding which of the algorithms can or can not be parallelized effectively and why. It is our hope that the results obtained here regarding some specific algorithms can lead to generalizations or provide insight into the following important question: "Why do some sequential algorithms parallelize well whereas others do not?" In order to resolve this question it seems certain that specific algorithms will have to be explored in detail.

We applied the "standard" parallelization approach to each of the sequential algorithms. The difficult part of this research was to classify the parallel complexities of the resultant algorithms. Like $\mathcal{NP}$-completeness results $\mathcal{P}$-completeness theorems are often difficult to obtain. We proved that natural decision problems based on several of the algorithms are $\mathcal{P}$-complete. Fast parallel algorithms exists for the others. Thus, the underlying sequential algorithms appear similar but their parallelizations differ markedly in complexity, assuming $\mathcal{NC}$ does not equal $\mathcal{P}$.

Before proceeding with the preliminaries, we describe some of the related work on the maximum acyclic subgraph problem (MASP). MASP is to find a subgraph H of a directed graph G with the properties that H is acyclic and has as large a cardinality as possible (usually with respect to the number of edges). This problem has been well studied [11, 16, 5, 2]. An equivalent formulation of the problem called the *feedback arc set problem* was proved $\mathcal{NP}$-complete [11]. A similar problem involving vertices instead of arcs called the *feedback vertex set problem* was also proved $\mathcal{NP}$-complete [11, 5]. There are *weighted* versions of both of these problems as well. These types of problems have applications in the study of *feedback systems* and in *deadlock detection* [18]. Because natural decision problems based on MASP are $\mathcal{NP}$-complete, approximation algorithms for it are very important.

There are several $\mathcal{P}$-completeness results known for variants of MASP [3, 15, 14, 6, 17, 16]. There are also random $\mathcal{NC}$ algorithms for some related problems [2, 15]. Recently, an $\mathcal{NC}$ approximation algorithm was developed that guarantees finding an approximate acyclic subgraph containing at least half of the edges [1]. Our approach is markedly different than these. None of the previous approaches focus on categorizing the sequential algorithms with respect to their parallel complexities. The $\mathcal{P}$-completeness results we obtain, which do not rely on edge or vertex weights, are new and contribute to the growing number of $\mathcal{P}$-complete problems [10].

The remainder of the paper is outlined below. In the next section we present some preliminary definitions and references for obtaining background material. In the third section we describe the sequential algorithms. We present theorems analyzing the parallel complexities of the different algorithms in the fourth section. Conclusions and directions for further work are described in the last section.

BACKGROUND

For a discussion of $\mathcal{NP}$ and $\mathcal{NP}$-completeness theory the reader is referred to [5]. Preliminary material on $\mathcal{NC}$, $\mathcal{P}$, $\mathcal{P}$-completeness theory and the importance of these concepts can be found in [10]. To obtain preliminary information about parallel algorithms the reader may consult [12]. Discussions concerning approximation algorithms for $\mathcal{P}$-complete and $\mathcal{NP}$-complete problems can be found in [5, 10].

We make use of the following terminology. Let $|S|$ denote the cardinality of the set S. For an input graph $G = (V, E)$ we assume the vertices in V are specified in a particular order $v_1, \ldots, v_{|V|}$. This can be thought of as a vertex numbering. We use the terms ordering and numbering interchangeably. For an ordering/numbering, we write the vertices (edges) from smallest to largest as $v_1, v_2, \ldots, v_{|V|}$ ($e_1, e_2, \ldots, e_{|E|}$). Some of the algorithms examined are based on edge numberings. We assume the input graphs are not multi-graphs and contain no self-loops. Since we allow two cycles in our graphs, the best approximation algorithms can find maximum acyclic subgraphs of size $1/2|E|$ [2].

Given a directed graph $G = (V, E)$ and a subset of nodes $V' \subseteq V$, $G' = (V', E')$ is the induced subgraph of G, where $E' = \{(u, v) \mid u, v \in V' \text{ and } (u, v) \in E\}$. To simplify notation we sometimes write $G' = (V', E)$ and it is understood that G' contains only those edges of E induced by V'. We also discuss subgraphs induced by a set of edges. Our focus will be on directed graphs. For the undirected case a maximum acyclic subgraph consists of a spanning tree and there is an $\mathcal{NC}^2$ algorithm for finding a spanning tree [4].

$\mathcal{P}$-complete Problems Used in Reductions

There are three $\mathcal{P}$-complete problems we need to describe for our reductions. The first is the *NOR circuit value problem* (NOR CVP) [10]. It is well-known that NOR CVP is $\mathcal{P}$-complete. We assume the gates in an instance of NOR CVP are numbered in topological order from 1 to n, are restricted to fan-out at most 2, and are such that no gate receives both its inputs from a single gate. When referring to NOR CVP, we consider this restricted version.

We also make use of the *NAND circuit value problem* (NAND CVP) [10]. It is known that the following restricted version of NAND CVP is $\mathcal{P}$-complete. Gates have a fan-out restriction of two; gates are numbered in topological order; inputs are restricted to having fan-out 1. When talking about NAND CVP, we are referring to this restricted version.

The last problem we need is the *order high degree vertex removal problem* [7]. The problem is defined below; it is $\mathcal{P}$-complete (see [7] for the reduction).

Definition 1 *Ordered High Degree Vertex Removal Problem*
Instance: An undirected graph $G = (V, E)$ with a numbering on the vertices in V and two designated vertices u and w.
Problem: Determine if there is an elimination order on V, $v_1, v_2, \ldots, v_{|V|}$, satisfying the following two properties:

1. *u is eliminated before w, and*

2. *for $1 \leq i \leq |V|$, v_i is the lowest numbered vertex of maximum degree in the $(i-1)$-th remaining subgraph of G.*

THE SEQUENTIAL APPROXIMATION ALGORITHMS

In this section we describe several classes of sequential approximation algorithms for MASP. Nearly all of the algorithms have been studied previously and their quality as approximation algorithms has also been addressed [2]. Our concern is with how well the algorithms parallelize. If we can not parallelize an algorithm efficiently, then our goal is to prove the algorithm is inherently sequential. The input and output specifications for the algorithms are as follows:

Input: A directed graph $G = (V, E)$ with a numbering on the vertices $v_1, \ldots, v_{|V|}$ and an ordering on the edges $e_1, \ldots, e_{|E|}$.

Output: An approximate maximum acyclic subgraph.

The first two algorithms we consider are *maximal* algorithms. Algorithm 1, the standard greedy algorithm, is shown below. It computes a maximal vertex induced subgraph.

ALGORITHM 1

> **begin**
>
> > $V' \leftarrow \emptyset$;
> >
> > **for** $i \leftarrow 1$ **to** $|V|$ **do**
> >
> > > **if** the induced subgraph $(V' \cup \{v_i\}, E)$ is acyclic **then** $V' \leftarrow V' \cup \{v_i\}$;
> >
> > **return** (V', E)
>
> **end.**

Algorithm 2 is depicted below. The algorithm adds an edge to the subgraph if the edge does not add a cycle to the graph being considered. Otherwise, the edge is placed in a different set. The graph induced by the larger of the two edge sets is returned. Note, if G is a multi-graph then $|F|$ may be larger than $|T|$.

ALGORITHM 2

> **begin**
>
> > $T \leftarrow \emptyset$;
> >
> > $F \leftarrow \emptyset$;
> >
> > **for** $i \leftarrow 1$ **to** $|E|$ **do**
> >
> > > **if** $(V, T \cup \{e_i\})$ is acyclic **then** $T \leftarrow T \cup \{e_i\}$ **else** $F \leftarrow F \cup \{e_i\}$;
> >
> > **if** $|T| \geq |F|$ **then return** (V, T) **else return** (V, F)
>
> **end.**

The second class of algorithms we present is based on an algorithm of Berger and Shor [2]. All of these algorithms work by processing the vertices in some designated order. Algorithm 3 processes vertices based on their overall degree. That is, the sum of the incoming plus outgoing edges. For a given vertex if the number of incoming edges is larger (smaller) than the number of outgoing edges, then we keep the incoming (outgoing) edges and delete the outgoing (incoming) edges.

ALGORITHM 3

    begin

        $K \leftarrow \emptyset$;

        $G_1 \leftarrow G$;

        for $i \leftarrow 1$ **to** $|V|$ **do** {

            $v \leftarrow$ a maximum degree vertex in G_i;

            $I \leftarrow$ the set of incoming edges in G_i of v;

            $O \leftarrow$ the set of outgoing edges in G_i of v;

            if $|I| \geq |O|$ **then** $K \leftarrow K \cup I$ **else** $K \leftarrow K \cup O$;

            $G_{i+1} \leftarrow G_i - v$ }

        return (V, K)

    end.

Algorithm 4 is a variant of Algorithm 3. In this case instead of removing the edges to keep as well as the edges to delete from the graph, we simply mark the edges to keep without removing them. The algorithm is more concerned with manipulating edges rather than nodes. A lemma proved in [8] shows that Algorithm 4 does in fact compute an acyclic subgraph. The exact quality of the approximation this algorithm computes is an open question. We find the method of computation used by Algorithm 4 interesting. Notice, the subgraphs computed by Algorithms 3 and 4 are not necessarily related.

ALGORITHM 4

    begin

        $K \leftarrow \emptyset$;

        $G_1 \leftarrow G$;

        for $i \leftarrow 1$ **to** $|V|$ **do** {

            $I \leftarrow$ the set of incoming edges of v_i in G_i;

            $I' \leftarrow I - K$;

            $O \leftarrow$ the set of outgoing edges of v_i in G_i;

            $O' \leftarrow O - K$;

            if $|I| \geq |O|$ **then** $\{K \leftarrow K \cup I; \ G_{i+1} \leftarrow G_i - O' \}$

                else $\{K \leftarrow K \cup O; \ G_{i+1} \leftarrow G_i - I' \}$ }

        return (V, K)

    end.

The idea behind Algorithm 5 is to process each vertex and keep either all incoming or all outgoing edges depending on which set is larger [2]. The difference between this algorithm, and Algorithms 3 and 4, is how G_i is maintained. Algorithms 3 and 5 appear nearly identical.

ALGORITHM 5

> **begin**
>> $K \leftarrow \emptyset$;
>>
>> $G_1 \leftarrow G$;
>>
>> **for** $i \leftarrow 1$ **to** $|V|$ **do** {
>>> $I \leftarrow$ the set of incoming edges for v_i in G_i;
>>>
>>> $O \leftarrow$ the set of outgoing edges for v_i in G_i;
>>>
>>> **if** $|I| \geq |O|$ **then** $K \leftarrow K \cup I$ **else** $K \leftarrow K \cup O$;
>>>
>>> $G_{i+1} \leftarrow G_i - v_i$ }
>>
>> **return** (V, K)
>
> **end.**

The last algorithm we present processes the edges in some designated order. The ordering of the vertices plays a significant role in the computation as well. Algorithm 6 works by laying out all vertices on a line and then putting edges in R (L) that go to the "right" ("left") on the line [2]. It is easy to see that both subgraphs (V, R) and (V, L) are acyclic. The approximation can be taken as the larger of the two graphs. Notice the similarities between Algorithms 2 and 6. The difference is in the conditional part of the if-statement.

ALGORITHM 6

> **begin**
>> $R \leftarrow \emptyset$;
>>
>> $L \leftarrow \emptyset$;
>>
>> **for** $i \leftarrow 1$ **to** $|E|$ **do**
>>> **if** "left endpoint of e_i" $<$ "right endpoint of e_i" **then** $R \leftarrow R \cup \{e_i\}$
>>>
>>>> **else** $L \leftarrow L \cup \{e_i\}$;
>>
>> **if** $|R| \geq |L|$ **then return** (V, R) **else return** (V, L)
>
> **end.**

We have described six sequential approximation algorithms in this section. Although several of the algorithms are quite similar, we prove in the next section that they have different parallel complexities, assuming $\mathcal{NC}$ does not equal $\mathcal{P}$.

THE PARALLEL COMPLEXITIES OF ALGORITHMS 1 – 6

A standard technique in complexity theory for measuring the difficulty of an algorithm is to examine the complexity of a natural decision problem that incorporates the algorithm. This is the approach we adopt here. We begin by defining a natural decision problem based on Algorithm 1 and prove it is $\mathcal{P}$-complete.

Definition 2 *Problem 1*
Given: A directed graph $G = (V, E)$ with an ordering on the vertices $v_1, \ldots, v_{|V|}$ and a designated vertex u.

Problem: Is u contained in the subgraph of G computed by Algorithm 1?

Theorem 1 *Problem 1 is $\mathcal{P}$-complete under log-space reducibility.*

PROOF

Algorithm 1 is easily seen to run in polynomial time. The acyclic property is polynomial time testable, hereditary and non-trivial on directed graphs. Therefore, the result follows from an application of a theorem due to Miyano [13].   ∎

The theorem shows Algorithm 1 is inherently sequential. The subgraph computed by Algorithm 1 is often referred to as the lexicographically first maximal acyclic subgraph. Below we define decision problems based on Algorithms 2, 3, and 4.

Definition 3 *Given: A directed graph $G = (V, E)$ with a numbering on the vertices $v_1, \ldots, v_{|V|}$, an ordering on the edges $e_1, \ldots, e_{|E|}$, and a designated edge e.*
Problem 2: Is e contained in the edge set T computed by Algorithm 2?
Problem 3: Is e contained in the edge set K computed by Algorithm 3?
Problem 4: Is e contained in the edge set K computed by Algorithm 4?

First, we consider the parallel complexity of Problem 2. The following theorem indicates Algorithm 2 is inherently sequential. Thus, it cannot be parallelize effectively, unless $\mathcal{NC}$ equals $\mathcal{P}$.

Theorem 2 *Problem 2 is $\mathcal{P}$-complete under log-space reducibility.*

PROOF

We reduce NOR CVP to the problem. Let α denote an instance of NOR CVP and g_{out} the output gate of α. The idea is to replace NOR gates with a gadget so that the ordering of the edges within each gadget allows us to compute the value of the corresponding gate in the circuit.

Figure 1 shows how inputs are represented. The vertex labeled $i(\text{bot})$ is the node that a gadget's "mid" node $g(\text{mid})$, which is defined below, connects to. The edges corresponding to the wires of the circuit's inputs are connected to the gadget's node $g(\text{top})$ as shown in the figure. This is done so that for TRUE (FALSE) inputs the corresponding edge is put in T (F) by Algorithm 2.

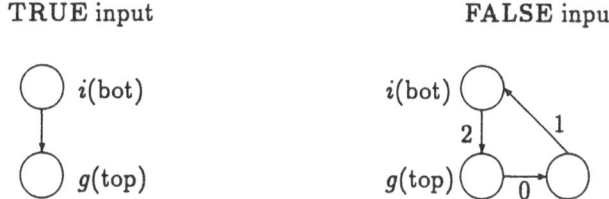

TRUE input   FALSE input

Figure 1. The representation of circuit inputs in Theorem 2. The numbering of the FALSE input gadget illustrates the relative order the edges occur in.

Suppose NOR gate g has inputs from gates i_1 and i_2, and outputs to gates o_1 and o_2. Figure 2 depicts the gadget replacing g. The vertices are labeled from top to bottom $g(\text{top})$, $g(\text{mid})$ and $g(\text{bot})$. The five *upward* pointing edges $(g(\text{top}), i_1(\text{mid}))$, $(g(\text{top}), i_2(\text{mid}))$, $(g(\text{mid}), i_1(\text{bot}))$, $(g(\text{mid}), i_2(\text{bot}))$, and $(g(\text{bot}), g(\text{top}))$

are ordered so that each one gets placed in the set T by Algorithm 2. If a gate input comes from an input to the circuit, then the corresponding gadget's connection from $g(\text{top})$ is omitted. Edges $(g(\text{bot}), o_1(\text{top}))$ and $(g(\text{bot}), o_2(\text{top}))$ carry the output value of gate g. That is, they will be placed in T (F) if and only if g evaluates to TRUE (FALSE). Two additional nodes are added to "ground" the outedges from the gadget corresponding to g_{out}. These nodes each have an edge to $g_{out}(\text{mid})$ that gets placed in T. Both have an incoming edge from $g_{out}(\text{bot})$. There are certain edges that need to get placed in T for the simulation to work. They are edges for TRUE inputs, the edges labeled 0 and 1 in Figure 1 for the FALSE input gadget, and all upward pointing edges. A numbering, based on the original topological numbering of the circuit and the number of gates in the circuit, can be constructed to obtain this ordering.

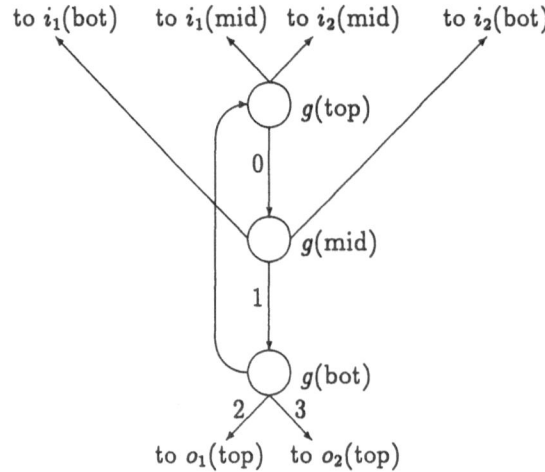

Figure 2. The representation of NOR gate g having inputs numbered i_1 and i_2, and outputs o_1 and o_2. The relative ordering of the downward pointing edges within the gadget is indicated by the labels 0 through 3.

The correctness of the reduction follows from Lemma 1 whose proof is given in [8].

Lemma 1 *Edges labeled 2 and 3 of the gadget corresponding to gate g in the instance of NOR CVP are put in the set T (F) constructed by Algorithm 2 if and only if gate g evaluates to TRUE (FALSE).*

It is easy to check that the reduction is log-space. By taking the designated edge in our instance of Problem 2 to be the one labeled 3 in the gadget corresponding to g_{out}, it follows from the lemma that this edge is placed in T if and only if the circuit evaluates to TRUE. Thus, Problem 2 is $\mathcal{P}$-complete. This completes the proof of Theorem 2. ∎

We observe that for each gadget and each input representation a majority of edges are placed in T. Thus, the decision problem "Is e contained in the subgraph computed by Algorithm 2?" is also $\mathcal{P}$-complete. The reduction also holds for graphs that are restricted to having indegree and outdegree of at most three. Before proceeding with Problems 3 and 4, we consider the following decision problem that is stated more along the lines of the original $\mathcal{NP}$-complete decision problem for the feedback arc set problem [11].

Definition 4 *Edge Maximal Acyclic Subgraph Problem*
Given: A directed graph $G = (V, E)$ with an ordering on the edges $e_1, \ldots, e_{|E|}$ and an integer k.
Problem: Is the edge maximal acyclic subgraph computed by Algorithm 2 of size at least k?

The theorem proved below shows that this problem is $\mathcal{P}$-complete.

Theorem 3 *The edge maximal acyclic subgraph problem is $\mathcal{P}$-complete under log-space reducibility.*

PROOF

The problem is clearly in $\mathcal{P}$. We modify the construction given in Theorem 2. Let l be the number of TRUE inputs, m the number of FALSE inputs, and n the number of NOR gates in an instance of NOR CVP. It is not hard to see that the reduction given in Theorem 2 constructs a graph that has at most $2m + 9n + 4$ edges and has at least $m + 6n + 2$ edges put in T by Algorithm 2.

The reduction given in Theorem 2 is modified by adding $d = m + 3n + 3$ additional dummy nodes. The dummies each have an edge directed to them from $g_{out}(\text{bot})$ and an edge directed to $g_{out}(\text{mid})$. This adds $2d$ edges to the graph. The edges to $g_{out}(\text{mid})$ are ordered so that they get placed in T by Algorithm 2. The other edges are ordered so they are considered last. Notice, the edges from $g_{out}(\text{bot})$ to the dummy nodes are either all placed in T or are all placed in F depending on whether edge $(g_{out}(\text{mid}), g_{out}(\text{bot}))$ is in F or T respectively.

Let $k = 3m + 12n + 6$. Using the new graph, if the circuit evaluates to FALSE then Algorithm 2 will put at most $k - 1$ edges in T. If the circuit evaluates to TRUE then the algorithm will place at least k edges in T. We remark that T always contains a majority of the edges. Thus, the circuit evaluates to TRUE if and only if at least k edges are placed in T. We omit the proof of correctness and the proof that the reduction is log-space. ∎

Theorems 2 and 3 indicate that Algorithm 2 is inherently sequential. Next we show that Problem 3 presented in Definition 3 is $\mathcal{P}$-complete.

Theorem 4 *Problem 3 is $\mathcal{P}$-complete under log-space reducibility.*

PROOF

Algorithm 3 clearly runs in polynomial time. We reduce the ordered high degree vertex removal problem to Problem 3 via a log-space reduction. Let $\langle H = (V, E), u, w \rangle$ denote an instance of the ordered high degree vertex removal problem. We transform this instance into a new instance $\langle G, e = (u, w) \rangle$, where e is placed in K if and only if u is removed before w in the instance $\langle H, u, w \rangle$.

The first step in the reduction is to direct all edges in H. From u and w direct all edges outward. For all other vertices direct edges any way consistent with this. For every vertex v other than u and w, we introduce three dummy vertices and direct edges from v to them. This introduces $3|V| - 6$ new nodes and the same number of edges. For u and w we introduce two dummy nodes apiece. u has directed edges to its dummy nodes; w has directed edges to its dummy nodes. This creates four more edges and four more dummy nodes. In the overall vertex order all dummy nodes appear after all of the original vertices. The vertices in V maintain their original ordering. Finally, an edge is introduced going from u to w.

We argue the correctness of the reduction. The individual degree of all vertices in V was increased by the same amount in the construction of the graph G. Additionally, the vertices were ordered in G so that they would be considered in the same order as in H by the natural high degree vertex removal algorithm [7]. If u is eliminated before w in the instance $\langle H, u, w \rangle$, then $e = (u, w)$ is put in K since u has more outgoing edges then incoming edges. If e is placed in K then it was put there when u was visited. Note, if w was visited before u then e would have been placed in T because w has more outgoing edges than incoming edges.

It is easy to check that the reduction can be performed in log-space.   ∎

We now focus on Problem 4 given in Definition 3. The following theorem shows that Algorithm 4 is inherently sequential.

Theorem 5 *Problem 4 is $\mathcal{P}$-complete under log-space reducibility.*

PROOF

Algorithm 4 runs in polynomial time. We reduce NAND CVP to it. Let α be an instance of NAND CVP and let g_{out} denote the output gate. From α we construct an instance $\langle G, e \rangle$ such that g_{out} evaluates to TRUE if and only if e is placed in the set K constructed by Algorithm 4 on input graph G.

The graph G we construct from α has the same basic structure as the circuit with gates becoming nodes in the graph and wires becoming edges. All wires in α are directed toward g_{out}. If there are "dangling" wires in the circuit then new vertices are added in G so the wires can be "grounded." Edge e is a ground of gate g_{out}. Inputs are handled differently. For each TRUE input in α connected to gate g, a vertex is introduced and connected by a directed edge to the vertex corresponding to gate g in G. No vertices are introduced for FALSE inputs. The order of the original topological numbering of α is maintained except nodes corresponding to inputs are ordered after the node representing g_{out}. Nodes introduced as grounds are ordered after the last "original input." It is clear that the reduction described above is a log-space reduction. The correctness of the reduction follows from the lemma stated below whose proof was given in [8].

Lemma 2 *An edge is placed in K by Algorithm 4 on input graph G if and only if the corresponding wire in α carries the value TRUE. The only possible exception is for single TRUE inputs.*

From Lemma 2 it follows that edge e is placed in K if and only if the output of gate g_{out} is TRUE. This completes the proof of Theorem 5.   ∎

Note, the maximum indegree of nodes in the reduction was two as was the maximum outdegree. Thus, the problem remains $\mathcal{P}$-complete with these restrictions. Two additional interesting decision problems are stated below.

Definition 5 *Algorithm 3 (4) Acyclic Subgraph Problem*
Given: A directed graph $G = (V, E)$ with an ordering on the vertices $v_1, \ldots, v_{|V|}$ and an integer t.
Problem: Is the edge set K computed by Algorithm 3 (4) of size at least t?

We suspect the problems in Definition 5 are $\mathcal{P}$-complete but have not been able to prove it. Alternative $\mathcal{P}$-complete problems may need to be used to demonstrate this. Although there are many $\mathcal{NP}$-complete problems based on the size of an object, there seem to be very few $\mathcal{P}$-completeness results of this nature [10]. This is in part what makes the proof of Theorem 3 interesting.

Thus far, we have shown that numerous decision problems based on Algorithms 1 through 4 are $\mathcal{P}$-complete. It is known that Algorithms 5 and 6 parallelize well [2]. We state the following theorem in contrast to the results presented so far.

Theorem 6 *Let $G = (V, E)$ be a directed graph. There are EREW PRAM algorithms that run in time $O(\log |V|)$ using $|E|$ processors, and compute the approximations found by Algorithms 5 and 6.*

CONCLUSIONS

Our goal was to try and advance the understanding as to why some sequential algorithms parallelize well. This is a difficult problem. The results we obtained for a specific group of related sequential algorithms were rather surprising. Although the classes of algorithms explored had similar structures, several of the algorithms were proved inherently sequential while others had $\mathcal{NC}$ implementations. Results of this nature have been obtained before [9] and are a step towards understanding the nature of parallelization. The results suggest it will be useful to try and parallelize a series of sequential algorithms when looking for a fast parallel algorithm for a problem. The $\mathcal{P}$-completeness results contribute to the growing number of such problems (see [10]) that can help a researcher decide whether or not a problem is likely to be efficiently parallelizable. An interesting open questions is whether or not general results can be established indicating when a particular algorithm can be parallelized efficiently.

ACKNOWLEDGEMENTS

I would like to thank the referees for their helpful suggestions.

REFERENCES

[1] B. Berger. The fourth moment method. In *Proceedings of the Second Annual ACM-SIAM Symposium on Discrete Algorithms*, pages 373–383. Association for Computing Machinery, 1991.

[2] B. Berger and P. Shor. Approximation algorithms for the maximum acyclic sub-graph problem. In *Proceedings of the First Annual ACM-SIAM Symposium on Discrete Algorithms*, pages 236–243. Association for Computing Machinery, 1990.

[3] D.P. Bovet, S. De Agostino, and R. Petreschi. Parallelism and the feedback vertex set problem. *Information Processing Letters*, 28(2):81–85, June 1988.

[4] S.A. Cook. A taxonomy of problems with fast parallel algorithms. *Information and Control*, 64(1-3):2–22, 1985.

[5] M.R. Garey and D.S. Johnson. *Computers and Intractability: A Guide to the Theory of NP-Completeness*. H. Freeman, San Francisco, 1978.

[6] L. M. Goldschlager, R. A. Shaw, and J. Staples. The maximum flow problem is log space complete for *P*. *Theoretical Computer Science*, 21:105–111, 1982.

[7] R. Greenlaw. Ordered vertex removal and subgraph problems. *Journal of Computer and System Sciences*, 39(3):323–342, 1989.

[8] R. Greenlaw. The parallel complexity of approximation algorithms for the maximum acyclic subgraph problem. Technical Report 91-13, University of New Hampshire, 1991.

[9] R. Greenlaw. A model classifying algorithms as inherently sequential with applications to graph searching. *Information and Computation*, to appear.

[10] R. Greenlaw, H.J. Hoover, and W.L. Ruzzo. A compendium of problems complete for *P*: Parts I and II. Technical Report 91-11, University of Alberta, and Technical Report 91-05-01, University of Washington, to appear.

[11] R.M. Karp. *Reducibility Among Combinatorial Problems*, pages 85–103. Plenum Press, New York, 1972.

[12] R.M. Karp and V. Ramachandran. Parallel algorithms for shared-memory machines. In *Handbook of Theoretical Computer Science*. MIT Press, 1990.

[13] S. Miyano. The lexicographically first maximal subgraph problems: P-completeness and NC algorithms. *Mathematical Systems Theory*, 22(1):47–73, 1989.

[14] V. Ramachandran. The complexity of minimum cut and maximum flow problems in an acyclic network. *Networks*, 17:387–392, 1987.

[15] V. Ramachandran. Fast and processor-efficient parallel algorithms for reducible flow graphs. Technical Report UILU-ENG-88-2257, ACT-103, University of Illinois at Urbana-Champaign, November 1988.

[16] V. Ramachandran. Finding a minimum feedback arc set in reducible flow graphs. *Journal of Algorithms*, 9(3):299–313, 1988.

[17] A. Shamir. A linear time algorithm for finding minimum cutsets in reducible graphs. *SIAM Journal of Computing*, 8(4):645–55, 1979.

[18] C.C. Wang, E.L. Llyod, and M.L. Soffa. Feedback vertex sets and cyclically reducible graphs. *Journal of the ACM*, 32(2):296–313, April 1985.

ON THE DENSITY OF THE PROBABILISTIC POLYNOMIAL CLASSES

José D. P. Rolim

Centre Universitaire d'Informatique
Université de Genève
12, rue du Lac
CH-1207 Genève
Switzerland

1 Introduction

There are many results on which intractable problems can be solved quickly using randomized algorithms, starting with the classical paper by Rabin [10]. Comparisons of probabilistic and deterministic performances have stimulated several possibilities for randomization by considering the structure of the probabilistic classes [8]. The study of expected complexity has been developed from two basic points of view [13] . In the first one, the so called *distributional approach*, the input probability must be known and the theory is developed under these input assumptions. The second one, called the *randomized approach*, allows stochastic moves in the computations. In this paper, we study a distributional randomized approach. By defining density for probabilistic machines, we consider probability on the inputs and we adopt the probabilistic Turing machine as our formal model of computation.

The notion of *density* of a complexity class has been initially connected to the concept of sparseness [6], tally sets [3] and polynomial approximations [9]. The existence of sets of low density in $NP - P$ has long been conjectured [6]. By supposing that all words of the same length have the same probability, a density function can be related to the size of computable sets. The density notion can work as a measure of "efficiency", when it measures the "degree" of an approximation, as well as a measure of intractability of a set, e.g., the density of sets in $NP - P$. Lately the concept of density has been enlarged to deal with any probability distribution on the inputs [11]. But in all of these previous cited articles, the concept of density has been restricted to non-stochastic models of computation.

In this paper, we incorporate the notion of density to the complexity classes of a probabilistic Turing machine. We associate a density function $d(n)$ to the number of words that can be probabilistically computed within certain bound $f(n)$. Hence, the computation allows words to exceed bound $f(n)$, beyond accepting the inherent errors to a random process of computation.

We strength Gill's hierarchy of probabilistic polynomial classes [4], by showing that the basic inclusion relations are valid for any non-trivial density. Namely, we show that:

$$P(d(n)) \subseteq R(d(n)) \subseteq \left\{ \begin{array}{c} NP(d(n)) \\ \\ BPP(d(n)) \end{array} \right. \subseteq PP(d(n)) \subseteq PSPACE(d(n))$$

where $d(n)$ is a density function, R is the random polynomial time class, BPP the bounded polynomial time class, PP the probabilistic polynomial time class and P, NP and $PSPACE$ are the worst-case polynomial classes. Note that this is a considerable strengthing over the polynomial hierarchy of probabilistic languages, since for $d(n)$ very close to zero we allow languages of extreme difficulty to be included in the classes. Such languages are very sparse in the polynomial bounds and can be even non-bounded on some words.

We start by recalling some basic concepts on probabilistic Turing machines. In section 3, we define the probabilistic bound measures and we investigate the several concepts of polynomial probabilistic classes. In section 4, we define the concept of density functions. We extend the probabilistic complexity classes to embody densities. We give an interpretation of density 1 as the probabilistic classes without density and we extend the probabilistic polynomial classes to any density. We conclude in section 5, by pointing out some open questions and indicating some lines of research.

2 Probabilistic Computations

We adopt the *probabilistic Turing machine* as our formal model for probabilistic algorithms. We recall some basic concepts about this kind of machine [4].

A probabilistic Turing machine M is a deterministic multitape Turing machine with the ability to take random decisions. It has a special set of internal states, called *coin-tossing* states. The specification of M allows two possible next states for each coin tossing state. The decision on which should be the next state is taken based on the tossing of an unbiased and fair coin. The computation of M is *deterministic* except for the random decisions taken by M in the coin-tossing states. Furthermore, the tosses are independent of previous tosses and thus the probability of a computation path is of half to the power of the total number of coin tossing states encountered in the path.

The definition of probabilistic Turing machines can be extended by allowing that *biased* random decisions are made, that is the probability of getting heads can be different from the probability of getting tails. The resulting model has the same computational power as the unbiased model [12].

The output of machine M on input w is a random variable representing the possible computations of M on w. Thus, we define $M(w)$ as follows.

Definition 2.1 Let M be a probabilistic Turing machine and let w be an input to M. We define $M(w)$ as a random variable denoting the outputs of possible computations of M on w.

We denote by $Pr[M(w) = y]$ the probability of the output of the computation of M on w being y. In general, a probabilistic Turing machine computes a random function;

for each input w, the machine M produces output y with probability $Pr[M(w) = y]$. We say that M *converges to* y on input w if $Pr[M(w) = y] > \frac{1}{2}$. Despite the fact that the output of a probabilistic Turing machine is not in general uniquely determined by the input, we can define the partial function computed by a probabilistic machine in terms of cutpoint $\frac{1}{2}$ as follows.

Definition 2.2 The partial function f computed by a probabilistic Turing machine M is defined by:

$$f(w) = \begin{cases} y & \text{if there exists y for which M converges to on input w} \\ undefined & \text{if no such y exists} \end{cases}$$

We are primarily interested in Turing machines computing the partial characteristic functions of languages (i.e. $0, 1$-valued functions). A probabilistic Turing machine computing the partial characteristic function of a language L is said to *recognize L*.

Definition 2.3 A probabilistic Turing machine M is said to accept language L and we denote this by $L = L^P(M)$ if for all inputs w, $M(w) \in \{0,1\}$ and $Pr[M(w) = 1] > \frac{1}{2}$ if and only if $w \in L$.

A probabilistic Turing machine can accept a language L and have a non-zero probability of rejecting words that belong to L, for example. Therefore, we should be capable of expressing these cases by defining error probability as follows.

Definition 2.4 The error probability of probabilistic machine M recognizing language L is the function e defined by:

$$e(w) = \begin{cases} Pr[M(w) = 0] & \text{if } w \in L \\ Pr[M(w) = 1] & \text{if } w \notin L \text{ and } Pr[M(w) = 0] > \frac{1}{2} \\ undefined & \text{if } w \notin L \text{ and } Pr[M(w) = 0] \leq \frac{1}{2} \end{cases}$$

A useful probabilistic algorithm should have small probability of error. At the very least, the error probability should be uniformly bounded below $\frac{1}{2}$ for all inputs.

Definition 2.5 A probabilistic Turing machine M accepts language L with bounded error probability if there exists a constant $k < \frac{1}{2}$ such that $e(w) \leq k$ for every input w.

3 Probabilistic Complexity Classes

It is well known that the ability to make random decisions does not increase the computational power of Turing machines [4]. However, one question that is raised often is whether probabilistic machines can compute more efficiently than deterministic machines, that is using less time or tape. Therefore, it is important to have an agreeable definition of bounded computations for probabilistic Turing machines.

Definition 3.1 The *Blum run time* T_B and the *Blum space* S_B of probabilistic Turing machine M on input w are defined by [5]:

$$T_B(w) = \begin{cases} \text{least i such that } Pr[M(w) = y \text{ in time } i] > \frac{1}{2} & \text{if M converges on w to y} \\ \infty & \text{otherwise} \end{cases}$$

$$S_B(w) = \begin{cases} \text{least i such that } Pr[M(w) = y \; in \; space \; i] > \frac{1}{2} & \text{if M converges on w to y} \\ \infty & \text{otherwise} \end{cases}$$

In terms of acceptance of languages by probabilistic Turing machines, Definition 3.1 works as follows.

Definition 3.2 Let L be accepted by probabilistic Turing machine M. We define:

$$T_{BL}(w) = \begin{cases} \text{least i: Pr[M accepts w in time i]} > \frac{1}{2} & \text{if } w \in L \\ \text{least i: Pr[M rejects w in time i]} \geq \frac{1}{2} & \text{if } w \notin L \text{ and Pr[M(w)]} = 0 > \frac{1}{2} \\ \infty & \text{if } w \notin L \text{ and Pr[M(w)]} = 0 \leq \frac{1}{2} \end{cases}$$

$$S_{BL}(w) = \begin{cases} \text{least i: Pr[M accepts w in space i]} > \frac{1}{2} & \text{if } w \in L \\ \text{least i: Pr[M rejects w in space i]} \geq \frac{1}{2} & \text{if } w \notin L \text{ and Pr[M(w)]} = 0 > \frac{1}{2} \\ \infty & \text{if } w \notin L \text{ and Pr[M(w)]} = 0 \leq \frac{1}{2} \end{cases}$$

Gill [4] has shown that the definitions in 3.1 have the property of being Blum complexity measures [2] . That is, given an arbitrary probabilistic Turing machine M computing the partial function f, $T_B(w)$ ($S_B(w)$) is defined if and only if $f(w)$ is defined. In addition, there exists a recursive predicate of w and i that is true if Pr[M(w)=f(w) in time (space) i] $> \frac{1}{2}$ and false otherwise.

The complexity classes yielded by languages recognized by probabilistic Turing machines can be defined as follows.

Definition 3.3 Let $g(n) : N \to N$ be a recursive function. We define:

(i) $PRTIME(g(n))$ is the class of languages recognized by probabilistic Turing machines that have $T_{BL}(w) \leq g(|w|)$ for all inputs w.

(ii) $PRSPACE(g(n))$ is the class of languages recognized by probabilistic Turing machines that have $S_{BL}(w) \leq g(|w|)$ for all inputs w.

We define *polynomial bounded* probabilistic Turing machine as follows.

Definition 3.4 A probabilistic Turing machine M is polynomial time bounded if there exists a constant $c > 0$ such that *every* computation on any input w halts within time $|w|^c$.

Using this definition, we define complexity classes as follows.

Definition 3.5 We define:

(i) PP is the class of languages recognized by polynomial bounded probabilistic Turing machines.

(ii) BPP is the class of languages recognized by polynomial bounded probabilistic Turing machines with bounded error probability.

(iii) R is the class of languages recognized by polynomial bounded probabilistic Turing machines which have zero error probability for inputs not in the language.

The class R is also known as ZPP or RP in the literature. Notice that the definitions above *do not* use the Blum run time to define polynomial bounded machines. For example, we alternatively could say that a probabilistic Turing machine is polynomial bounded if there exists a polynomial $p(|w|)$ such that $T_{BL}(w) \leq p(|w|)$ for all inputs w. It is an open problem if the definition above and Definition 3.4 converge for *every* polynomial bounded complexity class. Obviously, the classes PP are the same under both definitions. It can easily be shown that the classes R converge under both definitions. However, there is no trivial proof whether the class BPP does contain the same languages under both definitions or not.

The polynomial classes mentioned above were shown by Gill to satisfy the following relations [4]:

$$P \subseteq R \subseteq \left\{ \begin{array}{c} NP \\ \\ BPP \end{array} \right. \subseteq PP \subseteq PSPACE$$

There has been some research about space bounded simulation of probabilistic machines by deterministic ones. It s known that $PRSPACE(f(n)) \subset DSPACE(f(n)^6)$ [7]. For time bounds the results already known yield only exponential simulations [1].

4 Density Functions and Probabilistic Classes

Let Σ denote a finite input alphabet, Σ^n denote words in Σ^* of length n and let X be a random variable taking values in Σ^*. We assume that we are given the conditional probability $Pr[X = w/n]$ of X taking value w in Σ^n given that X takes a value in Σ^n. Therefore, for any fixed value of n, we know how the words are distributed within this fixed length n. Thus, $Pr[X = w/n]$ can be seen as a generic probability distribution on n and $\sum_{w \in \Sigma^n} Pr[X = w/n] = 1$ for every n. If, for example, we assume a uniform distribution, i.e. $Pr[X = w/n] = |\Sigma|^{-n}$, we can move back to the standard complexity theory without probability. Otherwise, we suppose that this family of probability distributions is known. We suppose that this probability distribution is positive, i.e. every word w of length n has a non-zero probability of occurrence, $Pr[X = w/n] > 0$ for all w and n.

We say that a machine M respects the time bound $g(n)$ for word w if there is no computation of M on input w that takes more than $g(n)$ steps. We say that w respects the space bound $g(n)$ for M if there is no computation of M on w using more than $g(n)$ working tape cells. We extend the concept of bounded computation to include sets with density functions as follows.

Definition 4.1 Let $Pr[X = w/n]$ be positive. Let M be a probabilistic Turing machine.

(1) We say that M is a $g(n)$ time bounded Turing machine with density function $d(n)$ and probability distribution $Pr[X = w/n]$ if

$$d(n) \leq \sum_{w : M \text{ respects time bound } g(|w|) \text{ for } w} Pr[X = w/n]$$

(2) We say that M is a $g(n)$ space-bounded Turing machine with density function $d(n)$ and probability distribution $Pr[X = w/n]$ if

$$d(n) \leq \sum_{w : M \text{ respects space bound } g(|w|) \text{ for } w} Pr[X = w/n].$$

We say that machine M is of time(space) complexity $g(n)$ with density $d(n)$ if there exists a positive probability distribution $Pr[X = w/n]$ over the input alphabet of M for which M is of time(space) complexity $g(n)$ with density $d(n)$ and probability distribution $Pr[X = w/n]$. We can define probabilistic complexity classes as follows.

Definition 4.2 Let $0 \leq d(n) \leq 1$ and $Pr[X = w/n]$ be positive everywhere.

(i) $PRSPACE(g(n), d(n), Pr[X = w/n])$ is the class of languages recognized by $g(n)$ space bounded probabilistic Turing machines with density function $d(n)$ and probability distribution $Pr[X = w/n]$.

(ii) $PRTIME(g(n), d(n), Pr[X = w/n])$ is the class of languages recognized by $g(n)$ time bounded probabilistic Turing machines with density function $d(n)$ and probability distribution $Pr[X = w/n]$.

The definitions above were based on whether a machine M halts or not for *every* possible computation of M on input w. Definition 3.3 was based on the Blum run time of machine M on input w. However, the next result says that the two definitions are equivalent for density function 1.

Theorem 4.1 *Let $g(n)$ be total recursive and $Pr[X = w/n]$ be positive everywhere. Then*
$$PRTIME(g(n)) = PRTIME(g(n), 1, Pr[X = w/n]).$$

Proof: We claim that $PRTIME(g(n), 1), Pr[X = w/n] \subset PRTIME(g(n))$. Let L be a probabilistic language in $PRTIME(g(n), 1, Pr[X = w/n])$. Then there is a probabilistic Turing machine accepting L that halts for every input w in bound $g(|w|)$. Thus the Blum run time of such machine on every input w is bounded by $g(|w|)$. Therefore, L is in $PRTIME(g(n))$.

On the other hand, we also claim that $PRTIME(g(n)) \subset PRTIME(g(n), 1, Pr[X = w/n])$. Let L be in $PRTIME(g(n))$. So consider machine M accepting L with $T_{BL}(w)$ bounded by $g(|w|)$ for any input w and $k > 0$. We define a probabilistic machine M' that simulates machine M on input w by at most $g(|w|)$ steps. If the computation of M' on w exceeds $g(|w|)$ steps, then M' rejects w. Otherwise, when M does not exceed $g(|w|)$ steps, M' accepts w if and only if M accepts w.

The language accepted by M' is $L(M)$, since $Pr[M(w) = 1 \text{ in time } g(|w|)] > \frac{1}{2}$ for any word w in L, by the definition of $T_{BL}(w)$. Similarly, if w is not in L, then M rejects w in time $g(|w|)$ with probability greater than $\frac{1}{2}$ and thus, M' rejects w within time $g(|w|)$. Therefore, M and M' accept the same language. Thus, L belongs to $PRTIME(g(n), 1, Pr[X = w/n])$, since machine M' respects the bound $g(|w|)$ for any input w. $\diamond$

Note that the above result implies also in the convergence of definitions based on Blum run time and definitions based on bounds on every computation for the class $PRTIME(g(n))$. Similarly, we can prove the analogous result for space bounds.

Theorem 4.2 *Let $g(n)$ be total recursive and $Pr[X = w/n]$ be positive everywhere. Then*
$$PRSPACE(g(n)) = PRSPACE(g(n), 1, Pr[X = w/n]).$$

A probabilistic Turing machine M is said to be polynomial bounded with density $d(n)$ if there is a polynomial $p(n)$ such that M is of time complexity $p(n)$ with density

$d(n)$. Consider the uniform probability distribution on the inputs of size n. We enlarge the concept of probabilistic classes as follows.

Definition 4.3 Let $0 \leq d(n) \leq 1$. We define:

(i) $PP(d(n)) = \cup_{k>0} PRTIME(n^k, d(n), \frac{1}{\Sigma^n}) = \{$ L: there exists probabilistic Turing machine M accepting L in time n^k with density $d(n)$, for some $k > 0$ and uniform probability distribution $\}$.

(ii) $BPP(d(n)) = \{$ L: there exists probabilistic Turing machine M accepting L with bounded error probability such that M operates in time n^k with density $d(n)$, for some $k > 0$ and uniform probability distribution$\}$.

(iii) $R(d(n)) = \{$ L: there exists probabilistic Turing machine M accepting L with zero error probability for any w, $w \notin L$, such that M operates in time n^k with density $d(n)$, for some $k > 0$ and uniform probability distribution $\}$.

Obviously, Definitions 3.6 and 4.3 converge for the complexity classes with density function 1.

Theorem 4.3 *(i)* $PP = PP(1)$;

(ii) $BPP = BPP(1)$;

(iii) $R = R(1)$.

The following relations among the classes defined above and the classes $P(d(n))$, $NP(d(n))$ and $PSPACE(d(n))$ are valid.

Theorem 4.4 *Let* $0 < d(n) \leq 1$. *Then:*

$$PP(d(n)) \subset PSPACE(d(n))$$

Proof: Let L be in $PP(d(n))$. Then L is accepted by some probabilistic Turing machine M with k working tapes, that operates in time n^c with density $d(n)$, for some $c > 0$.

Consider a word w that respects the bound n^c for machine M. Each computation path of M on w is deterministic and can be simulated using time n^c. Hence, each path uses at most n^c working tape cells, since it is time bounded by n^c.

Consider machine M' that acts on any input w as follows. M' on tape T_0 records the sum of the probability of accepting paths and on tapes T_i, $1 \leq i \leq k$, simulates all possible paths of M on w. M' simulates each computation path of M, one at a time for at most n^c time steps, using always the same cells. If all the computations paths of M on w halt within n^c time steps, then M' accepts w if and only if the total probability recorded on T_0 is greater than $\frac{1}{2}$. If the word w respects the bound n^c for M, then the simulation is over. Otherwise, when M does not respect the bound n^c on w, then machine M' must continue simulating machine M on w until a decision is reached. But now M' simulates one step of each computation at a time, since M may have a non-halting computation path on input w. M' accepts w if and only if M accepts w.

For words w that respect the bound n^c for machine M, the number of cells used on tapes T_i, $1 \leq i \leq k$, is bounded by n^c. But each computation path has probability at least $\frac{1}{2^{n^c}}$, since n^c bounds the longest computation path for these words. But this number can be recorded using n^c cells on tape T_0. Therefore M' is of space complexity $2n^c$, sum of the cells scanned on tapes T_i, $0 \leq i \leq k$, with density $d(n)$. Thus L is in $PSPACE(d(n))$. ◇

Theorem 4.5 *Let $0 < d(n) \leq 1$. Then:*

$$BPP(d(n)) \subset PP(d(n))$$

Proof: This is a straightforward consequence of the definitions of $BPP(d(n))$ and $PP(d(n))$. ◊

Theorem 4.6 *Let $0 < d(n) \leq 1$. Then:*

$$R(d(n)) \subset NP(d(n))$$

Proof: Let L be in $R(d(n))$. Thus there is a probabilistic machine M recognizing L such that if w does not belong to L, then M does not have any computation path accepting w, or otherwise M would have non-zero error probability for some input not in the language. Hence M when viewed as a non-deterministic machine does not accept w either. If w is in L, then M has at least one accepting path, which suffices for the acceptance on the non-deterministic case. Thus, M viewed as a non-deterministic machine accepts L.

Furthermore, all words w for which probabilistic machine M respects the bound n^c, for some $c > 0$, have no computation path exceeding n^c time steps. Therefore, for these words the running time of non-deterministic machine M on w is at most n^c. So, L belongs to $NP(d(n))$. ◊

Theorem 4.7 *Let $0 < d(n) \leq 1$. Then:*

$$R(d(n)) \subset BPP(d(n))$$

Proof: Suppose that L is in $R(d(n))$. Consider a probabilistic Turing machine M accepting L with zero error probability for inputs not in L, that operates within time n^k with density $d(n)$.

Notice that if M has an accepting path for w, then w must be in L. This must happen because machine M does not have accepting computations when w is not in L, by definition of the complexity class $R(d(n))$.

Thus consider machine M' accepting L such that on input w of length n, M' sequentially simulates n times the behavior of machine M on w by at most n^k steps each time. If M has a computation that does not halt within n^k steps, then machine M' simulates the behavior of M on w without any time bound; M' accepts w if and only if M accepts w. If at some point M has an accepting path, then M' halts and accepts w. Otherwise, if all n computations halt and are rejecting computations, then M' rejects w.

If w is not in L, then w is not in $L(M')$ with zero error probability, since M has only rejecting paths for w. If w is in L, then M' must have accepting paths on w with probability greater than $\frac{1}{2}$, since machine M has such paths. For w in L, M' can make a mistake only when the n simulations of M on input w yield only rejecting paths. But machine M rejects inputs w in L with at most probability $\frac{1}{2}$. Thus M' have a probability of error bounded by $\frac{1}{2^n}$, since it simulates n machines M. Therefore, M' recognizes L with bounded error probability, $e(w) \leq \frac{1}{2^n} \leq \frac{1}{4} < \frac{1}{2}$, for all $n \geq 2$ and $w \in \Sigma^n$.

Furthermore, for words w that respect the bound n^k for machine M, all computations paths of M' on w halt computation in time n^{k+1}, since M always halts in time n^k for these words. Thus L is in $BPP(d(n))$. ◊

Theorem 4.8 *Let $0 < d(n) \leq 1$. Then:*

$$P(d(n)) \subset R(d(n))$$

Proof: A deterministic machine is a special case of a probabilistic Turing machine that makes no use of its randomness capacity and that makes no mistakes for any input. ◇

Theorem 4.9 *Let $0 < d(n) \leq 1$. Then:*

$$NP(d(n)) \subset PP(d(n))$$

Proof: Let L be in $NP(d(n))$. Let M be a non-deterministic machine accepting L within time bound n^k with density $d(n)$, for some $k > 0$. First, note that we can assume that M has a binary choice at every step and that all computations paths at least reach the bound n^k. Therefore, the computation tree of M on inputs w that respect the bound n^k has 2^{n^k} leaves.

Consider probabilistic machine M' that proceeds on input w as follows. First, M' tosses enough coins to get three computations paths. The first one is an accepting computation and has probability $[\frac{1}{2} - \frac{1}{8^{n^k}}]$. The second one is a rejecting computation and has probability $\frac{1}{8^{n^k}}$. The third one has probability $\frac{1}{2}$, and in this path M' simulates M but it also incorporates a time counter for n^k. If M' gets an answer just at n^k time steps, it halts with the answer of M with probability $\frac{1}{2} \cdot \frac{1}{2^{n^k}} = \frac{1}{4^{n^k}}$. If the path does not halt at n^k, M' simulates deterministically the behavior of M on input w. Since M may not halt on w, M' simulates each step of each computation path of M on w one at a time.

Hence in all cases, if w is in L an accepting path will be added to M' with at least probability $\frac{1}{4^{n^k}}$. If w is not in L, then there is no accepting path of M on w and a rejection probability of $\frac{1}{2}$ is added on this computation path. Thus, M' probabilistic recognizes L with at least probability $\frac{1}{2} + \frac{1}{4^{n^k}} > \frac{1}{2}$, for any input w of length n.

Furthermore, all inputs w for which M respects the bound n^k have the bound n^k respected by probabilistic machine M'. Thus, $L \in PP(d(n))$. ◇

5 Conclusions

We can summarize the inclusions above as follows.

$$P(d(n)) \subseteq R(d(n)) \subseteq \begin{cases} NP(d(n)) \\ \\ BPP(d(n)) \end{cases} \subseteq PP(d(n)) \subseteq PSPACE(d(n))$$

It has been conjectured that neither $BPP \subset NP$ nor $NP \subset BPP$ [4] . Thus much less $BPP(d(n)) \subset NP(d(n))$ nor $NP(d(n)) \subset BPP(d(n))$.

We could have defined an equivalent class to ZPP with density. ZPP stands for the class of languages accepted by probabilistic Turing machines with zero probability of error in average polynomial time. But since we allow some inputs to be unbounded, we do not expect to always have finite averages. If we restrict the average to be taken among the bounded words, then the notion of density is of little meaning, and the problem can be trivially reduced to manipulation of the class ZPP. We decide, instead, not to define the class $ZPP(d(n))$.

The study of the polynomial classes with density has taken in consideration only the uniform distribution. Notice that all the proofs shown here can be immediately translated to any *positive* everywhere probability distribution. For the sake of clarity of the notation, we have decided to omit $Pr[X = w/n]$ on the polynomial classes.

References

[1] M. Ajtai and A. Wigderson. Deterministic simulation of probabilistic constant depth circuits. In *Proceedings 26th Annual Symposium on Foundations of Computer Science*, pages 11–19, Portland, Oregon, 1985.

[2] M. Blum. A machine-independent theory of the complexity of recursive functions. *J. ACM*, 14(2), 1967.

[3] R. Book. Tally languages and complexity classes. *Information and Control*, 26:186–193, 1974.

[4] J. Gill. Computational complexity of probabilistic turing machines. *SIAM Journal of Computing*, (6):675–695, 1977.

[5] J. T. Gill. *Probabilistic Turing Machines and Complexity of Computation*. PhD thesis, Dept. of Mathematics, University of California, Berkeley, 1972.

[6] J. Hartmanis. On sparse sets in NP-P. *Information Processing Letters*, 16:55–60, 1983.

[7] J. W. Hunt. *Topics in Probabilistic Complexity*. PhD thesis, Stanford University, 1979.

[8] D. S. Johnson. The NP-completeness column: An ongoing guide. *Journal of Algorithms*, (5):433–447, 1984.

[9] K. Ko and D. Moore. Completeness, approximation and density. *SIAM Journal of Computing*, 10:787–796, 1981.

[10] M. O. Rabin. Probabilistic algorithms. In J. F. Traub, editor, *Algorithms and Complexity: New Directions and Recent Results*, pages 21–39. Academic Press, New York, 1976.

[11] J. Rolim and S. Greibach. On the IO-complexity and approximation languages. *Information Processing Letters*, 28(1):27–31, 1988.

[12] E. S. Santos. Probabilistic turing machines and computability. In *Proceedings American Mathematical Society*, 1969.

[13] A. C. Yao. Probabilistic computation: Toward a unified measure of complexity. In *Proceedings 18th Annual Symposium on Foundations of Computer Science*, pages 222–227, 1977.

Computer Architecture and Networks

MODELLING AND SIMULATION OF A PSEUDOSYSTOLIC PROCESSOR FOR MATRIX ALGORITHMS

Miguel E. Figueroa and Jaime H. Moreno

Departamento de Ingeniería Eléctrica
Universidad de Concepción
Casilla 53-C, Concepción, Chile
BITNET: mfigueroa%uconce@uchcecvm

ABSTRACT

We describe the modelling and simulation of a pseudosystolic processor for matrix algorithms. The processor follows the decoupled access/execute model of computation, and is therefore composed of two programmable units: an Access Unit (AU) and a Processing Unit (PU). Both units work independently and synchronize their operation through queues.

The modelling and simulation are based on a formal specification of the processor written in Verilog HDL, a high level language for hardware description. Such a specification describes the processor at the behavioral level (instruction set architecture) and at the structural level (register transfer architecture). Performance measures can be obtained through the simulation, making it possible to evaluate tradeoffs in the instruction set design as well as in lower levels of the architecture.

Hardware modelling and simulation are helping us to find bottlenecks in the architecture. Moreover, they are allowing us to evaluate the effectiveness of several features and their impact on overall system performance, thus proving to be an important tool in the development of complex digital systems.

INTRODUCTION

Hardware modelling and simulation play an important role in the design of a complex digital system. They help evaluating design tradeoffs and detecting errors at different levels of the system, from high level architecture to implementation. They also reduce time and cost in the design process. Frequently, a high level hardware description language (HDL) is used for hardware specification, while another language is used for system simulation. Unfortunately, it is hard to have a uniform approach if the two languages are different, and often consistency problems arise from this situation. As a result, HDLs and design tools have been developed for the compilation and simulation directly from the hardware description of a system [1, 2].

Among their features, HDLs allow structural and behavioral descriptions of a design, thus enabling the designer to describe and simulate the system at different levels of abstraction. In this way, a modification to the system (such as a new instruction in a processor) can be first simulated on the model at a high level, using a behavioral description, to test its effectiveness. When the results are satisfactory, the new feature can be simulated at a lower level, using a structural description, to study its implementation within the system. Currently, the most prominent HDLs are VHDL and Verilog* HDL. Both languages are widely used and have become standards for digital design [2, 3].

One example of complex digital systems are systolic-type arrays. Since the introduction of the concept [4], extensive research has been performed on the design and implementation of dedicated arrays for specific algorithms (specially for real-time signal processing) as well as on methods to systematically carry out the design and mapping tasks. Particularly, much research has focused on the efficient execution of matrix algorithms on processor arrays [5, 6], due to the importance of these algorithms in the resolution of scientific and engineering problems.

In recent publications, we have proposed a class-specific linear pseudosystolic array for partitioned execution of matrix algorithms [7, 8]. This array is well suited to (and was derived through) the MMG Method, a data-dependency graph-based mapping technique described in [9]. In this article, we present the development of a formal description of the processing elements in the pseudosystolic array, whose architecture uses the decoupled access/execute model of computation. This description is being written in Verilog HDL, at two different levels of abstraction: a behavioral level, which simulates the instruction set architecture of the processor; and a structural level, which simulates the register transfer architecture. Both descriptions allow the evaluation of design tradeoffs and the collection of performance measurements at different stages in the design process.

Hardware modelling and simulation are proving to be vital tools in the design of the processor. They are allowing us to find bottlenecks in the architecture, and optimize its performance through the evaluation of several features at both the behavioral and the structural level.

THE PSEUDOSYSTOLIC PROCESSOR

We describe now the architecture of the pseudosystolic processor for the linear array proposed in [7], supporting it with fragments of the Verilog HDL description. First, we briefly describe the architecture and main features of the array.

The array is a linear structure of K processing elements (PEs), as shown in Figure 1 for $K = 4$; two additional pseudoprocessors (PPEs) are used to simplify data transfers but do not perform computations. The array has support for external I/O from/to a host through chains of register/memory modules (the IR and OR blocks in the figure), and memory modules external to the cells. The data transfer rate is lower than the computation rate. Each memory module is associated to one cell and is accessed as a FIFO queue, so that there is no need for address generation; these memory modules have a capacity of $O(n)$ words, where n is the dimension of the matrix.

Input data for executing an algorithm are stored in the input modules (IRs), which are also accessed as FIFO queues; the host computer must transfer the data in the order in which they will be used. Such input data are pipelined through the IR modules until reaching their destination, where they wait until needed by the corresponding cell.

---

*Verilog is a trademark of Cadence Design Systems, Inc.

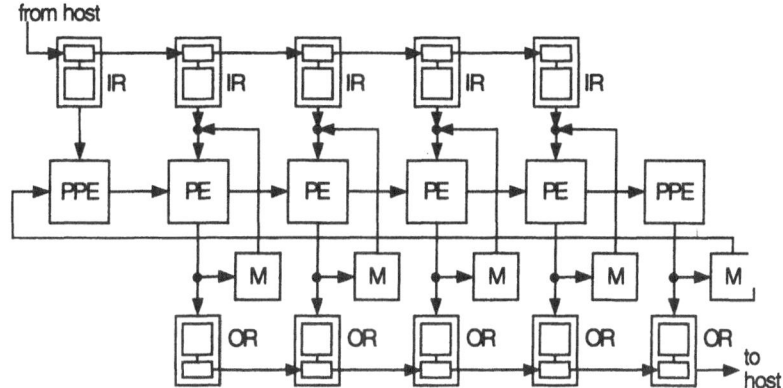

Figure 1. The linear pseudosystolic array

```
// Module Header

module mmg_cell( Xin_bus, cell_read, cell_rack,
                 Xout_bus, cell_wreq, cell_wack,
                 Yin_bus, mem_read, mem_rack, ir_read, ir_rack,
                 Yout_bus, mem_write, mem_wack, or_write, or_wack,
                 prog_load, reset, phi1, phi2 );

    input [wsize-1:0] Xin_bus, Yin_bus;    // input data busses
    input cell_rack, mem_rack, ir_rack;    // handshaking control signals
    output cell_read, mem_read, ir_read;   // handshaking control signals
    output [wsize-1:0] Xout_bus, Yout_bus; // output data busses
    input cell_wreq, mem_wack, or_wack;    // handshaking control signals
    output cell_wack, mem_write, or_write; // handshaking control signals
    input prog_load, reset, phi1, phi2;    // clock and control signals

    parameter Tpd = unit_delay;            // parameter and default value

/***************************************
 *  Verilog-HDL specification goes here: *
 *           ...                         *
 ***************************************/

endmodule
```

Figure 2. Module header for the processor

```
// Definition of internal components: processing unit, access unit, queues
// Module Header goes here

module mmg_cell( [ports] );
    // Input/output ports declaration
    // Internal signals declaration
    // Begin component instantiation and signal mapping
    processing_unit PU( [ports] );
    access_unit     AU( [ports] );
    queue           Xin_queue( [ports] ), Yin_queue( [ports] ),
                    Xout_queue( [ports] ), Yout_queue( [ports] );
    initial begin
        // initial state of the processor is defined here
    end
endmodule

// The following module overrides default parameters for components
module annotate;
    defparam
        // parameter values
endmodule
```

Figure 3. General structure of the processor

Similarly, output data are stored in the output modules (OR) waiting to be transferred to the host; these transfers are pipelined through the modules. All data transfers are unidirectional and take place concurrently with the execution of operations in the cells.

Cells in this array have an external interface which is described by the Verilog HDL module header depicted in Figure 2. Such a description shows the two input and the two output ports, along with their handshaking lines.

The architecture of the cells follows the decoupled access-execute model of computation [10]. This model decomposes the processing tasks into two parts, namely

- access operands and store results; and
- execute the operations that generate the results.

These tasks are carried out in separate units which run independent programs concurrently; the two units synchronize their execution through queues. This organization is shown in Figure 4, and is reflected in the Verilog HDL description given in Figure 3.

As depicted in Figures 3 and 4, cells consist of an *access unit (AU)* and a *processing unit (PU)*. AU transfers operands from and to memory, IR/OR modules and neighbor cells, through two input and two output channels (X_{in}, X_{out}, Y_{in}, Y_{out}); PU executes the arithmetic operations in a pipelined functional unit (FU), and has a register and two buffers to store data. Queues attached to input ports can deliver one word per time-step to PU, while queues attached to output ports can receive one word per time-step.

The processing unit

The processing unit (PU) performs the arithmetic operations on the operands read from the input queues. It also delivers the results to the output queues or stores them

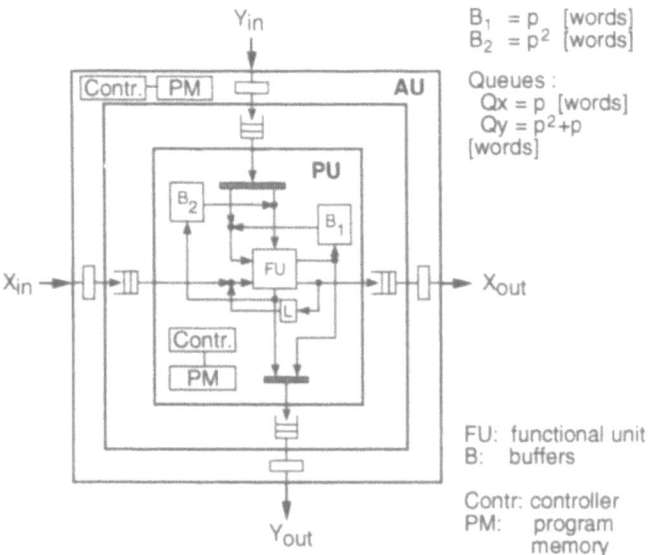

B$_1$ = p [words]
B$_2$ = p^2 [words]

Queues :
  Qx = p [words]
  Qy = p^2+p
[words]

FU: functional unit
B: buffers

Contr: controller
PM: program
     memory

Figure 4. Decoupled access-execute processor

in internal buffers for later reutilization. The Verilog HDL behavioral description of PU consists of a set of procedures that represent the various functions that the unit performs during program execution: instruction fetch, decoding, arithmetic operations, program control flow, etc. These procedures are invoked from a process that performs the scheduling of operations during the unit machine cycle. The structure of the behavioral description of PU is given in Figure 5.

Internally, PU is composed of a data section and a control section. The data section consists of a pipelined functional unit, plus a register L and two buffers (B_1, B_2) which are used to store intermediate data. These buffers operate as FIFOs, so that they don't require addressing. This internal structure is modeled in Verilog HDL through a register-transfer level description, as shown in Figure 6.

The schedule of operations obtained through the MMG mapping method [8] determined the features of the control section and instruction set of PU, which have been targeted to support the most frequently performed functions. Consequently, this unit supports the execution of single-instruction loops with no overhead, and the nesting of two block loops with just one overhead instruction each (setting the loop range and starting address). All instructions are executed in a single cycle. There are five different instruction types, as follows:

    a)   arithmetic operations,
    b)   call/return,
    c)   loop control,
    d)   seed values for division and square-root, and
    e)   access to FU registers.

An instruction type (a) is executed once and can be repeated L_1 times, corresponding to a single instruction loop. On the other hand, any instruction can determine the end of either of the two block loops.

To illustrate the execution of the three nested loops, Figure 7 shows a fragment of the behavioral description of the PU controller, corresponding to the instruction fetch and next-PC computation sequence.

```
module processing_unit( Xin, xin_rd, xin_rack, Xout, xout_wr, xout_wack,
                        Yin, yin_rd, yin_rack, Yout, yout_wr, yout_wack,
                        yout_dst, prog_load, reset, phi1, phi2 );

    input [wsize-1:0] Xin, Yin;
    input xin_rack, yin_rack;
    output xin_rd, yin_rd;
    output [wsize-1:0] Xout, Yout;
    input xout_wack, yout_wack;
    output xout_wr, yout_wr, yout_dst;
    input prog-load, reset, phi1, phi2;

    // aliases declaration
    'define   wsize       32
    'define   opcode      IR[wsize-1:wsize-6]
    'define   endL3       IR[6]
    'define   endL2       IR[5]
    'define   L1_count    IR[4:0]
    // ...
    // named events declaration

    initial begin
        // definition of initial state of PU
    end

    always @reset begin
        // reset sequence
    end

    always @prog_load begin
        // internal program load sequence
    end

    always @(posedge phi1 or posedge phi2) begin
        // behavioral description of PU
    end

    // tasks and functions definition

endmodule
```

Figure 5. Behavioral description of PU

```
// Components definition: functional unit, register, counter, table
// Same module header as behavioral description

module processing_unit( [ports] );
    // Input and output ports declaration
    // Internal signals declaration
    // Begin component instantiation and signal mapping

    func_unit    FU( [ports] );
    register     TL( [ports] ), MR1( [ports] ), MR2( [ports] ),
                 AR( [ports] ), L( [ports] );
    queue        B1( [ports] ), B2 ( [ports] );
    table        div_tab( [ports] ), sqr_tab( [ports] );

    initial begin
        // initial state
    end

    always @reset begin
        // reset sequence
    end

    always @prog_load begin
        // program load sequence
    end

    always @(posedge phi1 or posedge phi2)
    begin : controller
        reg [cntsize-1:0] LpCnt1, LpCnt2, LpCnt3, LpRng2, LpRng3;
        reg [memsize-1:0] LpAdr2, LpAdr3, PC;
        reg [wsize-1:0] IR;

        // control of PU is specified here
    end

    // tasks and functions definition

endmodule
```

Figure 6. Register transfer level description of PU

425

```
if( LpCnt1 == 0 ) begin
        // read next instruction and new count for internal loop
    IR <= #Tpd L1_count;
        // verify external loops and load new PC
    update_externals(LpCnt2, LpCnt3, PC, IR);
    end
else
        // decrement count for internal loop
    decrement(LpCnt1);
    // decode and execute contents of instruction register
execute_instruction(IR);
    // etc.
    // ...

/**** definition of related tasks ***/

task update_externals(LpCnt2, LpCnt3, PC, IR);
    input IR;
    inout LpCnt2, LpCnt3, PC;
    begin
        // check for end of loop L2 and execute loop L3 if necessary
    if( LpCnt2 == 0 )
        update_L3(LpCnt3, PC, IR);
        // update LpCnt2 if instructions determines end of L2
    case ( endL2(IR) )
        0:  increment(PC);
        1:  decrement(LpCnt2);
            PC <= #Tpd LpAdr2;
    endcase
    end
endtask

// ...
// update_L3 performs a similar task for loop L3
```

Figure 7. Instruction fetch and next-PC computation in PU

The access unit

The access unit (AU) transfers the operands and results between the external modules and the I/O queues. It is composed of four independent controllers that perform the data transfers associated to each port of the cell. The input controllers are used to access operands from external sources in advance to their utilization by PU; data are prefetched by the controllers and stored in the input queues until needed by PU. Similarly, results from PU are stored in the output queues and sent by the output controllers to the external modules, at a rate determined by the cell bandwidth.

Only the controller associated to Y_{in} is programmable, since it must prefetch data from two different sources (the IR module and the external memory) as required by the execution of the algorithm. The other controllers perform a much simpler task, and therefore they are just finite state machines. The X_{in} and X_{out} controllers transfer data between the queues and the neighbor cells. The Y_{out} controller sends data to the corresponding external memory and OR module. For this purpose, PU stores the data in the queue together with a flag (a bit) indicating the destination. Consequently, the controller sends out each data element as soon as the corresponding destination module is ready to accept it.

Figure 8 shows the Verilog HDL behavioral description of AU. This description is composed of four concurrent processes (one for each I/O channel), which use several procedures and functions to perform the different operations required during data transfer.

Internally, AU consists of a data section and a control section. The data section is quite simple, because it is composed of four registers located between each input or output cell port and the corresponding queues. On the other hand, the control section contains four independent controllers, one for each of the four channels (two inputs and two outputs). Figure 9 shows the Verilog HDL register transfer level description of AU. Since the Y_{in} controller is programmable, it is described as a different module.

Similarly to PU, the Y_{in} controller supports the execution of three nested loops: a single-instruction internal loop executed with no overhead, and two external loops which introduce one overhead (non-data transfer) instruction each (setting up loop range and starting address). The internal loop is used to read a block of data from the same module, while the two external loops are used to read consecutive blocks of data, as required by the algorithm.

The instruction set in AU is quite simple. It provides data transfer instructions (which indicate the source of the operand and, potentially, a single-instruction loop) and loop initialization instructions. Any data transfer instruction can determine the end of an external loop. To illustrate the data transfer mechanism, Figure 10 shows a fragment of the Verilog HDL behavioral description of the X_{in} controller.

CURRENT STATE OF DEVELOPMENT

We are currently developing a complete model of the processor using the structures presented above. Our goal is to obtain performance and utilization measures for the processor executing different matrix algorithms. These measures include code efficiency, FU utilization, mean length of queues and traffic in I/O busses. The next step is to model and simulate the linear array; measures of interest in this case include intercell communication bandwidth, load balance and data transfer rate to/from the host. This model will also be used as a target machine for an automatic code generator (based on the MMG method) currently under development.

```verilog
module acess_unit( [ports] );
    // aliases and named events declarations

    initial begin
        // initial state definition
    end
    always @reset
        // reset sequence
    end
    always @prog_load
        // program load for Yin controller sequence
    end

    always @(posedge phi1 or posedge phi2)
    begin : Xin_controller
        // behavioral description
    end

    always @(posedge phi1 or posedge phi2)
    begin : Yin_controller
        // behavioral description
    end

    always @(posedge phi1 or posedge phi2)
    begin : Xout_controller
        // behavioral description
    end

    always @(posedge phi1 or posedge phi2)
    begin : Yout_controller
        // behavioral description
    end

    // tasks and functions definitions

endmodule
```

Figure 8. Behavioral description of AU

```
// Components definition: port controller, programmable controller

module access_unit( [ports] );
    // Input and output ports declaration
    // Internal signals declaration
    initial begin
        // initial state definition
    end

    // Begin component instantiation and signal mapping
    port_controller Xin_cont( [ports] ),
                    Xout_cont( [ports] ),
                    Yout_cont( [ports] );

    prog_controller Yin_cont( [ports] );

endmodule
```

Figure 9. Register transfer level description of AU

```
// The process is activated by the clock
fork
    issue_request(cell_read);          // request datum from previous cell
    end_write(Xin_queue);              // end write cycle on input queue
join
wait(cell_rack);                       // wait for acknowledge
Xin_register <= #Tpd read_datum(Xin_bus); // read datum from port
fork
    remove_request(cell_read);         // end read cycle
    start_write(Xin_queue);            // begin write cycle on input queue
join
wait(Qxin_wack);                       // wait for acknowledge

// The process repeats on the next clock edge
```

Figure 10. Data transfer mechanism in the Xin controller

Table 1. Code efficiency for four matrix algorithms.

Algorithm	Efficiency
Matrix Multiplication	0.94
LU-decomposition	0.91
BA^{-1}	0.94
Choleski decomposition	0.92

Analytical results obtained up to now for a group of representative algorithms (matrix multiplication, LU decomposition, BA^{-1} and Choleski decomposition) show very good code efficiency in the processor; only 6% to 10% of the instructions executed are required for overhead tasks such as flow control, while the rest are used to perform operations required by the algorithm. Consequently, the processing element can deliver between 90% to 94% of its peak computing capacity. The results obtained are summarized in Table 1 for a problem of size 100 executed on an array with 10 cells.

ACKNOWLEDGEMENTS

This research has been supported in part by FONDECYT, Grant No. 0379-91 "Processor arrays for matrix algorithms."

REFERENCES

[1] R. Lipsett, E. Marschner, and M. Shahdad. VHDL – The Language. *IEEE Design and Test of Computers*, pages 28–41, April 1986.

[2] E. Sternheim, R. Singh, and Y. Trivedi. *Digital Design with Verilog HDL*. Automata Publishing Company, Cupertino, CA, 95014, 1990.

[3] D.R. Coelho. VHDL: a call for standards. In *25th ACM/IEEE Design Automation Conference*, pages 40–47, 1988.

[4] H.T. Kung. Why systolic architectures? *IEEE Computer*, 15(1):37–46, January 1982.

[5] M. Annaratone, E. Arnould, T. Gross, H.T. Kung, M. Lam, O. Menzilcioglu, and J.A. Webb. The Warp computer: Architecture, implementation and performance. *IEEE Transactions on Computers*, C-36(12):1523–1538, December 1987.

[6] J.G. Nash, K.W. Przytula, and S. Hansen. The systolic/cellular system for signal processing. *IEEE Computer*, 20(7):96–97, July 1987.

[7] J.H. Moreno, M.E. Figueroa, and T. Lang. Linear pseudosystolic array for partitioned matrix algorithms. *To be published in Journal of VLSI and Signal Processing*, 1991.

[8] J.H. Moreno and M.E. Figueroa. A decoupled access/execute processor for matrix algorithms: architecture and programming. In *International Conference on Application-Specific Array Processors*, Barcelona, Spain, September 1991.

[9] J.H. Moreno and T. Lang. Matrix computations on systolic-type meshes: An introduction to the multi-mesh graph (MMG) method. *IEEE Computer*, 23(4):32–51, April 1990.

[10] J.E. Smith. Decoupled access/execute computer architectures. *ACM Transactions on Computer Systems*, 2(4):289–308, November 1984.

THE CARACAS MULTIPROCESSOR SYSTEM

Mauricio Campo; José Sabino Carrizales;
Jorge H. Gonçalves R.; Francisco Landaeta R.

IBM Caracas Scientific Center
Apdo. 64778, Caracas 1060, Venezuela
E-Mail: goncalve at caracas1.vnet.ibm.com

ABSTRACT

This paper presents the Caracas Multiprocessor (CMPS) System design, which is a current project of the IBM Caracas Scientific Center. The main characteristic of the CMPS is the combination of a bus architecture with a point-to-point interconnection network. The bus system is based on the Microchannel architecture. The processing elements are provided with an Intel 80286 processor, a dual-port memory, four transputer link adaptors, and some control logic. The communication between PEs can be established via bus by memory-to-memory block transfers and directly via serial links. The links are commuted with help of a programmable switch network. The host is connected via a Microchannel bus, and can be a system such as the IBM PS/2* or the IBM RISC SYSTEM/6000* computers.

INTRODUCTION

It is well known that the microprocessors are widely used for their low cost, small size and wide range of processing and control capabilities, however some of them are not fast, or powerful enough to keep up with real-time applications. The use of many cheap micro-

---

* (Microchannel, PS/2 and RISC SYSTEM/6000 are trademarks of International Business Machines Corporation)

processors working in parallel each executing a different task compensates the speed drawback by increasing the system throughput.

The Caracas Multiprocessor System (CMPS) is a hybrid architecture with the following features:

- Low Cost
- Configurable by Software
- Two communication levels: Point-to-Point via serial links and via memory transfers by using dual-port memories.
- The CMPS bus system is based on the Microchannel Architecture.

It is an hybrid architecture since it combines a cluster architecture with a software configurable array processor architecture. The processing units are based on the Intel 80286 microprocessor [1]. The reasons for using the Intel 80286 as a node processor are the availability of hardware/software development tools and its hardware's low cost.

The cluster buses are based on the Microchannel architecture and are connected to a Microchannel host system. The communication between any two processors in this scheme takes place through dual-port memories or via point-to-point communication links. Memory is distributed in the system since each processing unit has its own local memory. The processing units which are interconnected to the Microchannel based cluster buses have dual-port memories, which are part of a host computer memory map and are used for booting and memory-to-memory communication purposes.

This design does not attempt to compete with other multiprocessor systems in terms of its computational performance capabilities, since the microprocessor used does not have a high speed of computation. However, the system performance may be improved in the future by adding processing elements with Intel 80486s or inmos transputers [2]. This will be always possible without changing the hardware design since via transputer link adaptors one can connect processors with different computation speeds.

The array architecture is software configurable. In order to do that, every four PEs are connected to a inmos C004 crossbar switch [2]. The four PEs and the C004 switch conform a basic construction module. An array is then constructed by combining many of these modules.

The use of the Microchannel architecture for memory-to-memory transfers with the configurable point-to-point communication links make this design an interesting hybrid architecture. The next section gives an overview of the architecture. The subsequent sections describe the main construction modules more in detail.

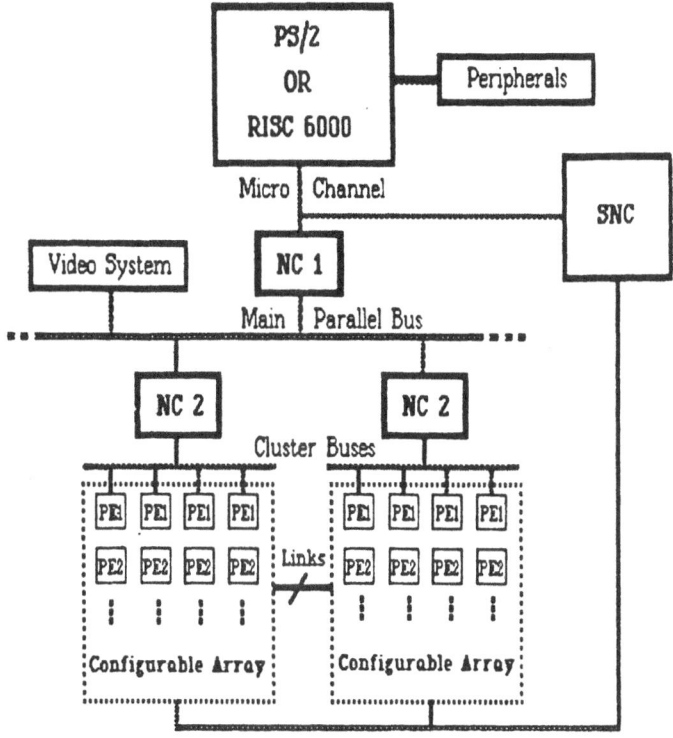

Figure 1. The CMPS Block Diagram.

ARCHITECTURE GENERAL DESCRIPTION

The block diagram of the CMPS is given in Figure 1. It shows a hierarchical architecture where

- a host computer is connected at the top of the hierarchy and
- Configurable processor arrays are connected at the bottom end of the hierarchy via a main parallel bus, which is also used to permit array-array communications. Figure 2 shows the inner structure of the arrays

  - The first row of Processing elements in the arrays are connected to the host system via a Microchannel based cluster bus and dual-port memories. The cluster buses and the inter-array communication bus constitute a hierarchical bus system. These PEs may be connected to adjacent PEs via 4 serial interconnection links.
  - The rest of the processing elements constitute a software configurable array processor.

So there are two interconnection media. One is the hierarchical bus system, which is a cluster architecture. The other interconnection media are interconnection links which are commuted by means of an array of crossbar switches.

The interconnections of the different bus systems involved are controlled with Network Controller Interfaces. The architecture is software configurable since many computational structures can be set by a programmable switch array controller. Serial interconnections between processing elements are achieved via transputer link adapters. The Processing elements are provided with four links. There is a Network Controller 1 which interconnects the parallel system to a host machine. There are different clusters attached to an intercluster parallel bus. Every cluster is connected to the rest of the system through a Network Controller 2. The intercluster parallel bus is similar to the Microchannel bus, but with some additional control lines. The Cluster bus is also similar to the Microchannel bus, however with more control lines but fewer address lines. The host computer is an IBM PS/2. The Microchannel architecture has better throughput and multiprocessing capabilities than the AT architecture.

The Processing Elements 1 (PE1s) are attached to the cluster bus via their dual-port memories, while the PE2s use only the serial interconnection links to communicate with their outside world. The NC2s are used to control the memory-to-memory communications between PE1s which attached to the same cluster bus. The memory-to-memory communication between PE1s in different clusters is controlled by the NC2s involved and the NC1.

The point-to-point communication links are established by using the Switch Network Controller (SNC), which is connected direct to the host via an adaptor card. A point-to-point communication is controlled by the two processing elements involved.

THE PROCESSING ELEMENT

The processing element is based on the Intel 80286 microprocessor, and is shown in Figure 3. The 80286 has a complex instruction set which makes the system a general purpose parallel computational system with the possibility of implementing a wide range of applications.

Besides the Intel 80286 microprocessor, a processing element is provided with an Intel 8207 dual-port controller, a dual-port memory of 256 kbytes, four transputer link adaptors and an I/O address decoder (for the selection of the link adaptors). There is an interrupt controller to manage interruptions when data is coming through one of the links and some other interrupt signals are used for synchronization.

Each dual-port memory may be accessed by two processors at a time: the local processor, and an external processor which writes a message into the dual-port memory using a DMA controller. The memory map of every dual-port memory has two predefined memory blocks destined to the in- and out-mailboxes, for sending and receiving messages. The rest of the dual-port memory is used by the local processor as instruction and data memory. Flags

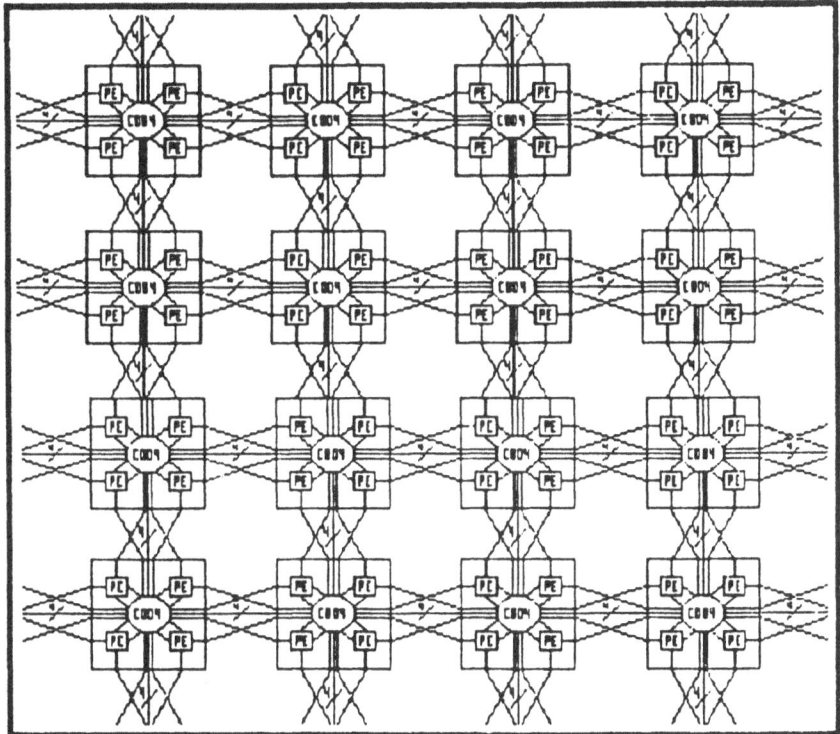

Figure 2. Inner Structure of the cluster array.

indicate unsent or unreceived messages. The memories are 256 kbyte dynamic RAMs constructed in two blocks, each of 128 kbytes.

The four serial links are implemented with transputer link adaptors C012. These link adaptors are connected to the local data bus and are selected to be read or written with addresses of the I/O-address space.

THE NETWORK CONTROLLERS

There are three different types of communications between PEs:

1. The communication between two PEs belonging to the same cluster via dual-port memories,

2. The data transfer between two processing elements belonging to different clusters via dual-port memories, and

3. Communication between two PEs via serial links

Data transfer inside the same cluster is controlled by the network controller NC2. If a processing element requires its cluster bus, a bus request signal must be sent to Network Con-

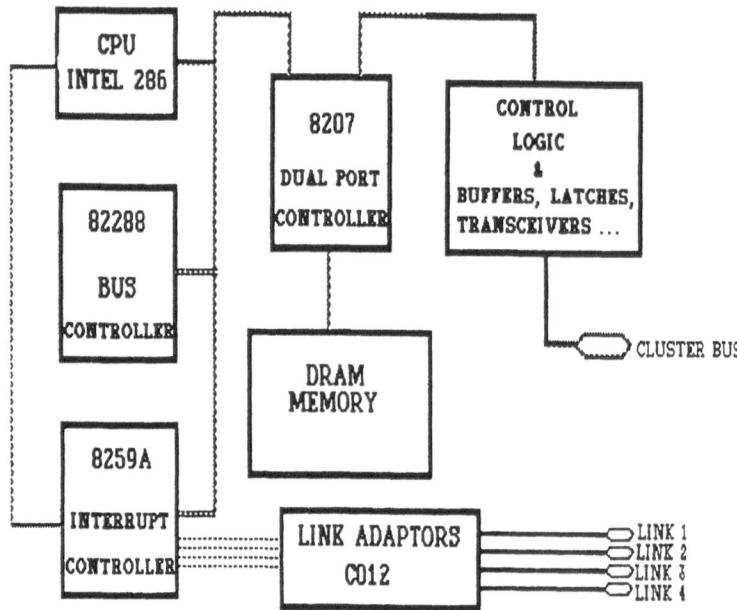

Figure 3. Processing element.

troller 2 where this signal is processed and prioritized by a Programmable Interrupt Controller; if this PE has the highest priority its bus request signal will interrupt the CPU which will send the DMA Controller the necessary instructions to perform the data transfer.

Data transfer between PEs belonging to different clusters is done using the first level Network Controller (NC1). In this type of transfer the NC2 is transparent and allows that the NC1 controls the cluster bus.

NC1 is composed by (see Figure 4):

1. support logic to POS (Programmable Option Select) protocol,
2. Microchannel signals adapting circuitry,
3. a 80286 CPU,
4. a 8259A Programmable Interrupt Controller,
5. a 82288 Bus Controller,
6. a masking interrupt logic,
7. a 82258 DMA Controller,
8. RAM and ROM memories,
9. latches and transceivers.

The NC2 is identical with NC1 with the exception of POS and signal adapting logic, these are not in NC2. A NC2 has two interrupt controllers: one for local PE-PE communication bus petitions, and another one for the inter-array communication bus requests.

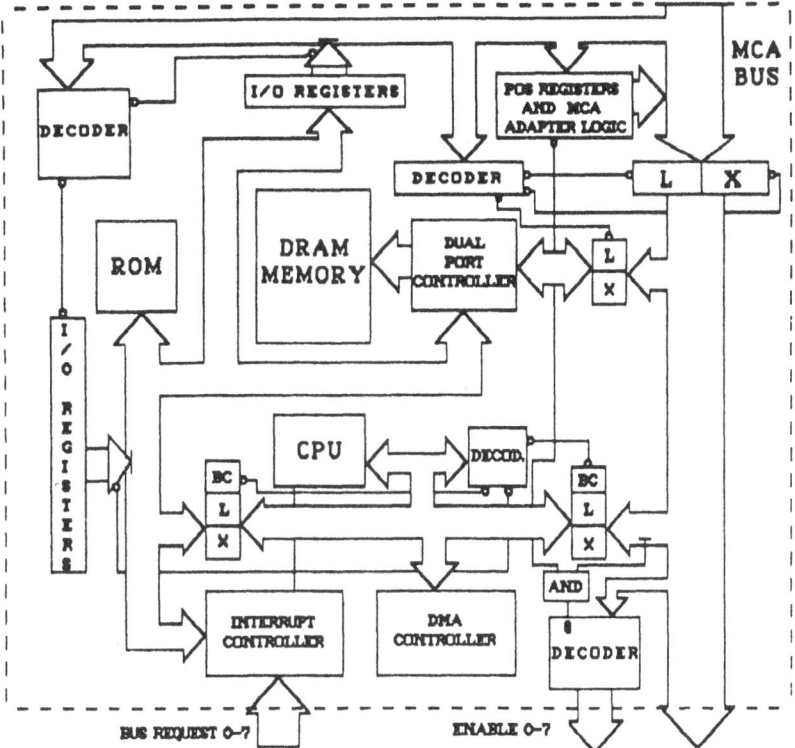

Figure 4. Network Controller 1 (NC1).

Additionally, block transfers between NC1-NC2 or NC2-PE are possible in case any NC1 or any PE should be booted after an error.

The buses are mainly be used for processor initialization when the executable programs are loaded, and for fast block transfer between processing elements.

The use of serial links allows the construction of more complex computer topologies. The serial links are connected by using a configurable switch array.

The design and implementation of a switch lattice allows different processor topologies to be established. Some interesting features of this design are:

1. It is configurable before and during the execution. This permits an optimal correspondence between the program and hardware topologies.
2. The combination of different processor types is possible since the communication through the links is asynchronous and serial.

The switch array is controlled in two modes using a centralized switch controller, or in a distributed manner.

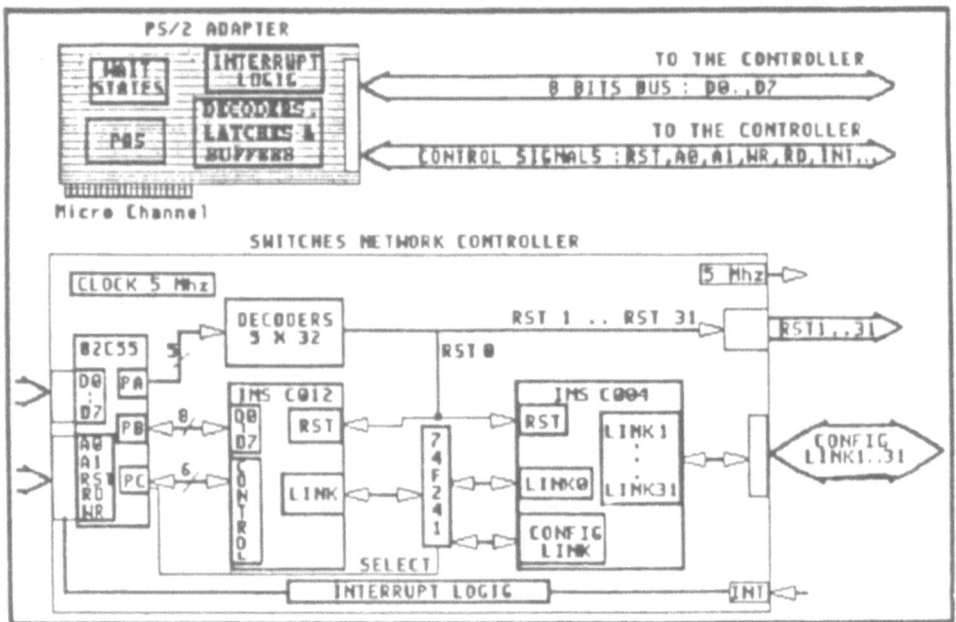

Figure 5. Switch Network Controller.

The centralized switch controller is designed to be connected to a Microchannel bus, so that the host of the multiprocessor system can be a PS/2 or a RISC SYSTEM/6000 workstation (see Figure 5). The network controller can be interrupted from any of the basic modules in case of error or for communication synchronization. The module status may be read directly from the host via link through the controller card.

The processor array is divided into basic hardware modules, which consist of a C004 accompanied by four processing elements (see Figure 2). The diameter of the network, which is the maximum distance between a pair of PEs, is one link, due to point-to-point connections, which can be established between any pair of nodes. The time delays are minimized due to the C004 bit-time delay, which is only a 1.75 bit-time delay on the signal. The resulting network is also flexible because different cubes and $k_{4,4}$ topologies can be embedded. The 4-cube topology may be easily implemented. There are unused links which can upgrade the performance and the reliability of the implementation by adding some extra strategic paths to the 4-cube topology. The switch configuration is performed using a centralized switch controller. Some extra logic for accessing the configuration link of each C004 in a decentralized mode is planned; so that each basic module programs its local switch. This is important when the computational array is used to implement a message passing architecture where communication tokens are routed by a local PE in every basic module.

438

FINAL REMARKS

We implemented our multiprocessor architecture with Intel 80286 node processors because of the availability of hardware/software development tools and the hardware's low cost. The high-speed communication technique has advantages in multiprocessing systems, and can be adopted for communication in multiprocessing systems based on powerful micro-processors. Processor nodes operating at different speeds and different word lengths could be combined in the same multiprocessor system. The dual-port memories allow the same memory to be used as working storage and for communication between nodes. With help of the dual-port memories, the arrays can be booted from the host by using memory block transfers. A host-PE communication is very simple since the dual-port memories are in the memory map of the host computer. A fully duplexed asynchronous and zero buffered communication scheme can be implemented by using the configurable switch array to establish point-to-point communication paths. The status of the PEs is shared with the corresponding NC2s. The NC2s share their status with the NC1 so that error transparency can be achieved. Parallel to design of the hardware architecture we are working on an operating system kernel. In order to do this, different distributed operating systems were analyzed, such as AMOEBA, MACH, Trollius and Helios [3,4,5,6]. As a result of this analysis, the new operating systems is going to share some design principles adapted to the CMPS architecture.

REFERENCES

1. Intel 80286 Hardware Reference Manual 1987.
2. inmos Product Information: The Transputer Family (1986).
3. Tanenbaum, A.; Renesse, R.: Distributed Operating System, Computing Surveys, 1986.
4. Mach Networking Group, Network Server Design, CMU, Aug. 1989.
5. Trollius Reference Manual for C Programmers, The Ohio University, Enero, 1990.
6. The Helios Operating System, Perihelion Software, Prentice-Hall, 1989.

A NEW COMMUNICATION SYSTEMS ARCHITECTURE

SUPPORTING MIGRATION TO OSI

Geert M. Solvie

Institute of Telematics
University of Karlsruhe
7500 Karlsruhe, Germany

ABSTRACT

Analysis of existing approaches supporting migration to OSI communication systems and comparison with user requirements proved that an important handicap to use of OSI is inadequate support of migration from existing to OSI communication systems. Existing approaches do not pay enough attention to the differing application services offered by existing proprietary communication systems and OSI communication systems. Moreover they are not flexible enough to encounter future changes in communication systems technology and user requirements. Therefore a new communication systems architecture based on the OSI architecture, the *eXtended OSI architecture*, supporting migration to OSI is introduced in this paper.

INTRODUCTION

The need for communication between applications located at different computers increases. Communication systems perform the task of connecting computer systems to render possible communication between applications. They offer application (communication) services to the applications transferring data, accessing remote files, initiating remote operations, etc. Internally communication systems use a set of rules and formats for exchange of information, called the protocol.

For different computer systems different communication systems were introduced, offering different services and using different protocols. Therefore communication between different computers was restricted to computers of the same type with the same communication system. To offer communication between different computers also, gateways, bridges etc. were introduced. But these facilities are very complex and often fail to offer the complete set of services for application support of the interconnected communication systems. In addition to that any two different communication systems require a special gateway or bridge, resulting in a great number of them and in case of changing protocols of one communication system, each gateway offering connection to this communication system has to be changed also.

COMPUTER SCIENCE, Edited by R. Baeza-Yates
and U. Manber, Plenum Press, New York, 1992

To overcome the problems presented and to make users more independent of manufacturers the International Organization for Standardization (ISO) defined a communication system architecture for *Open Systems Interconnection* (OSI). It was published in 1984 in the reference model.[1] This architecture offers communication between any two computer systems (endsystems in OSI terminology) conforming to the OSI architecture and the associated standards. The OSI architecture defines 7 layers—physical layer, data link layer, network layer, transport layer, session layer, presentation layer and application layer—each performing a specific task, offering specific services and using a specific standardized protocol. An overview with emphasis on the three topmost layers, the application oriented layers, is given by Henshall and Shaw.[2]

Up to now OSI communication systems are not as much in use as was suggested some years ago. Two reasons may be given for this delay. First standardization of application services, the communication services offered to the application, is slow. Second, and most important, the process of migration from existing non-OSI communication systems to OSI communication systems is not supported sufficiently.

Nevertheless OSI communication systems will increase in number inevitably because of strategies of mandatory usage of OSI communication systems in government agencies of various countries,[3] e.g. the USA with GOSIP,[4] europe with EPHOS,[5] the United Kingdom, Sweden and Canada. Companies communicating with government agencies have to work at migration to OSI. If some of them use OSI as a basis for communication their communication partners have to work at migration also, and so on. So everyone not living on a communication island will be affected by migration to OSI. Therefore effort is made moving existing networks to OSI networks, like EARN,[6] or at least interconnect existing networks with OSI networks. An example of an existing network to be connected to the OSI world is SNA. Approaches for interconnecting SNA with OSI are presented in Sy et al.[7] and Tillman and Yen.[8]

Despite the advantages of OSI, introducing OSI communication systems results in the same problems as introducing any other new communication system architecture. *Different services* are offered, making new applications necessary, *different protocols* are used, hindering interconnection to existing communication systems, and probably new infrastructure is required. Migration to OSI is even worse than introducing a new communication system existing in parallel to the old ones because existing communication systems used prior to migration period shall stop to exist, making existing applications useless. Otherwise different communication systems would have to be managed in parallel, an annoying task.

The following section presents existing approaches claiming support of migration. They are analyzed with respect to application user requirements in a section on *Estimation of existing approaches supporting migration to OSI*. Since none of them satisfies all requirements a new communication system architecture, the eXtended OSI architecture XOSI, satisfying all user requirements is presented after that. Finally the use of XOSI supporting migration to OSI is presented.

EXISTING APPROACHES FOR SUPPORT OF MIGRATION TO OSI

Approaches supporting communication with applications using OSI application services offered in OSI networks may be classified as follows:

- approaches proceeding in use of existing non-OSI communication systems and communicating with OSI applications by means of *protocol conversion*,[9, 10]
- approaches proceeding in use of existing non-OSI communication systems or using new OSI communication systems offering OSI and non-OSI services by means of *service interface conversion*,[11]
- approaches using OSI protocols supporting OSI applications communicating with OSI applications and using appropriate non-OSI protocols to support communication between non-OSI applications.

In this section a short introduction to existing approaches which are sometimes proposed for use in support of migration will be given. The approaches are described in more detail in several publications.[12-15] The approaches will be analyzed in a following section.

Dual-Stack Approach

The dual-stack approach is the simplest of the presented approaches, an example is a dual-stack system for OSI and TCP/IP.[12-14] The dual-stack approach is based on coexistence of two or more complete communication systems. In this way OSI services as well as services of other communication systems are offered in parallel with unrestricted functionality. But each of the communication systems requires its own network infrastructure and there is no interconnection between them. The dual-stack approach belongs to the class of approaches using OSI protocols supporting communication between OSI applications and using appropriate non-OSI protocols to support communication between non-OSI applications.

Figure 1 illustrates an endsystem affected by migration to OSI using the dual-stack approach. This endsystem offers OSI as well as non-OSI application services. OSI applications may communicate with other OSI applications via an OSI network, non-OSI applications may communicate with other non-OSI applications via a non-OSI network.

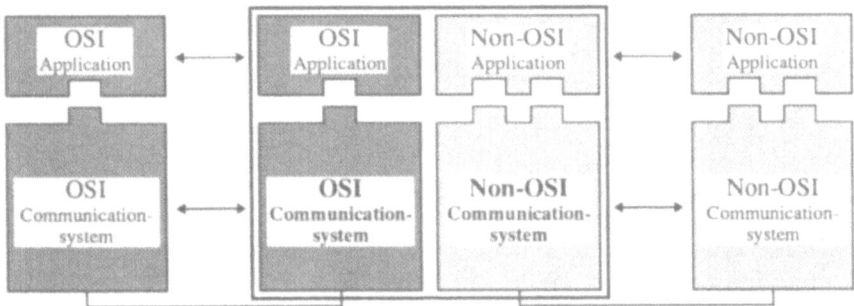

Figure 1. An example for the Dual-Stack approach. The endsystem affected by migration to OSI is enclosed in the box with bold lines.

Application-Layer Gateways

An application-layer gateway belongs to the class of approaches based on protocol conversion. Protocol data units (PDU) of one communication systems application layer are transformed to PDUs of another application layer and vice versa.[12-14] Therefore interconnection between different communication systems is supported, especially OSI—non-OSI. Even though major drawbacks are associated with this approach. Most important the loss of functionality and information because of the complexity and number of different application layer protocols which can not be transformed all completely in a gateway.[13] Also no OSI application services are offered in the non-OSI system.

Figure 2 presents an endsystem affected by migration to OSI using an application-layer gateway for communication with OSI applications. In the non-OSI network up to the gateway non-OSI protocols are used. They are transformed in the application layer gateway to OSI protocols rendering possible communication with OSI applications.

Transport-Layer Gateways

A transport-layer gateway transforms transport PDUs of one communication system to those of another communication system, especially OSI—non-OSI.[12-14] Therefore it belongs to the class of approaches based on protocol conversion. Transformation at transport level supports interconnection of different communication systems but does not support commu-

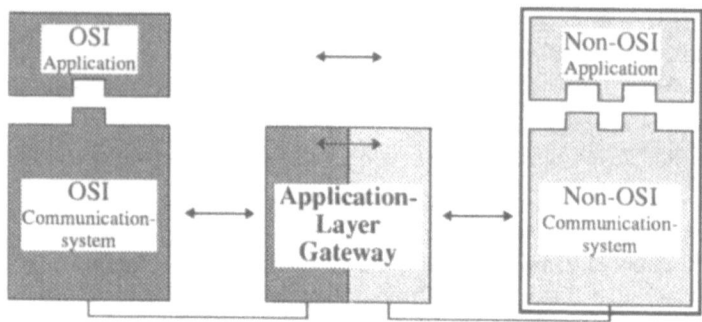

Figure 2. Example for an Application-Layer Gateway. The non-OSI endsystem affected by migration to OSI is enclosed in the box with bold lines.

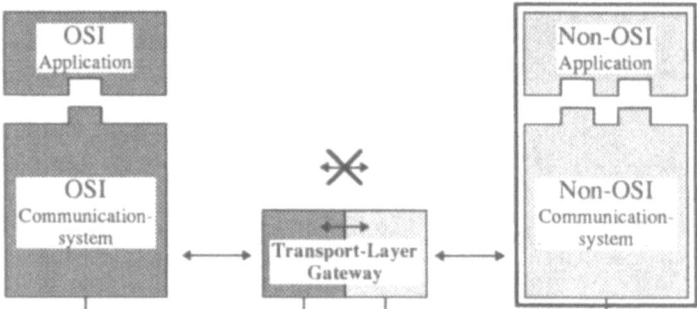

Figure 3. A Transport-Layer Gateway supporting migration to OSI. No support is given for transformation of application oriented protocols. Therefore the OSI and Non-OSI applications can not communicate.

nication between OSI and non-OSI applications because of missing application layer protocol transformation, see figure 3. Application services may be added but this results in an application-layer gateway.

Application-Service Adaption

If the application-service adaption approach is used, no application layer PDUs are to be transformed. Instead application services are to be converted.[11] Therefore it is an approach based on service interface conversion. Having migration to OSI in mind, an OSI communication system is the basis in this approach. If other application services than OSI application services are required, a service conversion function is required for transformation of services. A complete transformation at application service level is not always possible because of the differences of the services offered. Therefore this approach may result in loss of functionality and information.

Figure 4 presents an endsystem affected by migration to OSI, enclosed in the box with bold lines, using an OSI communication system to offer OSI application services and additional application-service converters to offer non-OSI application services.

Universal Application-Service Interface

An universal application-service interface (illustrated in figure 5) is a standardized interface offering application services independent of the used communication system. As an example, this approach is intended in IBM's Systems Application Architecture (SAA)[16] with the Common Programming Interface offering access to the Common Communications Support

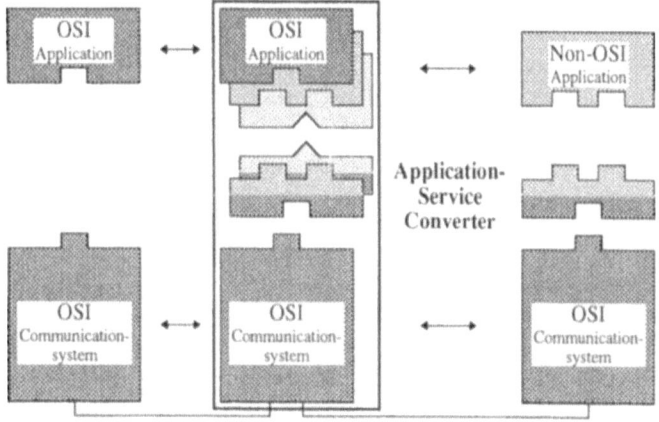

Figure 4. The Application-Service Adaption approach. OSI and Non-OSI applications may communicate by using Application-Service Converter.

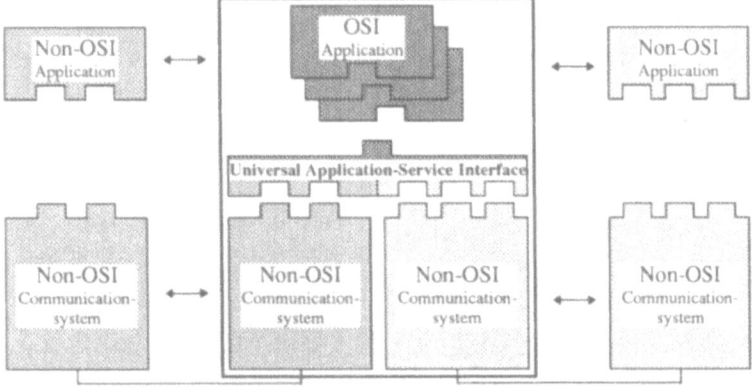

Figure 5. An example for an Universal Application-Service Interface offering OSI services on top of two different communication systems.

(CCS). The drawback of an universal application-service interface is that it is not suitable for already existing applications. Although this approach is favorable for future applications if a really universal interface is defined and standardized, especially one offering the complete OSI functionality.

Transport-Service Adaption

Opposite to the other approach based on transport level, the transport-layer gateway, transport-service adaption does not base on protocol conversion but on service interface conversion. On top of an existing transport system a conversion function is implemented, offering OSI transport services. This is much easier than at application service level because of the small number of transport services and their similarities in different communication systems. Therefore transport-service adaption does not result in loss of functionality or information. Figure 6 presents an example configuration for a transportconverter offering OSI transport services to OSI application oriented layers, which offer OSI application services to an OSI application. In Rose and Cass[15] conversion functions for OSI transport services on top of TCP are presented.

Interconnection with an OSI network may be obtained by simply copying the OSI transport PDUs in a bridge node. For more details see the characterization of a Transport-Service Bridge by Rose.[12] It was first implemented in ISODE.[17] Communication between OSI and non-OSI applications is not possible because either OSI application oriented protocols or non-OSI protocols are used. To offer different application services in a single endsystem a combination with the dual-stack approach is required.

Network-Service Adaption

Just so as transport-service adaption, network-service adaption offers the same (OSI) transport services to both communication partners. Contrary to the former approach the latter bases on service adaption at network layer, see figure 7. In general this is very simple because the non-OSI services used may be considered as a data-link service (OSI layer 2). Routing is handled by the OSI network protocol. Interconnection with an OSI network may be obtained by simply copying the OSI network PDUs, as described for Network Tunnels.[12] The major drawback of network-service adaption is that offering different application services requires combination with the dual-stack approach.

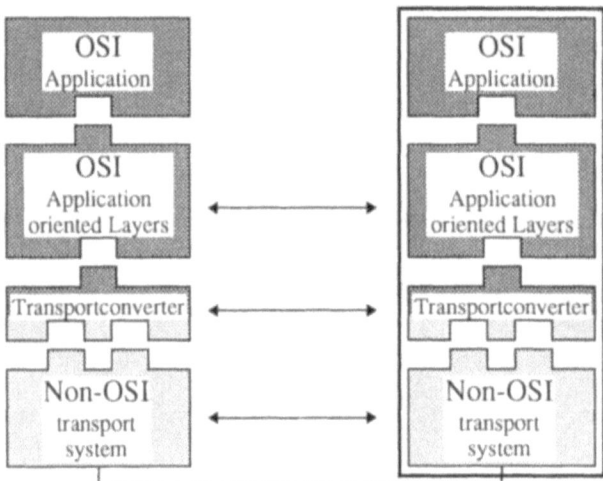

Figure 6. An example for the Transport-Service Adaption approach using OSI application oriented layers on top of a non-OSI transport system.

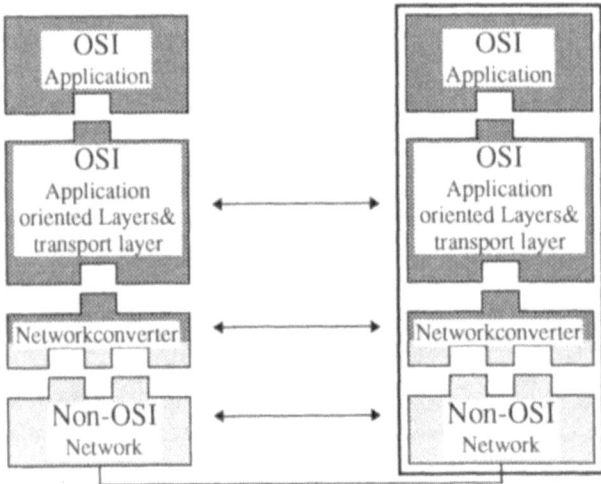

Figure 7. An example for the Network-Service Adaption approach using OSI application oriented layers on top of a non-OSI network.

ESTIMATION OF EXISTING APPROACHES SUPPORTING MIGRATION TO OSI

Performing migration to OSI is a long-term process. One of the main reasons for delay of OSI, is insufficient support of user requirements for migration to OSI. The requirements will be presented following. After that the existing approaches presented in the previous section will be examined whether satisfying user requirements or not.

User Requirements for Support of Migration

Users do not care for protocols, gateways or other technical details. They want their application to act in the expected manner and perform necessary communication transparently. Therefore application users require support of migration to:

a) ensure continuous operation,

b) guarantee no (additional) errors in the application program,

c) protect investments in complex application programs,

d) do not make training of users on new application programs necessary,

e) offer powerful OSI application services to be used in new applications.

Requirements a)-d) will be met perfectly if the unchanged application program is used during migration period and after migration to OSI is complete. An application program interacts with the communication system through communication system *application services* only. Those are the communication services offered by the communication system to the application at the application interface. Examples of application services are execution of remote operations and access and manipulation of remote files. Modifications to the application program are not necessary if the existing application services, offered by communication systems to be replaced by OSI, are preserved during migration to OSI. Therefore a resulting requirement for an architecture supporting migration to OSI, satisfying requirement e) too, is *coexistence of unchanged application services* of existing communication systems and OSI communication systems.

Analysis of Existing Approaches

From the presented requirements for support of migration to OSI five criteria are derived:

Support of existing applications: If support of existing applications is offered, applications using non-OSI conforming application services may be used in the endsystem affected by migration without any modifications of existing applications being necessary.

Support of OSI applications: If support of OSI applications is offered, OSI application services are offered. Therefore new applications using OSI services are supported by the endsystem affected by migration.

Loss of functionality or information: Loss of functionality indicates whether the complete set of functions offered by an ordinary OSI or non-OSI system is offered in the endsystem affected by migration also. Loss of information may occur if at least one of the communication systems involved in communication does not support all presentation functionalities used by the sender. E.g. a sender uses the multi-media facilities of MHS. If the text-oriented SMTP is to be used between sender and receiver, multi-media information will be lost.

Existing network infrastructure sufficient: Today non-OSI networks are used to support communication of non-OSI applications. If the existing network infrastructure is sufficient, the existing non-OSI networks may be used to support OSI applications also, at least until migration is complete. Otherwise an OSI network has to be installed additional to the existing network, resulting in management overhead.

447

Adaptability to changed environment: During migration period and after migration is complete the environment may change. Those changes may be the network used, new versions of protocols, etc. User requirements demand adaptability to changed environment with acceptable costs to protect investments.

An analysis of the presented approaches supporting migration to OSI with respect to the introduced criteria is given in table 1.

Table 1. Comparison of approaches supporting migration to OSI.

Criteria	migration approach						
	Dual-Stack	Application-Layer Gateway	Transport-Layer Gateway	Application-Service Adaption	Universal Application-Service Interface	Transport-Service Adaption	Network-Service Adaption
support of existing applications	yes	yes	no*	yes	no	no*	no*
support of OSI applications	yes	no	no	yes	yes†	no*	no*
loss of functionality or information	no	yes	yes	yes	yes	no	no
existing network infrastructure sufficient	no	yes	yes	no	no	yes	yes
adaptability to changed environment	no	no	no	yes	yes	yes	yes

*No support at application service level but at transport level.
†If standardized with respect to OSI

Analyzing table 1 manifests that approaches based on protocol conversion—application-layer gateways and transport-layer gateways—often result in loss of functionality or information. This is because of the complexity of application protocols and important differences between those of several communication systems. Another deficiency of approaches based on protocol conversion is that the endsystem affected by migration to OSI does not support OSI application services. Therefore these approaches are improper for migration.

Approaches based on service interface conversion—application-service adaption, universal application-service interface, transport-service adaption and network-service adaption—either result in potential loss of functionality or information, if conversion takes place at application service level, or do not offer application services.

The dual-stack approach belongs to the class of approaches using OSI protocols to offer OSI application services and appropriate other protocols to offer other application services. This approach is the only one of the already existing approaches satisfying the application requirements for coexistence of complete OSI and non-OSI application services. Two essential problems are connected with this approach. First, every communication system of which application services are supported results in a complete communication system, and network probably too, to be implemented and managed. Producing an enormous overhead and costs of multiple implemented services, protocols and networks. Second, any changes in the network, e.g. migration to an OSI-transport system, will be supported only if every communication system in the dual-stack system supports these changes.

As a conclusion, approaches based on protocol conversion are not proper to support migration to OSI because they do not offer OSI application services and result in loss of functionality or information. Approaches based on service interface conversion are suitable for support of the migration process at transport level. But they lack of application services.

The only approaches satisfying application user requirements are those using appropriate protocols to offer application services. But these approaches require an OSI transport system in parallel to the existing non-OSI transport system and changes of the environment are cumbersome.

XOSI—AN ARCHITECTURE FOR A FLEXIBLE COMMUNICATION SYSTEM

As a result of the analysis of existing approaches, a communication system supporting migration to OSI must offer the required application services, an OSI application service, any specific proprietary non-OSI application service (e.g. SNA) or any other application supporting communication service by using appropriate protocols (e.g. to offer SNA application services use SNA protocols). At transport level other than the original transport protocols corresponding with the application oriented protocols may be used because service conversion is acceptable here (see network-/transport-service adaption approaches). A suitable communication system architecture results of combining the dual-stack approach restricted to the application oriented layers (5-7) with an approach based on service conversion at transport service level. This is illustrated in figure 8.

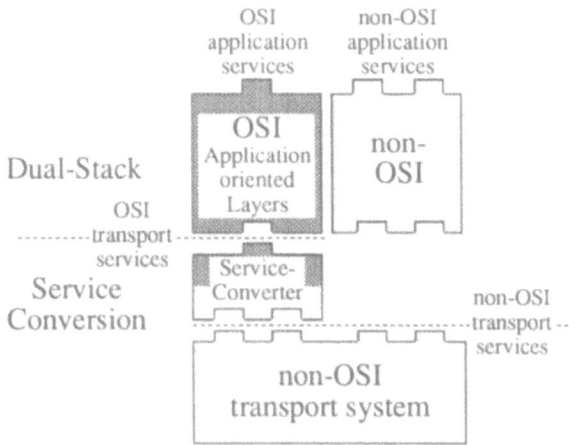

Figure 8. A combination of the dual-stack and service conversion approaches.

A problem with this architecture is overhead as well as its inflexibility with respect to changes at the application oriented layers. This results from the dual-stack approach used at these layers. A more *flexible architecture* would support changes and reduce overhead.

Configuration of Services and Protocols

Flexibility of a communication system may be reached by generation of services and protocols satisfying application requirements best. The most general approach rendering possible generation is by deriving an implementation from a formal specification of the communication requirements. A formal specification for a non-trivial communication service and protocol would be very complex and nearly unmanageable. Today no system generates a complete implementation of a complex protocol from its specification only, if at all a formal specification for complex protocols exists. Therefore this approach is not practicable, at least not today.

A practicable approach to generate services and protocols satisfying application requirements with low overhead is configuration of implemented basic components. The components must be as general as possible to be applicable for different service requirements and as simple as possible to reduce overhead of not used functionality of a component. As a result there may be defined and implemented a lot of basic components, some of them perhaps just slightly different. But the set of defined and implemented components does not result in overhead for an implementation of a flexible communication system because implementations of actually unnecessary components may be stored anywhere, e.g. components of general interest (for instance OSI components, SNA components) on a fileserver. Only the components necessary to satisfy specific communication requirements are used in the flexible communication system.

An absolutely necessary requirement for basic components is their mutual independence. Dependencies between components result in restrictions for selection of components. ISO defined an approach for configuration of application services at OSI application layer.[18] In this approach no independence of the to be configured components is mandatory, e.g. see mapping rules of ACSE[19] and CCR[20] which directly map onto presentation layer services[21] and RTSE[22] which directly maps onto ACSE services[23] and presentation layer services. This results in predefined dependencies of components and restricts selection of components. For example selection of a better service element for association management than ACSE in connection with RTSE is not possible because of the dependencies.

The set of basic components and rules for coordination of their interaction to offer an application service will be called a *context*. A *context specification* is used to specify the selection of appropriate basic components and the coordination of their interaction. The selected components, satisfying specific communication requirements, have requirements for transfer of their PDUs also. Therefore each component defines a new context for its to be transferred PDUs. Based on the resulting context specification further basic components are selected and so on. The selection process continues until all communication requirements are satisfied by a basic transport service. This concept of *hierarchical context specifications* results in a most flexible configuration of arbitrary basic components.

The eXtended OSI Architecture

A new communication system architecture offering flexibility and minimum overhead is the *eXtended OSI architecture*, XOSI. In XOSI flexibility is obtained by configuration of basic components, the *autonomous service-elements*. Independence of autonomous service-elements favors usage of them in different configurations, each of them satisfying application requirements best.

The eXtended OSI architecture is restricted to the application oriented layers—session layer, presentation layer and application layer in OSI terminology—because the existing approaches supporting migration at transport level proved to be sufficient. Therefore the basic transport service for PDUs to be sent on behalf of an autonomous service element is the service offered by the transport system. The separation between transport system and application support is at all most desirable because application support must be independent of the transport system to favor migration to OSI.

Besides the autonomous service-elements two additional components are used in the XOSI architecture, the *coordinator* and the *contextmanager*. They are responsible for performing and controlling configuration. Figure 9 gives an overview of the architecture and its components. The components are explained in detail in the following sections.

Autonomous Service-Elements. The service offered by an autonomous service-element must be self-contained. Therefore an autonomous service-element has to be independent of other service-elements. Even though services of other service-elements are used to transfer PDUs. But an autonomous service-element itself does not specify the service-element of which the service has to be used. It does not know anything about other autonomous service-elements or adjacent layers offering services.

Autonomous service-elements are derived from complex protocols by splitting. OSI and non-OSI protocols are split into autonomous service-elements taking into account the independence of resulting service-elements. Splitting is not limited within OSI application oriented layers. There may result autonomous service elements, especially non-OSI, involving func-

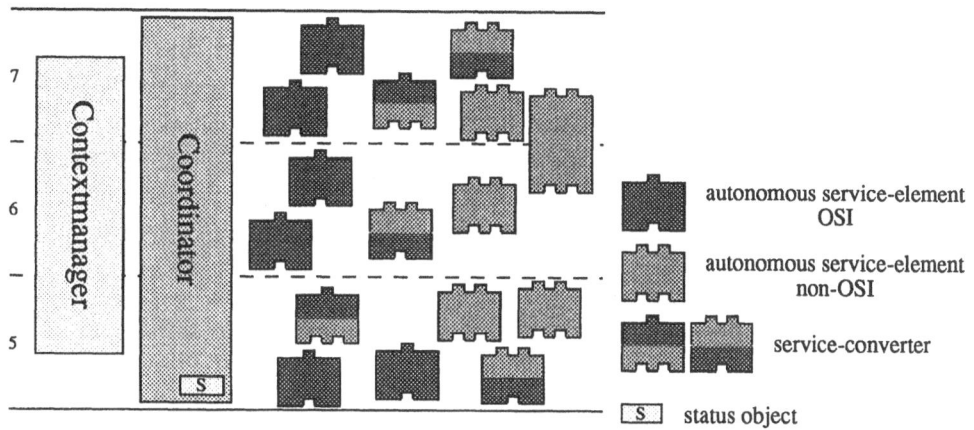

Figure 9. The extended OSI architecture.

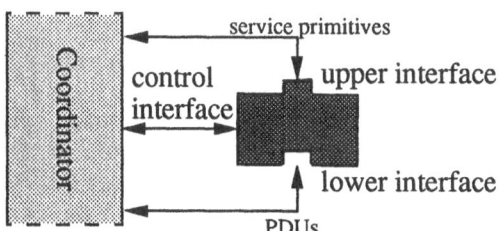

Figure 10. The interfaces of an autonomous service-element.

tions of more than one OSI layer. Autonomous service elements may be configured in any way resulting in a composed protocol, especially an OSI conforming protocol or a protocol conforming to a vendor specific communication system. But even new composed protocols may result, satisfying application requirements better than existing protocols. New service-elements applying protocols not used in existing communication systems may be used also, if special application requirements must be satisfied and OSI conformity may be ignored. A special kind of autonomous service-elements are service-converter. Examples for service-converters have been presented in the transport-service adaption and the network-service adaption approaches. Service-converters may be selected any time the required services differ from the supported services, e.g. OSI transport services required and TCP services offered.

The only interface of an autonomous service-element is the interface to the coordinator. It is divided into an *upper interface*, a *lower interface*, and a *control interface* (see figure 10). The upper interface offers services to the user of the service-element, via the coordinator. Service primitives are exchanged here. At the lower interface PDUs are exchanged. Any additional information necessary for correct behavior of an autonomous service-element is supplied by the coordinator. An example for additional information is the presence and ownership of tokens (session layer). Access to these information is offered through the control interface.

The Coordinator. Coordination of autonomous service-elements is done by the coordinator component. It is the only interface for communication among autonomous service-elements, and between autonomous service-elements and upwards the application and downwards the transport system. It is the only entity responsible for routing of PDUs and service primitives within the XOSI architecture.

Routing is specified by rules. With $X, Y \in S$ (service set), $Z_n, Z_{n+1} \in Z$ (state set of the status object), $\alpha, \beta \in A$ (autonomous service-element set) and $X.req, X_{RC}, Y_{RI} \in I$ (incoming event set) these rules are of the form:

$$Z_n, X.req \quad \rightarrow \quad \alpha$$
$$Z_{n+1}, X_{RC} \quad \rightarrow \quad \alpha$$
$$\cdots$$
$$Z_{n+1}, Y_{RI} \quad \rightarrow \quad \beta$$

The confirmed service X may be initiated in state Z_n with the service primitive X.req. This service primitive is routed to the autonomous service-element α. For a confirmed service in general no other service may be initiated until confirmation. Therefore the only rule accepting a service primitive in state Z_{n+1}, resulting from the initiation of X.req, is the confirmation X_{RC}. However communication may be aborted any time by some error. For that reason an event Y_{RI} indicating this kind of error must be permitted in state Z_{n+1} also. This PDU is routed to service-element β.

The rules required for routing in the coordinator are derived from the *context* selected for a connection (in application layer: association). Specifying a context conforming to the OSI protocol specification results in an OSI conforming protocol. Specifying a context conforming to any vendor specific communication system an appropriate protocol will result, eventually up to the point where mapping onto OSI services is performed. The responder is informed of the selected autonomous service elements and routing rules during connection establishment. If it does not support all of the proposed service elements it will reject connection establishment.

To manage information that may be accessed and manipulated by more than one autonomous service-element the coordinator uses a *status object*. Information managed in the status object are the connection state (*connection idle, connection establishing, connection established, connection releasing*), the transaction state (*TA idle, TA active, TA ending*), the presence and ownership of tokens, etc. Although some states of autonomous service-elements are used in the status object no duplication of the states of the service-elements used occurs. A change of the state in the status object occurs only when an externally visible change is performed. E.g. when a transaction is in the termination phase several service primitives and PDUs are used. No other services and PDUs are allowed until the transaction is complete. Therefore the autonomous service-element supporting transactions (e.g. CCR) changes the state from *TA active* where execution of remote operations is allowed to *TA ending* where no execution of remote operations is allowed. After completion of the transaction the state is changed to *TA idle*. Then orderly release of the connection is permitted.

An example for the explicit use of the status object by an autonomous service-element is the requirement for the ownership of the (session layer) *Data Token* for transfer of data (PDUs) on a half-duplex session connection. The autonomous service-element offering the session layer data transfer asks the status object via the coordinator whether the *Data Token* is owned by the initiator of the data transfer service. If true, a session data PDU will be generated. It is returned to the coordinator which is responsible for routing it to a suitable transfer service (e.g. data transfer service of the transport system). If the *Data Token* is not owned, an error notification is returned to the coordinator and no session data PDU is sent.

Further tasks of a coordinator are concatenation of PDUs, interface to the application and unique identification of service primitives and PDUs.

The Contextmanager. The contextmanager is the component selecting suitable autonomous service-elements and generating rules for routing of service primitives and PDUs within the coordinator. The rules are derived from a context specification.

First the application specifies a context (level 1) according to its communication requirements. The contextmanager selects one or more autonomous service-elements offering the specified context and thereby satisfying the application requirements. The selection is done by comparison of the required services, specified in the context, and the services offered by autonomous service-elements, specified for each service-element. According to the context specification rules for coordination of the selected service-elements are generated.

To satisfy communication requirements of the selected autonomous service-elements each service-element specifies a context for its to be transferred PDUs. The resulting contextspecifications of level 2 are handled by the contextmanager similar to the specification of level 1, but with respect to the interrelation of the selected service-elements. The selection process continues until all communication requirements, specified in a context at level n, are satisfied by the services offered by the transport system (hierarchical context specification).

A very simple contextspecification omitting parameters looks like this:

connection-establishment(...);

transaction-begin(...);

{execute-remote-operation(...);}*

transaction-end(...);

connection-release(...);

This is a simple specification for a connection oriented service for execution of any number of remote operations which are entirely enclosed in a transaction.

Analysis of XOSI

The presented communication system architecture XOSI has to be compared with the existing approaches. This will be done with respect to the criteria already presented in section *Analysis of Existing Approaches*.

An XOSI communication system offers *support of existing applications* as well as *support of OSI applications*. Neither *loss of functionality* nor *loss of information* may occur because appropriate protocols may be used any time. *Existing infrastructure is sufficient* for there may be used any transport system. If necessary, adaption is done by service conversion at transport of network layer. Because of its flexibility an XOSI communication system may *adapt to changed environment* easily.

As a result, the XOSI architecture is the approach satisfying support of migration to OSI best. None of the other approaches satisfies all user requirements.

XOSI SUPPORTING MIGRATION TO OSI

Supporting migration to OSI requires OSI and non-OSI application services to be offered and OSI as well as non-OSI application oriented protocols to be configurable. Therefore OSI as well as to be supported non-OSI protocols have to be split into autonomous service-elements. The simplest splitting results in one autonomous service-element for each communication system. Usage of these service-elements then trivially results in an OSI or non-OSI conforming protocol and OSI or non-OSI application services.

A better approach for splitting, reducing overhead, consists of a number of autonomous service-elements with universal functionality, which may be used in other configurations also. Criteria for splitting are:

- an OSI-conforming or non-OSI conforming proprietary protocol must be configurable by selection of appropriate autonomous service elements and coordination rules,
- functionalities with strong interrelation shall be gathered in the same autonomous service-element, those with weak or no interrelation in different service-elements,
- the resulting autonomous service-elements shall be as universal as possible,
- the information to be managed in the status object of the coordinator shall be minimal.

Splitting OSI Protocols

An essential aspect of the XOSI architecture is its ability to offer OSI conforming protocols. A simple splitting of OSI protocols results in one autonomous service-element for each layer. But this splitting results in service-elements with great implementation overhead of unused functionalities and not universal applicability. This section presents an example of how the OSI conforming protocols of the application oriented OSI layers may be split, according to the presented criteria.

Session Layer. OSI session layer standards[24, 25] specify 12 functional units. One or more of them may be negotiated during connection establishment, always including the *Kernel* functional unit. Examination of the functional units manifests that the services are nearly optimally combined with the exception of services for token management, being used several times. A splitting of the session layer protocol, according to the principles presented above, results in the following autonomous service-elements:

Kernel offers services for connection management and data transfer,

Expedited data offers services for expedited data transfer,

Typed data offers services for transfer of typed data,

Capability data offers services for capability data transfer,

Minor synchronize offers services for setting of minor synchronization points,

Major synchronize offers services for setting of major synchronization points,

Resynchronize offers services for resynchronization,

Exceptions offers services for exception reports,

Activity management offers services for management of activities,

Token management offers services for management of tokens.

Information to be managed in the status object of the coordinator is the presence and ownership of tokens. Every service-element offering a service requiring or modifying the ownership of a token (e.g. *major synchronize, minor synchronize, token management*) must have access to the status object, managed by the coordinator.

Presentation Layer. Analogous to session layer, presentation layer standards[24, 25] specify functional units which may be negotiated during connection establishment phase. Here only three functional units are specified. One mandatory (kernel) and two optional (context management and context restoration) functional units. Splitting the presentation layer protocol two autonomous service-elements result:

Kernel offers services for connection management and data transfer, (including encoding and decoding of transfer syntax),

Context management and restoration offers services for altering the defined set of presentation contexts and resynchronization.

The information to be managed in the status object is the defined set of presentation contexts. This information may be accessed by both service-elements. The *kernel* service-element negotiates the defined set of presentation contexts and requires presentation context information for encoding/decoding of transfer syntax, and the *context management and restoration* service-element may alter the defined presentation contexts.

In an environment where use of the context restoration functional unit is rare a splitting of the *context management and restoration* service-element in two service-elements for *context management* and *context restoration* may be clever to reduce implementation overhead. The disadvantage of this splitting is that context restoration information must be managed in the status object of the coordinator additionally.

Application Layer. For OSI application layer the structure is defined in an additional document.[18] Within this structure different *application service elements* are standardized, e.g. ACSE, ROSE, CCR, RTSE, FTAM; Bever[26] presents an overview. They may be selected and combined according to rules specified in those standards, e.g. RTSE uses ACSE services for association management.

The OSI application service elements are defined with respect to the interrelation of services, e.g. ACSE[23,19] offers services for association management, ROSE[27,28] offers services for the execution of remote operations. They do not have to be split and may be taken as an autonomous service-element, ignoring the dependencies between some of them. However there are more complex application service elements which may be split into several autonomous service-elements, e.g. FTAM.

Splitting Non-OSI Protocols

Non-OSI protocols have to be split the same way as OSI protocols. Splitting non-OSI protocols sometimes is more complex because they are not always strictly layered as the OSI layers and service dependencies are more complex.

Configuration of OSI and Non-OSI Conforming Protocols

The presented autonomous service-elements, resulting from a splitting of OSI protocols, may be configured in a way that an OSI conforming protocol results. This is possible because the autonomous service-elements have been selected with respect to the negotiable OSI functional units. An example for a configuration offering services for execution of remote operations could consist of the ROSE and ACSE autonomous service-elements, the presentation *kernel* autonomous service-element and the session *kernel* autonomous service-element. If half-duplex transfer is required also, the session *token management* autonomous service-element would be selected additionally.

Such as OSI protocols may be configured, the autonomous service-elements resulting from a splitting of non-OSI protocols may be configured in a way that a specific non-OSI conforming protocol results, offering non-OSI application services.

Having migration to OSI in mind an XOSI communication system today must offer regular OSI services along with specific proprietary application services of communication systems used today. This avoids changes of existing applications using application services and supports new OSI applications. Changes of the protocols used and the transport system offering data transfer must be transparent. Figure 11 and figure 12 present example configurations for migration to OSI using an XOSI communication system. At an early stage existing non-OSI transport systems may be used. Non-OSI applications may use non-OSI application services offered by appropriate non-OSI protocols using the non-OSI transport system. If OSI application services have to be offered, OSI application oriented protocols are used (figure 11 left tower of autonomous service-elements). They require for OSI transport services. These are offered by the non-OSI transport system by using transport-service adaption. An autonomous service-element realizing a transportconverter is used in XOSI to offer OSI transport services on top of a non-OSI transport system. Thereby no loss of functionality or information results. Interconnection with an OSI transport system is possible via a transport-service bridge, again without loss of functionality or information.

At the end of migration process, OSI transport systems will be used. Therefore another autonomous service-element is required, offering non-OSI transport services on top of an OSI transport system. These non-OSI transport services may be used by appropriate non-OSI application oriented protocols, offering non-OSI application services (figure 12 middle tower of autonomous service-elements). The OSI application oriented layers use the OSI transport services directly (figure 12 left tower of autonomous service-elements). There are no changes at application service level visible. Further changes at the transport system, e.g. high-speed networks, are transparent to the application also. New versions of protocols at application

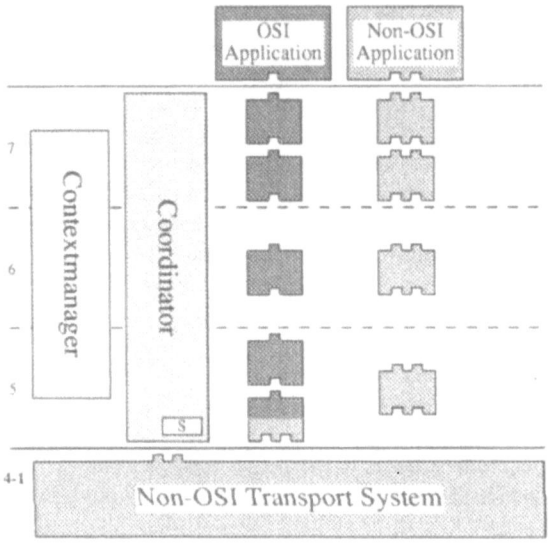

Figure 11. An example configuration using a non-OSI transport system.

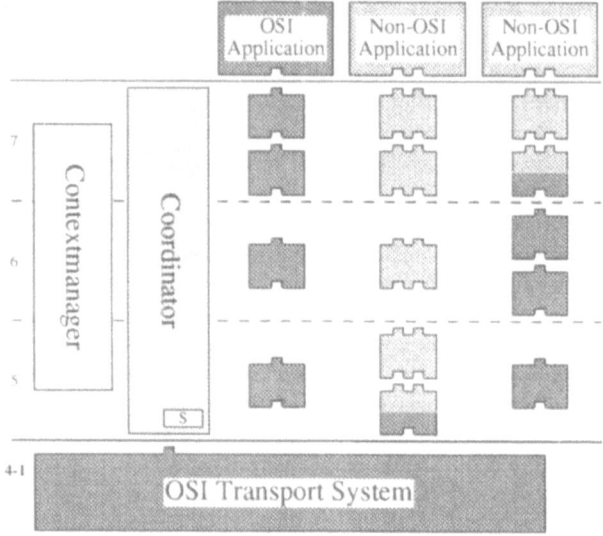

Figure 12. An example configuration using an OSI transport system.

oriented layers may be used in parallel to the old ones, offering new and old services.

Even if existing networks are to be used for local environments simultaneous to OSI networks the XOSI communication system architecture may be used. According to the application requirements protocols are configured and an appropriate transport system is selected, eventually an autonomous service-element for transport service conversion is used.

To reduce overhead of application oriented layers for different communication systems, mapping onto OSI services may be performed at a higher level than transport layer, for an example see figure 12 right tower of autonomous service-elements. The level where mapping is performed depends on the similarities and differences between required services for transport of non-OSI PDUs and capabilities of offered OSI services. Mapping in the topmost layer reduces non-OSI protocols to a minimum and along with it the non-OSI protocol overhead is low. Mapping done in lower layers offers a common base of non-OSI services for various higher layer non-OSI protocols of the same non-OSI communication system, reducing the overhead of mapping for different protocols. Where mapping is performed best depends on the number of applications for the non-OSI services, the number of different protocols in one non-OSI communication system and the differences between the required non-OSI services and the offered OSI services. Again no loss of functionality or information is associated with mapping because of the flexibility of the architecture.

CONCLUSION

Analysis of existing approaches supporting migration to OSI manifests that none of them satisfies all user requirements. Therefore the new communication system architecture— eXtended OSI—, restricted to the application oriented layers and using an existing approach at transport level, was introduced. It offers capabilities perfectly satisfying the requirements of application support for migration to OSI.

The flexibility of the presented architecture is useful not exclusively for migration. The capabilities of configuring arbitrary services and protocols using any autonomous service-elements makes the eXtended OSI architecture support specific application requirements not satisfied by OSI protocols. Some of these requirements result from innovative applications, e.g. multi media applications, and innovative transport technology, e.g. high speed networks. Although all those non-OSI scopes OSI conforming protocols may be used any time.

REFERENCES

1. ISO7498-1;Information processing systems - Open Systems Interconnection - Basic Reference Model. International Standard, October 15 1984.

2. J. Henshall and S. Shaw. *OSI Explained; End-to-End Computer Communication Standards.* Ellis Horwood Series Computer Communications and Networking, second edition, 1990.

3. Rebecca Nitzan and Phill Gross. The role of the U.S. GOSIP. *Computer Networks and ISDN Systems,* 19:270–274, 1990.

4. U.S. Government Open Systems Interconnection Profile (GOSIP), April 1989. DRAFT Version 2.0.

5. L. Caffrey. EPHOS: Towards a european GOSIP. *Computer Networks and ISDN Systems,* 19:265–169, 1990.

6. Paul Bryant. The migration of EARN to use ISO protocols. *Computer Networks and ISDN Systems,* pages 201–203, 1987.

7. K. K. Sy, M. O. Shiobara, M. Yamaguchi, Y. Kobayashi, S. Shukuya, and T. Tomatsu. OSI-SNA interconnections. *IBM Systems Journal,* 26(2):157–173, 1987.

8. Matthew A. Tillman and David (Chi-Chung) Yen. SNA and OSI: Three strategies for interconnection. *Communications of the ACM,* 33(2):214–224, February 1990.

9. Paul E. Green. Protocol conversion. *IEEE Transactions on Communications,* COM-34(3):257–268, March 1986.

10. Simon S. Lam. Protocol conversion. *IEEE Transactions on Software Engineering,* 14(3):353–362, March 1988.

11. Gregor von Bochmann. Deriving protocol converters for communications gateways. *IEEE Transactions on Communications,* 38(9):1298–1300, September 1990.

12. Marshall T. Rose. Transition and coexistence strategies for TCP/IP to OSI. *IEEE Journal on selected areas in communications,* 8(1):57–66, January 1990.

13. David Simpson. 5 routes to coexistence. *Systems Integration,* pages 82–88, April 1990.

14. Marshall T. Rose. *The Open Book.* Prentice-Hall, 1990.

15. Marshall T. Rose and Dwight E. Cass. OSI transport services on top of the TCP. *Computer Networks and ISDN Systems,* 12(3):159–179, 1986.

16. V. Ahuja. Common communications support in systems application architecture. *IBM Systems Journal,* 27(3):264–280, 1988.

17. Julian Onions. ISODE: In support of migration. *Computer Networks and ISDN Systems*, 17:362–366, 1989.

18. ISO 9545; Information technology - Open Systems Interconnection - Application Layer Structure. International Standard, December 15 1989.

19. ISO8650; Information processing systems - Open Systems Interconnection - Protocol Specification for the Association Control Service Element. International Standard, December 15 1988.

20. ISO9805; Information technology – Open Systems Interconnection – Protocol Specification for the Commitment, Concurrency, and Recovery service element. International Standard, November 15 1990.

21. ISO8822; Information processing systems - Open Systems Interconnection - Connection oriented presentation service definition. International Standard, August 15 1988.

22. ISO9066-2; Reliable Transfer, Part2: Protocol Specification. International Standard, 1989.

23. ISO8649; Information processing systems - Open Systems Interconnection - Service Definition for the Association Control Service Element. International Standard, December 15 1988.

24. ISO8326; Information processing systems - Open Systems Interconnection - Basic connection oriented session service definition. International Standard, August 15 1987.

25. ISO8327; Information processing systems - Open Systems Interconnection - Basic connection oriented session protocol specification. International Standard, August 15 1987.

26. Martin Bever. OSI Application Layer. Tutorial ITG/GI-Fachtagung, Stuttgart, February 1989.

27. ISO9072-1; Remote Operations, Part 1: Model, Notation and Service Definition. International Standard, November 15 1989.

28. ISO9072-2; Remote Operations, Part 2: Protocol Specification. International Standard, November 15 1989.

MODELLING AND ANALYSIS OF TIME CRITICAL
APPLICATIONS ON LOCAL AREA NETWORKS

Marcos A. G. Brasileiro[1], James A. Field[2] & J. Antão B. Moura[3]

[1]DEE/CCT/UFPb - Brasil
[2]U. of Waterloo - Canada
[3]DSC/CCT/UFPb
Av. Aprigio Veloso, 882 - Bodocongó
58100 Campina Grande, PB. - Brazil

ABSTRACT

For the purpose of resource sharing, various applications may be integrated in a communication system. Some of these applications may have extreme or critical requirements on the system performance. Such applications are said to be Critical Applications. This paper deals with the characterization and analytical modelling of Critical Applications on Local Area Networks (LANs). Criteria for judging the criticalness of an application with respect to the performance of a LAN, are also discussed.

INTRODUCTION

The wide interest in Local Area Networks (LANs) is due to their potential use in a large spectrum of applications (e.g, office automation, process control, distributed processing, etc.). This traffic integration is economically justified[1] . Most of the networks in operation today were designed for data applications such as interactive computing or file transfer. For these applications, the relevant performance measures are usually the average values of some probability distributions (e.g. average delay versus throughput).

In a more realistic scenario, applications other than the data processing mentioned above, may compete for the communication subnetwork. Each competing application has different requirements. Particularly, some applications may have extreme requirements on the network performance. For example, in a digitized voice transmission, the number of packets whose delay has exceeded a given time limit must be kept small, if high quality of the voice reconstruction at destination is desired. Therefore knowing only the averages of probability distributions is insufficient to precisely analyze the performance of integrated applications.

A model which captures the integration of applications and also provides the relevant measures pertinent to each application, is needed to study the performance of integrated LANs.

Applications placing extreme requirements on the network performance are called *Critical Applications*. It is specifically for those applications that the model mentioned above has to provide means to study the network performance. Therefore, for studying integrated applications in a LAN, a formal specification for Critical Applications is necessary. Based on this specification and the solution for the integration model, we give a formal criteria for judging the criticalness of a given application.

In this paper we focus on Critical Applications requiring an Upper Bound Limit on time delay on Token Passing LANs. For these Critical Applications, the relevant measure is $\Pr[t > T_1]$, the probability that the time delay exceeds T_1, where T_1 is a characteristic parameter pertinent to the application. To find $\Pr[t > T_1]$ we need the time delay probability distribution. This requires the solution of the communication subnetwork model of the Token Passing LAN.

The criteria for judging the criticalness of a given application consists on the determination of $\Pr[t > T_1]$ and its comparison to the acceptable probability (*tolerance probability*) which is specified on the application specification.

This article is organized as follows: first, we show a formal characterization for a Critical Application with Upper Bound Limit Measure. Next, we present the model and solution for the integrated communication subnetwork of a Token Passing LAN, and the criteria for judging the criticalness of an application. Following, we present a case study. Finally, we show the conclusions and comments.

FORMAL SPECIFICATION FOR CRITICAL APPLICATION WITH UPPER BOUND LIMIT MEASURE

In many applications the performance of the systems is satisfactory provided some probability of a specified parameter needing a given bound is small. In this section we give general formal definitions for such systems. For convenience we consider only upper bounds but the definition is easily extended to include lower bounds and ranges[2].

The performance requirements for a given application present on a LAN may be characterized by a set $\{m\}$ of performance measures:

$$\{m\} = \{m_1, m_2, m_3, ..., m_k\}$$

where $m_i(1 \leq i \leq k)$ is a measure relevant to the application. For example, in a file transfer application, m_i and m_j could be the time delay and throughput, respectively.

Let $[m_i]$ be a value of m_i. Now, for each set $\{m\}$ there exists a bounds set $\{M\}$:

$$\{M\} = \{ [M_1], [M_2], [M_3], \ldots, [M_k] \}$$

whose elements are the bound values for each measure in $\{m\}$. For instance, in digitized voice traffic transmission, $[M_i]$ could be the maximum permissible delay per packet. Associated with each $[M_i] \in \{M\}$, there exists a *tolerance probability* defined by:

$$f_i = \Pr ([m_i] > [M_i])$$

Let us denote $\{f\}$ as the set of tolerance probabilities associated with each $[M_i] \in \{M\}$.

For a given LAN, there exists a probability density function $p_i(m_i)$ associated with each measure $m_i \in \{m\}$. Consequently, for each set $\{m\}$, there exists a set $\{p\}$ given by:

$$\{p\} = \{p_1(m_1), p_2(m_2), p_3(m_3), \ldots, p_k(m_k)\}$$

An application with upper bound measures specified by the sets $\{m\}$, $\{M\}$ and $\{f\}$ is said to be critical with respect to a LAN characterized by $\{p\}$ if there is a measure $m_i \in \{m\}$ such that the following expression holds:

$$\lim_{x \to \infty} \int_{[M_i]}^{x} p_i(m_i) \, d[m_i] = f_i^* = f_i - \varepsilon \tag{1}$$

The set $\{f^*\}$ whose elements are f_i^*s, which satisfy the equations above, is denominated *set of critical tolerance probability*. The knowledge of this set is important for judging the criticalness of a given application with respect to the LAN performance. Thus, an application is critical if there exists at least one $f_i \in \{f\}$ such that $f_i = f_i^* - \varepsilon$, $\varepsilon \to 0$, for each $f_i^* \in \{f^*\}$. Therefore, a given LAN is suitable for an application if $f_i \geq f_i^*$ for each $f_i \in \{f\}$ and $f_i^* \in \{f^*\}$. When at least one $f_i < f_i^*$, the considered LAN does not satisfy the application performance requirements.

In order to judge the criticalness of an application, we need its formal specification, i.e. the knowledge of the sets $\{m\}$, $\{M\}$, $\{f\}$. Also it is necessary to determine the sets $\{p\}$ and $\{f^*\}$ which characterize the LAN. These last sets depend on the topology, speed of the transmission medium, communication protocols, etc. To find the sets $\{p\}$ and $\{f^*\}$ we need to solve the model for the communication subnetwork. As we mentioned, the solution has to provide the pdf of each relevant measure of an application.

In the following section we present the model and solution for the communication subnetwork of an Integrated Token Passing LAN.

MODEL FOR ANALYZING TIME CRITICAL APPLICATION

We present in this section a model for the Token Passing LAN which captures the integration of applications. Following, we show the criteria for judging the criticalness of a given application.

Network Model

Let us consider a Token Passing LAN supporting a heterogeneous user population, depicted in Figure 1.

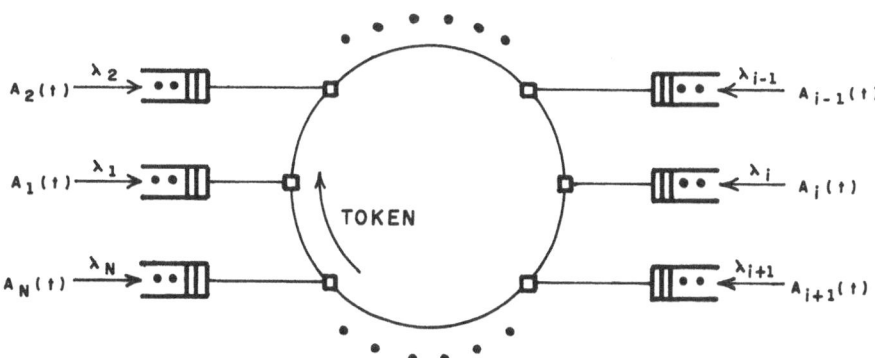

Figure 1. Logical Token Passing Ring

Each interface may have a different traffic arrival pattern and a different service time distribution. Packets arrive at interface i according to a general and independent process GI, with PDF $A_i(t)$, and average λ_i packets/s. The service process is FCFS with PDF $B_i(t)$, and average b_i seconds. We assume that each interface has an unlimited buffer space and that the arrival and service processes are independent and stationary.

Due to the mathematical intractability of most cyclic service queue problems, some simplifying assumptions must be made[3,4]. One of most common assumptions is the independence of the stochastic processes. We will consider the solution of non-exhaustive cyclic service queues, i.e. for each token visit to a given interface (queue), only one packet is transmitted. Furthermore, we will include in the solution for the Token Passing LAN model, the concept of *conditional of token cycle*, in order to better reflect the reality on the considered model[5].

The solution of Token Passing LAN model is similar to those of cyclic service queues. These type of queues have been extensively investigated in the literature[5,6,7,8,9,10,11,12].

For interface i, we are assuming that the relevant measure for the process $A_i(t)$ is an Upper Bound Limit Measure. Therefore, a derivation of the time delay PDF $D_i(t)$, is needed.

According to the communication protocol for Token Passing LANs, when an interface receives a free token it has the right for transmission. After the transmission of one packet from interface i, a free token is issued by this interface and transmitted downstream to the interface $i+1$. The elapsed time between the emission of a free token and its reception by the adjacent interface on the Logical Ring, is a random variable with independent PDF, $C_i(t)$ and average c_i.

Particularly, for interface i, the elapsed time between a transmission of a packet until the visit of a new free token, is a random variable which is specified as a sum of independent random variables, and is given by:

$$\tilde{R}_{i_1} = N \tilde{C}_i + \sum_{j=0}^{\tilde{n}} \tilde{B}_j \qquad (2)$$

where $\tilde{C}_i$ and $\tilde{C}_j$ are random variables related to $C_i(t)$ and $B_i(t)$, respectively. The random variable ñ, represents the number of active interfaces during a free token cycle on the Logical Ring. An interface is active if it has a packet to be transmitted when it receives the token. The random variable $\tilde{R}_{i_1}$ is defined as the *free token cycle* for interface i when it is active.

Based on the considerations above and on Figure 1 interface i may be modelled as a gated server as shown in Figure 2. The gate opening is a random variable defined by:

$$\tilde{R}_{i_o} = N \tilde{C}_i + \sum_{\substack{j=0 \\ j \neq 1}}^{\tilde{n}} \tilde{B}_j \qquad (3)$$

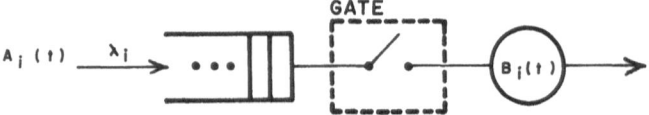

Figure 2. Interface Model

When the gate is closed, the effective service time for a packet in interface i is given by $\tilde{R}_{i_1}$, which has a general PDF. Therefore, interface i may be modelled like a gated GI/G/1 queue.

It should be mentioned that the integration of applications phenomenon, i.e. the influence of others interfaces $j \neq i$ on interface i, is expressed by Equations (2) and (3).

Our goal is to obtain from the solution of the proposed model, the pdf $p_i(m_i)$ mentioned before, which in this case is exactly the time delay pdf $D_i(t)$, since we are considering Time Critical Applications. In[13], the Laplace Transform - LT of the queueing time PDF for a GI/G/1 queue is shown. The spectral solution to Lindley's integral equation is used. Following the steps of the above solution, we derive the expression for the queueing time, given by:

$$w_i(s) = \frac{1}{\Psi_i + (s)} \cdot \lim_{s \to 0} \frac{\Psi_i + (s)}{s} \tag{4}$$

where $\Psi_i+(s)$ is a complex function which depends on the arrival and service processes and its determination is reported in[13].

Since the random variables associated with service and queueing times are statistically independent the LT of the time delay PDF is given by:

$$D_i(s) = B_i(s) \cdot W_i(s) \tag{5}$$

The inverse transform of $s \cdot D_i(s)$ is $D_i(t)$, which is the time delay pdf.

Successively using the spectral solution mentioned above and Equations (4) and (5), for each interface on the network, we determine the set $\{D_i(t)\}(1 \leq i \leq N)$, which is the set $\{p\}$ as mentioned before.

The queueing time PDF given by Equation (4) depends on $A_i(t)$, $B_i(t)$, R_{i0} and R_{i1}. Let us define $\tilde{R}_{i_0}$ and $\tilde{R}_{i_1}$ as the conditional token cycle without and with a packet transmission, respectively. Therefore, the knowledge of the Laplace Transform of those random variables is important for determining $W_i(s)$ in Equation (4).

Equation (2) may be written as:

$$\tilde{R}_{i_1} = N\tilde{C}_i + \sum_{j \neq i} [\alpha_{ij}^1 \tilde{B}_j + (1 - \alpha_{ij}^1) \cdot 0] + \tilde{B}_i \tag{6}$$

where $\alpha^1{}_{ij}$ is the probability of serving one packet of interface $j \neq i$, during a token cycle in which one packet of interface i was served. Similarly, Equation (3) can be written:

$$\tilde{R}_{i_0} = N\tilde{C}_i + \sum_{j \neq i} [\alpha_{ij}^0 \tilde{B}_j + (1 - \alpha_{ij}^0) \cdot 0] \tag{7}$$

where $\alpha^0{}_{ij}$ is the probability of serving one packet of interface $j \neq i$, during a token cycle without the service of one packet of interface i.

Let $R_{i0}(t)$ and $R_{i1}(t)$ be the PDFs associated to $\tilde{R}_{i_0}$ and $\tilde{R}_{i_1}$, respectively. The LT for those PDFs are:

$$R_{i_0}(s) = \prod_{j=i}^{N} c_i(s) \cdot \prod_{j \neq i} [\alpha_{ij}^0 B_j(s) + (1 - \alpha_{ij}^0)] \tag{8}$$

$$R_{i_0}(s) = \prod_{j=i}^{N} c_i(s) \cdot \prod_{j \neq i} [\alpha_{ij}^1 B_j(s) + (1 - \alpha_{ij}^1)] \cdot B_i(s) \tag{9}$$

where $B_j(s)$ and $C_i(s)$ are the LT of $B_i(t)$ and $C_i(t)$, respectively. Equations (8) and (9) follow directly when considering R_{i0} and R_{i1} as a sum of independent random variables.

For the unconditional token cycle R we find from the law of total probabilities

$$R(s) = (1 - \alpha_i)\, R_{i_0}(s) + \alpha_i\, R_{i_1}(s) \tag{10}$$

where α_i is the probability that interface i is active upon a visit of a free token.

Based on Equations (8), (9) and (10) and on the Laplace Transform properties, we derive the average values of $R_{i0}(t)$, $R_{i1}(t)$ and $R(t)$, respectively given by:

$$\overline{R}_{i_0} = \overline{C}_0 + \sum_{j \neq i} \alpha_{ij}^0\, b_j \tag{11}$$

$$\overline{R}_{i_0} = \overline{C}_0 + \sum_{j \neq i} \alpha_{ij}^1\, b_j + b_i \tag{12}$$

$$\overline{R} = (1 - \alpha_i)\, \overline{R}_{i_0} + \alpha_i\, \overline{R}_{i_1} \tag{13}$$

$\overline{C}_0$ is the average token cycle when no packets are served during this cycle. Additionally, the probabilities α_{ij}^0 and α_{ij}^1 are given by:

$$\alpha_{ij}^0 = \lambda_i\, \overline{R}_{i_0} \tag{14}$$

$$\alpha_{ij}^1 = \lambda_i\, \overline{R}_{i_1}\ ,\ j \neq 1 \tag{15}$$

The probabilities above are the probabilities that a token meets at least one packet in interface j ($j \neq i$) and are identical with the average number of packets served in that interface during the R_{i0} and R_{i1} cycles, respectively. Analogously, the probability α_i is:

$$\alpha_i = \lambda_i\, \overline{R} \tag{16}$$

Inserting (14) and (15) in (11) and (12), respectively, we find:

$$\overline{R}_{i_0} = \frac{\overline{c}_0}{1 - \rho_0 + \rho_i} \tag{17}$$

$$\overline{R}_{i_1} = \frac{\overline{c}_0 + b_i}{1 - \rho_0 + \rho_i} \tag{18}$$

where $\rho_0 = \rho_1 + \rho_2 + \ldots + \rho_N$ defines the total server (network) utilization and $\rho_i = \lambda_i b_i$ ($1 \leq i \leq N$) is the server utilization by interface i only. It should also be mentioned that the solution (17) and (18) holds only as long as $\alpha_{ij}^1 \leq 1$. This condition is always fulfilled in case of symmetrical load[5]. Inserting (16), (17) and (18) in (13) we find the expression for the average token cycle, $\overline{R}$.

Following, we present the criteria for judging the criticalness of a Time Critical Application.

Criteria for Judging the Criticalness of a Time Critical Application

Above, we showed the expression for the G1/G/1 time delay by Equations (4) and (5). We also outlined, a formal specification for applications with Upper Bound Limit Measure, specifically Time Critical applications. For the particular interface i under consideration, the formal specification is as follows:

$$\{m_i\} = \{m_1 = t_i, (t_i = time\ delay)\ \}$$

where $\{m_i\}$ is the set of relevant measures to the application in interface i. In this case, there is one relevant measure only. The set of bound values is:

$$\{M_i\} = \{[M_1] = T_{1i}\}$$

Additionally, the set of tolerance probabilities is given by:

$$\{f_i\} = \{f_1 = Pr\ [t_i > T_{1i}\ ]\}$$

Finally, the set of pdfs associated to relevant measures is:

$$\{p_i\} = \{p_i(m_i) = D_i(t_i)\}$$

We say that the application in interface i is critical if $f_1 = f_1^* - \varepsilon$ for $\varepsilon \to 0$. In order to judge the criticalness of a Time Critical application, the set of critical tolerance probabilities $\{f_i^*\} = \{f_1^*\}$, is needed. Basically, this determination consists on solving Equation (1) for f_1^*.

$$\lim_{t \to \infty} \left[\int_{T_{1i}}^{t} D_i\ (t_i)\ dt_i \right] = f_1^* \tag{19}$$

One possible method for solving (19) is to evaluated the inverse transform of $s \cdot D_i(s)$ (see Equation (5)) to give $D_i(t_i)$ and then integrate as above. Unfortunately, $D_i(s)$ usually has a complicated expression and its inverse transform cannot be evaluated from a LT entry table directly. Then, some numerical inversion technique must be used[14,15]. Another possible way for solving the equation (19) is to solve the integral in the s domain.
Equation (19) can be written also, as:

$$\lim_{t \to \infty} \left[\int_{0}^{t} u(t_i - T_{1i}) \cdot D_i\ (t_i)\ dt_i \right] = f_1^*$$

where $u(t)$ is the step function. From a general form of Parseval's formula, the last equation can be written:

$$f_1^* = \int_{0}^{\infty} u(t_i - T_{1i}) \cdot D_i\ (t_i)\ dt_i = \frac{1}{2\pi i} \int_{c-i\infty}^{c+i\infty} u(-s)[sD_i(s)]\ ds \tag{20}$$

for $t_i \geq 0$ and $\alpha < c < \beta$; this interval is the strip of convergence of the Laplace integral. The integration in the complex s-plane is taken to be a stright-line integration parallel to the imaginary axis and lying within the strip of convergence. The usual means for carrying out this integration is to make use of the Cauchy residue theorem as applied to the integral in the complex domain around a closed contour. Usually, the determination of residues is not straightforward, specially when $D_i(t_i)$ is a general fdp.

From Equation (19), we see that f_1^* is exactly the integral of the tail of $D_i(t_i)$ for $t_i > T_{1i}$. In literature, there exist some inequalities, namely: Markov, Chebyschev and One-Sided; that could be used to estimate f_1^* more easily[16,17,18,19]. Since we are interested in calculating the tail of $D_i(t_i)$ for $t_i > T_{1i}$, the One-Sided inequality is more suitable to give us this estimate. The One-Sided naquality is expressed as follows[19]:

$$\Pr[t_i > T_{1i}] \leq \frac{\tau^2 D_i}{\tau^2 D_i + (T_{1i} - \bar{D}_i)^2} \; , \; T_{1i} > \bar{D}_i \tag{21}$$

$$\Pr[t_i \leq T_{1i}] \leq \frac{\tau^2 D_i}{\tau^2 D_i + (T_{1i} - \bar{D}_i)^2} \; , \; T_{1i} < \bar{D}_i \tag{22}$$

where $\bar{D}_i$ and $\tau^2 D_i$ are the average and variance of $D_i(t)$, respectively. Thus, f_1^* may be estimated by Equation (21).

Any of the outlined methods of calculating f_1^* could be used. In this paper we will compare the methods reported, through a case study. To show the criteria for judging the criticalness of an application, we present in the next section, an example of a hypothetical Token Passing LAN, whose interfaces are identical and modelled as M/G/1 queues. However, we should mention that the model and solution presented before are valid for a generic interface as the GI/G/1 queue.

CASE STUDY

Let us consider a Token Passing LAN with the following characteristics: there are ten M/M/1 identical interfaces (N=10), with $\lambda_i = \lambda = 1.0$ packet/sec, and $b_i=b=1.0$ ms ($1 \leq i < 10$); the token service time is constant, $c_i = c = 0.1$ ms; the service discipline is the FCFS; the relevant application is that with Upper Bound Limit Measure, specified by the sets, $\{m\} = \{t=Time\ Delay\}$, $\{M\} = \{[M_1] = T_1\}$ and $\{f\} = \{\Pr[t > T_1] = f_1\}$.

In order to find the sets $\{p\} = \{D(t)\}$ and $\{f^*\} = \{f_1^*\}$. which characterize the network, we need the time delay fdp given by Equation (5):

$$D(s) = W(s) \cdot B(s)$$

In this case, the transmission time has an Exponential fdp with average b, and Laplace Transform:

$$B(s) = \frac{1}{s+1}$$

Based on the considerations made above, a given interface may be modelled as a gated M/G/1 queue (see Figure 2) with an effective service FDP given by $R_1(t)$ in Equation (9) (for ease of reading we suppress the subscript i in the following treatment).

We assume that the queueing system is in the stationary state. Let K be the number of waiting packets in a given interface, at the scan instant (free token visit). We are interested in the stationary distribution

$$P_k = P\{K=k\}, \quad k=1,2,3, ... \tag{23}$$

Because of the memoryless property of the arrival process, the system state of the considered interface forms an embedded Markov chain at the discret set of scan instants (renewal points). The stationary distribution satisfies the equation[13]:

$$P_k = P_0 P_{ok} + \sum_{m=1}^{K+1} P_m P_{mk} \ , \ K = 1,2,\dots \tag{24}$$

where the transition probabilities P_{mk} are given by

$$P_{mk} = \begin{cases} \int_{t=0}^{\infty} \frac{(\lambda t)^{(k-m+1)}}{(k-m+1)!} \cdot dR_1(t) \ , \ m > 0 \\ \int_{t=0}^{\infty} \frac{(\lambda t)^k}{k!} \cdot dR_0(t) \ , \ m = 0 \end{cases} \tag{25}$$

Together with the normalizing condition

$$\sum_{k=0}^{\infty} P_k = 1 \tag{26}$$

the stationary probabilities of state at the scan instants are completely determined by the set of Equations (24), (25) and (26).

Analogously, we can find the state distribution at departure instants. The knowledge of those two state distribution leads us to finally derive the queueing time Laplace transform expression, given by[2]:

$$W(s) = \frac{1 - \lambda \overline{R}_1}{\overline{R}_0} \cdot \frac{1 - R_0(s)}{s - \lambda [1 - R_1(s)]} \tag{27}$$

where $\overline{R}_0$ and $\overline{R}_1$ are the mean values of $R_0(t)$, in Equation (17) and (18), respectively. From (27) we find for the mean queueing time:

$$\overline{W} = -\frac{d}{ds} W(s) \bigg|_{s=0} = \frac{\overline{R}_0^2}{2 \overline{R}_0^2} + \frac{\lambda \overline{R}_1^2}{2(1 - \lambda \overline{R}_1^2)} \tag{28}$$

$\overline{R}_0^2$ and $\overline{R}_1^2$ are the second moments of $R_0(t)$ and $R_1(t)$, derived from (8) and (9), respectively. Higher order moments of $W(t)$ can be derived using Takacs' M/G/1 recurrence formula[20].

Inserting the specified parameter values in (17) and (18), we find:

$$\overline{R}_0 = \frac{1}{1 - 9\lambda} \ ; \quad \overline{R}_1 = \frac{2}{1 - 9\lambda}$$

From Equation (15) and the condition $\alpha_{ijl} \le 1$, we can find the stability condition for the queueing system under consideration, which is $\lambda < 1/11$ packets/ms.

Referring to Equations (8), (9), (14) and (15), we find:

$$R_0(s) = e^{-s} \left[\frac{\lambda}{1 - 9\lambda} \cdot \frac{1}{s+1} + \frac{1 - 10\lambda}{1 - 9\lambda} \right]^9 \tag{29}$$

$$R_1(s) = e^{-s} \left[\frac{2\lambda}{1-9\lambda} \cdot \frac{1}{s+1} + \frac{1-11\lambda}{1-9\lambda} \right]^9 \cdot \left(\frac{1}{s+1} \right) \tag{30}$$

From (27), the queueing time LT is:

$$W(s) = (1 - 11\lambda) \cdot \frac{[1-R_0(s)]}{s - \lambda[1 - R_1(s)]} \tag{31}$$

and

$$D(s) = \frac{(1 - 11\lambda)}{s + 1} \cdot \frac{[1-R_0(s)]}{s - \lambda[1 - R_1(s)]} \tag{32}$$

In order to calculate f_1^* any of the methods mentioned, namely: the LT inversion of $D(t)$ in (19); the complex integral solution using Cauchy residue theorem in (20); and the estimation by means of the One-Sided inequality, could be used. For the case study under consideration, $D(s)$ is a rather complex function. Actually, its denominator is a transcendental function. Because of the limitations of our computing system in determining complex zeros of transcendental function, we were not able to find f_1^* using Cauchy residue theorem in (20). Due to the complexity of $D(s)$, the determination of f_1^* using (19) consisted in numerically

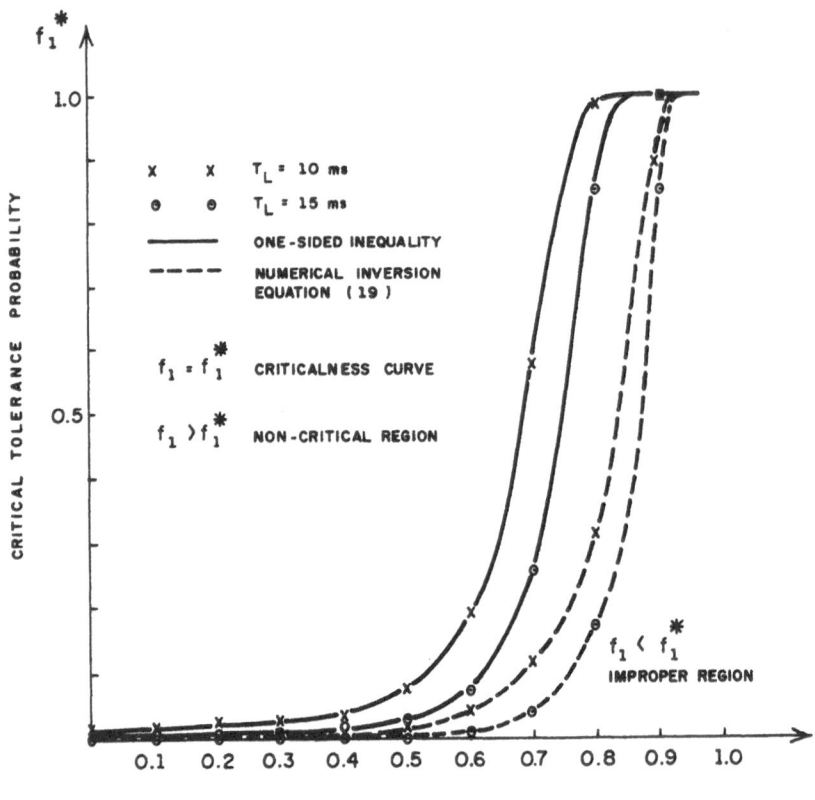

Figure 3. Critical Tolerance Probability

finding the inverse LT and then numerically integrate as in (19) using the Cautious Romberg Extrapolation algorithm with a 10-3 accuracy. The numerical LT inversion algorithm used was that reported in[15]. The results for f_1^*, with $T_1 = 10$ ms and $T_1 = 15$ ms, for the LT inversion method, together with the One-Sided estimation[2], are depicted in Figure 3.

For the considered case study, given the formal application specification, namely: the bound limit value T_1, and the tolerance probability f_1, we can determine from Figure 3, the critical total server utilization ρ_0^*. For example, for $T_1 = 15$ ms and $f_1 = 0.2$, we determine $\rho_0^* = 0.67$ for the One-Sided estimation, and $\rho_0^* = 0.81$ for the numerical inversion method. Following, we find the critical arrival rate $\lambda^* = \rho_0^*/10$. Then, for any $\lambda < \lambda^*$ the application is not critical. The non-critical region is $f_1 > f_1^*$ and the improper region for an application is $f_1 < f_1^*$.

As we can observe, the One-Sided estimation overestimates the criticalness of a given application. Nevertheless it leads to a relatively easy evaluation of f_1^*, and should be used when the accuracy for judging the criticalness is not extreme. It should also be mentioned that the non-critical region determined by the One-Sided estimation is inside the non-critical region

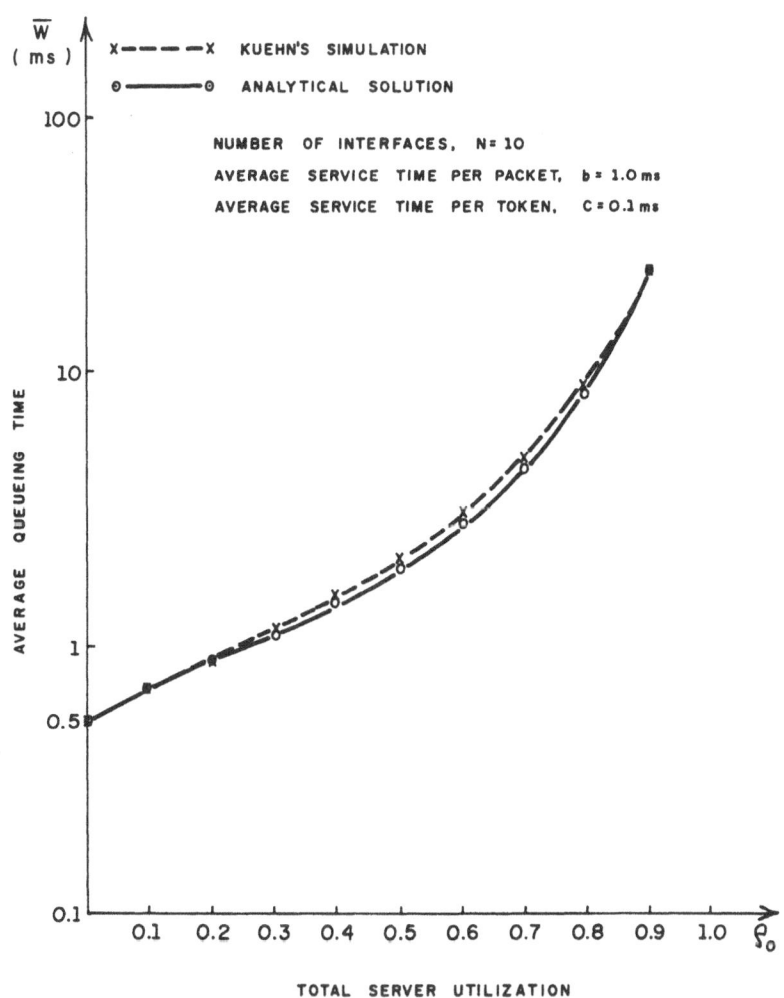

Figure 4. Average Queueing Time

found by the numerical inversion method. Therefore, any application found as non-critical by the One-Sided estimation is actually a non-critical application with respect to a given Token Passing LAN.

It should be mentioned that the accuracy of the criteria for judging the criticalness of a given application, depends on the model and solution adopted to find the relevant measure fdp. To validate our model, we show in Figure 4 the simulation results for the average queueing time $W(t)$, performed by Kuehn[5], compared to results provided by Equation (28). The simulation results have a 95% confidence level. As we can observe, from Figure 4, the analytical results and simulation agree closely. However, this validation is not complete, since other moments should be compared and even that is not sufficient for a complete validation since successive token cycle times are not independent of each other; for a more complete validation, some covariance measure should be considered, too. We observe a very good accuracy for low traffic since the independence assumption is asymptotically exact for zero arrival rate, as well as for heavy traffic since each of the interfaces contributes in the limit with a full service time to the token cycle times become independent of each other again.

CONCLUSION

This paper provides a new concept which is the "Time Critical" specification for a given network application. In addition, the criteria for judging the criticalness of this application with respect to the network performance, is reported. To determine this criticalness, was observed that an estimation by means of a probability inequality allows a relatively easy evaluation of numerical results. However, this method should be used with caution when a good accuracy is needed for a refined criticalness judgement, other two methods are outlined.

For judging the criticalness of a given application, a generic model for an Integrated Token Passing Local Network is suggested and the accuracy of its approximate solution is validate by another author's computer simulation.

The analysis reported in this article, can give a better insight in studing new Integrated Token Passing Local Network, as will as can be used to analyze the existing netwoks performance when new applications are added to the actual and future user population.

REFERENCES

1. I. Gitman, and H. Frank; "Economic Analysis of Integrated Voice and Data Networks: A Case Study", *Proceedings of the IEEE*, Vol.66, No.11, November.
2. M. A. G. Brasileiro; "Modelagem de Aplicações Críticas no Tempo em Redes Locais com Passagem de Ficha". *Tese de Doutorado*, Departamento de Engenharia Elétrica da UFPb, Campina Grande, Brasil (1987).
3. M. A. Leibowitz; "An Approximate Method for Treating a Class of Multiqueue Problems", *IBM Journal*, 5, 204(1961).
4. S. Halfin; "An Approximate Method for Calculating Delays for a Family of Cyclic Type Queues", *B.S.T.J.*, 54, 1733 (1975).
5. P. J. Kuehn; "Multiqueue Systems with Nonexhaustive Cyclic Service", *B.S.T.J.*, Vol.58, 671 (1979).
6. B. Avi-Itzhak, W.L. Maxwell, and L.W. Miller; "Queueing with Alternating Priorities", *Opns. Res.*, 13, 306 (1965).
7. L. Takács; "Two Queues Attended by a Single Server", *Opns. Res.*, 16 639 (1968).
8. R. B. Cooper, and G. Murray; "Queues Served in Cyclic Order", *B.S.T.J.*, 48, 675 (1969).
9. M. Einsenberg; "Queues with Periodic Changeover Times", *Opns. Res.*, 19, 386 (1971).
10. O. Hashida; "Analysis of Multiqueue", *Review of the Electr. Comm. Laboratories*, Nippon Telegraph and Telephone Public Corp., 20, 189 (1972).
11. H. Takagi, L. Kleinrock; "Analysis of Polling Systems", *JSI Research Report*, TR87-0002, 01/08/85.
12. P. Tran-Gia, and T. Raith; "Multiqueue Systems with Finit Capacity and Nonexhaustive Cyclic Service", *Proceedings of the IFIP*, Tokyo, 213 (1985).

13. L. Kleinrock; "Queueing Systems, Volume I: Theory", John Wiley & Sons, New York (1975).

14. D. Jagerman; "An Inversion Technique for the Laplace Transform with Application to Approximation", *B.S.T.J.*, 57, 669 (1978).

15. H. Stehfest; "Algorithm 368- Numerical Inversion of Laplace Transform", *Comm., of ACM* - 13, 47 (1970).

16. H. Cramér; "Mathematical Methods of Statistics", Princeton Univ. Press, Princeton, New Jersey (1964).

17. A. Papoulis; "Probability, Random Variables and Stochastic Process", McGrawHill Book Company, New York (1965).

18. W. Feller; "An Introduction to Probability Theory and Its Applications", 3rd Edition, Vol.1, Willey, New York (1968).

19. A. O. Allen; "Probability, Statistics, and Queueing Theory with Computer Science Applications", Academic Press, New York (1978).

20. L. Takács; "A Single-Server Queue with Poisson Input, *Opns. Res.*, 10 (1962).

MATRIX MULTIPLICATION ON DIGITAL SIGNAL PROCESSORS AND HIERARCHICAL MEMORY SYSTEMS

Ismael Palacios, Mario Medina and Jaime Moreno

Departamento de Ingeniería Eléctrica
Universidad de Concepción
Casilla 53-C, Concepción, Chile
BITNET: mmedina%uconce@uchcecvm.bitnet

ABSTRACT

We discuss mapping the matrix multiplication algorithm onto a two-level hierarchical memory system which incorporates DMA capabilities between levels, as available on Digital Signal Processors (DSPs). We show that it is possible to hide the hierarchical nature of the memory system from the processor, so that computations can proceed at the processor's speed. This is accomplished by the use of a block algorithm, and by prefetching data from the slower second-level memory into the faster but smaller first-level memory under DMA control. The Texas Instruments TMS 320C30 Digital Signal Processor is used as an example, and performance estimates for different memory timings are given. These results are also compared to the performance of executing the matrix multiplication algorithm without exploiting the DMA capabilities.

INTRODUCTION

Digital Signal Processors (DSPs) are specialized microprocessors suitable for the execution of numerically intensive applications[1]. They have been successfully used in real-time areas such as speech recognition, digital audio, telecommunications, as well as in areas traditionally dominated by conventional processors (medical imaging, graphics generation, simulation). Digital signal processors achieve their high performance by integrating features such as floating-point multiply-and-add operators, pipelined and/or parallel functional units, parallel and multilevel memory systems (small and fast on-chip memory, large external memory), multiple busses, and direct memory access (DMA) controller. The effective utilization of the capabilities of a DSP, specially the concurrent execution features, imposes an important burden on code development, sometimes forcing the use of assembly language. On the other hand, the demand for easily-understood, quick and reliable code forces the use of high-level languages, which in turn place the burden of effective resource utilization on the compiler and the compiler writer.

Matrix algorithms are a frequently used mathematical tool in digital signal processing[2]. Many applications of matrix algorithms in digital signal processing are based on DSPs, as a result of their specialized features. The generation of efficient code for matrix computations, especially for large size matrices, requires careful management of the processor resources as well as the memory. This is particularly true in DSPs with a multilevel (hierarchical) memory, due to the potential degradation in performance resulting from high memory bandwidth requirements arising from the distribution of matrix data throughout the memory levels.

The problem of allocating matrix data to memory and accessing such data in memory has been studied extensively. In fact, matrix algorithms for general-purpose computers have been developed around classes (levels) of basic linear algebra subprograms (BLAS)[3]. There are three levels of BLAS, each class exploiting the locality (reuse of data elements) of the problem differently. The higher level BLAS have more locality and therefore are better suited for systems with memory hierarchies[4]. Consequently, using BLAS to write code for a matrix algorithm in a general-purpose processor has certain similarities with code generation for a Digital Signal Processor with a multilevel memory system. It should be noted that the direct use of BLAS on DSPs is not recommended, as in a dedicated environment better matching between algorithm and architecture can be achieved than what is possible with BLAS. In particular, the DMA capabilities of a DSP allow prefetching data, feature that cannot be exploited under BLAS because such an approach uses a demand-based model of data transfers.

In this paper, we discuss mapping the matrix multiplication algorithm onto Digital Signal Processors (or two-level hierarchical memory systems), considering that the bandwidth of the first level of memory matches the processor throughput while the second level of memory has lower bandwidth (longer access time), and that it is possible to transfer data between these two levels via a DMA controller. The Texas Instruments TMS 320C30 Digital Signal Processor[5] is used as an example. Estimates of the execution time resulting from the mappings are given. The results included here show that it is possible to keep the processor always busy, in spite of the slower second level memory. In other words, it is possible to program the matrix multiplication algorithm in such a way that the entire memory system appears as a large fast first level. This is possible by taking advantage of the on-chip DMA controller existing in DSPs.

MANAGING THE MEMORY HIERARCHY IN DIGITAL SIGNAL PROCESSORS

The memory system in DSPs usually consists of a small and fast first level, and a larger but slower second level of memory. The first level is normally built into the DSP to speed up memory accesses, and may include cache memories, parallel memory modules and/or multiport memories. For the purposes of this work, we shall consider a model of a DSP whose memory is organized as two internal blocks, each one supporting two simultaneous accesses every cycle.

The execution of matrix algorithms on DSPs generally requires the storage of large size matrices in external memory, which is normally slower than the processor. Consequently, accessing data elements directly from external memory degrades performance. Although a system with large fast external memory may be designed, its cost would be prohibitive. Moreover, as we will show here, it is possible to program a DSP in such a way that the impact of slow external memory is not significant.

The key to efficient use of a DSP's resources lies in using the DMA controller to transfer data into internal memory while the processor is busy executing useful operations, thus freeing the CPU from the data transfer task. Once data is loaded into internal memory, it must be reused as many times as possible to avoid reloading data from external memory.

This concurrent operation of DMA and CPU can be regarded as a two stage pipelined structure, as shown in Figure 1.

– The first stage corresponds to data transfers from external into internal memory under DMA control.

– The second stage corresponds to the execution of arithmetic operations by the CPU, on data resident in internal memory.

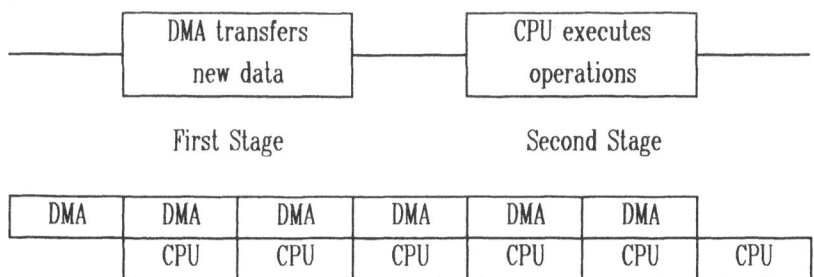

Figure 1. Data transfer and execution pipeline

For this pipelined structure to be efficient, the loss of valuable CPU cycles just waiting for DMA data transfers to finish must be avoided. That is, the first stage must take less or equal time than the second stage. In other words, time spent in the transfer of a new block of data via DMA must be less than the time taken by the processor in performing operations on the previous block of data. As long as the processor remains busy doing useful computations, it doesn't matter if the DMA controller is idle.

By this scheme, data needed by the processor is always transferred to fast internal memory before the processor needs it. Memory appears to the CPU as composed only of fast memory blocks, whose speed matches the processor's capabilities. The use of this scheme requires the specification and scheduling of data transfers from external to internal memory, as discussed in the next section.

MAPPING THE MATRIX MULTIPLICATION ALGORITHM

Let's consider the multiplication of matrices A and B, of sizes n_1 by n_2 and n_2 by n_3 respectively, and its addition to matrix C of dimensions n_1 by n_3 (C <- C + A*B). This algorithm consists of three nested loops; the innermost loop calculates the inner product between a row of A and a column of B, and the other two loops control which row and column must be operated upon.

For i = 1 to n_1
    For j = 1 to n_3
        For k = 1 to n_2
            $c_{i,j} = c_{i,j} + a_{i,k} * b_{k,j}$

The matrix multiplication algorithm can be represented by an homogeneous complete graph, where each node corresponds to a multiply-and-add operation, as shown in Figure 2. This type of representation has been called a MultiMesh Graph[6]. Matrices A and B enter the graph in the horizontal and vertical axes, while the resulting matrix C is calculated depthwise.

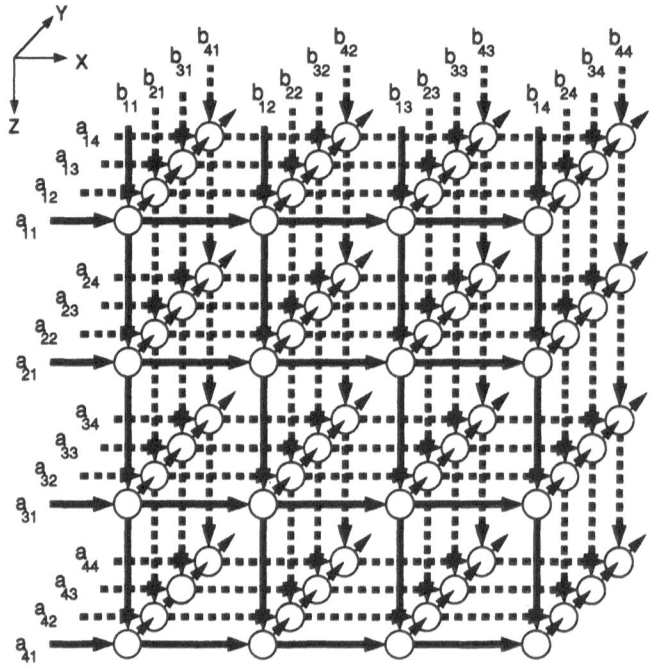

Figure 2. Matrix Multiplication Multimesh Graph

The conventional execution of the algorithm corresponds to traversing the graph depthwise, in the direction of calculated data. Each node must read three operands from memory, execute a multiply-and-add instruction and store the result, which totals four memory accesses. If data resides in internal memory, the algorithm can proceed at the processor's speed. On the other hand, if data must be read from external memory, which is larger but slower, the algorithm's timing will be linked to the speed of the slow external memory.

As internal memory size is small and cannot contain a complete matrix, matrix multiplication must be expressed as a block algorithm. It is well known that block algorithms improve performance on hierarchical memory systems, as data loaded into the first memory level can be reused, avoiding excessive movement of data to and from the second memory level. Level 3 BLAS[3,4,7] has been designed to speed up matrix algorithms by taking advantage of this fact. BLAS3, however, does not consider the effect of prefetching data into the first memory level under DMA control. This drawback of BLAS3 has led us to develop the alternative model described next.

Let A, B and C be partitioned into submatrices of dimensions m_1 by m_2, m_2 by m_3 and m_1 by m_3, respectively, in such a way that the data involved in each block can be stored in the first level of memory. The algorithm for obtaining matrix C is as follows:

```
For i = 1 to k₁
    For j = 1 to k₃
        For k = 1 to k₂
            Ci,j = Ci,j + Ai,k*Bk,j
```

where $n_1 = k_1*m_1$, $n_2 = k_2*m_2$ and $n_3 = k_3*m_3$, and k_1, k_2 and k_3 are positive integers.

Since the block operations $C_{i,j} = C_{i,j} + A_{i,k}*B_{k,j}$ possess a large amount of data locality, the algorithm proceeds by dedicating the DSP's full resources to each of the block operations in turn.

Several issues about the algorithm above must be addressed. These are:
- The loop ordering used to compute each block update
- The algorithm used for multiplying $A_{i,k}$ and $B_{k,j}$
- The method by which data transfers will occur
- The sizes of the submatrices

Concerning the first issue, the three loops may be interchanged leading to different sweeps of the matrices. To choose a loop ordering, the data transfers needed to compute a block are examined. Each block reads submatrices $A_{i,k}$ and $B_{k,j}$ once, but must access submatrix $C_{i,j}$ twice (first to read its data and then to store the result). If the loop ordering shown above is used, and submatrix $C_{i,j}$ is stored in internal memory during the innermost loop execution, data transfers are minimized as each submatrix $C_{i,j}$ must be read and stored exactly once.

Actually, each block operation $C_{i,j} = C_{i,j} + A_{i,k}*B_{k,j}$ is itself a matrix multiplication performed on data residing in internal memory. There are three basic generic approaches to perform these computations, which correspond to different choices of loop ordering. They are called the outer, middle, and inner product methods due to the fundamental kernels used.

The outer product scheme updates matrix C by computing m_2 outer products between columns of A and rows of B, as follows:

```
Outer Product:
For i = 1 to m₂
    C = C + aᵢ*bᵢᵀ
```

The kernel of the middle product calculation is the product of A by columns of B, operation that is repeated m_3 times, as follows:

```
Middle Product:
For i = 1 to m₃
    cᵢ = cᵢ + A*bᵢ
```

The inner product approach multiplies both matrices by performing $m_1 * m_3$ inner products. This is the kernel of choice for Digital Signal Processors, because they incorporate features such as multiply-and-add instructions, delayed branches and block repeat capabilities which speed up inner product computations. This kernel is described as follows:

Inner Product:
For i = 1 to m_3
    For j = 1 to m_1
        $c_{i,j} = c_{i,j} + \underline{a}_i^{T} * \underline{b}_j$

Normally, every kernel computation has associated a startup time t_s, which must be considered $m_1 * m_3$ times for the inner product scheme, but only m_3 times for the middle product and m_2 times for the outer product kernel.

To make efficient use of the processor's resources, all submatrices $A_{i,k}$ and $B_{k,j}$ must be transferred into internal memory under DMA control, as described earlier. While the CPU performs a block operation, the DMA controller must transfer the data corresponding to the next submatrix product into internal memory. This pipelined operation can be repeated for each block being calculated, effectively eliminating a large amount of overhead from the algorithm's execution. This procedure is depicted in Figure 3.

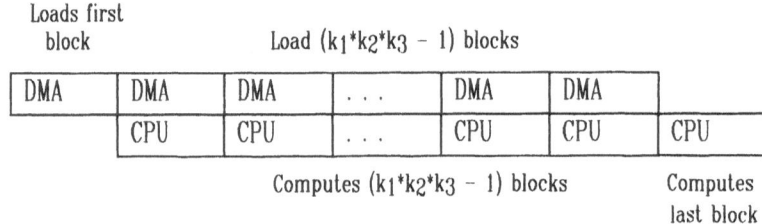

Figure 3. Parallel DMA and CPU operation

For this scheme to be successful, internal memory must be divided in two modules, each storing completely the data required to compute a block and allowing two simultaneous accesses. That is, each module must be big enough to store all data needed to update a complete $C_{i,j}$ submatrix. This memory distribution and its data allocation are shown in Figure 4.

PERFORMANCE ANALYSIS OF THE MAPPING

In order to determine the block sizes m_1, m_2, m_3, the various factors affecting the performance of the algorithm can be studied according to the decoupling methodology proposed in[7]. The total time T required to perform a given algorithm may be written as:

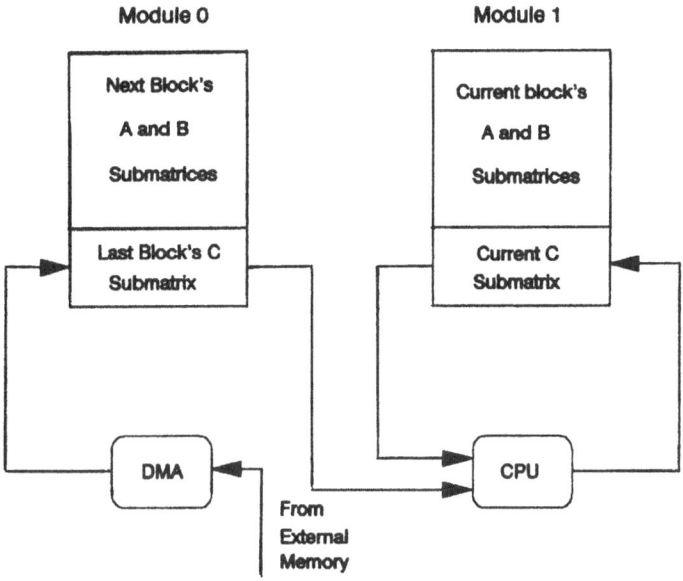

Figure 4. Data allocation in first memory level

$$T = T_a + T_l + T_s = n_a{}^*t_a + n_l{}^*t_l + n_s{}^*t_s$$

where:

T_a : arithmetic time (computation time if all operands reside in first memory level)
T_l : data transfer time (time spent transferring data between memory levels).
T_s : kernel startup time.
n_a : number of arithmetic operations.
n_l : number of data loads.
n_s : number of inner products computed per block.
t_a : average time for arithmetic operations (processor–dependent).
t_l : average time for data transfers (processor–dependent).
t_s : average startup time of an inner product (processor–dependent).

These parameters are derived considering the calculation of the total number of blocks, $k_1{}^*k_2{}^*k_3$. Each block consists of $m_1{}^*m_2{}^*m_3$ multiply–and–add operations, so that

$$n_a = k_1{}^*k_2{}^*k_3{}^*(m_1{}^*m_2{}^*m_3) = n_1{}^*n_2{}^*n_3$$

each block must read a submatrix $A_{i,k}$ and a submatrix $B_{k,j}$. However, each submatrix $C_{i,j}$ will be accessed exactly twice, once to read its data and once to write the results. Consequently,

$$n_l = k_1{}^*k_2{}^*k_3{}^*(m_1{}^*m_2) + k_1{}^*k_2{}^*k_3{}^*(m_2{}^*m_3) + k_1{}^*k_3(2{}^*m_1{}^*m_3)$$
$$= n_1{}^*n_2{}^*n_3/m_3 + n_1{}^*n_2{}^*n_3/m_1 + 2{}^*n_1{}^*n_3$$

The average data transfer time t_l is determined by the pipelined scheme proposed. Since every element of $C_{i,j}$ is computed one at a time, it must be read and written under CPU control. On the other hand, submatrices $A_{i,k}$ and $B_{k,j}$ are transferred into internal memory under DMA control in parallel with CPU computations. So, excepting for the transfer of the first pair of submatrices, the transfer of the following $(k_1{}^*k_2{}^*k_3 - 1)$ pairs of submatrices does not increase the data transfer time. Since the time required to transfer the first pair of submatrices is small, it can be neglected. If the time needed to transfer a single element from external into internal memory under CPU control is t_{CPU}, the average data transfer time t_l is:

$$t_l = [t_{CPU}{}^*(2{}^*m_1{}^*m_3){}^*k_1{}^*k_3]/n_l = (2{}^*t_{CPU}{}^*n_1{}^*n_3)/n_l$$

As the startup overhead affects every inner product computation in each of the $k_1{}^*k_2{}^*k_3$ blocks, it follows that

$$n_S = k_1{}^*k_2{}^*k_3{}^*(m_1{}^*m_3) = n_1{}^*n_2{}^*n_3/m_2$$

Therefore, the total execution time for the complete matrix operation is:

$$T = T_a + T_l + T_s = n_a{}^*t_a + n_l{}^*t_l + n_s{}^*t_s$$
$$= (t_a + t_s/m_2){}^*n_1{}^*n_2{}^*n_3 + (2{}^*t_{CPU}){}^*n_1{}^*n_3$$

From the expression above one can infer that, in order to minimize the total execution time, m_2 should be maximized. The problem of obtaining the optimum block sizes m_1, m_2 and m_3 is equivalent to the solution of the maximization problem:

max $\{m_2\}$
subject to:
$2(m_1{}^*m_2 + m_1{}^*m_3 + m_2{}^*m_3) <=$ memory size
$t_{DMA}{}^*m_2{}^*(m_1 + m_3) <= t_a{}^*m_1{}^*m_2{}^*m_3 + t_s{}^*m_1{}^*m_3$

The first constraint shows that internal memory must fully contain the data necessary to compute two blocks. The second constraint indicates that the time needed to transfer submatrices $A_{i,k}$ and $B_{k,j}$ under DMA control must be less or equal to the time the CPU spends calculating a whole block.

PERFORMANCE ESTIMATES FOR THE TMS 320C30

The Texas Instruments TMS 320C30 Digital Signal Processor is used to illustrate the advantages of the proposed approach. The processor's memory system consists of an internal memory formed by two 1Kx32 RAM modules, each supporting two simultaneous accesses every instruction cycle. The processor also includes a parallel multiply/add instruction which executes in a single cycle. The computation of an inner product using multiply/add instructions has a startup time of one cycle. The time needed to transfer an element from external into internal memory under DMA control is $(3+W)$ where W corresponds to the external memory's wait states, whereas an element is transferred under CPU control in $(1+W)$ cycles[8]. It follows that, for the TMS 320C30,

$t_{DMA} = (3 + W)$
t_s : 1 cycle.
t_a : 1 cycle.

so the maximization problem to be solved is:

max $\{m_2\}$
subject to:
$m_1{}^*m_2 + m_1{}^*m_3 + m_2{}^*m_3 <= 1024$
$(3+W)^*m_2{}^*(m_1 + m_3) <= m_1{}^*m_2{}^*m_3 + m_1{}^*m_3$

and the total algorithm's execution time is:

$t = (1 + 1/m_2)^*n_1{}^*n_2{}^*n_3 + 2^*(1+W)^*n_1{}^*n_3$

The optimum block sizes m_1, m_2 and m_3, obtained by solving this optimization problem are shown in Table 1 as a function of the number of wait states W.

Table 1. Optimum block sizes for the TMS 320C30.

W	m_1	m_2	m_3
0	6	82	6
1	8	60	8
2	10	46	10
3	12	36	12
4	14	29	14
5	16	24	16
6	18	19	18
7	19	17	19

Using the results shown in Table 1, estimates for the algorithm's execution time as a function of matrix order and the number of wait states W have been obtained. Figure 5 shows performance estimates of the execution of the matrix multiplication algorithm according to the scheme proposed, for square matrices of order less than 1000 and different number of wait states. For the sake of comparison, the performance of the conventional approach is also shown. As can be seen, execution time can be made independent of external memory's wait states, if the processor's DMA capabilities are taken advantage of, and an order of magnitude improvement over the conventional scheme can be achieved.

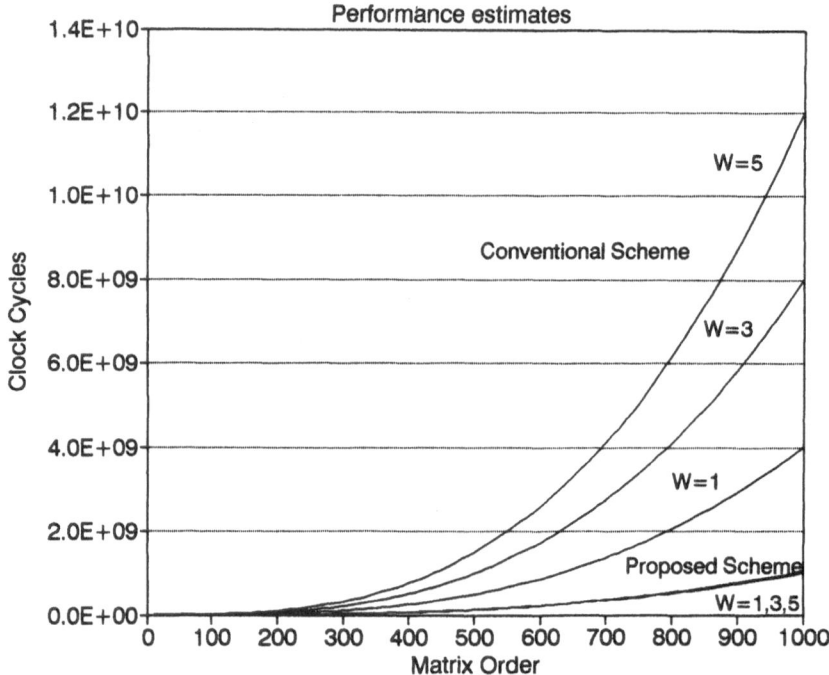

Figure 5. Performance Estimates For The TMS 320C30

SUMMARY

The projection of the matrix multiplication algorithm onto a Digital Signal Processor has been illustrated. We show a block algorithm that makes use of the DMA capabilities of DSPs to prefetch data into the first level of memory in parallel with CPU computations. We show performance estimates for the block algorithm, and obtain the block sizes that minimize the algorithm's total execution time.

A comparison between performance estimates of the conventional approach and the proposed scheme indicates that the proposed scheme offers significant speed advantages over the conventional approach, leads to programs with lower overhead and effectively uncouples external memory timing from program execution speed. The results derived from this work have been derived for the TMS 320C30 processor, but may easily be applied to other digital signal processors, or to other systems that include a two-level hierarchical memory system and DMA capabilities.

ACKNOWLEDGEMENTS

This research has been supported in part by FONDECYT, Grant 0379-91, "Procesor arrays for matrix algorithms."

REFERENCES

1. E. A. Lee, Programmable DSP Architectures, Parts I & II, IEEE *ASSP Magazine* 4:19, October 1988; 4:11, January 1989.
2. M. Speiser and H. Whitehouse, A Review of Signal Processing with Systolic Arrays, *in* "SPIE Real-Time Processing Vi", 2:6, August 1983.
3. K. A. Gallivan, R. J. Plemmons and A. H. Sameh, Parallel Algorithms for Dense Linear Algebra Computations, SIAM *Review* 54:135, March 1990.
4. J. J. Dongarra, J. Du Croz, S. Hammarling and I. Duff, A Set of Level 3 Basic Linear Algebra Subprograms, ACM *Trans. Math. Softw.*, 1:17, March 1990.
5. P. Papamichalis and R. Simar, Jr., The TMS 320C30 Floating-Point Digital Signal Processor, IEEE *Micro* December 1990.
6. J. H. Moreno and T. Lang, Matrix Computations on Systolic-Type Meshes, IEEE *Computer* 32:51, April 1990.
7. K. Gallivan, W. Jalby and U. Meier, The Use of BLAS3 in Linear Algebra on a Parallel Processor with a Hierarchical Memory, SIAM *J.Sci.Stat.Comput.*, 1079:1084, November 1987.
8. Texas Instruments, Inc. "TMS 320C3x User's Guide", 1990.

Author Index

Subject Index